Lecture Notes in Computer Science   11632

Commenced Publication in 1973
Founding and Former Series Editors:
Gerhard Goos, Juris Hartmanis, and Jan van Leeuwen

More information about this series at http://www.springer.com/series/7410

Xingming Sun · Zhaoqing Pan ·
Elisa Bertino (Eds.)

Artificial Intelligence and Security

5th International Conference, ICAIS 2019
New York, NY, USA, July 26–28, 2019
Proceedings, Part I

 Springer

Editors
Xingming Sun (ID)
Nanjing University of Information
Science and Technology
Nanjing, China

Zhaoqing Pan (ID)
Nanjing University of Information
Science and Technology
Nanjing, China

Elisa Bertino (ID)
Purdue University
West Lafayette, IN, USA

ISSN 0302-9743   ISSN 1611-3349   (electronic)
Lecture Notes in Computer Science
ISBN 978-3-030-24273-2   ISBN 978-3-030-24274-9   (eBook)
https://doi.org/10.1007/978-3-030-24274-9

LNCS Sublibrary: SL4 – Security and Cryptology

This Springer imprint is published by the registered company Springer Nature Switzerland AG
The registered company address is: Gewerbestrasse 11, 6330 Cham, Switzerland

Preface

The 5th International Conference on Artificial Intelligence and Security (ICAIS 2019), formerly called the International Conference on Cloud Computing and Security (ICCCS), was held during July 26–28, 2019, at New York University, New York, USA. Over the past four years, ICAIS has become a leading conference for researchers and engineers to share their latest results from research, development, and applications in the fields of artificial intelligence and information security.

We used the Microsoft Conference Management Toolkits (CMT) system to manage the submission and review processes of ICAIS 2019. We received 1529 submissions from 20 countries and regions, including USA, Canada, UK, Italy, Ireland, Japan, Russia, France, Australia, South Korea, South Africa, India, Iraq, Kazakhstan, Indonesia, Vietnam, Ghana, China, Taiwan, and Macao, etc. The submissions cover the areas of artificial intelligence, big data, cloud computing and security, information hiding, IoT security, multimedia forensics, encryption and cybersecurity, and so on. We thank our Technical Program Committee members and external reviewers for their efforts in reviewing papers and providing valuable comments to the authors. From the total of 1,529 submissions, and based on at least three reviews per submission, the Program Chairs decided to accept 230 papers, yielding an acceptance rate of 15%. The volume of the conference proceedings contains all the regular, poster, and workshop papers.

The conference program was enriched by a series of keynote presentations, and the keynote speakers included: Nasir Memon, New York University, USA; Edward Colbert, Virginia Tech Hume Center for National Security and Technology, USA; Quanyan Zhu, New York University, USA; Zhihua Xia, Nanjing University of Information Science and Technology, China; Tom Masino, TradeWeb, USA; etc. We thank them for their wonderful speeches.

There were 45 workshops organized at ICAIS 2019, covering all the hot topics in artificial intelligence and security. We would like to take this moment to express our sincere appreciation for the contribution of all the workshop chairs and their participants. We would like to extend our sincere thanks to all authors who submitted papers to ICAIS 2019 and to all Program Committee members. It was a truly great experience to work with such talented and hard-working researchers. We also appreciate the external reviewers for assisting the Program Committee members in their particular areas of expertise. Moreover, we want to thank our sponsors: Nanjing University of Information Science and Technology, Springer, New York University, IEEE Broadcast Technology Society (BTS) Nanjing Chapter, ACM China, Michigan State University, Taiwan Cheng Kung University, Taiwan Dong Hwa University, Taiwan Providence University, Nanjing University of Aeronautics and Astronautics, State Key Laboratory of Integrated Services Networks, and the National Nature Science Foundation of China.

May 2019

Xingming Sun
Zhaoqing Pan
Elisa Bertino

Organization

General Chairs

Yun Q. Shi	New Jersey Institute of Technology, USA
Mauro Barni	University of Siena, Italy
Xingang You	China Information Technology Security Evaluation Center, China
Elisa Bertino	Purdue University, USA
Quanyan Zhu	New York University, USA
Xingming Sun	Nanjing University of Information Science and Technology, China

Technical Program Chairs

Aniello Castiglione	University of Salerno, Italy
Yunbiao Guo	China Information Technology Security Evaluation Center, China
Suzanne K. McIntosh	New York University, USA
Zhihua Xia	Nanjing University of Information Science and Technology, China
Victor S. Sheng	University of Central Arkansas, USA

Publication Chair

Zhaoqing Pan	Nanjing University of Information Science and Technology, China

Workshop Chair

Baowei Wang	Nanjing University of Information Science and Technology, China

Organization Chairs

Edward Wong	New York University, USA
Zhangjie Fu	Nanjing University of Information Science and Technology, China

Technical Program Committee

Saeed Arif	University of Algeria, Algeria
Anthony Ayodele	University of Maryland University College, USA

Zhifeng Bao	Royal Melbourne Institute of Technology University, Australia
Zhiping Cai	National University of Defense Technology, China
Ning Cao	Qingdao Binhai University, China
Paolina Centonze	Iona College, USA
Chin-chen Chang	Feng Chia University, Taiwan, China
Han-Chieh Chao	Taiwan Dong Hwa University, Taiwan, China
Bing Chen	Nanjing University of Aeronautics and Astronautics, China
Hanhua Chen	Huazhong University of Science and Technology, China
Xiaofeng Chen	Xidian University, China
Jieren Cheng	Hainan University, China
Lianhua Chi	IBM Research Center, Australia
Kim-Kwang Raymond Choo	University of Texas at San Antonio, USA
Ilyong Chung	Chosun University, South Korea
Robert H. Deng	Singapore Management University, Singapore
Jintai Ding	University of Cincinnati, USA
Xinwen Fu	University of Central Florida, USA
Zhangjie Fu	Nanjing University of Information Science and Technology, China
Moncef Gabbouj	Tampere University of Technology, Finland
Ruili Geng	Spectral MD, USA
Song Guo	Hong Kong Polytechnic University, SAR China
Jinsong Han	Xi'an Jiaotong University, China
Mohammad Mehedi Hassan	King Saud University, Saudi Arabia
Debiao He	Wuhan University, China
Russell Higgs	University College Dublin, Ireland
Dinh Thai Hoang	University Technology Sydney, Australia
Wien Hong	Nanfang College of Sun Yat-Sen University, China
Chih-Hsien Hsia	National Ilan University, Taiwan, China
Robert Hsu	Chung Hua University, Taiwan, China
Yongjian Hu	South China University of Technology, China
Qiong Huang	South China Agricultural University, China
Xinyi Huang	Fujian Normal University, China
Yongfeng Huang	Tsinghua University, China
Zhiqiu Huang	Nanjing University of Aeronautics and Astronautics, China
Patrick C. K. Hung	University of Ontario Institute of Technology, Canada
Farookh Hussain	University of Technology Sydney, Australia
Hai Jin	Huazhong University of Science and Technology, China
Sam Tak Wu Kwong	City University of Hong Kong, SAR China
Chin-Feng Lai	Taiwan Cheng Kung University, Taiwan, China
Loukas Lazos	University of Arizona, USA

Sungyoung Lee	Kyung Hee University, South Korea
Bin Li	Shenzhen University, China
Chengcheng Li	University of Cincinnati, USA
Feifei Li	Utah State University, USA
Jiguo Li	Hohai University, China
Jin Li	Guangzhou University, China
Jing Li	Rutgers University, USA
Kuan-Ching Li	Providence University, Taiwan, China
Peng Li	University of Aizu, Japan
Xiaolong Li	Beijing Jiaotong University, China
Yangming Li	University of Washington, USA
Luming Liang	Uber Technology, USA
Haixiang Lin	Leiden University, The Netherlands
Xiaodong Lin	University of Ontario Institute of Technology, Canada
Zhenyi Lin	Verizon Wireless, USA
Alex Liu	Michigan State University, USA
Guangchi Liu	Stratifyd Inc., USA
Guohua Liu	Donghua University, China
Joseph Liu	Monash University, Australia
Mingzhe Liu	Chengdu University of Technology, China
Pingzeng Liu	Shandong Agricultural University, China
Quansheng Liu	University of South Brittany, France
Xiaodong Liu	Edinburgh Napier University, UK
Yuling Liu	Hunan University, China
Zhe Liu	University of Waterloo, Canada
Wei Lu	Sun Yat-sen University, China
Daniel Xiapu Luo	Hong Kong Polytechnic University, SAR China
Junzhou Luo	Southeast University, China
Xiangyang Luo	Zhengzhou Science and Technology Institute, China
Suzanne K. McIntosh	New York University, USA
Nasir Memon	New York University, USA
Sangman Moh	Chosun University, South Korea
Yi Mu	University of Wollongong, Australia
Jiangqun Ni	Sun Yat-sen University, China
Rongrong Ni	Beijing Jiao Tong University, China
Rafal Niemiec	University of Information Technology and Management, Poland
Zemin Ning	Wellcome Trust Sanger Institute, UK
Shaozhang Niu	Beijing University of Posts and Telecommunications, China
Srikant Ojha	Sharda University, India
Jeff Z. Pan	University of Aberdeen, UK
Wei Pang	University of Aberdeen, UK
Rong Peng	Wuhan University, China
Chen Qian	University of California Santa Cruz, USA
Zhenxing Qian	Fudan University, China

Chuan Qin	University of Shanghai for Science and Technology, China
Jiaohua Qin	Central South University of Forestry and Technology, China
Yanzhen Qu	Colorado Technical University, USA
Zhiguo Qu	Nanjing University of Information Science and Technology, China
Kui Ren	State University of New York, USA
Arun Kumar Sangaiah	VIT University, India
Zheng-guo Sheng	University of Sussex, UK
Robert Simon Sherratt	University of Reading, UK
Yun Q. Shi	New Jersey Institute of Technology, USA
Frank Y. Shih	New Jersey Institute of Technology, USA
Biao Song	King Saud University, Saudi Arabia
Guang Sun	Hunan University of Finance and Economics, China
Jiande Sun	Shandong Normal University, China
Jianguo Sun	Harbin University of Engineering, China
Jianyong Sun	Xi'an Jiaotong University, China
Krzysztof Szczypiorski	Warsaw University of Technology, Poland
Tsuyoshi Takagi	Kyushu University, Japan
Shanyu Tang	University of West London, UK
Xianping Tao	Nanjing University, China
Jing Tian	National University of Singapore, Singapore
Yoshito Tobe	Aoyang University, Japan
Cezhong Tong	Washington University in St. Louis, USA
Pengjun Wan	Illinois Institute of Technology, USA
Cai-Zhuang Wang	Ames Laboratory, USA
Ding Wang	Peking University, China
Guiling Wang	New Jersey Institute of Technology, USA
Honggang Wang	University of Massachusetts-Dartmouth, USA
Jian Wang	Nanjing University of Aeronautics and Astronautics, China
Jie Wang	University of Massachusetts Lowell, USA
Jing Wang	Changsha University of Science and Technology, China
Jinwei Wang	Nanjing University of Information Science and Technology, China
Liangmin Wang	Jiangsu University, China
Ruili Wang	Massey University, New Zealand
Xiaojun Wang	Dublin City University, Ireland
Xiaokang Wang	St. Francis Xavier University, Canada
Zhaoxia Wang	A-Star, Singapore
Sheng Wen	Swinburne University of Technology, Australia
Jian Weng	Jinan University, China
Edward Wong	New York University, USA
Eric Wong	University of Texas at Dallas, USA

Q. M. Jonathan Wu	University of Windsor, Canada
Shaoen Wu	Ball State University, USA
Shuangkui Xia	Beijing Institute of Electronics Technology and Application, China
Lingyun Xiang	Changsha University of Science and Technology, China
Shijun Xiang	Jinan University, China
Yang Xiang	Deakin University, Australia
Yang Xiao	The University of Alabama, USA
Haoran Xie	The Education University of Hong Kong, SAR China
Naixue Xiong	Northeastern State University, USA
Xin Xu	Wuhan University of Science and Technology, China
Wei Qi Yan	Auckland University of Technology, New Zealand
Aimin Yang	Guangdong University of Foreign Studies, China
Ching-Nung Yang	Taiwan Dong Hwa University, Taiwan, China
Chunfang Yang	Zhengzhou Science and Technology Institute, China
Fan Yang	University of Maryland, USA
Guomin Yang	University of Wollongong, Australia
Ming Yang	Southeast University, China
Qing Yang	University of North Texas, USA
Yuqiang Yang	Bohai University, USA
Ming Yin	Purdue University, USA
Xinchun Yin	Yangzhou University, China
Shaodi You	Australian National University, Australia
Kun-Ming Yu	Chung Hua University, Taiwan, China
Yong Yu	University of Electronic Science and Technology of China, China
Gonglin Yuan	Guangxi University, China
Mingwu Zhang	Hubei University of Technology, China
Wei Zhang	Nanjing University of Posts and Telecommunications, China
Weiming Zhang	University of Science and Technology of China, China
Xinpeng Zhang	Fudan University, China
Yan Zhang	Simula Research Laboratory, Norway
Yanchun Zhang	Victoria University, Australia
Yao Zhao	Beijing Jiaotong University, China
Linna Zhou	University of International Relations, China

Organizing Committee

Xianyi Chen	Nanjing University of Information Science and Technology, China
Yadang Chen	Nanjing University of Information Science and Technology, China
Beijing Chen	Nanjing University of Information Science and Technology, China

Huajun Huang	Central South University of Forestry and Technology, China
Jielin Jiang	Nanjing University of Information Science and Technology, China
Zilong Jin	Nanjing University of Information Science and Technology, China
Yan Kong	Nanjing University of Information Science and Technology, China
Yiwei Li	Columbia University, USA
Yuling Liu	Hunan University, China
Lirui Qiu	Nanjing University of Information Science and Technology, China
Zhiguo Qu	Nanjing University of Information Science and Technology, China
Guang Sun	Hunan University of Finance and Economics, China
Huiyu Sun	New York University, USA
Le Sun	Nanjing University of Information Science and Technology, China
Jian Su	Nanjing University of Information Science and Technology, China
Lina Tan	Hunan University of Commerce, China
Qing Tian	Nanjing University of Information Science and Technology, China
Yuan Tian	King Saud University, Saudi Arabia
Zuwei Tian	Hunan First Normal University, China
Xiaoliang Wang	Hunan University of Science and Technology, China
Lingyun Xiang	Changsha University of Science and Technology, China
Lizhi Xiong	Nanjing University of Information Science and Technology, China
Leiming Yan	Nanjing University of Information Science and Technology, China
Hengfu Yang	Hunan First Normal University, China
Li Yu	Nanjing University of Information Science and Technology, China
Zhili Zhou	Nanjing University of Information Science and Technology, China

Contents – Part I

Cloud Computing

Cloud Computing

Fuzzy Clustering: A New Clustering Method in Heterogeneous Medical Records Searching

Zhenyu Zhang[1], Wencheng Sun[1], Zhiping Cai[1(✉)], Ningzheng Luo[2], and Ming Wang[2]

[1] National University of Defense Technology, College of Computer, Changsha 410073, China
zpcai@nudt.edu.cn
[2] Shenzhen Ningyuan Technology Co., Ltd,, Shenzhen 518052, China

Abstract. Clustering of heterogeneous medical records plays an extremely important role in understanding pathology, identifying correlations between medical records, and adjuvant treatment of medical records. In view of the instability of the existing medical record clustering algorithm in the processing of heterogeneous medical record data, this paper proposes a medical record clustering algorithm based on fuzzy matrix for integrated structure and unstructured data. Firstly, the algorithm de-correlates the initial data based on the Spearman correlation coefficient to avoid the data correlation error of subsequent analysis. Second, this paper introduces the posterior probability theory for stability weighting, comprehensive structure and unstructured data. Finally, according to fuzzy transitive closure principle, the medical records are clustered from the perspective of relationship transformation. Compared with the existing partial clustering algorithm, the algorithm proposed in this paper improves the clustering accuracy. In addition, it also solves the dynamic and hierarchical problems of medical record clustering to some extent.

Keywords: Medical record clustering · Spearman correlation · Posterior probability · Fuzzy transfer closure · Level clustering

1 Introduction

Please note that the first paragraph of a section or subsection is not indented. The first paragraphs that follows a table, figure, equation etc. does not have an indent, either. With the application of digital technology in the medical field, hospitals and medical centers produce and process large amounts of medical data every day, including medical records, electronic medical records, various medical images and inspection reports by the widespread use of PACS (Picture Archiving and Communication Systems) and HIS (Hospital Information System) systems. How to extract the available information from these large amounts of heterogeneous data is of great research value and application prospect [1]. The clustering of heterogeneous medical records is such a technology. By clustering a large number of heterogeneous medical records, it is helpful for understanding all kinds of pathology and identification of the relationship between the diseases in addition to clinical disease adjuvant treatment.

© Springer Nature Switzerland AG 2019
X. Sun et al. (Eds.): ICAIS 2019, LNCS 11632, pp. 3–15, 2019.
https://doi.org/10.1007/978-3-030-24274-9_1

The existing classical clustering algorithms, including K-means algorithm [2], mean shift clustering, genetic algorithm, DBSCAN algorithm [3], etc., are clustering algorithms by clustering isomorphic data based on distance. However, these algorithms have obvious shortcomings in clustering medical records due to the heterogeneity of medical record data. The medical record data generally contains disease data information of various structures, including structural data [4], text data, image data, etc. Different information has complementarity and correlation. The complementarity makes the information complete, and the correlation leads to the imbalance of data characteristics. The existing clustering algorithm often has a large clustering error due to the correlation between data when considering a variety of structural data. At present, the clustering technology of heterogeneous medical records need further analysis.

This paper comprehensively considers the structural data and non-structural data in the medical record information. By de-correlation operation and weighting processing of two types of data, the concept of the medical record distance index is proposed based on two aspects of information. Thus, the medical record distance relation matrix is established. Aiming at the obtained relation matrix, a medical record clustering algorithm based on fuzzy relation correlation principle is designed. The algorithm has higher clustering accuracy, and the multi-level clustering structure can be obtained through the selection of different thresholds [5], which solves the hierarchical problem of clustering to some extent.

2 Problem Description

Accurate description of medical records is the basis of medical record clustering. This paper uses the graph structure to describe the relationship between the medical records [6], and uses $WG = (V, E, T, S)$ to represent the medical record relationship, in which, V is the set of graph nodes, indicating the medical records; E is the graph edge collection, indicating the relationship between the medical records; T is the graph node structure information, indicating the structural data of medical records; and S is the non-structural information of the graph node, indicating the non-structural data of the medical record. Therefore, we separate the structural and non-structural medical record information to describe the overall medical record to enrich and arrange the original information of the medical record cluster, which lays a foundation for the improvement of clustering accuracy.

$$T = \left[t_i^j \right]_{n \times m'} = \begin{bmatrix} t_1^1 & t_1^2 & \cdots & t_1^{m'} \\ t_2^1 & t_2^2 & \cdots & t_2^{m'} \\ \vdots & \vdots & & \vdots \\ t_n^1 & t_n^2 & & t_n^{m'} \end{bmatrix} \quad S = \left[s_i^j \right]_{n \times m} = \begin{bmatrix} s_1^1 & s_1^2 & \cdots & s_1^m \\ s_2^1 & s_2^2 & \cdots & s_2^m \\ \vdots & \vdots & & \vdots \\ s_n^1 & s_n^2 & & s_n^m \end{bmatrix}$$

Medical record clustering is a kind of intrinsic topological characteristic of medical record. It is naturally divided into some medical record groups, which makes two medical records in the same medical record group more similar than two medical records in different medical records. In order to discover or identify a medical record category, the cluster structure is uniquely determined if it can be determined whether any two medical records are in the same category. The matrix is described as $P = [p_{ij}]_{n \times n}$, where $p_{ij} \in \{0, 1\}$, 0 means that two medical records are in different categories and 1 means that two medical records are in the same category. It should be pointed out that the medical record with itself must be in the same category. If A and B are in the same category, B and A are in the same category, and vice versa. If A and C are in the same category and B and C are in the same category, B and C are also in the same category.

The above three conditions in the matrix P can be symbolized as follows: $p_{ii} = 1$, namely the reflexivity is satisfied; $p_{ij} = p_{ji}$, namely the symmetry is satisfied; if $p_{ij} = 1$ and $p_{jk} = 1$, $p_{ik} = 1$, namely the transitivity is satisfied. Therefore, the matrix P reflecting the cluster of medical records is a common equivalence matrix [7].

Thus, the problem can be described as follows:

$$f(T, S) = P \qquad (1)$$

where T represents the structural information of the medical record, S represents the non-structural information of the medical record, P represents the clustering structure which is a common equivalence matrix, and the function f represents the mapping relationship between the information of the heterogeneous medical record and the clustering structure.

3 Fuzzy Clustering

3.1 Medical Record Distance Measure

As mentioned in the previous problem modeling, this paper obtains the cluster structure of the medical record through a series of mapping relationships from the complete information of the medical record. First, we need to pre-process data on the two structural information of the medical record. In order to avoid the clustering result being affected by the correlation between two medical records, this section conducts correlation analysis and de-correlation processing [8]. Simultaneously, based on the designed stability weighting method, the concept of medical record distance is proposed, and the two kinds of structural information are combined to cluster the medical records.

3.1.1 Correlation Analysis of Medical Record Information
The original data of the medical record considered in this paper is divided into two types: structured key-value data and unstructured key-text data. The structured data can be directly represented by the model mentioned above. The unstructured data needs to be preprocessed with data. The text data is extracted based on the medical corpus, and converted into structured data. Thus, the original medical record data is converted into a data format conforming to the model.

The characteristics of the medical records in the cluster structure are considered as follows: the similarity of the features of the same type of medical records is relatively high, and the similarity of the characteristics of different types of medical records is relatively low. Therefore, compared with the medical record feature value, the feature similarity can better reflect the clustering of the medical record. This paper describes the feature similarity by Euclidean distance.

The structural data and unstructured data in the medical record data are highly correlated because of their different sources of information. When the medical record is clustered based on the full information, the correlation between two medical records is a non-negligible influence factor. Otherwise, it will bring the superposition effect to the later comprehensive discussion. At present, there is no unified standard in the quantification of medical records. The quantization error will make the relational data deviate from the theoretical normal distribution, resulting in the overall distribution type of the attribute unknown. Thus, this paper uses the Spearman correlation coefficient to measure the correlation between two medical records, which is used to describe the association of data that does not obey the normal distribution, the grade data, and the data whose overall distribution type is unknown.

Spearman correlation coefficient is applied to measure the correlation between two medical records. X and Y sets are taken to perform the corresponding values in the matrices W and N, and each set has n^2 elements, X_i, Y_i are the $i(0 < i \leq n^2)$ element in the corresponding set, and X and Y are respectively sorted (ascending or descending at the same time). The corresponding sorted set x and y, Spearman correlation coefficient are:

$$\rho = 1 - \frac{6}{n^2(n^4 - 1)} \cdot \sum_{i=1}^{n^2} d_i^2 \tag{2}$$

$$d_i = x_i - y_i \tag{3}$$

where x_i and y_i are the number of sorts of X_i in set X and the order of Y_i in set Y, respectively.

Based on the above analysis, similarity and decorrelation processing is performed by the following operations:

$$n'_{ij} = 1 - \sqrt{\frac{1}{m} \sum_{k=1}^{m} (s_i^k - s_j^k)^2} \tag{4}$$

$$w_{ij} = 1 - \sqrt{\frac{1}{m'} \sum_{k=1}^{m'} (t_i^k - t_j^k)^2} \tag{5}$$

$$n_{ij} = n'_{ij} - \frac{\rho \cdot \sqrt{\sigma_W}}{\sqrt{\sigma_{N'}}} \cdot w_{ij} \tag{6}$$

where n'_{ij} is the non-structural medical record similarity, w'_{ij} is the structural medical record similarity, ρ is the correlation coefficient, σ_W is the variance of W, and σ_N is the variance of N'. The resulting intensity-independent attribute matrix is: $N = [n_{ij}]_{n \times n}$.

Hence, the correlation process in this paper to solve the problem is as follows:

$$f_1(T, S) = (W, N) \tag{7}$$

where W is a structural relationship matrix, N is a non-structural relationship matrix, and function f1 is a correlation culling function, which is a function of function f.

3.1.2 Medical Record Distance Index

(1) Stability empowerment

The difficulty of the problem studied in this paper is how to determine the degree of influence on the cluster structure on caused by the two types of data information. Currently [9], for the comprehensive analysis of unrelated variables, there are several solutions. However, the weights in most methods require subjective endowment. Due to the lack of relevant theoretical knowledge in the clustering of medical records, it is difficult to obtain the weight of the influence on the clustering structure based on the mechanism model. Therefore, this type of method is more subjective in the clustering of medical records. Therefore, this paper proposes a weight assignment method with higher precision based only on the original data.

We design a weight-fitting method based on data stability to synthesize multiple influencing factors and solve the subjective problems that are often encountered in the process. This method is based on the idea of posterior probability in information theory [10]. The posterior probability refers to the probability that the receiver knows that the message originated from a sender after receiving a message. This is an idea based on the distribution of the results of the discussion conditions. The result set is relatively stable to a certain extent. Therefore, the abruptness of the factors with an influence on the formation of the result should be limited, which shows factors with a greater impact on the results are relatively stable. According to this principle, we achieve the stability of the results by limiting the abruptness of the factors with a greater impact on the results. Therefore, the influence weight of the medical record structure data and the non-structural data on the cluster structure is positively correlated with its own stability. Its stability can be reflected by the variance.

The variances of two uncorrelated variable sequence sets $A_t = \{a_1, a_2 \cdots a_t\}$ and $B_t = \{b_1, b_2 \cdots b_t\}$ are denoted by σ_A and σ_B, respectively. Two variable sequences can be combined by the above method to obtain $C_t = \{c_1, c_2 \cdots c_t\}$:

$$c_i = \frac{\sigma_B}{\sigma_A + \sigma_B} a_i + \frac{\sigma_A}{\sigma_A + \sigma_B} b_i \tag{8}$$

(2) Two-degree distance in cluster

In the previous sections, we have only analyzed the impact of the direct relationship between the two medical records on the formation of clustering structure. The clustering structure is usually a collection of many medical records. The clustering coefficient of the internal medical records is very high, and the clustering coefficient is reflected by the indirect relationship between the medical records. Considering this nature of the cluster structure, this paper regards the indirect relationship between the two medical records as another influencing factor of the cluster structure [11]. Specifically, the clustering relationship between medical records is not only determined by the direct relationship of the medical records, but also influenced by the indirect relationship of the two neighbors. The two neighbors refer to medical records that require two steps to arrive [12]. The difference between the distance of the two medical records and the other medical records is used to measure the impact factors of the two neighbors:

$$\lambda_{ij} = \sqrt{\frac{1}{n} \sum_{k=1}^{n} [1 - (w_{ik} - w_{jk})]^2} \tag{9}$$

This paper processes the concept of "medical record distance". Based on the above analysis, by comprehensive stability weighting and clustering coefficient operation, according to formulas (8) and (9), the medical record distance reflecting the clustering situation of the two medical records is defined as follows:

$$l_{ij} = \frac{1}{\sqrt{n}} \times \left(\frac{\sigma_N \cdot w_{ij}}{\sigma_N + \sigma_W} \cdot \sqrt{\sum_{k=1}^{n} [1 - (w_{ik} - w_{jk})]^2} + \frac{\sigma_W \cdot n_{ij}}{\sigma_N + \sigma_W} \cdot \sqrt{\sum_{k=1}^{n} [1 - (n_{ik} - n_{jk})]^2} \right) \tag{10}$$

where σ_N is the matrix N element variance, σ_W is the matrix W element variance, and l_{ij} is the medical record distance between medical record i and medical record j. The disease distance matrix is obtained as $L = [l_{ij}]_{n \times n}$.

Hence, this paper processes the following process to solve the problem:

$$f_2(W, N) = L \tag{11}$$

where W is the structural relationship matrix, N is the non-structural relationship matrix, L is the medical record distance matrix, function f_2 is the medical record distance function, and is the function of the function f.

3.2   Medical Record Distance Measure

As mentioned in the previous problem modeling, the cluster structure finally obtained in this paper is a common equivalence relation. The community distance matrix $L = [l_{ij}]_{n \times n}$ that has been obtained so far is also a representation of the relationship. Therefore, the process of medical record clustering is essentially the process of relationship transformation, which is the process of transforming from a normal relationship to an equivalence relationship. The fuzzy relation theory can solve this problem very well, and it can complete the transformation of the relationship through a series of fuzzy operations. This section analyzes the processed medical record data based on the fuzzy relation to cluster the medical records.

3.2.1 Fuzzy Equivalence of Medical Record Distance

The medical record distance matrix $L = [l_{ij}]_{n \times n}$ is represented as a fuzzy relation in the node set $V \times V$. Since the L value interval is (0, 1), the matrix L can reflect the corresponding fuzzy relation value. In the fuzzy relation, $l_{ij} \in [0, 1]$, $l_{ii} = 0$, $l_{ij} = l_{ji}$, and the fuzzy relation only satisfies the symmetry. To solve the problem, the fuzzy relation needs to be processed to satisfy both reflexivity and transitivity.

To make the relationship satisfy the reflexivity, we deal with the medical record distance matrix as follows: if $l_{ii} = 1$, then $l_{ij} \in [0, 1]$, $l_{ij} = l_{ji}$, $l_{ii} = 1$. The matrix, a fuzzy similar matrix, satisfies both symmetry and reflexivity.

To make the relationship satisfy the transitivity, we use the transitive closure method in fuzzy mathematics to process the medical record distance matrix L. Since the medical record distance matrix L is a fuzzy similar matrix [13], its power matrix is continuously increasing and the convergence index is (n–1), which satisfies $L \subseteq L^2 \subseteq L^3 \cdots \subseteq L^{n-1} = L^n$. Hence, for any fuzzy matrix $L \in F_{n \times n}$, the transitive closure of the matrix L satisfies the transitivity, which means that the matrix is a fuzzy equivalent matrix. The max-min product and transitive closure between fuzzy matrices are as follows [14]:

$$d_{ij} = \bigvee_{1 \le k \le p} (a_{ik} \wedge b_{kj}) = \max_{1 \le k \le p} (a_{ik} \wedge b_{kj}) \tag{12}$$

$$T_c(L) = \bigcup_{k=1}^{\infty} L^k = L^{n-1} \tag{13}$$

The essence of fuzzy equivalence of the medical record distance matrix is that the max-min product of the power of the matrix L is transformed into a fuzzy equivalence matrix according to the principle of fuzzy transit closure.

Hence, for the solution of the problem, this paper processes the following process:

$$f_3(L) = L^{n-1} \tag{14}$$

where L is the medical record distance matrix, L^{n-1} is the (n–1) times max-min product of L, and function f_3 is the fuzzy transfer closure function, which is the function of function f.

3.2.2 Fuzzy Relation Determination

In this paper, we need to obtain a common equivalence matrix that can reflect the clustering structure. We also need to convert the fuzzy equivalence matrix with the value interval (0, 1) into a common equivalence matrix with the value {0, 1}. The truncation relation operation in fuzzy mathematics can complete the transformation, and L is the fuzzy relation in $V \times V$. For any $\alpha \in [0, 1]$, the characteristic function of the α-cut relationship is:

$$\mu_{L_\alpha}(x,y) = \begin{cases} 1 & \mu_L(x,y) \geq \alpha \\ 0 & \mu_L(x,y) < \alpha \end{cases} \tag{15}$$

Thus, under the premise of no change in the equivalence of the relationship, the fuzzy relation is transformed into a certain relation. Finally, a clear medical record division relationship is obtained - medical record clustering. It is necessary to point out that there are different clustering structures based on different intercept values, that is, the clustering of the medical record has multiple levels.

Hence, for the solution of the problem, this paper processes the following process:

$$f_4(L^{n-1}) = P \tag{16}$$

where L^{n-1} is the (n-1) times max-min product of L, P is the cluster structure matrix, and function f4 is the truncation function, which is the function of function f.

4   Algorithm Description and Analysis

4.1   Algorithm Description

Based on the above methods, this paper proposes a new concept of medical record distance from the full information of the medical records by the correlation analysis and weighting of the structural medical record information and the non-structural medical record information. Through the fuzzy relationship related theory to cluster medical record, this paper presents a new method for clustering medical records. The algorithm model is as follows.

$$f(T,S) = f_4(f_3(f_2(f_1(T,S)))) = P \tag{17}$$

where T is the structural information of the medical record, S is the non-structural information of the medical record, and P is the clustering structure of the medical record. The function f represents the mapping relationship between the medical information and the cluster structure. The function f1 is the correlation culling function, the function f2 is the medical record distance function, the function f3 is the fuzzy transitive closure function, and the function f4 is the truncation operation function.

The specific description of the medical record clustering fuzzy relation algorithm is as follows.

Medical record clustering fuzzy relational algorithm

Input: Structure matrix T, unstructured matrix S
Output: Medical record clustering structure P
(1) for all(Medical record group)
(2)   n ← European distance
(3) define D ← Sorting difference
(4) define ρ ← Spearman Correlation coefficient (D)

(5) for all(Medical record group) $n_{ij} = n'_{ij} - \rho \cdot \sqrt{\sigma_W} \cdot w_{ij} / \sqrt{\sigma_{N'}}$

(6) for all(Medical record group)
(7)   for all(Medical record)

(8)   define $\lambda_{ij} = \lambda_{ij} + [1 - (w_{ik} - w_{jk})]^2 / n$

(9)   define $\gamma_{ij} = \gamma_{ij} + [1 - (n_{ik} - n_{jk})]^2 / n$

(10) define σ_W ← (W variance); σ_N ← (N variance)

(11) $\sigma_W = \sigma_N / (\sigma_W + \sigma_N)$; $\sigma_N = \sigma_W / (\sigma_W + \sigma_N)$

(12) for all(Medical record group)
(13)   define $l_{ij} = \sigma_W \lambda_{ij} w_{ij} + \sigma_N \gamma_{ij} n_{ij}$

(14) for all(Medical record)
(15)   for all(Medical record group)

(16) $l_{ij} = \bigvee_{1 \le k \le p} (l_{ik} \wedge l_{kj}) = \max_{1 \le k \le p} (l_{ik} \wedge l_{kj})$

(17) define a ← input
(18) if($l'_{ij} \ge \alpha$): $p_{ij} = 1$
(19) else: $p_{ij} = 0$
(20) if(P== expected): over
(21) else: turn(17)
(22) return P

The algorithm flow is shown in Fig. 1. By the medical record information, the structural data and text data in the medical record information are obtained. Feature is extracted from the text data to obtain structural data. The modified structure matrix is obtained from the correlation analysis of two matrices to remove the correlation and avoid correlation errors. The two correction matrices are weighted to obtain the full information matrix of the medical record distance, and the new medical record distance effectively avoids the subjective drawbacks of empowerment. The fuzzy equivalent closure process is performed on the medical record distance matrix to obtain a fuzzy equivalence matrix. Based on the truncation relationship, a common equivalence matrix that reflects the structure of the medical record category is obtained. Through these operations, the process from the full information of the medical record to the clustering of the medical record is realized.

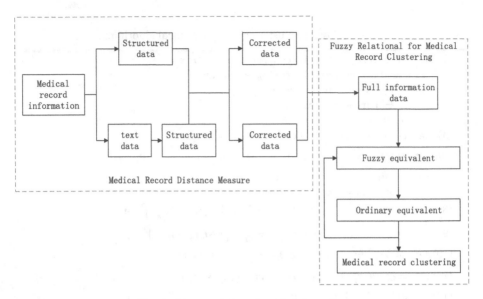

Fig. 1. Fuzzy relation algorithm flow chart

4.2   Algorithm Analysis

The program clustering algorithm proposed in this paper is programmed and compared based on the data sets of heterogeneous medical records and classical algorithms. This article uses the actual medical record data of a medical data center. The clustering evaluation index uses the standard mutual information Normalized Mutual Information (NMI) and the Adjusted Rand Index (ARI) [15, 16]. Specifically, the Rand Index, by giving the actual category information, uses the ratio of the sum in all pairs of elements whose actual and the consequential values are the same and different. However, under the random result, the Rand index is not close to 0. Therefore, the Rand index is adjusted by normalization. NMI is a normalized mutual information that measures the degree of coincidence between algorithmic partitioning results and real results. Experiments are conducted through the medical record data set. The distribution of NMI and ARI, and the time complexity comparison of each algorithm based on different data amounts are shown in Figs. 2, 3 and Table 1.

Under different medical record amounts, the ARI of the cluster structure obtained by the algorithm in this paper is higher and not sensitive to community parameters (Fig. 2). Under different medical record amounts, the NMI of the cluster structure obtained by the algorithm in this paper is higher and more sensitive to the size of the medical record, which shows a faster decline when the medical record size is larger (Fig. 3). The time complexity of the algorithm in this paper is relatively high and not suitable for real-time large-scale medical record clustering, which is also the direction that should be paid attention to and improved in the future work (Table 1).

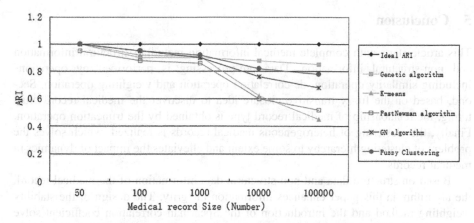

Fig. 2. ARI of each algorithm under different medical record amounts.

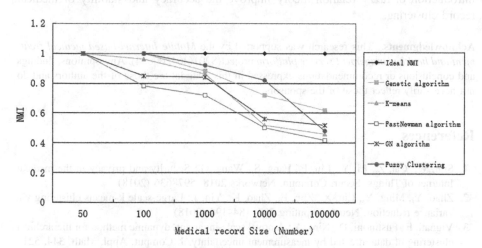

Fig. 3. NMI of each algorithm under different medical record amounts.

Table 1. Time complexity of each algorithm.

GN	Fast-Newman	Genetic algorithm	K-means	Fuzzy clustering
$O[m^2 n]$	$O[n^2]$	$O[dg(n + t)^2]$	$O[(n + t) \lg^2 n]$	$O[n^2 \lg n]$

In general, the algorithm with high accuracy and stability in this paper has a relatively high time complexity compared with other algorithms, which is not sensitive to the size of the medical record. It is suitable for medical record clustering of small-scale, medium-scale and large-scale medical records with low real-time requirements.

5 Conclusion

This article starts with complete medical information including structural information and non-structural information. Data pre-processing is performed by operations including similarity operation, de-correlation operation and weighting operation. Second, based on the fuzzy transitive closure idea to discover the medical record clustering, the relationship of medical record type is obtained by the truncation operation. Finally, the clustering of heterogeneous medical records is realized, which solves the problem of clustering hierarchy to some extent and alleviates the impact of dynamics in medical records.

Based on structure data and non-structural data information of the medical record, the algorithm in this paper enhances information integrity. The design of the stability weighting method and the introduction of the Spearman correlation coefficient solve the information interference problem. The concept of medical record distance and the introduction of fuzzy relation theory improve the accuracy and stability of medical record clustering.

Acknowledgments. This research was supported by the *Mobile Internet-based medical treatment and health management service platform* project(S2016I64200024). Any opinions, findings and conclusions or recommendations expressed in this material are those of the authors and do not necessarily reflect those of the sponsors.

References

1. Sun, W., Cai, Z., Li, Y., Liu, F., Fang, S., Wang, G.: Security and privacy in the medical Internet of Things. Secur. Commun. Networks **2018**, 5978636 (2018)
2. Zhao, Y., Ming, Y., Liu, X., Zhu, E., Zhao, K., Yin, J.: Large-scale k-means clustering via variance reduction. Neurocomputing **307**, 184–194 (2018)
3. Vignati, F., Fustinoni, D., Niro, A.: A novel scale-invariant, dynamic method for hierarchical clustering of data affected by measurement uncertainty. J. Comput. Appl. Math. **344**, 521–531 (2018)
4. Sun, W., Cai, Z., Li, Y., Liu, F., Fang, S., Wang, G.: Data processing and text mining technologies on electronic medical records: a review. J. Healthcare Eng. **2018**, 1–9 (2018)
5. Chen, Y., Tang, S., Bouguila, N., Wang, C., Du, J., Li, H.: A fast clustering algorithm based on pruning unnecessary distance computations in DBSCAN for high-dimensional data. Pattern Recogn. **83**, 375–387 (2018)
6. Dasari, P.R., Chidambaram, M., Seshagiri Rao, A.: Simple method of calculating dynamic set-point weighting parameters for time delayed unstable processes. IFAC PapersOnLine **51** (1), 395–400 (2018)
7. Fan, X., Lu, H., Zhang, Z.: Direct calibration transfer to principal components via canonical correlation analysis. Chemometr. Intell. Lab. Syst. **181**, 21–28 (2018)
8. Boixader, D., Recasens, J.: On the relationship between fuzzy subgroups and indistinguishability operators. Fuzzy Sets Syst. (2018)
9. Fang, S., et al.: Feature selection method based on class discriminative degree for intelligent medical diagnosis. CMC Comput. Mater. Continua **55**, 419–433 (2018)
10. Liu, D.: The equivalence relationship of matrix and the corresponding equivalence classes. Appl. Mech. Mater. **3512**, 651–653 (2014)

11. Xiong, Z., Shen, Q., Wang, Y., Zhu, C.: Paragraph vector representation based on word to vector and CNN learning. CMC Comput. Mater. Continua **055**(2), 213–227 (2018)
12. Friston, K.J., Penny, W.: Posterior probability maps and SPMs. Neuroimage **19**(3), 1240–1249 (2003)
13. Vinh, L.T., Lee, S., Park, Y.-T., d'Auriol, B.J.: A novel feature selection method based on normalized mutual information. Appl. Intell. **37**(1), 100–120 (2012)
14. Rotshtein, A.P.: Ranking of system elements based on fuzzy relation of influence and transitive closure. Cybern. Syst. Anal. **53**(1), 57–66 (2017)
15. Wu, X., Song, Z.: Simplification of the Tsukamoto method for solving the max-min fuzzy relation equation. J. Luoyang Inst. Technol. (Nat. Sci. Ed.) **27**(02), 79–82 + 93 (2017)
16. Steinley, D., Brusco, M.J., Hubert, L.: The variance of the adjusted Rand index. Psychol. Methods **21**(2), 261 (2016)

NOAA-LSTM: A New Method of Dialect Identification

Shuai Ye, Cuixia Li$^{(\boxtimes)}$, Ruoyan Zhao, and Weidong Wu

Software and Applied Science and Technology Institute of Zhengzhou
University, Zhengzhou, China
qyliying@126.com

Abstract. Dialect Identification (DID) is a particular case of general Language Identification (LID). Due to the high similarity of dialects and similar phonetic features in adjacent areas, DID is a more challenging problem. Long Short-Term Memory (LSTM) networks tend to be used and do well in LID tasks in recent years, but do not have a good performance on DID tasks. In this paper, NOAA (New One-against-all) binary classifier based on OAA (One-against-all) binary classifier obtained proposed, and a new dialect recognition method was combining NOAA with LSTM networks was offered under the guidance of Chinese humanities. The new approach achieves better performance on a DID task than a single LSTM network. The experiment was conducted based on six major dialects in China, and trained under the acoustic characteristics of log Mel-scale filter banks energies (FBANK). Experimental results on six dialects recognition tasks indicate that the accuracy of the new method is higher than that of a single LSTM network.

Keywords: Dialect Identification · LSTM · Binary classifier

1 Introduction

Chinese Dialect Identification (DID) is a technology that can determine the dialect by a segment of speech [1]. During the past several decades, researchers at home and abroad have made continuous breakthroughs in the real-time, accuracy and multilingual aspects of Language Identification (LID). However, Dialect Identification (DID) is a virtually unexplored field in Language Identification (LID). DID is a much more challenging task than Mandarin identification owing to the similarity between regional dialects [2–4].

Chinese DID can be widely used in Multilanguage information processing, machine translation, assisted manual consultation and many other fields. Besides, it can also be used for military information retrieval and forensic identification. Dialect Identification was first studied in Taiwan [5], and then scholars participate in research work in Singapore [6]. At the present stage, there is much related research work in China [7]. How to solve the accent, that is, the Dialect Identification (DID) problem, has become the focus of competition in the next stage of speech recognition.

Chinese dialects not only use a common way of writing and vocabulary, but also share an extraordinarily similar pronunciation system, but the same language has

© Springer Nature Switzerland AG 2019
X. Sun et al. (Eds.): ICAIS 2019, LNCS 11632, pp. 16–26, 2019.
https://doi.org/10.1007/978-3-030-24274-9_2

different intonations, and parts of these intonations are so different that they are difficult to understand. This prosodic information in the dialects of neighbouring regions has numerous similarities, and human perception experience believes that prosodic information in these intonations is important for dialect classification [8]. The concept of Chinese dialect can be traced back to the Zhou Dynasty in 2500 years ago [9]. Due to the customs of different regions and the long-term migration habits of people in different regions, the rhythm information in the dialects of neighbouring regions is similar, luckily, in distant areas is very different. So the dialects can be identified and classified according to the differences of rhythm information between the dialects.

In the research of Language Identification (LID), common algorithms including Deep Neural Networks (DNNs) [10], Convolutional Neural Networks (CNNs) [4], Recurrent Neural Networks (RNNs) [11], and Long Short-Term Memory (LSTM) networks [12]. These algorithms have achieved excellent results in LID, but are not satisfactory in the performance of DID. This paper proposes a new method of DID. In the identification process, the dialects far away from each other are grouped to expand their diversities, so that the features between dialects are enormously visible, and then enter the next the LSTM networks classifies these dialects. The improved OAA(One-against-all) binary classifier combined with LSTMs according to the historical factors of Chinese humanities achieve better identification performance than single Long Short-Term Memory (LSTM) networks.

2 Related Works

2.1 Long Short-Term Memory (LSTM) Networks

Deep learning [13] is an extremely effective method to extract data characteristics in recent years. Speech is a typical sequential signal, and Recurrent Neural Networks (RNNs) is a model suitable for handling sequence data. Besides, it is based on the recurrent network structure and can use the sequence information of the data itself to discover the internal rules and characteristics of the sequence. Recurrent Neural Networks (RNNs) add the "memory" component to the Fully Connected (FC) DNN layers. The calculation of the current state depends on only the current input, but the results of the previous time [14]. However, due to the existence of "loop" structure, Recurrent Neural Networks (RNN) is easy to sink into the problem of gradient vanishing or gradient explosion when dealing with long sequence speeches. For the sake of solving the long-term dependency problem in RNNs, Schmidhuber and others proposed Long Short-Term Memory Networks (LSTM) [15].

For the standard Recurrent Neural Networks (RNNs), the current hidden layer state is composed of the input information at this time and all previous hidden layer state information. The hidden layer of standard RNN has only one cell state, that is h. The volume limitation of memory cells leads to exponential decay of early memory, which is more sensitive to short-term input. LSTM model adds a memory unit named c based on the original short-term memory unit named h to achieve the goal that maintains long-term memory. In order to control the long-term state named c, the LSTM leads into three gate controllers: input gate, forget gate and output gate. The gate controller determines the proportion of information that can be transmitted [12] (see Fig. 1).

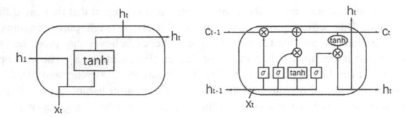

Fig. 1. LSTM improvements for RNN (Three more door controllers and one memory unit C_t)

Generation of Temporary Memory Units. As shown in formula (1). Before the new memory unit C_t is generated, a temporary memory unit c' is generated. The input layer neurons at time t and the hidden layer cells at time $t - 1$ are linearly combined with their respective weighting matrices, followed by the nonlinear activation function of $tanh()$, and the output c'_t of the temporary memory unit at time t is obtained.

$$c'_t = tanh\left(W^{(c)}x_t + U^{(c)}h_{t-1}\right) \tag{1}$$

Input Gate. There is an input gate before the generation of memory unit C. Its function is to judge the effectiveness of memory information stored in temporary memory unit c'. According to the input layer and the last hidden layer unit, we can estimate whether the temporary memory unit is retained or not, as to determine the extent to which it is involved in building the final memory, as shown in formula (2).

$$i_t = \sigma\left(W^{(i)}x_t + U^{(i)}h_{t-1}\right) \tag{2}$$

Forget Gate. The forget gate is similar to the input gate in mathematical form, it determines the importance of previous memory units to current memory units. Similarly, the information received by the input neuron and the storage of the previous hidden unit determines whether the previous memory unit is retained.

$$f_t = \sigma(W^{(f)}x_t + U^{(f)}h_{t-1}) \tag{3}$$

Generation of Final Memory Unit. As shown in formula (4), the generation of the final memory unit C_t of the current time t depends on the memory unit C_{t-1} of the past time $t - 1$ that controlled by the forget gate f_t and the temporary memory unit c'_t controlled by the input gate it, add the output of these two outputs to get the final memory unit.

$$c_t = f_t \cdot c'_t + i_t \cdot c'_t \tag{4}$$

Output Gate. The function of output gate is to distinguish memory unit from hidden layer unit, in memory unit C_t, a great quantity of information is stored, not only a short-term memory of temporary memory units but also a long-term memory of previous memory units. A large number of information is redundant, and all the information of the memory unit flows into the hidden layer as the final output, which will affect the capability of the model. The mathematical form of the output gate is propinquity to the input gate and forget gate, as shown in formula (5). The memory cell passes through a nonlinear function *tanh()*, and then filters the information of the output gate, for the iteration of the hidden layer cell, as shown in formula(6).

$$o_t = \sigma(W^{(o)}x_t + U^{(o)}h_{t-1}) \tag{5}$$

$$h_t = o_t\, tanh(c_t) \tag{6}$$

Input the training data to LSTM network, the output of the LSTM network is received through the forward calculation of the logical framework, that is hidden layer element $h \in R^{D_h}$, D_h indicates the number of neurons in the hidden layer. For the classification problem, we can map to a linear output layer whose weight matrix is $W^{(s)}$, and calculate the probability distribution of the classification results following the *softmax* function, then the LSTM network cost function is calculated according to formula (8).

$$y'_t = softmax\left(W^{(S)}h_t\right) \tag{7}$$

$$J^{(t)}(q) = -\sum_v y_{t,j} \times \log_2(y'_{t,j}) \tag{8}$$

In the above formula, v represents the number of classifications, $y_{t,j}$ represents the true probability of belonging to class j at time t. $y'_{t,j}$, indicates the training accuracy of class j under time t.

2.2 Improved OAA(One-Against-All) Binary Classifier

Binary or two item classification is a task that based on classification rules to classify the elements of a given set into two groups. In practical applications, the multi-classification problem is more common than binary classification problem, constructing a multi-classifier by combining multiple binary classifiers is a common way [16]. There are three binary classification algorithms: One-against-all (OAA), One-against-one (OAO) and Directed Acyclic Graph (DAG). These three binary classification methods all exist the problem that with the increase of the number of classes, the number of sub-classifiers is larger at the same time the training time and testing time is much longer. To solve this problem, improving the OAA classification method, which is called NOAA (New One-against-all). It combines several binary classifiers to construct a multi-classifier, and then uses a strategy to determine the final class of the output sample. In the OAA binary classifier, for a k-classification problem, one class is distinguished each time, and all classes are obtained through k-1 steps [17]. For the NOAA binary classifier, when solving a k-classification problem, if k is an even, the k/2 classes are regarded as one big class and the remaining k/2 classes as another big class, and so forth, until the final classification results are obtained. If k is an odd number, then (k + 1)/2 classes are taken as one big class and the remaining (k − 1)/2 classes are taken as another big class. The final classification result is obtained by the same method.

Compared with OAA algorithm, NOAA (New One-against-all) algorithm has the advantages of fewer classification steps, fewer repetitive operations and higher classification speed. In the process of classification and combination, according to the actual situation, the category with lower similarity can be selected and combined into a large category to distinguish, which enlarges the difference of the combination category, reduces the difficulty coefficient of classification in the subsequent process, and improves the classification accuracy. The framework of the OAA (One-against-all) classification algorithm and the NOAA (New One-against-all) classification algorithm are shown in Figs. 2 and 3, respectively.

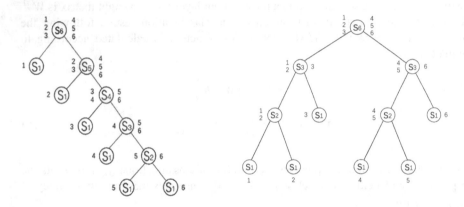

Fig. 2. The framework of OAA

Fig. 3. The framework of NOAA

2.3 Combination of NOAA Binary Classifier and Long Short-Term Memory Networks

Describe the whole training process, for the convenience of calculation and code reading, each dialect is corresponding to a label, the label is in the shape of 1_2_..._n cut the label, and the first digit represents the first category, the second digit represents the second category, and the last digit represents the final category. First of all, the extracted dialect features are put into the constructed network model Network0. Then select the second network that will be entered according to the first target tag. If the first label value is 0, then put it into network1 for further training. Otherwise, it will be put into the network2 for further training. Network1 and Network2 will be trained according to the second target tag, and so on until the final classification results are obtained. The overall structure of network0, network1 and network2 is the same, but the input voice features are different, so the feature weights obtained by each network training are different. In each training network, the speech features first pass through the LSTM networks layer, then through two fully connected layers, and softmax layer, finally, output the networks. The network structure used in each classification process is the LSTM network, while in the selection process, the ideology of binary classifier is used. Finally formed the network structure that uses the LSTM network to classify each node, while using the binary classifier as the whole framework.

Take the four-classification as an example, the whole recognition process is described as the following. A speech is extracted features and put into some repeated models in the LSTM networks, the last model outputs the output vectors of LSTM networks. Then pass two full connected layers and one softmax layer to get the prediction label 1 of this voice, and then selecting the next network to be entered according to the value of this prediction label, if the value of predicted label 1 is 0, the voice features are tested in network1. Otherwise they are tested in network2, output the feature vector and get the final prediction result. The process that a voice experiences after extracting features is shown in the following Fig. 4.

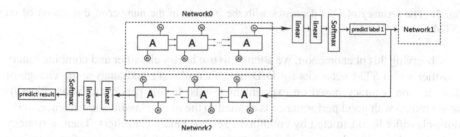

Fig. 4. The framework of NOAA with LSTM

3 Experiment

The experiment is based on six major dialects in China, including Sichuan dialect, Shanghai dialect, Changsha dialect, Nanchang dialect, Hokkien dialect and Hakka dialect. Each dialect includes an average of 6 h of reading style voice data, covering 35 speakers. Data are collected from various types of smartphones, and the recording environment contains quiet environment and noisy environment. Data are stored in PCM format with a sampling rate of 16000 Hz and 16 bits quantization.

This paper uses log Mel-scale filter banks energies (FBANK) acoustic characteristics to train. The enhanced data set adopts the method of increasing noise and separating the left and right channels, in order to achieve the goal of achieving steady performance through limited data resources. The training environment is python2.7 version, pytorch 0.4.0 version.

It is found that the accuracy of classification decreases with the increase of the number of dialect types when LSTM is used alone. After a large number of experiments, this law is confirmed. For the binary classification problem, the LSTM networks can achieve 0.99 accuracy, but only 0.79 in the six classification problem. The experimental results are shown in Fig. 5.

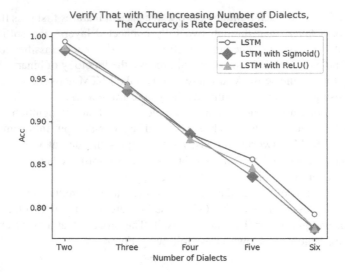

Fig. 5. The accuracy of DID decreases with the increase of the number of dialects based on LSTM

Observing this phenomenon, we attempt to use binary classifier and combine binary classifier with LSTM networks for DID task, then observe and analyse the change of classification accuracy based on experiment results. In this paper, the binary classification model with good performance is applied to the multi-classification science, and a multi-classifier is constructed by combining several binary classifiers. Then, a strategy is used to determine the class of the output sample, each binary classifier is trained independently. OAA(One-against-all) binary classifier requires more discrimination steps, longer training and testing time, so we prove OAA (One-against-all) binary classifier, and named it New OAA (New One-against-all) binary classifier. In order to verify the effectiveness of New OAA (New One-against-all) binary classifier, based on three frameworks, namely LSTM, OAA with LSTM and NOAA with LSTM, we carry out a large number of experiments. The experimental results are shown in Table 1.

Table 1. Comparison of average accuracy of three algorithms

Number of dialects	LSTM	OAA with LSTM	NOAA with LSTM
2	0.9937	0.9937	0.9937
3	0.9436	0.9599	0.9543
4	0.8854	0.9099	0.9140
5	0.8536	0.8755	0.8874
6	0.7924	0.8299	0.8342

The experimental results explain that the classification accuracy is low when the binary classifier is not used. After using OAA binary classifier and NOAA binary classifier, the classification accuracy is improved, and the accuracy difference between them is small. The experimental result is drawn as a line chart as shown in Fig. 6 below.

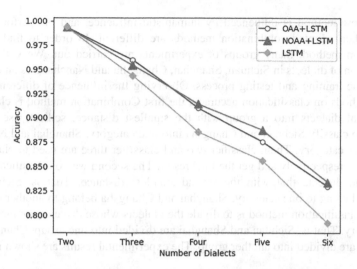

Fig. 6. The results of experiments based on the three models

Compared to the results of using OAA (One-against-all) binary classifier and NOAA (New One-against-all) binary classifier, discovering that they have similar effects on improving classification accuracy, but the training time is different. To explore the changes in training time, we measured the training time for two, three, four, five and six classification problem, the results are shown in Fig. 7 below. Observed and analysed the experimental results, finding that NOAA adopts better performance in training time compared to OAA. Especially when there are massive kinds of dialects, this performance difference becomes more apparent.

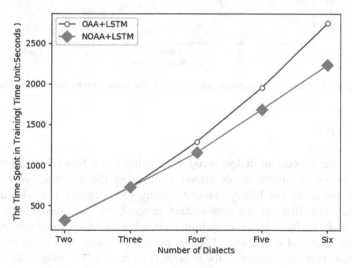

Fig. 7. Comparison of training time of two algorithms.

This new method is influenced by humanistic influence, and the performance is distinct when adopted combination methods are different. In order to find the best combination method, many groups of experiments are carried out. We will take the classification of dialects in Sichuan, Shanghai, Changsha and Nanchang as an example, showing the training and testing process. Observing the influence of different combination methods on classification accuracy, the first Combination method is classifying the regional dialects into a group with the smallest distance, scilicet, use the first classifier to classify Sichuan and Changsha into one category, Shanghai and Nanchang into another category. Then, classifier two and classifier three are used to classify the four dialects respectively and get the final result. The second way of classification is to classify the dialects that with the second smallest distance. That is, Sichuan and Nanchang belong to one category, Shanghai and Changsha belong to another category. The third classification method is to divide the dialects whose distance are farthest into one category. That is, Sichuan and Shanghai are divided into one group, Changsha and Nanchang are divided into another group. The experimental results are shown in Fig. 8.

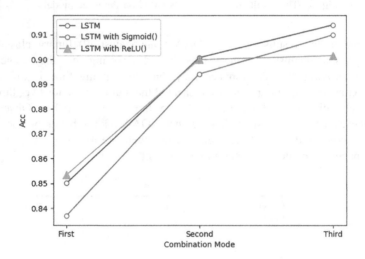

Fig. 8. The results of experiments based on the three combination methods

4   Conclusion

In this paper, the process of dialect recognition using Long Short-Term memory networks and binary classifiers has described. Comparing the difference of recognition accuracy of not using the binary classifier, using OAA binary classifier and using NOAA binary classifier, in the combination process, the well-designed use of the feature that dialectal features far away from each other are much more obvious, that is enhancing the dialectal differences. Finally, we have proved the effectiveness of the new identification method based on the experimental results. The model can be applied to not only the domain of dialect recognition and classification but also other domains related to classification problems. It is of great significance of machine learning that widely existed classification problems.

Acknowledgment. This research was financially supported by the key Technology R&D Program projects of Henan Province (172102210003), College Students Innovation and Entrepreneurship Training Program of Henan Province (S201810459069) and College Students Innovation and Entrepreneurship Training Program of Zhengzhou University (201810459069).

References

1. Xia, W., et al.: Chinese dialect identification based on gender classification. In: 2011 International Conference on Wireless Communications and Signal Processing (WCSP). IEEE (2011)
2. Ali, A., et al.: Automatic dialect detection in arabic broadcast speech. arXiv preprint arXiv: 1509.06928 (2015)
3. Khurana, S., et al.: QMDIS: QCRI-MIT advanced dialect identification system. In: Proceedings of Interspeech 2017, pp. 2591–2595 (2017)
4. Najafian, M., et al.: Exploiting convolutional neural networks for phonotactic based dialect identification. In: 2018 IEEE International Conference on Acoustics, Speech and Signal Processing (ICASSP). IEEE (2018)
5. Chang, W.-W., Tsai, W.-H.: Chinese dialect identification using segmental and prosodic features. J. Acoust. Soc. Am. **108**(4), 1906–1913 (2000)
6. Lim, B.P., Li, H., Ma, B.: Using local & global phonotactic features in Chinese dialect identification. In: IEEE International Conference on Acoustics, Speech, and Signal Processing, 2005. Proceedings (ICASSP 2005), vol. 1. IEEE (2005)
7. Mingliang, G., Yuguo, X., Yiming, Y.: Semi-supervised learning based Chinese dialect identification. In: 9th International Conference on Signal Processing, 2008. ICSP 2008. IEEE (2008)
8. Ma, B., Zhu, D., Tong, R.: Chinese dialect identification using tone features based on pitch flux. In: IEEE International Conference on Acoustics, Speech and Signal Processing, 2006. ICASSP 2006 Proceedings. 2006, vol. 1. IEEE (2006)
9. Zhang, M.-H., et al.: Phonemic evidence reveals interwoven evolution of Chinese dialects. arXiv preprint arXiv:1802.05820 (2018)
10. Richardson, F., Reynolds, D., Dehak, N.: A unified deep neural network for speaker and language recognition. arXiv preprint arXiv:1504.00923 (2015)
11. Mikolov, T., et al.: Extensions of recurrent neural network language model. In: 2011 IEEE International Conference on Acoustics, Speech and Signal Processing (ICASSP). IEEE (2011)
12. Sak, H., Senior, A., Beaufays, F.: Long short-term memory recurrent neural network architectures for large scale acoustic modeling. In: Fifteenth Annual Conference of the International Speech Communication Association (2014)
13. LeCun, Y., Bengio, Y., Hinton, G.: Deep learning. Nature **521**(7553), 436 (2015)
14. Wu, S., et al.: Modeling asynchronous event sequences with RNNs. J. Biomed. Inf. **83**, 167–177 (2018)
15. Hochreiter, S., Schmidhuber, J.: Long short-term memory. Neural Comput. **9**(8), 1735–1780 (1997)

16. Takenouchi, T., Ishii, S.: Binary classifiers ensemble based on Bregman divergence for multi-class classification. Neurocomputing **273**, 424–434 (2018)
17. Kumar, A.M., Gopal, M.: Fast multiclass SVM classification using decision tree based one-against-all method. Neural Process. Lett. **32**(3), 311–323 (2010)

Evaluation Method of Teachers' Teaching Ability Based on BP Neural Network

Pengchao Niu[1,2], Yuan Sun[1,2(✉)], Wei Song[1], and Shijiao Zhang[1,2]

[1] School of Information Engineering, Minzu University of China,
Beijing 100081, China
tracy.yuan.sun@gmail.com
[2] Minority Language Branch, National Language Resource and Monitoring
Research Center, Minzu University of China, Beijing 100081, China

Abstract. The evaluation of teachers' teaching ability is an important part of educational activities, and a reasonable evaluation method plays an important role in improving teachers' ability. At present, most of the evaluation methods used by schools and educational institutions are manually formulated some evaluation indicators. These methods are usually influenced by the personal preferences and the implementation is time-consuming. According to these problems, this paper proposes a method to evaluate teachers' teaching ability based on BP neural network. Through constructing the templates, we extract teachers' information and establish the knowledge base. Then a BP neural network is used to teaching ability evaluation. Finally, the experimental results prove the proposed method is effective.

Keywords: Evaluation method · Teachers' teaching ability ·
Information extraction · BP neural network

1 Introduction

Teachers' teaching ability refers to the individual psychological characteristics which are necessary for teachers to complete teaching activities smoothly and directly affect the efficiency and effectiveness of teaching activities [1, 2]. Teachers' teaching ability directly affects the quality of teaching and its development [3, 4]. Most of the current teaching ability evaluation methods use peer evaluation, expert evaluation and student evaluation [5].

Evaluation index system is the compass of teachers' teaching practice, teachers will constantly revise their own teaching practice according to the evaluation index. Reasonable methods will stimulate teachers' self-improvement motivation, and unreasonable methods will directly lead to the distortion of teaching ability evaluation [6].

The traditional teaching evaluation method has great shortcomings. First, it is greatly influenced by the students' personal preferences, which can not reflect the teachers' teaching ability truly and objectively. Secondly, this kind of evaluation is time-consuming, so it becomes a mere formality in the end, and all the teachers get similar scores, which can not reflect the actual teaching ability of teachers very well [7].

X. Sun et al. (Eds.): ICAIS 2019, LNCS 11632, pp. 27–38, 2019.
https://doi.org/10.1007/978-3-030-24274-9_3

In the information age, new evaluation methods are needed to make the evaluation process more natural and the results more authentic [8].

This paper introduces a teaching ability evaluation method based on BP neural network. The evaluation method quantifies and classifies the teacher information extracted based on template, to realize the evaluation of teachers' teaching ability.

2 Related Works

Teachers and students are the two major elements of the teaching system. In the past, people only considered students as an element and evaluate the learning effect of students, but ignored teachers as an element. In recent years, educational scholars began to realize that they should consider teachers as an element too. They put forward requirements for teachers' teaching ability, and formulated a series of traditional evaluation methods. As time goes by, the shortcomings of these methods have become more and more obvious, the function of this method has also been ineffective. With the development of computer technology, the method of combining computer technology with teachers' ability evaluation begins to appear. The evaluation method of teachers' teaching ability based on BP neural network is the product of the combination of machine learning algorithm and teachers' ability evaluation.

2.1 Evaluation Method of Teachers' Teaching Ability

In recent years, the academic circles began to use quantitative analysis method to evaluate teachers' teaching ability, and made some progress. Jiajia Liu calculated the weight of each index of teaching ability of university teachers by AHP, and put forward some strategies to improve teachers' teaching ability. Zhihua Wu constructed an evaluation index system of teachers' teaching ability by means of single sample T test, cluster analysis and principal component factor analysis [9].

With the development of computer technology, machine learning algorithms such as SVM, Bayes and Decision Tree are widely used in teaching evaluation. SVM is usually used to find the optimal classification plane in nonlinear space, and ultimately divide the sample data into several labels, to achieve the purpose of intelligent classification [10]. This method realizes the evaluation of teachers' ability through classification.

2.2 Information Extraction

The process of information extraction is mainly to find valuable information from a large number of plain texts, which is difficult to process directly and convert into structured data [11]. At present, there are two main types of text information extraction methods: statistical-based information extraction and rule-based information extraction [12, 13]. The basis of statistical-based information extraction is Statistical model. For example, HMM, maximum entropy, etc. The advantage of HMM-based information extraction is that it is supported by statistical theory. The weakness is that a large amount of training data is needed. Maximum entropy was proposed by E.T. Jaynes in the 1950s and applied to natural language processing in the 1990s [14]. The advantage is that the feature selection is flexible. The weakness is that the convergence speed of the algorithm is slow and the running time is long. In recent years, natural language processing technology has also been applied to information extraction, and natural language semantic construction improves natural language comprehension ability and analytical skills of the machine [15].

Template-based information extraction technology is widely used in information retrieval systems, such as medical, mechanical dynamics, astronomy, news and other professional retrieval. Information extraction technology based on template matching has been studied for a long time at home and abroad, and the famous template matching methods include SemInt, Cupid, LOLITA, ATRANS and so on [16]. Template-based information extraction has the characteristics of simple operation, high extraction accuracy, easy technical implementation and convenient cooperation with other technologies.

3 Framework

The process of model building is mainly divided into three parts: the construction of information knowledge base, construction of BP neural network and teacher evaluation. The process is shown as Fig. 1.

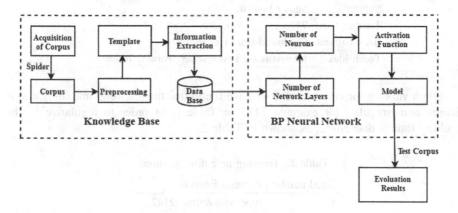

Fig. 1. Framework of model building.

(1) Building a knowledge base. Crawlers are used to crawl the corpus, and ICTCLAS is used for preprocessing. For the information that can not be extracted directly in the process of information extraction, the template is constructed to extract this information. Finally, the extracted information is stored in the database.

(2) Constructing BP neural network. Based on the teacher information stored in knowledge base, the template is constructed. The number of network layers, the number of neurons in each network layer and the activation function are determined according to the template. Finally, a BP neural network model is generated.

(3) Based on the previously constructed model, this paper classifies and evaluates some teachers' corpus.

4 Evaluation Method

4.1 Information Extraction Technology Based on Template

Template-based information extraction technology focuses on the construction of templates. The template construction is determined by the purpose of the information extraction and the structural characteristics of the original text. First, analyze the text characteristics to determine which information need to be obtained. Secondly, through the analysis of the sentence structure of the original text, we have found the characteristics of the required information and whether there is any correlation between all the required information, such as the relationship between sentence structure and part of speech. Finally, the information extraction template is constructed according to the characteristics of the extracted information. A teacher information crawled are shown in Table 1.

Table 1. Teacher information.

Key	Value
Id	1
Name	Lei qi
Image	201110312320351422844537_big.jpg
Point	5
Subject	Senior English
Teacher Time	7175
Back Ground	Graduated from Heilongjiang…
Teach Idea	Interest is the best teacher, learning in joy…

When viewing the crawl results, we have found that the teaching time (in hours) is chaotic and irregular, for example 7175 in Table 1. In order to regularize it, the teaching time is discretized, as shown in Table 2.

Table 2. Teaching time discretization.

Serial number	Partition interval
1	time>=0&&time<2142
2	time>=2142&&time<5068
3	time>=5068

The extracted data is stored in the Mysql database. After analyzing the corpus, we have found that the extracted attributes are not perfect for describing the data and cannot be directly used to display the teaching ability of teachers in the knowledge base. The attributes that have been extracted are name, photo, subject, and time of teaching. Because the background part is still in the form of a large text corpus. the background part needs to be further extracted. We will extract three attributes, university, degree and honor, from the background part. We use ICTCLAS as a tool of corpus segmentation and part-of-speech tagging and manual proofreading to ensure accuracy.

The attributes are universities, degrees, and honors that we need to extract in the background corpus. Through the analysis of Back Ground corpus, we have found that the degree attribute has "Bachelor", "Master" and "Doctorate" in the corpus, thus, the keyword matching can be performed. For the university attribute part, after analyzing many background parts, we use the combination of the speech part and named entities to construct a template for information extraction as shown in Table 3.

Table 3. Template of university.

Templates	Example
n+n+n+university	"beijing"/n "aviation"/n "aerospace"/n university
n+n+university	"china"/n "agricultural"/n university
n+university	"shandong"/n university
n+n+college	"beijing"/n "relation"/n college
s+n+university	"northeast"/s "petroleum"/n university
s+university	"southwest"/s university
n+m+n+college	"beijing"/n "second"/m "foreign language"/n college
v+n+college	"Disaster prevention"/v "technology"/n college

The table covers almost all the characteristics of the college name in the corpus. The constructed template is used to match each background corpus, and the information is extracted and stored in the database. For the honor part, after analyzing many teachers' honors, we have found that some verbs and nouns can represent the honor, as shown in the Table 4. The template is used to match the background corpus, the matched phrases are extracted and stored in the database, and then information is proofread to prevent duplicate of information.

Table 4. Template of honor.

Field template	Example
"excellent"/a "teacher"/n	Excellent teacher of new oriental education technology group
"editor-in-chief"/n	Editor-in-Chief of "Zhengheng" magazine
"prize"/n	High score prize
"obtain"/v	Received the new oriental outstanding teacher award

After obtaining university template and honor template, template-based matching in the background corpus is used to extract the required information. Since almost every corpus in this paper contain three attributes, the template-based information extraction technology can be used, and the efficiency of information extraction is high.

4.2   Construction of Knowledge Base

After the above text information extraction, we can get eight attributes of each teacher. Based on these attributes, we make a comprehensive analysis of teachers' teaching situation.

In this paper, a teacher's information is defined as a corpus. And the vector of a corpus is represented by five dimensions subject, teaching grade, educational background, teaching time and honor. Among them, subjects include English, Chinese, Mathematics, etc. Grades include junior 1, junior 2, junior 3 and senior 1, etc. Educational background includes bachelor, master, doctorate; The teaching time is normalized. Word of vector has been used to represent document in a matrix form, also can be used to generate the vector space model [17].

As shown in Table 5, for the characteristic value of subject, we stipulate that it is set to 1 when the value of subject in the corpus is Chinese, Math or English, and the other is set to 0. For grade, it will be known as junior high school when the value is the first, second, third in junior high school and senior high school entrance examination, and the value is set to 0. Senior 1, Senior 2, Senior 3 and College Entrance Examination collectively referred to as Senior High School, and set to 1. Some teachers are both junior high school teachers and senior high school teachers, we set these characteristics as 2. For teacher's educational background, bachelor is set to 1, master is set to 2, and doctorate to 3. Some teachers do not have educational background information and set the value of this type of teacher's educational background to 0. The value of teaching time is calculated from this equation of (time-min)/(max-min). For honors, the honored teacher has a value of 1, otherwise the value is set to 0. Here is an example, San Zhang, teaching subject is English, teaching grade is junior two, teaching time is 7300, education background is master and honor is Beijing new oriental outstanding teacher, so the vector of this corpus is (1, 0, 0.53, 2, 1).

Table 5. Eigenvalue vector analysis.

Eigenvalues		Process
Subject	Chinese&&Mathematics&&English	1
	Other	0
Honor	Received honor	1
	Other	0
Grade	Junior High School	0
	Senior High School	1
	All	2
Educational background	Bachelor	1
	Master	2
	Doctorate	3
	Other	0
Teaching time		(time-min)/(max-min)

The teacher's teaching situation is now divided into four categories, continued-maintenance, cheering, need to improve, and efforts to improve. If the score is between 5 and 10, it is the class of continued maintenance; the score between 4 and 5 is in the cheering category; if the score is between 2.5 and 4, it belongs to need to improve class; if scores between 0 and 2.5, it belongs to efforts to improve class. In the simulation experiment, we add the values of each dimension in the vector as the score, and in the real environment, the score is given by the judges. Based on score, each corpus is labeled manually.

4.3 Construction of BP Neural Network

It can be carried out in the next step that teachers' teaching situation prediction based on BP neural network according to the data obtained from the preprocessing. Construction of BP Neural Network is the Key Step, it is divided into the construction of the model and the adjustment of the parameters.

Construction Method of BP Neural Network. There must be an input layer, and an output layer in the network, and one or more hidden layers are required. At the same time, the number of neurons in each layer of the neural network needs to be determined. Activation function is an important part of BP neural network, which usually adopts S-type logarithm or tangent function. BP neural network designed in this paper adopts tansig activation function in both hidden layer and output layer, and its corresponding expression is shown in Eq. (1).

$$f(x) = \frac{2}{1 + e^{-2x}} - 1 \tag{1}$$

Parameters Adjustment. There are a lot of parameters in the BP neural network model, and the quality of parameter setting has a great impact on the prediction results.

Through the experiment of single hidden layer and double hidden layer, we have found that the effect will be better if we use double hidden layer. And we set the number of iterations to 600, the learning rate to be 0.01. The number of neurons in the hidden layer is determined according to the Eq. (2).

$$n_z = \sqrt{n_x + n_y} + m \tag{2}$$

The n_z refers to the number of neurons in the hidden layer, n_x and n_y refer to the number of neurons in the input layer and the output layer respectively, and m refers to a constant of zero to ten. The dimension of each corpus vector in the input layer is 5, the dimension of the classification is 1, so the number of neurons in the input layer is 6. The result of the output layer is the category, and the dimension is 1, so the number of neurons in the output layer is 1. When the corpus belongs to class of continued maintenance, the output result is 1. When the corpus belongs to class of cheering, the output result is 2. When the corpus belongs to class of need to improve, the output result is 3. When the corpus belongs to class of efforts to improve, the output result is 4. Through continuous experiments, the optimal number of neurons each hidden layer is determined to be 14.

5 Experiments

5.1 Experiment on Information Extraction

The corpus in this paper comes from the Internet. First, New Oriental is selected from various educational websites, because the website has rich teacher information, the URL is http://souke.xdf.cn/TeacherList.aspx of New Oriental. Then through the web crawler, we extracted relevant information about the teacher from the website.

In order to verify the effect of the constructed template, 612 corpus were manually labeled, and 312 corpus were used as training corpus. The template was continuously generalized and revised during the training process. The remaining 300 are used as test corpus. It can be seen from the result that template-based information extraction has a high accuracy. However, the automation level is low because templates need to be constructed manually and need manual participation in the process of generalization and continuous adjustment of the model. After extracting the required information, the results of verifying the effectiveness of the constructed template are shown in Table 6.

Table 6. Template inspection results.

Attribute category	Number(piece)			Percent (%)		
	Total	Identified	Correct	Precision	Recall	F1
University	155	132	128	96.97%	82.58%	89.20%
Degree	204	152	150	98.68%	73.53%	84.27%
Honor	97	65	54	83.08%	55.67%	66.67%
Summary	456	349	332	95.13%	72.81%	82.48%

The calculation method of Precision is shown in Eq. (3).

$$\Pr ecision(A, B) = \frac{|A \cap B|}{|A|} \tag{3}$$

The calculation method of Recall is shown in Eq. (4).

$$Recall(A, B) = \frac{|A \cap B|}{|B|} \tag{4}$$

A refers to the positive sample set of the model output, and B refers to the true positive sample set. The F1 value is an evaluation index that combines these two indicators, and F1 is shown in Eq. (5).

$$F1 = 2P * R/(P + R) \tag{5}$$

Prefers to the precision rate and R refers to the recall rate.

5.2   Experiment on BP Neural Network

The corpus is trained by the BP neural network designed above. There are 612 corpus in this paper, 412 of them were used as train samples, and the remaining samples were used as test samples.

When experiments are done with MATLAB, the results are shown in Table 7. The test corpus is 200 items, and the correct predictive result is 177 items, the correct rate is 88.5%.

Table 7. Experimental results.

Type	Number			Percent (%)		
	Total	Identified	Correct	Precision	Recall	F1
Efforts to improve	65	61	57	93.44%	87.67%	90.48%
Need to improve	60	57	49	85.96%	81.67%	83.76%
Cheering	41	46	38	82.61%	92.68%	87.36%
Continued maintenance	34	36	33	91.67%	97.06%	94.29%

The simulation result is shown in Fig. 2. Red is the real classification, and green is the classification of the prediction. It can be clearly seen from the figure that the contact ratio is high between the real result and the predictive result.

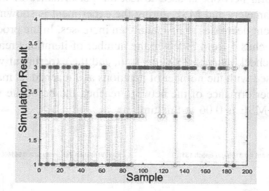

Fig. 2. Simulation result.

A graphical representation of the absolute error and the percentage error are shown as Fig. 3. The absolute error and the percentage error are 0 for most predicted samples, indicating that the neural network model has a higher correct rate.

When the experiment stops, Gradient Validation Checks, Learning Rate and the number of iterations are shown in Table 8.

As can be seen from the table, the experiment was stopped when the value of validation checks reaches 6. At this point, the error has reached the optimal, the error may increase or the phenomenon of over-fitting will appear if retraining, so when the value of validation checks reaches 6, the experiment was stopped. In this process, the optimal gradient is 0.036, the optimal learning rate is 1.315 and the number of iterations is 100.

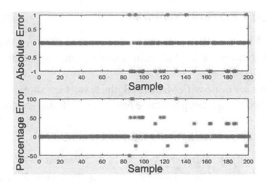

Fig. 3. Absolute error and percentage error.

Table 8. Attribute change.

Gradient	Validation checks	Learning rate	Epoch
0.313	6	0.051	131

MSE in BP neural network is used to test the performance of this network. The variation of the parameters and MSE during the experiment is shown as Fig. 4. From the figure, the gradient decreases at first, and then increases. In the process, the value of validation check reaches 5 from 3. When the number of iterations reached to 120, the value of validation check increased sharply to 6, and the experiment was stopped. The learning rate increased with the number of iterations and reached its maximum between 100 and 120. The performance of the network reached the best state when iterating to 124 times, and the MSE is 0.06 at this time.

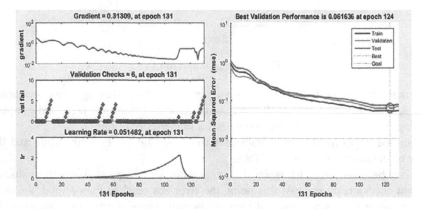

Fig. 4. Variation of the parameters and MSE.

In order to prevent over-fitting of data, BP neural network will divide the samples into training samples, validation samples and test samples. In these three parts, training samples is used to train, validation samples and test samples are used to test, and then regression analysis is carried out. The correlation coefficients at the end of the experiment is shown in Table 9.

Table 9. Correlation coefficient of regression test.

Training	Validation	Test	All
0.96	0.96	0.96	0.96

The change of the correlation coefficient during the experiment is shown as Fig. 5, in which the abscissa represents the true value of the classification and the ordinate represents the output value of the neural network. It can be seen that the correlation coefficient is very high, and the fitting curve is almost on the diagonal, thus the prediction accuracy is extremely high.

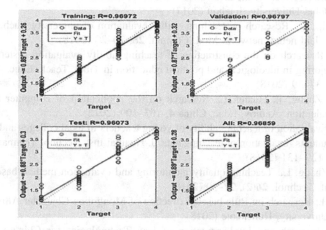

Fig. 5. Change of correlation coefficient during experiment.

6 Conclusion and Future Work

In this paper, through the analysis of the existing evaluation methods of teachers' teaching ability, we have found that there are great shortcomings. Based on this, this paper proposes a new and reasonable evaluation method of teachers' teaching ability. This method is based on BP neural network, extracts teachers' information through template, constructs knowledge base and trains neural network model, and finally evaluates teachers' teaching ability through classification. In the process of evaluating, the influence of individual factors on the results has been removed, which not only makes the evaluation process more reasonable, but also makes the evaluation more efficient.

In the future, we will consider the influencing factors of teachers' teaching ability more comprehensively. Based on this method, we can make a more objective evaluation of teachers' teaching ability in all aspects.

Acknowledgments. This work is supported by National Nature Science Foundation (No. 61501529), National Language Committee Project (No. ZDI125-36).

References

1. Lin, Y.: On the constitution and cultivation of teachers' teaching ability in colleges and universities. Educ. Occup. **9**, 99–110 (2008)
2. Ma, Y.: Research on the Components of Chemistry Teachers' Teaching Ability in Excel. Shandong Normal University, Jinan (2017)
3. Liu, J.: Model building and promotion strategy of the teaching ability of university and college teachers. J. Changsha Univ. Sci. Technol. (Soc. Sci.) **3**, 133–137 (2015)
4. Chunlan, Yu.: International comparison of teachers' performance evaluation system in higher vocational colleges and its enlightenment to China. Mod. Commun. **21**, 32–34 (2018)
5. Gao, X.: The Research of the Evaluation Method of Teachers' Teaching Ability Based on Emotion. Bohai University, Jinzhou (2017)
6. Wang, H., Li, Q.: Research on teaching ability evaluation of university teachers based on discrete hopfield neural network. Mod. Comput. **28**, 20–23 (2018)
7. Wang, Q.: Research on the construction of teaching ability evaluation system for young teachers majoring in ideological and political education in Tibet. Teach. Educ. (High. Educ. Forum) **18**, 37–39 (2018)
8. Zhang, B., Zhang, J., Huang, L.: Research on the application of computer modeling in teaching evaluation. Audiov. Educ. China **4**, 103–109 (2013)
9. Zhao, W.: Evaluation of teaching ability of young teachers in local colleges and universities based on students' evaluation of teaching data. J. Huaihai Inst. Technol. (Humanit. Soc. Sci. Ed.) **16**(9), 129–131 (2018)
10. Yang, B., Zhang, L.: Teaching quality monitoring and evaluation method based on SVM. Comput. Inf. Technol. **26**(2), 27–30 (2018)
11. Mengjun, H.: Research on Rule-based Extraction of Mongolian Character Attributes. Inner Mongolia University, Huhehaote (2018)
12. Yang, Y.: Research and Implementation of Key Technologies for Chinese Information Extraction. Beijing University of Posts and Telecommunications, Beijing (2008)
13. Li, X., Miao, Z.: Free text information extraction technology. Inf. Sci. **7**, 815–821 (2004)
14. Zhao, L.: Research on Comment Information Extraction Based on Maximum Entropy Method. Shanghai Jiaotong University, Shanghai (2009)
15. Wang, S., et al.: Natural language semantic construction based on cloud database. Comput. Mater. Continua **57**(3), 603–619 (2018)
16. Li, D.: Information Extraction Algorithm Based on the Template Matching in Traffic Standards. Chang'an University (2017)
17. Xiong, Z., Shen, Q., Wang, Y., Zhu, C.: Paragraph vector representation based on word to vector and CNN learning. Comput. Mater. Continua **55**(2), 213–227 (2018)

Research on the Promotion of Tibetan New Words and Platform Design

Hao Li[1,2], Yuan Sun[1,2(✉)], Wei Song[1], and Jie Qin[1,2]

[1] School of Information Engineering,
Minzu University of China, Beijing 100081, China
tracy.yuan.sun@gmail.com
[2] Minority Languages Branch, National Language Resource and Monitoring
Research Center, Minzu University of China, Beijing 100081, China

Abstract. With the rapid development of the country's technology and culture, more and more Tibetan new words appear, which add vitality to the language. This paper investigates the current usage of Tibetan new words by questionnaire and statistics of relevant websites. We find there exist some problems including time delay, non-standard form of expression and the publishing approach is too single. These problems bring great barriers to communicate and use Tibetan new words. To solve these problems, we design a platform for the promotion of Tibetan new words in the website, which can make the Tibetan new words become more standardized and effective, and we can get statistics on the usage of new words. Meanwhile, it is conducive to the spread of new words in Tibetan, and the platform can also collect effective data to serve the related work of Tibetan new words.

Keywords: Minority language · Tibetan new words · Language promotion · Learning platform

1 Introduction

China has 56 ethnic groups and many different languages. Tibetan is the language used by the Tibetan people. It is used by more than 6 million people in China, and is distributed in Tibetan, Qinghai, Sichuan, Gansu and Yunnan provinces [1]. With the development of society, the frequency of new words in Tibetan has become more and more frequent. However, there are dialects in the five provinces of Tibetan, the lag of standardization work, and the lack of uniform and standardized translation, these brings great challenges to the development of Tibetan.

The development of language has a decisive influence on education. For the Tibetans in different Tibetan areas, the research on their familiarity and habitual expressions of new words is conducive to promote Tibetan new words.

At present, the release way of new words in Tibetan is mainly published by some traditional paper documents and the government, which are relatively scattered and the real-time performance is poor. It takes a good platform to promote the Tibetan new words. At present, the website development technology is already in a mature stage. The educational resources are gradually running in the form of cloud services in cloud

X. Sun et al. (Eds.): ICAIS 2019, LNCS 11632, pp. 39–50, 2019.
https://doi.org/10.1007/978-3-030-24274-9_4

personal learning environments and devices such as smart phones, pads, and e-book bags [2]. Based on this background, the construction of a new words learning and promotion platform for minority languages can be a method and a way to promote new words in minority languages. Starting from the actual research, the author decided to start this work from the Tibetan first, in order to meet the needs of the Tibetan compatriots represented by the majority of young students.

2 Related Works

The study of Tibetan new words began as early as the 1950s. Today, nearly 70 years later, the work related to Tibetan new words has made great achievements, at the same time there are some problems. After entering the Internet era, the traditional way of promoting new words has been transformed from audio media and offline media into Internet and mobile Internet media. This allows the promotion to have new developments in this era.

2.1 Tibetan New Words

The progress of the times and society is always accompanied by the development of language. And the emergence of new words in different languages has a great relationship with the socio-economic, political and cultural. Natural Language Processing is a major branch of artificial intelligence [3]. The application of machine learning in the field of natural language processing has also led to the development of new words [4]. For example, for the study of Chinese and English new words, firstly, it is carried out by an authoritative department such as the Standardization Committee of the International Standardization Committee, at the same time, Xinhua News Agency and the authoritative publications of "China Translation" also regularly compile the translated names of some new English nouns, secondly, the definition and translation of some new words are given by the English-Chinese dictionary and the new words dictionary. All of the above methods have certain lags and are not comprehensive, so the translation and naming of many new words must be done by individual translators. There are two ways of transliteration and paraphrases.

From the 70s to the 80s, the number of Tibetan new words began to expand, which greatly enriched the vocabulary of Tibetan, and the Tibetan new words also existed [5]. Since then, from the end of the 1980s to the beginning of the 21st century, all parties have invested a great deal of energy to solve the problem of standardization of Tibetan new words and achieved positive results. Since 1999, the Office of the Standardization and Validation Committee for Tibetan Words in Qinghai Province has published the "Tibetan Terminology Bulletin" every year. The new words are translated by experts from various universities and related language research centers, and has good normative and authoritative. In the academic research of information on Tibetan new words. In 2011, Jia Jiji of Northwest University for Nationalities compiled more than 5000 new words in the reference books such as the New Word Terminology Dictionary and the Chinese-English New words Dictionary translated by the Chinese National Translation Center. Through the processing of the corpus, a new vocabulary related to the Tibetan news page is established, which includes 3017 new words, and contains additional information such as part of speech, word length, and word class of the new word [6].

In words of Tibetan new words, the translation of the three major dialect districts in the five provinces is based on their local language habits, such as publishers and information networks.

2.2 New Words Platform

The promotion of new words in English is mainly carried out by various paper and electronic reading materials. At the same time, the dictionary is also an important means of promoting the new words in English. For example, the Webster English Dictionary includes a word or phrase that is widely used within a certain period of time, or is quoted by multiple publications. The editors of the dictionary spend hours reading various paper and electronic versions of the readings every day in order to discover new words and new usages in time. The words that have been marked by the editors will be stored in a computer system. The promotion of Chinese new word words does not seem to have a systematic promotion platform, but it is always spread in China in the form of Weibo, WeChat, Forum, Baidu Encyclopedia and News.

In words of Tibetan, the release of new terminology on the Internet is more limited, most of which are published in the form of pictures in each issue of the Tibetan Terminology Bulletin, they cannot fully display all new words. And there are a few new words published on the Tibetan version of several major websites, such as People's Daily, Xinhuanet Tibetan Channel and China Tibet. The Tibetan Department of Gansu National Normal University has published some new words in Tibetan through the website, but the latest one was published in September 2015, and the website entrance is not easy to find. In addition, the Tibetan-Chinese bilingual website is still a Tibetan learning website that is still running, which is rich in functions, including Tibetan grammar, Tibetan encyclopedia, Tibetan calligraphy and Tibetan vocabulary. But after using, the author found that the site's lexical information is too old. New words such as "WeChat", "Alipay" and "Chinese Dream" have not been found. Even the words "online" and "internet" that are common in Chinese are not included.

3 Preliminaries

In order to better understand the status of Tibetan new words. The author conducted two aspects of research: first, the author conducted a questionnaire of more than 100 Tibetan students in an ethnic university, second, in view of the existing Tibetan new word words, the author counts the word frequency of the mainstream news website in Tibetan in recent years.

The research mainly contains two aspects, one is questionnaires among Tibetan students, and the other is statistical analysis of Tibetan websites. Participants were 104 Tibetan students from an ethnic university. Students are a representative group of Tibetans, they from different regions have different expressions in the use of new words and replace Tibetan expressions with Chinese. Therefore, the investigation of Tibetan new words in Tibetan students can be used to some extent to understand the use of new words in Tibetan. In addition, in view of the existing Tibetan new words, the author counts the frequency of words in the mainstream news websites of Tibetan in recent years, and analyzes the use of new words.

3.1   Collection of Tibetan New Words

Based on great deal of investigation and material, the author collected a total of 1,841 Tibetan new words from 2011 to 2016, mainly from People's Daily Online, China Tibetology Network and the National Committee for the Validation of Tibetan New Word Words, as the new words library for Tibetans. The specific composition is shown in Table 1.

Table 1. Number of new words in each year.

Years	2011	2012	2013	2014	2015	2016
Quantity	141	304	819	444	74	59
Total	1841					

3.2   Questionnaire Design

Questionnaire survey is a common method used by researchers to collect data in empirical research. It uses language as the medium and uses strictly designed questions or tables to collect data of research objects [7]. In designing the questionnaire, we followed the relevant theories of questionnaire survey method and consulted senior professors of ethnic linguistics to ensure the rationality and objectivity of questionnaire setting [8, 9].

The rigor of the choice of words. The Tibetan new words involved in the questionnaire mainly comes from the mainstream formal website.

The first part of the questionnaire about the background is mainly to know the influence of the region on the use of Tibetan new words in Tibetan students. The subjective questions are set to know their subjective willingness to some significant problems. The second part is about the familiarity of 70 Tibetan new words in order to know their familiarity with them. The third part of the topic is set to know the current non-standardization of new words.

3.3   Tibetan Corpus from Internet

This study uses the machine method to complete the word frequency statistics of 1841 Tibetan new words. The survey database is a collection of news corpora obtained from four Tibetan websites, including four websites: Qinghai Lake Network, Qinghai Tibetan Broadcasting Network, China Tibet News Network, and Xinhuanet Tibet Channel. The corpus totals 74,284 texts with a size of 568.9. MB, as shown in Table 2.

Table 2. Corpus composition table.

Website name	Number of texts						Size (MB)
	2011	2012	2013	2014	2015	2016	
Qinghai Lake Network	1953	1273	1697	1544	999	451	89.8
China Tibet news network	126	33	3408	31	1564	5439	104
Qinghai Tibetan radio network	3699	1729	4278	12290	17115	13570	351
Xinhuanet Tibet channel	41	188	397	763	1294	402	24.1
Total	74284						568.9

4 Data Analysis

4.1 Questionnaire Data Analysis

Analysis on the Awareness of New Words. The author made statistics on the familiarity degree of 70 new words in Tibetan in the second part of the questionnaire, and divided into five levels according to the degree of familiarity, and the value ranges from 1 to 5 points. The awareness score takes the average of 70 new words scores. The questionnaire survey issued 107 questionnaires and 103 valid questionnaires were retrieved. The Tibetan college students who participated in the questionnaire came from four provinces (Tibet, Gansu, Qinghai and Sichuan) among the five major provinces and regions of Tibetan language in China. As shown in Table 3. It can be seen from the data in the figure that the overall average score of all Tibetan students participating in the questionnaire is 3.64, which indicates that the respondents' overall familiarity with new words in Tibetan is quite good. From a regional point of view, the Tibetan students from the Qinghai region have a relatively high level of cognition, which can reach 3.76. The Tibetan students in Tibetan and Sichuan areas are close to the overall level and are slightly lower. Tibetan students in the Gansu region score relatively lowest.

Table 3. Number of participants from different regions.

	Tibet	Gansu	Qinghai	Sichuan	Total
Number of people	41	13	29	20	103
Average score	3.61	3.48	3.76	3.58	3.61

Analysis of Different Expressions of Tibetan New Words. For a Chinese neologism, a term corresponds to multiple Tibetan expressions, in the third part of the questionnaire, we set 30 questions to investigate the customary expressions of new words. The options include various Tibetan, Chinese and English forms of new words. The statistical results are shown in Table 4. It can be seen that most of the respondents prefer to use the Tibetan form to express new words.

Table 4. The situation of different expressions of new words.

Form	Tibetan	Chinese
Percentage	65.61%	34.39%

Respondents responded to "the use of other ways to express the reasons for the new terminology of Tibetan," the two highest rates of the reasons for the "cross-regional exchange barriers" and "the lack of unified expression of the language of the nation", accounting for 35.58%. Both options reflect the existence of non-standardized words in Tibetan new words. Among them, "barriers exist in inter-regional communication" are caused by the non-standard new words of Tibetan, and "the lack of unified expression of national language" is the root cause.

Analysis of Tibetan New Words' Lagging Condition and the Tibetan University Students' Expectation. Among respondents, more than 75% of them expected to have the expression of new words in Tibetan within a short time after the emergence of the Chinese new words. However, more than 89% of the respondents believe that there are still more than half a year lags in the expression of words in Tibetan.

Nearly 60% of Tibetan college students in the questionnaire survey learned new words through the Internet, such as chat tools, blogs, and public numbers. This result is in line with the trend that college students can better use the Internet.

Regarding "whether it is expected to have a special platform to learn the words of Tibetan new words", 89.42% of the fillers chose very much to expect, and 57.6% of fillers expect to obtain the words of Tibetan new words through the website and APP. The specific situation is shown in Table 5.

Table 5. Lag time and publish way of Tibetan new words.

Lag time	Less than half a year	Half a year	1 year	1–2 years	More than 2 years
Percentage	11.54%	31.73%	27.88%	20.19%	8.65%
Tolerance	Synchronization	Short time	Long time	Don't care	
Percentage	39.05%	38.10%	16.19%	6.67%	

4.2 Internet Data Analysis

Through analysis, among the 1841 Tibetan new words, 18.70% of new words appears in the database text, and 81.30% of new words appear in the text as 0. The specific situation is shown in Table 6 and Fig. 1.

From the statistical analysis of questionnaire results and the 1841 new words comparisons on the four mainstream Tibetan news websites, it can be seen that Tibetan college students have a better overall understanding of the words of Tibetan new words, but there are also some problems. Summarized as follows.

Table 6. Tibetan new words frequency distribution table

Frequency segment	Number of words	Percentage (%)	Examples words
0	1497	81.31	ད་ཕྲུག་རྒྱས་སྐད་(clenbuterol) ཆུ་བོར་དཔལ་འཛིར་(bubble economy)
1-10	184	9.99	རང་འརེགས་ཡུལ་སྐོར་(self-help travel) ནག་དུང་(unregistered citizens)
11-50	78	4.24	བཙོན་སྐྱོན་ཉུང་གཏོང་(energy-saving reduction) ནང་སྐྱེས་རྩལ་ནུགས་(endogenous power)
51-100	20	0.92	མཉན་གྲོགས་(buddy) ཉིའོ་ཡུལ་སྐྱེང་ཟུན་(Diaoyu islands)
101-500	37	1.09	ནུགས་བསྐྱར་བ་(power)
501-1000	8	0.43	ཡུལ་སྒོལ་(tacky)
>=1000	17	1.09	ཀུང་གོའི་ཕུགས་འདུན་(The Chinese dream) ཁྲིང་(Qin)
total	1841	100	

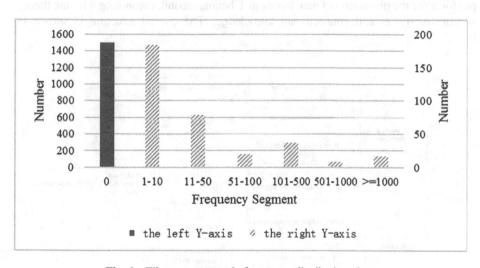

Fig. 1. Tibetan new words frequency distribution chart

First, there is a lag phenomenon in new words in Tibetan. Second, Tibetan students are more inclined to use the Tibetan form to express new words, but there are irregularities in the form of Tibetan expression. Third, the Internet has become a common way for Tibetan college students to obtain new words, and early 60% of Tibetan college students mainly use the Internet to obtain new words. In the survey of expected ways of the new word words promotion platform, the proportion of expressing expectations through the Internet has reached 57.6%.

According to the conclusions of the survey, the author proposes to build a platform for the promotion of Tibetan new words to meet the Tibetan students' learning needs.

5   Design of a Platform for Promoting New Words in Tibetan

5.1   Design Ideas and Principles of the Platform

Design Principles. It is a process of learning new knowledge for Tibetan college students to master new words. In the process, we follow the constructivist theory to build an extension platform that allows Tibetan students to spontaneously learn new words of Tibetan through the promotion platform under the guidance of existing experience and knowledge [10].

At the same time, combining with the theory of communication, the promotion platform is not just promoting the terminology of new words, but also can collect some information feedback from platform learners.

Function of Target System. Tibetan new words promotion platform design considering two parts, first of all, the author analyzes the status quo and main users of the platform for the promotion of new words in Tibetan, second, combining with the theory of constructivism and connectivism knowledge. The overall structure is shown in Fig. 2.

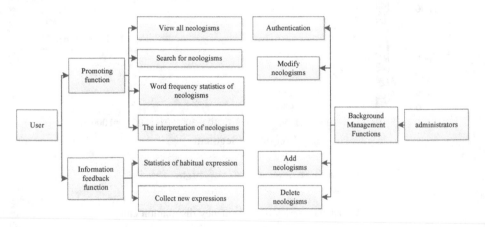

Fig. 2. Promotion platform function char.

(1) Tibetan new words display function. This function is the core function of the promotion platform and is used to satisfy users' needs for knowing new words in Tibetan. In addition to the basic Tibetan-Chinese counterpart, the platform also has detailed information on the new words, such as explanations, time of occurrence, and so on.

(2) Search function. This function allows users to query the Tibetan new words based on their own needs. Based on the non-standard phenomenon expressed in words of Tibetan new words, the search function is designed to be an accurate search.

(3) Information feedback function. For the polysemy term of Tibetan new words, the platform can record the user's choices, at the same time, the user can also supplement the expressions of the new words in Tibetan.

(4) Network frequency display function. This function provides users with data support for word analysis and research. The platform uses a line chart to display the number of new words in each Tibetan word appearing on the web text in the past five years. At the same time, it provides small function buttons such as screenshots to facilitate users to save data.

(5) Show all words of Tibetan new words by time. The platform provides the ability to display all new words, and allows users to view the screening criteria at the boundary of the year so that users can understand the Tibetan new words that appear in different years.

5.2 Description of the Website

The page design of the website refers to the style of Baidu Encyclopedia. The home page contains a search box and provides access to popular words, views of all new words, and more. The search results page displays details of new words, including Chinese, Tibetan, time of occurrence, feedback, and Chinese interpretation. In addition, the page also contains the word frequency statistics of the word on the four Tibetan news websites for the past five years.

Promotion Function Module. The homepage display is divided into Chinese and Tibetan versions, which can be achieved by clicking the button in the upper right corner of the page. The page is implemented using PHP code. As shown in Fig. 3. The user clicks the View All New words button to access all new words pages. This page is also divided into Tibetan and Chinese versions. As shown in Fig. 4. After performing the search operation, the user enters the new words detail page, and displays information including Tibetan-Chinese translation, appearance time, information feedback, word interpretation, and word frequency trend information. As shown in Fig. 4.

Information Feedback Function Module. Teaching quality is a key factor influencing student achievement [11]. In the new words details page, the author added an information feedback module. The collection of information including usage habits, the selection of different Tibetan forms, and the use of the frequency in the past five years (2011–2016) on the four news websites (Qinghai Lake Network, Qinghai Tibetan Broadcasting Network, China Tibet News Network, Xinhuanet Tibet Channel). As shown in the Fig. 5.

དབྱིན   汉语

藏语新词术语

	搜 索

热门新词:

- 瘦肉精   · 餐车   · 借记卡
- 乘务员   · 形象大使   · 给力
- 热线   · 安乐死   · 自助游
- 知名品牌   · 微博   · 黑户
- 安乐死   · 火车   · 地沟油

查看所有新词

Fig. 3. Chinese version of the home page.

藏语新词术语

新词音气

2016 2015 2014 2013 2012 2011

形象大使	2011
微博	2011
瘦肉精	2011
弱势群体	2011
热线	2011
借记卡	2011
黑作坊	2011
地沟油	2011
乘务员	2011
车次	2011

« 1 2 3 4 … 3 »

Fig. 4. All new words display page.

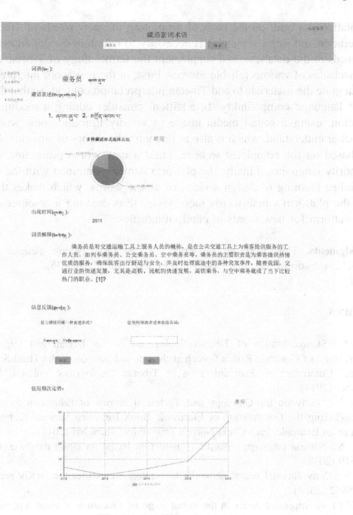

Fig. 5. Search results page.

6 Conclusions

Through a questionnaire survey of Tibetan students in Minzu University of China, and a survey of new words on four Tibetan-language news websites, this paper proposes that there are problems such as irregular expression and time lag in the promotion of Tibetan new words, so this paper build a platform for the promotion of new words in Tibetan, users can view the new words in all directions, and also provide feedback on the platform, which satisfies the Tibetan students' learning needs for Tibetan new words. Meanwhile, it promotes the promotion of Tibetan new words.

The author designed the platform based on the educational theories of constructivism, connectivity, new constructivism, and modern educational technology.

The platform is built on the basis of promoting the new words of Tibetan. In the future operation and improvement, it is necessary to maintain the continuous updating of new words in the database, and supplement the terminology of Tibetan new words from the websites of various reliable sources. First, in the new word interpretation part, we can integrate the materials to add Tibetan interpretation content, so that the platform has better language compatibility. In addition, consider adding a module for video interpretation, using a sound media image to vividly introduce new words to help learners better understand, which is also in line with the theory of situational cognition. Second, based on the completed website, build a new words promotion website for other minority languages. Finally, the platform can be combined with the current hot MOOC online learning to design a video of a new words, which makes the interpretation of the platform's new words more vivid, thus creating a resource-rich online learning platform for new words of ethnic minorities.

Acknowledgments. This work is supported by National Nature Science Foundation (No. 61501529), National Language Committee Project (No. ZDI125-36).

References

1. Qiao, C.: Standardization of Tibetan Neologisms is "an Urgent and Urgent Task" – Interpretation of Comrade Redi's Speech at the Second Session of the Third Session of the National Committee on Standardization of Tibetan Neologisms, vol. 04. China Tibet Publisher (2014)
2. Zhihe, Y.: Study on the Ontology and Technical Norms of Education Resource Cloud Service-Taking the Construction of Electronic Book Resource Service Technical Specification as an Example. East China Normal University, Shanghai (2012)
3. Wang, S.: Natural language semantic construction based on cloud database. CMC **57**(3), 603–619 (2018)
4. Kim, Y.: Convolutional neural networks for sentence classification. arXiv preprint arXiv: 1408.5882 (2014)
5. Wei, Z.: Five important nodes in the initial stage of Tibetan new word terminology work. Chin. J. Tibetology **S1**, 164 (2016)
6. Jia, Y.: Research on New Words in Tibetan News Pages. Northwest University for Nationalities, Lanzhou (2011)
7. Tao, Y.: Precautions in the application of questionnaire method. China Urban Econ. **20**, 305 (2011)
8. Hao, X., Yin, Z.: Study on the minority language life in China in the past ten years. Stud. Ethnic Educ. **01**(28), 74–80 (2017)
9. Wu, M.: A Survey of Language Use and Language Attitudes of Minority College Students in Beijing. Minzu University of China, Beijing (2007)
10. Zhi, C.: The application of constructivism learning theory in network education. J. Guangzhou Univ. (Soc. Sci. Ed.) **11**, 90 (2002)
11. Wang, T., Wu, T., Ashrafzadeh, A.H., Hc, J.: Crowdsourcing-based framework for teaching quality evaluation and feedback using linguistic 2-tuple. CMC **57**(01), 81–96 (2018)

A Classification Model for Drug Addicts Based on Improved Random Forests Algorithm

Tianyue Chen[1](✉) [iD] and Haiyan Gu[2](✉) [iD]

[1] Beihang University, Haidian, Beijing 100191, China
cty7002@126.com
[2] Jiangsu Police Institute, Nanjing 210031, Jiangsu, China
ghy7388@126.com

Abstract. To accomplish the rapid screening of drug addicts and to meet the requirements of modern police work, this research employs a data-mining technology that utilizes real samples of drug addicts as well as non-drug addicts. The aim is to construct a classification model based on pulse wave data. After the pre-processing of pulse wave data, the original random forest classification model is initially established with high accuracy, but with a relatively low recall rate and F1 score. To resolve this issue, an improved classification model is henceforth proposed. The improved model mainly involves three improvement strategies: firstly, perform cross-validation by dividing multiple training sets and test sets to obtain generalization errors; secondly, balance the sample distribution using down-sampling techniques; and finally, select model parameters based on multi-criteria analysis. According to the evaluation results of accuracy, precision, recall rates, and F1 scores, the performance of the improved random forest classification model has demonstrated its superiority and robustness via experiments using different datasets.

Keywords: Pulse wave · Data preprocessing · Random forest · Classification model

1 Introduction

Presently, the screening methods of drug addicts domestically and internationally are mostly relying on chemical-testing methods, particularly blood testing and urine testing. Notwithstanding the high accuracy derived from the use of these testing methods, the processes are extremely demanding in terms of both testing equipment as well as operators. Additionally, the noncompliant behavior of some drug addiction suspects can also be a challenging commission. Therefore, conventional testing methods no longer meet the requirements of the rapid screening of drug addicts in modern police work. To combat drug crimes and maintain social stability, a feasible solution is the use of mobile terminals for quick discrimination of drug suspects after collecting and analyzing their pulse waves.

As a non-invasive detection method, pulse wave detection has been applied in medical and clinical examinations for years [1, 2]. Related research studies involving the analysis of the physiological characteristics of drug users have been reported since

© Springer Nature Switzerland AG 2019
X. Sun et al. (Eds.): ICAIS 2019, LNCS 11632, pp. 51–62, 2019.
https://doi.org/10.1007/978-3-030-24274-9_5

2001 [3]. However, these studies were mainly focused on medical pathology analysis. Research progresses on the use of pulse wave characteristics for the detection of drug addicts are relatively scarce. In view of this, this research proposes a big data analysis method for rapid screening as assistance to modern public security practice.

The discrimination of drug suspects is a typical binary classification problem. As a conventional classification model, a simple decision tree is prone to over-fitting that can result in high variance and bias. To mitigate this issue with decision trees, a more efficient and accurate classification model, the Random Forest (RF), was proposed by Breiman in 2001 [4]. This model has been widely used in various fields since that time. This paper utilizes the age, gender, and pulse wave data collected from drug addicts as well as non-drug addicts as the dataset. The goals is to establish and improve a drug suspects classification model based on the random forest algorithm, by which the discrimination of drug addicts can be easily achieved with high efficiency.

2   Data Preprocessing for Model Establishment

In this research, the pulse wave data was collected from 912 drug addicts and nearly 10,000 non-drug addicts using the Healthme pulse acquisition and analysis system. Samples aged no more than 40 years old were selected for the dataset because people in this age group are in relatively good physical condition and are less likely to be affected by diseases. The data set included the pulse wave data of 300 drug addicts and 1293 non-drug addicts, totaling 1593 cases.

According to the pause wave characteristics, 11 variables such as age, gender and pulse wave characteristics like SlopeU, PWTT, AWX and WaveWidth were selected as model features for model construction. The definitions of some of the features are shown in Table 1, where the values of SlopeU, PWTT, AWX and WaveWidth are the average values during the acquisition period.

Table 1. Definitions of some of the model features.

Name of feature	Data type	Definitions
Gender	Factor	Gender (1 for male and 0 for female)
SlopeU	Numeric	The rising slope of the pulse wave
PWTT	Numeric	The transit time of the pulse wave from the heart to the branch of the femoral artery
AWX	Numeric	The height difference between the main peak and reflection point
WaveWidth	Numeric	The duration of more than 60% of the main peak

2.1   Multicollinearity Test

Multicollinearity refers to the significant correlations between the feature variables which may lead to the distortions or inaccuracy in model estimations [5]. The multi-colinearity test was performed on the 10 numerical variables x1, x2, x3, x4, x5, x6, x7, x8, x9 and x10, including those mentioned above. The absolute values of the correlation coefficients between the numerical feature variables are less than 0.7, indicating that the linear correlations between the model features were insignificant and these features could be applied for the construction of random forest model.

2.2 Skewness Correction

During the modeling process, data transformation is performed in the cases where the continuous response variable does not obey the normal distribution [6]. Skewness is a numerical feature measuring the direction and the extent to which the statistical data distribution skews [8]. Due to the high skewness of the 10 numerical variables, the Box-Cox transform was applied for skewness correction so that the transformed characteristic variables could be closer to the normal distribution than the original ones. The general form of the Box-Cox transformation is:

$$y(\lambda) = \begin{cases} \frac{y^{\lambda}-1}{\lambda}, & \lambda \neq 0 \\ lny, & \lambda = 0 \end{cases} \quad (1)$$

In this formula, $y(\lambda)$ is a new variable obtained after the Box-Cox transformation while y is the original numerical variable and λ is the transformation parameter. The transformation parameter λ was estimated using the original data itself, usually through the maximum likelihood estimation or Bayesian method, to determine the transformation that should be performed to form a normally distributed dataset.

2.3 Data Standardization

For a specific model, the different base units of different features will lead to the model being more biased towards features with larger base unit [7]. Only after data standardization can each feature in the model be considered with justified weights [8]. Therefore, the means and standard deviations of the 10 numerical variables were closer to 0 and 1 respectively after the Box-Cox transformation for data standardization.

3 Analysis and Construction of the Random Forest Model

3.1 Principles of the Random Forest Algorithm

On the basis of a single decision tree, a random forest consists of several decision trees whose results are aggregated into one final result through random resampling techniques and random node splitting techniques. It is essential that there is no correlation between each decision tree. The result of each decision tree in the forest is calculated and the class with the largest number of votes is the classification result of the sample. The basic instruction for random forests is to reduce the overfitting effect through combining multiple parallel estimators and averaging the results to find an optimized classification. The specific steps of the algorithm are as follows: [9]

1. Randomly extract the training data subsets. In the original training dataset, apply the bootstrap method to randomly extract M new sample subsets $S_i(i = 1, 2\ldots, M)$ so that each subset has the same number of samples in Si. Each sample is randomly chosen and replaced.
2. Randomly extract the feature variables. N feature variables are randomly selected as the model feature of each tree, where N is no more than the total number of all feature variables.
3. Node splitting, the core step of random forests algorithm. Following the principles of Gini impurity, select the optimal feature subset in which the Gini impurity value reaches its minimum for the growth of the branches. Each tree grows to their maximum depth without any pruning.
4. The classification result is determined by the largest number of votes. According to the above methods, a random forest is generated by M decision trees and result of each tree would count toward the final judgment.

3.2   Construction of a Classification Model

After data preprocessing, the feature variables were well prepared for model construction. The random forest algorithm was employed to construct the classification model for drug addicts. The specific steps taken are listed as follows:

1. The number M of characteristic variables in a feature subset of a single decision tree was set to 3, 5, and 7, respectively.
2. The number of decision trees N was set to 10, 50, 100, and 500, respectively.
3. The Cartesian product of the number of feature subsets and the number of trees were calculated to obtain the parameter combination $[M, N]$.
4. Each combination of parameters was used to fit the random forest model and obtain a total of $3 \times 4 = 12$ Random Forest models.
5. The out-of-bag accuracy of each random forest model was calculated, and the pair with the highest accuracy was selected as the optimal parameter combination.
6. The random forest model was fitted with the optimal combination of parameters and all data sets.

The out-of-bag accuracy of each random forest model is shown in Table 4.

Table 2. The out-of-bag accuracy of random forest models.

Parameter combination [M,N]	[3, 10]	[3, 50]	[3, 100]	[3, 500]	[5, 10]	[5, 50]
	85.62%	86.00%	85.81%	85.56%	85.82%	85.50%
Parameter combination [M,N]	[5, 100]	[5, 500]	[7, 10]	[7, 50]	[7, 100]	[7, 500]
	85.73%	85.69%	84.93%	85.12%	85.12%	85.19%

The data in Table 2 demonstrates that when the number of characteristic variables of the character subset is 3 and the number of trees in the random forest is 50, the fitted model has the highest out-of-bag accuracy of 86.00%. Therefore, the parameters of the first random forest classification model are determined.

3.3   Analysis of the Test Results

Definitions of Model Performance Indicators

Generally, TP represents the proportion of actual positives that are correctly identified while FP represents the proportion of actual positives that are falsely identified. TN indicates the proportion of actual negatives that are correctly identified while FN indicates the proportion of actual negatives that are falsely identified. In this paper, drug addicts were referred to as positive samples while non-drug addicts were negative samples.

- Accuracy rate = (TP + TN)/(TP + TN + FN + FP); among all people to be tested, the percentage of people whose prediction results were consistent with reality.
- Precision rate P = TP/(TP + FP); among all people predicted to be drug addicts, the percentage of those who were actual drug addicts.
- The recall rate R = TP/(TP+FN), also known as sensitivity; among all actual drug users, the percentage of people who were correctly identified.
- F1 = (2×P×R)/(P+R). F1 Score is an indicator used to measure the accuracy of the binary classification model in statistics. F1 Score considers both the accuracy rate and recall rate of the classification model [10] with a maximum value 1 and a minimum 0. The F1 score can be regarded as a weighted average of the model's accuracy and recall rate. It is a more comprehensive indicator for evaluation of the model's performance.
- The ROC curve (Receiver Operating Characteristic curve) is a kind of curve of a certain model plotted with the true positive rate (sensitivity) as the ordinate and the false positive rate (1- specificity) as the abscissa. If ROC curve is much closer to the upper left corner, the accuracy of the test will be much higher. The AUC (Area Under Curve) is the area under the ROC curve. The higher AUC value is, the better classification performance of the model will be.

Evaluation of Model Performance

By conducting further analysis of the random forest model with parameter combination [3, 50], it could be found that the precision of the model is 73.61%, the recall rate is 40.00%, and F1 is 51.84%. The corresponding ROC curve is shown in Fig. 1. The AUC valve is 0.87.

Although the accuracy of the random forest classification model for drug addicts is very high (86%), given that the number of positive and negative sample in this case is unbalanced, the ratio of which is around 1:4, merely the accuracy rate would not be sufficient to prove the model's classification performance.

Since the number of negative samples was much larger than that of positive samples, the fitted model was more inclined to predict positive samples as negative samples; the relatively low recall rate (40%) means that such model would probably miss a large number of actual drug addicts. Moreover, the F1 score is 51.84%, indicating that the overall performance of the model was not satisfactory, either.

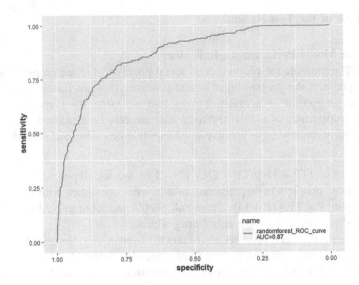

Fig. 1. The ROC curve and AUC value of the random forest model with the parameter combination [3, 50].

3.4   Problems in the Model Construction

Although the random forest model can process high-dimensional data and can be quickly established even without feature selection [11], a model which is constructed following the previous steps has the following problems:

- The evaluation of the performance can only be based on the results of out-of-bag estimations. Usually, for the random forest models, researchers use the out-of-bag estimate method to obtain an unbiased estimation of the error so that it would not be necessary to conduct cross-validation on independent test sets for error generalization. In cases when the data set is small and difficult to divide into training sets and test sets, it is effective to adopt the out-of-bag estimate for performance evaluation [12], but will introduce estimation bias, which would probably lead to an optimistic estimation of the model's generalization ability.
- When the sample is unbalanced, the prediction results tend to be the majority among all classes. During the process of constructing a random forest model, the weight on each sample is the same due to the definition of loss function. Since the weights of positive and negative samples are the same, when the number of negative samples is far more than that of the positive samples, the model will tend to judge a sample as a negative one during the optimization process of loss function. Therefore, when the sample is unbalanced, the performance of the model will be negatively affected. This will lead to a problem that the classifiers tend to be biased towards the majority [13, 14]. In real life, drug addicts, who are regarded as the minority, are far fewer in number than non-drug addicts. The previous model was not specifically designed to identify the minority.

- If the accuracy is taken as the only indicator, the evaluation of the model's performance would not be reliable since the emphases in different cases vary greatly. The analysis of the previous model has shown that single evaluation standard in parameter selection will result in an optimistic estimate of model's performance with poor actual applicability.

In summary, the model constructed using the conventional algorithm has significant defects, which needs to be improved to enhance its practical applicability.

4   Construction and Analysis of an Improved Random Forest Classification Model

4.1   Main Strategies for Constructing an Improved Classification Model

According to the problems which have been analyzed above, the construction of the classification model will be improved three aspects: performance evaluation, sample balancing and parameter selection.

4.2   Construction of the Improved Model

Division of the Training Set and Test Set
In order to obtain a more realistic evaluation of the model's generalization ability, three different combinations of training set and test set with the same number are generated from the original dataset by division. The division ratio of the training set and the test set in each combination will be set to 3:1. The values of the out-of-bag estimation in the following Tables 3, 4, 5 and 6 refer to the average out-of-bag estimation results on the three training sets, which differs from the out-of-bag estimation of the overall data in the original model.

Sample Balancing
Because the optimal parameters were determined based on the training data but the problem of unbalanced sample was still not solved, it is necessary to further improve the construction of the random forest model on the balanced data set with the assistance of downsampling algorithm [15]. The specific operation process of downsampling is as follows:

1. Employ one of the combinations with training set X and test set C.
2. Separate the drug users from the normal people in the training set X to construct a drug addict training sample set X_x and a normal training sample set X_z.
3. Conduct random sampling on the normal training sample set X_z till the number of sample set X_{z1} is consistent with that of X_x.
4. Combine X_{z1} and X_x to obtain a new training set X_1 with balanced sample categories.
5. Perform model fitting on training sets X_1, X_2, X_3.

Optimal Parameter Selection

1. Calculate the out-of-bag F1 scores of the three training sets respectively. The average value was used as the evaluation indicator to perform the first round of parameter selection. The out-of-bag F1 scores of the random forest models under all parameter combinations are shown in Table 3.

Table 3. The out-of-bag F1 scores for the first round of parameter selection.

Parameter combination [M,N]	[3, 10]	[3, 50]	[3, 100]	[3, 500]	[5, 10]	[5, 50]
	48.95%	50.12%	49.87%	50.10%	52.53%	52.19%
Parameter combination [M,N]	[5, 100]	[5, 500]	[7, 10]	[7, 50]	[7, 100]	[7, 500]
	50.16%	52.59%	50.23%	49.95%	49.83%	49.53%

The maximum value of F1 is 52.59% and the standard deviation is 1.22%, so the range within 1.5 standard deviations below the maximum is 50.76%–52.59%. The candidate parameter combinations such as [5, 10], [5, 50] and [5, 500] were selected for the next round.

2. Calculate the out-of-bag accuracy of the three training sets respectively in the second round. The out-of-bag accuracy of the random forest models with selected parameter combinations are shown in Table 4.

Table 4. The out-of-bag accuracy for the second round of parameter selection.

Parameter combination [M,N]	[5, 10]	[5, 50]	[5, 500]
	85.84%	85.57%	86.12%

Because the maximum accuracy is 86.12%, and the standard deviation is 0.27%, the range within 1.5 standard deviations below the maximum is 85.71%–86.12%. Therefore, the candidate parameter combinations such as [5, 10] and [5, 500] were selected for the next round.

3. Calculate the out-of-bag AUC value of the three different training sets respectively in the third round. The out-of-bag AUC value of the random forest models with selected parameter combinations are shown in Table 5.

Table 5. The out-of-bag AUC value for the third round of parameter selection.

Parameter combination [M,N]	[5, 10]	[5, 500]
	0.8471	0.8491

Because the maximum AUC value is 0.8491, and the standard deviation is 0.0014, the range within 1.5 standard deviations is 0.847–0.8491. The candidate parameter combinations such as [5, 10] and [5, 500] were selected for the next round.

4. Calculate the out-of-bag F1 score of the three different training sets respectively in the final round. The out-of-bag F1 score of the random forest models with selected parameter combinations are shown in Table 6.

Table 6. The out-of-bag F1 score for the fourth round of parameter selection.

Parameter combination [M,N]	[5, 10]	[5, 500]
	0.4946	0.5263

As is shown in Table 6, when the number of feature variables in a feature subset is 5 and the number of trees in the forest is 500, random forest model with the best performance can be constructed.

4.3   Construction Flowchart

The complete construction process is shown in Fig. 2:

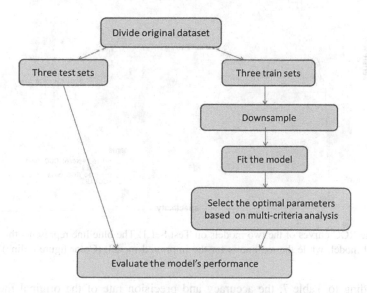

Fig. 2. Construction flowchart.

4.4   Tests and Comparisons of the Improved Model

After completing the dataset division and sample balancing mentioned above, three different combinations of training sets and test sets were generated based the previous dataset. The original model, also known as the previous model, and the improved model were tested on these dataset combinations respectively. Table 7 shows the accuracy, precision rate, recall rate, and F1 scores of the two models on the three test sets. Figure 3 displays the ROC curves of the two models on Test Set 1.

Table 7. Comparison between performances of the two models on three test sets.

		Accuracy	Precision	Recall	F1 score	AUC
Test set 1	Before improvement	84.59%	66.67%	36.67%	0.4731	0.89
	After improvement	82.39%	52.13%	81.67%	0.6364	0.90
Test set 2	Before improvement	86.79%	73.68%	46.67%	0.5714	0.90
	After improvement	81.45%	50.50%	85.00%	0.6335	0.90
Test set 3	Before improvement	83.33%	60.61%	33.33%	0.4301	0.85
	After improvement	82.70%	52.81%	78.33%	0.7833	0.86

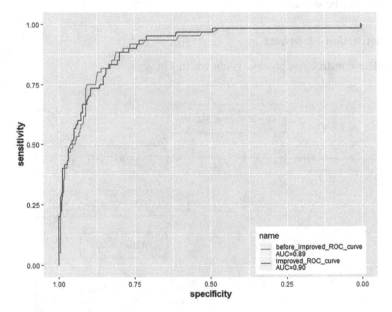

Fig. 3. The ROC curves of the two models on Test Set 1. The blue line represents the result of the original model, while the red line is for the improved model. (Color figure online)

According to Table 7, the accuracy and precision rate of the original model are slightly higher than those of the improved model while the recall rate and F1 scores of the improved model are obviously much higher than that of the original model.

Generally, accuracy is the primary evaluation indicator of a classification model if the sample distribution is balanced. However, in practical police work, the recall rate and F1 score are of much higher significance to achieving the discrimination of drug addicts than the other indicators since the police should correctly identify as many actual drug addicts as possible. As the most common indicator, AUC describes the overall performance of the model; the F1 score is the harmonic mean of the precision and recall rates, which can effectively reflect the ability of the model to identify the minority class. Therefore, the improved model can better meet actual need.

Furthermore, both the results of Table 7 and Fig. 3 show that the AUC value of the improved model is slightly higher than that of the original model while the ROC curves are almost the same. The ROC curves and AUC values of the model on Test Set 2 and Test Set 3 are similar to those of Test Set 1, which demonstrates the model's high robustness and generalization ability on different datasets.

From the above analysis, it can be summarized that the prediction ability of the improved model was greatly enhanced concerning the problem of the biased model. In special cases where the dataset is unbalanced and the minority class should be effectively identified, more weight should be assigned on the F1 score to evaluate the practical performance of the model. Therefore, the overall performance of the improved model is superior to the original model as it can identify actual drug addicts more accurately.

5 Conclusion

In this research, an original classification model based on random forest algorithm for drug addicts is initially constructed by training on pulse wave data from real samples of drug addicts and non-drug addicts. In view of defects of the original model, three kinds of improvement strategies are proposed:

1. Dividing multiple training sets and test sets in the construction process of random forest model and perform cross-validation to obtain a more generalized model performance evaluation, which can solve the problem of optimistic estimation caused by only relying on the out-of-bag estimation.
2. Downsampling method is applied to balance the data set, which can mitigate the potential risk of a majority-biased model.
3. Multiple evaluation indicators such as F1 score, accuracy rate and AUC value are adopted to select the optimal parameters of the model.

On the basis of these improvements, a new random forest classification model is constructed. According to the test results of improved classification model, the performance evaluation indicators such as the recall rate and F1 score, which are most essential for the special case of drug addicts discrimination, have been raised greatly. The improved model shows significant superiority to the original one, providing a more reliable technical solution for rapid screening in modern police work.

In recent years, methods applying deep learning to solve classification problems have emerged in an endless stream. However, the existing deep learning algorithms focus on analyzing digital image and natural language problems while there are few specific algorithms for problems with low-dimensional data. In addition, models based on deep learning are less interpretable and are more likely to be overfitting. At this stage, the amount of dataset in this paper has not met the requirements for deep learning training, but this method provides a direction for further research.

References

1. Li, S., Zhang, F.: Point-contact type FBG dynamic pressure sensor and its application in the measurement of pulse information. Optoelectron. Laser 27(10), 1017–1022 (2016)
2. Xiaorui, S., Aike, Q.: Evaluation of cardiovascular health based on pulse wave detection technology. J. Med. Biomech. 30(5), 468–473 (2015)
3. Chen, M., Cai, K.: A modern spectrum analysis method for pulse abnormalities of drug abusers. J. Chongqing Univ. (Nat. Sci. Ed.) 24(4), 98–102 (2001)
4. Breiman, L.: Random forests. Mach. Learn. 54(1), 5–32 (2001)
5. Ming, L.: The solution of multicollinearity: a new standard to rule out variables. Stat. Decis. Mak. 5, 82–83 (2013)
6. Zhang, Y., Gong, H.: Approximate linear Bayesian estimation of skewness coefficient. Stat. Decis. Mak. 78–81 (2017)
7. Sun, H., McIntosh, S.: Analyzing cross-domain transportation big data of New York City with semi-supervised and active learning. Comput. Mater. Continua 57(1), 1–9 (2018)
8. Chen, Y., Zhou, J., Du, J.: Credit evaluation method based on transaction data. Comput. Appl. Softw. 35(5), 168–171 (2018)
9. Feifei, S., Zhuo, C., Xiaolei, X.: Application of an improved random forest based classifier in crime prediction domain. J. Intell. 33(10), 148–152 (2014)
10. Hao, H., Xianhui, W.: Maximum F1-score criterion based discriminative feature compensation training algorithm for automatic mispronunciation detection. Acta Electronica Sin. 43(7), 1294–1299 (2015)
11. Verikas, A., Gelzinis, A., Bacauskiene, M.: Mining data with random forests: a survey and results of new tests. Pattern Recognit. 22(2), 330–349 (2011)
12. Zhihua, Z.: Machine Learning. Tsinghua University Press, Beijing (2016)
13. Yin, H., Hu, Y.: Unbalanced feature selection algorithm based on random forest. J. Sun Yat-Sen Univ. (Nat. Sci. Ed.) 53(5), 59–65 (2014)
14. Shishi, D.: Analysis of random forest theory. Integr. Technol. 2(1), 1–7 (2013)
15. Wu, X., Zhang, C., Zhang, R., et al.: A distributed intrusion detection model via nondestructive partitioning and balanced allocation for big data. CMC Comput. Mater. Continua 56(1), 61–72 (2018)

Studying L-Diversity and K-Anonymity Over Datasets with Sensitive Fields

Franck Seigneur Nininahazwe[✉]

School of Computer and Software,
Nanjing University of Information Science and Technology, Nanjing, China
seigneurinuyasha777@yahoo.fr

Abstract. Data mining has been popular for its possibilities and what it has to offer. There is a need to consider the privacy of the people which data will be used when publishing datasets. The main issue is to be able to publish datasets without compromising privacy of the people in them. That's when techniques like k-anonymity and l-diversity can be used to protect privacy of every tuple in those datasets. There are a lot of techniques which would help protect the privacy of a given dataset, but here only two techniques were considered, l-diversity and k-anonymity. In this paper, first the two main techniques were introduced. Secondly, experimentations comparing k-anonymity to l-diversity over 3 main possible attacks scenario were run: the prosecutor scenario, the journalist scenario and the marketer scenario. Those experimentations considered datasets with sensitive data and quasi-identifier. In the end the author offers a conclusion stating which one of the two techniques is the best regarding the security and the utility of the dataset.

Keywords: Privacy Preserving Data Mining (PPDM) · K-anonymity · L-diversity

1 Introduction

Nowadays, many company or organization publish a lot of data. It can be any sort of data: medical data, customer data, census… While publishing those data, there is a need to protect the privacy of people in them. Publishing data and putting individuals in them at risk of privacy breach is unacceptable. In order to prevent that, some techniques have been developed.

In this paper, the author is going to discuss two of them in particular. K-anonymity and l-diversity are well known techniques for privacy preserving while publishing data. Sweeney [1] proposed k-anonymity in order to reduce the privacy breach in data when they were published. This technique works by using generalization and suppression to make an individual record identical to at least k − 1 other records in the anonymized dataset. L-diversity was proposed to tackle k-anonymity weaknesses concerning homogeneity and background knowledge. Homogeneity attack becomes possible when equivalence class lacks diversity, and on the case of background knowledge the attacker is aware of a relationship between quasi-identifiers and sensitive attributes [2].

© Springer Nature Switzerland AG 2019
X. Sun et al. (Eds.): ICAIS 2019, LNCS 11632, pp. 63–73, 2019.
https://doi.org/10.1007/978-3-030-24274-9_6

Although those techniques have been used for few years now, and there is other many anonymization based techniques like t-closeness or M-Varience, the author chose to study k-anonymity and l-diversity because they are the most popular ones and also the ones with the most available algorithms. The goal here is to perform our own experimentation in order to be sure which one is the best or which one has the less weak point. In the end, the author will discuss his findings and make a conclusion on which one is the best.

2   Related Works

Privacy preserving data mining techniques have been discussed in some papers, some doing review about a selected number of techniques and doing research on their pros and cons [2], or evaluating the actual state of things and doing some predictions for the future [3], others showing proposed methods [4].

In more specific cases, papers have been written about k-anonymity, its weak points what it brings and how it is generally used [1]. L-diversity has also some papers discussing what it brings, why it should be used and some even stating that it's the solution to k-anonymity weaknesses [4, 5].

Those techniques aren't the only ones [6]. Due to the recent exponential increase in data, many techniques were made to protect users' privacy. They are classified either based on data distributions, level in mining process, and how data is manipulated. Which gives us three main categories: randomization based techniques (random noise addition, condensation,…), anonymization based techniques (k-anonymity, l-diversity, …) and cryptography based techniques (homomorphic encryption, secret sharing,…) [7]. Many other techniques are being developed in order to ensure that data mining is done without violating the privacy of the people those data belong to.

It's by reading those literatures that the author decided to make his own experimentations and choose two of the anonymization based techniques k-anonymity and l–diversity and see which one is the best between the two.

3   Data Mining

In short, data mining is the process of finding patterns in large datasets and extract those patterns, it's also the action of extracting information from a dataset and transform it into an understandable structure for further use. The ultimate goal of data mining is prediction, and predictive data mining is the most common type of data mining and one that has the most direct business applications. The process of data mining consists of three stages [2, 8]:

- **The initial exploration:** This stage usually starts with data preparation which may involve cleaning data, data transformations, selecting subsets of records and in case of datasets with a large numbers of variable, you may need to perform some preliminary feature selection operations in order to reduce the amount of variables so you can have a number of variables you can deal with (depending on the statistical methods which are being considered).

- **Model building or pattern identification with validation/verification:** This stage involves considering various models and choosing which one is the best considering how they perform when they tasked a prediction task (i.e., explaining the variability in question and producing stable results across samples). This may sound like a simple operation, but in fact, it sometimes involves a very elaborate process. In that operation, people uses many types of techniques based on a procedure called "competitive evaluation of models," which is using different models on the same sample of that and according to the results choose which you may use.
- **Deployment:** this last stage consists on using the selected method on the data so you can generate some prediction about the results or at least have an idea about what kind of outcome you should expect.

4 Privacy Preserving Data Mining

In order to mine data people needs methods but also a way to protect sensible information that's why preservation of privacy in data mining has emerged as an absolute prerequisite for exchanging confidential information in terms of data analysis, validation, and publishing [8, 9].

There are two main considerations of PPDM.

Firstly, sensitive raw data like identifiers, names, addresses and so on, should be modified or trimmed out from the original database, in order for the holder of the data to not be able to deduce anyone private information or put at risk such kind of information. The sensitivity of a function, denoted Δf is defined by:

$$\Delta f = \max \|f(D_1) - f(D_2)\| \tag{1}$$

Secondly, if by using data mining you can mine some sensitive information then those data should also be excluded, because those type of data can really compromise data privacy. With that knowledge it can be said that privacy preservation has two major categories: users' personal information and information concerning their collective activity. The former is referred to as individual privacy preservation and the latter is referred to as collective privacy preservation.

Individual Privacy Preservation: The primary goal of data privacy is the protection of personally identifiable information. In general, information is considered personally identifiable if it can be linked somehow to an individual person which means indirectly or directly. Thus, when we use data mining techniques on personal data, the attribute values which can link to a person are private and need to be protected. Miners are then able to learn from global models rather than from the characteristics of a particular individual.

Collective Privacy Preservation: Protecting personal data may not be enough. Sometimes, we may need to hide the ability of learning from sensitive data representing the activities or behavior of a group. We refer to that kind of protection of sensitive data as collective privacy preservation. Here, the objective is quite the same to that one for statistical databases, in which security control mechanisms provide aggregate infor-mation about groups and, at the same time, should prevent disclosure of confidential information about individuals.

However, unlike as is the case for statistical databases, another objective of col-lective privacy preservation is to preserve strategic pattern that are paramount for strategic decisions, rather than minimizing the distortion of all statistics.

In other words, the goal here is not only to protect information that can lead to an identification of a person but also some patterns and trends that are not supposed to be discovered. Some group privacy can be achieved by applying the following formula for D1 and D2 differing on c items:

$$\Pr[A(D_1) \in S] \le \exp(\varepsilon c) \times \Pr[A(D_2) \in S] \qquad (2)$$

Privacy Preservation in Data Mining has some limitations: Privacy Preservation Data Mining techniques do not mean perfect privacy, for example, a given data mining computation which won't reveal the sensitive data, but the data mining result will enable all parties to estimate the value of the sensitive data. It isn't that the PPDM was "broken", but that the result itself violates privacy.

Although many methods have a lot in common, they also have their differences and it's those differences which make someone use this method instead of the other one according to his objectives and results he/she wants to achieve.

As mentioned before, there are many PPDM techniques but the author chose to discuss only two of them for reasons already explained. The next point will discuss those two techniques.

5   Analysis of the Two Chosen Techniques

5.1   K-anonymity

K-anonymity is an anonymization technique which uses generalization and suppression by doing so try to protect against identity disclosure. For k-anonymity, the protected micro-data table T' is said to satisfy k-anonymity if and only if each combination of quasi-identifiers (QI) attributes in T' occurs at least k times [1].

It was created as an attempt to solve the problem: "Given person-specific field-structured data, produce a release of the data with scientific guarantees that the indi-viduals who are the subjects of the data cannot be re-identified while the data remain practically useful".

For the given parameter k and the quasi-identifier $QI = \{A_{i1}, A_{i2}, .., A_{il}\}$, a table T is said to be k-anonymous if for each tuple t ε T, there exist at least another (k − 1) tuples $t_1, t_2, \ldots, t_{k-1}$ such that those t tuples have the same projection on the quasi-identifier [1]:

$$t_1(A_{i1}, .., A_{il}) = t_2(A_{i1}, .., A_{il}) = \ldots = t_{k-1}(A_{i1}, .., A_{il}) \qquad (3)$$

A dataset which is going to be anonymized is divided into different types of attributes [1]:

- **Explicit identifiers** which are set of attributes that explicitly identify a person such as an ID, name or social security ID.
- **Quasi-identifiers** which are set of attributes which if combined can help re-identify a tuple. For example birth date, gender and address can be considered as quasi-identifiers.
- **Sensitive attributes** are attributes that contain some sensitive information about a person, for example a disease, a salary.
- And finally **Non-sensitive attributes** are set of attributes which cannot cause any harm.

While using k-anonymity those types of attributes will need to be considered according to the dataset in question because not all of them contains the same thing. The following tables are just an example of how it works (Tables 1 and 2).

Table 1. A dataset example

Name	Gender	Age	Job
John	Male	20	Cashier
Anna	Female	56	Teacher
Elisabeth	Male	25	Inventor
Gael	Female	52	Researcher

Table 2. An example of a k-anonymized dataset

Name	Gender	Age	Job
*	Male	20>=age<=30	Cashier
*	Female	>=50	Teacher
*	Male	20>=age<=30	Inventor
*	Female	>=50	Researcher

This data has 2-anonymity with respect to the attributes 'Gender' and 'Age' since for any combination of these attributes found in any row of the table there are always at least 2 rows with those exact attributes. The attributes available to an adversary are called "quasi-identifiers". Each "quasi-identifier" tuple occurs in at least k records for a dataset with k-anonymity.

Because k-anonymization does not include any randomization, attackers can still make inferences about data sets that may harm individuals. For example, if the 56 years old female Anna is known to be in the database above, then it can be reliably said that she is either a researcher or a teacher.

5.2   L-diversity

L-diversity applies anonymization by using a group based system in order to preserve privacy in datasets by reducing granularity of a data representation.

Let a q*-block be a set of tuples such that its non-sensitive values generalize to q*. A q*-block is l-diverse if it contains l well represented values for the sensitive attribute S. A table is l-diverse, if every q*-block in it is l-diverse [4, 5].

L-diversity is defined in three different ways [4, 5]:

- **Distinct l-diversity** which ensures that there is at least l different sensitive value in each q-block.
- **Recursive (c, l)-diversity** for which in a given q*-block, let r_i denotes the number of times the ith most frequent sensitive value appears in that q*-block. Given a constant c, the q*-block satisfies recursive (c, ℓ)-diversity if $r_1 < c(r_l + r_{l+1} + \ldots + r_m)$. A table T* satisfies recursive (c, ℓ)-diversity if every q*block satisfies recursive ℓ-diversity.
- **Entropy l-diversity,** for it, a table is said to be entropy l-diverse if:

$$-\sum_{s \varepsilon S} p_{(q*,s)} \log \left(p_{(q*,s')} \right) \geq \log(l) \tag{4}$$

Where $p_{(q*,s)} = \frac{n_{(q*,s)}}{\sum_{s' \varepsilon S} n_{(q*,s')}}$ is the fraction of tuples in the q*-block with sensitive attribute value equal to S.

The following is an example of how it works (Tables 3 and 4):

Table 3. An example of a medical dataset

Name	Age	Condition
Arya	25	VIH
John	33	Cancer
Josephine	22	Cancer
Erica	38	Heart disease
Emma	26	Cancer
Alex	35	Viral infection

Table 4. 2-diverse anonymized medical dataset

Name	Age	Condition
*	<=29	VIH
*	<=29	Cancer
*	<=29	Cancer
*	>=30	Viral infection
*	>=30	Cancer
*	>=30	Heart disease

6 Type of Attacks

Privacy of datasets which are going to be published can be diminished or destroyed by many types of attacks. Here the author concentrated on three major attacks, which are prosecutor model attack, journalist model attack and marketer model attack.

For example, we can use the next formula, where I $(\cdot)$ is the indicator function and f_j is the size of equivalence class j in the dataset and t a given threshold.

$$R_a = \frac{1}{n} \sum_{j \in J} f_j \times I(\theta_j > t) \tag{5}$$

6.1 Prosecutor Model

We assume that the intruder is trying to re-identify the record belonging to a specific person. This specific person is known to the intruder. For example, this specific target person may be the intruder's neighbor or a famous person. The intruder has some background information about that target, and then uses this background information to search for a matching record in the disclosed database [2, 9, 10].

If any of the three following conditions are true, then prosecutor risk is a threat [2, 9]:

- The disclosed dataset represents the whole population (e.g., a population registry) or has a large sampling fraction. If the whole population is being disclosed then the intruder would have certainty that the target is in the disclosed data set. Also, a large sampling fraction means that the target is very likely to be in the disclosed data set.
- The dataset is not a population but is a sample from a population, and if it can be easily determined who is in the disclosed dataset. For example, the sample may be a data set from an interview survey conducted in a company and it is generally known who participated in these interviews because the participants missed half a day of work. In such a case it is known within the company, and to an internal intruder, who is in the disclosed data set.
- The individuals in the disclosed data set self-reveal that they are part of the sample. For example, subjects in clinical trials do generally inform their family, friends, and even acquaintances that they are participating in a trial. One of the acquaintances may attempt to re-identify one of these self-revealing subjects. Individuals may also disclose information about themselves on their blogs and social networking site pages which may self-reveal that they are part of a study or a registry. However, it is not always the case that individuals do know that their data is in a dataset. For example, for studies where consent has been waived or where patients provide broad authorization for their data or tissue samples to be used in research, the patients may not know that their data is in a specific dataset, providing no opportunity for self-revealing their inclusion.

In the above conditions the term population is used loosely. It does not mean the population of a geographic area, but the group of people who have a specific known characteristic. For example, a data set of all patients with renal cancer for a province would be a renal cancer population registry since everyone with renal cancer would be in that registry.

6.2   Journalist Model

The intruder does not care which individual is being re-identified, but is only interested in being able to claim that it can be done. In this case the intruder wishes to re-identify a single individual to discredit the organization disclosing the data [11].

An intruder gets hold of an identification database with 100 records. The intruder then attempts re-identification by matching an arbitrary record against the records in a medical database by comparing for example age or gender. In our example, once an arbitrary individual is re-identified, the intruder will know which disease that individuals suffer from.

However, a smart intruder would focus on the records in equivalence classes with the highest probability of re-identification. Equivalence classes with the smallest value have the highest probability of being re-identified, and therefore we assume that a smart intruder will focus on these.

Furthermore, an intruder may commit illegal acts to get access to population registries. For example, privacy legislation and the Elections Act in Canada restrict the use of voter lists to running and supporting election activities. There is at least one known case where a charity allegedly supporting a terrorist group has been able to obtain Canadian voter lists for fund raising [11].

6.3   Marketer Model

The attacker doesn't target a person in particular. The attacker aims at re-identifying a high number of individuals. It is only considered successful if a high number of tuples can be re-identified. It doesn't matter who is re-identified as long as all tuples which could be re-identified are re-identified then that's the only thing which interest the attacker. The intruder may be doing that just to harm the company or the holder of the dataset or just to harm as many people as possible. The motivation could also be about money.

6.4   Comparison

The following table is a small comparison between the three different types of attacks (Table 5).

Table 5. Comparison of the three attacks

Model	Background knowledge	Targeted tuple	Tuples on highest risk only
Prosecutor model	Yes	Known	No
Journalist model	No	Any	Yes
Marketer model	No	Several	No

7 Experimentations and Results on Datasets with Sensitive Fields

In our experimentations, we used UTD anonymization tool and ARX anonymization tool. All of that was done on a computer running windows with 8 GB of memory and an Intel double core of 2.30 GHz.

We ran our experimentations on different datasets, one containing the disease of the person as the sensitive field, the second one containing the profession of the person as the sensitive field and finally for the last one what was decided to be the sensitive field was the project each one was working on and their medical status. Those datasets where found on public repository and modified or merged according to what was needed.

In the following graphics, we considered the number of records at highest risk and success rate of each kind of attack, the results are the average value for the different tables and are expressed in percentages. The author used different size datasets, the settings where different according to the size, 4-anonymity or 4-diversity for small size datasets and up to 100-anonymity or 100-diversity for really large datasets

8 Discussion

From the results in Fig. 1 you can see the number of values at highest risk depends from one technique to another, it also seemed that more the number of tuples were high more easy it was to reduce that number.

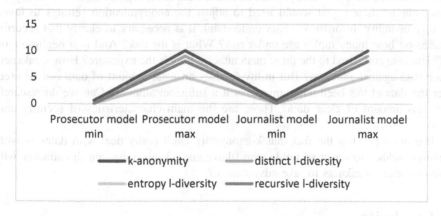

Fig. 1. The amount of values on highest risk

In Fig. 2 the entropy l-diversity seems to be the one which performed the best against attacks. Although that's the case it doesn't perform well when it comes to utility compared to the others. The more a dataset is secured the more its utility is diminished.

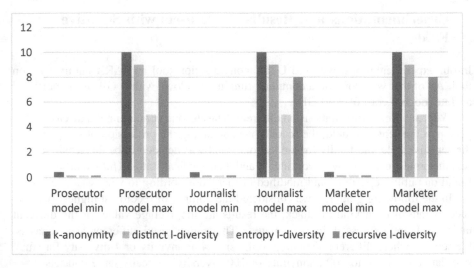

Fig. 2. The average success rate of each attack

The experimentations proved that there are no perfect solutions. Each technique has its pros and cons. Whether you want security or utility, you must choose what you prefer in order to choose a suitable technique. The security or utility is easily manageable when faced with small size datasets, the more a dataset is large the more difficult it is to manage security over utility or vice versa. With that said it is clear that utility is the opposite of security, you can't have both at the highest level, depending on what your needs are, you would need to adjust the anonymization settings to favor security or utility. In order to better understand, it is necessary to clarify that security focuses on how many tuples are under risk? What is the risk? And is it negligible or not? But also compared to the three main attacks, how is the exposure? How weakened is the data against attackers? But utility focuses on what amount of data can be used after the dataset has been anonymized, is it a sufficient amount? Can we do research over this amount of clear data? Those are the main characteristics of security and utility.

The other point is the fact that k-anonymity can't really deal with datasets with sensitive fields, the sensitive fields won't have enough diversity and the attacker will have one more weakness to take advantage of.

9 Conclusion

In this paper, two PPDM techniques were presented which are k-anonymity and l-diversity. Those two methods were defined and an explanation on how they work was given. Examples were added for a better understanding.

The second part concerned his findings. Although, it's now clear that in matter of security l-diversity is better than k-anonymity for datasets with sensitive fields, things are not that simple. There is other criteria you need to consider like what kind of dataset you want to have after anonymization, how utile do you want it be, or do you prefer security over utility and so on.

As a conclusion, we found that there is no better method unless you consider some criteria like security, or utility. In that case, if the dataset contains sensitive fields then l-diversity is the best solution.

References

1. Sweeney, L.: K-anonymity: a model for protecting privacy. Int. J. Uncertain. Fuzziness Knowl. Based Syst. **10**(05), 557–570 (2002)
2. Senosi, A., Sibiya, G.: Classification and evaluation of privacy preserving data mining: a review. In: 2017 IEEE AFRICON, pp. 849–855. IEEE (2017)
3. Malik, M.B., Ghazi, M.A., Ali, R.: Privacy preserving data mining techniques: current scenario and future prospects. In: 2012 Third International Conference on Computer and Communication Technology (ICCCT), pp. 26–32. IEEE (2012)
4. Ye, Y., Wang, L., Han, J., Qiu, S., Luo, F.: An anonymization method combining anatomy and permutation for protecting privacy in microdata with multiple sensitive attributes. In: 2017 International Conference on Machine Learning and Cybernetics (ICMLC), vol. 2, pp. 404–411. IEEE (2017)
5. Machanavajjhala, A., Gehrke, J., Kifer, D., Venkitasubramaniam, M.: L-diversity: privacy beyond K-anonymity. In: Proceedings of the 22nd International Conference on Data Engineering, ICDE 2006, p. 24. IEEE (2006)
6. Wang, X., Xiong, C., Pei, Q., Qu, Y.: Expression preserved face privacy protection based on multi-mode discriminant analysis. CMC Comput. Mater. Contin. **57**(1), 107–121 (2018)
7. Xiong, L., Shi, Y.: On the privacy-preserving outsourcing scheme of reversible data hiding over encrypted image data in cloud computing. CMC Comput. Mater. Contin. **55**(3), 523–539 (2018)
8. Mendes, R., Vilela, J.P.: Privacy-preserving data mining: methods, metrics, and applications. IEEE Access **5**, 10562–10582 (2017)
9. Raj, R., Kulkarni, V.: A study on privacy preserving data mining: techniques, challenges and future prospects. Int. J. Innov. Res. Comput. Commun. Eng. **3**(11) (2015)
10. Li, N., Li, T., Venkatasubramanian, S.: t-closeness: privacy beyond K-anonymity and L-diversity. In: IEEE 23rd International Conference on Data Engineering, ICDE 2007, pp. 106–115. IEEE (2007)
11. El Emam, K., Dankar, F.K.: Protecting privacy using k-anonymity. J. Am. Med. Inform. Assoc. **15**(5), 627–637 (2008)

Power System Transient Stability Prediction Algorithm Based on ReliefF and LSTM

Bo Li[1(✉)], Ting Wen[2], Chao Hu[3], and Bo Zhou[3]

[1] Electric Power Dispatching and Control Center of Guangdong
Power Grid Co., Ltd., Guangzhou 510600, China
18665676787@163.com
[2] Management Science Research Institute of Guangdong Power Grid Co., Ltd.,
Guangzhou 510600, China
[3] NARI Information & Communication Technology Co., Ltd.,
Nanjing 210033, China

Abstract. The stability of the power system has great significance to the national economy, and the sudden situation of the power system will bring great losses. The prediction of the transient stability of the power system can be helpful for coping with the sudden situation of the power system. In order to predict the transient stability of power system, this paper proposes an algorithm based on ReliefF and LSTM network. We first use the ReliefF algorithm to filter features to obtain the most relevant ones, and then the optimal parameters of the LSTM neural network are obtained through iteration, and the trained neural network is used to make a transient prediction of the power network. Compared with the traditional method and SVM algorithm, our algorithm is superior in the aspects of efficiency and accuracy.

Keywords: Transient stability prediction · LSTM · ReliefF · Power system

1 Introduction

With the rapid development of the national economy and the gradual penetration of renewable energy, the power system has formed complex characteristics such as large power systems, ultra-high voltage, long distance, heavy load, large-area networking, AC-DC combined transmission in decade. The safe and stable operation of the power system has always been a core issue in the power field. The more complex junction and behavior characteristics of the power system pose new challenges for the safe and stable operation of the power system. Many large-scale blackouts have had a huge impact on people's daily lives.

Power system stability means that the power system can still maintain stable operation after being disturbed [1]. The stability of the power system is divided into three categories: power angle stability, voltage stability and frequency stability.

The traditional methods of power system transient stability analysis mainly include the following three aspects

(1) Time domain simulation method [1]: This is a mature transient stability analysis method widely used in power systems. The time domain method mathematically

© Springer Nature Switzerland AG 2019
X. Sun et al. (Eds.): ICAIS 2019, LNCS 11632, pp. 74–84, 2019.
https://doi.org/10.1007/978-3-030-24274-9_7

models the whole system according to the physical properties and topological relations of power system components, fully retaining The nonlinear characteristics and dynamic response characteristics of the system are used as the initial value of the system. The state of the system state quantity is calculated by time-series and solving the differential equation form.

(2) Direct method [2]: The transient stability problem is mainly analyzed by using system energy and its transformation. The calculation speed is greatly improved compared with the time domain simulation method. At the same time, the direct method can also provide information such as the stability margin of the system.

(3) Hybrid method [3]: Combining time domain simulation and transient energy function method, taking into account the advantages of both. It first obtains the system's variable curve by time domain method simulation, and then calculates it according to the system energy, thus obtaining transient stability data.

With the development of computer technology, it is possible to obtain national synchronized measurement data in real time in the power grid dispatching center, which provides an opportunity for machine learning training through data and stable prediction of power system. On the one hand, the transient stability domain boundary can be regarded as a nonlinear function of a system state variable. Because the function is too complicated, it is difficult to directly obtain an analytical solution. On the other hand, machine learning is a natural data analysis tool that can be used to find the connection between system state variables and stability domain boundaries. In theory, if there is a nonlinear relationship, then the machine learning method can be used to fit this relationship to predict the power system transients. In 1999, Liu et al. [4] proposed a new radial basis neural network based on fuzzy clustering to predict the stability of power systems. In 2007, Wu et al. [5] proposed a transient stability prediction algorithm based on least squares support vector machine. According to the idea of block matrix inversion, the standard algorithm was improved and the calculation speed was improved. In 2013, Wang et al. [6] proposed a power system transient stability evaluation method based on response trajectory and core vector machine. Compared with the previous method, the proposed method has lower time and space complexity and higher evaluation accuracy.

Machine learning generally falls into two broad categories [7], supervised learning and unsupervised learning. The difference between the two is whether the provided training set is labeled, and the application of machine learning is wide [8, 9]. Unlike expert systems, machine learning automatically trains a model through an algorithm that allows output prediction of unknown input samples. With the development of computer science, machine learning faces the problem of "curse of dimensional" [10], that is, there will be some redundant features affecting the results of the algorithm. Similar problems exist in the power network transient prediction algorithm. When the characteristics of the power network can be provided enough, we must consider how to more rationally screen out the most relevant features to ensure more accurate training. A more generalized predictive model. The ReliefF algorithm [11] is a feature selection algorithm extended from the Relief algorithm [12, 13]. The Relief algorithm solves the problem of two classifications, and ReliefF is an extension to multiple classifications. There are many transient states of the power system, so our ReliefF algorithm can well screen the most relevant features. Then the training of the predictive model is performed. The LSTM network is a cyclical network that is a variant of RNN, and an we all know, LSTM has a wide range of applications [14–16]. We know that the transient prediction of the power system is not an independent process, but a timing-related process. Therefore, it is reasonable to use the LSTM network to predict the transient state of the power system.

The next sections of this paper are organized in the following structure. The second section of this paper introduces the basic knowledge of ReliefF and LSTM network. The third section introduces the power system transient stability prediction algorithm based on ReliefF and LSTM networks. Next, in Sect. 4, experiments and analysis were performed to evaluate the performance of the algorithm. The last section discusses and summarizes the algorithm.

2 Preliminary Knowledge

2.1 ReliefF Algorithm

The ReliefF algorithm was proposed in 1994 by Kononeill [11]. The ReliefF algorithm is an extension of the multi-class problem of the Relief algorithm. Relief is an algorithm developed by Kira and Rendell in 1992 that takes a filter-method approach to feature selection that is notably sensitive to feature interactions [12, 13]. First we collect the labelled data, which is divided into two categories. We then randomly select a sample from these data to find the closest samples to the random sample. The closest sample in the same class is called Near-hit, and the closest sample in the different class is called Near-miss. Then we update the weight vector with the weight update rule according to Near-hit and Near-miss. Repeat the above steps T times. At this point, we get a final weight vector, and divide this final weight vector by T to get the average of a weight vector. We will select the feature based on it and a pre-set threshold, which is typically an empirical value. Features that are greater than the threshold will be considered as related features being selected, and features that are less than the threshold will be considered as non-related features and discarded. In this way, we will eventually get a set of features that we can use to do the work of machine learning, the flow of the algorithm is as follows in Fig. 1.

The Relief algorithm is relatively simple, but it has high efficiency and satisfactory results, it is widely used, its limitation is that it can only process two types of data. Kononeill has extended it to handle multi-category problems. When dealing with multiple types of problems, the ReliefF algorithm randomly takes a sample R from the training sample set, and then finds the k neighbor samples (near Hits) from the R-like sample set, from the different classes of each R. In the sample set, find k neighbor samples (near Misses), and then update the weight of each feature.

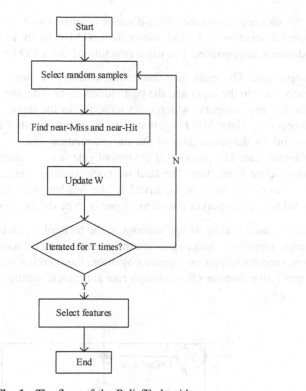

Fig. 1. The flow of the ReliefF algorithm

2.2 LSTM Neural Network

LSTM was proposed in 1997 by Sepp Hochreiter and Jürgen Schmidhuber [17] and improved in 2002 by Felix Gers' team [18]. LSTM is a variant of RNN, which is shown in Fig. 2, RNN is mainly processed sequentially over time. Long-term information needs to traverse all cells sequentially before entering the current processing unit, which causes vanishing gradients. As a result, the LSTM network has emerged, which can bypass the unit to remember longer time steps and eliminate some of the problem of gradient disappearance. The LSTM unit consists of a memory unit, an input gate, an output gate, and a forgotten gate. A schematic diagram of the LSTM unit is shown in Fig. 3 below, the unit remembers values in any time interval, and three gates control the flow of information into and out of the unit.

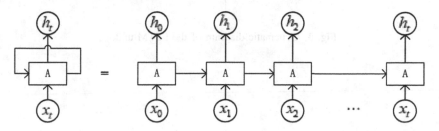

Fig. 2. The algorithm process of RNN

RNN can only remember short-distance information in a sequence of information. The special structure of LSTM allows the LSTM network to have the ability to store long distance information. The main structure of the LSTM network is as follows:

(1) Input gate: The input gate determines whether the input value is worth retaining according to the input and the past hidden layer state, thereby making a constraint on the new memory, which is an indicator of the input information update.
(2) Forgetting Gate: The Forgotten Gate evaluates whether the past memory unit is useful for the calculation of the current memory unit.
(3) Output gate: The purpose of the output gate is to separate the final memory from the hidden layer state. The final memory contains a large amount of information that does not need to be saved in the hidden layer state. This threshold can evaluate which part of the memory needs to be displayed in the hidden layer state.

LSTM has a variety of applications in the technology field. LSTM-based systems can learn translation languages, control robots, image analysis, document summarization, speech recognition image recognition, handwriting recognition, control of chat bots, predictive disease, click-through rate and stock, synthetic music, and more.

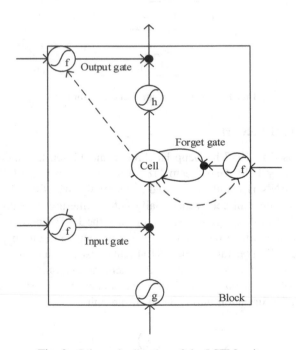

Fig. 3. Schematic diagram of the LSTM unit.

3   Power System Transient Stability Prediction Algorithm Based on ReliefF and LSTM

The overall flow chart of the power system transient stability prediction algorithm is shown in the following figure. It can be divided into three parts.

(1) Data preparation: the data preparation phase of the algorithm is divided into two parts, namely data acquisition and processing and obtaining the most relevant features of the power system through the ReliefF algorithm;

(2) Model training: The training part of the model includes two parts: training and accuracy verification. Firstly, the LSTM is used to train the transient stability model of the power network. After the training, the accuracy of the model is verified. If the preset criteria are not met, continue training until the engineering use standard is reached, and the prediction model is obtained;

(3) Result feedback: The feedback part of the results includes two parts: power system transient stability prediction and prediction result feedback. The obtained prediction model is put into the data to be predicted, and the power network transient stability prediction result is obtained. Next, we will explain the algorithm in detail, the algorithm is based on the following specific steps, and the flow of our algorithm is shown in Fig. 4.

Step 1. First, the power transient data is collected, and some of the error fields are processed or deleted, and some data is labeled to obtain tagged input data.

Step 2. The ReliefF algorithm is then used to filter features to obtain the most relevant ones, and use these features to facilitate the next classification task.

Step 2-1. Set all the feature weights to 0,

Step 2-2. Then randomly select one sample R from the N labeled sample data, after that, we can find the k nearest neighbors H_j (j = 1, 2,..., k) of R from the same sample set of R, and find k nearest neighbors $M_j(C)$ from each different class of sample set, the formula is as follows

$$
\begin{aligned}
W_{i+1} = W_i &- \sum_{j=1}^{k} diff(i, R, H_j)/mk \\
&+ \sum_{C \neq class(R)} \left[\frac{p(C)}{1-p(class(R))} \right] \sum_{j=1}^{k} diff(i, R, M_j(C))/mk
\end{aligned}
\tag{1}
$$

Step 3. Repeat the above steps T times until the final correlation vector of the feature is obtained and the most relevant feature is filtered according to the preset threshold.

Step 4. Calculate the output value of each neuron in the forward direction. According to the steps, the forgetting gate f_t, the candidate gate c_t, the output gate o_t and the output s_t are respectively calculated.

Step 4-1. The forgetting gate can be implemented by the activation function shown in Eq. 2.

$$
f_t = \sigma(W_f^T \times s_{t-1} + U_f^T \times x_t + b_f)
\tag{2}
$$

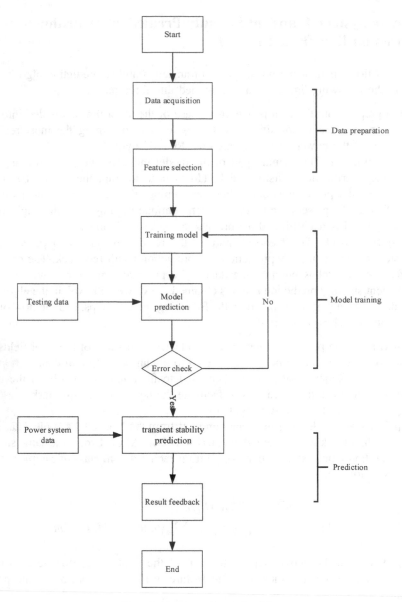

Fig. 4. Process of our algorithm.

Where σ represents the activation function, which is usually sigmoid. W_f^T represents the forgotten gate weight matrix, U_f^T is the weight matrix between the input layer and the hidden layer of the forgetting gate, and bf represents the offset of the forgetting gate. The subscript "f" here is the first letter of "forget".

Step 4-2. Then we calculate the candidate gate which is responsible for the current input information and past memory information.

$$C_t = \tanh(W_c^T \times s_{t-1} + U_c^T \times x_t + b_c) \tag{3}$$

Here the activation function is replaced by tanh, which regulates the output value between -1 and 1.

Step 4-3. Then we use Eq. 4 to calculate the output gate

$$O_t = \sigma(W_o^T \times s_{t-1} + U_o^T \times x_t + b_o) \tag{4}$$

Here the activation function is still using sigmoid. As you can see from the previous introduction, sigmoid will regularize O_t to a weight value between 0 and 1.

Step 4-4. Finally, we use Eq. 5 to calculate the output s_t and use these parameters to construct the LSTM unit.

$$s_t = O_t \times \tanh(C_t) \tag{5}$$

Step 5. Determine the optimization objective function. In the early stages of training, the output value and the expected value will be inconsistent, so the error term value of each neuron can be calculated, thereby constructing a loss function.

Step 6. The network weight parameter is updated according to the gradient guidance of the loss function. Similar to traditional RNN, the backpropagation of the LSTM error term consists of two levels: one is spatially level, and the error term is propagated to the upper layer of the network. The other is the time level, which propagates back in time, that is, from the current t time, the error of each moment is calculated.

Step 7. Then jump to step 1 and repeat steps 4, 5, and 6 until the network error is less than the threshold. At this point we can get a model that meets the industrial requirements, and we can use this model to predict the transient stability of the new power system data.

Step 8. Transient stability prediction: We collect the data to be detected and preprocess these data, and then the most relevant features are extracted using the ReliefF algorithm. Input these processed data into the model obtained in the previous step to predict the transient stability of the power system, and the results obtained are recorded.

Step 9. Feedback of prediction results: The predicted records are analyzed. If the transient stability of the power system is destroyed, the data can be further analyzed and checked according to the predicted data, and the reasons for the transient stability of the power system network are obtained.

4 Experiment and Analysis

We will experiment from the two aspects of accuracy and efficiency. This algorithm selects the traditional power system transient prediction method and SVM [6] transient prediction algorithm to compare with this algorithm. The comparison results will be explained in the following subsections.

4.1   Accuracy Analysis

First, let's analyze the accuracy of the algorithm. Table 1 and Fig. 5 clearly show the accuracy of traditional methods, SVM algorithms and our algorithms.

Table 1. Accuracy of three methods (%).

	1	2	3	4	5	6	7	8	9	10
Traditional method	81.5	78.8	79.2	76.3	73.3	76.7	76.2	83.7	72.5	80.8
SVM	83	79.4	83.5	81.6	87.1	87.6	86.8	81.8	81.4	81.7
Ours	88.6	92.1	94.5	89.2	88.7	91.7	93.2	89.6	87.3	88.4

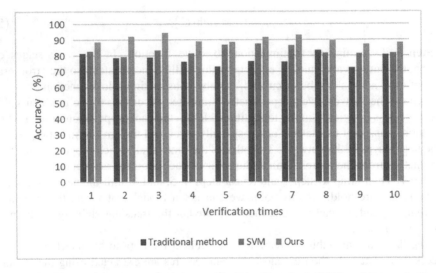

Fig. 5. The accuracy comparison among Traditional method, SVM, and our method.

From the graphs and tables, we can see that the accuracy of the traditional method is the lowest, and the accuracy of the SVM algorithm is slightly higher than the traditional transient prediction method. The accuracy of our proposed algorithm is higher than that of traditional transient prediction methods and SVM algorithms. Therefore, our algorithm is superior in accuracy to traditional methods and SVM algorithms.

4.2   Efficiency Analysis

Next we analyze the efficiency of the algorithm. The efficiency of the algorithm is the time spent on transient prediction. The longer the time, the lower the efficiency, and vice versa. Table 2 and Fig. 6 clearly show the efficiency comparison between the traditional transient prediction method, the SVM algorithm and our proposed algorithm.

Table 2. Time consumption of three methods (s).

	1	2	3	4	5	6	7	8	9	10
Traditional method	83	91	88	87	85	87	89	92	91	87
SVM	65	67	66	71	72	65	74	66	71	68
Ours	40	46	41	45	44	42	46	44	50	48

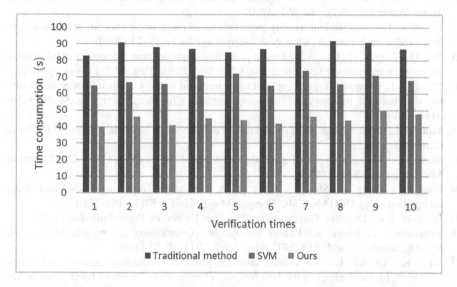

Fig. 6. Comparison of time consumption among Traditional method, SVM, and our method.

It can be clearly seen from the graph and table that the traditional method takes the most time. Therefore, the efficiency of the traditional method is the lowest, and the SVM algorithm transient prediction takes less time than the traditional method. Our proposed algorithm takes the lowest time to perform power system transient prediction. Therefore, our proposed algorithm has the highest efficiency.

5   Conclusion

With the continuous development of power systems, there is an increasing demand for safe and stable operation of power systems. Timely and correct predictions of the transients of the power system can help professionals control the risks that can occur in the power system. How to quickly and accurately predict the transient state of the power system has attracted wide attention of researchers. We propose a power system transient prediction algorithm based on ReliefF and LSTM networks, first screening the most relevant features, and then training an efficient and accurate prediction algorithm based on the most relevant features selected. In this paper, we compare the proposed algorithm with the traditional method and the SVM algorithm, and analyze it from the two aspects of accuracy and efficiency. The comparison results show that our algorithm not only achieves accuracy or efficiency. Very good results, better than the other two algorithms.

References

1. Tang, Y., Wang, Y.T., Tian, F., et al.: Research and development of stability analysis, early warning and control system for huge power grid. Power Syst. Technol. **36**(7), 1–11 (2012)
2. Wan, Q.L., Shan, Y.D.: Re-understanding of the application of direct method to analyze the transient stability of power system. Autom. Electr. Power Syst. **22**(9), 13–15 (1998)
3. Maria, G.A., Tang, C., Kim, J.: Hybrid transient stability analysis power systems. IEEE Trans. Power Syst. **5**(2), 384–393 (1990)
4. Liu, Y.T., Lin, F.: Transient stability prediction based on phasor measurement technique and fuzzy radial basis network. Chin. Soc. Electr. Eng. **20**(2), 19–23 (2000)
5. Wu, Q., Yang, Y.H., Liu, W.Y.: Online prediction of power system transient stability based on least squares support vector machine. Chin. Soc. Electr. Eng. **27**(25), 38–43 (2007)
6. Wang, Y.J., Wang, B., Tang, F., et al.: Online transient stability evaluation of power system based on response trajectory and core vector machine. Chin. Soc. Electr. Eng. **34**(19), 3178–3186 (2014)
7. Mohri, M., Rostamizadeh, A., Talwalkar, A.: Foundations of Machine Learning. MIT Press, Cambridge (2012)
8. Meng, R.: A fusion steganographic algorithm based on Faster R-CNN. CMC Comput. Mater. Contin. **55**(1), 1 (2018)
9. Fang, W., Zhang, F., Sheng, V.S., et al.: A method for improving CNN-based image recognition using DCGAN. CMC Comput. Mater. Contin. **57**(1), 167–178 (2018)
10. Bellman, R.E.: Dynamic Programming. Princeton University Press, Princeton (1957)
11. Kononenko, I., Šimec, E., Robnik-Šikonja, M.: Overcoming the myopia of inductive learning algorithms with RELIEFF. Appl. Intell. **7**(1), 39–55 (1997)
12. Kira, K., Rendell, L.: The feature selection problem: traditional methods and a new algorithm. In: Proceedings of the 10th National Conference on Artificial Intelligence. AAAI Press, San Jose (1992)
13. Kira, K., Rendell, L.: A practical approach to feature selection. In: Proceedings of the Ninth International Workshop on Machine Learning, pp. 249–256. Morgan Kaufmann Publishers, San Francisco (1992)
14. Shi, X., Chen, Z., Wang, H., et al.: Convolutional LSTM Network: a machine learning approach for precipitation nowcasting. In: International Conference on Neural Information Processing Systems, pp. 802–810. MIT Press, Cambridge (2015)
15. Graves, A., Jaitly, N., Mohamed, A.R.: Hybrid speech recognition with deep bidirectional LSTM. In: 2013 IEEE Workshop on Automatic Speech Recognition and Understanding, pp. 273–278. IEEE, Olomouc (2013)
16. Ordóñez, F.J., Roggen, D.: Deep convolutional and LSTM recurrent neural networks for multimodal wearable activity recognition. Sensors **16**(1), 115 (2016)
17. Graves, A.: Long short-term memory. In: Supervised Sequence Labelling with Recurrent Neural Networks. SCI, vol. 385, pp. 37–45. Springer, Heidelberg (2012). https://doi.org/10.1007/978-3-642-24797-2_4
18. Gers, F.A., Schmidhuber, J., Cummins, F.: Learning to forget: continual prediction with LSTM. In: International Conference on Artificial Neural Networks, ICANN 2002, pp. 850–855. IET (2002)

A No-Pairing Proxy Re-Encryption Scheme for Data Sharing in Untrusted Cloud

Xin Qian[1,2(⊠)], Zhen Yang[1,2], Shihui Wang[3], and Yongfeng Huang[1,2]

[1] Department of Electronic Engineering, Tsinghua University,
Beijing 100084, China
qianxl16@mails.tsinghua.edu.cn
[2] Tsinghua National Laboratory for Information Science and Technology,
Beijing 100084, China
[3] School of Computer Science and Information Engineering, Hubei University,
Wuhan 430062, China

Abstract. To protect data sharing from leakage in untrusted cloud, proxy re-encryption is commonly exploited for access control. However, most proposed schemes require bilinear pair to attain secure data sharing, which gives too heavy burden on the data owner. In this paper, we propose a novel lightweight proxy re-encryption scheme without pairing. Our scheme builds the pre-encryption algorithm based on computational Diffie–Hellman problem, and designs a certificateless protocol based on a semi-trusted Key Generation Center. Theoretical analysis proves that our scheme is Chosen-Ciphertext-Attack secure. The performance is also shown to achieve less computation burden for the data owner compared with the state-of-the-art.

Keywords: Proxy re-encryption · No pairing · Certificateless ·
Cloud data sharing

1 Introduction

Booming cloud computing has been developing very fast for many years, which brings convenience for billions of users all over the world. However, widely used cloud service has also caught the attention of attackers which have conducted many cloud security accidents, especially cloud data leakage. Accumulating data leakage in cloud environment makes cloud service untrusted for users.

To protect cloud data from leakage, encryption access control mechanisms has been introduced for secure data sharing [16], including proxy re-encryption.

The notion of proxy re-encryption (PRE) was first introduced by Blaze et al. [1] in 1998, and they promoted the first bidirectional PRE scheme based on a simple modification of the El Gamal encryption scheme [13]. Proxy re-encryption (PRE) is a cryptographic scheme which efficiently solve the problem of delegation of decryption

Supported by the National Key Research and Development Program of China (No. 2016YFB0801301, No. 2016YFB0800402); the National Natural Science Foundation of China (No. U1405254, No. U1536207).

© Springer Nature Switzerland AG 2019
X. Sun et al. (Eds.): ICAIS 2019, LNCS 11632, pp. 85–96, 2019.
https://doi.org/10.1007/978-3-030-24274-9_8

rights. It allows a semi-trusted proxy with re-encryption keys, generated by the dele-gator, to transform a ciphertext under a given public key of the delegator into a ciphertext of the same message under a different public key the delegatee, while learning nothing about the encrypted message. PRE schemes have many practical applications due to its transformation property, such as cloud storage [2], distributed file systems, encrypted email forwarding [1], outsourced filtering of encrypted spam and so on.

Most of the PRE schemes in practical applications are constructed based on either traditional Public Key Infrastructure (PKI) or Identity-Based Encryption (IBE) setting. In the PKI setting, the authenticity of a user's public key is assured by Digital Cer-tificates, which is digitally signed and issued by a trusted third party called the Cer-tification Authority (CA). It is the management of certificates, which is a costly and a cumbersome process including the revocation, storage, distribution of certificates and so on, that inherently makes PRE schemes based on PKI setting inefficient. In the IBE setting, the secret keys of all the users are generated by a third party called the Private Key Generator (PKG), therefore brings the key-escrow problem.

To solve both certificate management problem in the PKI setting and key-escrow problem in the IBE setting, certificateless public key encryption (CLPKE) was first introduced by Al-Riyami and Paterson [4] in 2003. CLPKE combines the advantages of PKI and of IBE, while does not suffer from the aforementioned problems, therefore indicates a new direction for the construction of the PRE schemes. The notion of certificateless proxy re-encryption (CLPRE) was introduced by Sur et al. [5] in 2010.

We propose a lightweight proxy certificateless proxy re-encryption(CLPRE) scheme for data sharing in untrusted cloud. Our scheme builds the pre-encryption algorithm based on computational Diffie–Hellman problem, and designs a certificate-less protocol based on a semi-trusted Key Generation Center. Compared with the proxy re-encryption schemes state-of-the-art, our CLPRE scheme can be more lightweight for data owner and achieve same security against Chosen Ciphertext Attack (CCA).

2   Related Work

Since the first bidirectional PRE scheme was promoted by Blaze et al. [1] in 1998, there have been lots of works and promotions about PRE scheme. Ateniese et al. [3] proposed a unidirectional PRE schemes in 2005, which is the first unidirectional PRE scheme based on bilinear pairings and achieves CPA-secure (chosen-plaintext attack, CPA).

Canetti et al. [6] and Libert et al. [7] proposed the first bidirectional multi-hop and the first unidirectional single hop scheme both achieve RCCA-secure (replayable chosen ciphertext attack) in the standard model. For greater security, the construction of CCA-secure (chosen-ciphertext attack, CCA) PRE scheme has become an significant issue. In 2008, Deng et al. [8] proposed a bidirectional CCA secure PRE scheme without the bilinear pairings. Later, Hanaoka et al. [9] proposed a generic construction of CCA secure PRE scheme in the standard model.

All the PRE schemes are constructed based on either traditional Public Key Infrastructure (PKI) or Identity-Based Encryption (IBE) setting. In order to avoid both certificate management problem in the PKI setting and key-escrow problem in the IBE setting, certificateless public key encryption (CLPKE) first introduced by Al-Riyami and Paterson [4] in 2003 is considered in the construction of the PRE schemes. In 2010, Sur et al. [5] first introduced the notion of CLPRE and proposed a CCA secure CLPRE scheme in the random oracle model, which was shown to be vulnerable to chosen ciphertext attack by Zheng et al. [10]. In 2013, a CLPRE scheme using bilinear pairings proposed by Guo et al. [11] satisfies RCCA-security in the random oracle model. A lot of works have been proposed during these years [17]. Unfortunately, construction of CLPRE schemes has so far depended on the costly bilinear pairings.

In 2005, Baek et al. [12] proposed an efficient certificateless public key encryption (CLPKE) scheme that does not rely on the bilinear parings. In 2014, Yang et al. [14] addressed a CLPRE scheme without bilinear pairing, which claimed to be CCA-secure in the random oracle model, yet was shown to be vulnerable to chain collusion attack in by Srinivasan et al. [15] in their work proposed in 2015. In that work, they proposed the first CCA-secure unidirectional certificateless PRE scheme without bilinear pairing under the Computational Diffie-Hellman (CDH) assumption in the random oracle model.

3   Model

In order to describe our lightweight proxy re-encryption scheme for data sharing in untrusted cloud more figurative and in details, Fig. 1 gives an overview of entities and their activities in this framework.

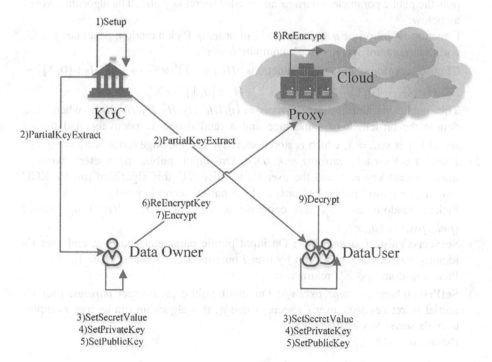

Fig. 1. Model architecture of our lightweight proxy re-encryption scheme.

Data Owner: Owner encrypts his data and uploads the ciphertext to the Cloud. Owner decides which users are authorized to share data from cloud by generating re-encryption keys for those authorized to transform the ciphertext.

Data User: Authorized users can share data from cloud by download the transformed ciphertext from cloud and decrypt by their own.

Proxy: Proxy is a semi-trusted third party in untrusted cloud. It re-encrypt the ciphertext in cloud under the private key of data owner into a ciphertext of the same message under given private keys of authorized users, while learning nothing about the encrypted data.

KGC: Key Generation Center is a semi-trusted fourth party, which means it is honest but curious. KGC initialize the whole system, and generate partial keys for everyone in the system. Users can generate his own public key and private key from partial keys generated by KGC and secret value chosen by himself. At the same time, KGC does not have any information about the secret value generated by the user and hence cannot decrypt any ciphertext.

4 CLPRE Scheme

The detailed construction of our CLPRE scheme are as follows. User i and user j represent the data owner and the authorized user respectively.

(1) **Setup** (1^κ): In the setup phase, on input a security parameter 1^κ, the Probabilistic Polynomial Time (PPT) algorithm run by the Key Generation Center (KGC) outputs the public parameters *params* and master secret key *msk*. The algorithm works as below:

Generate a k-bit prime q and a group $\mathbb{G}$ of order q. Pick a random generator $g \in \mathbb{G}$, and then randomly pick $s \in \mathbb{Z}_q^*$, compute $h = g^s$;

Choose cryptographic hash functions $H_1 : \{0,1\}^* \times \mathbb{G} \to \mathbb{Z}_q^*$, $H_2 : \{0,1\}^* \to \mathbb{Z}_q^*$, $H_3 : \mathbb{G} \to \{0,1\}^{l+l_0}$, $H_4 : \mathbb{G} \to \mathbb{Z}_q^*$, $H_5 : \{0,1\}^* \to \mathbb{Z}_q^*$.

The public parameters are $params = \{q, l, l_0, H_1, H_2, H_3, H_4, H_5\}$, where l, l_0 denote the bit-length of a message and a randomness respectively, and master secret key is $msk = s$, which is stored secretly. The message space is $\mathcal{M} = \{0,1\}^l$.

(2) **PartialKeyExtract** $(params, msk, ID_i)$: On input public parameters *params*, master secret key *msk* and the user i's identity ID_i, this algorithm run by KGC outputs the partial public key ppk_i and the partial secret key psk_i.

Pick a random $\alpha_i \in \mathbb{Z}_q^*$, and compute $a_i = g^{\alpha_i}$, $x_i = \alpha_i + sH_1(ID_i, a_i)$, return $(ppk_i, psk_i) = (a_i, x_i)$.

(3) **SetSecretValue** $(params, ID_i)$: On input public parameters *params*, and user i's identity ID_i, this algorithm run by user i outputs user i's secret value v_i.

Pick a random $z_i \in \mathbb{Z}_q^*$, return $v_i = z_i$.

(4) **SetPrivateKey** $(params, psk_i, v_i)$: On input public parameters *params*, user i's partial secret key psk_i, user i's secret value v_i, this algorithm run by user i outputs user i's secret key sk_i.

Return $sk_i = (x_i, z_i)$.

(5) **SetPublicKey** $(params, ppk_i, v_i)$: On input public parameters $params$, user i's partial public key ppk_i, user i's secret value v_i, this algorithm run by user i outputs user i's public key pk_i.

Compute $u_i = g^{z_i}$, return $pk_i = (a_i, u_i)$.

(6) **ReEncryptKey** $(params, ID_i, (pk_i, sk_i), ID_j, pk_j)$: On input public parameters $params$, user i's identity ID_i, user i's cryptographic key pair (pk_i, sk_i), user j's identity ID_j and public key pk_j, this algorithm run by user i outputs a re-encryption key $rk_{i \to j}$ from user i to user j.

Parse pk_i as (a_i, u_i), sk_i as (x_i, z_i) and pk_j as (a_j, u_j), compute $V_j = a_j h^{H_1(ID_j, a_j)}$, and $W_{ij} = H_5\left(r_j^{z_i} \| u_j^{x_i} \| ID_i \| pk_i \| ID_j \| pk_j\right)$. Then compute $B_i = (x_i H_4(u_i) + z_i)$, return $rk_{i \to j} = B_i W_{ij}$.

(7) **Encrypt** $(params, m, pk_i)$: On input public parameters $params$, data $m \in \mathcal{M} \left(\mathcal{M} = \{0, 1\}^l\right)$, and user i's public key pk_i, this algorithm run by user i outputs a second level ciphertext c_i.

Parse pk_i as (a_i, u_i), pick a randomness $\sigma \in \{0, 1\}^{l_0}$, compute $V_i = a_i h^{H_1(ID_i, a_i)}$, $r = H_2(m \| \sigma \| ID_i \| u_i)$, then compute $c_1 = g^r$, $c_2 = (m \| \sigma) \oplus H_3(A_i^r)$, in which $A_i = V_i^{H_4(u_i)} \cdot u_i$. Return $c_i = (c_1, c_2)$.

(8) **ReEncrypt** $(params, c_i, rk_{i \to j})$: On inputs public parameters $params$, a second level ciphertext c_i, a re-encryption key $rk_{i \to j}$, this algorithm run by proxy outputs a first level ciphertext c_j.

Parse $c_i = (c_1, c_2)$, compute $c_1' = c_1^{rk_{i \to j}}$, $c_2' = c_2$, in which $rk_{i \to j} = B_i W_{ij}$, $B_i = (x_i H_4(u_i) + z_i)$. Return $c_j = (c_1', c_2')$.

(9) **Decrypt** $(params, pk_i, c_i)$: On input public parameters $params$, user i's public key pk_i, and a ciphertext c_i, this algorithm run by user i outputs either a plaintext $m \in \mathcal{M}$ or an error symbol $\perp$.

   i. **Decrypt2** $(params, pk_i, c_i)$: The algorithm is run by the data owner user i.

     Parse pk_i as (a_i, u_i), sk_i as (x_i, z_i), $c_i = (c_1, c_2)$, compute $(m \| \sigma) = c_2 \oplus H_3\left(c_1^{(x_i H_4(u_i) + z_i)}\right)$, then compute $r = H_2(m \| \sigma \| ID_i \| u_i)$.

     Check if the equation holds: $g^r = c_1$.

     Return m if it holds: $(m \| \sigma) = c_2 \oplus H_3\left(c_1^{(x_i H_4(u_i) + z_i)}\right)$.

     Otherwise return $\perp$, which implies the ciphertext c_i is wrongful.

   ii. **Decrypt1** $(params, pk_i, c_i)$: The algorithm is run by the authorized user j.

     Parse pk_i as (a_i, u_i), sk_i as (x_i, z_i), $c_i = (c_1', c_2')$, compute $V_j = a_j h^{H_1(ID_j, a_j)}$, $W_{ji} = H_5\left(V_j^{z_i} \| u_j^{x_i} \| ID_i \| pk_i \| ID_j \| pk_j\right)$ and $(m \| \sigma) = c_2' \oplus H_3\left(c_1'^{1/W_{ji}}\right)$, $r = H_2(m \| \sigma \| ID_j \| u_j)$.

     Check if the equation holds: $\left(V_j^{H_4(u_j)} \cdot u_j\right)^{r W_{ji}} = c_1'$.

     Return m if it holds: $(m \| \sigma) = c_2' \oplus H_3\left(c_1'^{1/W_{ji}}\right)$.

     Otherwise return $\perp$, which implies the ciphertext c_i is wrongful.

5 Correctness

5.1 Correctness of PartialKey

As we can see from the **PartialKeyExtract** algorithm, $a_i = g^{\alpha_i}$, $x_i = \alpha_i + sH_1(ID_i, a_i)$, the equation $g^{psk_i} = g^{x_i} = g^{\alpha_i + sH_1(ID_i, a_i)} = a_i h^{H_1(ID_i, a_i)} = ppk_i h^{H_1(ID_i, ppk_i)}$ will hold, if the partial cryptographic key pair $(ppk_i, psk_i) = (a_i, x_i)$ is properly generated by KGC.

5.2 Correctness of Ciphertext2

As we can see from the **Encryt** algorithm, $c_1 = g^r$, $c_2 = (m \parallel \sigma) \oplus H_3(A_i^r)$, the

equation $g^r = g^{H_2(m\parallel\sigma\parallel ID_i\parallel u_i)} = g^{H_2\left(c_2 \oplus H_3\left(c_1^{(x_i H_4(u_i) + z_i)}\right) \parallel ID_i \parallel u_i\right)} = c_1$ will hold, if $c_i = (c_1, c_2)$ is a correctly second level ciphertext generated by user i.

5.3 Correctness of Ciphertext1

As we can see from the **ReEncryt** algorithm, $c_1' = c_1^{rk_{i \to j}} = (g^r)^{rk_{i \to j}}$, in which

$rk_{i \to j} = B_i W_{ij}$, $c_2' = c_2 = (m \parallel \sigma) \oplus H_3\left(A_j^r\right)$, the equation $c_1' = g^{rB_j W_{ji}} = A_j^{rW_{ji}} = \left(V_j^{H_4(u_j)} \cdot u_j\right)^{H_2(m\parallel\sigma\parallel ID_j\parallel u_i)W_{ji}} = \left(V_j^{H_4(u_j)} \cdot u_j\right)^{H_2\left(c_2' \oplus H_3\left(c_1'^{1/W_{ji}}\right)\parallel ID_j\parallel u_i\right)W_{ji}}$ will hold, if $c_i = (c_1', c_2')$ is a correctly first level ciphertext generated by the proxy.

5.4 Correctness of Decrypt2

As mentioned above, $c_1 = g^r$, $c_2 = (m \parallel \sigma) \oplus H_3(A_i^r)$, hence $(m \parallel \sigma) = c_2 \oplus H_3(A_i^r) = c_2 \oplus H_3(g^{B_i r}) = c_2 \oplus H_3(c_1^{B_i}) = c_2 \oplus H_3\left(c_1^{(x_i H_4(u_i) + z_i)}\right)$, in which $A_i = V_i^{H_4(u_i)} \cdot u_i$, $B_i = (x_i H_4(u_i) + z_i)$.

5.5 Correctness of Decrypt1

As mentioned above, $c_1' = c_1^{rk_{i \to j}}$, $c_2' = c_2 = (m \parallel \sigma) \oplus H_3\left(A_j^r\right)$, hence $(m \parallel \sigma) = c_2' \oplus H_3\left(A_j^r\right) = c_2' \oplus H_3(g^{B_j r}) = c_2' \oplus H_3\left(c_1^{B_j}\right) = c_2' \oplus H_3\left(c_1'^{1/W_{ji}}\right)$.

5.6 Correctness of the Whole Scheme

For all $m \in \mathcal{M}$ and all users' cryptographic key pair (pk_i, sk_i), (pk_j, sk_j), these algorithms should satisfy the following conditions of correctness:

(a) $\text{Decrypt}_2(params, sk_i, \text{Encrypt}(params, ID_i, pk_i, m)) = m$
(b) $\text{Decrypt}_1(params, sk_j, \text{ReEncrypt}(params, rk_{i \to j}, c_i)) = m$
    where $c_i = \text{Encrypt}(params, ID_i, pk_i, m)$, $rk_{i \to j} = \text{ReEncryptKey}(params, ID_i, (pk_i, sk_i), ID_j, pk_j)$.

6 Security Proof

Two types of adversaries, Type I adversary $\mathcal{A}_I$ and Type II adversary $\mathcal{A}_{II}$ are considered for a CL-PRE. $\mathcal{A}_I$ models an attacker from the outside (i.e. anyone except the KGC) without access to the master secret key msk but may replace public keys of entities (i.e. user i or user j) with values of its choice. $\mathcal{A}_{II}$ models an honest-but-curious KGC who has access to the master secret key msk, but is not allowed to replace public keys of entities. In our model, Type I adversary $\mathcal{A}_I$ is not considered since

Here we focus on the Type II adversary $\mathcal{A}_{II}$ only and prove the chosen ciphertext security of first level ciphertext.

Definition (CLPRE-CCA Security). We say a CLPRE scheme is CLPRE-CCA secure if the scheme is 1st-IND-CLPRE-CCA secure and 2nd-IND-CLPRE-CCA secure.

Theorem 1 (1st-IND-CLPRE-CCA security). The proposed CLPRE scheme is 1st-IND-CLPRE-CCA secure against Type-II adversary $\mathcal{A}_{II}$ in the random oracle model, if the CDH assumption holds in $\mathbb{G}$.

Lemma 1. Assume that H_1, H_2, H_3, H_4, H_5 are random oracles, if there exists a 1st-IND-CLPRE-CPA Type I adversary $\mathcal{A}_{II}$ against the proposed CLPRE scheme with advantage ϵ when running in time t, making at most q_{pk} public key request queries, at most q_{pak} partial key extract queries, at most q_{sk} private key extract queries, at most q_{pkr} public key replacement queries, at most q_{rk} re-encryption key extract queries, at most q_{re} re-encryption queries, q_{dec_2} decrypt2 queries, q_{dec_1} decrypt1 queries, and q_{H_i} random oracle queries to $H_i (1 \leq i \leq 5)$. Then, for any $0 < v < \epsilon$, there exists an algorithm $\mathcal{C}$ to solve the (t', ϵ')-CDH problem in $\mathbb{G}$ with

$$t' \leq t + (q_H + 2q_{H_1} + 2q_{H_2} + q_{H_3} + q_{H_4} + q_{H_5} + q_{pk} + q_{pak} + q_{sk} + q_{rk} + q_{re}$$
$$+ q_{dec_2} + q_{dec_1}) \mathcal{O}(1) + (2q_{pk} + q_{pak} + 2q_{sk} + 5q_{rk} + 6q_{re}$$
$$+ 2q_{dec_2} + 5q_{dec_1})t_e$$

$$\epsilon' \geq \frac{1}{q_{H_3}} \left(\frac{2(\epsilon - v)}{e\left(1 + q_{pak} + q_{rk}\right)} - \tau \right)$$

where e is the base of the natural logarithm, we denote the time taken for exponentiation operation in group $\mathbb{G}$ as t_e, and τ denotes the advantage that $\mathcal{A}_{II}$ can distinguish the incorrectly-formed re-encryption keys in our simulation from all correctly-formed re-encryption keys in a "real world" interaction.

Theorem 2 (2nd-IND-CLPRE-CCA security). The proposed CLPRE scheme is 2nd-IND-CLPRE-CCA secure against Type-II adversary $\mathcal{A}_{II}$ in the random oracle model, if the CDH assumption holds in $\mathbb{G}$.

Lemma 2. Assume that H_1, H_2, H_3, H_4, H_5 are random oracles, if there exists a 2nd-IND-CLPRE-CPA Type I adversary $\mathcal{A}_{II}$ against the proposed CLPRE scheme with advantage ϵ when running in time t, making at most q_{pk} public key request queries, at most q_{pak} partial key extract queries, at most q_{sk} private key extract queries, at most q_{pkr} public key replacement queries, at most q_{rk} re-encryption key extract queries, at most q_{re} re-encryption queries, q_{dec_2} decrypt2 queries, q_{dec_1} decrypt1 queries, and q_{H_i} random oracle queries to $H_i(1 \le i \le 5)$. Then, for any $0 < v < \epsilon$, there exists an algorithm C to solve the (t', ϵ')-CDH problem in $\mathbb{G}$ with

$$t' \le t + (q_H + q_{H_1} + q_{H_2} + q_{H_3} + q_{H_4} + q_{H_5} + q_{pk} + q_{pak} + q_{sk} + q_{rk} + q_{re}$$
$$+ q_{dec_2} + q_{dec_1}) \mathcal{O}(1) + (2q_{pk} + q_{pak} + 2q_{sk} + 5q_{rk} + 6q_{re}$$
$$+ 2q_{dec_2} + 5q_{dec_1})t_e$$

$$\epsilon' \ge \frac{1}{q_{H_3}} \left(\frac{2(\epsilon - v)}{e\left(1 + q_{pak} + q_{rk}\right)} - \tau \right)$$

where e is the base of the natural logarithm, we denote the time taken for exponentiation operation in group $\mathbb{G}$ as t_e, and τ denotes the advantage that $\mathcal{A}_{II}$ can distinguish the incorrectly-formed re-encryption keys in our simulation from all correctly-formed re-encryption keys in a "real world" interaction.

Proof. We show how to construct an algorithm C which can solve the (t', ϵ')-CDH problem in group $\mathbb{G}$.

Suppose C is given a CDH challenge tuple $(g, g^a, g^b) \in \mathbb{G}^3$ with random unknown $a, b \in \mathbb{Z}_q^*$ as input. The goal of C is to compute the g^{ab}. C act as challenger and play the 2nd-IND-CLPRE-CPA "Game II" with adversary $\mathcal{A}_{II}$ as follows.

"Game II": This is a game between $\mathcal{A}_{II}$ and the challenger C.

$\mathcal{A}_{II}$ has access to the master secret key msk, but is not allowed to replace public keys of entities.

Setup. C takes a security parameter 1^κ, runs Setup(1^κ) algorithm to generate the system parameter params $= \{q, l, l_0, H_1, H_2, H_3, H_4, H_5\}$, and a master secret key msk $=$ s. C gives params to $\mathcal{A}_{II}$ while keeping msk secret.

Random Oracle Queries. H_1, H_2, H_3, H_4, H_5 are random oracles controlled by C, who maintains six hash lists Hlist, H_1list, H_2list, H_3list, H_4list, H_5list. Whenever $\mathcal{A}_{II}$ request access to any hash function, C responds as follows:

H queries: On receiving a query $(<Q>, \alpha)$, C searches Hlist and returns α as answer if found. Otherwise, chooses $\alpha \in_R \mathbb{Z}_q^*$ and returns α. C adds $(<Q>, \alpha)$ to the Hlist.

H_1 queries: On receiving a query $(<ID,a>, X)$, C searches H_1list and returns X as answer if found. Otherwise, chooses $X \in_R \mathbb{Z}_q^*$ and returns X. C adds $(<ID,a>, X)$ to the H_1list.

H$_2$ queries: On receiving a query $(<m, \sigma, ID, u>, R)$, $\mathcal{C}$ searches H$_2$list and returns R as answer if found. Otherwise, chooses $R \in_R \mathbb{Z}_q^*$ and returns R. $\mathcal{C}$ adds $(<m, \sigma, ID, u>, R)$ to the H$_2$list.

H$_3$ queries: On receiving a query $(<t, u>, A)$, $\mathcal{C}$ searches H$_3$list and returns A as answer if found. Otherwise, chooses $A \in_R \mathbb{Z}_q^*$ and returns A. $\mathcal{C}$ adds $(<t, u>, A)$ to the H$_3$list.

H$_4$ queries: On receiving a query $(<u>, B)$, $\mathcal{C}$ searches H$_4$list and returns B as answer if found. Otherwise, chooses $B \in_R \mathbb{Z}_q^*$ and returns B. $\mathcal{C}$ adds $(<u>, B)$ to the H$_4$list.

H$_5$ queries: On receiving a query $\left(<k_1, k_2, ID_i, pk_i, ID_j, pk_j>, W\right)$, $\mathcal{C}$ searches H$_5$list and returns W as answer if found. Otherwise, chooses $W \in_R \mathbb{Z}_q^*$ and returns W. $\mathcal{C}$ adds $\left(<k_1, k_2, ID_i, pk_i, ID_j, pk_j>, W\right)$ to the H$_5$list.

Phase1. $\mathcal{A}_{II}$ issues any one of the following queries adaptively.

Partial Key Compute. $\mathcal{A}_{II}$ computes the partial private key pair (ppk_{ID_i}, psk_{ID_i}) for any ID_i of its choice, by computing compute $a_i = g^{\alpha_i}$, $x_i = \alpha_i + sH_1(ID_i, a_i)$, $(ppk_i, psk_i) = (a_i, x_i)$. $\mathcal{C}$ maintains a list of partial keys computed by $\mathcal{A}_{II}$ in a partial key list $\left(ID_i, ppk_{ID_i}, psk_{ID_i}\right)$.

Public key request queries. On input ID by $\mathcal{A}_{II}$, the challenger $\mathcal{C}$ searches whether there exists a tuple $(ID, pk_{ID}, coin) \in$ pklist. If not, $\mathcal{C}$ runs algorithm **SetPublicKey** to generate the public key pk_{ID} for entity ID, then adds the tuple $(ID, pk_{ID}, coin)$ to the pklist and return pk_{ID} to $\mathcal{A}_{II}$. Otherwise, $\mathcal{C}$ returns pk_{ID} to $\mathcal{A}_{II}$. The value of coin is decided the challenger $\mathcal{C}$'s strategy.

Private key extract queries. On input identity ID by $\mathcal{A}_{II}$, the challenger $\mathcal{C}$ searches whether there exists a tuple $(ID, pk_{ID}, coin) \in$ pklist. If coin $\neq \perp$, $\mathcal{C}$ runs algorithm **SetPrivateKey** to generate the private key sk_{ID} for entity ID. If coin $= \perp$, $\mathcal{C}$ returns "Reject".

Re-encryption key extract queries. On input (ID_i, ID_j) by $\mathcal{A}_{II}$, the challenger $\mathcal{C}$ searches whether there exists a tuple $(ID_i, pk_{ID_i}, coin_i) \in$ pklist. If $coin_i \neq \perp$, $\mathcal{C}$ responds by running algorithm **ReEncryptKey** to generate the re-encryption key $rk_{ID_i \rightarrow ID_j}$ for entity ID_i, ID_j. Otherwise, $\mathcal{C}$ returns "Reject".

Re-encryption queries. On input $(ID_i, ID_j C_{IDi})$ by $\mathcal{A}_{II}$, the challenger $\mathcal{C}$ searches whether there exists a tuple $(ID_i, pk_{ID_i}, coin_i) \in$ pklist. If $coin_i \neq \perp$, $\mathcal{C}$ responds by running algorithm **ReEncrypt** to convert the second level ciphertext c_{ID_i} into the first level ciphertext c_{ID_j}. Otherwise, returns "Reject".

Decryption queries for second level ciphertext. On input (ID, c) by $\mathcal{A}_{II}$, if c is a second level ciphertext, $\mathcal{C}$ responds by running algorithm **Decrypt$_2$** using the related private key to decrypt the C and returns the result to $\mathcal{A}_{II}$. Otherwise, returns "Reject".

Decryption queries for first level ciphertext. On input (ID, c) by $\mathcal{A}_{II}$, if c is a first level ciphertext, $\mathcal{C}$ responds by running algorithm **Decrypt$_1$** using the related private key to decrypt the c and returns the result to $\mathcal{A}_{II}$. Otherwise, returns "Reject".

Challenge. Once the adversary $\mathcal{A}_{II}$ decides that Phase 1 is over, it outputs the challenge identity ID_*, and two equal length plaintexts $m_0, m_1 \in \mathcal{M}$. Moreover, $\mathcal{A}_{II}$ is restricted to choose a challenge identity ID_* that trivial decryption is not possible. $\mathcal{C}$ searches a tuple $\left(ID_*, pk_{ID_*}, coin_*\right) \in$ pklist, then picks a random bit $\delta \in \{0, 1\}$, and computes the challenge ciphertext $c_* = $ Encrypt $\left(params, ID_*, pk_{ID_*}, m_\delta\right)$, and returns c_* to $\mathcal{A}_{II}$.

Phase2. The adversary $\mathcal{A}_{II}$ continues to query any of the above mentioned oracles with the restrictions defined in the IND-CLPRE-CCA "Game II".

Guess. Finally, the adversary $\mathcal{A}_{II}$ outputs a guess $\delta' \in \{0, 1\}$ and wins the game if $\delta' = \delta$.

We define the advantage of $\mathcal{A}_{II}$ in "Game II" as $\text{Adv}_{\text{GameII}, \mathcal{A}_{II}}^{\text{IND-CLPRE-CCA}}(k) = \left|\Pr[X' = X] - \frac{1}{2}\right|$.

A CLPRE scheme is said to be (t, ϵ)-2nd-IND-CLPRE-CCA secure if for any t-time 2nd-IND-CLPRE-CCA Type-II adversary $\mathcal{A}_{II}$ we have $\text{Adv}_{\text{GameII}, \mathcal{A}_{II}}^{\text{IND-CLPRE-CCA}}(k) = \left|\Pr[X' = X]\right| < \epsilon$. We simply say that a CLPRE scheme is 2nd-IND-CLPRE-CCA secure if t is polynomial with respect to security parameter k and ϵ is negligible.

7   Performance Evaluation

We make comparison between our scheme and Sur et al.'s scheme, Yang et al.'s scheme and Srinivasan et al.'s scheme, in terms of computational cost and ciphertext size. The number of "bignum" operations that CLPRE schemes need to perform are considered, other operations like addition or multiplication in group, XOR operation and conventional hash function evaluation is omitted, since the computation of these operations is efficient and far less than that of exponentiations or pairings. two modular exponentiations and the three modular exponentiations can be computed at a cost of about 1.17 and 1.25 exponentiations respectively, using simultaneous multiple exponentiation algorithm mentioned in [23]. The Map-To-Point hash function is special and far more expensive than conventional hash operation so it cannot be omitted.

From the Tables, we can find that all of our five algorithm listed in the table are much more computation efficient than Sur et al. [5]'s scheme and Yang et al. [14]'s scheme. Our encrypt algorithm and ciphertext size of the first and second level ciphertext are more efficient than those in Srinivasan et al. [15]'s scheme (Table 1).

Table 1. Comparison of CLPRE schemes' performance.

Schemes	Sur [5]	Yang [14]	Srinivasan [15]	Our CLPRE scheme
Encrypt	$5.08t_e$	$3.25t_e$	$3t_e$	$2.25t_e$
SetReEncKey	$4.08t_e$	$2.17t_e$	$2t_e$	$2.17t_e$
ReEncrypt	$6t_p$	$2.17t_e$	t_e	t_e
Decrypt$_2$	$2t_p+3.08t_e$	$3.17t_e$	$2t_e$	$2t_e$
Decrypt$_1$	t_p+4t_e	$4.25t_e$	$4t_e$	$4.25t_e$
$|c_i|$	$3|G_1|+|m|+|\sigma|$	$2|G|+|\mathbb{Z}_q^*|+|m|$ $+|\sigma|$	$2|G|+|\mathbb{Z}_q^*|+|m|$ $+|\sigma|$	$|G|+|m|+|\sigma|$
$rk_{i \to j}$	$3|G_1|$	$|\mathbb{Z}_q^*|$	$|\mathbb{Z}_q^*|$	$|\mathbb{Z}_q^*|$
$|c_j|$	$|G_1|+2|G_2|+|m|$ $+|\sigma|$	$|G|+|m|+|\sigma|$	$3|G|+|m|+|\sigma|$	$|G|+|m|+|\sigma|$
Pairing-Free	×	✓	✓	✓
Map-To-Point-Free	×	✓	✓	✓
Assumption	p-BDHI	CDH	M-CDH	CDH

8 Conclusion

We provide a lightweight proxy certificateless proxy re-encryption (CLPRE) scheme without pairing. We also prove security of our CLPRE scheme against Type II adversary $\mathcal{A}_{II}$ under the CDH assumption in the random oracle model, and make comparison with representative CLPRE scheme. The results show that our scheme is much more computational and communicational efficient than Sur et al.'s scheme and Yang et al.'s scheme, and outperform Srinivasan et al.'s scheme in terms of space efficiency.

References

1. Blaze, M., Bleumer, G., Strauss, M.: Divertible protocols and atomic proxy cryptography. In: Nyberg, K. (ed.) EUROCRYPT 1998. LNCS, vol. 1403, pp. 127–144. Springer, Heidelberg (1998). https://doi.org/10.1007/BFb0054122
2. Xu, L., Wu, X., Zhang, X.: CL-PRE: a certificateless proxy re-encryption scheme for secure data sharing with public cloud. In: Proceedings of the 7th ACM Symposium on Information, Computer and Communications Security, pp. 1–10 (2012)
3. Ateniese, G., Fu, K., Green, M., Hohenberger, S.: Improved proxy re-encryption schemes with applications to secure distributed storage. ACM Trans. Inf. Syst. Secur. (TISSEC) 9(1), 1–30 (2006)
4. Al-Riyami, S.S., Paterson, K.G.: Certificateless public key cryptography. In: Laih, C.-S. (ed.) ASIACRYPT 2003. LNCS, vol. 2894, pp. 452–473. Springer, Heidelberg (2003). https://doi.org/10.1007/978-3-540-40061-5_29

5. Sur, C., Jung, C.D., Park, Y., Rhee, K.H.: Chosen-ciphertext secure certificateless proxy re-encryption. In: De Decker, B., Schaumüller-Bichl, I. (eds.) CMS 2010. LNCS, vol. 6109, pp. 214–232. Springer, Heidelberg (2010). https://doi.org/10.1007/978-3-642-13241-4_20
6. Canetti, R., Hohenberger, S.: Chosen-ciphertext secure proxy re-encryption. In: Proceedings of ACM CCS 2007, pp. 185–194 (2007)
7. Libert, B., Vergnaud, D.: Unidirectional chosen-ciphertext secure proxy reencryption. IEEE Trans. Inf. Theory **57**(3), 1786–1802 (2011)
8. Deng, R.H., Weng, J., Liu, S., Chen, K.: Chosen-ciphertext secure proxy re-encryption without pairings. In: Franklin, M.K., Hui, L.C.K., Wong, D.S. (eds.) CANS 2008. LNCS, vol. 5339, pp. 1–17. Springer, Heidelberg (2008). https://doi.org/10.1007/978-3-540-89641-8_1
9. Hanaoka, G., et al.: Generic construction of chosen ciphertext secure proxy re-encryption. In: Dunkelman, O. (ed.) CT-RSA 2012. LNCS, vol. 7178, pp. 349–364. Springer, Heidelberg (2012). https://doi.org/10.1007/978-3-642-27954-6_22
10. Zheng, Y., Tang, S., Guan, C., Chen, M.-R.: Cryptanalysis of a certificateless proxy re-encryption scheme. In: 2013 Fourth International Conference on Emerging Intelligent Data and Web Technologies (EIDWT), pp. 307–312. IEEE (2013)
11. Guo, H., Zhang, Z., Zhang, J., Chen, C.: Towards a secure certificateless proxy re-encryption scheme. In: Susilo, W., Reyhanitabar, R. (eds.) ProvSec 2013. LNCS, vol. 8209, pp. 330–346. Springer, Heidelberg (2013). https://doi.org/10.1007/978-3-642-41227-1_19
12. Baek, J., Safavi-Naini, R., Susilo, W.: Certificateless public key encryption without pairing. In: Zhou, J., Lopez, J., Deng, R.H., Bao, F. (eds.) ISC 2005. LNCS, vol. 3650, pp. 134–148. Springer, Heidelberg (2005). https://doi.org/10.1007/11556992_10
13. El Gamal, T.: A public key cryptosystem and a signature scheme based on discrete logarithms. In: Blakley, G.R., Chaum, D. (eds.) CRYPTO 1984. LNCS, vol. 196, pp. 10–18. Springer, Heidelberg (1985). https://doi.org/10.1007/3-540-39568-7_2
14. Yang, K., Xu, J., Zhang, Z.: Certificateless proxy re-encryption without pairings. In: Lee, H.-S., Han, D.-G. (eds.) ICISC 2013. LNCS, vol. 8565, pp. 67–88. Springer, Cham (2014). https://doi.org/10.1007/978-3-319-12160-4_5
15. Srinivasan, A., Rangan, C.P.: Certificateless proxy re-encryption without pairing: revisited. In: Proceedings of the 3rd International Workshop on Security in Cloud Computing, pp. 41–52. ACM (2015)
16. Liu, Y., Peng, H., Wang, J.: Verifiable diversity ranking search over encrypted outsourced data. CMC Comput. Mater. Contin. **55**(1), 037–057 (2018)
17. Tang, Y., Lian, H., Zhao, Z., Yan, X.: A proxy re-encryption with keyword search scheme in cloud computing. CMC Comput. Mater. Contin. **56**(2), 339–352 (2018)

E-Sports Ban/Pick Prediction
Based on Bi-LSTM Meta Learning Network

Cheng Yu[1], Wan-ning Zhu[1](✉), and Yu-meng Sun[2]

[1] Institute of Software Engineering, Jinling Institute of Technology,
Nanjing 211169, Jiangsu, China
zhuwanning@jit.edu.cn
[2] Department of Business English, Jiangsu University of Technology,
Changzhou 213001, China

Abstract. With the continuous development of e-sports, the application of data analysis in e-sports has been widely concerned. In this paper, we introduce the important process before the MOBA e-sports game: the bans and picks (BP). In order to solve the problem, we propose the improved meta-learning network structure. Our model uses Bi-LSTM as the controller to increase the link between past and future sequences. The modified cosine measure is used to replace the cosine measure to make the similarity determination more accurate. The simulation results show that the proposed structure has achieved good results in the e-sports BP prediction problem, and the accuracy rate is about 84%.

Keywords: Meta learning · Bi-LSTM · LSTM · Series forecasting · E-sports

1 Introduction

In recent years, e-sports has developed rapidly as an emerging industry of inter-net + competitive sports [1–3]. As the center of the e-sports industry, the decisive factors of the e-sports competition began to attract the attention of researchers. It turns out that data analysis is more important than early talent, skills and experience in the competition [4].

At present, the main research issues in the field of e-sports data analysis can be divided into two categories: 1. The prediction problem of the winning rate of e-sports games. This problem generally obtains various data from the open source data inter-face, using the characteristics of the data and adopting different models to obtain the victory rate after data preprocessing [5–7]. 2. E-sports advantage role combination mining [8, 9].

The multiplayer online battle arena (MOBA) is one of the most popular e-sports game now. Like League of Legends, DOTA2, etc. Our research team specializes in data analysis tasks for MOBA games. In the previous study, the team solved the problem of e-sports video data export and role session recognition [10–12]. This paper discusses e-sports BP prediction model, and proposes a more accurate solution based on previous research [8, 9].

© Springer Nature Switzerland AG 2019
X. Sun et al. (Eds.): ICAIS 2019, LNCS 11632, pp. 97–105, 2019.
https://doi.org/10.1007/978-3-030-24274-9_9

We have found that the pre-match tactical arrangement has an indispensable link, namely the hero bans and picks (BP). And BP's results even affect the outcome of the game.

Take DOTA2 as an example. Each hero has different strengths and weaknesses, different battlefield positions (partially biased towards attacking the enemy, partial favoring teammates, etc.), and different role types (Melee, Long-Range, etc.). How to balance these differences, or give the team an advantage in the preparation stage of the game is an urgent issue.

This important problem is solved very poorly with the existing deep learning network [13–16]. Because the data set has the characteristic that the category is much, the sample is little. Therefore, in this paper, an e-sports BP prediction algorithm based on Bi-LSTM meta-learning is proposed. Taking DOTA2 as an example, the Bi-LTSM memory network is adopted as the controller, the memory matrix reads (save) weights, and the modified cosine similarity measure keys are used to solve the problem that the existing deep learning network fails to solve well. The final simulation experiment shows that this algorithm has a correct rate of about 80%, which is 10–15% higher than the previous LSTM model adopted by bp(draft) algorithm [8].

2 Preliminary Knowledge

2.1 Introduction to Meta-learning

Metacognition usually refers to a situation where the agent learns at two levels, each with a different time scale. Rapid learning occurs in a task, for example, learning how to precisely classify data sets. This kind of learning is guided by knowledge, and the metacognition based on memory enhancement neural network gradually accumulates in the task, which captures the differences among task structures in different target areas. Given that it has two levels, this form of meta-learning is often described as 'learning to learn'.

2.2 Introduction to Model Prediction Task (Ban-Pick Prediction)

DOTA2 contains 114 characters (often referred to as heroes). Each team will ban unselected heroes in certain order and without repetition, every team bans 6 heroes. At the same time, team will select unbanned and unpicked heroes in a certain order, and the pick limit of each team is 5.

Table 1. DOTA2 BAN-PICK process

	B	B	B	B	B	B	P	P	P	P	B	B	B	B	P	P	P	P	B	B	P	P
Radiant	■			■	■			■	■				■		■	■		■		■		■
dire		■	■			■	■			■	■	■		■			■		■		■	■

As shown in Table 1, the ban-pick process in DOTA2 is performed by the two factions, radiant and dire(antithesis).

E-sports ban-pick prediction is a new research problem, which has great research value and application value. The solution of this problem has a great influence on the preparation of e-sports and the strategy of improving the role selection in the competition. Although the problem is important, it has not been solved so far [13], According to features of the BP problem, this problem is transformed into a kind of time series prediction problem [15], give $\{x(t_i)\}_{i=1}^{j}$, get $x(t_{j+1})$.

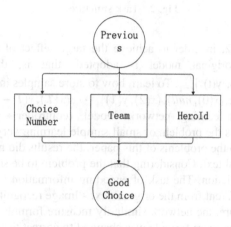

Fig. 1. Selective impact

More specifically, as shown in Fig. 1, BP is based on the result of the previous selection (Choice number, team, heroId) to predict a good choice. Given data set $D = \{x(t_i)\}_{i=1}^{j} = \{(x(t_i^{Choice}), x(t_i^{Team}), x(t_i^{Hero}))\}_{i=1}^{j}$ to predict $x(t_{j+1}) = (x(t_{j+1}^{Choice}), x(t_{j+1}^{Team}), x(t_{j+1}^{Hero}))$, $\{x(t_i)\}_{i=1}^{j}$ represents the bp data from the beginning of the i to the end of the j (Choice number, team, heroId).

To solve this problem, this paper proposes to use Bi-LSTM [18] meta-learning network for e-sports BP prediction. The goal of the task is: Given data set is D, loss of learning is ζ, Select learning parameters θ make $\theta^* = \arg\min_\theta E_{D \sim P(D)}[\zeta(D; \theta)]$.

Given that BP's sample collection was taken from each DOTA2 season, each season had a short cycle time and few matches. As a result, the training sample categories are large and the sample size of each category is small. As a consequence, the results of traditional deep learning network learning solve this problem are not satisfactory. Therefore, this paper proposes a BP prediction model based on meta-learning, which solves this problem well.

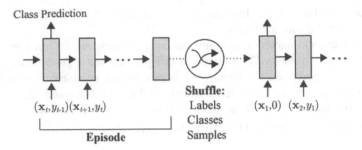

Fig. 2. Task structure

As shown in Fig. 2, in order to achieve the target effect of the model, the task architecture in the original model is adopted, that is, the given data set $D = \{x(t)\}_{t=1}^{T} = \{(x(t), y(t))\}_{t=1}^{T}$, To learn how to store samples in memory, the model actually sees the input: $(x(0), null), (x(2), y(1)), \cdots, (x(T), y(T-1))$.

LSTM-based meta-learning network model (controller + read-write memory module) [16, 17] solves the problem of small sample learning very well, but when the solution was applied to the problems of this paper, the results did not achieve the effect shown in of the original text. Considering that the problem to be solved in this paper is a sequence-based prediction. The task of encoding information is independent of the sequence, which is different from the original text - Image recognition, and the result is not very ideal. Therefore, the network similarity measure formula was adjusted in this paper, and the cosine measure formula was changed to correct the cosine formula [19].

At the same time, the sequence reaches the length of 22, and the effect of LSTM is not very ideal, so we adopt Bi-LSTM to replace LSTM. Unlike traditional LSTM, Bi-LSTM considers both past features (extracted through forward processes) and future features (extracted through backward processes). Two-way LSTM is equivalent to two LSTM, one is a forward input sequence, the other is a reverse input sequence, and the output of both is combined as the final result, which makes the connection between the past and the future stronger. Therefore, the result of this paper is better.

3   BP Prediction Network Model Based on Bi-LSTM Meta Learning

3.1   Memory Enhancement Network Model Based Bi-LSTM Meta Learning

The structure of LSTM is shown in Fig. 3. $x(t)$ is the input data at time t, define u represents the user(team), U represents a collection of all users. $f(t)$, $i(t)$, $o(t)$ are input gates at time t, output gates, forget gates. $c(t)$, $c(t-1)$ respectively represent the hidden layer output at time t and time $t - 1$. The expression is as follows:

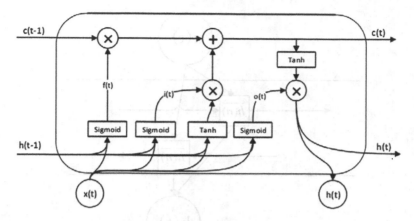

Fig. 3. LSTM Network cell structure

$$i(t) = sigmoid(W_{xi}x(t) + W_{hi}h(t-1) + b_i) \tag{1}$$

$$f(t) = sigmoid(W_{xf}x(t) + W_{hf}h(t-1) + b_f) \tag{2}$$

$$o(t) = sigmoid(W_{xo}x(t) + W_{ho}h(t-1) + b_o), \tag{3}$$

W_x is the input weight matrix, W_h represents the state weight matrix of the hidden layer at time $t - 1$, is the bias constant. t time $c(t)$ and $h(t)$ expression (Fig. 4):

$$c(t) = f(t) \cdot c(t-1) + i(t) \cdot \tanh(W_{xc}x(t) + W_{hc}h(t-1) + b_c) \tag{4}$$

$$h(t) = o(t) \cdot \tanh(c(t)) \tag{5}$$

Figure 5, it is presented in this paper: Bi-LSTM Meta-learning structure k_t is the key value generated by Bi-LSTM,

$$k_t = softmax(W_{\overrightarrow{h}k} * \overrightarrow{h(n)} + W_{\overleftarrow{h}k} * \overleftarrow{h(n)} + b_k) \tag{6}$$

(6) stored in the matrix M_t or compared to M_t stored values), Represents the i row of the matrix. When start measuring k_t and the data stored in $M_t(i)$, then Modified cosine similarity evaluation was used

$$K(k_{u,t}, M_{u,t}(i))$$
$$= \frac{\sum (k_{u,t} - \overline{M_u(i)})(M_{u,t}(i) - \overline{M_u(i)})}{\sqrt{\sum_{u \in U}(k_{u,t} - \overline{M_u(i)})}\sqrt{(M_{u,t}(i) - \overline{M_u(i)})^2}} \tag{7}$$

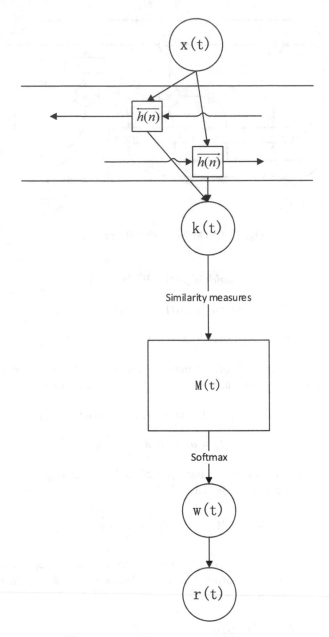

Fig. 4. A Bi-LSTM meta-learning structure

$k_{u,t}$ represents the predicted value of user u at time t, $M_{u,t}(i)$ represents the predicted value matrix of user u at time t, $\overline{M_u(i)}$ represents the row average of user u's predicted value matrix.

Since the sample set is small due to the limited number of games played each season, it is particularly important to judge the sample similarity more accurately. Taking into account the problem in this paper, the prediction of time series is affected by user evaluation criteria. In esports, each team has a different understanding of bp for each esports season. It is not hard to see, then, that when they conduct the bp process the evaluation (criteria) are different, that is, each team has a different evaluation scheme. The cosine similarity in original model is difficult to embody this characteristic of data (The cosine similarity calculation method is only limited to the case that the scale of the score is basically the same for different users).

The modified cosine similarity measure improves the above defects by subtracting the user's average score for the project. So we use the modified cosine similarity. Therefore, the modified cosine similarity is used to replace the cosine similarity of the original text $K(k_t, M_t(i)) = \frac{k_t \cdot M_t(i)}{\|k_t\| \|M_t(i)\|}$.

(7) Perform softmax to generate a read weight vector w_t^r,

$$w_t^r = \frac{\exp(K(k_t, M_t(i)))}{\sum_j \exp(K(k_t, M_t(j)))} \tag{8}$$

(8) Produces a classified output r_t, $r_t = \sum_i w_t^r(i) M_t(i)$ or to softmax and as additional input to the state of the next controller.

4 Experiment

4.1 Data Set

DOTA2 is an open source game of data, and tournament information can be obtained directly. We used machtId to call the open interface to obtain the data, and accumulated the data of 4000 games in the past year, which included including the records of 18 teams of different games, with an average of about 220 games for each team. While each team usually has to compete with 10+ teams, so the data sets conform to the characteristics of multiple categories and small samples.

The data set is randomly divided into training, verification and test set by 6:2:2.

4.2 The Experimental Contrast

In order to better show the advantages of the algorithm in this paper, LSTM, RNN and LSTM-based ML models, which are good at processing sequential tasks, were selected for comparison experiments with Bi-LSTM Meta Learning model in this paper (Table 2).

Table 2. Model accuracy

Model	Training accuracy	Test accuracy
LSTM	66%	64%
RNN	61%	59%
ML-LSTM	72%	74%
ML-Bi-LSTM	84%	86%

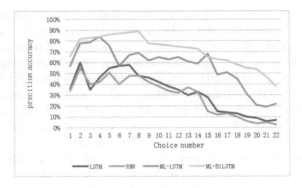

Fig. 5. Train TOP-3 accuracy

As shown in Table 1, the algorithm in this paper has achieved good results in this problem.

Figure 5 shows the comparison of the accuracy of top-3 in model training. It can be seen that this model solves this problem well compared with other algorithms. However, as the step length becomes longer, the accuracy of the algorithm decreases. We consider that in the process of bp, when one party gets the position selection of local suppression, the later bp is more diversified and there are more choices, so it is more difficult to learn.

5 Summary

Because the BP prediction is an important problem which has not been well solved has not been very good solution, this paper proposes a e-sports BP prediction algorithm based on meta learning, DOTA2, for example, USES the LTSM memory type network as the controller, memory read (save) weight matrix, modified cosine similarity measure method of key value ingeniously solved the existing deep learning network fails to solve the problem. The final simulation experiment shows that this algorithm has a correct rate of about 78%, which is 10–15% higher than the single LSTM model adopted by the previous bp algorithm. This result provides great reference value for e-sports data analysis, and it can better target the conventional bp hands in terms of tactical arrangement.

Acknowledgment. This article is funded by the Jinling Institute of Science and Technology, a high-level talent research startup fund, and a web user behavior analysis and research project based on quantum algorithms (No. jit-b-201624).

References

1. Wang, Y., et al.: Analysis on the development status and prospect of China e-sports industry. Financ. Times **2018**(18), 313 (2018)

2. Li, Q., et al.: Research on the key influencing factors of e-sports industry development in China. Beijing University of Posts and Telecommunications (2018)
3. Yang, B.: Six e-sports will be featured in Jakarta Asian games industry still needs regulation. 21st century business herald, 2018-05-15 (2017)
4. Ren, Y., et al.: Analysis of the winning factors of Chinese e-sports hero league in S5 season. Northwest Normal University (2016)
5. Rioult, F., et al.: Mining tracks of competitive video games. AASRI Procedia **8**, 82–87 (2014)
6. Andono, P.N., Kurniawan, N.B., Supriyanto, C.: DotA 2 bots win prediction using Naive Bayes based on AdaBoost algorithm. In: Proceedings of the 3rd International Conference on Communication and Information Processing, pp. 180–184. ACM (2017)
7. Chen, Z., et al.: Modeling Game Avatar Synergy and Opposition through Embedding in Multiplayer Online Battle Arena Games (2018). arXiv preprint: arXiv:1803.10402
8. Summerville, A., Cook, M., Steenhuisen, B.: Draft-analysis of the ancients: predicting draft picks in DotA 2 using machine learning. In: Twelfth Artificial Intelligence and Interactive Digital Entertainment Conference (2016)
9. Zhu, Y.: Research on association rule algorithm and its application in e-sports. Guilin University of Electronic Science and Technology (2017)
10. Yu, C., Zhu, W., Li, L., et al.: Research on e-sports session identification. In: MATEC Web of Conferences. EDP Sciences, vol. 189, p. 10011 (2018)
11. Li, L., Zhu, W., Yu, C., et al.: Esports analysis data acquisition algorithm based on convolutional neural network. In: MATEC Web of Conferences. EDP Sciences, vol. 189, p. 03003 (2018)
12. Yu, C., Zhu, W.: Tactical analysis of MOBA games based on hotspot map of battlefield. Comput. Sci. **2018**(S2), 149–151+175 (2018)
13. Lecun, Y., Bengio, Y., Hinton, G.: Deep learning. Nature **521**(7553), 436 (2015)
14. Levine, S., et al.: Learning hand-eye coordination for robotic grasping with deep learning and large-scale data collection. Int. J. Robot. Res. **37**(4–5), 421–436 (2018)
15. Cheng, J., Xu, R., Tang, X., Sheng, V.S., Cai, C.: An abnormal network flow feature sequence prediction approach for DDoS attacks detection in big data environment. CMC Comput. Mater. Contin. **55**(1), 095–119 (2018)
16. Nie, Q., Xuba, X., Feng, L.Y., Zhang, B.: Defining embedding distortion for intra prediction mode-based video steganography. CMC Comput. Mater. Contin. **55**(1), 059–070 (2018)
17. Li, H., et al.: An overview of feature representation and similarity measurement in time series data mining. Comput. Appl. Res. **30**(05), 1285–1291 (2013)
18. Greff, K., Srivastava, R.K., Koutník, J., et al.: LSTM: a search space Odyssey. IEEE Trans. Neural Netw. Learn. Syst. **28**(10), 2222–2232 (2016)
19. Santoro, A., Bartunov, S., Botvinick, M., et al.: One-shot learning with memory-augmented neural networks. In: Proceedings of the 33rd International Conference on Machine Learning. JMLR: W&CP, vol. 48 (2016)

Bottlenecks and Feasible Solutions of Data Field Clustering in Impact Factor, Time Resolution, Selecting Core Objects and Merging Process

Hong Zhang, Hanshuo Wei, Youchen Shen,
Hui Wang, and Qiumei Pu[✉]

School of Information Engineering, Minzu University of China, Beijing, China
puqiumei@muc.edu.cn

Abstract. Data field Clustering is a method to group datasets by virtue of the theory data field which sees every data object as a point with evaluated mass, gets the core data objects, iteratively merges them via simulating the mutual interactions and opposite movements hierarchically. However, there exist some bottlenecks and problems where it may restrict the use and application extending to real areas widely. The determination of impact factor-sigma, the evaluation mass process for every object, the selection of the core objects according to their masses, the ratio of sample initially, time resolution as well as the process of the merging core objects are all crucial to the effectiveness and efficiency of the algorithm results. Through analyzing the main process of data field clustering as well as doing experiment with 2 dimensions data sets, a number of problems are found and several feasible measures to improve the data field clustering is put forward. Using test data sets as example, it is preliminary proven that the improved algorithm obtains a favorable result. Furthermore, the improved method contributes to the further application of data field cluster in Intrusion Detection Systems.

Keywords: Data field clustering · Impact factor · Selecting core object · Time resolution · Merging process

1 Introduction

Nowadays, the form of data, from easy to difficulty, can be extended to many varieties which include numerical value, sound, image, video information and so on. Clustering is one of methods in machine learning which groups a set of data into different clusters or categories according to their features so that it maximizes the similarity within clusters and simultaneously minimizes the similarity between every two different cluster [1, 2]. Other than classification in statistics, clustering, an unsupervised technique, cannot know the number of clusters at the beginning and what causes the grouping [3, 4]. The purpose of clustering is to discover overall distribution patterns and interesting correlations in data sets [5], further to uncover knowledge in specific areas. Having applied to various research fields such as data extraction, geographic

© Springer Nature Switzerland AG 2019
X. Sun et al. (Eds.): ICAIS 2019, LNCS 11632, pp. 106–120, 2019.
https://doi.org/10.1007/978-3-030-24274-9_10

information system and recommending system, Yang [6] propose a novel combination algorithm based on unsupervised Density-Based Spatial Clustering of Applications with Noise (DBSCAN) density clustering. The clustering analysis is also applied to the satellite image segmentation. [7] clustering plays an important role in machine learning as well as artificial intelligence.

Existing clustering algorithms are classified into more than six groups on the whole including hierarchy-based algorithms, partition-based algorithms, density-based algorithms, grid-based algorithms, constraint-based algorithms, subspace-based algorithms etc. [8]. These algorithms have its own characteristics respectively and are suitable for different conditions with different parameters vary in all kinds of data. Some of them are easier to implement while they have more computation complexity such as k-means which belongs to partition-based algorithms. Some of them possess the ability to handle arbitrary shapes but they need too many parameters for a user to input. The purpose of research on clustering is let it adapt to varieties of data existing nowadays better.

For the sake of adapting diverse demands in a way of effectiveness and efficiency, clustering especially needs to statisfy some basic conditions followed. (1) generating arbitrary shapes of clusters rather than be confined to some particular shape; (2) being immune to the effects of order of input patterns. (3) decreasing the reliance of algorithms on users-dependent parameters; (4) detect and remove possible outliers and noise; (5) provide some insight for the number of potential clusters without prior knowledge [9].

Inspiration from physical field, data field is proposed to characterize the interaction between objects for extracting the interested patterns; then, by simulating their mutual interactions and opposite movements, clusters are come into being hierarchy by hierarchy. Eventually, a novel algorithm is proposed by Wang Shuliang, Gan Wenyan and Li Deyi. Experiments show that it performs better than K-means, BIRCH (Balanced Iterative Reducing and Clustering using Hierarchies), CURE (Clustering Using Representatives) and CHAMELEON [8]. In spite of its good performance, some bottlenecks and problems are emerged behind at the same time. This paper, sufficiently, analyzes the process of the data field for hierarchical clustering algorithm; in addition, bottlenecks and problems are found and some feasible measures are proposed to solve them as much as possible.

Intrusion Detection is a process to detect intrusion activities at Internet and provide effective prevention measures. Detection is classified into three major categories: Signature-based Detection (SD), Anomaly-based Detection (AD) and Stateful Protocol Analysis (SPA). The Intrusion Detection System (IDS) is the software or hardware system to automate the intrusion detection process [14]. Data field clustering technology can be used to AD methods [15]. Therefore, the improvement of data filed clustering is crucial to its further application in IDS.

The rest of this paper is going to be structured as follows. First, related work is introduced in Sect. 2. Then, more details about the realization of data field clustering as well as key steps of it are listed. Advantages of Data field clustering is presented in Sect. 3, which is our impetus to explore the algorithm. Next, Bottlenecks and Problems, emphatically, are analyzed, which accounts for a large part of this paper. Also, methods to solve the problems are given then. Furthermore, we show some experiments we have done to illustrate the idea improving the algorithm we proposed. Finally, conclusion and further study are discussed.

2 Related Work

In data field clustering, Wang have proposed a set of theory of Data Field for Hierarchical Clustering. Inspired by the field in physical space, data field is put forward to describe the mutual relationship between one object and others (i.e. mutual interactions and opposite movements). Then, clusters are discovered hierarchy by hierarchy through the core objects' merging.

Based on data field theory, Wang and Chen designed HASTA clustering algorithm. It models the dataset as a data field by assigning all the data objects into quantized grids. After determining the clustering centers and the edges of cluster, the full size of arbitrary shaped clusters can be detected [10].

In feature selection field, which is the precondition of clustering, forming the important features (objects) for the clustering process, a novel feature selection with data field is proposed by Han. It evaluates the importance of different feature subset through constructing an entropy measure to uncover the optimal feature subset. It is independent of specific clustering algorithm [11].

A method of automatically calculating the threshold value for the clustering algorithm, which is based on the principle is put forward by Wang [12].

The problem of finding fixed threshold values for different datasets has been solved by using data field.

As is shown above, data field clustering is implied in a variety of fields. As a result, it is necessary to improve the algorithm by further exploration.

3 Key Steps of Data Field Clustering

3.1 Mathematical Model

In data space $\Omega \subseteq R^P$, let dataset $D = \{X_1, X_2, ..., X_n\}$ denote a P-dimensional independent random sample, where $X_i = (X_{i1}, X_{i2}, ..., X_{ip})^T$ with $i = 1, 2, ..., n$. Each data object x_i is taken as a particle with mass m_i, X_i radiates its data energy and is also influenced by others simultaneously. A virtual field called data field is created only if the necessary conditions are characterized, i.e. short-range, with source and temporal behavior [8]. If there exists an arbitrary point $x = (x_1, x_2, ..., x_P)^T$ in Ω, the scalar potential function of data field on x_i is defined as Eq. (1).

$$\varphi(x) = m_i \times K\left(\frac{\|x - x_i\|}{\sigma}\right) \tag{1}$$

where $m_i \left(m_i \geq 0, \sum_{i=1}^n m_i = 1\right)$ is treated as the mass of data object x_i, and it represents the strength of data field from x_i. $K(x)$ that satisfies $\int K(x)dx = 1, \int xK(x)dx = 0$ is the unit potential function to express the law that x_i always radiates its data energy in the same way in its data field. $\|x - x_i\|$ is the distance between data object x_i and the point x in the field. $\sigma \in (0, +\infty)$ is an impact factor that controls the interacted distance between objects.

Each data object x_i in D has its own data field in the data space Ω. All the data fields will be superposed on the point x. In other words, any data object is affected by all the other objects in the data space. So, the potential value of the arbitrary point x in the data fields on D in Ω is defined as

$$\varphi(x) = \sum_{i=1}^{n} m_i \times K\left(\frac{\|x - x_i\|}{\sigma}\right) \tag{2}$$

Because the gradient of a potential function is the strength function of the corresponding force field, the data field vector at x is:

$$\overrightarrow{F(x)} = \nabla\varnothing(x) = \sum_{i=1}^{n}\left((x_i - x) \times m_i \times K\left(\frac{\|(x_i - x)\|}{\sigma}\right)\right) \tag{3}$$

As is mentioned above, the purpose of clustering is to maximize the similarity within clusters and simultaneously minimize the similarity between every two different cluster. Thus, we take the form of short-range, nuclear field strength function as the field strength function. Therefore, the K(x) will be defined followed:

$$K(x) = e^{-\left(\frac{\|x - x_i\|}{\sigma}\right)^2} \tag{4}$$

3.2 Estimating Masses

According to the reference of [8], the procedure of optimizing impact factor is ahead of estimating masses in this part. Indeed, every object's potential value needs to be calculated in the process of optimizing impact factor (Eq. (5)). Consequently, the former contains the latter. As a result, we should figure out the estimating masses problem first.

The principle and specific process can be found at reference [8]. The result of estimating masses is that a small number of data objects which are called core data objects in intensive areas have bigger masses while most of the far apart objects have less mass or even the mass is zero. Thus, the core data objects with bigger masses represent the whole datasets in the next step.

3.3 Optimizing Impact Factor-Sigma (σ)

In the context of Mathematical Model, the impact factor, a crucial parameter, whose value has a great impact on the spatial distribution of data field, controls the interacted distance between data objects. It is no exaggeration to say that the value of impact factor determines whether we can obtain a well clustering result at last. Based on the theory of entropy, potential entropy is defined as Eq. (5):

$$H = -\sum\nolimits_{i=1}^{n} \frac{\varphi_i}{z} \log\left(\frac{\varphi_i}{z}\right) \tag{5}$$

Where $Z = \sum_{i=1}^{n} \varphi_i, 0 \leq H \leq \log(n)$. Also, the definition of φ_i is equal to Eq. (1). If the masses of data have been evaluated, entropy H is the function of σ. Through the process of minimize H, we get the appropriate σ. Moreover, if all the data being considered to compute the optimal entropy H, the total time complexity of the process will be $O(n^2)$. If n is very big, the algorithm's efficiency will be very low. As a result, in practice, a sample will be constructed random drawing from the original data sets by an empirical threshold.

3.4   Determination the Core Objects and Initially Partitioning

In Sect. 3.2, we obtain all the masses of data objects. The mass of data ranges from very small even zero to relatively large possible near 1 (under the condition of data normalization). But how to choose the core objects? The reference offers a method that choose the nonzero ones from the whole data.

Initially partitioning is to assign every none-core object to the core object via simulating its oppositely moving trend in the data field. When data objects are initially partitioned, the initial clusters can be hierarchically merged by interactively simulating the mutual interaction among core objects.

4   Advantages of Data Field Clustering

4.1   Higher Efficiency

Taking no account of the step of optimizing impact factor, the time complexity can be calculated as followed. Estimating the masses of objects by solving the problem on constrained quadratic programming will costs O(nsample2), with randomly sampling size nsample $\ll$ n. If the number of the core objects is ncore, the average time complexity of initially partitioning is O(ncore(n-ncore)). In addition, the average time complexity of iteratively merging clusters is O(ncore2). In summary, the total time complexity is O(nsample2 + ncore(n-ncore) + ncore2) $\approx$ O(n). Comparing it with other clustering, the time complexity of O(n) is outstanding and remarkable [8].

4.2   Ability to Handle Different Geometric Shapes

On the whole, absorbing some excellent characters of physical field, the data field algorithm holds the ability of finding different kinds of shapes and densities via assigning core objects to go deep into any cluster center.

By getting rid of the data objects without 3σrange, the algorithm can remove the outliers as much as possible. The experiment result show that most of the noisy data are not amalgamated into their neighboring clusters separately.

5   Bottlenecks and Problems

In spite of the advantages of data field algorithm, there exists a certain of bottlenecks and problems in the specific implementation as well as application in practical fields. These drawbacks will be analyzed sufficiently next.

For convenience, some definitions and statements are given followed for the rest of the paper.

(1)   Dataset $D = \{X_1, X_2 \ldots, Xn\}$, $D \subseteq R^p$ where $X_i = (X_{i1}, Xi_2 \ldots, Xip)^T$ with i = 1, 2 ..., n;

(2) n_{sample} random drawing from n, $n_{sample} \ll n$;

(3) D_{sample} random drawing from D, $D_{sample} \ll D$;

5.1   Impact Factor (Sigma) Restriction-Hard to Determine

The main ideal of data field clustering is to find the core area with larger potential value to form the cluster center. Also, the potential function $\varphi(x)$ which contains variable σ plays a decisive role in the whole data field distribution. Thus, the value of impact factor influences the whole distribution of data field indirectly. Although, data field algorithm, in the entire process, seems no input user-dependent, the parameter impact factor-sigma-which is estimated by optimizing it according to entropy theory varies in different datasets. And furthermore, the optimal value may not the best one to choose which needs to adjusted by multiply a parameter c, 'if σ is optimized too much, the clustering may be vulnerable to the impact of noise or outlier data [8]. In practical, via a mass of experiments, c is not easy to determine which leads to the inaccuracy of the whole algorithm.

The relationship between entropy H and σ can be generally described by their curve graphic (Fig. 1).

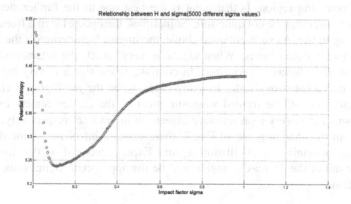

Fig. 1. Relationship between H and σ in ideal condition

But, at most circumstance, the curve of H and σ may not as regular as Fig. 1. Two kinds of experimental datasets are randomly chosen from numerous datasets to depict the relationship between H and σ in general (Fig. 2).

(a) 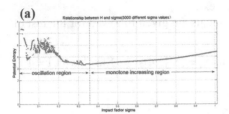   **(b)**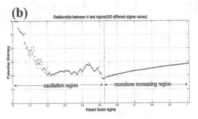

Fig. 2. (a) 5000 different sigma values, (b) 500 different sigma values

As is obviously depicted followed, the whole curve can be roughly separated into two parts what is called oscillation region and monotone increasing region. Oscillation region locates in the beginning of the abscissa which represents impact factor from zero. The main law of oscillation region is its choppy characteristic which contains countless peaks and bottoms. More precision point or bigger datasets corresponds to more peaks and bottoms bringing about in this region.

Monotone increasing region locates after oscillation region. Just as its name, the changing law is its character of monotone increasing with the increasing impact factor. It can be easily proved through experiments that this region will be sustained to the positive infinity.

Optimizing impact factor, the reference proposed, is to find the nadir of the whole curve where the ordinate corresponding to the most appropriate impact factor (min-Sigma) is the minimal value of potential entropy. Via large amounts of experiments, the nadir will be gotten just at the junction of the two region or at the starting of the monotone increasing region. Is that point is the best one to the further step of clustering? The answer may be not quite sure. Sometimes, the optimal sigma from the nadir will be too big to use. As we mentioned above, the impact factor controls the interacted distance between data objects. When sigma is very small, the interaction distance between two data objects is very short. In contrast, when sigma is very big, the data objects are interacted strongly [8]. In many cases, when the minSigma is chosen, the equipotential lines will be formed wrapping most of the cluster centers in one sets instead of wrapping every representative objects in its own set respectively.

Seen from the changing law of Fig. 2, there exists a bit of monotone decreasing region at the beginning of Oscillation region. Experiments tell us that the minimal value at the tail of the decreasing region will be the appropriate sigma value to depict the interactions.

5.2   Evaluation Mass Result-Not Seems so "Good"

In order to find a small number of core objects in datasets, a constrained quadratic programming problem whose time complexity is $O(n^2)$ has been put forward. It's very interesting that the principle of evaluation mass conforms to 20–80 rule originated from Italian economist Vilfredo Pareto. The rule discovered that about 80% of the wealth in most countries was controlled by a consistent minority - about 20% of the people [13]. Analogizing the rule, a minority of data objects we called core objects are given biggish masses to guide the clustering process.

Nevertheless, the distribution of evaluated masses in core objects is not very balanced whose result is not hoped. Observing Fig. 3 (drawn from an evaluation masses of a dataset), a few of core objects in the most intensive region of the dataset are given masses much larger than others. As a result, the very few extraordinary objects (defined exob), whose total mass roughly accounts for 80% or more, control the whole distribution of datasets. Surrounding the exob, the equipotential lines are very intensive while others relative sparse even it is obviously a kind of cluster. That is to say, the evaluation assigns much mass unduly to exob ignoring the influence except for that. However, clustering, indeed, is to discover every clusters not only one or two with high density. The bias of evaluation for minority core objects often leads to some inaccuracies and errors in the next steps. Spontaneously, adjusting the parameter of sigma to change the bias case is the only choice. Surely, it is practicable. But, meanwhile, another problem how to determine this value emerges.

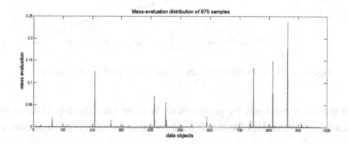

Fig. 3. Mass-evaluation distribution of 975 samples under minimal entropy

On the other hand, only samples which are randomly chosen from the entire datasets are evaluated. Let n represents the total number of the datasets, the number of samples is quite less than n. The accuracy decreases with the lack of adequate numbers. Thus, evaluation mass seems not a perfect procedure which gives rise to an unsatisfactory result.

5.3   Selection of the Core Objects-Incomplete and Difficulty to Select

With the purpose of reducing the total time complexity of data field algorithm, core objects are selected after evaluation masses. Every element in D_{sample} instead of D will be evaluated, which can largely decrease the complexity. However, some of important elements, unfortunately, are not chosen which results in ignoring some clusters. The incompleteness characteristic may lead to an unsatisfactory result.

Besides, in any case, a small portion of core objects will be selected from the D_{sample}. Two methods can be easily gotten: by proportion and by a threshold.

The former is to extract a number of elements as core objects by proportion for instance 10%. The latter selects core objects by a given threshold i.e. elements' mass which greater than threshold (thr) value were seen as core objects.

The reference offers the latter one and stipulates thr = 0. In real computation, in fact, the evaluation mass may be very small rather than equal to zero. Masses approaches to zero are further studied through Fig. 4 with one dataset detailed values of mass distribution. As shown in Fig. 4, the 736 mass evaluation values (account for about 75%) in the latter part of 975 samples range from 0.0001 to 0.001. Obviously, all the 736 objects with relatively small mass are greater than 0; Thus, setting the threshold 0 loses the efficacy. In consequence of this fact, thr > 0. If thr = 0.001 i.e. filter out all the 736 objects, a number of characteristics are ignored at the same time. So, determination of thr becomes a necessary step. However, there are large gaps between different datasets to determine thr.

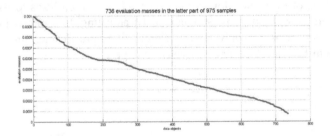

Fig. 4. 736 evaluation masses in the latter part of 975 samples

Consider the other methods by proportion. We can take the top 10% or smaller 5% data objects as core objects. But the result may cause some rather small masses coming in.

5.4   Problems in Merging Core Objects

The last step of data field clustering hierarchically is via simulating mutual interactions and opposite movements among core objects. To be specific, core objects selected will be moved by uniformly acceleration motion. When the distance of arbitrary two objects are very near, they will be merged and form a new data object. Basic formulas in this process are given followed [9].

$$\overrightarrow{a^{(t)}}\left(x_i^*\right) = \sum_{x_i^* \in D_{new}}^{n}\left(m_j^*(t) \times \left(x_j^*(t) - x_i^*(t)\right) \times e^{-\left(\frac{\left\|x_j^*(t) - x_i^*(t)\right\|}{\sigma}\right)^2}\right) \tag{6}$$

$$\overrightarrow{x_i^*(t+\Delta t)} = \overrightarrow{x_i^*(t)} + \frac{1}{2}\overrightarrow{a^{(t)}}(\Delta t)^2 \tag{7}$$

$$d_{min} = min \left\| x_j^*(t) - x_i^*(t) \right\|, (i \neq j) \tag{8}$$

$$a_{max} = max \left\| a^t \left(x_i^* \right) \right\| \tag{9}$$

$$\Delta t = \frac{1}{f} \sqrt{\frac{2d_{min}}{a_{max}}} \tag{10}$$

Focus on the only uncertainty parameter f which is called time resolution, problem is showed up. According to Eq. (10), a little time Δt is in inverse proportion to acceleration size i.e. $f \propto 1/\Delta t$. Besides, by Eq. (7), f is in inverse proportion to displacement $x_i^*(t)$ i.e. $f \propto 1/ x_i^*(t)$ and $f \propto F$ (F represents the force acts on one data object). In fact, the size of f determines unit mobile distance objects moving. When f is very small, the distance of core objects moving in one time will be very long. When f is very big, the distance of core objects moving in one time will be very short. External manifestations of unit mobile distance is core objects' speeds. However, the whole merging efficiency is not easily equal to the object speed. Fast movement does not means high merging efficiency. Just the opposite, too fast speed may give rise to inaccuracy. Figure 5 presents a common case during merging process under two velocities vividly.

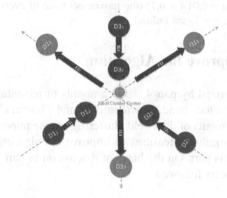

Fig. 5. Different position result from two velocities in one-time iteration.

Supposing Dij represents core data object Di on position j and Fij represents a force on Di with sequence j. Three core data objects D1, D2 and D3 are ready to move by virtue of Eqs. (6)–(10). On one condition, Fij is very small (Fi1). After a unit moving, Di1 moves to Di2 (D12, D22, D32). As a result, three core data objects will be merged in next iteration with the satisfying merging condition (11)–(12). Eventually, they are merged on the ideal cluster center with forming a new core data object. On the other condition, Fij is rather big (Fi2). After a unit moving, Di1 moves to Di3 directly with a longer distance. The next iteration will be full of variables rather than merge on the ideal center. By virtue of relationship between force F and time resolution f above, iteration time will be increased under too big value of f. What is more, it may bring about an incorrect result needless to say that it reduces the whole algorithm efficiency.

$$m^*_{new}(t) = m^*_i(t) + m^*_j(t) \tag{11}$$

$$x^*_{new}(t) = \frac{m^*_i(t) * x^*_i(t) + m^*_j(t) * x^*_j(t)}{m^*_i(t) + m^*_j(t)} \tag{12}$$

As is clear from Fig. 6a and b, an inappropriate parameter f can lead to a bad merging result.

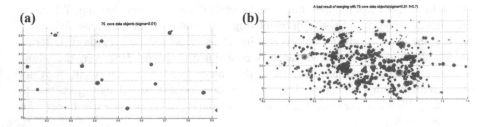

Fig. 6. (a) Original 75 core data objects (sigma = 0.01), (b) A chaotic result of merging with 75 core data objects (sigma = 0.01 f = 0.7) (the movement trace of every 75 data objects is all described by blue point) (Color figure online)

6   Measures to Improve the Algorithm

On one hand, as summarized by part 4, large amounts of advantages in the data field clustering exist. On the other hand, shortcomings and "barriers" is inherent of this algorithm. Anyhow, the merits of data field clustering are the impetus for us to research ways to enhance the algorithm. Measures to improve the algorithm are explored and studied preliminary in this part. On the basis of discussion in part 5, improvement can be realized by three aspects followed.

6.1   Impact Factor-Fetch Less Than the "Optimized"

Determining the value of impact factor sigma (σ) which is the most important parameter need to be evaluated is the first step to do. Aiming at searching for the very appropriate parameter σ, entropy concept is brought in, with the structuring relationship between σ and entropy. As the result shows, the nadir of the curve is not often the suited place. Via lots of experiments, we find that the end of first monotonous decreasing region in oscillation region can get the optimal sigma (Fig. 7).

Oscillation characteristic is taken into consideration in first region (Fig. 2), a new simple heuristics method is put forward to find the optimal sigma. Pseudocode is given followed.

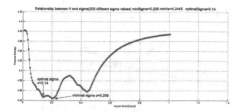

Fig. 7. Ways to find optimal sigma

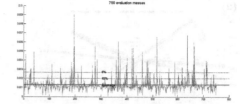

Fig. 8. 750 evaluation masses, sigma = 0.01

Algorithm: simple heuristic method of finding optimal impact factor (sigma) (SHGetOpSigma)

Input: data sets(dts), start sigma probe value(startSigma), interval(gapV), detection number(osp)

Output: optimal sigma σ^*

Generally speaking, for most datasets in 2-dimension, the startSigma take no more than 0.01, and the gapV take range from 0.005 to 0.01 due to different datasets with detection number(osp) taking no more than 5. The most advantage of this SHGetOpSigma is easy to construct with relatively high efficiency under just search in a small area of whole interval. Additionally, it is without losing accuracy.

6.2   Filter Mass by Size

All links link with one another. An appropriate sigma value is serviceable to the next step of mass evaluation and core objects selection. Via 6.1 step, an excellent mass evaluation can be obtained. Using better evaluation sigma, a relatively better evaluation masses are gotten which is shown followed by Fig. 8.

Figure 8 gives 750 samples with their masses evaluated by optimal sigma, as well as three-line added in. The first line is the average mass of all objects. The second and third line denote the top 6% and 10% mass size respectively.

Because the values of masses vary in size ranging from zero to one, given a dataset, it is hard to select core data objects by one given threshold. It is feasible to select them by proportion. Experiments demonstrate the reasonable interval is 6% to 10%.

6.3   Ways to Choose Time Resolution

As part 5.4 analyzing, time resolution f controls the unit mobile distance which is directly proportional to the velocity of moving for one iteration. For another, high velocity does not mean high efficiency and sometimes it may lead to error. So, a proper value of f, except to sigma, is crucial to the final merging result.

For a data set in 2-dimension, after normalization process, f takes 0.75 to 1.

Figure 9, 7 core objects unit opposite movement path at a period time, (Using solid circle represents data, the size of circle represents mass size. Bigger circle means greater mass e.g. data 1's mass is bigger than 6.)

(a)   **(b)**

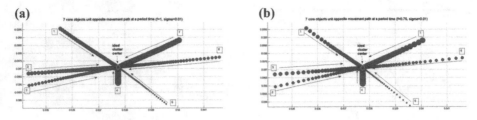

Fig. 9. (**A**) (f = 1, sigma = 0.01), (**B**) (f = 0.75, sigma = 0.01)

A comparison between different time resolutions has been done, showing 7 core data objects opposite movement trace in a period in Fig. 9. It is clear that unit movement distance at Fig. 9B is farther than Fig. 9A and both the two conditions get the same result which clusters them at the ideal cluster center. Figure 9B is superior to Fig. 9A because the former gets a relative fast speed with good performance.

7   Experiments

In fact, the core data objects' moving trace is not just along straight line. They are attracted by data field gravitation and sometimes do curve motion (Fig. 10).

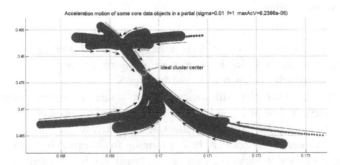

Fig. 10. Acceleration motion of some core data objects in a partial (sigma = 0.01 f = 1. Arrow direction is the direction of objects' moving, and they come together at the ideal cluster center.)

According to the theory in Part 6, which offers several measures to improve the data field for Hierarchical clustering, some experiments are done and we got some excellent results. Using 399 data and 3100 data as examples, a more efficient process is gotten (Fig. 11).

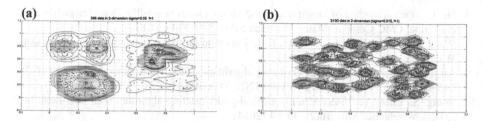

Fig. 11. (A) 399 data in 2-dimension (sigma = 0.05 f = 1), (B) 3100 data in 2-dimension (sigma = 0.05 f = 1)

8 Conclusion

Data field Clustering is an eminent algorithm more outstanding than K-means, BIRCH, CURE, Chameleon methods in some case [8]. In spite of its advantages, there exist bottlenecks or problems which restrict the use and application extending to real areas widely in it. Simply analyzing the basic process of data field clustering and its superiorities, this paper places emphasis on analyzing and dissecting the problems and barriers of the data field clustering in four aspects such as determination of impact factor sigma, mass evaluation, selection core objects as well as core data merging process. It is found that it is hard to determined impact factor, evaluating mass, selecting core objects and time resolution in the data field clustering algorithms. These problems analyzed, several feasible methods are put forward to solve them preliminarily. By improving, the method of data field clustering, which can be applied to IDS, has been enhanced. And the improved aspects contribute to the further application of data field clustering to AD measures.

Acknowledgments. Thanks to vice Professor ZhangHong for proof-reading and great help of refining this paper. He provides biggest support with great patience all the time.

References

1. George, K., Han, E.H., Chameleon, V.K.: A hierarchical clustering algorithm using dynamic modeling. IEEE Comput. **27**(3), 329–341 (1999)
2. Li, X., Zhang, S.C., Wang, S.L.: Advances in data mining applications. Int. J. Data Warehouse. Min. **2**(3), i–iii (2006)
3. Song, M., Hu, X.H., Yoo, I., Koppel, E.: A dynamic and semantically-aware technique for document clustering in biomedical literature. Int. J. Data Warehouse. Min. **5**(4), 44–57 (2009). https://doi.org/10.4018/jdwm.2009080703
4. Silla Jr., C.N., Freitas, A.A.: A survey of hierarchical classification across different application domains. Data Min. Knowl. Disc. **22**, 31–72 (2011). https://doi.org/10.1007/s10618-010-0175-9
5. Gan, W., Li, D.: Dynamic clustering based on data fields. In: Proceedings of the Eleventh International Fuzzy Systems Association World Congress, vol. III (2005)
6. Yang, K., Tan, T., Zhang, W.: An evidence combination method based on DBSCAN clustering. CMC Comput. Mater. Continua **57**(2), 269–281 (2018)

7. He, L., et al.: A method of identifying thunderstorm clouds in satellite cloud image based on clustering. CMC Comput. Mater. Continua **57**(3), 549–570 (2018)
8. Wang, S.L., Gan, W.Y., Li, D.Y., Li, D.R.: Data field for hierarchical clustering. Int. J. Data Warehouse. Min. **7**(2), 43–63 (2011)
9. Xu, R., Wunsch, D.: Survey of clustering algorithms. IEEE Trans. Neural Networks **16**(3), 645–678 (2005). https://doi.org/10.1109/TNN.2005.845141
10. Wang, S., Chen, Y.: HASTA: a hierarchical-grid clustering algorithm with data field. Int. J. Data Warehouse. Min. **10**(2), 39–54 (2014)
11. Yuan, H., Wang, S., Li, Y., Fan, J.: Feature selection with data field. Chin. J. Electron. **23**(4), 661–665 (2014)
12. Wang, S., Wang, D., Li, C., Li, Y., Ding, G.: Clustering by fast search and find of density peaks with data field. Chin. J. Electron. **25**(3) (2016)
13. http://c2.com/cgi/wiki?EightyTwentyRule
14. Liao, H.-J., et al.: Intrusion detection system: a comprehensive review. J. Netw. Comput. Appl. **36**(1), 16–24 (2013)
15. Han, S., et al.: Research on application of date site in information security. Comput. Digit. Eng.

Detection of Microblog Overlapping Community Based on Multidimensional Information and Edge Distance Matrix

Chunhui Deng[1], Huifang Deng[2(✉)], and Youjun Liu[2]

[1] School of Computer Engineering, Guangzhou College,
South China University of Technology, Guangzhou 510800, China
dengch@gcu.edu.cn
[2] School of Computer Science and Engineering,
South China University of Technology, Guangzhou 510006, China
hdengpp@qq.com

Abstract. The traditional community detection algorithms are often based on the network structure, without considering the unique characteristics of weibo (microblog) network. In this paper we proposed a weibo overlapping community detection algorithm, called MIEDM. It takes weibo network as research object and is based on multidimensional information and edge distance matrix. First, we established the weighted network topology graph integrating the weibo multidimensional information such as weibo user relationship, user behavior, weibo theme, and geographic location. Second, based on the edge-node-edge random walk model, we constructed the edge distance matrix. The matrix not only considers the distance of adjacent edges but also the distance of non-adjacent edges. Then, we improved the existing density peak clustering algorithm, and employed the improved algorithm to identify the initial communities with the edge distance matrix considered. In addition, the initial discovered communities are merged and optimized according to the modularity increment. Final, the results of experiments on the weibo network and real networks show that this algorithm yields higher accuracy, stability and generality.

Keywords: Multidimensional information · Edge distance matrix ·
Random walk · Density peaks clustering algorithm ·
Weibo (microblog) overlapping community detection

1 Introduction

Weibo, also known as micro-blog, is a platform for information sharing, dissemination and collection based on user relationships [1]. Users can form individual community through the WEB, WAP and various clients, and share the updated information in real-time. According to China Sina Finance and Economics statistics [2], as of December 2016, weibo monthly active users have reached 313 million.

The Study of weibo topics mainly includes link prediction, community detection, user influence analysis, topic detection, and information dissemination. One of the important purposes of weibo network research is to find the user sets having the same

© Springer Nature Switzerland AG 2019
X. Sun et al. (Eds.): ICAIS 2019, LNCS 11632, pp. 121–136, 2019.
https://doi.org/10.1007/978-3-030-24274-9_11

interest preferences or frequent communications from the huge weibo network and group them reasonably. Those kinds of sets are normally called communities. The ultimate goal is to achieve the precise marketing push of product or service. Community detection is an effective method to find the above sets.

So far, for the study of community detection, the researchers have suggested many community detection algorithms from different approaches, such as the method based on graph-partitioning, the method based on hierarchical clustering, the method based on modularity and so on. However, these traditional community detection methods are often based the network structure, without considering the unique characteristics of weibo network, such as user tags or labels, forward (re-post), praise (thumbs-up), comment and other multidimensional information which brings about inaccuracy in community detection. In addition, in weibo network the user may usually has multiple interests, such as user who is interested in music is also interested in dance, which leads to a result that the same node (user) may belong to different communities. Therefore, the traditional non-overlapping community discovery algorithm cannot truly depict the microscopic features of weibo social network.

From this view, this paper proposes an overlapping community detection algorithm taking weibo network as research object. This algorithm not only considers the multiple dimensions or components of weibo information, but also calculates the similarity of adjacent and non-adjacent edges. And it also considers the overlapping feature of community structure, which can achieve more accurate and real weibo community detection.

The rest of the paper is organized as follows. Section 2 briefly introduces related works. Section 3 presents the process of weibo multidimensional information model construction. In Sect. 4, we develop our algorithm called MIEDM. In Sect. 5, we show experiments on MIEDM, compare with some other algorithms, and discuss the influence of parameters on the results of the experiments. In Sect. 6, we conclude our work.

2 Related Works

At present, the researches on community detection at home and abroad are mainly divided into non-overlapping and overlapping community detections. For non-overlapping community detection, the communities that are identified are all non-overlapping, namely each node only can belong to a community, as shown in Fig. 1 (left). The typical algorithms are based on hierarchical clustering algorithm, based on modularity algorithm, based on information entropy algorithm and so on. The hierarchical clustering algorithm is divided into divisive and cohesive. The Girvan-Newman (GN) algorithm [3] is a typical divisive. Its main idea is to divide a social network into independent and different communities by constantly removing the edges that have higher "edge betweenness". Clauset proposed a fast greedy algorithm [4], which first regards each node as a community, and then gathers those communities of high similarity into a larger community. Duch and Arenas [5] proposed a novel method to find the community structure in complex networks based on an extremal optimization of the value of modularity. Argerich [6] presented a community detection algorithm based on information entropy and random walk model. But, in the real network, a node often belongs to different communities simultaneously, namely the community structure is overlapping with each other in the network, as shown in Fig. 1 (right). Therefore, in recent years, many researchers proposed some overlapping community detection algorithms, such as, clique percolation algorithm, local extension and optimization algorithm, label propagation algorithm and so on. Clique percolation algorithm is one of the most classic overlapping community detection approaches. In 2005, Palla et al. [7] proposed an overlapping community detection algorithm based on clique percolation algorithm and applied it to the weighed network. In 2010, Evans [8] proposed a clique graph (CG) algorithm based on clique percolation algorithm. It shows how to construct a clique graph through clique percolation algorithm. Fortunato et al. [9] presented the first algorithm that finds both overlapping communities and the hierarchical structure. It is based on the local optimization algorithm.

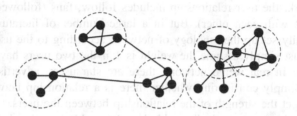

Fig. 1. Non-overlapping (left) and Overlapping (right)

However, the traditional community detection algorithms are mainly aimed at the network topology analysis and research instead of the weibo network natures. At present some scholars use the characteristics of weibo network to improve the traditional community detection algorithm for enhancing the accuracy of the weibo network community detection. In these studies, there are several main ideas adopted more widely: (1) the interest themes posted by weibo users; (2) the attributes of weibo users; (3) the interactive behavior between weibo users. For example, Yan et al. [10] and Wang et al. [11] provided community detection algorithms based on the weibo users theme similarity and network structure. The main procedure is as follows: first, retrieve users theme from their weibo; then cluster the similar users based on Link relations between users; and finally, get the communities. Cai et al. [12] proposed a weibo community detection algorithm based on users interactive behavior similarity, which can solve the problem of sparseness of weibo social network. Beginning with users theme and interaction, Darmon et al. [13] proposed a weibo community detection algorithm based on the traditional order statistics local optimization method (OSLOM).

3   Weibo Multidimensional Information Model

A weibo user generally exhibits multiple information components, such as: follow, followed (fans), weibo information posted, interactions, personal labels and so on. In the existing weibo user researches, the researchers tend to focus on weibo user relationships [10], interactions between weibo users [13], weibo user theme interest similarity [14], and weibo user geographical location [15, 16]. And many research results show that these information components play an important role in seeking weibo user sets with the same interest. But, most researchers use only one or another component for community detection. With the increase in weibo network users and diversification in interactions between users, integration of multiple information components can improve the quality and accuracy of community detection. Therefore, this paper combines weibo user relationship, user interaction behavior, user theme interest (according to user labels and weibo information published) and user geographical location to construct the weibo multidimensional information model. The following introduces processing method of each information component.

3.1 User Relationship

In weibo network, the user relationship includes follow, fans (followed), and follow each other (fans with each other). But in a large number of literature studies, the researchers usually set up the topology of network according to the user relationship directly. They just simply assume the weight is 1 if the two users have relationship, otherwise 0. But in real weibo network, there are star users, advertising users and isolated users. Simply considering whether there is a relationship between the users cannot fully reflect the strength of the relationship between the users.

Therefore, in this paper, in dealing with the relationship between the users, we first delete the isolated, star and advertising nodes. Second, for the case of "only one followed by another" between two users (nodes), we think that the degree of interest is half of that for the case of "both two followed with each other". Thus, the formula for dealing with the relationship between users is extended as follows:

$$sim\_con(i,j) = \begin{cases} 1 & i \ and \ j, \ both \ "follow" \ with \ each \ other \\ 0.5 & i \ or \ j, \ either \ one \ "followed" \ by \ another \\ 0 & others \ (no \ "follow") \end{cases} \quad (1)$$

From (1), the topological structure acquired after processing the follow relationship between users intuitively represents the weighted adjacency matrix A of the network. Any element $a_{ij} = sim\_con(i,j)$ of A represents the strength of interest between the user i and j.

3.2 User Theme Interest

Weibo user often exhibits a certain interest preferences in the release of weibo and their own labels. Digging into these preferences can help analyze user theme interest similarity. We derive the strength of user theme interest similarity from the user exhibited weibo information and tags.

User Weibo Information Processing. Common approach is used to deal with user released weibo information: first, we use ICTCLAS system (Institute of Computing Technology, Chinese Lexical Analysis System) [17] to segment weibo texts; second, we use TF•IDF (Term Frequency•Inverse Document Frequency) to extract the feature terms; and third, we calculate the similarity of the feature terms between any two users based on the cosine similarity. In this paper, we extract the features of each user's top 10 terms, calculate the similarity $sim\_tw(t_i, t_j)$ between feature term t_i of user i and feature term t_j of user j (where t_i, t_j = 1, 2, 3, .., 10; i, j = 1, 2, 3, .., N, N is the total number of weibo users), and get a 10×10 matrix:

$$sim\_t(i,j) = \begin{bmatrix} sim\_tw(1_i, 1_j) & \cdots & sim\_tw(1_i, 10_j) \\ \vdots & sim\_tw(t_i, t_j) & \vdots \\ sim\_tw(10_i, 1_j) & \cdots & sim\_tw(10_i, 10_j) \end{bmatrix} \quad (2)$$

In (2), each row represents the similarities between a given feature term of user i and all 10 feature terms of user j respectively, and each column represents the similarities between all 10 feature terms of user i and a given feature term of user j respectively.

As the larger the similarity of feature terms between users is, the larger the similarity of weibo information posted by users is, considering this, in this paper, we first find the average maximum similarities sim_wbi_{col} and sim_wbi_{row} in following way:

$$sim\_wbi_{col} = \frac{1}{10} \sum_{i=1}^{10} \max(sim\_tw(t_i, t_1), \ldots, sim\_tw(t_i, t_{10})) \quad (3a)$$

$$sim\_wbi_{row} = \frac{1}{10} \sum_{j=1}^{10} \max(sim\_tw(t_1, t_j), \ldots, sim\_tw(t_{10}, t_j)) \quad (3b)$$

Because the average maximum similarity sim_wbi_{col} (3a) is normally different from sim_wbi_{row} (3b), we then take their arithmetic mean to deal with the difference, i.e.:

$$sim\_wb(i,j) = \frac{1}{2}(sim\_wbi_{col} + sim\_wbi_{row}) \quad (4)$$

In this way we get the overall averaged maximum similarity $sim\_wb(i,j)$ between user i and j regarding their feature terms.

User Labels Processing. A weibo user can choose 10 short labels (tags) at most. Therefore, in this paper we calculate labels (l_i, l_j) similarity $sim\_lw(l_i, l_j)$ for each user using the same weight and get a 10×10 matrix:

$$sim\_l(i,j) = \begin{bmatrix} sim\_lw(1_i, 1_j) & \cdots & sim\_lw(1_i, 10_j) \\ \vdots & sim\_lw(l_i, l_j) & \vdots \\ sim\_lw(10_i, 1_j) & \cdots & sim\_lw(10_i, 10_j) \end{bmatrix} \quad (5)$$

In (5), each row is the similarity between a given label of user i and all 10 labels of user j respectively, and each column is the similarity between all 10 labels of user i and a given label of user j respectively. We use the same way as getting (3) to first find the average maximum similarities sim_lbi_{col} and sim_lbi_{row} respectively, and then deal with the difference in them by taking their arithmetic average to get the overall averaged maximum similarity between user i and user j regarding their labels, i.e.:

$$sim\_lb(i,j) = \frac{1}{2}(sim\_lbi_{col} + sim\_lbi_{row}) \tag{6}$$

The users posted weibo information and chosen labels are processed according to the (4) and (6) respectively, and by integrating two we can obtain users' theme interest similarity $sim\_tl(i,j)$ according to [18], as follows:

$$sim\_tl(i,j) = \log_2(\frac{1}{2}(sim\_lb(i,j) + sim\_wb(i,j)) + 1) \tag{7}$$

Where the purpose of adding 1 to this right hand side of (7) is to prevent a negative value from occurrence.

3.3   User Interaction Behavior

In study of user interaction behavior, in this paper we follow the way given in [18] to deal with user interaction information such as forward, comment, praise, and mention (@), i.e., we evaluate corresponding similarity $F(i,j)$, $C(i,j)$, $P(i,j)$ and $A(i,j)$ as follows:

$$F(i,j) = \frac{2 \times fd(i,j)}{fd_{i \to all} + fd_{all \to j}} \tag{8}$$

$$C(i,j) = \frac{2 \times com(i,j)}{com_{i \to all} + com_{all \to j}} \tag{9}$$

$$P(i,j) = \frac{2 \times pra(i,j)}{pra_{i \to all} + pra_{all \to j}} \tag{10}$$

$$A(i,j) = \frac{2 \times at(i,j)}{at_{i \to all} + at_{all \to j}} \tag{11}$$

where, $fd(i,j)$, $com(i,j)$, $pra(i,j)$ and $at(i,j)$ respectively represent the number of times that user i has forwarded, commented, praised, and @ (referred) onto user j, and $fd_{i \to all}$, $com_{i \to all}$, $pra_{i \to all}$ and $at_{i \to all}$ represent the number of times that user i to all users respectively, and $fd_{all \to j}$, $com_{all \to j}$, $pra_{all \to j}$, $at_{all \to j}$ respectively represent the number of times that all users have forwarded, commented, praised and @ (referred) onto user j. Integrating (8), (9), (10) and (11) we obtain user interaction behavior evaluation formula as follows:

$$sim\_action(i,j) = \delta_f F(i,j) + \delta_c C(i,j) + \delta_p P(i,j) + \delta_a A(i,j) \qquad (12)$$

Because the importance of forward, comment, praise and @ is different from each other, based on the hierarchical analysis method, we set δ_f, δ_c, δ_p and δ_a to be 0.35, 0.15, 0.15 and 0.35 as the weighted factor of each interaction behavior respectively.

3.4   User Geographical Location

In this paper we scale user's geographic location as three different levels: country, province and city, and quantize it as follows: if two users stay in the same country, but not in the same province and city, the similarity $sim\_lbs(i,j)$ between user i and user j is set to be 0.2 (the third level); if they are found in the same country and same province, but not in the same city, the similarity is set to be 0.5 (the second level); if they are located in the same country, same province and same city, the similarity is set to be 1 (the top level), i.e.,:

$$sim\_lbs(i,j) = \begin{cases} 0.2 & c_i = c_j \\ 0.5 & c_i = c_j \text{ and } p_i = p_j \\ 1 & c_i = c_j \text{ and } p_i = p_j \text{ and } ct_i = ct_j \end{cases} \qquad (13)$$

Where, c_i, p_i, and ct_i respectively represent country, province and city of user i.

So far, we have proposed the way of processing the weibo user's relationship, theme interest, interaction behavior and geographic location, and particularly showed how to calculate the interest similarity between user i and user j for each information component. Now let us construct our weibo multidimensional information model. The main idea is that we determine the weibo network topology graph based on weibo user relationship, and weight each edge in the network graph to show the strength of user relationship according to user's theme interest, interaction behavior and geographical location. This way, we can obtain a weighted matrix $W = [w_{i,j}]$ of the weibo network, where each component $w_{i,j}$ is determined, as follows:

$$w_{i,j} = \lambda_1 sim\_con(i,j) + \lambda_2 sim\_tl(i,j) \\ + \lambda_3 sim\_action(i,j) + \lambda_4 sim\_lbs(i,j) \qquad (14)$$

Where parameters λ_1, λ_2, λ_3 and λ_4, represent the different impacting factors of different information contributors, which must satisfy $\lambda_1 + \lambda_2 + \lambda_3 + \lambda_4 = 1$, whose specific values are discussed in the experiment section.

4   MIEDM Algorithm

The task of this paper is to design an overlapping community detection algorithm for weibo networks. Based on previous discussions, the design ideas of the algorithm follow three steps:

(1) According to the edge-node-edge random walk model, we create the edge distance matrix. This matrix not only takes into account adjacent edges but also non-adjacent edges.

(2) We use improved density peak clustering algorithm conducting the initial community detection based on the edge distance matrix established in the above step (1)

(3) We merge and optimize the initially discovered communities to further improve the quality of community detection

4.1 Edge Distance Matrix

Since we have already got the weighted weibo network topology graph and its weighted matrix W in Sect. 3, now we can define the weighted network as $G = (V, E, W)$ where V denotes the node set and E is the edge set. In this paper, the edge distance matrix is created according to the edge-node-edge random walk model.

According to the description of the edge-node-edge random walk model in [19], for a given unweighted network $G = (V, E)$ we define the random process on it as follows: Suppose the "walker" is on a node in the G, it randomly walks from an edge of this node to the other adjacent edge, and then choose a node of this adjacent edge as a new starting point, and repeats the process.

Now let $p1(e_{i,j}, e_{m,n})$ as the transfer probability of one walking step from edge $e_{i,j}$ to edge $e_{m,n}$:

$$
p1(e_{i,j}, e_{m,n}) = \begin{cases} \frac{1}{2}\frac{w_{m,n}}{\sum_{h=1}^{k} w_{m,h}} + \frac{1}{2}\frac{w_{m,n}}{\sum_{h=1}^{k} w_{n,h}} & \{m,n\} \cap \{i,j\} = \{m,n\} \\ \frac{1}{2}\frac{w_{m,n}}{\sum_{h=1}^{k} w_{m,h}} & \{m,n\} \cap \{i,j\} = \{m\} \\ \frac{1}{2}\frac{w_{m,n}}{\sum_{h=1}^{k} w_{n,h}} & \{m,n\} \cap \{i,j\} = \{n\} \\ 0 & other \end{cases}
\tag{15}
$$

Where k is the degree of node h, i.e., the number of edges or other nodes directly connected to this node (h) (the larger the number/degree, the greater the importance of this node in the network); m, n and r denote any one node of the network map. 1/2 is the probability of selecting any one node of an edge, $w_{m,n}$ is the weight of edge $e_{m,n}$ as given in (14), $\sum_{h=1}^{k} w_{m,h}$ is the weighted sum of edges h ($h = 1, 2, .., k$) connected with node m, and $w_{m,n}/\sum_{h=1}^{k} w_{m,h}$ represents the probability of selecting node n connected with node m.

Now let us define $p^l(e_{m,n})$ as the probability of reaching edge $e_{m,n}$ through l randomly walking steps as follows:

$$p^l(e_{m,n}) = \sum_{r \neq m} p^{l-1}(e_{r,n}) \cdot p1(e_{r,n}, e_{m,n})$$
$$+ \sum_{s \neq n} p^{l-1}(e_{m,s}) \cdot p1(e_{m,s}, e_{m,n}) + p^{l-1}(e_{m,n}) \cdot p1(e_{m,n}, e_{m,n}) \tag{16}$$

Where the first term, second term and the third term on the right hand side of (16) represent the probability of reaching the edge $e_{m,n}$ from edges of nodes r connecting to node n, from edges of nodes s connecting to node m and from the edge $e_{m,n}$ itself, respectively, from previous step $l - 1$ to step l; $p^{l-1}(e_{r,n})$ is the probability of reaching the edge $e_{r,n}$ at step $l - 1$. Upon taking into account each step of the "walker" in the calculation of the local random walk (LRW) similarity, we can get the equation to calculate the superposed random walk (SRW) similarity as follows:

$$S_{e_{m,n},e_{i,j}}^{SRW}(Sn) = \begin{cases} C(e_{m,n}) \sum_{l=1}^{Sn} p^l(e_{m,n}) + C(e_{i,j}) \sum_{l=1}^{Sn} p^l(e_{i,j}) & otherwise \\ 1 & \{m,n\} \cap \{i,j\} = \{m,n\} \end{cases} \tag{17}$$

Where Sn is the step number of random walk; $C(e_{m,n})$ represents the clustering coefficient of edge $e_{m,n}$, which is used to measure the importance and aggregation of the edge in network and given by:

$$C(e_{i,j}) = \frac{N(e_{i,j}) + 1}{\min(k_i - 1, k_j - 1)} \tag{18}$$

Where $N(e_{i,j})$ represents the number of triangles actually containing the edge $e_{i,j}$ in the network; $\min(k_i - 1, k_j - 1)$ gives the number of triangles that can form most possibly with the edge $e_{i,j}$ contained and obviously this number depends on the degree $k_{i\ or\ j}$ of node i or j in the network; And plus 1 in the numerator of (18) is to prevent 0 from occurrence.

Now let us define the distance $d(e_{m,n}, e_{i,j})$ between any two edges, say, $e_{m,n}$ and $e_{i,j}$ in the network as follows:

$$d(e_{m,n}, e_{i,j}) = 1 - S_{e_{m,n},e_{i,j}}^{SRW} \tag{19}$$

The theoretical ground is that the greater the similarity between any edges in the network, the smaller the corresponding edge distance. If we know the distances between all edges, we can construct an $E \times E$ edge distance matrix D of weibo network, E is the total number of the edges in the network.

4.2 Initial Community Detection Based on Density Peak Clustering Algorithm

Once obtaining the edge distance matrix D of the network, we need to obtain the membership of edges associated with communities. In this paper we introduce density peak clustering algorithm (DPCA) [20] to deal with edge distance matrix D. DPCA not only can cluster the networks of different shapes but also can find the cluster center. Its primary idea is to calculate the local density $\rho_{e_{i,j}}$ of each edge and the distance $\delta_{e_{i,j}}$ of each edge reaching the edges of higher local density. And both their magnitudes depend on the distances $d_{e_{i,j},e_{m,n}}$ between edges $e_{i,j}$ and $e_{m,n}$:

$$\rho_{e_{i,j}} = \sum_{e_{m,n}=1}^{n} \xi(d_{e_{i,j},e_{m,n}} - d_c) \tag{20}$$

$$\xi(d_{e_{i,j},e_{m,n}} - d_c) = \begin{cases} 1 & d_{e_{i,j},e_{m,n}} < d_c \\ 0 & otherwise \end{cases} \tag{21}$$

Where d_c is a cutoff distance and is usually constant which is determined by the value of the edge distance $d_{e_{i,j},e_{m,n}}$ corresponding to the sorting position of 2% counted from the end of the downward sorted distance list among all edges.

$\delta_{e_{i,j}}$ is obtained by computing the minimum distance between the edge $e_{i,j}$ and any other edges of higher local density:

$$\delta_{e_{i,j}} = \min_{\forall e_{m,n} \in E : \rho_{e_{m,n}} > \rho_{e_{i,j}}} (d_{e_{i,j},e_{m,n}}) \tag{22}$$

For the edge with the highest local density, we conventionally take $\delta_{e_{i,j}} = \max_{\forall e_{m,n} \in E} (d_{e_{i,j},e_{m,n}})$, and at the same time, take this edge as the cluster center.

DPCA determines the cluster center by observing decision graph which takes the local density $\rho_{e_{i,j}}$ as the horizontal axis and the minimum distance $\delta_{e_{i,j}}$ as the vertical axis, this is quite error prone. Thus, in this paper we improve the DPCA and define density distance $\gamma_{e_{i,j}}$ of each edge $e_{i,j}$ as follows:

$$\gamma_{e_{i,j}} = \rho_{e_{i,j}} \times \delta_{e_{i,j}} \tag{23}$$

We calculate density distances $\gamma_{e_{i,j}}$ for all edges $e_{i,j}(i,j = 1, 2, \ldots, N)$ and sort them in descending order. And then we take the ordinal number of each (downward sorted) density distance $\gamma_{e_{i,j}}$ of edge $e_{i,j}$ as the horizontal axis, $\gamma_{e_{i,j}}$ as the vertical axis. In this way, one could see that the larger the value $\gamma_{e_{i,j}}$, the greater the likelihood that $e_{i,j}$ is the center of the cluster. And moreover, $\gamma_{e_{i,j}}$ varies more smoothly at the non-clustered center, while jumps when transiting from non-cluster center to cluster center. Therefore, we define a transfer variable $\eta_{e_{i,j}}$ of edge $e_{i,j}$ to represent the cluster center which directly involves the jump:

$$\eta_{e_{i,j}} = \left| \gamma_{e_{i,j}+1} + \gamma_{e_{i,j}-1} - 2\gamma_{e_{i,j}} \right| \tag{24}$$

Obviously $\eta_{e_{i,j}}$ measures the change in the density distance $\gamma_{e_{i,j}}$ after downward sorting $\gamma_{e_{i,j}}$. And the larger the value $\eta_{e_{i,j}}$, the greater the change in $\gamma_{e_{i,j}}$, it implies that the edge $e_{i,j}$ is for sure the clustering center. After all possible cluster centers are identified which always have higher local density, each remaining edge is grouped into its nearest cluster center which has higher local density than it to complete the initial community detection.

4.3 Community Merging and Optimizing

We have conducted the initial community detection for any edge as above. If an edge is in a community, then its two nodes connected with each other must be in the same community. Based on this philosophy the case of the edge community can be transformed as the case of a node community.

However, since we adopted random walk model for initial community detection, the communities discovered in this way may be highly overlapped. Therefore, in this paper we use the modularity increment/variation before and after merging

$$\Delta Q_w = \frac{1}{w} \sum_{h=1}^{C} \sum_{v,u \in c_h} \frac{1}{N_v \cdot N_u} [w_{v,u} - \frac{k_v k_u}{w}] \tag{25}$$

to merge and optimize the possibly overlapped communities. Where N_v and N_u respectively represents the number of communities containing the node v and node u; c_h denotes the community h; C represents the total number of communities; w represents the weighted sum of all edges; $w_{v,u}$ represents the weight of edge $e_{v,u}$; k_v represents the degree of node v. If we get a result of $\Delta Q_w > 0$ then we merge these two communities, otherwise, it means that no further merging is required (i.e., the merging process is finished).

4.4 Extension of MIEDM Algorithm Applicability

Through the above description and analysis, we find that MIEDM algorithm, which is intentionally targeted at weibo network, is also applicable to general networks. For example, for a given network $G = (V, E)$, first we compute the edge distance matrix based on the edge-node-edge random walk model, then identify preliminary communities which could be overlapped based on the improved DPCA, and finally merge and optimize the overlapped communities based on the modularity increment (25). In this paper we call this applicability extended algorithm as EDME algorithm which is applicable to the general networks but without including the networks' multidimensional information as MIEDM does for weibo network.

5 Experiments

In order to verify the accuracy, stability and generality of the algorithm, we conduct the experiments on real networks and Sina weibo network respectively and use modularity Q to evaluate the quality of community detection:

$$Q = \frac{1}{2E} \sum_{v \in c_v, u \in c_u} \left[a_{v,u} - \frac{k_v k_u}{2E} \right] \tau(c_v, c_u) \qquad (26)$$

Where E is the total number of edges; c_v and c_u respectively represents the communities containing the node v and node u; $a_{v,u}$ is the element of adjacency matrix A, and if node v is directly connected with node u, $a_{v,u} = 1$, otherwise $a_{v,u} = 0$; $\tau(c_v, c_u)$ is defined as follows: if both node v and node u are contained in the same community, $\tau(c_v, c_u) = 1$, otherwise $\tau(c_v, c_u) = 0$.

At the same time, we compare our algorithm with other existing algorithms: LC [21] which only considers adjacent edge, LDM [22] which uses the fuzzy c-means algorithm (FCM), ELC [23] which calculates the similarity based on nodes, TPC [11] which only considers weibo theme, and the classic LFM algorithm [9].

5.1   Real Networks

The real networks used in this paper include Karate, Dolphin, Football, Power and Word-Association (WA). The related information about them are shown in Table 1.

Table 1. Data set of real networks

Network	Number of nodes	Number of edges
Karate	34	78
Dolphin	62	159
Football	115	613
Power	4941	6594
Word-Association	7205	31784

The Result and Analysis of Real Network Experiments. Form the experimental results shown in Table 2, we can see that increase in the scale of network has very minor effect on the experimental results (modularity Q). Compared with the LFM algorithm which is regarded to be efficient in community detection currently, the difference is very small. There is even a 16.38% improvement gained in the Word-Association network. And compared with LC, the algorithm of EDME proposed in this paper gives the maximum improvements. It can be seen that the EDME shows a good stability and generality.

Impact of Parameters l on Experimental Results. EDME algorithm only involves the random walk step number of l and with the increase in l, the probability $p^l(e_{m,n})$ of reaching $e_{m,n}$ gets smaller and smaller, so in this paper the maximum value of l is set as 6. We conduct experiments on the Dolphin and Word-Association (WA) networks respectively; the results are shown in the Fig. 2.

In Fig. 2, we can see that the quality of community detection shows the best when the random walk step number l takes 3. This is consistent with the findings from majority researches.

Table 2. Comparison of results (q) on real networks

Network\Algorithm\Modularity(Q)	Karate	Dolphin	Football	Power	WA
EDME (this paper)	0.687	0.671	0.643	0.695	0.682
LC	0.551	0.537	0.518	0.504	0.471
Improved (%) vs LC	**24.68**	**24.95**	**24.13**	**37.90**	**44.80**
LDM	0.631	0.643	0.678	0.563	0.603
Improved (%) vs LDM	**8.87**	**4.35**	**−5.16**	**23.44**	**13.10**
ELC	0.618	0.594	0.621	0.519	0.633
Improved (%) vs ELC	**11.16**	**12.96**	**3.54**	**33.91**	**7.18**
LFM	0.712	0.664	0.671	0.624	0.586
Improved (%) vs LFM	**−3.51**	**1.05**	**−4.17**	**11.38**	**16.38**

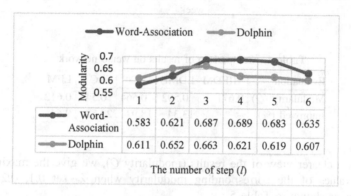

	1	2	3	4	5	6
Word-Association	0.583	0.621	0.687	0.689	0.683	0.635
Dolphin	0.611	0.652	0.663	0.621	0.619	0.607

The number of step (l)

Fig. 2. Impact of parameter l on the results

5.2 Sina Weibo Network

In this paper the Sina weibo data set is obtained through two ways: shared and collected, and the information details are given in Table 3.

The Result and Analysis of weibo Network Experiment. In Table 4, the MIEDM algorithm, which integrated weibo multidimensional information, improved the modularity by 13.34% compared with EDME algorithm which excluded weibo information and by 18.97% compared with TPC algorithm which only considers weibo theme. Thus, it can be seen that the quality of community detection can be improved appreciably when weibo multidimensional information are considered. Compared with the ELC algorithm calculating the similarity based on nodes, the MIEDM algorithm has showed an obvious superiority. It implies that the MIEDM is of high accuracy.

Impact of Factors λ on the Experimental Results. Now let us discuss the impact of parameters λ_σ (σ = 1, 2, 3, 4) occurred in constructing weibo multidimensional information model. As $\lambda_1 + \lambda_2 + \lambda_3 + \lambda_4 = 1$, from the analytic hierarchy process we know that λ_4 has the smallest proportion. So in the experiment we tried 0.1, 0.2 and 0.3 for λ_4 respectively.

Table 3. Data set of weibo network

Data item	Size	Description
Number of user	63641	Data set containing the number of weibo users
Number of weibo	78088	Total number of weibo posted in one week
Number of user relationship	1391718	The number of relationship between users
Number of weibo forward	25949	Total number of weibo forwarded (re-posted) in one week
Number of weibo comment	65357	Total number of weibo commented on in one week
Number of weibo praise	44432	Total number of weibo praised (thumbs-up) in one week
Number of weibo mention @	20203	Total number of weibo mentioned (referred) in one week

Table 4. Comparison of results on weibo network

Evaluation	MIEDM	EDME	TPC	ELC	LFM
Modularity (Q)	0.671	0.592	0.564	0.543	0.612
Improved (%)	–	13.34	18.97	23.57	9.64

And for a clearer view of the results (modularity Q), we give the maximum and minimum values of the corresponding modularity when λ_4 set 0.1, 0.2 and 0.3 respectively, as shown in Table 5.

Table 5. The experimental results when λ takes different values

λ_4	λ_3	λ_2	λ_1	Modularity (Q)
0.1	0.1	0.5	0.3	0.523
0.1	**0.3**	**0.4**	**0.2**	**0.679**
0.2	0.1	0.6	0.1	0.531
0.2	0.3	0.3	0.2	0.634
0.3	0.3	0.1	0.3	0.502
0.3	0.2	0.4	0.1	0.610

It can be seen that when λ_1, λ_2, λ_3 and λ_4 are, respectively, takes 0.2, 0.4, 0.3, and 0.1 we get the maximum modularity value of 0.679, which is the best result.

6 Conclusions

In this paper, we proposed a weibo overlapping community detection algorithm: MIEDM based on multidimensional information and edge distance matrix. First, we constructed the weibo multidimensional information model based on multidimensional information of weibo. Second, based on the edge-node-edge random walk model, we formulated the edge distance matrix. Third, we improved the original DCPA algorithm and used it to carry out the initial community detection. Fourth, we defined the modularity increment and use it to merge and optimize the initial discovery communities. Fifth, we described the general applicability of the extension of MIEDM algorithm to general network. And finally we demonstrated the accuracy, stability and generality of the MIEDM algorithm by experiments.

References

1. Xiong, X.B., Zhou, G., Huang, Y.Z., Jun, M.A.: Predicting popularity of tweets on Sina weibo. J. Inf. Eng. Univ. **13**, 496–502 (2012)
2. Sina Finance and Economics statistical report on weibo users of the second quarter of 2016. Sina Finance and Economics Network (2016). http://finance.sina.com.cn/stock/usstock/c/2017-02-23/us-ifyavvsk2753481.shtml
3. Girvan, M., Newman, M.E.J.: Community structure in social and biological networks. Proc. Natl. Acad. Sci. U.S.A. **99**(12), 7821–7826 (2002)
4. Clauset, A., Newman, M.E., Moore, C.: Finding community structure in very large networks. Phys. Rev. E **70**(6–2), 066111 (2004). https://doi.org/10.1103/physreve.70.066111
5. Duch, J., Arenas, A.: Community detection in complex networks using extremal optimization. Phys. Rev. E **72**, 027104 (2005). https://doi.org/10.1103/PhysRevE.72.027104
6. Argerich, L.: EntropyWalker, a fast algorithm for small community detection in large graphs. Comput. Sci. (2015)
7. Palla, G., Derényi, I., Farkad, I., Vicsek, T.: Uncovering the overlapping community structure of complex networks in nature and society. Nature **435**(7043), 814–818 (2005)
8. Evans, T.S.: Clique graphs and overlapping communities. J. Stat. Mech. Theory Exp. **2010**(12), 257–265 (2010). https://doi.org/10.1088/1742-5468/2010/12/p12037
9. Lancichinetti, A., Fortunato, S., Kertesz, J.: Detecting the overlapping and hierarchical community structure of complex networks. New J. Phys. **11**(3), 19–44 (2008)
10. Yan, G.H., Shu, X., Zhi, M.A., Li, X.: Community discovery for microblog based on topic and link analysis. Appl. Res. Comput. **30**(7), 1953–1957 (2013)
11. Wang, W.P., Fan, T.: Community discovery method based on users' interest similarity and social network structure. Syst. Appl. Comput. 108–113 (2013)
12. Cai, B.S., Chen, X.: Research on weibo community discovery based on behavior similarity. Comput. Eng. **39**(8), 55–59 (2013)
13. Darmon, D., Omodei, E., Garland, J.: Followers are not enough: a question-oriented approach to community detection in online social networks. Eprint arXiv (2014). https://doi.org/10.1371/journal.pone.0134860

14. Chen, X., Chen, X., Cheng, Y.: Community structure discovery and community topic analysis in microblog. In: Proceedings of International Conference on Information Management, Innovation Management and Industrial Engineering, vol. 1, pp. 590–595. IEEE (2014)
15. Brown, C., Nicosia, V., Scellato, S., Noulas, A., Mascolo, C.: The importance of being placefriends: discovering location-focused online communities. In: WOSN 2012 Proceedings of the 2012 ACM Workshop on Online Social Networks, pp. 31–36 (2012). https://doi.org/10.1145/2342549.2342557
16. Jiang, J.T.: Research and implementation of community detection based on geographical feature for social networks. Master's Dissertation, Beihang University (2014)
17. The system of ICTCLAS. http://ictclas.nlpir.org/
18. Wang, N.W.: Research on overlapping community detection in weibo networks. Master's Dissertation, Beijing Jiaotong University (2016)
19. He, D., Liu, D., Zhang, W.X., Jin, D., Yang, B.: Discovering link communities in complex networks by exploiting link dynamics. J. Stat. Mech. Theory Exp. **2012**(10), 10015 (2013). https://doi.org/10.1088/1742-5468/2012/10/P10015
20. Rodriguez, A., Laio, A.: Machine learning. Clustering by fast search and find of density peaks. Science **344**(6191), 1492 (2014). https://doi.org/10.1126/science.1242072
21. Ahn, Y.Y., Bagrow, J.P., Lehmann, S.: Link communities reveal multiscale complexity in networks. Nature **466**(7307), 761–764 (2010)
22. Zhang, G.J., Zhang, J.P., Yang, J., Xin, Y.: Overlapping community detecting based on link distance matrix. Appl. Res. Comput. **9**, 1–7 (2017)
23. Huang, L., Wang, G., Wang, Y., Blanzieri, E., Su, C.: Link clustering with extended link similarity and EQ evaluation division. PLoS ONE **8**(6), e66005 (2013). https://doi.org/10.1371/journal.pone.0066005

Research on Settlement Deformation of Asphalt Pavement Structure in Soft Soil Zone Based on Pavement Settlement Theory

Congrong Tang[1][(⊠)], Xin Xu[2], and Haiyan Ding[2]

[1] Nanjing Sutong Road and Bridge Engineering Co., Ltd.,
Nanjing 211200, China
tcr751101@163.com

[2] Kunshan Dengyun College of Science and Technology, Suzhou 215300, China
71159341@qq.com, 534468911@qq.com

Abstract. With the rapid development of highways, asphalt concrete pavements with semi-rigid bases have also been widely used in highway construction in China. Because asphalt concrete pavement has good mechanical properties and good road performance, it greatly improves the road performance and safety performance, and it has good comfort. As the project is in soft land, the weak layer of the foundation is thick, the strength of the roadbed is insufficient, and easy to produce post-construction settlement or uneven settlement, these reasons may cause deformation of the asphalt pavement structure during road operation, and affect the mechanical properties and road performance of the road surface. Simulating the settlement of subgrade pavement by using finite element software modeling, we will study the effects of soil thickness, pavement section location and consolidation time on the settlement deformation of pavement.

Keywords: Asphalt pavement · Finite element simulation · Settlement · Deformation numerical analysis

Uneven settlement of soft soil foundation or impact of vehicle load, the structure of the asphalt pavement will be damaged and deformed during the operation of asphalt pavement. thereby reducing the performance and integrity of the road surface, reducing the safety performance, easily leading to traffic accidents, increasing the degree of danger of the road surface and reducing the life cycle of the road surface [1, 2]. The soft base section has high water content, low strength, long consolidation time and easy rheology. It is easy to settle after completion during operation. These can cause cracks in the base layer and reflective cracks in the surface layer, leading to early and initial damage of the asphalt pavement, which seriously affects the comfort and safety of road driving [3, 4]. We conduct multi-faceted analysis and research on the settlement deformation of asphalt pavement in soft soil area, grasp the causes and influencing factors of settlement deformation of soft soil section, strengthen the design and preventive measures of pavement, reduce the influence of settlement deformation on pavement, and improve the road surface, thereby improving the road performance and life cycle of the road surface [5, 6].

© Springer Nature Switzerland AG 2019
X. Sun et al. (Eds.): ICAIS 2019, LNCS 11632, pp. 137–147, 2019.
https://doi.org/10.1007/978-3-030-24274-9_12

1 Project Overview

The road is in a soft soil area, the soft soil layer is thick, the road construction route is long, and the amount of engineering is large. It is easy to destroy the ecology when the construction is broken. There are neighboring residential houses and public facilities around the road. There are many municipal pipelines, transformers, electric poles, high-voltage lines and other facilities along the road, the height of the embankment is 6 m. The two layers of soft soil are muddy clay and silty clay, the width of the bottom surface is 80 m, the width of the surface is 26 m, and the total thickness is 26.59 m. The pavement and embankment are graded at 1:1.5. The surface is set to a water-permeable boundary, and both sides and the bottom are set to be impervious. The groundwater level is located 1 m below the surface; the thickness of the sand cushion is 0.5 m.

The structure of the road is shown in Fig. 1. It consists of five materials. The thickness and parameters of pavement and embankment are shown in Table 1.

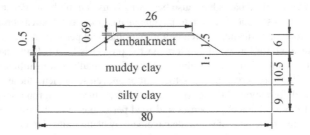

Fig. 1. Asphalt pavement structure model

2 Theory of Subgrade Settlement

In the study of settlement and consolidation of foundations, the widely used theoretical basis is the Taishaji theory and the Biot theory. However, for the study of subgrade settlement deformation, the time span is large and there are obvious lateral differences. Since the two theories of the Tassa Foundation theory and the stratified summation method are established under the premise of assumptions, the gap between theoretical and actual results is too big. So it is not applicable to the study of settlement deformation of roadbed with large time span and obvious lateral difference. The Biot theory studies the effects of foundation settlement and consolidation under consideration of deformation coordination, and compared with the actual situation, it can be used to simulate the consolidation settlement problem of actual engineering and carry out calculation analysis by means of numerical analysis techniques such as computer [5, 6]. Research and analysis of settlement involves primary consolidation settlement analysis, secondary consolidation settlement analysis and instantaneous settlement observation calculation. The formula is shown in Formula 1 [7].

Table 1. Pavement material properties

Structural layer	Material name	Thickness (cm)	Elastic modulus E (MPa)	Poisson's ratio (μ)	Bulk weight γ_d (kN/m³)
Surface layer	Asphalt mastic SMA	4	1400	0.35	24.2
Middle layer	Asphalt concrete AC20	6	1200	0.3	24.2
Below layer	Bitumen stabilized macadam ATB	24	1000	0.3	24.1
Upper base layer	Graded gravel GM	15	500	0.35	23.6
Lower base layer	Cement stabilized macadam CTB	20	1500	0.25	23.5

$$S(t) = Sd(t) + Sc(t) + Ss(t) \tag{1}$$

Sd(t): instantaneous settlement of a certain time period t;
Sc(t): main consolidation settlement of a certain time period t;
Ss(t): secondary consolidation settlement for a certain period of time t;
S(t):   total settlement for a certain period of time t.

3 Establishment and Detection of Asphalt Pavement Model

3.1 Establishment of Asphalt Pavement Model

The parameters established by the finite element analysis model of asphalt pavement are shown in Tables 2, 3 and 4.

Table 2. Drucker-Prager model parameters

Material type	γ_d (kN/m³)	c (kPa)	φ (°)	E (kPa)	μ	β (°)	k	ψ (°)
Embankment fill	18.5	30.1	35.3	20000	0.45	29.3	1.00	29.2
Muddy clay	17.9	7.8	23.9	2500	0.35	35.5	1.00	35.5

Table 3. Hardening parameters of the Drucker-Prager model

Embankment filling		Silt clay	
$\sigma_1 - \sigma_3$ (kPa)	ε_p	$\sigma_1 - \sigma_3$ (kPa)	ε_p
169.8	0.000	56.78	0.000
650.2	0.038	103.125	0.0079
740.8	0.045	178.70	0.025
800.8	0.075	283.10	0.053
850.0	0.090		

Table 4. Clay plasticity model parameters

Material type	γ_d (kN/m^3)	c (kPa)	φ (°)	k	υ	λ	M	α_0 (N/m^2)	β	K	e_1
Silty clay	18.2	23.1	31.7	0.02	0.32	0.08	1.26	0.00	1.00	1.00	1.03

The asphalt pavement structure is established by using the D-P model. The properties and parameters of the materials are shown in Tables 2 and 3. The two layers of soft soil of muddy clay and silty clay were established by D-P and C-P models respectively. The properties and parameters of the materials are shown in Table 4. According to the project overview: the width of the bottom surface is 80 m, the width of the surface is 26 m, and the total thickness is 26.59 m, the pavement and embankment are graded at 1:1.5, and the slope is 1:1.5. The surface is set to a water-permeable boundary, and both sides and the bottom are set to be impervious. The groundwater level is located 1 m below the surface; the thickness of the sand cushion is 0.5 m. According to the requirements of Table 1, the materials are set in order and the components of the model are materialized, then define the model seed and define the grid control to realize the division of the model grid, the main situation is shown in Fig. 2.

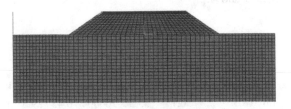

Fig. 2. Divided grid model

3.2   Detection of Asphalt Pavement Model

We use Result/Frame/Step in finite element to control the pavement of each embankment and pavement and operate to get the cloud map of the consolidation settlement after 75 days, 150 days, 225 days, 375 days, 675 days, 1125 days, 1800 days, 2812 days, 4331 days, 5475 days after the completion of the roadbed structure and road pavement. We use the Query information tool in the finite element to analyze the settlement in the cloud image and analyze the settlement difference based on the settlement. This is the difference in settlement between the shoulder and the road. The settlement cloud is shown in Fig. 3. 1–8 is the first layer of embankment paving and 30 days, the second layer of embankment is paved and 30 days, the third layer of embankment is paved and 30 days, the fourth layer of embankment paving and 120 days of settlement cloud map;

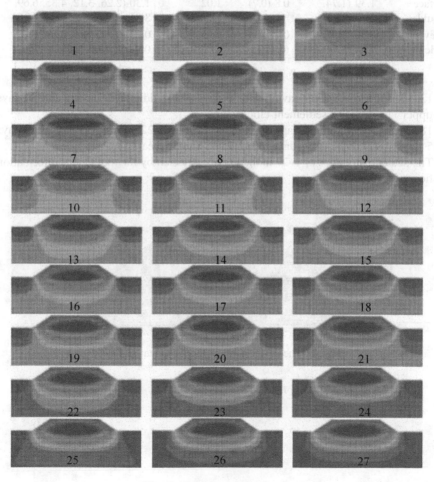

Fig. 3. Settlement cloud map

9–12 is the lower base layer paving and 20 days, the upper base layer paving and 20 days of settlement cloud map;

Table 5. Settlement values of asphalt pavement

Settlement detection	Location embankment (cm)	Subgrade (cm)	Pavement (cm)	Completion (days)
	1 layer (2–4 layers)	Lower layer (top)	Lower layer (middle)	75 (150, 225, 375, 675, 1125, 1800, 2812, 4332, 15 年)
Surface center point	2.35 (3.71, 4.97, 7.87)	1.53 (1.17)	1.67 (0.836)	1.56 (2.63, 3.58, 5.16, 7.47, 9.76, 11.75, 13.2, 14.06, 14.4)
Surface shoulder	1.39 (1.74, 2.13, 4.33)	0.8 (0.7)	1.02 (0.597)	1.30 (2.26, 3.12, 4.35, 6.69, 8.85, 10.75, 12.15, 13, 13.3)
Uneven settlement	0.96 (1.97, 2.84, 3.54)	0.73 (0.47)	0.65 (0.239)	0.26 (0.37, 0.46, 0.81, 0.78, 0.91, 1, 1.05, 1.06, 1.1)

13–17 is the lower layer paving and 30 days, the middle layer paving and 30 days, the upper layer paving settlement cloud map;

18–27 Settlement cloud maps of 75 days, 150 days, 225 days, 375 days, 675 days, 1125 days, 1800 days, 2812 days, 4332 days, and 15 years.

The settlement values of 1–27 in the Fig are detected by the tool Query information, as shown in Table 5.

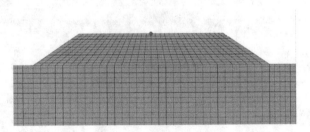

Fig. 4. The center point of the pavement surface

4 Numerical Analysis of Settlement Deformation of Asphalt Pavement

For the study of settlement deformation of asphalt pavement, we perform numerical analysis of the effects mainly from the influence of soil thickness, pavement section position and consolidation time on the settlement and deformation of pavement. The effects of fill thickness, pavement section and time on settlement deformation are shown in Figs. 4, 5 and 6.

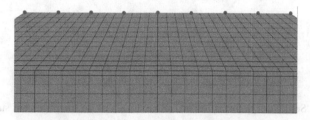

Fig. 5. The pavement surface of the embankment for 120 days

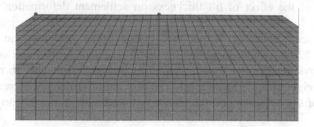

Fig. 6. The pavement surface after paving

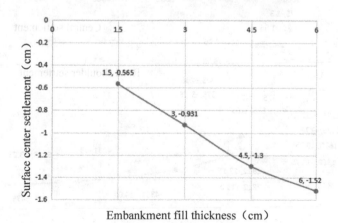

Embankment fill thickness（cm）

Fig. 7. Line diagram of the surface settlement of the pavement surface

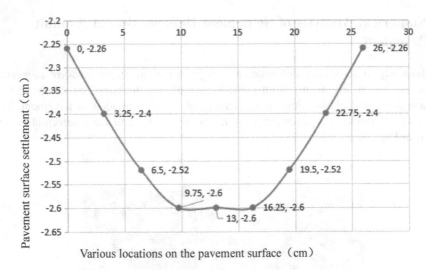

Fig. 8. Settlement deformation at various locations on the pavement surface

(1) The curve of the effect of fill thickness on settlement deformation

The curve of the effect of fill thickness on settlement deformation is shown in Fig. 7.

It can be seen from Fig. 7 that the surface center settlement increases from 0.565 cm to 1.52 cm, which increases by 0.955 cm, and the increase is 169%. The increase is obvious; the settlement decreases linearly with the increase of the embankment height of the embankment. The amount of settlement increases with the filling height of the embankment, the amount of settlement varies linearly.

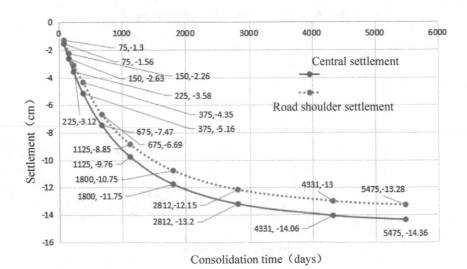

Fig. 9. Settlement varies with consolidation time

(2) The Curve of influence of settlement deformation of pavement section

The Curve of influence of settlement deformation of pavement section is shown in Fig. 8.

It can be seen from Fig. 8 that the closer the surface of the asphalt pavement is to the shoulder, the smaller the settlement, the closer the settlement is to the center, the difference between the shoulder and the center of the same pavement section is 0.34 cm, and the ratio of settlement difference and settlement is Between 13% and 15%, the difference in settlement among the surfaces of the road is not large.

(3) The Curve of the influence of time on settlement

The Curve of the influence of time on settlement is shown in Fig. 9.

It can be seen from Fig. 9 that the settlement amount of the asphalt pavement surface becomes larger with the increase of the consolidation time. The sedimentation amount changes gradually after 1125 days, and the sedimentation amount tends to be stable and the change is small after 15 years.

5 Conclusion

By using the asphalt pavement structure of expressway in soft soil area as the object, the date of filling process, settlement of soft soil foundation, lateral settlement of roadbed and settlement of pavement structure with consolidation time are modeled and simulated by finite element method, and detailed analysis and research are carried out. The conclusions are drawn as follows: The thickness of soft soil layer affects the change of settlement of soft soil foundation, and the settlement amount increases with the increase of thickness. The settlement at the center of the pavement surface is slightly larger than that of the shoulder, but it is not obvious. The settlement of the center of the pavement surface is the largest, but the difference in settlement between the shoulder and the pavement at the same pavement surface is small relative to the settlement of the entire pavement, However, the difference in settlement between the shoulder surface of the same road surface and the center of the road surface is compared with the entire road surface, and the settlement is small. The consolidation time is an external factor that affects the settlement of the asphalt pavement surface, but the impact on subsidence is very large, In a short time, the settlement amount changes obviously with the increase of consolidation time, but with the influence of external load and self stress, the roadbed and road surface become more and more stable, and the settlement of the road surface begins to be less and less affected by time.

Deformation analysis of asphalt pavement structure is a good way to solve the problem of early and initial damage of asphalt pavement structure on soft soil foundation. Therefore, on the basis of summing up the experience of using the existing structure in China, and making full use of the experience accumulated in the design and use of foreign structures. We need to refine the reasonable combination of asphalt pavement structure, and systematically study the asphalt pavement structure design method and graded gravel material design. After comprehensive analysis of the settlement law of soft soil foundation, the influence of the settlement amount of the roadbed on the internal structure, and the influence of the consolidation time on the settlement of the pavement structure, the design index and design method of asphalt pavement structure for soft soil area are summarized and proposed, and the simulation model is built by the software of limit software. The research results have great significance for the analysis of asphalt pavement structure deformation of expressway in soft soil area, which can solve the early damage problem of highway asphalt pavement structure in this area and avoid resource, manpower and economic waste. The solution is currently plaguing the difficulties and hot issues of China's transportation construction. The construction of road projects has been greatly promoted, which has also accelerated the economic development. The finite element calculation method is used to simulate the expressway in the soft soil area. The design of the asphalt pavement structure is a step-by-step and continuous improvement process.

Compared with conventional pavement structure design, the construction of high-grade asphalt roads in soft soil areas prone to disease is a very complicated and difficult technical problem, Soft soil foundations are full of variability and instability, which puts very high demands on designers. Although the elastoplastic model of finite element construction is similar to the actual road situation, there are many uncertainties in the reality, so the accuracy of the finite element model needs to be further improved. It is necessary to build a road section in combination with the actual pavement structure, and carry out long-term observation of pavement performance for further in-depth study.

References

1. Gao, W.: Research on asphalt pavement structure design method in soft soil area. Chongqing Jiaotong Univ. **1**(2), 7–8 (2012)
2. Song, Y., Liu, D., Wei, Y., et al.: Research on reliability of asphalt pavement structure based on finite element method. In: Proceedings of the 17th National Conference on Structural Engineering, pp. 400–403 (2008)
3. Jiao, T.: Reliability analysis of asphalt pavement structure and its finite element simulation. Inner Mongolia Univ. Technol. (5), 49–53(2007)
4. Deng, X.: Subgrade pavement engineering. Southeast Univ. (4), 377–418 (2008)
5. Shua, Z., Xiao, Z.: Characterization of loading rate effects on the interactions between crack growth and inclusions in cementitious material. Comput. Mater. Continua **57**(3), 417–446 (2018)
6. Shuren, Z., Wen, L., Jun, L., Jeong, U.K.: Improved VGG model for road traffic sign recognition. Comput. Mater. Continua **57**(1), 11–24 (2018)
7. Liao, G., Huang, X.: Application of Abaqus finite element software in road engineering. Southeast Univ. (12), 77–150 (2014)
8. Zhang, D., Huang, X., Zhao, Y., et al.: Skeleton composition and contact characteristics of asphalt mastic mixture material. J. Jilin Univ. (Eng. Ed.) **45**(2), 394–399 (2015)
9. Sun, Z., Huang, X.: Linear fatigue damage characteristics and deformation law of asphalt pavement. J. Southeast Univ. (Nat. Sci. Ed.) **42**(3), 521–525 (2012)
10. Zhao, N.: Structural stress analysis of asphalt pavement under longitudinal slope condition based on finite element analysis. Hebei Univ. Technol. (3), 8–9 (2010)

11. Hashiguchi, K.: Fundamentals in constitutive equation: continuity and Smoothness conditions and loading criterion. Soils Found. (3), 45–67 (2000)
12. Zhang, L., Qian, Z., Yang, L., et al.: Fractal expression of surface morphology and anti-sliding performance of asphalt concrete pavement. Highway (5), 85–88 (2013)
13. Chowdhury, E.Q., Nakai, T., Tawada, M., et al.: A model for clay using modified stress under various loading conditions with the application of subloading concept. Soils Found. (3), 65–87 (1999)
14. Meng, S.: Research on reasonable structure of asphalt pavement. Southeast Univ. (3), 62–69 (2005)
15. Asaoka, A., Nakano, M., Noda, T.: Superloading yield surface concept for highly structured soil Behavior. Soils Found. (3), 23–56 (2000)
16. Xie, Y.: Fatigue life prediction of graded gravel base asphalt pavement based on finite element method. Chongqing Jiaotong Univ. (1), 15–45 (2015)
17. Yang, D., Liu, T., Huang, W., et al.: Quality control technology for asphalt pavement aggregate processing. Highw. Traffic Technol. (4), 41–44 (2012)
18. Oka, F., Yashima, A., Tateishi, A., et al.: A cyclic elastic plastic constitutive model for sand considering a plastic strain dependence of the shear modulus. Geotechnique (3), 112–135 (1999)
19. Ashmawy, A.K., Bourdeau, P.L., Drnevieh, V.P., et al.: Cyclic response of geotextile reinforced soil. Soils Found. (3), 87–96 (1999)
20. Huang, G., He, Z., Huang, T., et al.: Analysis of dynamic creep viscoelastic properties of asphalt mixture. J. Southeast Univ. (Nat. Sci. Ed.) **42**(6), 121–176 (2012)
21. Huang, W., Song, T., He, Z., et al.: Study on the grading range of asphalt mixture engineering design. J. Chongqing Jiaotong Univ. (Nat. Sci. Ed.) **29**(5), 27–71 (2010)

Legal Case Inspection: An Analogy-Based Approach to Judgment Evaluation

Shang Li[✉], Bin Guo, Yilei Cai, Lin Ye, Hongli Zhang, and Binxing Fang

School of Computer Science and Technology,
Harbin Institute of Technology, Harbin 150001, China
ls@hit.edu.cn

Abstract. In the era of big data, enormous growth of various legal data leads to a huge burden on law professionals, which lies in the contradiction between the increasing number of legal cases and the shortage of judicial resources. This issue enlightens us to explore the key technologies in the computer-aided criminal case process lines. In this paper, we investigate an analogy-based method of legal case inspection. We use the document vector generated by Doc2Vec (semantics-based case feature, SCF) and the feature defined by the case judgement model (model-based case feature, MCF) as two ways to find similar cases. The measurement methods of similarity between two cases and the deviation of case judgment are also defined. Experimental results on a real-world dataset shows the effectiveness of our method. The recall rate of irrational cases when using the MCF is higher than that when using the SCF.

Keywords: Legal case inspection · Judgment evaluation · Analogy · Neural networks

1 Introduction

Legal case inspection (LCI) is an inspection mechanism for the trial work of the people's courts and judges at all levels. As the number of legal cases continues to grow in recent years, miscarriage of justice or judicial arbitrariness may come up in judicial practice, resulting from inconsistent judgment scale of different judges due to their different understandings and interpretation of the laws and cases, the mistakes of the judges at work, etc. The LCI aims to find irrational judicial decisions in order to avoid trial bias as far as possible. If the automated LCI process can be implemented, it can effectively prevent miscarriage of justice or judicial arbitrariness in the future, which is of great significance to the maintenance of judicial justice.

In this paper, we investigate the analogy-based LCI method, which is to evaluate the judgment rationality of the target case via the judgment results of its precedent similar cases. Formally, the input of the LCI method is the case text excluding the result of judgment, while the output is the deviation of prison term. The deviation needs to be measured by similar cases, while similar cases need to be determined by the similarity of the case features. Therefore, the LCI process can be divided into three steps: case feature generation, similarity measurement, and deviation measurement. Experimental

© Springer Nature Switzerland AG 2019
X. Sun et al. (Eds.): ICAIS 2019, LNCS 11632, pp. 148–158, 2019.
https://doi.org/10.1007/978-3-030-24274-9_13

results on a real-world dataset containing more than 40,000 judgment documents of theft cases shows the effectiveness of our method.

The rest of this paper is organized as follows. Section 2 overviews related work. The generation of two types of case feature is described in Sect. 3. In Sect. 4, we propose the LCI method. Evaluation results are presented in Sect. 5, and finally, Sect. 6 contains the concluding remarks.

2   Related Work

Several key issues have been studied in the field of artificial intelligence and law, such as the prediction of judgment result and the inference of relevant law articles.

The judgment prediction is an important combination point between artificial intelligence and law. Liu et al. [1, 2] use the KNN algorithm to classify 12 criminal cases in Taiwan, the former establishes a case-based reasoning system by defining various criminal rules in advance, while the latter implement a classifier that uses phrases to index. To obtain a better classification effect, Sulea et al. [3, 4] increased the number of classifiers, they combine with the output of multiple SVM (support vector machine) classifiers to predict the law area, ruling and sentence. Katz et al. [5] propose a model with the extreme random tree to predict the voting behavior of the US Supreme Court from 1953 to 2013. Lin et al. [6] achieve a deeper understanding of the factors of the case by adding some non-TF-IDF features. According to the three characteristics of relevant legal provisions, sentiment analysis of crime facts and prison term, Liu and Chen [7] use SVM algorithm to classify the judgment text automatically.

Inferring applicable law articles for a given case is also an important work. Aletras et al. [8] propose a binary classification model, and the target output is a practical judgment on whether there is a violation of a specific clause of the Human Rights Convention. Liu and Liao [9] convert this multi-label problem into a multi-category classification problem by considering a fixed set of legal provisions, and achieve satisfactory initial results in the classification of theft and gambling crimes. Liu et al. [10] propose a more optimized algorithm, they first use the SVM for preliminary articles classification, and then use the word-level features and co-occurrence tendencies in articles to reorder the results.

In summary, previous studies have considerably facilitated the advance in the field of artificial intelligence and law [11–18]. Nevertheless, legal case inspection remains a huge challenge. Our work in this paper aims to fill this gap.

3   Feature Generation

The LCI process is based on a set of similar cases of the target case, and the similarity measurement calls for calculable case features. In this section, we present the generation method of two types of case feature, i.e. the semantics-based case feature (SCF) and the model-based case feature (MCF).

3.1   Semantics-Based Case Feature

Considering that the inspection is an unsupervised process, the case feature used for inspection should be obtained without relying on the process of inspection. The training process of the full text through Doc2Vec is an unsupervised learning process, and the document vector is a one-dimensional vector, which can be directly calculated, so the document vectors are more suitable to construct the case feature.

For the SCF, the training process based on Doc2Vec is shown in Fig. 1. Firstly, each case is transformed into a long sentence. Then, texts of all the cases is used as a corpus and input into Doc2Vec for training. After training, the document vectors corresponding to each case can be obtained.

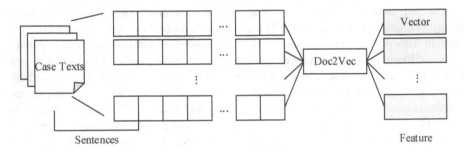

Fig. 1. Generation of SCF

3.2   Model-Based Case Feature

Taking the theft case as the research object in this paper, we need first build its judgment model according to relevant law articles, i.e. Article 264 in the Criminal Law of the People's Republic of China. Through the comprehensive analysis of Article 264 and the structure of judgment document, we can describe a theft case with 11 dimensions as the judgment model shown in formula (1): (a) the value of stolen items, (j) whether the defendant is juvenile, (d) whether the defendant is disabled, (b) whether the crime can be deemed as burglary (breaking in home), (w) whether the defendant carried lethal weapons, (p) whether the defendant is a pickpocket, (o) whether the crime involves other serious circumstances (including but not limited to: collision, arson, resistance to arrest, etc.), (r) whether the defendant is a recidivist, (c) whether the defendant returned stolen items or compensated the victim, (s) whether the defendant voluntarily surrendered and (t) the prison term.

$$C = (a, j, d, b, w, p, o, r, c, s, t) \tag{1}$$

Figure 2 briefly illustrates the generation process of the MCF based on GRU (Gated Recurrent Unit) network. When case text arrives, the feature generator divides it into sentences and deals with the sentences one by one. Through the Chinese word segmentation and word embedding step, words will be converted to distributed representations as the k-dimensional vector form. Then the GRU network takes the sequence of word vectors as input, and generates an output sequence of vectors through GRU units. Finally, the feature merging part averages the features of all the sentences to transform them into a single vector as the MCF.

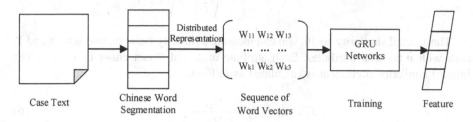

Fig. 2. Generation of MCF

4 Method

4.1 Similarity Measurement

Before performing LCI process, it is necessary to obtain similar cases of the target case. The key issue is how to measure the similarity between two judgment documents. Generally, vector-based similarity can be computed by one of these metrics: Euclidean distance, Manhattan distance, Minkowski distance, cosine similarity, and Jacquard similarity coefficient.

The Euclidean distance is the linear distance between two points in the Euclidean space and can be calculated as follows:

$$D(X, Y) = \sqrt{\sum_{i=1}^{n} (X_i - Y_i)^2} \tag{2}$$

The Manhattan distance is the sum of the absolute value of the difference between each dimension of the vectors as follows:

$$D(X, Y) = \sum_{i=1}^{n} |X_i - Y_i| \tag{3}$$

The Minkowski distance is a metric in a normed vector space which can be considered as a generalization of both the Euclidean distance and the Manhattan distance, which can be calculated as follows:

$$D(X, Y) = \left(\sum_{i=1}^{n} |X_i - Y_i|^k \right)^{\frac{1}{k}} \tag{4}$$

The cosine similarity is a measure of similarity between two non-zero vectors of an inner product space that measures the cosine of the angle between them as follows:

$$sim(X, Y) = \frac{X \cdot Y}{\|X\| \|Y\|} = \frac{\sum_{i=1}^{n} (X_i Y_i)}{\sqrt{\sum_{i=1}^{n} X_i^2} \sqrt{\sum_{i=1}^{n} Y_i^2}} \qquad (5)$$

The Jaccard similarity coefficient can measure similarity between two sets, X and Y, each with n boolean attributes. Each attribute of X and Y can either be 0 or 1. The Jaccard similarity coefficient is calculated as follows:

$$J(X, Y) = \frac{M_{11}}{M_{01} + M_{10} + M_{11}} \qquad (6)$$

where M_{11} is the total number of attributes where X and Y both have a value of 1, M_{01} and M_{10} represent the total number of attributes where the attribute of X is 0/1 and the attribute of Y is 1/0, respectively.

According to the definitions of Euclidean distance, Manhattan distance, and Minkowski distance, they focus on the absolute difference of each dimension in the vector. For the case features, since different dimensions represent different information, it is more suitable to measure the similarity by relative difference. Therefore, we select the cosine similarity to calculate the similarity between cases with SCF. As for cases with MCF, considering that the nine features except the value of stolen items are boolean values, the strategy is to multiply the similarity measured by the 9 boolean features and the value of stolen items, respectively. The similarity measured by the 9 boolean features is calculated as Eq. (7), that is, the number of attributes with the same boolean value is divided by the total number of attributes.

$$sim(X, Y) = \frac{|\{i | X_i = Y_i, i = 0, 1, 2 \cdots n\}|}{n} \qquad (7)$$

For SCF, it is necessary to multiply the similarity of the document vector by the similarity of the value of stolen items to obtain the final similarity. For MCF, it is necessary to multiply the similarity of boolean features by the similarity of the value of stolen items. Considering that the relative difference of theft value can better reflect the similarity degree than the absolute difference, the relative difference is selected to measure the similarity. Since the value of stolen items is mostly concentrated below 10,000 yuan, in order to have its value evenly distributed, we take its logarithm to when calculating the similarity. Therefore, the similarity of the value of stolen items is calculated as follows:

$$sim(x, y) = 1 - \frac{|\log(x) - \log(y)|}{\max(\log(x), \log(y))} \qquad (8)$$

In summary, the similarity between cases with SCF and MCF is calculated as Eqs. (9) and (10), respectively.

$$sim(X, Y) = sim_{docvec}(X_{docvec}, Y_{docvec}) \cdot sim_{money}(X_{money}, Y_{money}) \qquad (9)$$

$$sim(X, Y) = sim_{boolean}(X_{boolean}, Y_{boolean}) \cdot sim_{money}(X_{money}, Y_{money}) \qquad (10)$$

4.2 Deviation Measurement

In the LCI process, in order to evaluate whether the judgment result is rational or not and to compare the difference in the judgment rationality between different cases, the judgment deviation of a legal case should be defined to measure the likelihood of a certain case's misjudgment. The judgment deviation is calculated based on a set of similar cases to the target case, which are generated according to the similarity measurement. We hold the point that the judgment deviation of a case is closely related to judgment results of its similar cases, that is, if the judgment difference between a case and others exceeds a certain degree, the case's judgment may be irrational. The judgment deviation of the target case t is calculated as Eq. (11): firstly, the top K similar cases to t are selected, then the relative errors between t and each one of K cases are calculated, respectively, and finally, the average value of the relative errors is taken as the judgment deviation of the case t.

$$E_t = \frac{\sum_{i=1}^{K} \frac{|p_i - p_t|}{p_t}}{K} \qquad (11)$$

5 Experiments

In order to verify the effectiveness of the proposed LCI method, the SCF and the MCF are used in the experimental evaluation.

5.1 Evaluation of Semantics-Based Case Feature

In the evaluation, Dov2Vec is used to train the case text to construct features. The corpus used for training consists of 41,418 judgment documents, and the document vectors of 50, 100, 150, 200, 250 and 300 are trained, respectively. For each case, the similarities to the other cases are calculated according to the method presented in Sect. 4.1 with the six types of document vectors. After the similarity measurement, all the cases are sorted in descending order of the similarity to the target case.

Similarity has the following effect on the judgment deviation: the higher the similarity to the target case, the more realistic the deviation obtained, and vice versa. In order to obtain a reliable judgment deviation, it is necessary to select an appropriate document vector dimension to maximize the credibility of similarity measurement. Here, we employ the average relative error (ARE) of the judgment results of each case and its most similar case as the metric to compare the effects of different dimensional document vectors on similarity measurement. As is shown in Fig. 3, the ARE achieves the minimum value at 100 dimensions, indicating that the similarity calculated with the 100-dimensional document vector is more reliable than other dimensions, so the 100-dimensional document vector is selected as the SCF.

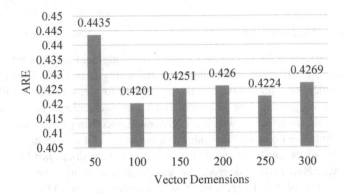

Fig. 3. Comparison of ARE on different vector dimensions

To obtain the judgment deviation of each case, we first select the top K similar cases to the target case ($K = 10, 20, ..., 100$), then calculate the relative error between each case and the target case, respectively, and finally, use the ARE as the judgment deviation of the target case. Here, we employ the number of cases with judgment deviation greater than 1.0 as the metric to evaluate the effects of different Ks on the effectiveness of LCI method. As is shown in Fig. 4, the number of cases with judgment deviation greater than 1.0 achieves the maximum value of 148 when $K = 10$.

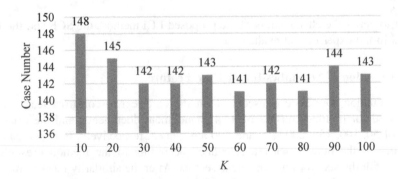

Fig. 4. Number of cases with deviation greater than 1.0 with different Ks

In order to validate whether the cases selected based on the judgement deviation are actually irrational, we manually read the cases with judgment deviation greater than 1.0 and make reference to relevant law articles. When K varies from 10 to 100, we get a total of 189 cases with judgment deviation greater than 1.0, 125 of which considered as actually irrational after manual validation. According to the number of actually irrational cases found with ten Ks, we calculate the recall rate, precision and the corresponding F1 score, respectively.

As is shown in Table 1, the highest recall rate is obtained when $K = 10$ or $K = 20$, the highest precision is obtained when $K = 50$, and the highest F1 value is obtained when $K = 20$. Considering that the inspection is more focused on finding irrational cases, the highest recall rate should be obtained as far as precision is acceptable. On the whole, when $K = 20$, the recall rate is the highest, and the precision is also higher. Therefore, it is best when $K = 20$, that is, supervise through 20 cases with the highest similarity to the target case.

Table 1. Comparison of recall rate, precision and F1 score with different Ks

K	Recall	Precision	F1
10	**0.8400**	0.7094	0.7692
20	**0.8400**	0.7241	**0.7777**
30	0.8080	0.7112	0.7565
40	0.8080	0.7112	0.7565
50	0.8320	**0.7272**	0.7761
60	0.8000	0.7092	0.7518
70	0.8000	0.7042	0.7490
80	0.7920	0.7021	0.7443
90	0.8240	0.7152	0.7657
100	0.8160	0.7132	0.7611

5.2   Evaluation of Model-Based Case Feature

The experimental setting of MCF evaluation is the same as the SCF evaluation. Let $K = 10, 20, ..., 100$, the numbers of cases with judgment deviation greater than 1.0 are shown in Fig. 5. The results show that the number of cases with judgment deviation greater than 1.0 is 156 at $K = 10$, and as the value of K increases, the number of cases gradually decreases, and finally, the minimum number of cases is 121 at $K = 100$.

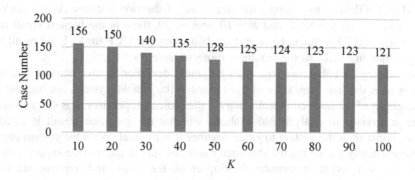

Fig. 5. Number of cases with deviation greater than 1.0 with different Ks

A total of 200 cases are collected from 10 sets of cases. After manual validation, 137 cases are considered to be actually irrational, and the other 63 cases were rational. As is shown in Table 2, when $K = 10$ or $K = 20$, the highest recall rate is 0.8029, and when $K = 90$, the highest precision is 0.7886, and when $K = 30$, the highest F1 score is 0.7870. Although the precision is lower at $K = 20$, the recall rate achieves the maximum value. In the judicial practice, the LCI task requires a higher recall rate, so the best effect can be achieved when $K = 20$.

Table 2. Performance with different Ks

K	Recall	Precision	F1
10	**0.8029**	0.7051	0.7508
20	**0.8029**	0.7333	0.7665
30	0.7956	0.7785	**0.7870**
40	0.7664	0.7777	0.7720
50	0.7226	0.7734	0.7471
60	0.7080	0.7760	0.7404
70	0.7080	0.7822	0.7432
80	0.7007	0.7804	0.7384
90	0.7080	**0.7886**	0.7461
100	0.6934	0.7851	0.7364

5.3   Case Study and Analysis

When using the SCF, the recall rate reaches the highest value of 0.8400 when the top 20 similar cases are used for LCI. When using the MCF, the recall rate reaches the highest value of 0.8029 when the top 20 similar cases are used for LCI. Intuitively, the effect of the former is better. However, due to the different experimental sets used to calculate the recall rate, the comparison results cannot correctly reflect the actual differences between the two features.

There are 254 cases with judgment deviation greater than 1.0, of which 157 irrational cases and 97 rational cases were found via manual validation. The 254 cases can be used as the dataset to compare the recall rate of the two features. As is shown in Fig. 6, when using the MCF and $K = 10$ or $K = 20$, there is the highest recall rate, whose value is 0.7006. It can be seen that when using the MCF for LCI, the recall rate is higher than the SCF, so the feature is more suitable for LCI.

Considering that the case with high judgment deviation is an irrational case that does not meet the judgment rules of most cases in the judicial system, but because the service object of the inspection technology is the judicial supervisor, it is still necessary for the supervisor to analyze and evaluate whether the judgment result is actually rational, rather than the system to judge whether it is rational. What the system can do is to automatically screen out the abnormal cases and submit them to the supervisors for review, so as to avoid supervisors looking at all the cases, and improve the work efficiency of supervisors. From this point of view, if the system can screen out the cases with problems as much as possible and submit them to the supervisors, the effect of

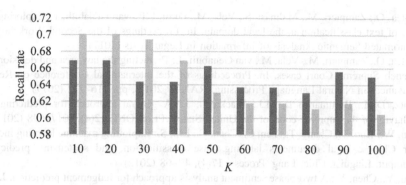

Fig. 6. Comparison of recall rates with two case features

automated inspection will be achieved. The experiments in this section show that under the optimal conditions, the inspection method defined in this paper can screen out 110 cases from 157 cases with problems, and realize the expected function to a certain extent, and initially achieve the automatic inspection.

6 Conclusion

In this paper, we investigated an analogy-based approach to legal case inspection. The SCF is trained via Doc2Vec, and the MCF is generated according to the judgment model of theft cases. Then, the similarity calculation methods of the two features are respectively defined, and the final similarity is the result of multiplying the feature similarity by the stolen goods value similarity. In order to quantify the deviation of the case, its calculation method is defined. The experimental results show that no matter which feature is used, the best results are obtained when using the top 20 similar cases of the target case, and the results of the two characteristics on the same dataset show that the recall rate based on the case model is the better, which is considered to be more suitable for LCI task. In future work, we will further validate and advance the proposed method on various types of criminal case.

Acknowledgment. This work is supported by the National Key Research and Development Program of China under grants 2018YFC0830902 and 2016QY03D0501, and the National Natural Science Foundation of China (NSFC) under grants 61723022 and 61601146.

References

1. Liu, C., Chang, C., Ho, J.: Case instance generation and refinement for case-based criminal summary judgments in Chinese. J. Inf. Sci. Eng. **20**(4), 783–800 (2004)
2. Liu, C.-L., Hsieh, C.-D.: Exploring phrase-based classification of judicial documents for criminal charges in Chinese. In: Esposito, F., Raś, Z.W., Malerba, D., Semeraro, G. (eds.) ISMIS 2006. LNCS (LNAI), vol. 4203, pp. 681–690. Springer, Heidelberg (2006). https://doi.org/10.1007/11875604_75

3. Sulea, O., Zampieri, M., Malmasi, S., Vela, M., Dinu, L.P., van Genabith, J.: Exploring the use of text classification in the legal domain. In: Proceedings of the Second Workshop on Automated Semantic Analysis of Information in Legal Texts (2017)
4. Sulea, O., Zampieri, M., Vela, M., van Genabith, J.: Predicting the law area and decisions of French Supreme Court cases. In: Proceedings of the International Conference on Recent Advances in Natural Language Processing (RANLP 2017), pp. 716–722 (2017)
5. Katz, D.M., Bommarito II, M.J., Blackman, J.: A general approach for predicting the behavior of the supreme court of the United States. PLoS ONE **12**(4), e0174698 (2017)
6. Lin, W., Kuo, T., Chang, T., Yen, C., Chen, C., Lin, S.: Exploiting machine learning models for Chinese legal documents labeling, case classification, and sentencing prediction. Comput. Linguist. Chin. Lang. Process. **17**(4), 49–68 (2012)
7. Liu, Y., Chen, Y.: A two-phase sentiment analysis approach for judgement prediction. J. Inf. Sci. **44**(5), 594–607 (2018)
8. Aletras, N., Tsarapatsanis, D., Preotiuc-Pietro, D., Lampos, V.: Predicting judicial decisions of the European Court of Human Rights: a natural language processing perspective. PeerJ Comput. Sci. **2**, e93 (2016)
9. Liu, C.-L., Liao, T.-M.: Classifying criminal charges in Chinese for web-based legal services. In: Zhang, Y., Tanaka, K., Yu, J.X., Wang, S., Li, M. (eds.) APWeb 2005. LNCS, vol. 3399, pp. 64–75. Springer, Heidelberg (2005). https://doi.org/10.1007/978-3-540-31849-1_8
10. Liu, Y., Chen, Y., Ho, W.: Predicting associated statutes for legal problems. Inf. Process. Manage. **51**(1), 194–211 (2015)
11. Meng, R., Rice, S., Wang, J., Sun, X.: A fusion steganographic algorithm based on faster R-CNN. CMC Comput. Mater. Continua **55**(1), 1–16 (2018)
12. Wang, R., Shen, M., Li, Y., Gomes, S.: Multi-task joint sparse representation classification based on fisher discrimination dictionary learning. CMC Comput. Mater. Continua **57**(1), 25–48 (2018)
13. Hochreiter, S., Schmidhuber, J.: Long short-term memory. Neural Comput. **9**(8), 1735–1780 (1997)
14. Cho, K., et al.: Learning phrase representations using RNN encoder-decoder for statistical machine translation. In: Proceedings of the 2014 Conference on Empirical Methods in Natural Language Processing (EMNLP 2014), pp. 1724–1734 (2014)
15. Palau, R.M., Moens, M.: Argumentation mining: the detection, classification and structure of arguments in text. In: Proceedings of the 12th International Conference on Artificial Intelligence and Law, pp. 98–107 (2009)
16. Hachey, B., Grover, C.: Extractive summarization of legal texts. Artif. Intell. Law **14**(4), 305–345 (2006)
17. Farzindar, A., Lapalme, G.: Legal text summarization by exploration of the thematic structures and argumentative roles. In: Proceedings of the Text Summarization Branches Out Workshop, pp. 27–38 (2004)
18. Galgani, F., Compton, P., Hoffmann, A.: Combining different summarization techniques for legal text. In: Proceedings of the Workshop on Innovative Hybrid Approaches to the Processing of Textual Data, pp. 115–123 (2012)

A Novel Noise Filter Based on Multiple Voting

Weiwei Zhu[1], Hao Yuan[1], Liang Wang[2], Ming Wan[2(✉)], Xing Li[1],
and Jingbin Ren[1]

[1] State Grid Gansu Electric Power Information and Communication Company,
Beijing, China
184089182@qq.com, 53816552@qq.com, 460105664@qq.com,
yh_yuanhao@126.com
[2] Nanjing Nari Information and Communication Technology Co. Ltd.,
Nanjing, China
{wangliang1, wanming}@sgepri.sgcc.com.cn

Abstract. Label noises exist in many applications, which usually add difficulties for data analysis. A straightforward and effective method is to detect and
filter out them prior to training. Ensemble learning based filter has shown
promising performances. We define an important parameter to improve the
performance of the algorithm. The proposed method is cost sensitive which
integrates the mislabeled training dataset and noise costs for learning. Finally,
the experimental results on the benchmark datasets show the superiority of the
proposed method.

Keywords: Label noise · Cost · Ensemble learning

1 Introduction

There are two types of errors in the training data: label error and feature error [1–3].
Label error means the label information is incorrect, while feature error means the
features are corrupted. Both errors are harmful. In this work, the label error is selected
to study.

Label errors are not rare in real applications. The quality of label is influenced by
both the labeling person and the information given to the person. If the person's
knowledge and understanding are not correct, the labeling errors are generated. On the
other hand, incorrect information to the experts can also lead to mislabeling.

The existence of label errors can degrade the performance of learning in many
aspects. Learning is to search for the best hypothesis in the hypothesis space. To
evaluate the goodness of a hypothesis, the label information is used in supervised
learning. Obviously, if label information contains errors, the selected hypothesis might
be not optimal, which consequently can reduce the classification performance, increase
the classifier complexity, etc.

There are mainly two types of approaches to deal with label noises: algorithm level
approaches and data level approaches. Algorithm level approaches do not handle label
noises explicitly. Instead, they focus on adding the robustness to the learning algorithms to alleviate the effects of label noises. Data level approaches explicitly handle

© Springer Nature Switzerland AG 2019
X. Sun et al. (Eds.): ICAIS 2019, LNCS 11632, pp. 159–170, 2019.
https://doi.org/10.1007/978-3-030-24274-9_14

label noises and one popular method is to recognize and remove the noises from the training dataset. Both approaches are suitable for certain problems. But usually data level approaches, especially noise filters are used more widely, which could bring improvements on the classification accuracy, model interpretability, etc.

Traditional noise filters include k nearest neighbors based [4–9], graph based, and rule based. Edited nearest neighbor (ENN) is a knn based noise filter, whose idea is to remove examples whose class differs from a majority of its k-nearest neighbors. For example, in Fig. 1, the instances consist of two classes according to the shapes: circle (C) and triangle (T). When the instance d1 is selected, firstly its k nearest neighbors are searched (suppose k = 5). Based on the Euclidean distance, its five nearest neighbors (N) include n1, n2, n3, n4, and n5. Four instances in N has C labels, while one instance in N has T label. Based on ENN, the instance d1 should be assigned the C label, which is different with its given label. Thus, d1 is regarded as noisy and removed.

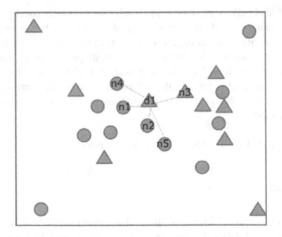

Fig. 1. Example of a mislabeled instance

When the above procedures are done repeated, it is called repeated edited nearest neighbor (RENN). A more condense dataset can be achieved by RENN (in Fig. 2).

In recent years, ensemble learning based filters (EnFilter) are proposed and show better performances compared to traditional methods [10–16]. In EnFilter, the ensemble learning method is employed since the voting of multiple classifiers is usually more accurate than a single classifier. Usually the randomness of training data permutation makes the diversities between different classifiers. Existing research has shown that the training data random permutation can be conducted once or more than once. And in the case of more than once, this kind of EnFilter is called multiple voting based filter (MVFilter), which outperforms single voting based filter (SVFilter) in most experiments.

In essence, MVFilter is the combination of multiple SVFilters, which treat a training sample as mislabeled if a certain number of SVFilters believe it is mislabeled. This "certain number" is actually a threshold, which determines the minimal number of

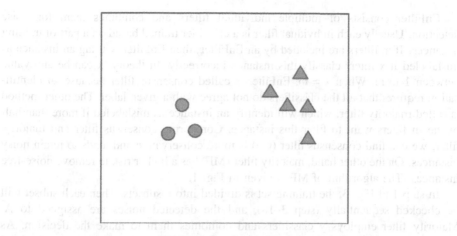

Fig. 2. A clean dataset after repeated edited nearest neighbor

SVFilters required to treat an instance mislabeled. When this number is extreme small (equal to one), then if one SVFilter treat an instance as mislabeled, MVFilter will also treat it as mislabeled. When this number if big (equal to the total number of SVFilters in MVFilter, denoted by t), then only when all the SVFilters treat an instance as mislabeled, then MVFilter will remove it. Obviously, these two extreme values are not reasonable for the real problem. For the former case, it is too easy to classify an instance as mislabeled, which has a high risk to remove the noise-free instances. For the latter, it is too conservative so the label noises are hard to remove. Thus, the key point in MVFilter is to select an optimal value for the threshold so that the performance of MVFilter can be maximized.

The empirical selection of MVFilter is effective in some sense, but it is not systematic. In this work, a novel approach is proposed to derive this optimal value of MVFilter. It considers not only the number of errors, but also the costs of errors since different cost errors might be different. Therefore, when a cost matrix is given, our proposed method aims to minimize the expected cost of MVFilter. The proposed method is tested on a set of experiments, which has different errors and different cost matrixes. The experimental results show that MVFilter based on our approach is better than existing approaches. The proposed approach is helpful to solve the mislabeled problems in many important areas, such as security [17, 18].

In the next section, we will briefly review the related works. Section 3 presents our proposed approach. The experimental evaluations are presented in Sect. 4. Section 5 concludes this work and presents future works.

2   Related Works

This work tries to predict the optimal threshold value in multiple voting based filters (MVFilter). MVFilter belongs to the category of ensemble learning based filter (EnFilter). The necessary background knowledge is presented in this section.

EnFilter consists of multiple individual filters and combines them for noise detection. Usually each individual filter is a classifier trained based on a part of training instances. If m filters are included by an EnFilter, then EnFilter will tag an instance as mislabeled if x filters classify this instance incorrectly. In theory, x can be any value between 1 to m. When x = m, EnFilter is called consensus filter because an identification requires that all the classifiers do not agree with a given label. The other method is called majority filter, which will identify an instance as mislabeled if more than half of the m filters want to filter this instance. Comparing consensus filter and majority filter, we can find consensus filter (CF) is more conservative and tends to retain noisy instances. On the other hand, majority filter (MF) has a higher risk to remove noise-free instances. The algorithm of MF is given in Fig. 1.

In step 1 of Fig. 3, the training set is divided into n subsets. Then each subset will be checked sequentially (step 3–18), and the detected noises are assigned to A. Majority filter employs y classifiers and combines them to make the decision. As shown in step 15, for an instance, if more than half of y classifiers do not agree the label of an instance, then this instance is regarded as mislabeled instance and added into A.

Algorithm 1 Majority Filter (MF)

Input: E (training set)
Parameters: n (number of subsets), y (number of learning
    algorithms), $A_1, A_2, \ldots, A_y$ (y learning algorithms)
Output: A (detected noisy subset of E)

  1: form n disjoint almost equally sized subsets of E_i, where
      $\bigcup_i E_i = E$
  2: $A \leftarrow \emptyset$
  3: **for** $i = 1\ldots n$ **do**
  4:    form $E_t \leftarrow E \backslash E_i$
  5:    **for** $j = 1, \ldots y$ **do**
  6:      induce H_j based on examples in E_t and A_j
  7:    **end for**
  8:    **for** every $e \in E_i$ **do**
  9:      $ErrorCounter \leftarrow 0$
10:      **for** j=1,\ldots,y **do**
11:        **if** $H_j$incorrectly classifies e **then**
12:          $ErrorCounter \leftarrow ErrorCounter + 1$
13:        **end if**
14:      **end for**
15:      **if** $ErrorCounter > \frac{y}{2}$, **then**
16:        $A \leftarrow A \cup \{e\}$
17:      **end if**
18:    **end for**
19: **end for**

Fig. 3. Majority filtering algorithm

The algorithm of consensus filtering is shown in Fig. 4. It is different with majority filtering in step 14. Here only when all the y classifiers do not agree with a label, then this label is taken out as a noise. So the decision of consensus filtering is more strict compared to majority filtering.

Algorithm 2: Consensus Filtering (MF)

Input: E (training set)
Parameter: n (number of subjects), y (number of learning algorithms), $A_1, A_2, \ldots, A_y$ (y kinds of learning algorithms)
Output: A (detected noisy subset of E)
(1) form n disjoint almost equally sized subset of E_i, where $\bigcup_i E_i = E$

(2) $A \leftarrow \emptyset$
(3) **for** $i = 1, \ldots, n$ **do**
(4) form $E_t \leftarrow E \setminus E_i$
(5) **for** $j = 1, \ldots y$ **do**
(6) induce H_j based on examples in E_t and A_j
(7) **end for**
(8) **for** every $e \in E_i$ **do**
(9) *ErrorCounter* $\leftarrow 0$
(10) **for** $j = 1, \ldots, y$ **do**
(11) **if** H_j incorrectly classifies e
(12) **then** *ErrorCounter* $\leftarrow$ *ErrorCounter* $+ 1$
(13) **end for**
(14) **if** *ErrorCounter* $= y$, **then** $A \leftarrow A \cup \{e\}$
(15) **end for**
(16) **end for**

Fig. 4. Consensus filtering algorithm

3   Our Approach

In Sect. 2, we have introduced two important ensemble learning based noise filtering approaches: majority filter and consensus filter. In essence, both of them utilize the single voting method. As shown in Fig. 5, in single voting method, the training dataset is divided into different subsets (subset[1], subset[2],..., subset[n]). Each subset will be checked individually. Finally the detected noises are removed. Because the division of training dataset is executed only for once, this is named as single voting method. In fact, the division of training dataset is a random process. Therefore, there is some randomness and uncertainty if the training dataset is divided for multiple times. The diversity of multiple times voting is expected to outperform the single voting. When the training dataset is divided for multiple times, the method is called multiple voting, which is should in Fig. 6.

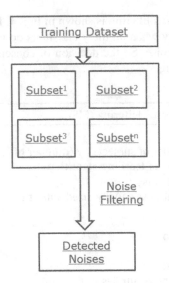

Fig. 5. The framework of single voting method

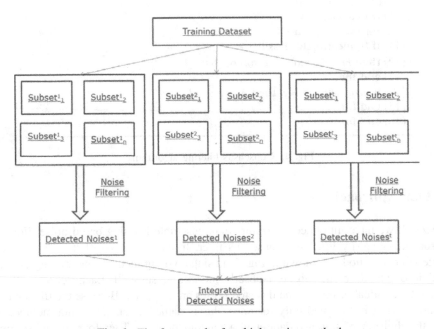

Fig. 6. The framework of multiple voting method

As shown in Fig. 6, a detected noise index is generated for each time of training dataset division. Finally different indexes (Detected Noise[1], Detected Noise[2],..., Detected Noise[t]) are merged to output the final noise index. In Fig. 6, we need to define an important parameter. If the number of index appears in different divisions is equally or above this parameter, the sample with this index is regarded as noises. Obviously, an appropriate setting of this parameter is crucial in multiple voting based filters. We call this parameter decision point. Empirically we can set this decision point based on the majority voting idea.

For example, if we have 9 single voting models which generated 9 different indexes. For a given index a, it has to appear in at least 5 models. When both single voting and multiple voting utilize majority filter, this algorithm is called MF_{MF} (majority voting majority voting) which is shown in Fig. 7. When single voting is based on majority voting, while multiple voting is based on consensus voting, this algorithm is called MF_{CF} (majority voting consensus voting). In this case, only if all the 9 different models believe an instance is noisy, then this instance is regarded as mislabeled and removed.

Algorithm 3: MajorityFiltering_MajorityFiltering (MF_{MF})

Input: E (training set)
Parameter: n (number of subsets), y (number of learning algorithms), t (number of times of subsets partitioning), $A_1, A_2, \ldots, A_y$ (y kinds of learning algorithms)
Output: A (detected noisy subset of E)
(1) **for** $p = 1, \ldots, t$ **do**
(2) form n disjoint almost equally sized subset of E_{pi}, where $\bigcup_i E_{pi} = E$
(3) $A^p \leftarrow \emptyset$
(4) **for** $i = 1, \ldots, n$ **do**
(5) form $E_t \leftarrow E \setminus E_{pi}$
(6) **for** $J = 1, \ldots y$ **do**
(7) induce H_{pj} based on examples in E_t and A_j
(8) **end for**
(9) **for** every $e \in E_{pi}$ **do**
(10) $ErrorCounter \leftarrow 0$
(11) **for** $j = 1, \ldots, y$ **do**
(12) **if** H_{pj} incorrectly classifies e
(13) **then** $ErrorCounter \leftarrow ErrorCounter + 1$
(14) **end for**
(15) **if** $ErrorCounter > \frac{y}{2}$, **then** $A^p \leftarrow A^p \cup \{e\}$
(16) **end for**
(17) **end for**
(18) **end for**
(19) $A \leftarrow \emptyset$
(20) **for** every $e \in E$ **do**
(21) $ErrorCounter \leftarrow 0$
(22) **for** $j = 1, \ldots, p$ **do**
(23) **if** $e \in A^p$
(24) **then** $ErrorCounter \leftarrow ErrorCounter + 1$
(25) **end for**
(26) **if** $ErrorCounter > \frac{p}{2}$, **then** $A \leftarrow A \cup \{e\}$
(27) **end for**

Fig. 7. Multiple voting with a fixed threshold

In this work, our mission is to select the optimal decision point. Given a noisy training dataset, it is easy to find this value by simply exploring all the possible values and selecting the value achieving the minimal number of errors. However, in the real problem, this is infeasible because our mission is to detect all the noises from the training dataset. Our core idea is to generate a simulated noisy training dataset to help the discovery of the optimal decision value. Here, the noise ratio is assumed to be prior knowledge which is known in advance. According to this noise ratio, the noises are randomly generated for a couple of times. Finally the optimal value will be made.

4 Experiments

In this section, we conduct a set of experiments to verify the performance of our proposed method. We will see whether our detected optimal threshold value can boost the performance of multiple voting based filters. We select two datasets from UCI repository, which are Heart dataset and Wdbc dataset. The Heart dataset consists of 14 features and 270 instances. Wdbc dataset consists of 30 features and 569 instances.

In the experiments, each benchmark dataset was divided into a training set and a test set. Training set includes mislabeled data. Each filter algorithm removes mislabeled data from the training set. Test set is only used by our approach for testing.

The performances of each algorithm are evaluated based on the cost value. To compute the cost value for each filter, each dataset D was processed as follows:

(1) Three trials derived from threefold cross-validation of D were used to evaluate the performance of each filter. During each trial, 2/3 of D, or Tr, was used as a training set. We artificially changed some labels that were originally correct in Tr, according to predefined mislabeled ratios to generate mislabeled data. We considered three different mislabeled ratios: 10%, 20%, and 30%. For example, if 10% mislabeled ratio is used, we randomly selected 10% of the samples from Tr and changed correct labels to incorrect labels.
(2) For each of three trials, the cost of errors for each filter is calculated. The average cost of each algorithm was obtained by averaging the costs of three trials.
(3) Considering that the partitioning of D and generated mislabeled data could influence the cost value, we executed each experiment 10 times and get 10 cost values (executed the previous two steps 10 times).
(4) Finally, the reported cost value was calculated as the average of these 10 values.

In the experiments, there are two important parameters: the noise ratio and cost information. We consider different combinations of noise ratios and the costs.

For the Heart dataset, we get the following results. In Fig. 8, we compare CF variants when noise ratio is 10%. Different costs are considered. Finally the mean cost values are shown in Fig. 8. Obviously our proposed method (CFOPD) achieves the minimal cost. When noise ratios change to 20% and 30%, our proposed method consistently gives the best results (Figs. 9, 10).

For the Wdbc dataset, we compare the performances of majority filtering variants because consensus filtering variants have been compared in the first dataset. We found that for all the noise ratios (Figs. 11, 12, and 13), our proposed method (MFOPD) is always the best one.

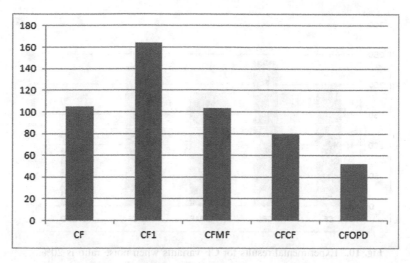

Fig. 8. Experimental results for CF variants when noise ratio is 10%.

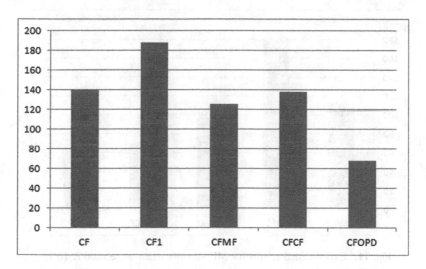

Fig. 9. Experimental results for CF variants when noise ratio is 20%.

Through the above experiments, we have the following observations:

(1) For both datasets, the multiple voting based methods are generally better than single voting based methods.
(2) Based on our proposed method, the performance of multiple voting can be further improved.
(3) When noise ratio is high, our proposed method can achieve more obvious improvements.

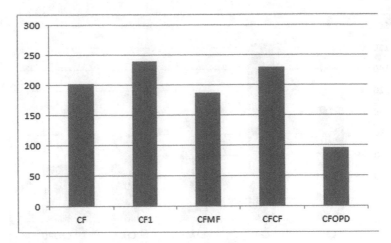

Fig. 10. Experimental results for CF variants when noise ratio is 20%.

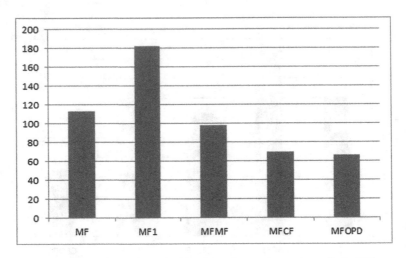

Fig. 11. Experimental results for MF variants when noise ratio is 10%.

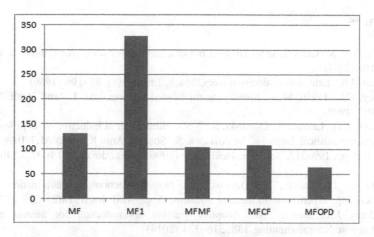

Fig. 12. Experimental results for MF variants when noise ratio is 20%.

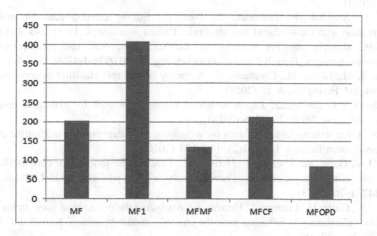

Fig. 13. Experimental results for MF variants when noise ratio is 30%.

5 Conclusions

In this work, we propose a novel method to improve the ensemble learning based filters. We focus on determining the optimal threshold value which has an obvious impact on the performance of filters. Our method considers the mislabeled data distribution and the cost of mislabeling simultaneously. Through the experiments on the benchmark datasets, the performance of proposed method is verified.

In this future, we will consider to incorporate more prior information to improve the performance of our approach.

References

1. Zhu, X., Wu, X.: Class noise vs. attribute noise: a quantitative study. Artif. Intell. Rev. **22**(3), 177–210 (2004)
2. Quinlan, J.R.: Induction of decision trees. Mach. Learn. **1**(1), 81–106 (1986)
3. Brodley, C.E., Friedl, M.A.: Identifying mislabeled training data. J. Artif. Intell. Res. **11**, 131–167 (1999)
4. Gamberger, D., Lavrač, N., Džeroski, S.: Noise elimination in inductive concept learning: a case study in medical diagnosis. In: Arikawa, S., Sharma, Arun K. (eds.) ALT 1996. LNCS, vol. 1160, pp. 199–212. Springer, Heidelberg (1996). https://doi.org/10.1007/3-540-61863-5_47
5. Gamberger, D., Lavrac, N., Dzeroski, S.: Noise detection and elimination in data preprocessing: experiments in medical domains. Appl. Artif. Intell. **14**(2), 205–223 (2000)
6. Rico-Juan, J.R., Inesta, J.M.: Adaptive training set reduction for nearest neighbor classification. Neurocomputing **138**, 316–324 (2014)
7. Calvo-Zaragoza, J., Valero-Mas, J.J., Rico-Juan, J.R.: Improving kNN multi-label classification in Prototype Selection scenarios using class proposals. Pattern Recogn. **48**(5), 1608–1622 (2015)
8. Kanj, S., Abdallah, F., Denoeux, T., Tout, K.: Editing training data for multi-label classification with the k-nearest neighbor rule. Pattern Anal. Appl. **19**(1), 145–161 (2015)
9. Roli, F.: Multiple classifier systems. In: Li, S.Z., Jain, A.K. (eds.) Encyclopedia of Biometrics. Springer, Boston (2015). https://doi.org/10.1007/978-1-4899-7488-4
10. Wozniak, M., Grana, M., Corchado, E.: A survey of multiple classifier systems as hybrid systems. Inf. Fusion **16**, 3–17 (2014)
11. Kuncheva, L.I., Rodriguez, J.J.: A weighted voting framework for classifiers ensembles. Knowl. Inf. Syst. **38**(2), 259–275 (2014)
12. Sun, S.: Local within-class accuracies for weighting individual outputs in multiple classifier systems. Pattern Recogn. Lett. **31**(2), 119–124 (2010)
13. Saez, J.A., Galar, M., Luengo, J., Herrera, F.: Tackling the problem of classification with noisy data using multiple classifier systems: analysis of the performance and robustness. Inf. Sci. **247**, 1–20 (2013)
14. Saez, J.A., Galar, M., Luengo, J., Herrera, F.: Analyzing the presence of noise in multi-class problems: alleviating its influence with the one-vs-one decomposition. Knowl. Inf. Syst. **38**(1), 179–206 (2014)
15. Barandela, R., Valdovinos, R.M., Sanchez, J.S.: New applications of ensembles of classifiers. Pattern Anal. Appl. **6**(3), 245–256 (2003)
16. Sanchez, J.S., Kuncheva, L.I.: Data reduction using classifier ensembles. In: ESANN, pp. 379–384 (2007)
17. Cui, J., Zhang, Y., Cai, Z., et al.: Securing display path for security-sensitive applications on mobile devices. CMC Comput. Mat. Continua **55**(1), 017–035 (2018)
18. Liu, Y., Peng, H., Wang, J.: Verifiable diversity ranking search over encrypted outsourced data. CMC Comput. Mat. Continua **55**(1), 037–057 (2018)

Fuzzy Control Method for Path Tracking System of Combine Harvester

Nan Qiao, Li-hui Wang$^{(\boxtimes)}$, Yue-xin Zhang, and Tang Xinhua

Key Laboratory of Micro-Inertial Instrument and Advanced Navigation Technology, Ministry of Education, School of Instrument Science and Engineering, Southeast University, Nanjing 210096, China
wlhseu@163.com

Abstract. The high-precision combine harvester path tracking system is a key to protect the efficiency and precision of harvesting. The speed and heading of combine harvester are the main factors influencing the accuracy of tracking, and the speed changes all the time according to the harvester's status. Traditional pure pursuit algorithm uses the constant look-ahead distance, cannot be adapted to the path tracking conditions of the combine harvester. The fuzzy control method for path tracking system was proposed to tune the look-ahead distance according to the speed and heading. Experiments showed that this method could restrain the maximum error from 0.142 m to 0.059 m, restrain the standard error from 0.042 m to 0.024 m, and improve the accuracy of harvest by 38.4%.

Keywords: Combine harvester · Automatic navigation · Path tracking system · Fuzzy control · Look-ahead distance

1 Introduction

It is necessary for agricultural productivity to keep the advances in mechanization and automation [1]. Agricultural automation has resulted in lower production costs, reduced reliance on manual labor, and increased product quality [2]. The automatic driving technology of the combine harvester is important for the development of Agricultural automation [3, 4]. The high-precision automatic driving system can effectively restrain the problem of repeating work and missing work. High-precision automatic driving system can also improve the efficiency and precision of harvesting [5]. The harvester with automatic driving can work all day, and is not subject to the low visibility or bad weather. In addition, it can also relieve the pressure of driver, while driver has to control the header, reel, cutter bar, grain conveyor, etc.

The basic automatic navigation process is such that the vehicle first obtains the positions and attitude of itself by sensors. Then the tracking system calculates the target plan to destination according to the surroundings. Finally, the vehicle drives itself autonomously by executing the necessary control command along the given path [6]. The path of a vehicle is described as the route that the vehicle would follow in an environment. Path tracking controllers are used to carry out the path following operations and minimal lateral distance.

© Springer Nature Switzerland AG 2019
X. Sun et al. (Eds.): ICAIS 2019, LNCS 11632, pp. 171–181, 2019.
https://doi.org/10.1007/978-3-030-24274-9_15

Path tracking, as a core part of automatic navigation control, directly affects the accuracy of navigation. Path tracking methods include intelligent control [7], PID control, optimal control and pure pursuit algorithm [8]. Besides, Fuzzy logic controller had been proposed to control a trajectory tracking for a wheeled mobile robot [9]. Among them, the pure pursuit algorithm is not based on the vehicle model, which can avoid the negative effect on the path tracking performance while the model is inaccurate or the model parameters change drastically.

As a geometric method, pure pursuit algorithm does not need complex control theory, and has less control parameters than other algorithm and simulates the driving behavior of human [10]. Pure pursuit can be dated back in history to the pursuit of missile to a target [11]. In this process, the missile velocity vector is always directed toward the instantaneous target position. Wallace et al. in 1985 were the first to develop pure pursuit strategy in the field of robotics, and they developed a method for estimating the steering necessary to maintain the vehicle on the road [12]. They achieved this by keeping the road centered in the image obtained from an onboard camera mounted on the vehicle. It was based on the concept that Amidi proposed a pure-pursuit method that follows explicit path [6]. The algorithm treats the lateral position deviation and the heading deviation as the algorithm input, calculates the target angle of the vehicle, and achieves the path tracking. However, it is currently used in small agricultural machineries such as tractors and transplanters, which are small volume and front wheel steering. Combine harvester is a large agricultural machinery, whose quality changes with time. Besides, its speed also changes with time according to the harvest conditions and it is a rear wheel steering system. Traditional pure pursuit algorithm is based on the constant look-ahead distance, and cannot meet the conditions of combine harvester. The objective of fuzzy logic control (FLC) systems is to control complex processes by means of human experience [13]. Moreover, Tang proposed a fuzzy control method to adjust the look-ahead distance, and verified the effect [14]. However, it was used for transplanters, and this method tuned the look-ahead distance according to the speed and lateral deviation. For combine harvester, the initial lateral deviation is 0, and the speed and heading error are the important factors.

We proposed a new fuzzy control model based on speed and heading error to achieve real-time adjustment of the look-ahead distance. GNSS receivers, angle sensors, controllers, hydraulic valves and other equipment were installed on the combine harvester. Experiments showed that the fuzzy control method could tune the look-ahead distance and improve the accuracy of harvesting.

2   Control Model

2.1   Path Tracking System

Path tracking is the process how to control the vehicle to follow a certain path at each instant of time. Its goal is to autonomously navigate and drive the vehicle along the path by continually generating speed and steering commands, which compensate for the tracking errors. The tracking errors mainly consist of vehicle's deviations in distance and heading from the path. Feedback and feedforward control mechanisms are used for this purpose, with a tradeoff between control effort and control error [6].

The harvester path tracking system is mainly composed of a position and heading collecting system, a tracking system and an automatic steering control system. The collecting system obtains the position and heading of harvester by GNSS dual antenna in real time and send it to tracking system. The tracking system calculates the target angle by pure pursuit algorithm, and send it to steering system. The steering system uses a feedback signal, collected by angle sensor, to drive the electro-hydraulic valves and adjusts the rear steering wheels to achieve path tracking. The operational principle of control system is shown in Fig. 1.

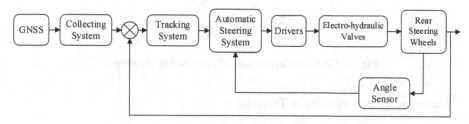

Fig. 1. Schematic diagram of the path tracking system

2.2 Pure Pursuit Algorithm

Pure pursuit algorithm establishes the path that the combine harvester needs to travel to reach the target position based on the lateral position deviation and the heading deviation [15, 16]. As shown in Fig. 2, the navigation coordinate system $(X^n - O - Y^n)$ and the carrier coordinate system $(X^v - O - Y^v)$ are established. (X_v, Y_v) is the coordinates of the target point in the carrier coordinate system; ρ is the radius of curvature, and it is a signed number. Combine harvester has a positive radius of curvature for counter-clockwise travel $(\rho > 0)$ and a negative radius of curvature for clockwise travel $(\rho < 0)$. R is the instantaneous turning radius of combine harvester. d is the lateral position deviation of combine harvester and is a signed number. And when the harvester is on the right side of target path, d is positive, on the left side d is negative. L_d is the look-ahead distance. ϕ_e is the error between the current heading of combine harvester and the heading of the target path. Φ is the change of heading angle when the combine harvester reaches the target point along the steering arc.

According to the figure, the horizontal and vertical coordinates of the target point in the carrier coordinate system are given by Eq. (1).

$$\begin{cases} X_v = -\frac{1}{\rho} + \frac{1}{\rho}\cos \Phi = \frac{\cos \Phi - 1}{\rho} \\ Y_v = -\frac{1}{\rho}\sin \Phi \end{cases} \tag{1}$$

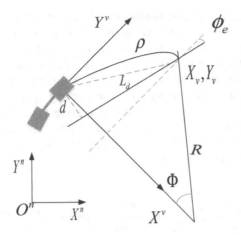

Fig. 2. Geometric expression of pure pursuit algorithm.

According to the Pythagorean Theorem:

$$X_v^2 + Y_v^2 = L_d^2 \tag{2}$$

ρ is given by Eq. (3) according to Eqs. (1) and (2).

$$\rho = -2\frac{X_v}{L_d^2} \tag{3}$$

So, X_v is given by Eq. (4).

$$X_v = -d\cos\phi_e + \sqrt{L_d^2 - d^2}\sin\phi_e \tag{4}$$

According to Eq. (3) and Eq. (4), ρ is given by:

$$\rho = -2\frac{X_v}{L_d^2} = 2\frac{\left(d\cos\phi_e - \sqrt{L_d^2 - d^2}\sin\phi_e\right)}{L_d^2} \tag{5}$$

According to the model of agricultural machinery kinematics, $\dot{\phi}$ is given by:

$$\dot{\phi} = \rho v = v\frac{\tan\delta}{L} \tag{6}$$

In this equation, L is the axis length of combine harvester. $\dot{\phi}$ is the heading change rate of combine harvester. v is the speed. δ is the target turn-angle of harvester. According to the Eqs. (5) and (6), δ is given by Eq. (7).

$$\delta = \arctan \frac{2L\left(d\cos\phi_e - \sqrt{L_d^2 - d^2}\sin\phi_e\right)}{L_d^2} \tag{7}$$

In Eq. (7), look-ahead distance is the only unknown parameter. It directly affects the accuracy of path tracking. When the look-ahead distance is large, the combine harvester will track along the smaller curvature path to the target point, the oscillation is smaller, but the tracking time is longer. When the look-ahead distance is small, the harvester will follow a larger curvature. This will reduce the tracking time, but it will cause a large oscillation.

2.3   Fuzzy Controller

The look-ahead distance in the pure pursuit algorithm is determined by factors such as the speed, lateral error and heading error of combine harvester. When combine harvester is working in the farm, the initial lateral error is 0, and the lateral error keep small during harvesting. Fuzzy control model was constructed with the speed and the heading error as the inputs, and the look-ahead distance as the output.

During harvesting, the speed has to change in real time according to many factors such as crop yield, feeding rate, cutting speed etc. Therefore, the speed must be treated as an input. Besides, the initial heading may have large deviation when the harvester turns around. Therefore, the fuzzy control model based on speed and heading deviation is consistent with the actual operation.

Firstly, the fuzzy sets should be constructed based on input and output variables according to the actual working state [16, 17]. The fuzzy controller designed has two inputs and signal output.

(1) Harvester speed v, basic domain is $[0, 3]$, this variable is in the fuzzy set (fuzzy domain) of $\{0, 0.75, 1.5, 2.25, 3\}$, and the corresponding linguistic variable set is $\{Z, S, N, L, VL\}$, quantization factor is 1.
(2) Heading error ϕ_e, basic domain is $[-10, 10]$, this variable is in the fuzzy set (fuzzy domain) of $\{-4, -2, 0, 2, 4\}$, and the corresponding linguistic variable set is $\{NL, NS, Z, PS, PL\}$, quantization factor is $2/5$.
(3) Look-ahead distance L_d, basic domain is $[0, 6]$, this variable is in the fuzzy set (fuzzy domain) of $\{0, 1, 2, 3, 4, 5, 6\}$, and the corresponding linguistic variable set is $\{Z, VS, S, N, L, VL\}$, quantization factor is 1.

According to the pure pursuit algorithm and harvesting conditions, fuzzy control rule should meet the following conditions [18]. The smaller the heading deviation is the larger forward distance should be. The faster harvester is the larger forward distance should be. The larger heading deviation is the smaller forward distance should be. The lower the harvester is the smaller forward distance should be.

The fuzzy rules are shown in Table 1, and the fuzzy control surface is shown in Fig. 3.

Table 1. Fuzzy control regulation

Heading deviation	Speed				
	Z	S	N	L	VL
NL	Z	VS	S	N	L
NS	Z	S	N	N	VL
Z	Z	S	N	L	VL
PS	Z	S	N	N	VL
PL	Z	VS	S	N	L

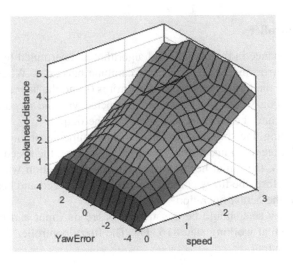

Fig. 3. Surface of fuzzy model

3 Simulation

We did the simulation in MATLAB to test the effect of fuzzy control method for path tracking system. The simulation conditions are as follows, initial position is (0,0), initial heading deviation is 5°, standard deviation of speed is 0.1 m/s, standard deviation of position error is 0.01 m, standard deviation of yaw error is 0.1°, standard deviation of turn-angle error is 0.2°, axle length of the car is 1 m, and the max turn-angle is 20°.

When the speed is 1 m/s, the tracking errors with constant look-ahead distance and fuzzy control method are compared in Fig. 4 and Table 2. When the speed is 3 m/s, the tracking error with constant look-ahead distance and fuzzy control method are compared in Fig. 5 and Table 3.

Table 2. Error statistics of path tracking (v = 1 m/s)

Look-ahead distance (m)	Mean error (m)	Standard error (m)	Maximum error (m)
0.3	0.0038	0.0048	0.023
0.6	0.0028	0.0036	0.025
Fuzzy control	0.0028	0.0035	0.022

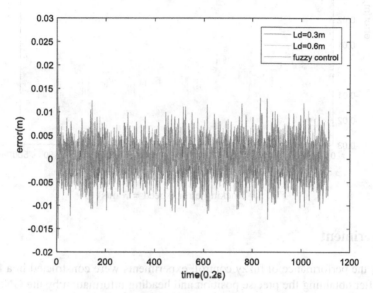

Fig. 4. Tracking error (speed = 1 m/s)

Table 3. Error statistics of path tracking (v = 3 m/s)

Look-ahead distance (m)	Mean error (m)	Standard error (m)	Maximum error (m)
0.9	0.0048	0.0064	0.054
1.5	0.0035	0.0059	0.063
Fuzzy control	0.0031	0.0045	0.051

With the look-ahead distance small, the maximum error could be restrained, but the standard error was large. In other words, the maximum offset of car was restrained, but the car had larger fluctuation. When the look-ahead distance is large, the standard error was restrained, but the maximum error is large. In other words, the car had smaller fluctuation, but its maximum offset was large. Fuzzy controller combined the advantages of both, the standard error and maximum error could be restrained at the same time, the accuracy of tracking were improved by 26% and 35% with low speed and high speed. This showed that fuzzy control was suitable for situations of high speed and low speed.

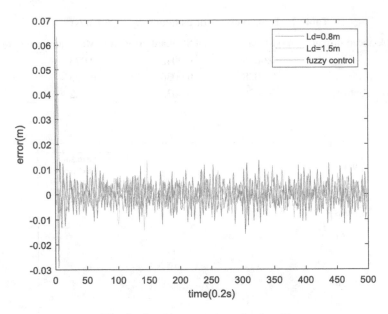

Fig. 5. Tracking error (speed = 3 m/s)

4 Experiment

To verify the performance of fuzzy control, experiments were constructed in a farm of China. After obtaining the precise position and heading information by the GNSS dual antenna (RTK) system, the target angle could be calculated by the path-tracking algorithm in tracking system. Automatic steering system controlled the turning angle in real time to follow the target angle, by driving hydraulic proportional with an angle sensor mounted on the rear wheel. Sampling frequency is 5 Hz, and the axis length of combine harvester is 3.75 m. In order to guarantee the harvesting efficiency, the speed was controlled at about 1.5 m/s. Figure 6 shows the Antenna installation, and Fig. 7 shows the result of path tracking.

Fig. 6. The photo of combine harvester   **Fig. 7.** Harvest result of path tracking

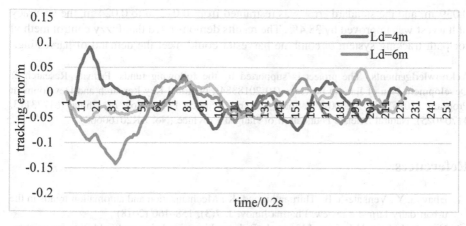

Fig. 8. Tracking error

Figure 8 shows the tracking error with the different look-ahead distances and the error statistics are shown in Table 4.

Table 4. Error statistics of path tracking

Look-ahead distance (m)	Mean error (m)	Standard error (m)	Maximum error (m)
6	0.039	0.042	0.142
4	0.028	0.033	0.091
Fuzzy control	0.024	0.024	0.059

The result demonstrated that fuzzy control could restrain the maximum error from 0.142 m to 0.059 m, and restrain the standard error from 0.042 m to 0.024 m. The accuracy of harvester was improved by 38.4%. It could be concluded that the proposed algorithm with fuzzy controller could tacked the aim path stably and accurately than the traditional path-tracking algorithm with constant look-ahead distance.

5 Conclusion

Combine harvester path-tracking system is an important aspect of precision agriculture. The path-tracking system can improve the efficiency of harvesting and relieve the pressure of driver. Pure pursuit is used to achieve path tracking. However, the traditional pure pursuit path-tracking method could not adapt to the changed speed of combine harvester, which had a bad effect on harvesting. To solve this problem, the fuzzy control method for path tracking system of combine harvester was studied. Fuzzy control model could adjust look-ahead distance according to speed and heading error, and improve the accuracy of harvesting. The experiment results showed that, compared with constant look-ahead distance, the maximum error was restrained from 0.142 m to

0.059 m, and the standard error was restrained from 0.042 m to 0.024 m, the accuracy of harvest was improved by 38.4%. The results demonstrated that fuzzy control method for path tracking system of combine harvester could meet the demand of harvesting.

Acknowledgements. The project is supported by the following funds: Primary Research & Development Plan of Jiangsu Province (BE2018384), National Key Research and Development Program (2016YFD0702000), National Natural Science Foundation of China (61773113, 41704025), Natural Science Foundation of Jiangsu Province (No. BK20160668).

References

1. Bhavya, Y., Venkatesh, B., Thirupathigoud, K.: Mechanization and automation trends in the urban dairy farms: a review. Pharma Innov. J. **7**(3), 158–160 (2018)
2. Han, X.Z., Kim, H.J., Kim, J.Y., et al.: Path-tracking simulation and field tests for an auto-guidance tillage tractor for a paddy field. Comput. Electron. Agric. **112**(Sp. Iss. SI), 161–171 (2015)
3. Rahman, M., Ishii, K.: Heading estimation of robot combine harvesters during turning maneuveres. Sensors **18**(5), 1390 (2018)
4. Hauglin, M., Hansen, E.H., Næsset, E., et al.: Accurate single-tree positions from a harvester: a test of two global satellite-based positioning systems. Scand. J. For. Res. **32**(8), 1–24 (2017)
5. Olivera, A., Visser, R.: Development of forest-yield maps generated from Global Navigation Satellite System (GNSS)-enabled harvester StanForD files: preliminary concepts. NZ J. Forest. Sci. **46**(1), 3 (2016)
6. Samuel, M., Hussein, M., Binti, M.: A review of some pure-pursuit based path tracking techniques for control of autonomous vehicle. Int. J. Comput. Appl. **135**(1), 35–38 (2016)
7. Dong, F., Heinemann, W., Kasper, R.: Development of a row guidance system for an autonomous robot for white asparagus harvesting. Comput. Electron. Agric. **79**(2), 216–225 (2011)
8. Li, T., Hu, J., Lei, G., et al.: Agricultural machine path tracking method based on fuzzy adaptive pure pursuit model. Trans. Chin. Soc. Agric. Mach. **44**(1), 205–210 (2013)
9. Zhou, Q., Qiu, Y., Li, L., et al.: Steganography using reversible texture synthesis based on seeded region growing and LSB. CMC Comput. Mat. Continua **55**(1), 151–163 (2018)
10. Hu, J., Gao, L., Bai, X., et al.: Review of research on automatic guidance of agricultural vehicles. Trans. Chin. Soc. Agric. Eng. **31**(10), 1–10 (2015)
11. Scharf, L., Harthill, W., Moose, P.: A comparison of expected flight times for intercept and pure pursuit missiles. IEEE Trans. Aerosp. Electron. Syst. **4**, 672–673 (1969)
12. Elbanhawi, M., Simic, M., Jazar, R.: Receding horizon lateral vehicle control for pure pursuit path tracking. J. Vib. Control **24**(3), 619–642 (2018)
13. Zhu, B.J., Hou, Z.X., Wang, X.Z., et al.: Long endurance and long distance trajectory optimization for engineless UAV by dynamic soaring. CMES Comput. Model. Eng. Sci. **106**(5), 357–377 (2015)
14. Tang, X., Tao, J., Zhiteng, L.I., et al.: Fuzzy control optimization method for stability of path tracking system of automatic transplanter. Trans. Chin. Soc. Agric. Mach. **49**(01), 29–34 (2018)

15. Saleh, A.I., Takieldeen, A., El-Sawi, A.R.: Aerospace vehicle simulation and analysis applying pure pursuit guidance method. Int. J. Comput. Appl. **155**(11), 19–21 (2016)
16. Takagi, T., Sugeno, M.: Fuzzy identification of systems and its applications to modeling and control. Readings Fuzzy Sets Intell. Syst. **15**(1), 387–403 (1993)
17. Zhang, D., Yan, X., Zhang, J., et al.: Use of fuzzy rule-based evidential reasoning approach in the navigational risk assessment of inland waterway transportation systems. Saf. Sci. **82**, 352–360 (2016)
18. Wan, M., Yao, J., Jing, Y., et al.: Event-based anomaly detection for non-public industrial communication protocols in SDN-based control systems. CMC Comput. Mat. Continua **55** (3), 447–463 (2018)

Research on Opinion Spam Detection by Time Series Anomaly Detection

Ye Wang[1,2], Wanli Zuo[1,2(✉)], and Ying Wang[1,2]

[1] College of Computer Science and Technology,
Jilin University, Changchun 130012, China
aiahwang@163.com, {wanli,wangying2010}@jlu.edu.cn
[2] Key Laboratory of Symbolic Computation and Knowledge Engineering,
Ministry of Education, Jilin University, Changchun 130012, China

Abstract. With the continuous development of e-commerce, buying online product has become a more desirable shopping option for modern people, but the product reviews which people need to consult when they buy goods are easily become the root cause of misleading consumption. Black profit chains of online sales make a lot of spam opinion makers flood the network who guide consumer's choice by writing deceptive and misleading spam opinions. In order to eliminate the impact of this black interest chain and safeguard the interests of the mass consumers, we propose a new model by using the time series anomaly detection, reducing the time complexity of spam opinion detection found by time series analysis, while improve the performance of spam detection. Based on time series anomaly detection, we analyze the content of reviews and the characteristics of reviewers and take experiments on real dataset that demonstrate advantages and effectiveness of the proposed approach.

Keywords: Time series · Abnormal point detection · Opinion spam detection · AR model

1 Introduction

With the gradual prevalence of e-commerce, opinion spam detection has attracted many researchers to conduct related research. At present, the research on the opinion spam detection can be divided into two aspects: (*i*) detection based on the contents of reviews and (*ii*) detection based on the commentator's behavior.

Jindal and Liu [1–3] first proposed the concept of spam detection in 2007, using Logistic regression algorithm and repetitive comment texts to find irrelevant reviews, non-commentary information and deceptive reviews. Mukherjee [4, 5] compared the experimental results based on the comment content and the commentator's characteristics on the Yelp data, and concluded that the recognition effect based on the feature of the reviewer is better. In the same year, he used the commentator feature to detect the spam opinions, and it's the first time who used unsupervised methods on this question. Mukherjee and Liu [6] analyzed the spam opinions by using the classification method and used the deceptive reviews generated by Amazon Mechanical Turk (AMT) as the effective annotation set. Ott [7, 8] combined linguistic features and psychological

© Springer Nature Switzerland AG 2019
X. Sun et al. (Eds.): ICAIS 2019, LNCS 11632, pp. 182–193, 2019.
https://doi.org/10.1007/978-3-030-24274-9_16

features to identify spam opinions and then studied the prevalence of spam opinions through an economical signal theory in the next few years, explaining the key role of prevalence of spam opinions. Feng [9] proposed a method based on syntactic structure to detect spam opinions. They used context free syntax parsing trees to extract information from data sets. Jindal and Liu [10] used individuals and groups by setting frequent rules. Patil [11] used language model based on SVM algorithm to detect the spam opinions. Chen [12] proposed deep-level language features, using information and inter-sentence information analysis and recognition of spam opinions. Bhalla [13] effectively exploited deceptive opinions through semantic analysis and comment content mining. And there were other researchers proposed semantic analysis methods [14, 15].

Methods based on commentator's behavior have also been explored for the opinion spam detection. Mukherjee [16, 17] dug out the characteristics of the spam group, classified the reviewers by group, and got a group of spammers with similar behavior through experiments. Lim [18] used the reviewers' scoring behavior feature to detect spam opinions. Li [19] detected spam opinions by comprehensive review content and commenter features, and the results indicated that commentary sentiment features have less impact on identifying deceptive reviews. Akoglu [20] used reviewers and the network effect of comment content to rate reviewers and reviews.

In the past, researchers have mainly identified spam reviews by analyzing commentator characteristics and comment content, ignoring the time characteristics. Xie and Ye [21, 22] respectively proposed a time-based spam detection method. The method of Xie S was mainly to catch singletons that spam reviewers with only a single review. The method of Junting Y proposed LOCALAR which used multivariate indicative signals but was only considered forward fitting and used square error as the method of calculating error.

In this work, we propose a time series anomaly detection model named *NPAR* used on opinion spam detection. This method has a certain degree of real-time, and can identify spam opinions in a timely and accurate manner, thereby preventing users from being misled by the spam opinions and improving the user's shopping experience. In summary, the main contributions of this paper are as follows.

1. We propose a new method based on AR algorithm to annotate time series anomaly points. The basic idea is using residuals statistics-based method and AR model for forward and backward fitting. And then use Gauss distribution statistic testing to find out the outlier.
2. We use the new time series anomaly detection method for opinion spam detection. By performing anomaly detection on the time series, the sub-feature is comprehensively analyzed in the time segment corresponding to the main feature in the time series, and it is determined whether the time segment should be identified as a spam review segment.
3. The proposed method can detect anomalies in real-time which is usable in practice and can identify spam reviews in a timely and accurate manner.

2 Feature Selection of Opinion Spam

In this paper, the comment data of the product is regarded as the time series, that is, each comment includes 4 parts, which are user name, user level, user rating, evaluation time, and then we generate time series by linking these metrics to time series. We use the following 6 identification sequences to analyze the spam time series (cf. Fig. 1).

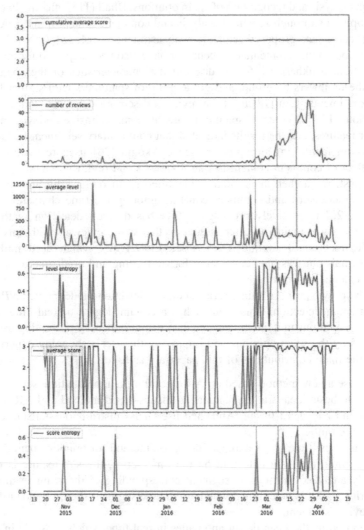

Fig. 1. Time series of product *a*

The main reason we chose the following indicators for detecting spam opinions is that can reflect the time series of the phenomenon when the brushing phenomenon occurs. When the time series is abnormally fluctuating, it is highly probable that a large amount of brushing behavior will occur at this time, so the spam opinions may be generated in the time period in which the time series is abnormal.

1. **Cumulative Average Score:** The cumulative average score refers to the average number of scores that the product has received since it was sold, and is a cumulative indicator. Over time, the cumulative average score is constantly changing. When there is a significant change in the cumulative average score, there may be a phenomenon of brushing. Let r_p^k denote the kth review rating of the item within the time period $[0, t * \Delta T]$, the total number of reviews for item p during this time period is $|r_p| = n$. Then,

$$R_p^t = \frac{1}{n} \sum_{k=1}^{n} r_p^k \qquad (1)$$

2. **Number of Reviews:** The number of reviews is the total number of reviews per ΔT time period for the item. When the number of reviews increases sharply, there may be a phenomenon of brushing. Let c_p^t denote the rating of the product p within the time period $[(t-1) * \Delta T, t * \Delta T]$. Then,

$$C_p^t = |c_p^t| \qquad (2)$$

3. **Average Level:** The average level is the average of rating per ΔT time period. The level of the spammers is mostly low, inasmuch as Taobao [21]. Most of the spammers need to use the alt account to brush. Let g_p^k denote the rank of the customer who evaluated the commodity p within the time period $[(t-1) * \Delta T, t * \Delta T]$, and the total number of reviews is $|g_p| = m$. Then,

$$G_p^t = \frac{1}{m} \sum_{k=1}^{m} g_p^k \qquad (3)$$

4. **Level Entropy:** The level entropy can reflect the confusion level per ΔT time period. When the customer's level is mostly distributed at a low level, the smaller the calculated result at this time, the more uneven the distribution. The customer level is divided into three levels, namely the heart level, the star level and the diamond level. Let er_p^k denote the ratio of each level of customers evaluated for the commodity p within the time period $[(t-1) * \Delta T, t * \Delta T]$. Then,

$$EA_p^t = - \sum_{k=1}^{3} er_p^k \cdot \log er_p^k \qquad (4)$$

5. **Average Score:** The average score can more directly reflect the customer's rating of the product p in each time period. This indicator affects the cumulative average score and has more obvious indication characteristics. Let $\bar{r}_p^k$ denote the kth comment score of the commodity p within the time period $[(t-1) * \Delta T, t * \Delta T]$, and the total number of reviews of the commodity p in the time period is $|\bar{r}_p| = n$. Then,

$$\bar{R}_p^t = \frac{1}{n} \sum_{k=1}^{n} \bar{r}_p^k \qquad (5)$$

6. **Score Entropy:** The score entropy is similar to the level entropy and can reflect the degree of confusion in the scores per ΔT time period. The customer's score is divided into 3 levels, which are good, middle and bad reviews. Then,

$$EG_p^t = -\sum_{k=1}^{3} eg_p^k \cdot \log eg_p^k \qquad (6)$$

3 Opinion Spam Detection

Taobao has been working hard to check the shops which hire spammers, through the use of related equipment and manual investigation to stop the brushing behavior and ensure the authenticity of online transactions [23]. However, it brings a lot of trouble for the opinion spam detection as the behavior of the spammers is closer to the normal customers, and the staff can't rely solely on the reviews to detect the spam opinions. In order to complete the brushing tasks, the brush will focus on the process for a period of time, and there will be a lot of deceptive opinions gathering.

We use the k-order ($k \in [1,5]$) AR model to fit the time series forward and backward. Mainly because the AR model has a simple structure and high fitting precision [24], it is suitable for studying stationary time series problems. Although the timing diagram in Fig. 1 has obvious trend, the time series is close to the stationary sequence in the adjacent time domain. Therefore, the spam opinions detection problem studied in this paper belongs to the stationary time series problem [25], so we propose a method based on the AR model to find anomaly points in the time series.

The research framework of time series anomaly detection and recognition model construction is shown in Fig. 2.

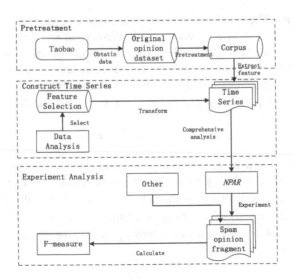

Fig. 2. Research framework

3.1 Time Series Analysis

Possible fragments of the spam opinions can be obtained by analyzing the time series anomaly fragments. The segment is more likely to be a spam opinion set when following occurs:

1. **Cumulative average score change:** In addition to increase the product rating, the purpose of the brushers is to edit the malicious bad opinion, and then decrease the score of the competitors. Finally, it will result in a decrease in the cumulative average score.
2. **Number of reviews increase:** Although there is no significant change in the cumulative average rating at this time, the seller may hire spammers to increase the number of praises in order to increase the number of opinions on the product and rise the ranking of the product.

In summary, we use the following steps for the analysis of abnormal time series:

Step 1. The cumulative average score and the number of reviews were respectively selected as the lead analysis indicator.

Step 2. When the lead indicator has an abnormal point, analyze whether the sub-features have corresponding changes. Because there may be other reasons result in the lead indicator change, such as changes in product quality may cause the true reviewer to write positive or negative reviews, further verification by the auxiliary identification is required. Take average level as an example, since creating a new account is convenient and fast, more importantly, the cost of old account being sealed is not small, thereby most of the spammers use the newly created account. When the number of reviews rises sharply and the average score of the commentators is low, then there may be a phenomenon of brushing. The reviews at this time should be possible spam reviews with the aim of improving product ratings and misleading consumers.

Step 3. If the lead feature and the sub-features meet the conditions shown in Table 1, the reviews within this time segment are marked as spam reviews. The conditional judgment of the auxiliary mark is judged by the rate of change in the forward window, that is, $\emptyset_t = t_i - t_{i-1}$, and the auxiliary change satisfies the condition when $|\emptyset_t| > \varphi$.

Table 1. Indicative signals

Name	Range	Condition
Cumulative average Score	[1, 3]	Change
Number of reviews	$[0, \infty]$	Increase
Average level	$[0, \infty]$	Decrease
Level entropy	$[0, \log_2 3]$	Increase
Average score	[1, 3]	Change
Score entropy	$[0, \log_2 3]$	Increase

3.2   The Change on Adjacent Interval

The change on adjacent interval refers to the change range of the data value in the time period before and after a certain time point. Let δ_t denote the change on adjacent interval, then,

$$\delta_t = |(t_i - t_{i-1})| + |(t_i - t_{i+1})| \tag{7}$$

δ_t is detected in the time series range, and set the threshold δ. If $\delta_t > \delta$, then the point is a time series abnormal point, otherwise it is identified as an unintended abnormal point, wherein the value of the threshold is obtained by weighting calculation.

3.3   NPAR Model

We propose a *NPAR* model (Near point auto regressive model) based on AR model and apply it to the detection of spam opinions. By determining the fitting residual of the forward and backward windows of the time by finding the value that minimized the residual, and comparing the likelihood residual probability distribution value with the threshold to obtain the time segment attribute, thereby determining whether the time segment should be marked as spam fragment.

The *NPAR* model is a p-order autoregressive model with forward and backward fitting at time point t. If the fitting window contains possible abnormal points, the point does not participate in the calculation, and the remaining non-probable abnormal points are shifted to the whole at time t and fill the window.

The forward fitting residual at time point t is:

$$\varepsilon_{1t} = x_t - \hat{x}_t, t \in T \tag{8}$$

$$\hat{x}_t = \sum_{i=1}^{p} \alpha_i x_{t-i} \tag{9}$$

The backward fitting residual at time point t is:

$$\varepsilon_{2t} = x_t - \hat{x}_t, t \in T \tag{10}$$

$$\hat{x}_t = \sum_{i=1}^{p} \beta_i x_{t-i} \tag{11}$$

Where $\alpha = (\alpha_1, \alpha_2, \cdots, \alpha_k)$ is the forward autoregressive coefficients, and $\beta = (\beta_1, \beta_2, \cdots, \beta_k)$ is the backward autoregressive coefficient,

$$\alpha_k = \frac{cov(x_t, x_{t-k})}{\sigma_t \sigma_{t-k}} \tag{12}$$

$$\beta_k = \frac{cov(x_t, x_{t-k})}{\sigma_t \sigma_{t-k}} \tag{13}$$

The fitting residual obtained at time t is:

$$\varepsilon_t = \varepsilon_{1t} + \varepsilon_{2t} \qquad (14)$$

The autocorrelation coefficients need to be estimated before the residuals are calculated. According to the Yule-Walker equation [26], take the former auto-regressive coefficients as an example.

$$\hat{r}_x(k) = \frac{1}{T} \sum_{i=0}^{T-1} x_{t-T+i} \times x_{t-T+i+k} \qquad (15)$$

Where $k = 0, 1, 2, \cdots, p$. And the backward autoregressive coefficient is similar to the forward autoregressive coefficient calculation method.

Based on the hypothesis testing theory, at a certain level of significance, the fitting residual ε_t approximates the Gaussian distribution $N(\mu, \sigma^2)$, and the probability density of the residual is:

$$f(\varepsilon) = \frac{1}{\sqrt{2\pi}\sigma} e^{-\frac{(\varepsilon-\mu)^2}{2\sigma^2}} \qquad (16)$$

Using maximum likelihood estimation, the likelihood function is:

$$L(\mu, \sigma^2) = \prod_{i=1}^{M} \frac{1}{\sqrt{2\pi}\sigma} e^{-\frac{(\varepsilon_i-\mu)^2}{2\sigma^2}} \qquad (17)$$

Respectively set,

$$\begin{cases} \frac{\partial}{\partial\mu} \ln L = 0 \\ \frac{\partial}{\partial\sigma^2} \ln L = 0 \end{cases} \qquad (18)$$

The maximum likelihood estimate obtained by calculation is:

$$\hat{\mu} = \frac{1}{M} \sum_{i=1}^{M} \varepsilon_i = \bar{\varepsilon} \qquad (19)$$

$$\hat{\sigma}^2 = \frac{1}{M} \sum_{i=1}^{M} (\varepsilon_i - \bar{\varepsilon})^2 \qquad (20)$$

Calculate the likelihood residual probability distribution $f(\varepsilon_i)$ for each sample point, and select the threshold F, then,

$$x_i = \begin{cases} f(\varepsilon_i) < F, & \text{abnormal} \\ f(\varepsilon_i) \geq F, & \text{else} \end{cases} \qquad (21)$$

Based on the above equations, the NPAR algorithm is as follows,

---

NPAR algorithm:

Input: Time points t_i, Abnormal points in the adjacent area NP,
          Time series length L, Residual fit threshold F

Output: Abnormal time points e_t^i

1	FOREACH $i \in [1, L]$ DO
2	IF $t_i \in NP$ THEN
3	$e_j = 1$
4	BREAK
5	FOREACH $k \in [1,5]$ DO
6	$x_{1t} = AR\left(t_{j-\Delta T}^j, k\right)$
7	$\hat{x}_{1t} = \sum_{j=1}^{k} \alpha_j x_{t+j}$
8	$\varepsilon_{1t} = x_{1t} - \hat{x}_{1t}$
9	$x_{2t} = AR\left(t_{j+\Delta T}^j, k\right)$
10	$\hat{x}_{2t} = \sum_{j=1}^{k} \beta_j x_{t+j}$
11	$\varepsilon_{2t} = x_{2t} - \hat{x}_{2t}$
12	$\varepsilon_t = \varepsilon_{1t} + \varepsilon_{2t}$
13	$k = k_{min}$
14	FOREACH $t_j \in [t_a - 2, t_i]$ DO
15	$x_{1t} = AR\left(t_{j-\Delta T}^j, k\right)$
16	$\hat{x}_{1t} = \sum_{j=1}^{k} \alpha_j x_{t+j}$
17	$\varepsilon_{1t} = x_{1t} - \hat{x}_{1t}$
18	$x_{2t} = AR\left(t_{j+\Delta T}^j, k\right)$
19	$\hat{x}_{2t} = \sum_{j=1}^{k} \beta_j x_{t+j}$
20	$\varepsilon_{2t} = x_{2t} - \hat{x}_{2t}$
21	$\varepsilon_t = \varepsilon_{1t} + \varepsilon_{2t}$
22	IF $f(\varepsilon_j) < F$
23	$e_j = 1$

The main idea of the NPAR algorithm is that, firstly, using the change on adjacent interval to detect the possible abnormal points. If the learning window contains possible abnormal points, the point does not participate in the fitting calculation, and the remaining non-probable abnormal points are shifted to the whole at time t to fill the window. For the time point t, the point to be measured uses the AR model for forward and backward fitting, finds the value k that minimized the fitting residual value in the window, and compares the residual corresponding to the value k with the threshold F to obtain the result. Lines 1–23 analyze the entire time series and traverse from the first segment; lines 2–4 determine whether there are possible abnormal points in the time segment, and if they exist, the point does not participate in the fitting calculation. The remaining non-probable abnormal points are shifted to the whole at time point t and fill the window; lines 5–12 calculate the fitting residuals for different value k; lines 15–21 calculate the fitting residuals corresponding to the minimum value k; finally, the fitting residual ε_t at time point t are calculated and the residual probability distribution $f(\varepsilon_i)$ is compared with the selected threshold F. If it is less than the threshold, then the point is determined as a time series abnormal point.

4 Experiment

4.1 Dataset

Taobao, as the largest online trading market in China, has generated thousands of transactions every day, and it also produced a huge amount of reviews with rich information. The experimental dataset used in this paper is derived from real product review, including three types of product, namely clothing, home appliances and toys, including 256,443 reviews. After preprocessing the data, a total of 87,546 similar reviews were found by calculating the similarity between sentences. Combined with the manual labeling method, a total of 90,431 spam opinions were selected.

4.2 Result

By analyzing the time series abnormal points of the number of reviews and comparing with other indicators in the same time segment, the time series of the commodity spam commentary shown in Fig. 1 is obtained.

As shown in Fig. 3, it can be found that most of the marked spam opinions are concentrated in the time anomaly fragments, and thus the problem proposed in this paper can be verified, that is, we can use *NPAR* algorithm to detect the spam opinions.

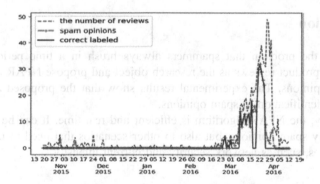

Fig. 3. Spam opinion distribution of product *a*

Table 2 shows the experimental results obtained by using the *NPAR* algorithm for the three types of data. It can be found that the more reviews, the better the results. In other words, the more reviews, the more obvious the spammers' operation in a certain time period, the easier it is to be discovered.

Table 2. The result on contrast experiments 1

Type	Correctly labeled	Annotated by NPAR	Actual spam opinions	Accuracy	Recall	F-measure
Clothing	41,972	49,379	53,124	85.00%	79.01%	81.89%
Home appliances	16,156	18,450	21,831	87.57%	74.00%	80.22%
Toys	10,868	12,479	15,476	87.09%	70.23%	74.59%

As shown in Table 3, the experimental results for all the data obtained by comparing the *NPAR* algorithm with the Patil [11], Chen [12], and Ye [22]. It can be found that the analogy based on the comment content, the commentator's behavior and time series analysis, the experimental result of the proposed *NPAR* algorithm is better, whether it is accuracy, recall or F-measure all higher than the results of other three algorithms.

Table 3. The result on contrast experiments 2

Algorithm	Correctly labeled	Annotated by others	Actual spam opinions	Accuracy	Recall	F-measure
NPAR	68,996	80,308	90,431	85.91%	76.30%	80.82%
Patil [11]	64,070	84,894	90,431	75.47%	70.85%	73.09%
Chen [12]	70,970	65,943	90,431	80.19%	75.48%	77.76%
Ye [22]	67,253	79,825	90,431	84.25%	74.37%	79.00%

5   Conclusion

According to the problem that spammers always brush in a time period, we take Taobao's real product reviews as the research object and propose NPAR algorithm to detect spam opinions. The experimental results show that the proposed algorithm is better in the identification of spam opinions.

Importantly, the NPAR algorithm is efficient and real-time. It can be applied not only to identify spam opinions, but also to other scenarios that need to identify time series anomalies, such as network security and current intensity.

References

1. Jindal, N., Liu, B.: Review spam detection. In: Proceedings of the 16th International Conference on World Wide Web, pp. 1189–1190. ACM (2007)
2. Jindal, N., Liu, B.: Analyzing and detecting review spam. In: Seventh IEEE International Conference on Data Mining (ICDM 2007), pp. 547–552. IEEE (2007)
3. Jindal, N., Liu, B.: Opinion spam and analysis. In: Proceedings of the 2008 International Conference on Web Search and Data Mining, pp. 219–230. ACM (2008)
4. Mukherjee, A., Venkataraman, V., Liu, B., et al.: What yelp fake review filter might be doing? In: ICWSM (2013)

5. Mukherjee, A., Kumar, A., Liu, B., et al.: Spotting opinion spammers using behavioral footprints. In: Proceedings of the 19th ACM SIGKDD International Conference on Knowledge Discovery and Data Mining, pp. 632–640. ACM (2013)
6. Mukherjee, A., Venkataraman, V., Liu, B., et al.: Fake review detection: classification and analysis of real and pseudo reviews. UIC-CS-03-2013. Technical report (2013)
7. Ott, M., Yejin, Ch., Claire, C., Jeffrey, T.H.: Finding deceptive opinion spam by any stretch of the imagination. In: Proceedings of the 49th Annual Meeting of the Association for Computational Linguistics (ACL-2011) (2011)
8. Ott, M., Cardie, C., Hancock, J.: Estimating the prevalence of deception in online review communities. In: Proceedings of the 21st International Conference on World Wide Web, WWW 2012. ACM New York (2012)
9. Feng, S., Banerjee, R., Choi, Y.: Syntactic Stylometry for Deception Detection. ACL (short paper) (2012)
10. Jindal, N., Liu, B., Lim, E.P.: Finding unusual review patterns using unexpected rules. In: Proceedings of the 19th ACM International Conference on Information and knowledge Management, pp. 1549–1552. ACM (2010)
11. Patil, M.S., Bagade, M.A.: Online review spam detection using language model and feature selection. Int. J. Comput. Appl. **59**(7), 33–36 (2013)
12. Chen, C., Zhao, H., Yang, Y.: Deceptive opinion spam detection using deep level linguistic features. In: Li, J., Ji, H., Zhao, D., Feng, Y. (eds.) NLPCC 2015. LNCS (LNAI), vol. 9362, pp. 465–474. Springer, Cham (2015). https://doi.org/10.1007/978-3-319-25207-0_43
13. Bhalla, R., Jain, P.: A model based on effective and intelligent sentiment mining: a review. Indian J. Sci. Technol. **9**(32) (2016)
14. Yuhong, Z., et al.: Sentiment classification based on piecewise pooling convolutional neural network. Comput. Mater. Contin **56**, 285–297 (2018)
15. Suzhen, W., et al.: Natural language semantic construction based on cloud database. Comput. Mater. Contin **57**, 603–619 (2018)
16. Mukherjee, A., Liu, B., Wang, J., et al.: Detecting group review spam. In: Proceedings of the 20th International Conference Companion on World Wide Web, pp. 93–94. ACM (2011)
17. Mukherjee, A., Liu, B., Glance, N.: Spotting fake reviewer groups in consumer reviews. In: Proceedings of the 21st International Conference on World Wide Web, pp. 191–200. ACM 2012
18. Lim, E.P., Nguyen, V.A., Jindal, N., et al.: Detecting product review spammers using rating behaviors. In: Proceedings of the 19th ACM International Conference on Information and Knowledge Management, pp. 939–948. ACM (2010)
19. Li, F., Huang, M., Yang, Y., et al.: Learning to identify review spam. In: IJCAI Proceedings-International Joint Conference on Artificial Intelligence, vol. 22, no. 3, p. 2488 (2011)
20. Akoglu, L., Chandy, R., Faloutsos, C.: Opinion fraud detection in online reviews by network effects. ICWSM **13**, 2–11 (2013)
21. Xie, S., Wang, G., Lin, S., et al.: Review spam detection via time series pattern discovery. In: International Conference on World Wide Web, pp. 635–636. ACM (2012)
22. Ye, J., Kumar, S., Akoglu, L.: Temporal opinion spam detection by multivariate indicative signals. arXiv preprint arXiv:1603.01929 (2016)
23. Zhongan Online. The black interest chain of Taobo is the part-time college student [DB/OL]. http://news.ubetween.com/2016/hotnews_0319/209152.html, 19 March 2016
24. Deng, F., Bao, C.: Speech enhancement based on AR model parameters estimation. Speech Commun. **79**, 30–46 (2016)
25. Chatfield, C.: The Analysis of Time Series: An Introduction. CRC Press, New York (2016)
26. Alkan, A., Yilmaz, A.S.: Frequency domain analysis of power system transients using Welch and Yule-Walker AR methods. Energy Convers. Manage. **48**(7), 2129–2135 (2007)

Application of Machine Learning Methods for Material Classification with Multi-energy X-Ray Transmission Images

Qingqing Chang, Weijiao Li, and Jiamin Chen[✉]

Criminal Investigation Technology Department,
The Third Research Institute of Ministry of Public Security, Shanghai, China
13621721332@139.com

Abstract. Automatic material classification is very useful for threat detection with X-ray screening technology. In this paper, we propose the use of machine learning methods to the problem of fine-grained classification of organic matters based on multi-energy transmission images, which has been overlooked by existing methods. The method which we propose consists three main steps: spectrum analysis, feature selection and supervised classification. We show detailed analysis of the relationship between feature dimension and material classification accuracy. Our method can also be used to find optimal X-ray configurations for material classification. We compare the performance of several machine learning models for the fine-grained classification task. For the task of classifying three categories of organic matters, we can obtain the classification accuracy higher than 85% with only X-ray measurements with the dimension of four. In conclusion, the results of our paper provide one promising direction for the automatic identification of organic contraband using multi-energy X-ray imaging techniques.

Keywords: Material classification · Machine learning · Multi energy

1 Introduction

X-ray image screening is widely used for aviation and transport security inspection across the world. The most widely deployed X-ray imaging technologies include transmission and backscatter technique. The ability of automatic material classification can be meaningful, which can improve efficiency and reduce the workload of human screeners.

X-ray transmission images usually have high resolution compared with backscatter images, which can reveal rich structural details of scanned baggage. Dual energy x-ray systems can provide additional information on the density and effective atomic number (Z_{eff}) of the material [1]. Current automatic inspection systems using machine learning techniques [2] mainly focus on detecting metallic contrabands such as handguns and knives from shapes and texture [3–5]. However, the problem of automatic detecting

Sponsored by the National Key Research and Development Program (Project No. 2016YFC0800904).

X. Sun et al. (Eds.): ICAIS 2019, LNCS 11632, pp. 194–204, 2019.
https://doi.org/10.1007/978-3-030-24274-9_17

organic materials such as explosives and drugs which have irregular shape and little texture has rarely been explored in existing systems [6, 7].

With dual energy X-ray imaging system, the measurement at each position is recorded by two different X-ray energies which represent the reduction of the intensity of an x-ray beam as it traverses matter (also known as attenuation). All objects can be classified into three categories using the effective atomic number as Fig. 1: metallic materials (Zeff > 20), inorganic materials (10 < Zeff < 20) and organic materials (Zeff < 10) [8]. The results of material classification are shown in pseudo-color as Fig. 2. Metallic materials are colored in blue; inorganic materials are colored in green, and organic materials are colored in orange. However, both everyday objects and contrabands can be classified into the same category of organic materials by such criteria. For example drugs (cocaine, heroin), drinks (water, milk) and flammable liquid (alcohol, TNT) have similar effective atomic number. In order to overcome the limitation of dual energy X-ray imaging, multi-energy X-ray imaging techniques can be applied for fine-grained organic material classification.

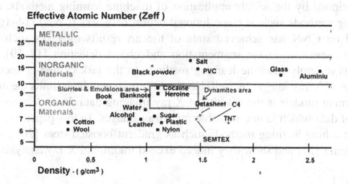

Fig. 1. Energy dependence of the mass attenuation coefficients of carbon and aluminum adapted from Iovea [9]

Fig. 2. Some example images of X-ray transmission images.

Several works have been proposed which make use of multi energy X-ray transmissions techniques for organic material identification [10]. A multi-energy system with multiple detectors, multiple spectrum and multiple generators for material discrimination was proposed in [11], which requires expensive specific hardware and thus made it not suitable for commercial use. Paulus et al. proposed one method which computed the material density and effective atomic number based on backscatter images using CdZnTe spectrometric probe [12]. However, their prototype system required very long acquisition time, which is also impractical for field application. Saverskiy et al. introduced the intra-pulse multi energy (IPME) method for material discrimination, which maintain a constant energy spectrum [13]. Their system required expensive multi-energy intra-pulse X-ray source. We aim to use the traditional X-ray detectors currently widely used in dual energy imaging systems and increase the measurement dimension to see if the fine-grained organic material classification is possible. Our method thus requires no special detectors and makes it possible for commercial application.

For the past several years, the area of computer vision and image processing has been revolutioned by the widely application of machine learning methods, especially deep learning methods such as convolutional neural networks (CNN) [14–16]. Recent work based on CNN has achieved state of the art results on tasks such as image classification, semantic image segmentation and object detection [17–19]. This has motivated us to apply machine learning methods to the task of fine-grained material classification of X-ray images as well. However, one issue which limits the application of deep learning models is the scarcity of X-ray imaging data. Deep learning methods need a lot of data which is not available for X-ray images. In this paper, we start with traditional machine learning methods such as gradient boosted trees [20] and support vector machines [21] and show they indeed exceed traditional X-ray analysis methods.

2   Methodology

In this paper, we propose to apply machine learning methods to the task of fine-grained organic matter classification with multi energy transmission (TS) images, which has been unexplored in traditional methods. Our method consists three steps: spectrum analysis, feature selection, and supervised classification. The schema of the overall system framework is shown in Fig. 3. Firstly, the energy spectrum of materials is acquired and each energy measurement is viewed as separate feature. Secondly all features from low energy to high energy is ranked by feature selection method. Lastly, various classification models are tested with the selected features. The details of each module is shown below.

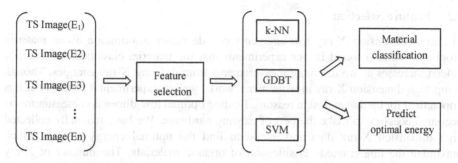

Fig. 3. A Schematic representation of the method framework.

2.1 Spectrum Analysis

With monochromatic X-ray source for security screening (typically 120–160 keV), without considering the effect of scattered radiation, the intensity of the material after transmission is

$$I_0 = N_0 \cdot e^{-\mu t} \tag{1}$$

Where N_0 is the transmission intensity of the material μ is the attenuation coefficient, which depends on the effective atomic number Z_{eff} and material density, and t is the thickness of the object.

In order to analyze the X-ray spectrum under different materials, we built a simulation model by Greant4 software, which included X-ray, multi-energy detector, and different materials as Fig. 4(a).By varying the properties, thickness and distance of the object to be examined, we obtain a series of energy spectrums as Fig. 4(b). The horizontal axis in represents X-ray energy, and the vertical axis represents the count under that energy, in units of 1000. It can be seen that although characteristic peaks of energy spectrums under different materials are similar, the energy attenuations varies greatly at low and high energies. Therefore, energy spectrum can be used as a feature of material classification and the reduction of dimension of energy spectrum will be the difficulty in hardware design.

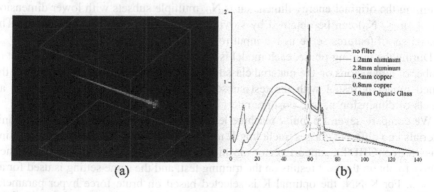

Fig. 4. X-ray energy spectrums. (a) shows the X-ray spectrum simulation model built by Greant4. (b) shows X-ray spectrums under different materials.

2.2   Feature Selection

The high dimension X-ray measurements encode richer information about material property. We also found in our experiments that the material classification accuracy indeed increases as we use more measurements from different X-ray energies. Though using high dimension X-ray measurements works well in experimental settings but it is impractical for hardware design reasons. Finding optimal low-dimension measurements become necessary to make the best of existing hardware. We have manually collected high dimension X-ray data and intend to find the optimal energy settings which maximize the fine-grained classification of organic materials. The number of X-ray measurement dimension depends on the tradeoff between hardware cost and material classification accuracy. The extreme situation is single or dual energy system for which only the top one or two optimal features are chosen.

According to the attenuation coefficients, X-ray energy is roughly divided into several energy domain: low energy, medium energy and high energy. Apart from pure data-driven methods for feature selection, we can also use this as prior knowledge to guide feature selection. In fact, we do find that the first several X-ray energies selected fall under different domains, which show consistency with current energy setting criteria. One problem with traditional methods is there is no way of finding the optimal energy setting for each domain. Nor can they find the optimal combinations of energy settings which is another highlight of our data-driven feature selection module.

Dimension reduction has been long studied in the area of pattern recognition and machine learning. But most dimension reduction aim to find the optimal dimension which may be composed by several features, such as principal component analysis (PCA) and independent component analysis (ICA). For our application, we want to select the optimal subset of features which correspond to actual X-ray measurement settings. In our framework, tree-based estimator is chosen to compute feature importance, which in turn can be used to retain the most relevant features. The features are ranked by discrimination power for material classification and the optimal one in each energy domain are selected for field application. The impact of feature dimension on the material classification accuracy is found by feeding the selected features to various classification module.

2.3   Classification Models

Assuming the original energy dimension is N_0, multiple subsets with lower dimension n ($1 \leq n \leq N_0$) can be obtained by varying the parameter of feature selection. The reduced set of features serve as the input to all classification models.

During the training phase, each model is trained separately to analyze the impact of number of dimensions on the material classification accuracy. During the test phase, the trained model is tested with the test subset and the accuracy is computed. For all subsets of dimension n, true positive rate (TPR) is calculated and compared.

We compare several popular machine learning methods to classify several organic materials into different classes, including K nearest neighbors (k-NN), gradient boosting decision tree (GBDT), support vector machines (SVM). For each model, we tune their settings to obtain the best results on the training test, and the same setting is used for all test sets. For K-NN, the optimal K is selected based on brute force hyper parameter searching. For gradient boosting decision tree, we found the optimal learning rate to be 0.05. The GBDT model is robust to overfitting, but we found the classification accuracy barely improve as the number of estimators exceed 200. For SVM models, we compared various settings and chose radial basis function as the kernel function.

3   Experiments and Results

3.1   Hardware Design and Data Collection

The multi-energy X-ray security scanner we use in our experiments is designed by the Third Research Institute of Ministry of Public Security, China. The detector used is Silicon photomultiplier array detector.

We collect one dataset which contains five common materials under different thickness. The objects used contain one iron step wedge (15 steps, each 0.2 mm difference, Z_{eff} = 26) as one metallic material and an aluminum step-wedge (15 steps, each 2 mm difference, Z_{eff} = 13) as inorganic material. There are three organic materials, including a Teflon (TFL, Z_{eff} = 8.34, ρ = 1.7 g/cm^3), a polymathic methacrylate (PMMA, Z_{eff} = 6.67, ρ= 1.18 g/cm^3) and a polypropylene material(Z_{eff} = 5.74, ρ = 0.92 g/cm^3) step wedge, which consist of 20 steps. All the step-wedges with various known thickness are examined radiographically as illustrated in Fig. 5. As thickness increases, the attenuation coefficients curve of materials at low energy (E_L) and at high energy (E_H) are shown in Fig. 6 [22].

A total 42 X-ray spectral channels are chosen ranging from 8 keV to 90 keV which generate 42-dimension X-ray scanning images for fine grained object classification. For given thickness of the same material, the transmission intensities under different X-ray energies can be counted by varying the parameters of X-ray detector. By increasing the value of X-ray source, we can obtain the integral energy-count (IEC) curve. According to different data collecting method, X-ray transmission integral IEC curves and energy spectrum can be measured for each material of different thickness as shown in Fig. 7.

Each X-ray image has the resolution of 1024 × 768 pixels. The raw detector output value ranges from 0 to 65535. We apply a min-max scaling to input raw data as the normalization pre-processing step. The scaling normalizes the input data to a fixed range between 0 and 1. For both feature selection and classification we use the scikit-learn package.

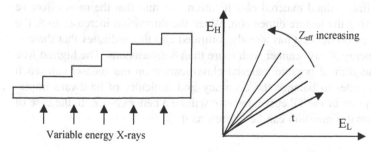

Fig. 5. One material step-wedge   **Fig. 6.** The attenuation coefficients curve of materials

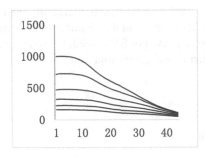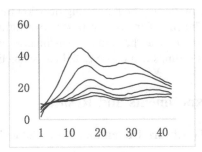

Fig. 7. The IEC curves and energy spectrum for one material of different thickness

3.2 Results

The ranking of feature importance of the 42-dimension features as the output of tree-based estimators is shown in Fig. 8. We can see that low energy measurements have relatively higher classification ability compared to high energy measurements. The features in the same energy domain are relevant as expected. According to the rank of importance, we can find the optimal n-dimension $(0 < n < N_0)$ subsets. Assuming the subset dimension is 5, the whole energy is divided into 5 domains equally. Each feature in the subset is the optimal one in the respective domain.

The true positive rate curve for material classification using gradient boosted trees is shown in Fig. 9. We can see that as the feature dimension increases, true positive rate first increases quickly, then gradually slows down until the classification accuracy reaches saturation. The results prove that using multiple energy measurements does improve material classification accuracy greatly. The results also show that when the feature dimension is 2, which correspond to traditional dual energy X-ray imaging systems which is widely used, metallic materials, inorganic materials and organic materials can be roughly classified but fine-grained organic material classification is not possible. Traditional methods compute the effective atomic number first and use it for further classification. Using gradient boosted trees, we do not need to compute the effective atomic number explicitly. We can directly perform category classification from the raw X-ray data. We also find out that using regression methods such as boosting or support vector regression, one can also regress the effective atomic number as well. The advantage of data-driven methods over traditional methods is that we can improve the system performance as we gather more data.

For the task of fine-grained material classification, we find that the most effective method is by increasing the feature dimension. When the dimension increases to 8, the classification accuracy on our test has already saturated and this indicates that there is no need for multi-energy X-ray scanner with more than 8 dimensions. The highest true positive rate for fine-grained organic material classification on our dataset can reach more than 85%. In order to balance the accuracy and difficulty of hardware implementation, the zero point of the TP curve derivate will be a better choice. In the case of our dataset, the optimal dimension can be chosen as 4.

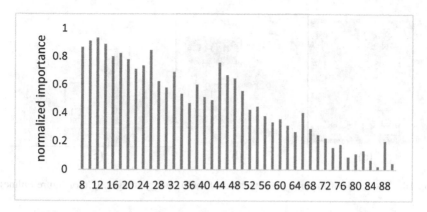

Fig. 8. The normalized importance of each energy dimension

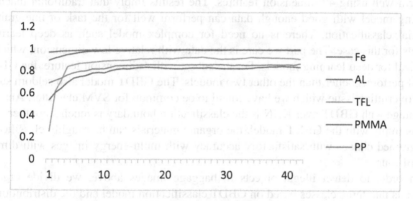

Fig. 9. The TPR curve of materials as energy dimension changes.

Table 1. TP rate for materials using three models

Model	Dimension	Material				
		Fe	AL	TFL	PMMA	PP
GBDT	42	1	0.99	0.93	0.85	0.86
KNN	42	1	0.98	0.91	0.83	0.84
SVM	42	1	0.98	0.92	0.92	0.85
GBDT	4	0.99	0.97	0.85	0.74	0.77
KNN	4	0.97	0.97	0.78	0.68	0.85
SVM	4	0.99	0.99	0.96	0.80	0.73

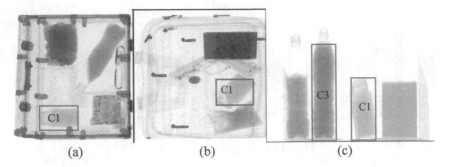

Fig. 10. The result of material classification of multi-energy images. (Color figure online)

The detailed classification accuracy of three models for two datasets with dimension of 42 and 4 respectively is shown in Table 1. It can be see that all three models perform well using 42-dimension features. The results imply that traditional machine learning model with good enough data can perform well for the task of fine-grained material classification. There is no need for complex model such as deep learning models for this case. The part we care is the data with relative low dimension, which is not ideal for deep learning models. For the subset with 4-dimension feature, the GBDT model performs better than the other two models. The GBDT model also seldom suffer from overfitting issue which we have found to be common for SVM classifier. Another advantage with GBDT over KNN is the classification boundary is much smoother. The results imply with the GBDT model, the organic materials can be roughly classified to fine-grained classes with satisfactory accuracy with multi-energy images with dimension of four.

In order to detect illegal objects in baggage images above, we divide organic materials into three classes based on GBDT classification model and the distribution of materials. Objects in class 1(C1) have similar properties as TFL, such as Heroin cocaine, and class 2(C2) presents daily used items such as water, sugar and so on, which are similar as PMMA. In the same way, light materials with low z_{eff} and density are labeled as class 3(C3), such as gasoline, alcohol. According to the national regulations on contraband in luggage, objects labeled C1 and C3 are marked with a red bounding box as Fig. 10. Although images features between different labels are indistinguishable, illegal objects can be labeled and detected by our method, especially for detection of flammable liquid.

4   Conclusion

In this paper, we introduce a framework for fine grained material classification based on multi-energy X-ray images. The main modules includes spectrum analysis, feature selection, and supervised classification. A data driven method can be applied to choose the optimal features. A novel dataset is collected and several machine learning methods have been compared to test their classification accuracy. Experimental results show the effectiveness of our methods. In the future we intend to extend the method for the task of detecting contrabands such as drugs and explosives.

For future work, we intend to investigate the problem of material overlap which now can only be solved by X-ray tomography. The application of deep learning methods for the task of material classification shall be investigated. From the dataset side, we intend to apply the method for the task of detecting contrabands such as drugs and explosives.

Acknowledgement. This research is Sponsored by the National Key Research and Development Program (Project No. 2016YFC0800904).

References

1. Wells, K., Bradley, D.A.: A review of X-ray explosives detection techniques for checked baggage. Appl. Radiat. Isot. **70**(8), 1729–1746 (2012)
2. Akcay, S., et al.: Transfer learning using convolutional neural networks for object classification within X-ray baggage security imagery. In: IEEE International Conference on Image Processing. IEEE (2016)
3. Krizhevsky, A., Sutskever, I., Hinton, G.: ImageNet classification with deep convolutional neural networks. NIPS. Curran Associates Inc. (2012)
4. He, K., Zhang, X., Ren, S., Sun, J.: Deep residual learning for image recognition. In: Proceedings of the IEEE Conference on Computer Vision and Pattern Recognition, pp. 770–778 (2016)
5. Mery, D., et al.: Modern computer vision techniques for X-ray testing in baggage inspection. IEEE Trans. Syst. Man Cybern. Syst. **47**(4), 682–692 (2017)
6. Baştan, M.: Multi-view object detection in dual-energy X-ray images. Mach. Vis. Appl. **26**(7–8), 1045–1060 (2015)
7. Singh, S., Singh, M.: Explosives detection systems (EDS) for aviation security. Signal Process. **83**(1), 31–55 (2003)
8. Wang, T.W., Evans, J.P.O.: Stereoscopic dual-energy X-ray imaging for target materials identification. IEE Proc. Vision Image Signal Process. **150**(2), 122–130 (2003)
9. Iovea, M., et al.: Portable and autonomous X-ray equipment for in-situ threat materials identification by effective atomic number high-accuracy measurement. In: Proceedings of SPIE - The International Society for Optical Engineering, vol. 8017, no. 2 (2011)
10. Caygill, J.S., Davis, F., Higson, S.P.J.: Current trends in explosive detection techniques. Talanta **88**, 14–29 (2012)
11. Maitrejean, S., Perion, D., Sundermann, D.: Multi-energy method: a new approach for measuring X-ray transmission as a function of energy with a Bremsstrahlung source and its application for heavy element identification. In: Proceedings of SPIE - The International Society for Optical Engineering, pp. 114–133 (1998)
12. Paulus, C., et al.: A multi-energy X-ray backscatter system for explosives detection. J. Instrum. **8**(4), P04003 (2013)
13. Saverskiy, A.Y., Dinca, D.C., Rommel, J.M.: Cargo and container X-ray inspection with intra-pulse multi-energy method for material discrimination. Phys. Procedia **66**, 232–241 (2015)
14. He, K., et al.: Mask R-CNN. In: IEEE International Conference on Computer Vision (ICCV). IEEE Computer Society (2017)

15. Ren, S., He, K., Girshick, R., Sun, J.: Faster R-CNN: towards real-time object detection with region proposal networks. In: Advances in Neural Information Processing Systems, pp. 91–99 (2015)
16. Cui, Q., McIntosh, S., Sun, H.: Identifying materials of photographic images and photorealistic computer generated graphics based on deep CNNs. Comput. Mater. Continua 55(2), 229–241 (2018)
17. Chen, L.-C., Papandreou, G., Kokkinos, I., Murphy, K., Yuille, A.L.: DeepLab: semantic image segmentation with deep convolutional nets, atrous convolution, and fully connected CRFs. IEEE Trans. Pattern Anal. Mach. Intell. 40(4), 834–848 (2018)
18. Liu, W., et al.: SSD: single shot multibox detector. In: Leibe, B., Matas, J., Sebe, N., Welling, M. (eds.) ECCV 2016. LNCS, vol. 9905, pp. 21–37. Springer, Cham (2016). https://doi.org/10.1007/978-3-319-46448-0_2
19. Fang, S., Cai, Z., Sun, W., et al.: Feature selection method based on class discriminative degree for intelligent medical diagnosis. Comput. Mater. Continua 55(3), 419–433 (2018)
20. Freund, Y., Schapire, R.E.: A decision-theoretic generalization of on-line learning and an application to boosting. J. Comput. Syst. Sci. 55(1), 119–139 (1997)
21. Cortes, C., Vapnik, V.: Support-vector networks. Mach. Learn. 20(3), 273–297 (1995)
22. Gorecki, A., Brambilla, A., Moulin, V., et al.: Comparing performances of a CdTe X-ray spectroscopic detector and an X-ray dual-energy sandwich detector. J. Instrum. 8(8), P11011 (2013)

Intra-class Classification of Architectural Styles Using Visualization of CNN

Rui Wang[1], Donghao Gu[1], Zhaojing Wen[1], Kai Yang[2,3(✉)],
Shaohui Liu[1], and Feng Jiang[1]

[1] School of Computer Science and Technology, Harbin Institute of Technology,
Harbin, Heilongjiang, China
[2] Post-Doctoral Scientific Research Station in Eastern War Area General
Hospital, Nanjing 210000, China
yangkai4545@163.com
[3] Aviation Machinery Department Army Air Force College,
Beijing 101123, China

Abstract. The classification of architectural style is one of the most challenging problems in architectural history due to its temporal inter-class relationships between different styles and geographical variation within one style. Previous computer version approaches have primarily focused on general classification of multiple architectural styles based on historical age, but very few studies have attempted deep learning to address intra-class classification problems according to geographical location, which might reveal the significance of local evolution and adaption of ancient architectural style. Therefore, we exemplified gothic architecture as a certain genre and leased a new dataset containing gothic architecture in three different countries: France, England, and Italy. Besides, a trained model is susceptible to overfitting due to fecundity of regional parameters and shortcoming of dataset. In this paper, we propose a new approach to accurately classify intra-class variance in the sense of their geographical locations: visualization of Convolutional Neural Network. Experimentation on this dataset shows that the approach of intra-class classification based on local features achieves high classification rate. We also present interpretable explanations for the results, to illustrate architectural indication of intra-class classification.

Keywords: Convolutional Neural Network ·
Architectural Style Classification · Visualization

1 Introduction

Architectural styles are phases of development that are characterized by diverse features like historical periods, regional character, and culture. Whereas most architecture can be generally classified within a chronology of styles, when a certain architectural style spread to other locations, each location developed its own unique characteristics and diverged from those of other countries [1]. Therefore, the intra-class classification according to regions is a tedious task that it has to identify distinguishable local features within common features of the same style.

© Springer Nature Switzerland AG 2019
X. Sun et al. (Eds.): ICAIS 2019, LNCS 11632, pp. 205–216, 2019.
https://doi.org/10.1007/978-3-030-24274-9_18

To the best of our knowledge, the majority of the existing research has been performed on the identification analysis of diverse architectural styles according to building age, and there is community interest in tackling this problem through CNN. Nevertheless, very few researches have further subdivided one style to veraciously define different genres through their local position and unique features. The major research challenge behind this work is whether we can automatically capture these unique local features by CNN based visualization and use them as criteria for intra-class classification. The intra-class classification confronts with an imbalance between the number of diverse local characteristics and the size of standard dataset, thus might cause overfitting of a trained neural network model.

Visualization tools intend to present features through recognizing properties of the input image that had the highest influence on providing the final prediction by the CNN. The essence of the method is that when moving deeper into the network, the feature maps are expected to concentrate on relevant information important for the classification task and discard irrelevant information disturbing the output. Therefore, last convolutional layer should contain the most relevant features (discriminative regional characteristics) to arrive at a particular decision (intra-class classification based on location).

The visualization of Gothic dataset shows that the most relevant elements that determine the output are some complex inter-class features, such as window, gateway, and proportion. Groups of lancet opening windows frequently are applied to English gothic architecture to stress perpendicularity in Fig. 1(a), the triple portal with rich decoration and large rose windows are typical for France to express its flamboyant characteristic in Fig. 1(b), and horizontality in facade proportion is specifically emphasized by Italy to maintain classical proportion in Fig. 1(c) [2]. These features as criterion of intra-class classification correspond with judgment by domain experts.

(a) English   (b) France   (c) Italy

Fig. 1. Gothic building dataset

Although the images are classified correctly, some irrelevant foreground objectives like trees are also regarded as decisive information. The main reason for this error is due to the small size of trained Gothic datasets, which causes network overfitting and further extracts the unrelated features that affect the correct classification of buildings.

In order to reduce overfitting, one method is to exclude pictures with foreground objectives during training. It requires precise visualization judgment of CNN to determine which picture ought to be discarded. For the classification of a small-size dataset, the presented article proposed a network, which extends the dataset, assists the bottom layers to extract architectural features without the interference of non-architectural features, and further capture the refined discriminative characteristics of Gothic architecture in the deeper layers. The results of the experiment have obtained high accuracy.

The contribution of this research is threefold: First, we compile a dataset of gothic buildings from different data sources which contain images from three different European countries and propose an effective network for intra-class classification of architecture in the case of a small size of dataset. Second, we explained the way network learns to detect relevant features for determination of output through convolutional network visualization and the cause of network model overfitting due to irrelevant information within a small number of datasets. Third, our research presents the most relevant cues detected by network visualization for intra-class classification of architecture based on distinguishable local features.

The paper is organized as follows: Sect. 2 discusses related work, Sect. 3 introduce the method of this article and explains theoretical analysis. In Sect. 4 describes results of experiments, and Sect. 5 contains our conclusion.

2 Related Works

2.1 Image Classification

Many recent research of various fields have applied deep learning to tackle image classification tasks. There are some general-purpose networks [3–9] with strong ability to extract features. The method of Dual-Branch Deep Convolution Neural Network [10] has been applied to polarimetric synthetic aperture radar (PolSAR) image classification through extracting polarization features from 6-channel real matrix and spatial information of RGB image. A method based on AlexNet [3] has been proved suitable for solving the microbial classification by Pedraza [11] in his research of Automated Diatom Classification (Part B): A Deep Learning Approach. Convolutional network can also be combined with Joint Bayesian for classification of view-invariant gait recognition [12]. In addition, in the context of medical image classification, there is the use of Transfer learning based on convolutional networks [13] with fine-tuning on already trained models to eliminate the work of training CNN from scratch.

For the classification of architectural style, previous works have adopted several different models. Shalunts [14] in Architectural Style Classification of Building Facade Towers first introduced the method of computer vision for classification of building facade towers, extracting Scale Invariant Feature Transform (SIFT) descriptors and exhibiting histogram of bag of visual words model. Another approach for use in Architectural Style Classification Using Multinomial Latent Logistic Regression [15]. The recent research by Llamas [16], Classification of Architectural Heritage Images Using Deep Learning Techniques, also applied deep learning to the classification of architectural styles, but its classification range is restricted to architecture with outstanding appearance and recognizable ornament, and the network models only use the conventional AlexNet [3] and ResNet [6] models showing that the availability of applying CNN as a method for building classification. Zeppelzauer [17] present a first convolutional neural network method for the automated age estimation of buildings from unconstrained.

2.2 Visualization Method

Although the convolutional network has achieved brilliant results in recent years, the deep understanding of convolutional networks is still limited. Visualization methods can be used to analyze how each color of the input maps to features on different layers. The multi-layered Deconvolutional Network with a novel visualization technique introduced by Zeiler [18] was a landmark approach, showing which parts of input stimuli are of high-performance contribution to classification and activate the feature map through non-parametric view of invariance. Dosovitskiy [19] adopted up-convolutional neural network to study image presentation, extracting input features for each layer into a reconstruction process. The network analyzes the information of the original image contained in each layer by comparing the color, the position and the squared Euclidean distance between the input image and the reconstructed one. Bojarski [20] used visualization method to explain the pavement features extracted by the network to influence the steering of the automatic driving. Recently Selvaraju [21] used the gradients of any target, flowing into final convolutional layer to produce a coarse localization map. And this approach is applicable to a wide variety of CNN model-families.

3 Approach

The intra-class classification of architectural styles is a challenging task because it requires not only to learn a particular type of object (e.g. gothic architecture) but also its local characteristics that distinguish it from other objects of the same style (e.g. gothic architecture of France vs. Gothic architecture of England). It is difficult to use convolutional visualization to form features that can distinguish Gothic buildings in different regions in the case of small-scale datasets because of the serious overfitting. In order to solve this problem, we propose a network structure with two discriminant abilities, which reduces over-fitting by introducing additional data by sharing underlying features.

Besides, we use visualization as an interpretation tool that helps to understand whether the network detects enough effective cues from the input image for classification task. The visualization of Gothic dataset shows the most relevant elements that determine the output. This approach can be regarded as an effective one if the result corresponds with complex inter-class features, such as the three-dimensional triple portals and large rose windows in France, the single portal with side gateways in England, and single gateway in Italy.

3.1 Network Structure

This method applied a double-branch network architecture, which has to complete two classification task simultaneously: determine if the picture is a Gothic building and which country the Gothic building is from. A double-branch network is closely related to visualization of convolution. Our dataset contains images of Gothic buildings from three countries with high resolution: English, France, and Italy. Although it is easy to achieve extremely high accuracy on the training dataset, convolution visualization shows a mismatch between output pixels that contribute most to the predictions made by the CNN and those expected to help classification. Some important pixels are even non-architectural information. This result indicts a serious overfitting problem.

To solve this problem, we propose an innovative network structure as shown in Fig. 2, which can reduce overfitting by introducing datasets that contains a wide range of Gothic buildings without further subdivision, and subsequently enable convolution visualization to detect regional characteristic. We adopted the method of convolution visualization in [20], which averages the feature map and estimates the contribution of each pixel to the final prediction through deconvolution [22] and point-wise multi-plication. The underlying idea of the point-wise multiplication is that pixels with a higher average of the feature maps at each scale are considered relevant pixels. With the use of this method, we have greatly reduced overfitting by sharing the features of bottom layers.

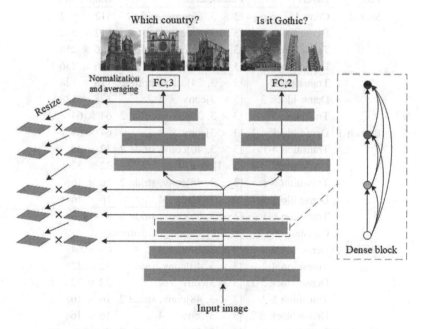

Fig. 2. The classification network structure proposed in this paper

In the right channel, we have ample datasets to solve the overfitting problem due to the easy access to images of Gothic buildings and non-Gothic buildings. When an image of a Gothic building is entered into the network, the pixels that play an important role in the bottom layer will fall on the building. In the left channel, we use subdivided Gothic building data for network training to distinguish typical features of Gothic architecture in different countries. Meantime, we perform visualization of convolution through the left channel. Through the process of sharing features by discriminator, in order to simultaneously satisfy the tasks of the two channels, the pixels with important contributions will be concentrated on the entire Gothic building. For the unique eigenvalues of the left channel, relevant pixels will focus on the most significant differences among Gothic architectures in different countries, whereas the common features of Gothic buildings will be ignored. For the multiplication in the visualization process, those common features will be ignored, but the features in bottom layers are used to greatly reduce overfitting.

For further enhancement of the prediction performance, we also adopted dense network [7] connection to obtain high accuracy of identification with a few feature maps, and thus enable the network less susceptible to overfitting. Specific network structure and parameters are shown in Table 1.

Table 1. The architecture and parameters of proposed network

Part	Layers	Parameters	Output size
Shared	Conv 1	[3 × 3, 8]conv, stride 1	512 × 512
	Dense block 1	[3 × 3]conv × 4	512 × 512
	Transition 1	[3 × 3, 8]conv, stride 2	256 × 256
	Dense block 2	[3 × 3]conv × 4	256 × 256
	Transition 2	[3 × 3, 24]conv, stride 2	128 × 128
	Dense block 3	[3 × 3]conv × 4	128 × 128
	Transition 3	[3 × 3, 32]conv, stride 2	64 × 64
Branch 1	Dense block 4-1	[3 × 3]conv × 4	64 × 64
	Transition 4-1	[3 × 3, 40]conv, stride 2	32 × 32
	Dense block 5-1	[3×3]conv × 4	32 × 32
	Transition 5-1	[3 × 3, 48]conv, stride 2	16 × 16
	Dense block 6-1	[3 × 3]conv × 4	16 × 16
	Transition 6-1	[3 × 3, 56]conv, stride 2	8 × 8
	Classification 1	3d fully-connected, softmax	
Branch 2	Dense block 4-2	[3 × 3]conv × 4	64 × 64
	Transition 4-2	[3 × 3, 40]conv, stride 2	32 × 32
	Dense block 5-2	[3 × 3]conv × 4	32 × 32
	Transition 5-2	[3 × 3, 48]conv, stride 2	16 × 16
	Dense block 6-2	[3 × 3]conv × 4	16 × 16
	Transition 6-2	[3 × 3, 56]conv, stride 2	8 × 8
	Classification 2	2d fully-conneted, softmax	

3.2 Training

For classification, we simply use cross-entropy loss, but the dual classification task makes the situation slightly complicated.

We define the cross-entropy loss of the left channel as follows, which is used to train the network to identify which country the Gothic architecture originated from.

$$L_{left} = -\log \frac{exp(leftout_{label})}{\sum_j exp(leftout_j)} \qquad (1)$$

The leftout is the output result of the left channel of the network structure, judging whether the image comes from Britain, France or Italy. The label represents the number of the real category.

We define the cross-entropy loss of the right channel as follows. It is responsible for training network learning to determine whether a picture is Gothic.

$$L_{right} = -\log \frac{exp(rightout_{label})}{\sum_j exp(rightout_j)} \qquad (2)$$

Since we train on small-scale data, it is necessary to use regularization to reduce over-fitting. We add L2 to our losses to punish:

$$L_w = \sum_{i=1}^{n} \|w_i\|^2 \qquad (3)$$

When we train the network, we use two data sets. One data set contains three national Gothic buildings, and the other includes two types: Gothic and non-Gothic buildings.

When training the pictures in the first data set, we train two classification tasks, and the final loss function is:

$$loss = L_{left} + L_{right} + \lambda \times L_w \qquad (4)$$

When we train the second data set, which includes non-Gothic architecture and Gothic architecture without knowing the source, we only train the right channel of the network structure to obtain better visualization results by sharing the underlying features. The loss function is as follows:

$$loss = L_{right} + \lambda \times L_w \qquad (5)$$

The λ is the coefficient of L2 penalty, and the value of λ is equal to 1×10^{-5}.

We use Adam optimizer [23] to train the network. The learning rate is set to 1×10^{-3}, batch size is set to 4, betas1 is set to 0.9, betas2 is set to 0.999, eps is set to 1×10^{-8}, and the network is trained 100000 times.

During the training process, we cut the input pictures into as large a square as possible, and adjust the size of the pictures to 512×512. Although the network is not fully convoluted, we can still visualize images of any size, because the visualization process does not involve full connectivity.

Because of the small size of the data sets, we enhance the data sets in training, including random image flipping, brightness and contrast adjustment.

3.3 CNN Visualization

We use the method in [20] to visualize convolution, and use normalization to improve the visualization effect. The method proposed is a process from coarse to fine, in which the average value of the feature map after rectified linear unit [24] is obtained. Finally, the average feature maps are enlarged by deconvolution and multiplied by the average feature map of the previous layer, and the process is repeated until input.

We make a slight improvement on this method, that is, normalize each scale of the feature map before calculating the average value of the feature map, so as to reduce the influence of the difference of magnification multiples between different channels on the average value. We will verify this effect in experiments.

4 Experiment

4.1 Dataset

We did not find the existing data set based on the national classification of Gothic architecture. We have produced a small data set for Gothic architecture classifications, including Gothic architecture in Britain, France and Italy. The data set includes 508 images, 196 from Britain, 217 from France and 95 from Italy. We divide the data group into training set and test set. The training set includes 375 pictures and the test set includes 133 pictures.

We have also produced another dataset, which is divided into two types: Gothic architecture and non-Gothic architecture. Among them, non-Gothic architecture is mostly modern architecture. This dataset is used to train whether the Gothic architecture is classified. Since there is no need to subdivide Gothic architecture, the dataset includes nearly 5000 pictures. As Fig. 3 shows, first row in the picture is Gothic architecture, and second row in the picture is non Gothic architecture.

Fig. 3. Gothic architecture and non-Gothic architecture

4.2 Visualization Result Analysis

We performed our intra-class classification experiment using dataset containing Gothic architecture from three different countries: English, France, and Italy. The results are mentioned in Fig. 4. The most relevant information captured by the CNN correspond with the distinguishable local clues used by domain experts for geographical classification. For English Gothic architecture, groups of lancet windows of very acute proportions on the building facades are captured as important indication clues. Experiment shows that French Gothic architecture are defined by the large rose windows, whereas the identifiable information for Italian Gothic architecture shows that they succeed the classical proportion of façade with a reduced size of rose windows and lack of emphasis on verticality.

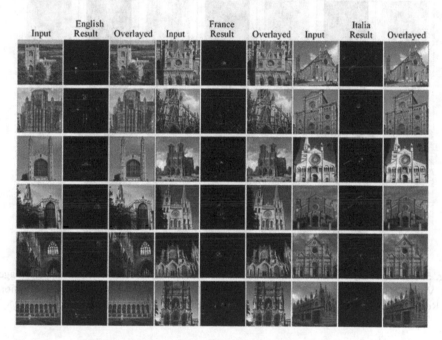

Fig. 4. Experimental results based on CNN visualization

4.3 Ablation Experiment

We use ablation experiments to verify the role of bifurcated network structures and normalization in visualization. Our ablation experiment consists of two parts: (1) training with a complete network, but in the visualization process, the normalized steps for each channel are removed; (2) training only for the left channel.

As shown in Fig. 5. Normalization plays some roles in the visualization of feature maps. The (b) in the figure is the result of normalization, (d) in the figure is not normalized. Although the results are highly similar in most regions, they are not visible in many light gray areas without normalization. Different channels of feature maps represent different features. If the average value is calculated directly without normalization, some large-scale feature maps will play a greater role in the visualization results, leading to some features may be ignored.

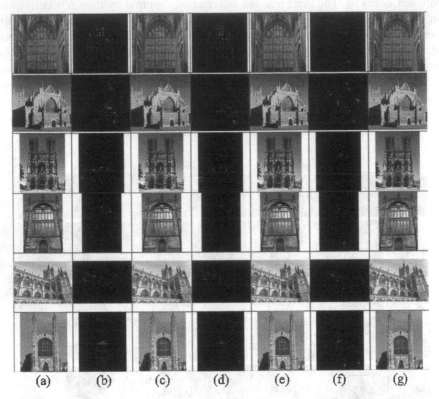

Fig. 5. Ablation experiment. (a) Image input. (b) Visualization result. (c) Overlapped image. (d) Visualization result without normalization. (e) Overlapped image without normalization. (f) Result without bifurcation network. (g) Overlapped image without bifurcation network.

4.4 Classification Accuracy

Although our main task is to find features through convolution visualization, the accuracy of classification is still an important indicator. We compare our network structure with VGG-16 and ResNet-18. It is worth mentioning that because of the small size of our data set, the number of network parameters and feature graphs is much smaller than both. We also compared the results of training set and test set to show the situation of over fitting. For our method, we also provide a version using only left channel training.

From the Table 2, we can see that the accuracy of our training set is lower than VGG-16 and ResNet-18 because of the small scale of our network. However, our network structure has a good performance on the test set. After introducing the second classification tasks to share the underlying features, it also alleviated the effect of over fitting.

Table 2. Comparison with different methods.

Algorithm	Training	Test
VGG-16	97.6%	77.4%
ResNet-18	98.4%	78.9%
Ours-left	96.5%	79.7%
Ours	94.6%	81.2%

5 Conclusions

The article presents with a method of intra-class classification of Gothic architecture according to geographical location. We introduce a method of visualizing identifiable parts of input image that have high influence on the output of CNN. And we propose a double-branch network that uses additional data sets to assist the network in extracting correct features, avoiding network overfitting due to small-scale data sets. The performance evaluation on a self-collected image database, including a variety of gothic architecture of different locations, reported acceptably high classification rate. Future work includes a similar method that can perform intra-class classification of other different architectural styles based on geography, and thus contribute to study of the local impact on the adaption of architectural styles in different countries.

References

1. Swanson, R.N.: The formation of English Gothic: architecture and identity. By Peter Draper. Heythrop J. **52**(3), 480–481 (2011)
2. Frankl, P., Crossley, P.: Gothic Architecture. Yale University Press (2000)
3. Krizhevsky, A., Sutskever, I., Hinton, G.E.: ImageNet classification with deep convolutional neural networks. In: Advances in Neural Information Processing Systems, pp. 1097–1105 (2012)
4. Simonyan, K., Zisserman, A.: Very deep convolutional networks for large-scale image recognition. arXiv preprint arXiv:1409.1556 (2014)
5. Szegedy, C., et al.: Going deeper with convolutions. In: Proceedings of the IEEE Conference on Computer Vision and Pattern Recognition, pp. 1–9 (2015)
6. He, K., Zhang, X., Ren, S., Sun, J.: Deep residual learning for image recognition. In: Proceedings of the IEEE Conference on Computer Vision and Pattern Recognition, pp. 770–778 (2016)
7. Huang, G., Liu, Z., van der Maaten, L., Weinberger, K.Q.: Densely connected convolutional networks. In: Proceedings of the IEEE Conference on Computer Vision and Pattern Recognition, pp. 4700–4708 (2017)
8. Zhou, S., Liang, W., Li, J., Kim, J.: Improved VGG model for road traffic sign recognition. CMC: Comput. Mater. Continua **57**(1), 11–24 (2018)
9. Cui, Q., McIntosh, S., Sun, H.: Identifying materials of photographic images and photorealistic computer generated graphics based on deep CNNs. CMC: Comput. Mater. Continua **055**(2), 229–240 (2018)
10. Gao, F., Huang, T., Wang, J., et al.: Dual-branch deep convolution neural network for polarimetric SAR image classification. Appl. Sci. **7**(5), 447 (2017)

11. Pedraza, A., Bueno, G., Deniz, O., et al.: Automated diatom classification (Part B): a deep learning approach. Appl. Sci. **7**(5), 460 (2017)
12. Li, C., Min, X., Sun, S., et al.: DeepGait: a learning deep convolutional representation for view-invariant gait recognition using joint bayesian. Appl. Sci. **7**(3), 210 (2017)
13. Tajbakhsh, N., Shin, J.Y., Gurudu, S.R., et al.: Convolutional neural networks for medical image analysis: full training or fine tuning? IEEE Trans. Med. Imaging **35**(5), 1299–1312 (2016)
14. Shalunts, G.: Architectural style classification of building facade towers. In: Bebis, G., et al. (eds.) ISVC 2015. LNCS, vol. 9474, pp. 285–294. Springer, Cham (2015). https://doi.org/10.1007/978-3-319-27857-5_26
15. Xu, Z., Tao, D., Zhang, Ya., Wu, J., Tsoi, A.C.: Architectural style classification using multinomial latent logistic regression. In: Fleet, D., Pajdla, T., Schiele, B., Tuytelaars, T. (eds.) ECCV 2014. LNCS, vol. 8689, pp. 600–615. Springer, Cham (2014). https://doi.org/10.1007/978-3-319-10590-1_39
16. Llamas, J., Lerones, P., Medina, R., et al.: Classification of architectural heritage images using deep learning techniques. Appl. Sci. **7**(10), 992 (2017)
17. Zeppelzauer, M., Despotovic, M., Sakeena, M., et al.: Automatic prediction of building age from photographs. In: Proceedings of the 2018 ACM on International Conference on Multimedia Retrieval, pp. 126–134. ACM (2018)
18. Zeiler, Matthew D., Fergus, R.: Visualizing and understanding convolutional networks. In: Fleet, D., Pajdla, T., Schiele, B., Tuytelaars, T. (eds.) ECCV 2014. LNCS, vol. 8689, pp. 818–833. Springer, Cham (2014). https://doi.org/10.1007/978-3-319-10590-1_53
19. Dosovitskiy, A., Brox, T.: Inverting visual representations with convolutional networks. In: Proceedings of the IEEE Conference on Computer Vision and Pattern Recognition, pp. 4829–4837 (2016)
20. Bojarski, M., Yeres, P., Choromanska, A., et al.: Explaining how a deep neural network trained with end-to-end learning steers a car. arXiv preprint arXiv:1704.07911 (2017)
21. Selvaraju, R.R., Cogswell, M., Das, A., et al.: Grad-CAM: visual explanations from deep networks via gradient-based localization. In: ICCV, pp. 618–626 (2017)
22. Noh, H., Hong, S., Han, B.: Learning deconvolution network for semantic segmentation. In: Proceedings of the IEEE International Conference on Computer Vision, pp. 520–1528 (2015)
23. Kingma, D.P., Ba, J.: Adam: a method for stochastic optimization. arXiv preprint arXiv: 1412.6980 (2014)
24. He, K., Zhang, X., Ren, S., et al.: Delving deep into rectifiers: Surpassing human-level performance on ImageNet classification. In: Proceedings of the IEEE International Conference on Computer Vision, pp. 1026–1034 (2015)

MSE-Net: Pedestrian Attribute Recognition Using MLSC and SE-Blocks

Miaomiao Lou, Zhenxia Yu$^{(\boxtimes)}$, Feng Guo, and Xiaoqiang Zheng

School of Computer Science, Chengdu University of Information Technology,
Chengdu, China
zhenxiayu@cuit.edu.cn

Abstract. Pedestrian attributes recognition draw significant interest in the field of intelligent video surveillance. Despite that the convolutional neural networks are remarkable in learning discriminative features from images, the learning of comprehensive features of pedestrians for fine-grained tasks remains an challenging problem. In this paper, we proposed a novel multi-level skip connections and squeeze-and-excitation convolutional neural network (MSE-Net), which is composed of multi-level skip connections (MLSC) and Squeeze-and-Excitation blocks (SE-Blocks). Additionally, the proposed MSE-Net brings unique advantages: (1) Multi-level skip connections (MLSC) obtain more meaningful fine-grained information from both the low-level and high-level features and can maintain gradient flow in the network. For fine-grained attributes, such as glasses and accessories, MLSC retains fine-grained information and local information from shallow layers; (2) Squeeze-and-Excitation blocks (SE-blocks) strengthen the sensitivity of the network to information, compress the features, and perceive global receptive field. It can select important feature channels, and then weights the previous features by multiplication and then recalibrates the original features in the channel dimension. Intensive experimental results have been provided to prove that the proposed network outperforms the state-of-the-art methods on RAP dataset, and the robustness against predicting positive and negative samples in each attribute.

Keywords: Pedestrian attributes recognition ·
Multi-level skip connections · Squeeze-and-Excitation block

1 Introduction

Analysing pedestrian attributes, such as gender, age and clothes types, have attracted great research attention due to the meaningful clues for smart video surveillance systems in recent years. For example, attributes can serve as mid-level representations of a pedestrian to improve the accuracy of re-identification effectively [1–4], and pedestrian retrieval [5].

Recently, deep convolutional neural networks (DCNNs) have been widely applied for pedestrian attribute recognition [6–10]. However, to enhance the performance of pedestrian attribute recognition, there are still a number of problems

© Springer Nature Switzerland AG 2019
X. Sun et al. (Eds.): ICAIS 2019, LNCS 11632, pp. 217–226, 2019.
https://doi.org/10.1007/978-3-030-24274-9_19

worthy of further studies. Firstly, fine-grained attributes (i.e., glasses and accessories) are directly hard to recognize due to the small size of positive samples. Secondly, the convergence speed of each attribute is different, which causes different attributes to affect the effect of identifying other attributes during the network training process. Thirdly, the large intra-class variations in attribute categories (e.g., appearance diversity and appearance ambiguity).

Considering the above difficulties, we proposed a novel multi-level skip connections and squeeze-and-excitation convolutional neural network (MSE-Net), which is composed of multi-level skip connections (MLSC) and Squeeze-and-Excitation blocks (SE-Blocks). In each original residual block of ResNet50 [11], the size of the feature map will gradually decrease due to the convolution of the stride, which means that the local information will be gradually lost. The MLSC module passes the features in each block to the next convolution layer through element-wise sum to the next convolutional layer, ensuring that the local features do not lose too much due to changes in the feature channels in the block. Simultaneously, it combines the characteristics of the first layer of feature information of each stage with the features of the last layer, retaining the fine-grained information of shallow layers, and retaining the local information of fine-grained attributes such as glasses and accessories.

Before classifying each attribute, we adopt a fully connected (FC) layer to isolate the impact between each attribute, avoiding the situation where each attribute converges differently during network training.

SE-Blocks fuse the scaled weighted features and the input feature in the block by element-wise sum, and then pass them to the next SE-Block. They strengthen the sensitivity of the network to attributes information, compress the attributes features, and perceive global receptive field. It can select important feature channels, and then weight the previous features by multiplication and then recalibrates the original features in the channel dimension, reducing inter-class variations between attributes due to network downsampling.

2   Related Work

The works of recognizing attributes of persons such as facial and clothing attributes have received great attention during the past few years. Most of existing pedestrian attribute recognition methods are directly based on the full human body. Layne et al. [12,13] uses support vector machines (SVM) to identify pedestrian attributes [12] such as backpacks and genders, and then uses these pedestrian attribute information to assist in pedestrian recognition. In order to solve the problem of attribute recognition in mixed scenes, Zhu et al. [14,15] introduced the Apis database and used boosting algorithm to identify pedestrian attributes. Deng et al. [16] utilized the intersection kernel SVM model proposed by Maji et al. [17] to recognize attributes. The Markov Random Field (MRF) was adopted to make a smooth on attribute prediction. However, these methods use manual extraction of pedestrian features, and manual extraction of features requires human experience. In addition, these methods also ignore the association between attribute features. With the development of convolutional neural networks (CNN), CNNs have achieved great success in pedestrian attribute recognition based on full body. ACN model proposed by Patrick et al. [18] to jointly learn all the attributes in a single model, and shows that parameter sharing can improve recognition accuracy over independently trained models. This routine is also adopted in the DeepMAR model proposed in [19].

Differ from above methods, other methods make use of part information to help improving the attribute recognition accuracy. In [20], part models like DPM and poselets are used for aligning input patches for CNNs. Gaurav et al. [21] propose an expanded parts model to learn a collection of part templates which can score an image partially with most discriminative regions for classification. The MLCNN [22] divides a human body into 15 parts and train CNN models for each of them, then choose part of the models to contribute to the recognition of an attribute, according to the spatial constraint prior of it. However the MLCNN could not cope well with the occlusion and large pose variance. The DeepMAR* model [23] takes three block images as input in addition to the whole body image, which correspond to the head-shoulder part, upper body and lower body of a pedestrian respectively. The WPAL-network [8] make use of flexible spatial pyramid pooling layers to help locating mid-level features of some attributes in only local patches rather than the whole image.

3   MSE-Net for Pedestrian Attribute Recognition

3.1   Network Architecture

The framework of the MSE-Net is illustrated in Fig. 1. The trunk convolution layers arc derived from the ResNet50 [11], which reaches a high accuracy for classification task with smaller number of layers. Considering the network prone to overfitting, the number of feature channels used in MSE-Net is half that of the original network.

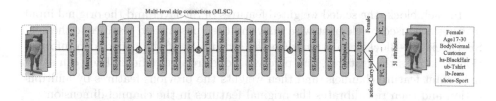

Fig. 1. Structure of the proposed network. The blue "S" denotes element-wise sum of feature maps. The green brace denotes MLSC modules. The red box represents the network's prediction of the pedestrian attributes. (Color figure online)

In the experiment, we use zero padding at each convolutional layer so that the size of the feature maps is only changed by stride convolutions. The PReLU activation function [24] is used in the network, which is a parameterized activation function. Each convolutional layer in the network is followed by an activation layer and batch normalization layer [25].

3.2 Squeeze-and-Excitation Block

As shown in Fig. 2, MSE-Net consists of two SE-Block, which are SE-Conv block and SE-Identity block. These blocks are identical in that a SE-layer [26] is added before element-wise sum. The difference between these blocks is that the size of original features are reduced by stride convolution in SE-Conv block. SE-layer can improve the representational power of a network by explicitly modelling the interdependencies between the channels of its convolutional features, which can learn to use global information to selectively emphasise informative features and suppress less useful ones.

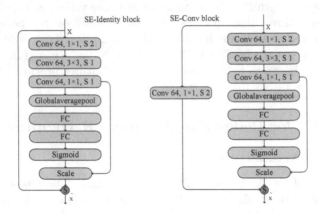

Fig. 2. Structure of SE-Block, which contains SE-Conv block and SE-Identity block. The blue "S" denotes element-wise sum of feature maps. (Color figure online)

In each block, the scaled weighted features of SE-layer and the original input features are fused by element-wise sum, and then pass mixed features to the next SE-Block. SE-Blocks can strengthen the sensitivity of the network to information, compress the features, and perceive global receptive field. They can select important feature channels, and then weights the previous features by multiplication and then re-calibrates the original features in the channel dimension.

3.3 Multi-level Skip Connections

In Fig. 1, the role of the MLSC module is to pass the features of SE-Conv block to the features of final SE-Identity block by element-wise sum. MLSC can reuse features so that local features in the block are not lost too much due to changes in feature channels caused by convolutional layers. More specifically, in each block, after reducing the size of the feature maps by stride convolution or maxpooling, we pass the resized feature maps to the end of SE-Identity block to reuse feature, obtains more meaningful fine-grained information from both the low-level and high-level features, and maintain gradient flow in the network.

In the end, we add a fully connected layer (FC), which outputs 128 dimensional feature vector. At this point, we split the network into 51 separate branches corresponding to the different attributes classification tasks. Finally, a fully connected layer is added to each of the branch to predict the each attributes classification task labels.

4   Experiments

4.1   Dataset

The RAP dataset is the largest pedestrian attribute dataset so far, including 41,585 samples with 72 attributes. As implemented in [23], 51 binary attributes are used for training and evaluating. In the experiment, images are zoomed to a fixed-size of 224×224 without resizing or warping. A few samples at different viewpoints in the dataset are shown in Fig. 3.

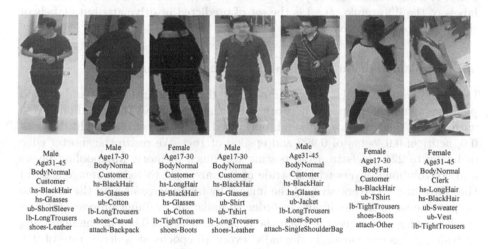

Fig. 3. Some samples at different viewpoints in RAP dataset.

4.2   Evaluation Protocols

We adopt the mean accuracy (mA) and the example-based criteria as evaluation metrics. MA calculates the ratio of the positive and negative sample pairs of each attribute separately, and then averages the accuracy of this attribute, and then averages all the attributes. The mA is formulated as:

$$mA = \frac{1}{N} \sum_{i=1}^{L} (\frac{|TP_i|}{|P_i|} + \frac{|TN_i|}{|N_i|}), \tag{1}$$

where N is the number of examples; L is the number of attributes; TP_i and P_i are correctly predicted positive examples and the number of positive examples; TN_i and N_i are correctly predicted negative examples and the number of negative examples.

The example-based evaluation criteria is defined as:

$$Accuracy_{exam} = \frac{1}{N} \sum_{i=1}^{L} \frac{|Y_i \bigcap f(x_i)|}{|Y_i \bigcup f(x_i)|} \tag{2}$$

$$Precision_{exam} = \frac{1}{N} \sum_{i=1}^{L} \frac{|Y_i \bigcap f(x_i)|}{|f(x_i)|} \tag{3}$$

$$Recall_{exam} = \frac{1}{N} \sum_{i=1}^{L} \frac{|Y_i \bigcap f(x_i)|}{|Y_i|} \tag{4}$$

$$F1 = \frac{2 * Precision_{exam} * Recall_{exam}}{Precision_{exam} + Recall_{exam}} \tag{5}$$

where N is the number of samples, Y_i is the set of ground-truth positive attribute labels of the ith sample, $f(x_i)$ is the set of predicted positive attribute labels of the ith sample, respectively.

4.3   Implementation Details and Parameter Settings

In the experiment, MSE-Net was implemented by keras framework and python packages. And the proposed network was trained on a NVIDIA GeForce M40 with 11 GB Memory by end-to-end, optimized by Adam with a weight decay of 0.0, $beta_1$ of 0.9, $beta_2$ of 0.999 and epsilon of 1e-8. We resize the shorter edge of image to 224 pixels to avoid costing too much memory. Maxpooling layers and convolutional layers with a stride of two are used to reduce image size. In the convolutional layers, we pad the images by filling zeros around the image to output the same size as input. In order to make the training process stable, a small learning rate is used to train the network, which is 0.001 at the beginning of training was exponentially degraded every 10 epochs at a decay rate of 0.9. The total epoch is 100 and the batch size is 64. In the training process, the loss function of each attribute uses a binary cross-entropy loss function, which is shown in (6). The total loss is the sum of the binary cross-entropy losses of the 51 attributes.

$$Loss = \frac{1}{N} \sum_{i=1}^{N} (-y_i^{truth} log y_i^{pred} - (1 - y_i^{truth}) log(1 - y_i^{pred})), \tag{6}$$

where N is the number of samples ($N = 8317$), y_i^{truth} is the ground truth of each attribute, y_i^{pred} is the probability of each attribute prediction.

4.4   Comparison with State-of-the-Art Automatic Methods

For comparisons, three approaches presented in [23] are used as benchmarks, including, the first three models are based on SVM classifier with hand-crafted features (ELF-mm [27,28]) and deep-learned features (FC7-mm and FC6-mm) respectively. DeepMAR [19] and WPAL-network [8] are CNN models that achieved good performances by joint training the multiple attributes.

The performance on the RAP dataset is listed in Table 1. The baseline ResNet50 and the proposed final model (MSE-Net) outperform the state-of-the-art methods in accuracy. We can find the MSE-Net performs quite well in terms of the metric of accuracy, precision, and f1-score, while shows some weakness as evaluated with mA. The higher accuracy means that our model can classify pedestrian attributes in all validation samples without considering positive and negative samples. When considering positive and negative samples, F1 score is the harmonic average of precision and recall, which can evaluate the classification effect and stability of the model. In terms of the mA criteria, which is less affected by true alarms on classes with fewer samples than their opposite class. Considering that an attribute contains a large number of negative samples, when the model make wrong prediction for negative samples, and correct prediction for positive samples, the precision is low, and the recall is very high. Thus $\frac{|TP|}{|P|}$ term is big, $\frac{|TN|}{|N|}$ is very small, so mA is very high, which can demonstrate the instability of the model. However, MSE-Net is a stability deep architecture, which can provide stable predictions on both positive samples and negative samples in an attribute.

Table 1. This table shows performance of 6 benchmark algorithms list in [8], the proposed network models without SE-blocks or MLSC modules and the proposed network models mentioned in this work, which evaluated on RAP dataset using mA and example-based evaluation criteria.

Methods	mA	Acc	Prec	Rec	F1
ELF-mm	69.94	29.29	32.84	71.18	44.95
FC7-mm	72.28	31.72	35.75	71.78	47.73
FC6-mm	73.32	33.37	37.57	73.23	49.66
Deep-Mar	73.79	62.02	74.92	76.21	75.56
WPAL-GMP	**81.25**	50.30	57.17	78.39	66.12
WPAL-FSPP	79.48	53.30	60.82	**78.80**	68.65
ResNet50	69.57	60.30	76.88	71.59	74.14
ResNet50(SE)	70.08	60.92	77.30	72.07	74.59
ResNet50(MLSC)	69.87	61.02	77.55	72.01	74.68
MSE-Net	71.12	**62.43**	**78.82**	72.94	**75.77**

As can be seen from the last four results from Table 1, the result of ResNet50 with SE-blocks or MLSC is better than the original ResNet50, and the MSE-Net based on ResNet50 is better than ResNet50 (SE) and ResNet50 (MLSC). In means that the MLSC and SE-Blocks have achieved the purpose of design, MSE-Net outperforms the state-of-the-art methods with higher accuracy and more stable precision and recall. In Fig. 4, we draw the score range of evaluation metrics of the mA and example-based criteria based on MSE-Net.

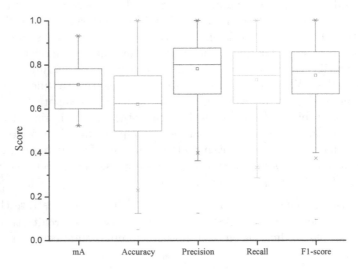

Fig. 4. Classification performance of the mA and example-based criteria based on MSE-Net.

Fig. 5. Some attributes recognition results from MSE-NET on testing RAP dataset.

Figure 5 shows some attributes recognition results from MSE-Net on testing RAP dataset. As can be seen from Fig. 5, the fifth column and the eighth column are the same image at different viewpoint, but MSE-Net can also make similar and correct predictions for this sample. The content below each image is the prediction of corresponding attribute, where the red attribute are represented as the fine-grained attribute, such as glasses, hats, and hair. MSE-Net retains fine-grained feature from shallow layers to correctly predict these fine-grained attributes by using MLSC.

5   Conclusion

In this paper, we present a novel deep architecture called MSE-Net with MLSC and SE-Blocks for pedestrian attribute recognition. MLSC can ensures that local features in the block does not excessively lost due to changes in feature channels. For fine-grained attributes, such as glasses and accessories, MLSC retains fine-grained information and local information from shallow layers. SE-Blocks can strengthen the sensitivity of the network to information, compress the features, and perceive global receptive field. Experimental evaluations have manifested the effectiveness of the MSE-Net compared with a wide range of state-of-the-art pedestrian attribute and multi-label classification methods. In the future, MSE-Net will be validated on other pedestrian datasets. We plan to conduct further research on this in the future.

References

1. Li, A., Liu, L., Wang, K., Liu, S., Yan, S.: Clothing attributes assisted person reidentification. IEEE Trans. Circuits Syst. Video Technol. **25**(5), 869–878 (2015)
2. Peng, P., Tian, Y., Xiang, T., Wang, Y., Huang, T.: Joint learning of semantic and latent attributes. In: Leibe, B., Matas, J., Sebe, N., Welling, M. (eds.) ECCV 2016. LNCS, vol. 9908, pp. 336–353. Springer, Cham (2016). https://doi.org/10.1007/978-3-319-46493-0_21
3. Reid, D.A., Nixon, M.S., Stevenage, S.V.: Soft biometrics; human identification using comparative descriptions. IEEE Trans. Pattern Anal. Mach. Intell. **36**(6), 1216 (2014)
4. Su, C., Zhang, S., Xing, J., Gao, W., Tian, Q.: Multi-type attributes driven multi-camera person re-identification. Pattern Recogn. **75**, 77–89 (2017)
5. Sun, Y., Zheng, L., Deng, W., Wang, S.: Svdnet for pedestrian retrieval. In: IEEE International Conference on Computer Vision, pp. 3820–3828 (2017)
6. Hall, D., Perona, P.: Fine-grained classification of pedestrians in video: benchmark and state of the art. In: Computer Vision and Pattern Recognition (2015)
7. Zhu, J., Liao, S., Lei, Z., Li, S.Z.: Multi-label convolutional neural network based pedestrian attribute classification. Image Vis. Comput. **58**(C), 224–229 (2017)
8. Zhou, Y., et al.: Weakly-supervised learning of mid-level features for pedestrian attribute recognition and localization. In: BMVC (2017)
9. Lin, Y.: Weighted sparse image classification based on low rank representation. Comput. Mater. Continua **56**(1), 91–105 (2018)
10. Fang, W., Zhang, F., Sheng, V.S., Ding, Y.: A method for improving CNN-based image recognition using dcgan. Comput. Mater. Continua **57**, 167–178 (2018)

11. He, K., Zhang, X., Ren, S., Sun, J.: Deep residual learning for image recognition. In: Proceedings of the IEEE Conference on Computer Vision and Pattern Recognition, pp. 770–778 (2016)
12. Layne, R., Hospedales, T.M., Gong, S.: Towards person identification and re-identification with attributes. In: Fusiello, A., Murino, V., Cucchiara, R. (eds.) ECCV 2012. LNCS, vol. 7583, pp. 402–412. Springer, Heidelberg (2012). https://doi.org/10.1007/978-3-642-33863-2_40
13. Layne, R., Hospedales, T.M., Gong, S., Mary, Q.: Person re-identification by attributes. In: BMVC, p. 8 (2012)
14. Zhu, J., Liao, S., Lei, Z., Yi, D., Li, S.Z.: Pedestrian attribute classification in surveillance: database and evaluation. In: IEEE International Conference on Computer Vision Workshops, pp. 331–338 (2013)
15. Zhu, J., Liao, S., Lei, Z., Li, S.Z.: Multi-label convolutional neural network based pedestrian attribute classification. Image Vis. Comput. **58**, 224–229 (2017)
16. Deng, Y., Luo, P., Chen, C.L., Tang, X.: Pedestrian attribute recognition at far distance. In: ACM International Conference on Multimedia. pp. 789–792 (2014)
17. Maji, S., Berg, A.C., Malik, J.: Classification using intersection kernel support vector machines is efficient. In: IEEE Conference on Computer Vision and Pattern Recognition, CVPR 2008, pp. 1–8 (2008)
18. Sudowe, P., Spitzer, H., Leibe, B.: Person attribute recognition with a jointly-trained holistic CNN model. In: IEEE International Conference on Computer Vision Workshop, pp. 329–337 (2015)
19. Li, D., Chen, X., Huang, K.: Multi-attribute learning for pedestrian attribute recognition in surveillance scenarios. In: 2015 3rd IAPR Asian Conference on Pattern Recognition (ACPR), pp. 111–115 (2015)
20. Zhang, N., Paluri, M., Ranzato, M., Darrell, T., Bourdev, L.: Panda: pose aligned networks for deep attribute modeling. In: Proceedings of the IEEE Conference on Computer Vision and Pattern Recognition, pp. 1637–1644 (2014)
21. Sharma, G., Jurie, F., Schmid, C.: Expanded parts model for human attribute and action recognition in still images. In: 2013 IEEE Conference on Computer Vision and Pattern Recognition, pp. 652–659 (2013)
22. Zhu, J., Liao, S., Yi, D., Lei, Z., Li, S.Z.: Multi-label CNN based pedestrian attribute learning for soft biometrics. In: International Conference on Biometrics, pp. 535–540 (2015)
23. Li, D., Zhang, Z., Chen, X., Ling, H., Huang, K.: A richly annotated dataset for pedestrian attribute recognition. arXiv preprint arXiv:1603.07054 (2016)
24. He, K., Zhang, X., Ren, S., Sun, J.: Delving deep into rectifiers: surpassing human-level performance on ImageNet classification. In: Proceedings of the IEEE International Conference on Computer Vision, pp. 1026–1034 (2015)
25. Ioffe, S., Szegedy, C.: Batch normalization: accelerating deep network training by reducing internal covariate shift. arXiv preprint arXiv:1502.03167 pp. 448–456 (2015)
26. Hu, J., Shen, L., Sun, G.: Squeeze-and-excitation networks. arXiv preprint arXiv:1709.01507 (2017)
27. Gray, D., Tao, H.: Viewpoint invariant pedestrian recognition with an ensemble of localized features. In: Forsyth, D., Torr, P., Zisserman, A. (eds.) ECCV 2008. LNCS, vol. 5302, pp. 262–275. Springer, Heidelberg (2008). https://doi.org/10.1007/978-3-540-88682-2_21
28. Prosser, B.J., Zheng, W.S., Gong, S., Xiang, T., Mary, Q.: Person re-identification by support vector ranking. In: BMVC, p. 6 (2010)

CBAM-GAN: Generative Adversarial Networks Based on Convolutional Block Attention Module

Bing Ma[1], Xiaoru Wang[1(✉)], Heng Zhang[1], Fu Li[2],
and Jiawang Dan[1]

[1] Beijing Key Laboratory of Network System and Network Culture,
Beijing University of Posts and Telecommunications, Beijing 100876, China
{bma,wxr,zh2015211203,type00a}@bupt.edu.cn
[2] Department of Electrical and Computer Engineering,
Portland States University, Portland, USA
lif@pdx.edu

Abstract. Generating images using generative adversarial networks (GAN) is one of the research hotspots. The traditional convolutional GAN treats spatial and channel-wise features equally, which causes the lack of flexibility in extracting features from the discriminator and the generator. To address the issue, we propose generative adversarial networks based on convolutional block attention module (CBAM-GAN) in this paper. CBAM-GAN adds the convolutional block attention module after some convolution operators to adaptively rescale spatial and channel-wise features, which can enhance salient regions and extract more detail features. We apply the network framework of CBAM-GAN to popular GAN models and do an empirical study on MNIST and CIFAR-10 datasets. Experiments show that our model can significantly improve the quality of generated images compared with the traditional convolutional GAN.

Keywords: Generative adversarial networks ·
Convolutional block attention module · Image generation

1 Introduction

Generative adversarial networks (GAN [1]) has become the most popular generative model since 2014. GANs can not only generate images with the same label (CGAN [2]), capture the semantic features of images (InfoGAN [3]), but also generate super-resolution images (SRGAN [4]), achieve image style transfer (CycleGAN [5]), generate clear images according to textual descriptions (StackGAN [6]) and so on. These image generation tasks can be implemented based on deep convolutional GAN (DCGAN [7]). It replaces the fully connected network in the original GAN with the convolutional network to train GAN model. DCGAN has a wide range of applications in the field of image processing, such as embedding image [31] and image recognition [31].

However, DCGAN still has the possibility of generating poor images. This is due to the limitations of the convolutional network itself. Firstly, the convolutional network is susceptible to the size of convolution kernels. Small convolution kernels are difficult to

X. Sun et al. (Eds.): ICAIS 2019, LNCS 11632, pp. 227–236, 2019.
https://doi.org/10.1007/978-3-030-24274-9_20

find dependencies across different images regions, while large convolution kernels increase network parameters and affect training efficiency [8]. Secondly, the convolutional network treats spatial and channel-wise features equally, which cannot capture critical information [9]. These reasons ultimately result in generating poor images.

The introduction of attention mechanism [10–13] can effectively capture global dependencies and improve the representation ability of the neural network. Self-attention [14, 15] calculates the response at a position in a sequence by attending to all positions within the same sequence. A^2-Nets [17] proposes the "double attention block" to aggregate and propagate informative global features from the entire spatiotemporal space of input images/videos, enabling subsequent convolution layers to access features from the entire space efficiently. In particular, the convolutional block attention module (CBAM [18]) can extract main features in both spatial and channel-wise dimensions, which enhances the representation of specific regions. Meanwhile, it will not obviously increase the parameters and computation.

Based on the analysis above, we propose generative adversarial networks based on convolutional block attention module (CBAM-GAN). To increase the flexibility of the convolutional network in extracting features, CBAM is added into the network of the discriminator and the generator. To demonstrate the effectiveness of our proposed model, the loss functions of popular GAN models (MM GAN, NS GAN, WGAN, WGAN GP, LS GAN) are exploited to compare the traditional convolutional GAN and CBAM-GAN. To objectively analyze the experimental results, Inception Score (IS) and Fréchet Inception Distance (FID) are taken to quantitatively evaluate the quality of generated images. The comparison experiments on MNIST and CIFAR-10 datasets show that CBAM-GAN can perform better than the traditional convolutional GAN in most popular GAN models.

2 Related Work

Generative Adversarial Networks. GAN [1] consists of the discriminator D and the generator G. G receives the random noise z to generate the fake image $G(z)$; D takes $G(z)$ and the real image x as inputs for binary discrimination. In the game problem of G and D, the goal of G is to make the distribution of generated data P_g close to the distribution of real data P_d; the goal of D is to correctly discriminate them. Together with the goals of D and G, the problem can be transformed into optimizing the value function $V(D, G)$ below.

$$min_G max_D V(D, G) = E_{x \sim P_d} log[D(x)] + E_{z \sim P_g}[log(1 - D(G(z)))] \tag{1}$$

GAN can be trained using the gradient descent method. In each iteration, optimizing D when fixing G and optimizing G when fixing D. The two networks train alternately until G can generate good images.

Popular GAN Models. Since the introduction of generative adversarial networks, many popular GAN models have improved the loss function of the original GAN [1]. WGAN [19] uses Wasserstein distance to fit the distribution between real data and generated data instead of JS divergence of the original GAN. WGAN GP [20] proposes an improved scheme to train WGAN. It replaces weight clipping with gradient penalty in the discriminator loss to prevent the vanishing or exploding gradient problem. LS GAN [21] is a kind of least squares GAN which uses a smooth, non-saturated L2 loss instead of log loss of the original GAN.

Together with MM GAN [1] and NS GAN [1] mentioned in the original GAN, the comparison of loss functions can be shown in Table 1.

Table 1. Comparison of discriminator and generator loss functions in MM GAN, NS GAN, WGAN, WGAN GP and LS GAN models.

GAN	Discriminator loss	Generator loss
MM GAN	$L_D^{MM\,GAN} = -E_{x \sim P_d} log[D(x)] - E_{z \sim P_g}[log(1 - D(G(z)))]$	$L_G^{MM\,GAN} = -L_D^{MM\,GAN}$
NS GAN	$L_D^{NS\,GAN} = L_D^{MM\,GAN}$	$L_G^{NS\,GAN} = -E_{z \sim P_g} log[D(G(z))]$
WGAN	$L_D^{WGAN} = -E_{x \sim P_d}[D(x)] + E_{z \sim P_g}[D(G(z))]$	$L_G^{WGAN} = -E_{z \sim P_g}[D(G(z))]$
WGAN GP	$L_D^{WGAN\,GP} = L_D^{WGAN} + \lambda E_{z \sim P_g}[\|\nabla D(\alpha x + (1 - \alpha G(z))\|_2 - 1]$	$L_G^{WGAN\,GP} = L_G^{WGAN}$
LS GAN	$L_D^{LS\,GAN} = E_{x \sim P_d}\left[(D(x) - 1)^2\right] + E_{z \sim P_g}[D(G(z))^2]$	$L_G^{LS\,GAN} = E_{z \sim P_g}[(D(G(z)) - 1)^2]$

Convolutional Block Attention Module. Convolutional block attention module (CBAM) is a recently introduced plug-and-play module to learn "what" and "where" to focus on the channel and spatial axes, respectively. The original convolution operations extract features by blending cross-channel and spatial information together, while CBAM can enhance meaningful features along both channel and spatial axes dimensions by sequentially applying channel and spatial attention modules with only a small computational cost [18].

CBAM can extract more detail features and improve the representation ability of the convolutional network. However, it has not yet been explored in the context of GAN. For GAN with two networks (discriminator and generator), whether CBAM can maintain its good characteristics in the process of gaming between the two networks needs to be verified by experiments.

3 CBAM-GAN Model

The traditional convolutional GAN exists some limitations mentioned above. Therefore, to increase the flexibility of the convolutional framework, we apply the CBAM mechanism to the discriminator and the generator of GAN. The network framework of CBAM-GAN is shown in Fig. 1.

In Fig. 1, both the generator and the discriminator use the Leaky Relu function except their last layer with the Tanh function and the Linear function, respectively. The size of all convolution and deconvolution kernels is 4×4 with stride = 2.

Note: CBAM should not be used in the last convolution layer of the generator because the generator will have generated the image after the last convolution layer.

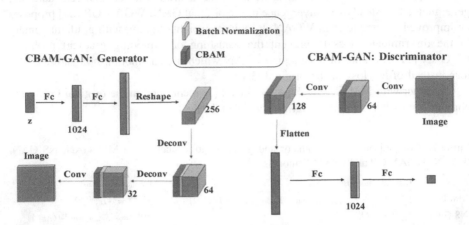

Fig. 1. Network framework of CBAM-GAN. The generator has five layers with two fully connected layers, two deconvolution layers and one convolution layer. The discriminator has four layers with two convolution layers and two fully connected layers.

Next, we define the specific theory and implementation details of CBAM in Fig. 1. Let $x \in \mathbb{R}^{H \times W \times C}$ denotes the feature map from previous layer, $x' \in \mathbb{R}^{1 \times 1 \times C}$ denotes the 1D channel attention map and $x'' \in \mathbb{R}^{H \times W \times 1}$ denotes the 2D spatial feature map. CABM can be designed as:

$$x'' = \left(x \otimes x'\right) \otimes x''$$

(2)

The operator $\otimes$ denotes element-wise multiplication and the $x''' \in \mathbb{R}^{H \times W \times C}$ denotes the redefined feature map after using CBAM [18]. Figure 2 depicts the complete process of CBAM. The refined feature maps will be seamlessly input into the next layer of the convolutional network.

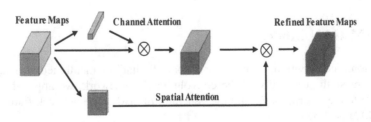

Fig. 2. Convolutional block attention module (CBAM). The operator $\otimes$ denotes element-wise multiplication.

Figure 3 depicts the specific details of CBAM with the channel attention spatial attention. For the channel attention, multi-layer perceptron (MLP) uses the Relu function. It has only one hidden layer with the size of C/r, which r is the reduction ratio.

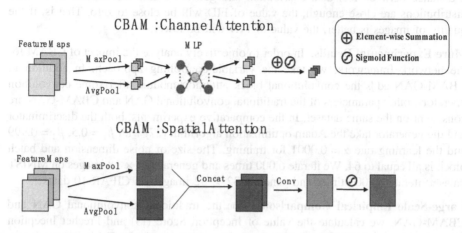

Fig. 3. CBAM with the channel spatial attention

The size of r relies on the number of channels in the previous layer. Suggesting that C/r should not be too small, otherwise the effect of the hidden layer will be weak.

4 Experiments

In this section, first, we introduce the experimental environments and datasets. Next, we take two evaluation metrics to quantitatively evaluate the quality of generated images. After making specific experimental details, we carry out large-scale empirical comparisons to prove the effectiveness of our proposed model.

Environments and Datasets. In this paper, all experiments about image generation are implemented on the TensorFlow1.8 GPU platform in SERVER Ubuntu 16.04 environment. We program both the convolutional GAN and CBAM-GAN based on the TF-GAN library in the TensorFlow1.8. A 1080Ti graphics card with 11G memory is enough for these experiments.

We use two classic image datasets, MNIST [22] and CIFAR-10 [23], to empirically demonstrate the effectiveness of our proposed model.

Evaluation Metrics. In this paper, Inception Score (IS) [24] and Fréchet Inception distance (FID) [25] are chosen to quantitatively evaluate the quality of generated images. IS measures the KL divergence between conditional class distribution and marginal class distribution using a pre-trained classifier. It can give a high score for good and diverse images. However, it only evaluates generated data distribution as an image generation model rather than its similarity to real data distribution.

Blunt violations like mixing in natural images from an entirely different distribution completely deceives the Inception Score [26]. Therefore, we also introduce FID because it has been shown to be more consistent with human evaluation in assessing the realism and variation of the generated samples [25]. FID measures the Wasserstein-2 distance between real data distribution and generated data distribution. If the two distributions are close enough, the value of FID will be close to zero. That is, if the quality of images is better, the value of FID will be lower.

More Experimental Details. In order to objectively analyze the impact of CBAM for the network framework, we take the variable-controlling approach. In addition to CBAM-GAN adds the convolutional block attention module after some convolution operators, other parameters of the traditional convolutional GAN and CBAM-GAN are consistent on the same dataset. In the comparative experiments, both the discriminator and the generator take the Adam optimization algorithm [27] with $\beta_1 = 0.5$, $\beta_2 = 0.999$ and the learning rate $\alpha = 0.0001$ for training. The size of noise dimension and batch block is all equal to 64. We iterate 6,000 times and generate 28×28 images on MNIST dataset; iterate 30,000 times and generate 32×32 images on CIFAR-10 dataset.

Large-Scale Empirical Comparisons. For the traditional convolutional GAN and CBAM-GAN, we calculate the value of Inception Score (IS) and Fréchet Inception distance (FID) on MNIST and CIFAR-10 datasets, respectively. Table 2 summarizes the comparative experiments results.

Table 2. Comparison of traditional convolutional GAN and CBAM-GAN using different loss functions from popular GAN models on MNIST and CIFAR-10 datasets. For CBAM-GAN, we fix the reduction ratio (named ratio in the table) to 1 or 2. The bold and underline fonts mark the best and second best results with higher IS and lower FID in the process of iterations, respectively.

Description	MNIST		CIFAR-10	
	IS	FID	IS	FID
MM GAN [1]	8.653	4.378	5.740	126.18
MM GAN + CBAM (ratio = 1)	8.720	4.224	6.443	117.68
MM GAN + CBAM (ratio = 2)	**8.843**	**3.163**	**7.113**	**115.47**
NS GAN [1]	8.739	4.873	5.739	118.38
NS GAN + CBAM (ratio = 1)	**8.806**	**3.386**	**6.518**	**115.82**
NS GAN + CBAM (ratio = 2)	8.618	5.053	5.931	117.59
WGAN [19]	8.635	4.337	6.552	108.30
WGAN + CBAM (ratio = 1)	8.722	**3.144**	7.028	107.79
WGAN + CBAM (ratio = 2)	**8.773**	4.335	**7.113**	**103.99**
WGAN GP [20]	**9.003**	4.610	4.633	139.72
WGAN GP + CBAM (ratio = 1)	8.864	3.710	6.075	**115.78**
WGAN GP + CBAM (ratio = 2)	8.960	**3.333**	6.318	122.93
LS GAN [21]	8.466	4.779	5.309	132.81
LS GAN + CBAM (ratio = 1)	8.533	5.320	**6.665**	**119.68**
LS GAN + CBAM (ratio = 2)	**8.726**	**2.653**	6.598	123.07

As shown in Table 2, when taking different loss functions, CBAM-GAN outperforms the traditional convolutional GAN except the IS (WGAN GP) comparative experiment on MNIST dataset. This is understandable because MNIST dataset is simple and IS evaluation metric has some limitations mentioned above.

For the more difficult CIFAR-10 dataset, we see that CBAM-GANs have significant improvements no matter IS or FID. Therefore, we have sufficient reasons to believe that our proposed model can generate higher quality images than the traditional convolutional GAN.

Figure 4 depicts the comparison of the traditional convolutional GAN and CBAM-GAN using WGAN GP loss function (a) and LS GAN loss function (b) on CIFAR-10 dataset. It shows that CBAM-GAN has faster and greater ability to increase the value of Inception Score (IS) and decrease the value of Fréchet Inception distance (FID). Besides, the curve of CBAM-GAN is also smoother than the curve of the traditional convolutional GAN, which means that our model is more stable during training.

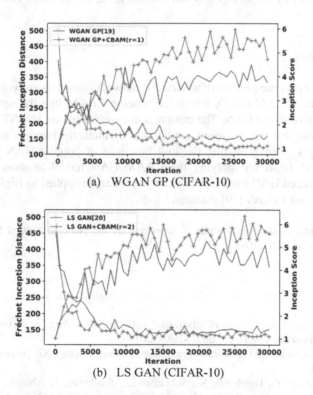

(a) WGAN GP (CIFAR-10)

(b) LS GAN (CIFAR-10)

Fig. 4. Comparison of IS and FID on CIFAR-10 dataset. The traditional convolutional GAN and CBAM-GAN use WGAN GP loss function (a) and LS GAN loss function (b). The curve with approximate upward trend represents the change of IS; with approximate downward trend represents the change of FID. The reduction ratio (named r in the fig.) is equal to 1 or 2 in WGAN GP+CBAM and LS GAN+CBAM, respectively.

Generated images on CIFAR-10 dataset can be found in Fig. 5. It shows that CBAM-GAN can generate clearer and more stable images compared with the convolutional GAN.

| WGAN [18] | WGAN+CBAM (ratio=1) | WGAN+CBAM (ratio=2) |
| (30k, FID=108.30) | (30k, FID=107.79) | (30k, FID=103.99) |

Fig. 5. Comparison of generated images on CIFAR-10 dataset. The traditional convolutional GAN and CBAM-GAN use WGAN loss function and iterate 30,000 times. Lower FID means better images.

5   Conclusion

In this paper, we propose generative adversarial networks based on convolutional block attention module (CBAM-GAN), which introducing CBAM into the network framework of the convolutional GAN. The comparison experiments on MNIST and CIFAR-10 datasets show that our proposed model can significantly improve the quality of generated images when exploiting the loss functions of popular GAN models. The future work will focus on applying the CBAM-GAN model to more challenging datasets in advanced GAN models. For example, it can be applied to BigGAN [28] on ImageNet [29] and CelebA [30] datasets.

Acknowledgments. This research study is supported by the National Natural Science Foundation of China (No. 61672108).

References

1. Goodfellow, I., et al.: Generative adversarial nets. In: Proceedings of Neural Information Processing Systems (NIPS), pp. 2672–2680 (2014)
2. Mirza, M., Osindero, S.: Conditional generative adversarial nets. arXiv preprint arXiv:1411. 1784 (2014)
3. Chen, X., Duan, Y., Houthooft, R., Schulman, J., Sutskever, I., Abbeel., P.: InfoGAN: interpretable representation learning by information maximizing generative adversarial nets. In: Proceedings of Neural Information Processing Systems (NIPS), pp. 2172–2180 (2016)
4. Ledig, C., et al.: Photo-realistic single image super-resolution using a generative adversarial network. In: Proceedings of Computer Vision and Pattern Recognition (CVPR), pp. 4681–4690 (2017)

5. Zhu, J.-Y., Park, T., Isola, P., Efros, A.A.: Unpaired image-to-image translation using cycle-consistent adversarial networks. In: Proceedings of International Conference on Computer Vision (ICCV), pp. 2242–2251 (2017)
6. Zhang, H., Xu, T., Li, H., Zhang, S., Wang, X., Huang, X., Metaxas, D.: StackGAN: text to photo-realistic image synthesis with stacked generative adversarial networks. In: Proceedings of International Conference on Computer Vision (ICCV), pp. 5908–5916 (2017)
7. Radford, A., Metz, L., Chintala, S.: Unsupervised representation learning with deep convolutional generative adversarial networks. arXiv preprint arXiv:1511.06434 (2015)
8. Zhang, H., Goodfellow, I., Metaxas, D., Odena, A.: Self-attention generative adversarial networks. arXiv preprint arXiv:1805.08318 (2018)
9. Zhang, Y., Li, K., Li, K., Wang, L., Zhong B., Fu, Y.: Image super-resolution using very deep residual channel attention networks. arXiv preprint arXiv:1807.02758v2 (2018)
10. Bahdanau, D., Cho, K., Bengio, Y.: Neural machine translation by jointly learning to align and translate. arXiv preprint arXiv:1409.0473 (2014)
11. Xu, K., et al.: Show, attend and tell: neural image caption generation with visual attention. In: Proceedings of International Conference on Machine Learning (ICML), pp. 2048–2057 (2015)
12. Yang, Z., He, X., Gao, J., Deng, L., Smola, A.J.: Stacked attention networks for image question answering. In: Proceedings of Computer Vision and Pattern Recognition (CVPR), pp. 21–29 (2016)
13. Gregor, K., Danihelka, I., Graves, A., Rezende, D.J., Wierstra, D.: Draw: a recurrent neural network for image generation. In: Proceedings of International Conference on Machine Learning (ICML), pp. 1462–1471 (2015)
14. Cheng, J., Dong, L., Lapata, M.: Long short-term memory-networks for machine reading. arXiv preprint arXiv:1601.06733 (2016)
15. Parikh, A.P., Täckström, O., Das, D., Uszkoreit, J.: A decomposable attention model for natural language inference. arXiv preprint arXiv:1606.01933 (2016)
16. Chen, Y.-P., Kalantidis, Y., Li, J.-S., Yan, S.-C., Feng, J.-S.: A^2-Nets: double attention networks. arXiv preprint arXiv:1810.11579v1 (2018)
17. Woo, S., Park, J., Lee, J.-Y., Kweon, I.S.: CBAM: convolutional block attention module. In: Ferrari, V., Hebert, M., Sminchisescu, C., Weiss, Y. (eds.) ECCV 2018. LNCS, vol. 11211, pp. 3–19. Springer, Cham (2018). https://doi.org/10.1007/978-3-030-01234-2_1
18. Arjovsky, M., Chintala, S., Bottou, L.: Wasserstein GAN. arXiv preprint arXiv:1701.07875 (2017)
19. Gulrajani, I., Ahmed, F., Arjovsky, M., Dumoulin, V., Courville, A.C.: Improved training of Wasserstein GANs. In: Advances in Proceedings of Neural Information Processing Systems (NIPS), pp. 5767–5777 (2017)
20. Mao, X., Li, Q., Xie, H., Lau, R.Y., Wang, Z., Smolley, S.P.: Least squares generative adversarial networks. In: Proceedings of International Conference on Computer Vision (ICCV), pp. 2813–2821 (2017)
21. The mnist database of handwritten digits. http://yann.lecun.com/exdb/mnist. Accessed 28 Oct 2018
22. The CIFAR-10 dataset. http://www.cs.toronto.edu/~kriz/cifar.html. Accessed 28 Oct 2018
23. Salimans, T., Goodfellow, I., Zaremba, W., Cheung, V., Radford, A., Chen, X.: Improved techniques for training GANs. In: Proceedings of Neural Information Processing Systems (NIPS), pp. 2234–2242 (2016)
24. Heusel, M., Ramsauer, H., Unterthiner, T., Nessler, B., Hochreiter, S.: GANs trained by a two time-scale update rule converge to a local nash equilibrium. In: Proceedings of Neural Information Processing Systems (NIPS), pp. 6626–6637 (2017)

25. Huang, G., et al.: An empirical study on evaluation metrics of generative adversarial networks. arXiv preprint arXiv:1806.07755v2 (2018)
26. Kingma, D.P., Ba, J.: Adam: a method for stochastic optimization. arXiv preprint arXiv: 1412.6980 (2014)
27. Brock, A., Donahue, J., Simonyan, K.: Large scale GAN training for high fidelity natural image synthesis. arXiv preprint arXiv:1809.11096 (2018)
28. IMAGENET. http://www.image-net.org. Accessed 28 Oct 2018
29. Large-scale CelebFaces Attributes (CelebA) Dataset. http://mmlab.ie.cuhk.edu.hk/projects/CelebA.html. Accessed 28 Oct 2018
30. Li, C.-L., Jiang, Y.-M., Cheslyar, M.: Embedding image through generated intermediate medium using deep convolutional generative adversarial network. CMC: Comput. Mater. Continua 56(2), 313–324 (2018)
31. Fang, W., Zhang, F., Sheng, V.S., Ding, Y.-W.: A method for improving CNN-based image recognition using DCGAN. CMC: Comput. Mater. Continua 57(1), 167–178 (2018)

A Novel Distributed Knowledge Reasoning Model

Yashen Wang[1]($\boxtimes$), Yifeng Liu[1], and Haiyong Xie[1,2]

[1] China Academy of Electronics and Information Technology, Beijing, China
yashen_wang@126.com, yliu@csdslab.net, haiyong.xie@ieee.org
[2] University of Science and Technology of China, Hefei, Anhui, China

Abstract. This paper proposes a novel model and device based on distributed knowledge reasoning, for predicting the environmental risk degree for an abnormal event (e.g., fire) in the Internet of Things (IoT) environment, which includes: (i) determining the predictive environmental information of the current node based on its historical environmental information and the predefined time-series prediction algorithm; (ii) determining the probability distribution function (PDF) of the environmental information obtained at each time corresponding to the historical environmental information; (iii) determining the deviated environment information based on the current environmental information and the probability distribution function mentioned above; and (iv) determining the environmental risk degree of the current node, based on the current environmental information, the predictive environmental information and the deviated environmental information. The wireless node of in the proposed model has the ability of perceiving and reasoning for the occurrence of an abnormal event. According to the current environmental information, the predictive environmental information and the deviated environmental information, the environmental risk degree of the current node could be determined jointly.

Keywords: Distributed knowledge reasoning · Internet of Things · Fuzzy logic

1 Introduction

Nowadays, the Internet of Things (IoT) [16,22] monitoring environment of wireless sensor networks, includes a number of intelligent wireless nodes (i.e., sensors) that can sense the emergence of an abnormal event (e.g., fire) [17,31]. Most of the mainstream knowledge reasoning systems based on the aforementioned wireless sensor networks are *centralized* systems [7,23], wherein the controlling site centralizes and processes the environment gathered by each sensor to complete knowledge reasoning. It is not only difficult to ensure the efficiency of knowledge reasoning, but also easy to cause that the number of the messages loaded on the whole network are too large. Moreover, the current mainstream system relies heavily on the type-I fuzzy logic model [29], while the model has obvious flexibility defects when it is applied to dynamic environment or when the construction of fuzzy logic rules contains uncertainty caused by local knowledge [4].

© Springer Nature Switzerland AG 2019
X. Sun et al. (Eds.): ICAIS 2019, LNCS 11632, pp. 237–247, 2019.
https://doi.org/10.1007/978-3-030-24274-9_21

To overcome the above-mentioned problems, this paper proposes a novel model and device based on distributed knowledge reasoning (KDR), for predicting the environmental risk degree for an abnormal event (e.g., fire) in Internet of Things (IoT) environment, which includes: (i) determining the predictive environmental information of the current node based on historical environmental information and predefined time-series prediction algorithm [3, 11]; (ii) determining the probability distribution function (PDF) [2] of the environmental information obtained at each time corresponding to historical environmental information; (iii) determining the deviated environment information based on the current environmental information and the probability distribution function mentioned above; and (iv) determining the environmental risk degree of the current node, based on the current environmental information, the predictive environmental information and the deviated environmental information.

The proposed model integrates the current environmental information, the predictive environmental information and the deviated environmental information, and integrates the short-term knowledge with the long-term knowledge to generate more complex and precise reasoning results for an abnormal event. Moreover, we adopts the widely-used Type-II fuzzy logic model [10, 20, 27] here to avoid the flexibility and accuracy defects of Type-I fuzzy logic model in modeling the uncertain local knowledge. Finally we adopts a knowledge-driven nodes clustering method, and this automatic clustering strategy of wireless nodes could reduce network load and enhance the modeling ability of uncertainties. Experimental results have demonstrated that, the proposed model could be applied in a wide range and could be widely applied in the environment of intelligent devices interconnection.

2   The Proposed Distributed Knowledge Reasoning Model

In the proposed distributed knowledge reasoning model, the wireless nodes of the monitoring environment of the Internet of Things, could perceive and reason the occurrence of an abnormal event (such as fire). Each node has the perception and calculation ability of reasoning localized knowledge (such as *whether there is fire or not* and *the degree of confidence*), and transmits the localized reasoning result to the network environment without manual intervention, i.e. the results are transmitted to its neighbor nodes or to the centralized information processing system (i.e. the controlling site).

The proposed distributed knowledge reasoning model for fire monitoring under a wireless sensor network environment, consists the following modules (as show in Fig. 1):

(1) The first determination module is used to **determine the predictive environment information** of the current node based on the historical environment information and the predefined time-series prediction algorithm.

(2) The second determination module is used to **determine the deviated environment information** according to the current environmental information and the probability distribution function. Wherein, the probability distribution function (PDF) of the environmental information obtained at each time is obtained according to the historical environmental information.

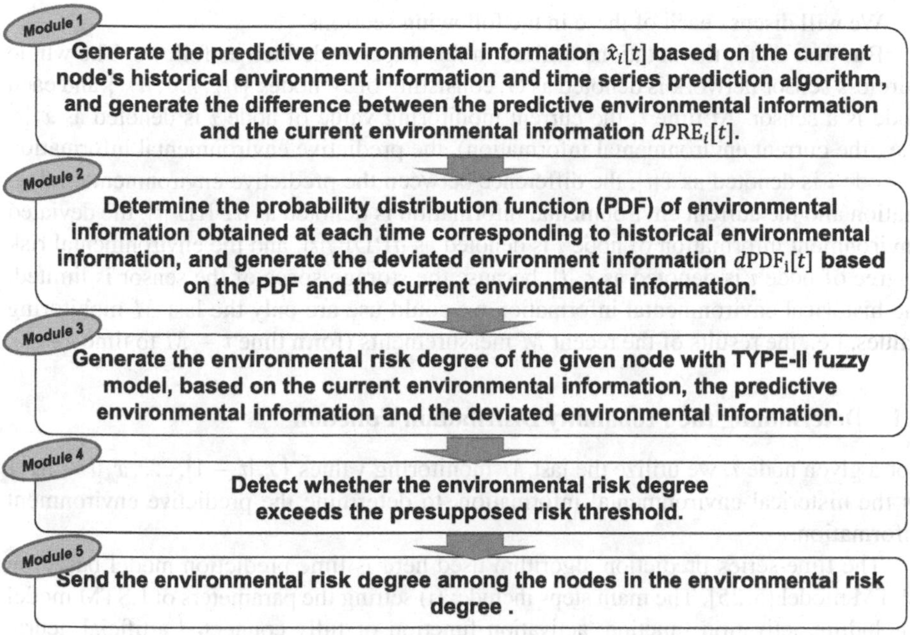

Module 1

Generate the predictive environmental information $\hat{x}_i[t]$ based on the current node's historical environment information and time series prediction algorithm, and generate the difference between the predictive environmental information and the current environmental information $d\text{PRE}_i[t]$.

Module 2

Determine the probability distribution function (PDF) of environmental information obtained at each time corresponding to historical environmental information, and generate the deviated environment information $d\text{PDF}_i[t]$ based on the PDF and the current environmental information.

Module 3

Generate the environmental risk degree of the given node with TYPE-II fuzzy model, based on the current environmental information, the predictive environmental information and the deviated environmental information.

Module 4

Detect whether the environmental risk degree exceeds the presupposed risk threshold.

Module 5

Send the environmental risk degree among the nodes in the environmental risk degree .

Fig. 1. The overall flow of the proposed Distributed Knowledge Reasoning Model.

(3) The execution module is used to **determine the environmental risk degree** of the given node according to the current environmental information, the predictive environmental information and the deviated environmental information.

(4) The detection module is used to **detect whether the environmental risk degree exceeds the predetermined danger threshold**.

(5) The transmission module is used to send the environmental risk degree to its the neighbor node, and more importantly to **send the environmental risk degree and/or alarm message to the head node of the cluster**, when the environmental risk degree of the current node exceeds the predetermined danger threshold.

In summary, this model integrates the current environmental information, the predictive environmental information and the deviated environmental information of a node. Therefore, each node needs to consider comprehensively both the **short-term knowledge** and the **long-term knowledge**:

- **short-term knowledge**: whether there is obvious deviation between the current environmental information and the predictive environmental information;
- **long-term knowledge**: the degree of deviation between the current environmental information and the current statistical distribution pattern (i.e., probability distribution function) of the node.

The combination of short-term knowledge and long-term knowledge can generate more complex and detailed reasoning results for an abnormal event.

We will discuss each of these in the following sections.

But first of all, the notations utilized in this paper is defined as follows: The whole wireless sensor network is denoted as G, consisting of N nodes $\{n_1, \ldots, n_N\}$ and each node is a sensor. At time t, the current monitoring value of node i is denoted as $x_i[t]$ (i.e., the current environmental information), the predictive environmental information of node i is denoted as $\hat{x}[t]$, the difference between the predictive environmental information and the current environmental information is denoted as $dPRE_i[t]$, the deviated environment information of node i is denoted as $dPDF_i[t]$, and the environmental risk degree of node i is denoted as $r_i[t]$. because the storage space of the sensor is limited, the historical environmental information we could use are only the last M monitoring values, i.e., the results of the recent M measurements (form time $t - M$ to time $t - 1$).

2.1 Determining the Probability Distribution Function

For a given node i, we utilize the last M monitoring values $\{x_i[t-1], \ldots, x_i[t-M]\}$ as the historical environmental information, to determine the predictive environment information.

The time-series prediction algorithm used here is time prediction model based on LSTM model [5,25]. The main steps include: (i) setting the parameters of LSTM model (including activation function, activation function of fully connected artificial neural network used for receiving all the LSTM outputs, rejection rate of each layer node, error calculation strategy, and iteration updating strategy of weight parameters, etc., [13,26]); (ii) training LSTM model with training dataset, and execute the prediction using trained models. With the aforementioned time-series prediction algorithm, we utilize the historical environmental information $\{x_i[t-1], \ldots, x_i[t-M]\}$ as input, and generate the predictive environmental information, denoted as $\hat{x}_i[t]$. In addition, it is required to satisfy this following constraint: $\mathbb{E}[\hat{x}_i[t] - x_i[t]] = 0$, wherein $x_i[t]$ is the actual monitoring value for node i at time t. With efforts above, we could generate the difference of the predictive environmental information ($\hat{x}_i[t]$) and the actual monitoring value $x_i[t]$ (i.e., the current environmental information) by $dPRE_i[t] = \|x_i[t] - \hat{x}_i[t]\|_2$. Wherein, $\| \cdot \|_2$ denotes the Euclidean norm.

2.2 Determining the Deviated Environment Information

Generally speaking, the probability distribution function of each node is unknown, and could be obtained based on a incremental learning strategy by utilizing the historical environmental information.

The incremental learning algorithm used here is Kernel Density Estimator algorithm [12,24]. The algorithm can generate an implicit distribution describing the past environmental information of a given node at each time. Through incremental learning of probability distribution function, the node can distinguish whether the current environmental information has significant deviation from the expected value of environmental information so far, that is, whether the instantaneous current environmental information does not conform to the inherent statistical distribution pattern of the node (i.e. probability distribution function). The aforementioned difference between the current environmental information and the expected value of environmental information, is called deviated environmental information (denoted as $d\text{PDF}_i[t]$) in this paper: if the estimated expectation of the monitoring value of node i at time t is denoted as $\mathbb{E}_i[x; t]$, and then $d\text{PDF}_i[t] = \|x_i[t] - \mathbb{E}_i[x; t]\|_2$. Wherein, $\|\cdot\|_2$ denotes the Euclidean norm [30].

2.3 Determining the Environmental Risk Degree

By fusing the current environmental information, the predictive environmental information and the deviated environmental information, the inference of an abnormal event is completed and the environmental risk degree is generated (the higher the value of the environmental risk degree, the higher the risk level). The fusion process is based on the **Fuzzy Reasoning Rule**s (**FRR**s) [9, 15], and the type-II fuzzy logic model [1, 19] is designed and implemented in this paper. For the application scenario of fire alarm, under the guidance of domain expert experience, the fuzzy reasoning rules designed here used three logical terms: low (numerical value close to 0), medium (numerical value close to 0.5), and high (numerical value close to 1). Note that: (i) each logical term corresponds to a numerical interval; and (ii) the current environmental information, the predictive environmental information and the deviated environmental information are mapped to corresponding logical terms through a mapping function.

The fuzzy reasoning rule designed in the proposed model is a non-linear among: (i) the current environmental information, $x_i[t]$; (ii) the difference between the predictive environmental information and the current environmental information, $d\text{PRE}_i[t]$; (iii) the deviated environment information, $d\text{PDF}_i[t]$; and (iv) the output, i.e., the environmental risk degree. The fuzzy reasoning rule designed in the proposed model could be described as follows, wherein operator $f(\cdot)$ denotes a specific function to map the logic term to interval:

- $\{f(x_i[t]) = high; f(d\text{PRE}_i[t]) = high; f(d\text{PDF}_i[t]) = high\} \rightarrow$
  $f(r_i[t]) = middle$
- $\{f(x_i[t]) = high; f(d\text{PRE}_i[t]) = high; f(d\text{PDF}_i[t]) = middle\} \rightarrow$
  $f(r_i[t]) = middle$
- $\{f(x_i[t]) = high; f(d\text{PRE}_i[t]) = high; f(d\text{PDF}_i[t]) = low\} \rightarrow$
  $f(r_i[t]) = high$
- $\{f(x_i[t]) = high; f(d\text{PRE}_i[t]) = middle; f(d\text{PDF}_i[t]) = high\} \rightarrow$
  $f(r_i[t]) = middle$
- $\{f(x_i[t]) = high; f(d\text{PRE}_i[t]) = middle; f(d\text{PDF}_i[t]) = middle\} \rightarrow$
  $f(r_i[t]) = high$
- $\{f(x_i[t]) = high; f(d\text{PRE}_i[t]) = middle; f(d\text{PDF}_i[t]) = low\} \rightarrow$
  $f(r_i[t]) = middle$
- $\{f(x_i[t]) = high; f(d\text{PRE}_i[t]) = low; f(d\text{PDF}_i[t]) = high\} \rightarrow$
  $f(r_i[t]) = middle$
- $\{f(x_i[t]) = high; f(d\text{PRE}_i[t]) = low; f(d\text{PDF}_i[t]) = middle\} \rightarrow$
  $f(r_i[t]) = high$
- $\{f(x_i[t]) = high; f(d\text{PRE}_i[t]) = low; f(d\text{PDF}_i[t]) = low\} \rightarrow$
  $f(r_i[t]) = middle$
- $\{f(x_i[t]) = middle; f(d\text{PRE}_i[t]) = high; f(d\text{PDF}_i[t]) = low/middle/$
  $high\} \rightarrow$
  $f(r_i[t]) = high$

- $\{f(x_i[t]) = middle; f(dPRE_i[t]) = middle; f(dPDF_i[t]) = low/middle/high\} \rightarrow$
  $f(r_i[t]) = middle$
- $\{f(x_i[t]) = middle; f(dPRE_i[t]) = low; f(dPDF_i[t]) = high\} \rightarrow$
  $f(r_i[t]) = low$
- $\{f(x_i[t]) = middle; f(dPRE_i[t]) = low; f(dPDF_i[t]) = low/middle\} \rightarrow$
  $f(r_i[t]) = middle$
- $\{f(x_i[t]) = low; f(dPRE_i[t]) = high; f(dPDF_i[t]) = middle/high\} \rightarrow$
  $f(r_i[t]) = middle$
- $\{f(x_i[t]) = low; f(dPRE_i[t]) = high; f(dPDF_i[t]) = low\} \rightarrow$
  $f(r_i[t]) = low$
- $\{f(x_i[t]) = low; f(dPRE_i[t]) = middle; f(dPDF_i[t]) = low/middle/high\} \rightarrow$
  $f(r_i[t]) = low$
- $\{f(x_i[t]) = low; f(dPRE_i[t]) = low; f(dPDF_i[t]) = high\} \rightarrow$
  $f(r_i[t]) = middle$
- $\{f(x_i[t]) = low; f(dPRE_i[t]) = low; f(dPDF_i[t]) = low/middle\} \rightarrow$
  $f(r_i[t]) = low$

2.4 Detection Module and Transmission Module

The detection module and the transmission module is implemented by a Knowledge-driven clustering process. And the knowledge-driven clustering process refers to the process of generating different clusters for all the nodes of G based on the environmental risk degree of each node. The member nodes in the same cluster hold similar views on whether the accident event occurs or not. The proposed model defines a plurality of clustering periods in advance, and carries out a knowledge-driven clustering process at each clustering period. In each cluster, one node is selected as the cluster-head node, while the other nodes are non-cluster-head nodes (i.e. cluster-member nodes).

The cluster-head node is responsible for aggregating the risk messages (i.e., environmental risk degree) of the cluster-member nodes, and then communicating with the controlling site. Therefore, under the communication strategy of the proposed model, the number of messages flowing through the whole wireless sensor network is significantly reduced, because there is no need for each node to communicate with the controlling site. The basic idea of the above-mentioned selection process of cluster-head node is described as following: (i) If a node generates a higher value of environmental risk degree than its neighbor node, then this node will be considered as the cluster-head node; (ii) Once a node is identified as the cluster-head node, the cluster-member nodes send their own risk messages (i.e., environmental risk degree) to the cluster-head node.

The procedure of the knowledge-driven automatic nodes clustering, is described as follows:

(1) Initially, some nodes are randomly selected as the cluster-head nodes.
(2) In each iteration, the cluster-head node is changed dynamically.
(3) When the number of iterations (or the exchanged messages) reaches the presupposed threshold, the cluster-head selection procedure terminates.

The procedure of dynamically changing the cluster-head nodes (the aforementioned step 2) could be described in details, as follows. For each node, the selection process needs a series of iterations [8, 21]. In each iteration, the node sends danger messages (i.e., environmental risk degree) to its neighbor nodes and also receives danger messages from neighbor nodes. For a node, by comparing its own risk with that of other nodes, the node with higher risk (i.e., higher value of the environmental risk degree) is selected as the cluster-head node, and the node with the highest risk becomes the cluster-head node: (i) the node with higher risk sends the risk message to its neighbors and becomes the cluster-head node; (ii) similarly, the nodes with less risk also send danger message to the neighbor. If the received message from other nodes indicates that the value of the environmental risk degree of other nodes is higher than that of the node itself, the neighbor is identified as a member of the cluster. In summary, in each round of iteration, a node is decided whether to become the cluster-head node according to the environmental risk degree.

If the value of the environmental risk degree exceeds the presupposed threshold, it indicates that there is a great danger hidden with relatively high confidence, i.e., the possibility of the occurrence of an abnormal event is high, in the current environment. It is necessary to send the environmental risk degree and/or alarm messages to the central node of the cluster where the current node is located (i.e., the cluster-head node). If the value of the environmental risk degree does not exceed the predetermined threshold, the danger and/or alarm messages can not be reported to the cluster-head node, and the current node only sends its own danger message to its neighbor nodes so that the neighbor nodes can reach a consensus on the dangerous situation.

After the current node sends danger message and/or alarm messages to the central node of the preset cluster in which the current node is located, the cluster-head node could integrate and send the danger degree of each node in the preset cluster to the controlling site regularly. By the way of interaction between the cluster-head node and the controlling site, the controlling site can not only know the environmental risk degree of each cluster, but also greatly reduce the load of the controlling site and therefore improve the system performance.

Note that, the central node of each cluster, i.e., cluster-head node, could be changed in real time. For example, the environmental risk degree of each node in a predetermined cluster is counted according to a predetermined time interval, and the node with the greatest risk is identified as the new cluster-head node in all the risk degrees. And take an another example, each node could set a selection probability [18, 28] according to its value of the own environmental risk degree, in which the selection probability indicates the probability that it becomes the central node, and determines that the node with the largest selection probability is the new cluster-head node. The proposed mechanism that adjusts the cluster-head node according to the environmental risk degree, can make the node in the most dangerous condition interact with the controlling site by adjusting the cluster-head node based on the environmental risk degree, and can get more attention from the controlling site.

3   Experiments and Results

We evaluate the proposed model in terms of the precision of fire alerts using real-data, and provide a comparative assessment with other knowledge reasoning models.

3.1   Datasets and Baselines

According to the experimental rules of Chinese SH_1-SH_4 standard fire, 20 sets of the indoor environmental parameters about 60 distributed sensors were collected under the conditions of standard no-fire and standard fire, respectively, and each sensor provide 1,000 measurements. The input is the sequential actual temperatures which is perceived by the distributed sensors, and the output is the judgment whether there exists a fire.

We compare the proposed distributed knowledge reasoning model (denoted as **DKR**) with the following alternative algorithms:

- **SM**: The most advanced single measurement (SM) algorithm alarms when a single environmental measurement value exceeds a predefined threshold. Obviously, it is a basic baseline.
- **AM**: Based on the historical environmental information of each sensor, an fire alarm is issued when the average measurement (AM) value exceeds a predefined threshold. Note that, This model implements a linear opinion base, wherein opinions are of equal weight, and the decision-making process of this model applies to every sensor.
- **CM**: the Type-II fuzzy logic model is utilized here, and we would like to compare with the Type-I fuzzy logic model. Therefore, we select the state-of-the-art fire-monitoring system with Type-I fuzzy logic model [6]. In the controlling site, Type-I fuzzy logic model is used to receive the measured values through the nodes, and controlling site is responsible for context event reasoning. This model combines the aggregated contextual data and predictive contextual values, the environmental risk degree is centrally inferred on the controlling site.
- **DDM**: [14] proposed a distributed data mining(DDM) system based on Grid environments to execute new distributed data mining techniques.

3.2   Results and Analysis

The experimental results are shown in Table 1. From the results, we could observe that, After the multi-type knowledge fusion of the proposed model, all kinds of the classifications (i.e., "fire" and "no-fire") are correct and the prediction accuracy is 100%. This phenomenon could explain as follow: The proposed **DKR** model continues to fuse the current environmental information, the predictive environmental information and the deviated environment information from rule patterns before inferring the abnormal events. Hence, in this way, our **DKR** model does not depend entirely on context values and infers an abnormal event, meanwhile taking into account historical context and similar future estimates. From Table 1, **SM** model and **AM** model are only based on a single predictive measurement of the given node, resulting in false alarms that exceed half of the total reasoning results. **CM** model has a negative impact on the identification of the abnormal events: In fact, it produces the least number of false alarms in the model being checked; however, high threshold may cause alarm loss, i.e. the abnormal event cannot be identified.

Table 1. The experimental results.

	#sample	SM		AM		CM		DDM		DKR (Ours)	
		#fire	#no-fire	#fire	#no-fire	#fire	#no-fire	#fire	#no-fire	#fire	#no-fire
Fire	20	12	8	16	4	20	0	18	2	20	0
No-fire	20	6	14	5	15	7	13	4	16	0	20

4   Conclusions

This paper provides a novel distributed knowledge reasoning technology in wireless sensor network environment (i.e., the process of data prediction), realizing distributed abnormal events (such as fire) reasoning based on local environmental knowledge. The proposed model could significantly reduce the message load in the whole wireless sensor network on the premise of improving the instantaneity and accuracy of reasoning procedure. Specifically, to achieve the above-mentioned purposes, this paper provides the a distributed knowledge reasoning model based on local fuzzy logic and knowledge-driven clustering a model for predicting environmental hazard: The model consists of several nodes (i.e., sensors), each node observes the same abnormal event (taking fire as an example), and infers whether the abnormal event occurs by persistently accepting environmental information data.

The processing process of the proposed model is carried out by each node itself, and the processing efficiency is high. There is no need to wait for the controlling site to return the calculation result, while the node itself could process. Therefore, the proposed framework can greatly reduce the number of responsible messages in the whole network and improve the framework's performance.

Acknowledgement. This work is funded by China Postdoctoral Science Foundation (No.2018M641436), and the Joint Advanced Research Foundation of China Electronics Technology Group Corporation (CETC) (No. 6141B08010102).

References

1. Almaraashi, M., John, R., Hopgood, A., Ahmadi, S.: Learning of interval and general type-2 fuzzy logic systems using simulated annealing: theory and practice. Inf. Sci. **360**, 21–42 (2016)
2. Beaulieu, N.C.: An infinite series for the computation of the complementary probability distribution function of a sum of independent random variables and its application to the sum of Rayleigh random variables. IEEE Trans. Commun. **38**(9), 1463–1474 (1990)
3. Cheng, J., Xu, R., Tang, X., Sheng, V.: An abnormal network flow feature sequence prediction approach for DDoS attacks detection in big data environment. CMC: Comput. Mater. Continua **55**(1), 095–119 (2018)
4. Coupland, S., John, R.: Geometric type-1 and type-2 fuzzy logic systems. IEEE Trans. Fuzzy Syst. **15**(1), 3–15 (2007)
5. Duan, Y., Lv, Y., Wang, F.Y.: Travel time prediction with LSTM neural network. In: IEEE International Conference on Intelligent Transportation Systems (2016)

6. Guo, L., Sun, Y., Li, J., Ren, Q., Ren, M.: A framework of fire monitoring system based on sensor networks. In: Wang, X., Zheng, R., Jing, T., Xing, K. (eds.) WASA 2012. LNCS, vol. 7405, pp. 398–410. Springer, Heidelberg (2012). https://doi.org/10.1007/978-3-642-31869-6_35

7. Hwang, T., Nam, Y., So, J., Na, M., Choi, C.: An energy-efficient data reporting scheme based on spectrum sensing in wireless sensor networks. Wireless Pers. Commun. **93**(4), 1–19 (2017)

8. Jiang, W., Sha, E.H.M., Zhuge, Q., Dong, H., Chen, X.: Optimal functional unit assignment and voltage selection for pipelined MPSoC with guaranteed probability on time performance. ACM Sigplan Not. **52**(4), 41–50 (2017)

9. Junior, F.R.L., Osiro, L., Carpinetti, L.C.R.: A fuzzy inference and categorization approach for supplier selection using compensatory and non-compensatory decision rules. Appl. Soft Comput. **13**(10), 4133–4147 (2013)

10. Karnik, N.N., Mendel, J.M., Liang, Q.: Type-2 fuzzy logic systems. IEEE Trans. Fuzzy Syst. **7**(6), 643–658 (1999)

11. Komijani, H., Parsaei, M.R., Khajeh, E., Golkar, M.J., Zarrabi, H.: EEG classification using recurrent adaptive neuro-fuzzy network based on time-series prediction. Neural Comput. Appl. **1**, 1–12 (2017)

12. Kristan, M., Leonardis, A.: Online discriminative kernel density estimator with Gaussian kernels. IEEE Trans. Cybern. **44**(3), 355–365 (2017)

13. Kucian, K., Loenneker, T., Dietrich, T., Dosch, M., Martin, E., Von Aster, M.: Impaired neural networks for approximate calculation in dyscalculic children: a functional MRI study. Behav. Brain Funct. **2**(1), 1–17 (2006)

14. Le-Khac, N.A., Aouad, L., Kechadi, M.T.: Toward a distributed knowledge discovery system for grid systems (2017)

15. Li, C., Gao, J., Yi, J., Zhang, G.: Analysis and design of functionally weighted single-input-rule-modules connected fuzzy inference systems. IEEE Trans. Fuzzy Syst. **26**(1), 56–71 (2018)

16. Liu, W., Luo, X., Liu, Y., Liu, J.: Localization algorithm of indoor Wi-Fi access points based on signal strength relative relationship and region division. CMC: Comput. Mater. Continua **55**(1), 071–093 (2018)

17. Lombardo, L., Corbellini, S., Parvis, M., Elsayed, A., Angelini, E., Grassini, S.: Wireless sensor network for distributed environmental monitoring. IEEE Trans. Instrum. Meas. **67**(5), 1214–1222 (2018)

18. Love, D.J.: On the probability of error of antenna-subset selection with space-time block codes. IEEE Trans. Commun. **53**(11), 1799–1803 (2005)

19. Mendez, G.M., Cavazos, A., Soto, R., Leduc, L.: Entry temperature prediction of a hot strip mill by a hybrid learning type-2 FLS. J. Intell. Fuzzy Syst. Appl. Eng. Technol. **17**(6), 583–596 (2006)

20. Nguyen, T., Nahavandi, S.: Modified AHP for gene selection and cancer classification using type-2 fuzzy logic. IEEE Trans. Fuzzy Syst. **24**(2), 273–287 (2016)

21. Piparo, G.B.L., Kisielewicz, T., Mazzetti, C., Rousseau, A.: Selection procedures for surge protective devices according to the probability of damage. Electr. Power Syst. Res. **146**, 321–330 (2017)

22. Razzaque, M.A., Milojevic-Jevric, M., Palade, A., Clarke, S.: Middleware for Internet of Things: a survey. IEEE Internet Things J. **3**(1), 70–95 (2017)

23. Saxena, M., Gupta, P., Jain, B.N.: Experimental analysis of RSSI-based location estimation in wireless sensor networks. In: 2008 International Conference on Communication Systems Software and Middleware and Workshops, COMSWARE, pp. 503–510 (2008)

24. Scott, D.W.: Kernel Density Estimation. Wiley, Hoboken (2018)

25. Selvin, S., Vinayakumar, R., Gopalakrishnan, E.A., Menon, V.K., Soman, K.P.: Stock price prediction using LSTM, RNN and CNN-sliding window model. In: International Conference on Advances in Computing (2017)
26. Shukla, D., Dawson, D.M., Paul, F.W.: Multiple neural-network-based adaptive controller using orthonormal activation function neural networks. IEEE Trans. Neural Netw. **10**(6), 1494–501 (1999)
27. Starczewski, J.T.: What differs interval type-2 FLS from type-1 FLS? Pamm **1**(1), 514–515 (2004)
28. Sun, J., Ling, B.: Software module clustering algorithm using probability selection. Wuhan Univ. J. Natural Sci. **23**(2), 93–102 (2018)
29. Turkdoganaydinol, F.I., Yetilmezsoy, K.: A fuzzy-logic-based model to predict biogas and methane production rates in a pilot-scale mesophilic UASB reactor treating molasses wastewater. J. Hazard. Mater. **182**(1), 460–471 (2010)
30. Volkov, V.V., Erokhin, V.I., Krasnikov, A.S., Razumov, A.V., Khvostov, M.N.: Minimum-Euclidean-norm matrix correction for a pair of dual linear programming problems. Comput. Math. Math. Phys. **57**(11), 1757–1770 (2017)
31. Zhao, H.D., Wang, H.Z., Liu, G.N., Li, C., Zhao, M.H.: The application of Internet of Things (IoT) technology in the safety monitoring system for hoisting machines. Appl. Mech. Mater. **209–211**, 2142–2145 (2012)

Research on Detection Method
of Abnormal Traffic in SDN

Yabin Xu[1,2]([⊠]), Chenxiao Cui[2], Ting Xu[2], and Yangyang Li[3]

[1] Beijing Key Laboratory of Internet Culture and Digital Dissemination
Research, Beijing 100101, China
[2] Beijing Information Science and Technology University,
Beijing 100101, China
xyb@bistu.edu.cn
[3] China Academy of Electronics and Information Technology,
Beijing 100041, China

Abstract. Compared with traditional network, the network architecture and equipment function of SDN have changed dramatically. Thus it is necessary to research more targeted network security strategies. Abnormal traffic detection is the foundation of intrusion detection and intrusion prevention. For this reason, This paper proposes a specific abnormal flow detection method aimed at SDN. The method makes full use of flow-table in SDN switch to extract the features of abnormal flows, and applies information entropy to process non-numerical features of a flow into numerical features. Finally, a BP neural network model previously trained by these numerical features are used for abnormal flows detection. The contrast experiment results show that, this method can detect abnormal traffic in SDN effectively.

Keywords: SDN · Abnormal traffic detection · Entropy · BPANN

1 Introduction

With the arrival of the "Internet+" era, new network applications emerge and make higher demands on the flexibility and convenience of network. Traditional network switch, because of the strong coupling between network control and data transmission, is strictly limit the development of these new network applications. In order to improve the status quo, researchers from Stanford University proposed an OpenFlow protocol [1] in 2008, and gradually extended it as Software Defined Network (SDN).

The core idea of SDN is to decouple network control from data transmission. The control function is provided by SDN controller. The SDN switch only has data transmission function and no control function, so as to simplify the design of switch. Due to the changes of network architecture, network devices and the functions of network device in SDN, the network security problems in SDN should be reconsidered, and a specific solution for SDN is needed. So far, data center network has been one of the main application areas for SDN. In data center network, the abnormal network flows can consume large network resources, making them unable to provide normal network service and even making data center suffer serious data loss. How to detect

© Springer Nature Switzerland AG 2019
X. Sun et al. (Eds.): ICAIS 2019, LNCS 11632, pp. 248–259, 2019.
https://doi.org/10.1007/978-3-030-24274-9_22

abnormal flows in data center network and take action to restrain them has become an urgent problem for network researchers and network managers. Therefore, the detection of abnormal flows in SDN makes sense.

2 Related Work and Our Idea

In traditional network, many detection methods of abnormal traffic are proposed. Huang [2], Zhu [3] and Kong [4] used some methods of machine learning to detect abnormal traffic in network. Cheng [5] defined a network flow abnormal index with the changing rules of new and old IP addresses, and set thresholds to detect DDOS attacks in big data environment. Chang [6] used flow as the basic unit for abnormal detection and a threshold is preset to decide whether the traffic belongs to anomaly. In traditional network, data transmission takes packet as the basic transmission unit. So sampling collection is needed for the method of traffic statistics, which result in extra overhead. In SDN, however, data transmission takes flow as basic transmission unit. So it is suitable for us to take flow as the detection unit whose information can be got directly from flow-table.

Wan [7] proposed an event-based anomaly detection approach which be installed in SDN switches to identify misbehaviors. They used the N-gram model and K-means algorithm to select feature and to extract event sequence, finally trained HMM to identify aberrant behaviors.

The number of successfully matched packets in flow-table of each switch is counted and a threshold is preset to detect abnormal traffic by Zhang [8]. This method is subjective because the threshold needs to be set upon experience and is lack of versatility. It can't dynamically change with the change of traffic.

Braga [9] proposed a detection method for DDoS attacks. The method uses the OpenFlow protocol to collect statistics of each data stream in the flow table and converts this information into a feature vector, finally inputs the data into the self-organizing mapping network. However, the selected data stream characteristics are relatively monotonous, and the distribution of IP addresses and port numbers in the switch is not considered.

Giotis [10] combined OpenFlow protocol with sFlow technology to extract flow-table information and carried out flow detection based on entropy. While this method proposed a static threshold to detect whether the flow is abnormal or not. So some error is inevitable in a dynamically changing network environment.

Several traditional flow detection methods are utilized under SDN architecture by Mehdi in literature [11]. But all these methods are using single traffic feature to classify flows, and they are only aiming at specific anomaly traffic.

Zuo [12] proposed an online traffic anomaly detection method (OpenTAD). The flow table statistic was collected from the controller online and generated the traffic matrix and sample entropy, finally used the PCA to detected the abnormal traffic. While this method also needs take static threshold to detect anomaly flow and cause little deviation for dynamically changing network traffic.

In summary, the research on detection technology of abnormal traffic in SDN architecture is not mature enough. Most existing methods which choose a threshold are relatively subjective and the detection results can be affected by the static threshold. Besides, existing research is not comprehensive enough in the selection of network traffic characteristics, resulting in a large deviation in the detection results. Faced with these problems, we take advantage of flow-table in SDN to extract versatile flow features, and employ the Artificial Neural Network model to detect abnormal flows.

3   Abnormal Traffic Detection System Design

Routers or switches in traditional network only contain information about the next forwarding node, so the concept of flow cannot be fully utilized to detect abnormal traffic. Under this condition, most of abnormal traffic detection methods utilize Net-Flow or sFlow to collect traffic statistics. While in SDN environment, every flow is transmitted according to the flow-tables in OpenFlow switches. So the information in flow-tables of OpenFlow switches can be used to extract the features about flows, and the abnormal traffic in network can be detected directly.

The network architecture of abnormal traffic detection scheme proposed by us is shown in Fig. 1.

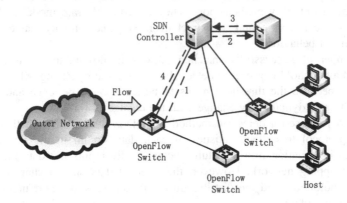

Fig. 1. Network architecture of abnormal traffic detection scheme in SDN

Three-layer network architecture is established in our solution. OpenFlow switches which correspond to the data layer in SDN architecture are in charge of data transmission. SDN controller in control layer collects flow-table information from data layer through the OpenFlow protocol and also provides the fundamental functions, such as topology discovery and flow-table management. Abnormal traffic detection server, which lies in the application layer, detects abnormal traffic by the detection model of abnormal traffic, taking parts of information from flow-tables uploaded by controller as features. The detection results will be sent back to SDN controller which can directly suppress the data forwarding of abnormal traffic.

The specific detection procedure of abnormal traffic (also shown in Fig. 1) is as follows:

(1) SDN controller collects information from each flow-table in OpenFlow switches.

(2) SDN controller transmits the flow-table information to the anomaly flow detection server. The anomaly flow detection server extracts flow features from the flow-table information and uses the machine learning method to detect whether there is abnormal traffic in OpenFlow switches.

(3) Anomaly flow detection server sends the detection results to SDN controller.

(4) SDN controller develops data forwarding control policy according to the detection result and allocates flow-tables to corresponding OpenFlow switch, so as to restrain the entrance of abnormal traffic and forward normal traffic.

4 Abnormal Traffic Features Selection and Processing

4.1 Flow Features Selection

As SDN controller can easily acquire flow-tables from every OpenFlow switches, we can determine whether the flow is abnormal according to the features implicit in the flow-table. Braga R in literature [9] choose a custom 6-tuple as the features of a flow to be detected, which consists of average of packets number per flow, average of bytes per flow, average of duration per flow, percentage of pair-flows, flows growth and ports growth. However, the implied features of the distribution of IP addresses and distribution of port numbers are not considered in this method. In order to describe the differences between normal traffic and abnormal traffic comprehensively, the flow features are described as a 8-tuple in this paper, which composed of number of packets per flow, average bytes per packet, duration time per flow, protocol type, source IP address, destination IP address, source port number and destination port number.

(1) Number of packets and average bytes per packet in one flow: Common abnormal traffic usually contains small amounts of packet. For example, about 3 packets constitute a flow during the DDoS attacks [13]. While normal traffic tends to transmit a large number of packets to complete the data communication task. Therefore, the number of packets of each flow can represent as one feature of abnormal traffic. Besides, normal traffic often carries large number of valuable data, so normal traffic contains a lot of bytes in each packet. On the contrary, abnormal traffic aim at sniffer or attacking, using only several bytes without real content, even its value is determined. Hence the average of bytes per packet can be chosen as another feature of the abnormal traffic and it can be calculated by formula (1):

$$\text{Average bytes in packet(Bytes)} = \frac{\text{number of transmitted bytes}}{\text{number of successfully matched packets}} \quad (1)$$

(2) Duration time and protocol type of a flow: In the data center network architecture of SDN, the features of a flow are obvious. Jouet [14], Noormohammadpour [15], Sasaki [16] showed in their researches most flows have shorter lifetimes and TCP protocol is widely utilized in data center network. On the contrast, anomaly flows

last longer time to keep generating harmful effects to network and use different protocols. For example, the Death of Ping and Worm Welchia use ICMP protocol, while DDoS attack usually use TCP protocol. In consideration of the flow features in data center network under the SDN architecture, duration time and protocol type of flow are used as parts of the features of a flow in this paper.

(3) Distribution of IP addresses and port numbers of flows: the distribution of IP addresses and port numbers are the important features to understand flows in network. In data center network, the distribution of IP addresses and port numbers of normal traffic are scattered, but abnormal traffic tends to focus traffic on one or more specific targets. For instance, DDoS attack will infect multiple puppet machines and launch concentrated attacks on a specific target. During an anomaly attack, several flow-table entries which consist of different source IP addresses and same destination IP address will emerge in a flow-table. Thus, the distribution of destination IP addresses tends to be centralized and the distribution of source IP address becomes more scattered.

4.2 Quantization Processing on Nonnumeric Flow Features

Since the distribution of IP addresses and port numbers of a flow cannot be described by numeric data directly and take part in the calculation, the theory of entropy is employed in this paper to process the distribution of IP addresses and port numbers into numeric data.

A flow F can be denoted as $\{F = A_{srcip}, A_{srcport}, A_{dstip...}\}$. The entropy of some features in a flow F is defined as $H(X) = -\sum_{i=1}^{n} P_i(x_i)log_2 P_i(x_i)$. Among them, $P_i(x_i)$ indicates the happening probability of event x_i.

For example, to calculate the entropy of source IP address, the formula is $H(SrcIP) = -\sum_{i=1}^{N} P_i(SrcIP)log_2 P_i(SrcIP)$. N denotes the total flow number of different source IP addresses, $P_i(SrcIP)$ denotes the ratio of the number of flows which contains ith source IP address to the number of total flows. It can be expressed as

$$P_i(SrcIP) = \frac{\text{dataflow number that contains SrcIP}}{\text{total dataflow number}} \tag{2}$$

Because the scale of dataset will affect the calculation of entropy, we normalize the entropy by dividing it with the maximum entropy value of the dataset, so the entropy can be described as:

$$H(SrcIP) = -\frac{\sum_{i=1}^{N} P_i(SrcIP)log_2 P_i(SrcIP)}{log_2 N} \tag{3}$$

So, the range of the entropy value can be normalized to the interval of (0, 1). For the destination IP address, the source port number and the destination port number can be obtained by the same calculation method for each entropy value.

By employing the concept of information entropy, the nonnumeric flow feature can be transmitted into numeric type. So the distribution of IP addresses and port numbers can be directly expressed and easily be calculated in abnormal traffic detection algorithm.

4.3 Quantization Processing on Nonnumeric Flow Features

In the process of selecting the features of abnormal flows, there may be the situation of which multiple features are related. For example, if feature A and feature B are related each other, then the feature vector of flows will make its importance strengthening in specific aspects because of the correlation of features A and B. Thus, it will weaken the importance of other features in the feature vector. Therefore, we must carry out consistency test before determining the feature vector of flows.

In order to improve the rationality and fairness of the model calculation, we utilize the feature redundant coefficient proposed by Wang [17] to estimate the redundancy among the features. The feature redundant coefficient can be calculated as:

$$t_{AB} = min\left(abs\left(\frac{\overline{A_S} - \overline{B_S}}{\overline{A_S} + \overline{B_S}}\right), abs\left(\overline{A_S} - \overline{B_S}\right) \right) \qquad (4)$$

$\overline{A_S}, \overline{B_S}$ respectively denotes the average entropy per second of feature A and feature B in a period of time. The more close to 1 t_{AB} is, the more irrelevant of feature A and feature B is. Otherwise, the two features are more relevant. In this paper, we set the threshold as 0.1. If $t_{AB} < 0.1$, these two features are considered as redundant. Then, one feature with smaller entropy should be deleted in this condition. For our selected features, the consistency test results indicate that the consistency of all the features does not exist.

5   Abnormal Traffic Detection in SDN

At present, BP Artificial Neural Network (BPANN) and Support Vector Machine (SVM) are two main machine learning models for abnormal traffic detection. Contrast experiments are needed in order to choose a better model.

SVM is a kind of machine learning method that based on the principle of structural risk minimization. It utilizes dataset to train the classification model, which maps the feature vector into high demission space and determines one maximum margin hyper plane to identify the classification of data. The bigger the margin is, the more accurate the results of classification are.

Supposing that the training dataset can be expressed as $(y_1, x_1), (y_2, x_2), \ldots, (y_i, x_i), \ldots, (y_l, x_l)$. Among them, $y_i = \{0, 1\}^l$ denotes the class label, 0 is the normal class and 1 is the abnormal class. $x_i \in R^n, i = 1, \ldots, l$, which denotes an n-dimensional feature vector. In the feature space, the linear equation of $\omega \cdot x + b = 0$ is used to make the margin distance maximum between hyper plane and the two classes. In this equation, ω presents the weight of vector and b is defined as an offset. The process of seeking the optimal separating hyper plane is the process of machine learning and the core problem is to solve the minimal solution of formula (5):

$$f(x) = sgn[(\omega \cdot x + b)] = sgn\left[\sum_{i=1}^{L}(\alpha_i^* y_i(x \cdot x_i) + b^*)\right] \qquad (5)$$

In this formula α_i^*, b^* are parameters of this optimal separating hyperplane. Different core function can be employed in formula (5) to construct different SVM model. Common used core functions are polynomial function, RBF core function and sigmoid core function. In this paper, we employ the RBF core function for its excellent overall performance.

BPANN is one kind of the artificial neural networks and has been applied in many fields. It is composed of multiple layer interconnected neuron. The neural model can be expressed as:

$$u_k = \sum_{i=1}^{n} w_{ik} x_i \qquad (6)$$

$$y_k = f(u_k + b_k) \qquad (7)$$

$x_i(i = 1, \ldots, n)$ is the input vector and $w_{ik}(i = 1, \ldots, n)$ is the weight of neuron k. The number of input vector is denoted by n. u_k is the linear combination output of input vector. b_k is denoted as the threshold value of a neuron. $f(x)$ is the activation function and y_k is the output of neuron.

The biggest advantage of BP Neural Network is that can adjust the artificial network model gradually so as to optimize the classification result through its self-learning ability by instant feedback process. An 8-tuple vector is chosen as the flow features in this paper and the output result is defined as flow classification. The corresponding BPANN construction is shown in Fig. 2.

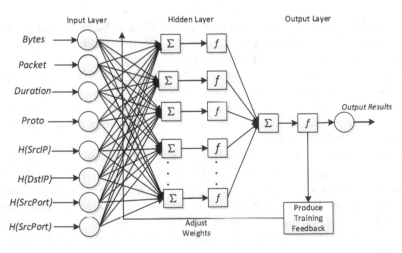

Fig. 2. BPANN structure for anomaly flow detection

6   Experiment and Evaluation

In order to evaluate the detection method of abnormal traffic in this paper, BPANN and SVM methods are used to detect the anomaly flows in dataset and the effects are compared. The dataset which we used is DARPA evaluating dataset from Lincoln Laboratory [18]. It is currently the most comprehensive attack test dataset at present. The DARPA dataset contains the simulating data from 5 week. The data of the first two weeks are provided as training data, and the data of the last two weeks are used as test data. The data from the first and the third week is normal flows without any attack. While several attack data are involved in the data from the second week.

In this paper, we use the precision (rate), recall (rate) and F-Measure as the evaluation criterions in contrast experiments. Formula (8) and (9) depict the formula to calculate precision rate and recall rate.

$$precision = \frac{tp}{tp + fp} \tag{8}$$

$$recall = \frac{tp}{tp + fn} \tag{9}$$

Among those formulas, tp denotes the number of attack flows that labeled as attack, fp is the legitimate flows that classified as attack, and fn denotes the attack flows that classified as legitimate flows. Because the restrictive relation exists between precision rate and recall rate, the detection effect of anomaly flows cannot be fully reflected by just using these two criterions. Therefore, F-measure is selected as a comprehensive evaluation criterion. F-measure can be calculated as:

$$F - measure = \frac{precision \times recall \times 2}{precision + recall} \tag{10}$$

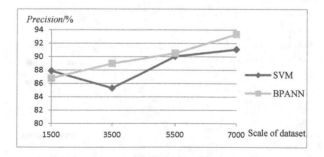

Fig. 3. Precision rate comparison between SVM and BPANN

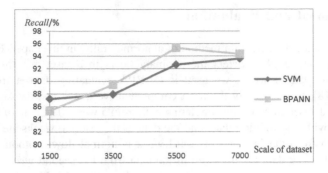

Fig. 4. Recall rate comparison between SVM and BPANN

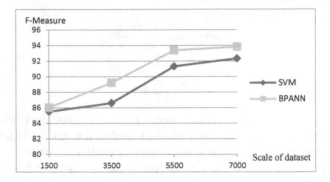

Fig. 5. F-measure comparison between SVM and BPANN

Contrast experimental results about the two kinds of machine learning methods are shown in Figs. 3, 4 and 5.

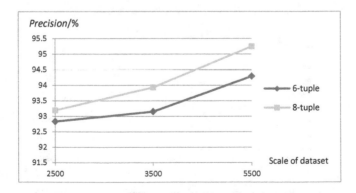

Fig. 6. Precision rate comparison between two methods

Figures 3, 4 and 5 show the comparison results of precision, recall and F-measure under the different scale of dataset. From the comparison figures we can see that, the detection model grow more rational and the performances of two model keep improving along with the expansion of the scale of dataset. Generally speaking, the precision rate of BPANN is higher than that of SVM. With the expansion of the scale of dataset, detection effect of BPANN gains a steady improvement. In recall rate, BPANN fluctuates in a relative acceptable range. The comparison results of F-measure between these two methods are shown in Fig. 5. As the size of dataset increases, the value of F-measure of both methods improves. But, in general, the value of F-measure of BPANN method is higher than that of SVM, which indicates that BPANN detection method perform better than SVM detection method. So BPANN model is selected as the detection method of abnormal traffic.

Since the detection methods of abnormal traffic in SDN are mostly aimed at DDoS attack at present, we take the BPANN method to detect DDoS attacks and compare the detection results with SOM method proposed by Braga R [9]. A DDoS attack generator called LOIC (LOIC) [19] is utilized in this contrast experiments. LOIC simulates the DDoS attack and generates the DDoS flows. During the whole experiment, 500 DDoS attack flows mixed with 5000 normal flows are evenly distributed. The contrast experiment results about precision rate, recall rate and F-measure are shown in Figs. 6, 7 and 8. In these figures, 6-tuple and 8-tuple respectively represents the method proposed by Braga R [9] and in this paper.

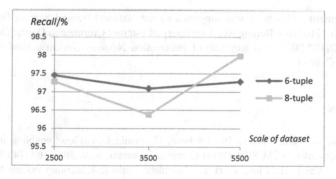

Fig. 7. Recall rate comparison between two methods

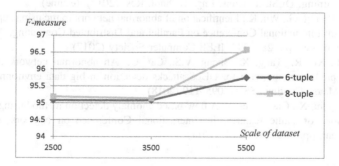

Fig. 8. F-measure comparison between two methods

From these figures it can be seen that precision rate and F-measure of these two methods are both improve along with the expansion of the scale of data flows. Although recall rate declines in the beginning, it shows a rapid upward trend when experimental data flows increase to a certain extent. Overall, every kinds of performance from the detection method based on 8-tuple proposed in this paper are much better than the detection method based on 6-tuple proposed by Braga R [9].

7 Conclusion

Taking advantage of forwarding data based on flows in SDN and obtaining information from flow-table in OpenFlow switches, this paper proposes a detection method of abnormal traffic based on a 8-tuple of flow features in SDN and BPANN. This method extracts data flow features from OpenFlow switches and uses BP neural network classification method to detect anomalies. As for the selection of the flow features, we utilize the 6-tuple features proposed by Braga R [9], and add the distribution of network IP addresses and port numbers. And we also use the information entropy theory to reflect the network traffic distribution in SDN with numerical data, so as to form more comprehensive and rational data flow characteristics. This paper uses the DARPA data set as the test data for the simulation experiment. The results of experiments shows, the detection model and features of abnormal flows proposed and used in this paper can effectively detect anomaly flows in SDN.

Acknowledgement. This work was supported by the National Natural Science Foundation of China Nos. 61672101, the Beijing Key Laboratory of Internet Culture and Digital Dissemination Research (ICDDXN004)* and Key Lab of Information Network Security, Ministry of Public Security, No. C18601.

References

1. McKeown, N., Anderson, T., Balakrishnan, H., et al.: OpenFlow: enabling innovation in campus networks. ACM SIGCOMM Comput. Commun. Rev. **38**(2), 69–74 (2008)
2. Huang, H., Deng, H., Chen, J., et al.: Automatic multi-task learning system for abnormal network traffic detection. Int. J. Emerg. Technol. Learn. (iJET) **13**(4), 4–20 (2018)
3. Zhu, M.-J., Guo, N.-W.: Abnormal network traffic detection based on semi-supervised machine learning. DEStech Trans. Eng. Technol. Res. (2017). (ecame)
4. Kong, L., Huang, G., Wu, K.: Identification of abnormal network traffic using support vector machine. In: International Conference on Parallel and Distributed Computing, Applications and Technologies, pp. 288–292. IEEE Computer Society (2017)
5. Cheng, R., Xu, R., Tang, X., Sheng, V.S., Cai, C.: An abnormal network flow feature sequence prediction approach for DDoS attacks detection in big data environment. CMC: Comput. Mater. Continua **55**(1), 095–119 (2018)
6. Chang, S., Qiu, X., Gao, Z., et al.: A flow-based anomaly detection method using sketch and combinations of traffic features. In: International Conference on Network and Service Management, pp. 302–305. IEEE (2011)

7. Wan, M., Yao, J., Jing, Y., Jin, X.: Event-based anomaly detection for non-public industrial communication protocols in SDN-based control systems. CMC: Comput. Mater. Continua **55**(3), 447–463 (2018)
8. Zhang, Y.: An adaptive flow counting method for anomaly detection in SDN. In: Proceedings of the Ninth ACM Conference on Emerging Networking Experiments and Technologies, pp. 25–30. ACM (2013)
9. Braga, R., Mota, E., Passito, A.: Lightweight DDoS flooding attack detection using NOX/OpenFlow. In: IEEE Local Computer Network Conference, pp. 408–415. IEEE Computer Society (2010)
10. Giotis, K., Argyropoulos, C., Androulidakis, G., et al.: Combining OpenFlow and sFlow for an effective and scalable anomaly detection and mitigation mechanism on SDN environments. Comput. Netw. **62**(5), 122–136 (2014)
11. Mehdi, S.A., Khalid, J., Khayam, S.A.: Revisiting traffic anomaly detection using software defined networking. In: Sommer, R., Balzarotti, D., Maier, G. (eds.) RAID 2011. LNCS, vol. 6961, pp. 161–180. Springer, Heidelberg (2011). https://doi.org/10.1007/978-3-642-23644-0_9
12. Zuo, Q., Chen, M., Wang, X., et al.: Online traffic anomaly detection method for SDN. J. Xidian Univ. (Nat. Sci.) **42**(1), 155–160 (2015). (in Chinese)
13. Chi, S., Zhou, S.: Research on defend against DDoS attacks. Netinfo Secur. (5), 27–31 (2012). (in Chinese)
14. Jouet, S., Perkins, C., Pezaros, D.: OTCP: SDN-managed congestion control for data center networks. In: Network Operations and Management Symposium, pp. 171–179. IEEE (2016)
15. Noormohammadpour, M., Raghavendra, C.S.: Datacenter traffic control: understanding techniques and trade-offs. IEEE Commun. Surv. Tutor. **20**(2), 1492–1525 (2017)
16. Sasaki, T., Pappas, C., Lee, T., et al.: SDNsec: forwarding accountability for the SDN data plane. In: International Conference on Computer Communication and Networks, pp. 1–10. IEEE (2016)
17. Wang, X., Shang, Z., Chen, L.: Feature selection algorithm toward abnormal traffic detection. Comput. Eng. Appl. **46**(28), 125–127 (2010). (in Chinese)
18. DARPA Intrusion Detection Data Sets. http://www.ll.mit.edu/ideval/data/index.html
19. LOIC: Low Orbit Ion Cannon. http://sourceforge.net/projects/loic/

Research on Constructing Technology of Implicit Hierarchical Topic Network Based on FP-Growth

Wentao Yu, Mianzhu Yi, and Zhufeng Li[(⊠)]

Zhengzhou Information Science and Technology Institute,
Zhengzhou 450001, China
20086538@qq.com

Abstract. Topic extraction for books is of great significance in the development of intelligent reading systems, question answering systems and other applications. Compared with the theme of microblog and science and technology literature, the topic of book has the characteristics of multi-themes, hierarchization, networking, and information sharing. Therefore, the topic extraction of books must be more complicated and difficult. This article is based on solving the problems such as quick positioning of the relevant contents of the answer, cross-topic retrieval, and other issues in the intelligent reading system. Based on the topic trees extracted from the novel text chapters using the TF-IDF algorithm, the FP-GROWTH algorithm is used to mine the topic words. The association relationship, in turn, analyzes the hidden relationship between topics, and proposes and constructs an implicit hierarchical subject network (IHTN) of the novel text. The experimental results show that this method can completely extract the thematic network of novel texts, effectively extract the chapter relationships, significantly reduce the answer retrieval time in the question answering system, and improve the accuracy of the answers.

Keywords: Book text · Topic extraction · FP-GROWTH algorithm · Implicit hierarchical topic network

1 Introduction

Information retrieval technology can enable people to accurately grasp the information they are concerned with in today's information explosion age. Information retrieval technology is widely used, mainly in search engines, question answering systems, and text intelligent reading. In the application of intelligent reading systems and question answering systems, instead of providing a large number of web pages like search engines for users to re-screen, users only need to ask questions in natural language to get the real answers to the questions. When searching for information in books, if the theme can be extracted from the text, the contents that users are interested in can be quickly located and returned. LDA theme model is a typical topic mining model in natural language processing. It can extract potential topics from text corpora and provide a method for quantifying research topics. It has been widely applied to various text processing fields, such as scientific literature topic discovery, online public opinion

© Springer Nature Switzerland AG 2019
X. Sun et al. (Eds.): ICAIS 2019, LNCS 11632, pp. 260–272, 2019.
https://doi.org/10.1007/978-3-030-24274-9_23

detection, and hotspot news topic analysis, information retrieval, text classification, etc., which has taken different text types, such as web pages and academic literature texts, into consideration.

In the application of intelligent reading system and QA system, when the source of the answer is a short text with a simple topic structure, for example, microblog, webpage or scientific document, topics can be quickly and accurately extracted through LDA model.

However, When the source of the answer is the book, because the text of the book presents the characteristics of multi-themes, there are still problems such as theme switching and information sharing between topics. The topic extraction method for microblogging and scientific literature will be inapplicable.

In this regard, this paper proposes an implicit hierarchical topic network model for novel text based on FP-GROWTH algorithm. Compared with the parallel theme extracted though the classic theme model LDA, the implicit hierarchical topic network can mine the semantic hierarchy hidden in the text, which can improve the positioning speed of the relevant content of the answer and allow the user's problem to involve multiple topics. The relationship between them improves the accuracy of answers in smart reading systems and question answering systems.

2 Research Status

The topic extraction model is developed from the semantic index model and can express the semantic information in the text accurately. The most used topic extraction model is the LDA model, which is widely used in text retrieval, machine learning and other fields. In recent years, the improvement and application of LDA algorithm in China has been a great success, widely used in microblog topic search, dynamic text topic mining and so on. literature [1] uses the MapReduce architecture to implement a parallel LDA model, which improves the computational efficiency of the LDA algorithm. The LDA model constructed by literature [2] can be used for topic extraction of dynamic texts. The work of foreign researchers on topic extraction is mostly concentrated on scientific literature: Van Eck and Waltman proposed a method for extracting scientific and technological literature topics using the SLMA clustering algorithm in literature [3]. This method is based on a direct-reference model and only contains documents that are components of direct-reference networks. And in the experiment of literature [4] 22 topics are provided and its coverage rate is 91.23%. Havemann et al. [5] proposed a new memetic type algorithm specifically designed to extract overlapping multi-level topics in scientific literature. Koopman and Wang [6] model data into semantic matrices by interpreting each cited bibliography or other metadata field as a semantic entity. In this experiment, two methods are provided using two different clustering algorithms (Louvain and K-means algorithms), and the coverage rate of the two methods has reached 100%. literature [7] adopts the hierarchical topic model (hLDA model) proposed by D. Blei to extract hierarchical topics and synonym mergers from the patent corpus to describe the technical structure hidden in the patent text and Technological evolution. Due to the limitations of the application scenario, this method also has certain problems. For example, the horizontal relationship between lower level topics is not taken into consideration; the hLDA model has a low accuracy in the retrieval of question answers. literature [8] has pioneered the topic forest model in 2003. However, this model, in order to facilitate transplant, does not involve semantics. Therefore, it has not attached enough importance to the hidden relationship between leaf nodes in novel text based intelligent reading system. At last, neural networks are often the top performers for addressing this problem, their usage is costly: they need to be trained, which is often very time-consuming, and their performance can vary from one task to an other depending on their objective function.

3   Implicit Hierarchical Topic Network

By mapping the topics of the same level in the chapter level topic tree to the same plane and using the association relation mining algorithm to calculate the association between the same plane topics, an implicit hierarchical topic network (IHTN) can be constructed on this basis. The implicit hierarchical topic network can solve the problem that the topic tree and topic forest models ignore potential relationships between leaf nodes.

3.1   Introduction to IHTN Model

Through extracting hierarchical topics from each chapter of the particular novel text, and then mining the relationship between these topics, the IHTN of a dialogue task is constructed. In fact, IHTN is not just a topic set. The elements of an IHTN set also include the relationships between topics. That is:

$$IHTN = \{\{T_1, T_2, R_{12}\}, \{T_1, T_3, R_{13}\}, \{T_2, T_n, R_{2n}\}, \ldots\}$$
$$T_1, T_2, T_3 \ldots T_n \in T, R_{12}, R_{13}, \ldots R_{2n} \ldots \in R,$$

T is the set composed of the leaf nodes of all the chapters in the specific novel text, and R is the set of topic relationships.

When the user's question involves topic related to multiple chapters, in order to meet the requirements of the answer extraction, this article establishes a one-to-many and many-to-many mapping from a number of topic words extracted from a specific question to multiple leaf nodes, thus improving the accuracy of answer extraction. And in order to facilitate answer extraction in the following steps, after the establishment of the IHTN, we need to search the leaf nodes that matches the problem topics according to a number of topic words extracted from the questions, and then, recommend those leaf nodes to users.

For example, if taking Jin Yong's famous martial arts novel *The Legends of the Condor Heroes* as the source text of answer extraction, the question "Why does the Seven Freaks of the South hunt down Duan Tiande?" is associated with numerous paragraphs. So it is impossible to get the detailed answer from a single chapter or paragraph. The main topics covered in this question include:

The relationship between topic words in such question sentences cannot be directly obtained from the topic tree of a chapter. It is necessary to obtain the chapter passages of the related different topic trees from the associations between the topic tree leaves of different chapters and submit them as the source of the answer extraction.

IHTN can represent the relationships between different topics, linking the topics of the chapters together into an interrelated whole. Figure 1 shows an example of a IHTN model with only four-level hierarchical topics (Fig. 2):

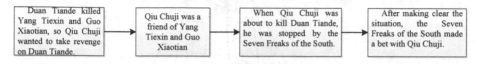

Fig. 1. The content of the question.

The node labeling rule in the figure is: $T_{a(b,c)}$, in which a represents the hierarchical topic tree to which the node belongs, b is the hierarchy, and c is the number of nodes in the current hierarchy.

When the topic words extracted from the question include two topics T_{q1}, T_{q2}, the inference engine of the session management first searches and matches the four-level topics according to T_{q1} and T_{q2} to determine the source of T_{q1} and T_{q2}. Since the source of T_{q1} and T_{q2} may be a hierarchical topic and may also come from two different hierarchical topics, it is divided into the following two cases:

(1) The source of T_{q1}, T_{q2} is a hierarchical topic. For example, T_{q1} and T_{q2} are finally matched with the sections corresponding to $T_{4(3,3)}$ and $T_{4(3,4)}$, but $T_{4(3,3)}$ and $T_{4(3,4)}$, at the same time are associated with $T_{3(3,4)}$. As a result, sections corresponding to $T_{4(3,3)}$, $T_{4(3,4)}$ and $T_{3(3,4)}$ will be submitted at the same time as the source of the answer extraction text.

(2) The sources of T_q1, T_q2 are two different levels of topics. For example, T_q1 and T_q2 eventually match the corresponding sections of $T_{1(3,3)}$ and $T_{3(3,5)}$. From the surface, we can see two different levels of topics, so if we do not consider the potential relationships between them, we can directly extract the answers from the questions, and the quality of the obtained answers will be difficult to satisfy the users. Through the IHTN model, the potential correlation between $T_{1(3,3)}$ and $T_{3(3,5)}$ can be tapped to improve the answer quality.

Using the topic hierarchy tree model can avoid the operation of searching the answer source text from the full text, and can greatly reduce the retrieval time, thereby reducing the response time of the question answering system and the intelligent reading system. In the process of mining the association relationship between topics, the topic is represented by a group of topic words, and the implicit relations between topics in the same plane can be derived through backward reasoning after mining frequent itemsets of topic words and determining the relationship between topic words.

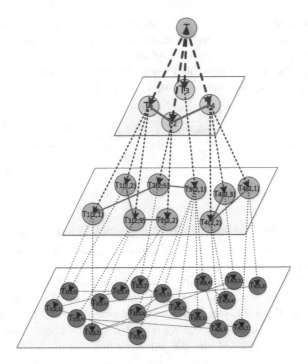

Fig. 2. IHTN model.

3.2   Implicit Hierarchical Topic Network Model Construction

3.2.1   Thematic Tree Hierarchy Extraction Based on TF-IDF

The core idea of TF-IDF can be understood as follows: if the word frequency of aword in the text is relatively large, i.e., the value of TF is relatively large, and the word frequency of other words in the corresponding corpus is relatively small, i.e., the value of IDF is relatively large, then the word can be believed having a good category distinguishing ability and it can be used as the topic word of the text. There are some problems in the algorithm for extracting text topic words, such as Topic Model. Its main problem is that the extracted keywords are generally too broad to reflect the theme of the article. The actual application effect of TextRank does not have obvious advantages over TFIDF. In order to increase the search speed, the TF-IDF algorithm is used to extract the topic words according to the level of chapter passages in text passages, and then build hierarchical topic trees.

TF = (the number of times the word appears in the article)/(the total number of words in the article)

IDF = log (total number of corpus documents/(number of documents containing the word + 1))

TF − IDF = TF * IDF

First of all, the text needs to be preprocessed through following steps: (1) Fragmentation. It means analyzing the marks of the text segmentation and carrying out segmentation according to the paragraph layout of the text chapters. (2) Word segmentation and stop words. Words are the basic unit to represent documents. Words are first segmented. After word segmentation, stop word processing is performed to reduce the influence of stop words on word mining results.

Secondly, we use TF-IDF to extract topic words from each chapter, taking the top ten most contributing topics as the topic T_1 of the current chapter; and then extract the topic word $T_{1(2,1)}$, $T_{1(2,2)}$, $T_{1(2,3)}$ for each section under this chapter; and finally extract the topic terms $T_{1(3,1)}$, $T_{1(3,2)}$, $T_{1(3,3)}$, $T_{1(3,4)}$, $T_{1(3,5)}$. After getting the theme of each level, according to the hierarchical relationship, the hierarchical topic tree of the chapter can be established, as shown in Fig. 3.

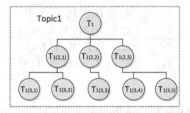

Fig. 3. Hierarchical topic tree.

On the basis of getting all hierarchical topic trees of the text, the topics of the same level in the topic trees can be mapped to the same plane (Fig. 4):

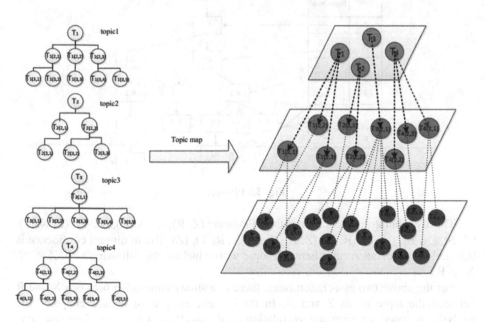

Fig. 4. Topic map.

3.2.2   Topic Association Relation Mining

Based on the FP-growth algorithm, this paper mines the relationships between nodes in the same plane. The main steps of the FP-growth algorithm include: building frequent pattern trees, constructing conditional pattern bases, and mining frequent patterns. The FP-growth algorithm is based on Apriori, but it uses advanced data structures to reduce the number of scans and greatly speed up the algorithm.

First, we construct a frequent pattern tree for topics within a plane. Taking the first level as an example, each topic is represented by eight topic words, with the topic words sorted according to the degree of contribution (Table 1).

Table 1. List of topics

Topics	Words
T_1	R, Z, H, J, P, X, Y, E
T_2	Z, Y, X, W, V, U, T, S
T_3	Z, S, F, X, R, T, I, Q
T_4	Z, R, Y, N, O, S, T, M

Then, we create an FP-tree for the theme on this plane with a minimum support of 2 (Fig. 5):

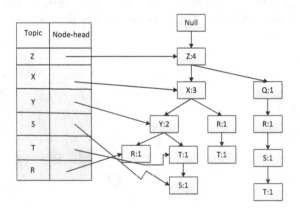

Fig. 5. FP-tree.

Thirdly, mining frequent item sets in FP-trees: (Z, R), (Z, X, R), (Z, T), (Z, X, Y), (Z, S), (X, R), (X, T), (R, T), (Z, R, T), (Z, X, R, T), (Z). The minimum confidence is 0.5, and the association rules between topic words include the following two: Z -> X, X -> R.

For the above two association rules, there is a strong correlation between X and R between the topic words Z and X. In the context analysis of textual chapters, the analysis is based on thematic correlation analysis. Thematic associations are also characterized by topic words. Therefore, by analyzing the topic-word association rules, the relationships between topics are analyzed. There is a topic word Z and X with a high degree of contribution in the topic T_2, but there is no topic word R having a strong relation with it; at the same time, there is a large contribution of the topic word Z, R in the topic T_4, but there is no topic word (i.e. R and X) which has a strong relationship with it. This phenomenon is not very valuable in user behavior analysis. However, in the contextual analysis of textual texts, especially the chapters, novels, research reports and other texts, due to the mutual influence of textual content, such as: The content of the text represented by topic T_2 has a certain influence on the topic word X. Due to the association rule X -> R, it can be inferred that the content in the chapter represented by topic T_2 will also affect the topic R and Z to a certain degree, while the topic R has a great contribution to the chapter represented by topic T_4. The influence of each other is especially evident when the topic is a novel hero. Therefore, it is determined that there is an implicit relationship between the chapters represented by the topic T_2 and the topic T_4, and thus a mark is added between the topic T_2 and the topic T_4 in the corresponding plane, as shown in Fig. 6.

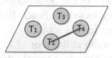

Fig. 6. Hidden relationship between topics.

According to the above method, the IHTN of the text can be obtained by mining and marking the implicit relation between all the plane topics.

4   Experimental Analysis

In this paper, the author uses the *"The Legends of the Condor Heroes"*, "The Condor Heroes", "The semi Gods and semi Devils", "Royal Tramp" as the test corpus to establish IHTN, first use the Python-based jieba word segmentation tool to preprocess the text. Then, each level of topic extraction is performed, and the TF-IDF algorithm is used to extract the theme for each chapter (without appendix and postscript), and the first ten keywords are used to represent the theme of each content; The paragraph is subject to topic extraction. Because each chapter has more paragraphs and the granularity is too small, the method of paragraph group is used in the experiment, that is, according to the content of the Storyteller of Mr. Zhang Shaozuo and other Storytellers, each storytelling is the subject of a paragraph group to extract theme.

4.1   Experiment

Experimental environment:

hardware: CPU 2 GHz, internal memory 8 GB, hard disk 1 TB.

Software environment: operating system Windows7. Programming language: Python2.7.0, implementation based on the Anaconda3.

Experimental methods: based on the questions raised, analyzing the sources of answers provided by the model. The specific indicators are the recall rate and the redundancy rate, in which the redundancy rate is: all entries in the result of unrelated items/results *100%, representing the proportion of invalid entries in the search results.

The topic extraction results are as follows:

The questions raised by the assessment included questions as to why, how, which and evaluation, etc. What and who problems were not considered due to the fact that there was less topic sharing. In the experiment, the indexing table, the topic tree method and the IHTN model were used to compare the retrieval time and recall rate. The results of the comparison between the topic tree method and the IHTN model on the redundancy rate were as follows (Table 2).

Table 2. Test problems.

ID	Questions
Why	1. Why did Seven Freaks of the South chase down Duan Tiande? 2. Why is Zhou Botong locked in Peach Blossom Island? 3. Why didn't Guo Jing have a squad? 4. Why is the ancient tomb at the foot of Zhongnan Mountain? 5. Why did Li Mochou become a female devil? 6. Why do Yang Guo and Xiao Long nv want to practice the jade heart? 7. Why did Yang Guo resent the Guo Jing couple? 8. Why did Zhou Botong was locked in Peach Blossom Island? 9. Why did Ah Zhu be beaten by Qiao Feng? 10. Why does Kangxi want to kill Aobai?
How	1. How did the Huang Pharmacist get the Jiuyin Zhenjing? 2. How does the Seven Freaks of the South teach Guo Jing? 3. How does Guo Jing tame the "Little Red Horse"? 4. How does Guo Jing become a golden knife emperor's son-in-law? 5. How does Huang Rong rectify Ouyang Ke? 6. How did the gang "Net Clothes School" develop? 7. How did Kangxi plan to kill Aobai? 8. How did Heaven and Earth develop? 9. How did Wei Xiaobao get the forty-two chapters? 10. How did Mao Dongzhu pretend to be Queen Mother?
Attributes	1. Which martial arts will Huang Rong? 2. What wishes did GuoXiang make with the three silver needles given by Yang Guo? 3. Who are the seven monsters in Jiangnan? 4. Who are the "East Evil, West poisonous, South king, North beggar and Mid Shentong"? 5. How many children does Guo Jing have? 6. What is the relationship between Qiu Qian ren and the ruthless valley master? 7. Where is the headquarters of Tiandihui? 8. What is the relationship between Muwangfu and Tiandihui? 9. How many wives does Wei Xiaobao have? 10. What kind of property did Wei Xiaobao get?

(continued)

Table 2. (*continued*)

ID	Questions
Evaluation	1. What is the relationship between Mu Nianci and Yang Kang?
	2. How is the relationship between Guo Jing and Torre?
	3. How is Guo Fu's character?
	4. How does Ouyang Feng treat Yang?
	5. How does the Golden Wheel King treat Guo Xiang?
	6. What kind of feelings does Qiao Feng have for Azi?
	7. Which wife does Wei Xiaobao like most?
	8. How is Huang Rong cooking?
	9. Is Kangxi a good emperor?
	10. How is Guo Jing in the heart of Tiemu?

(1) Retrieval time (Fig. 7)

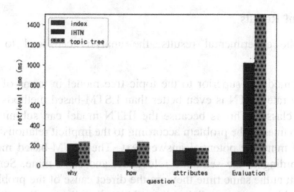

Fig. 7. Retrieval Time.

(2) Recall rate (Fig. 8)

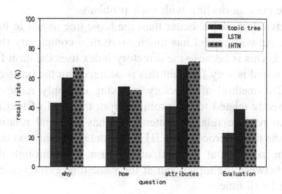

Fig. 8. Recall Rate.

(3) Redundancy rate (Fig. 9)

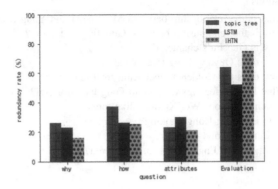

Fig. 9. Redundancy rate.

4.2   Analysis of Results

According to the experimental results, the analysis can lead to the following conclusions:

(1) The IHTN model is superior to the topic tree model in terms of recall rate and redundancy rate; IHTN is even better than LSTM-based methods for "why" and "attribute" classes. This is because the IHTN model can submit all the closely related storylines of the problem according to the implicit relationship between the topics, and mine the potential answer text. The LSTM-based method can only match according to the semantic relevance, and can't mine. Sentences are not relevant, but at the same time they are the direct cause of the problem. Therefore, for such problems as "cause", "pathway", "attribute", etc., the method can deeply dig the answers to the questions. However, for the "evaluation" category, the IHTN recall rate is inferior to the LSTM-based approach because evaluation questions generally involve less topic sharing and it is easy to get answers from a single sentence or a few sentences. Obviously, methods based on LSTM semantic relevance are good at dealing with such problems.

(2) The topic network model is better than the topic tree model in the retrieval time, but the topic network model has much more time complexity than the directory index method. This is because the directory index uses the hash function method, the retrieval speed is very fast, but this is achieved on the basis of sacrificing the recall rate. The method of directory indexing can only retrieve paragraphs or sentences directly related to the problem from the level of text and phrase. It is impossible to retrieve related content that has potential relationship with the problem. In the search process, the IHTN model mines the text that is not directly related to the problem at the text and phrase level through the hidden layer relationship between the topics, but at the same time extracts the answer greatly. So it takes a lot of time.

(3) It is worth noting that when dealing with the problem of evaluating related content such as question 3, the effect is not good, but the effect is better when asking questions about how, why, and which. This is because the evaluation category involves related techniques of emotional computing, and the IHTN model has not yet introduced the technique of emotional computing. Other methods also perform poorly on such issues for the same reason. When dealing with such problems, the IHTN model extracts content that is related or potentially relevant to the problem, so the redundancy rate is extremely high.

5   Conclusion

For applications such as smart reading and question answering systems, when dealing with long texts such as novel texts and research reports, due to the problems of information sharing among topics, multiple topics, etc., the resulting extraction of answers is not complete, the accuracy is not high. To resolve such kind of problems, this paper proposes to construct the IHTN model by establishing a topic tree and mining the implicit relationship between topics. The experimental results show that the model has better results in dealing with problem types that do not involve evaluation questions. However, due to the use of paragraph groups as leaf nodes in the process of text preprocessing, the granularity of this method is too large, which affects the accuracy. Therefore, the future study will focus on how the problems of how to find the right leaf node granularity.

References

1. Xue, X., Gao, J., et al.: Research on topic extraction algorithm based on MapReduce parallel LDA model. J. FuZhou Univ. (Nat. Sci. Ed.) **44**(5), 644–648 (2016)
2. Hu, J., Chen, G.: Mining and evolution of content topic based on dynamic LDA. Libr. Inf. Serv. **58**(2), 138–142 (2014)
3. Van Eck, N.J., Waltman, L.: Citation-based clustering of publications using CitNetExplorer and VOSviewer. In: Gläser, J., Scharnhorst, A., Glänzel, W. (eds.) Same Data – Different Results? Towards a Comparative Approach to the Identification of Thematic Structures in Science. Special Issue of Scientometrics (2017). https://doi.org/10.1007/s11192-017-2300-7
4. Velden, T., Boyack, K.W., Gläser, J., Koopman, R., Scharnhorst, A., Wang, S.: Comparison of topic extraction approaches and their results. In: Gläser, J., Scharnhorst, A., Glänzel, W. (eds.) Same Data—Different Results? Towards a Comparative Approach to the Identification of Thematic Structures in Science. Special issue of Scientometrics (2017)
5. Havemann, F., Gläser, J., Heinz, M.: Memetic search for overlapping topics based on a local evaluation of link communities. In: Gläser, J., Scharnhorst, A. Glänzel, W. (eds.) Same Data – Different Results? Towards a Comparative Approach to the Identification of Thematic Structures in Science. Special Issue of Scientometrics (2017). https://doi.org/10.1007/s11192-017-2302-5

6. Koopman, R., Wang, S.: Mutual information based labelling and comparing clusters. In: Gläser, J., Scharnhorst, A. Glänzel, W. (eds.) Same Data Different Results? Towards a Comparative Approach to the Identification of Thematic Structures in Science. Special Issue of Scientometrics (2017b). https://doi.org/10.1007/s1192-017-2305-x

7. Jing, C.L.Z., et al.: Application of hierarchical topic model on technological evolution analysis. Libr. Inf. Serv. **61**(5), 103–108 (2017)

8. Wu, X.J., Zheng, F., Xu, M.-X.: Topic forest based dialog management model. ACTA Autom. Sin. **29**(2), 275–283 (2003)

9. Erra, U., Senatore, S., Minnella, F., Caggianese, G.: Approximate TF-IDF based on topic extraction from massive message stream using the GPU. Inf. Sci. **292**, 143–161 (2015)

10. Haddi, E., Liu, X., Shi, Y.: The role of text pre-processing in sentiment analysis. Procedia Comput. Sci. **17**, 26–32 (2013)

11. Trstenjak, B., Mikac, S., Donko, D.: KNN with TF-IDF based framework for text categorization. Procedia Eng. **69**, 1356–1364 (2014)

12. Gimpel, K., et al.: Part-of-speech tagging for Twitter: annotation, features, and experiments. Carnegie-Mellon Univ Pittsburgh Pa School of Computer Science (2010)

13. Rill, S., Reinel, D., Scheidt, J., Zicari, R.V.: PoliTwi: early detection of emerging political topics on Twitter and the impact on concept-level sentiment analysis. Knowl.-Based Syst. **69**, 24–33 (2014)

14. Xiong, Z., Shen, Q., Wang, Y., Zhu, C.: Paragraph vector representation based on word to vector and CNN learning. CMC: Comput. Mater. Continua **055**(2), 213–227 (2018)

15. Wang, M., Wang, J., Guo, L., Harn, L.: Inverted XML access control model based on ontology semantic dependency. CMC: Comput. Mater. Continua **55**(3), 465–482 (2018)

PPD-DL: Privacy-Preserving Decentralized Deep Learning

Lei Song⬤, Chunguang Ma$^{(\boxtimes)}$⬤, Peng Wu⬤, and Yun Zhang⬤

College of Computer Science and Technology, Harbin Engineering University,
Harbin 150001, China
{songl,machunguang,wupeng,zhangy}@hrbeu.edu.cn

Abstract. Privacy is a fundamental challenge for the collection of massive training data in deep learning. Decentralized neural network enables clients to collaboratively learn a shared prediction model, which can protect clients' sensitive dataset without the need to centrally store training data. But distributed training process by iteratively averaging client-provided model updates will reveal each client's individual contribution (which can be used to infer clients' private information) to the server which maintains a global model. To address such privacy concern, we design privacy-preserving decentralized deep learning which we term PPD-DL. PPD-DL includes two non-collusion cloud servers, one for computing clients' local update safely based on homomorphic encryption, the other for maintaining a global model without the details of individual contribution. During the training and communications, PPD-DL ensures that no more information will be leak to the honest-but-curious servers and adversary.

Keywords: Privacy-preserving · Decentralized deep learning ·
Homomorphic encryption

1 Introduction

Due to the improvement of computing power and rich source of data, deep learning has found surprising applications in diverse domains such as pattern recognition, medical diagnosis, language translation, etc. [1]. The massive amounts of training data makes unprecedented accuracy of the resulting models which can outperform humans [2, 3].

The collection of the massive training data may raise the issue of privacy. The training dataset often involves personal behavior patterns, interests, photos, locations, health status and political leanings, etc. These personal privacy hidden behind the training dataset will cause immeasurable losses to the users.

To protect privacy, Google [4] investigates a learning technique called Federated Learning which allows clients to collectively gain the benefits of a shared model trained from this rich data. Clients hold their sensitive data locally without leaking information directly. However, the server can extract the data of individuals and infer clients'

This work was funded by the National Natural Science Foundation of China under Grant (No. 61472097).

X. Sun et al. (Eds.): ICAIS 2019, LNCS 11632, pp. 273–282, 2019.
https://doi.org/10.1007/978-3-030-24274-9_24

sensitive property when it is honest-but-curious, as shown in Fig. 1. [5] demonstrates that decentralized deep learning is vulnerable to inference attacks if adversary could obtain process parameters.

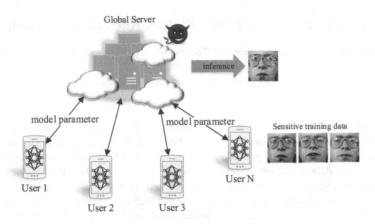

Fig. 1. The global server is the adversary in federated setting.

We present PPD-DL, a novel system which provides a more secure training for decentralized deep learning to protect clients' privacy over the honest-but-curious global server. PPD-DL includes two non-collusion cloud servers, namely a global server and an aggregation server. The aggregation server calculates the sum of all clients' updates on ciphertexts and then send it to the global server to update global state. During the whole process, no individual reveals its update in the clear to the aggregation server and global server only see the updates after they have been aggregated by aggregation server. Our solution is effective against both honest-but-curious global server and aggregation server.

Our contributions are summarized as follows: We present PPD-DL, providing a more secure way to aggregate data to calculate the global updates in federated setting. Even both global server and aggregate server are honest-but-curious, no more information will be leaked to them. Our system is robust to clients dropping out. When clients drop out, our system works well without additional operations. The auxiliary aggregation server provides a more secure and relatively simple manner to calculate, although it adds tolerable overhead.

2   Related Work

CryptoNets [6] can be applied to encrypted data for the privacy-preserving inference on a pre-trained neural network. Hesamifard et al. [7] attempt to improve [6] by low degree polynomial approximations on activation functions during the training. Mini-ONN [8] transformed from an existing neural network is an oblivious neural network supporting privacy-preserving predictions with reasonable efficiency. Because of the low efficiency, privacy-preserving neural networks based on homomorphic encryption usually are used in the prediction phase to protect client's private data.

Shokri and Shmatikov [9] present collaborative deep learning which enables multiple participants to learn neural network models on their own inputs, without sharing these inputs but benefitting from other participants who are concurrently learning similar models. Zhang et al. [11] exchange local gradients directly by using secure multiparty computation (SMC) in an oblivious manner. McMahan et al. [4] investigate Federated Learning, which learns a shared model using federated averaging algorithm. [10] attempts to improve [4] by SMC, presenting a practical protocol for securely aggregating data while ensuring that clients' inputs are only learned by the server in aggregate. Shamir's t-out-of-n Secret Sharing is used to against dropped-out clients. Kamp et al. [12] adapt dynamic averaging to the non-convex objectives of deep learning [13] and [14] propose algorithms for client sided differential privacy pre-serving federated optimization. Our system supports a simple but secure and robust to dropped-out clients without additionally operations.

3 Background and Preliminaries

3.1 Deep Learning

Deep learning is a kind of neural networks which aims to extract complex features from high-dimensional data and to build a model that relates inputs to outputs with multiple layers of nonlinear processing units. Figure 1 shows a typical neural network with two hidden layers. Training a deep neural network model is a process of optimizing parameters to minimize the error by iterative forward propagation and back propagation. In forward propagation, each successive layer uses the output from the previous layer as input, each neuron computes a sum weighted of its inputs and then applies a nonlinear activation function as the output. The output of i-th layer is $a_i = f(W_i a_{i-1} + b_i)$, where f is an activation function and W_i, b_i are weights and bias connecting layers i and $i + 1$. Common activation functions are Sigmoid $f(z) = (1 + e^{-z})^{-1}$, ReLu $f(z) = max(z, 0)$, etc. For classification task, the activation function of the last layer is usually softmax function. In back propagation, the error is propagated back through the network and weights are updated according to their gradients calculated by their contribution to the error. Stochastic gradient descent (SGD) is an effective algorithm to update weights. In each iteration, the coefficient w is updated as $w \leftarrow w - \eta \frac{\partial E}{\partial w}$, where η is the learning rate and E is the error computed over a minibatch. The training procedure can be generalized to decentralized deep learning, where multiple clients join together to learn a shared model maintained by the cloud server. In each update round, each client trains the model on its own data then sends local update w^j to the server; the server takes an average of all clients' updates to update the global model, the coefficient w is updated as

$w \leftarrow w - \eta \frac{\sum_{j=1}^{N} w^j}{N}$ (Fig. 2).

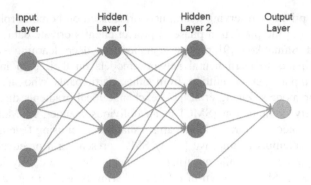

Fig. 2. A neural network with two hidden layers.

3.2 Homomorphic Encryption

Homomorphic encryption (HE) allows secure computation over encrypted data without knowledge of the secret key, the encrypted result matches the result of operations performed on the plaintext after being decrypted. An HE scheme has three main algorithms: key generation algorithm *keyGen*, encryption algorithm *Enc*, user decryption algorithm *Dec*. Fully homomorphic encryption (FHE) has the ability to perform addition and multiplication of two plaintexts using the corresponding ciphertexts. It holds the following properties: $m_1 + m_2 = Dec(Enc(m_1) \oplus Enc(m_2))$, $m_1 \times m_2 = Dec(Enc(m_1) \otimes Enc(m_2))$, where m is plaintext. Because of the low speed and expensive computational overhead, FHE is not feasible for practical applications currently. For the sake of efficiency, we adopt a renowned partial homomorphic encryption system called Paillier which supports addition over tiphertext. We can calculate $(Enc(m_1) \oplus Enc(m_2) \oplus Enc(m_3) \oplus \cdots \oplus Enc(m_n))$ using Paillier without knowing the plaintext message on the aggregation server.

The scheme of the Paillier cryptosystem works as follows:

$(pk, sk) \leftarrow keyGen(\cdot)$: select two equivalent length p and q which are two large prime numbers randomly and independently, compute $n = pq$, $\varphi(n) = (p-1)(q-1)$ then choose random integer g where $g \in \mathbb{Z}_{n^2}^*$, output $pk = (n, g)$ and $sk = (\varphi(n), \varphi(n)^{-1} \bmod n)$.

$c \leftarrow Enc(pk, m)$: given a plaintext message m, select random r where $0 < r < n$ and $r \in \mathbb{Z}_{n^2}^*$, output ciphertext $c = g^m \cdot r^n \bmod n^2$.

$m \leftarrow Dec(sk, c)$: given a ciphertext c, output $m = L(c^{\varphi(n)} \bmod n^2) \cdot \varphi(n)^{-1} \bmod n$, where $L(x) = \frac{x-1}{n}$.

3.3 Attack Model

In this paper, we assume that all the clients' datasets are sensitive and need protected against the servers. We further assume that the global server and the aggregation server are both honest-but-curious, also called semi-honest. It means that both servers will follow the protocol as specified without any deviations, but try to discover extra information from clients. Two cloud servers cannot be no collusion so that they can belong two independent cloud service providers. Based on the above assumption, we consider two kinds of attacks, namely *internal attack* and *outside attack*. Internal attack can be categorized into two cases, one internal attacker could be global server whose goal is to learn client's individual contribution and infer client's private data, the other internal attacker could be aggregation server whose goal is to obtain intermediate parameters of the learning process from clients and global server. Outside attacker utilizes communication channel to obtain intermediate results and private information.

We try to address the privacy-preserving problem of deep learning in federated setting. The security goals of our system are as follows.

Privacy of Data. Clients hold their sensitive data locally and reveal no more information to both cloud servers during the training process.

Channel Security. Even if the adversary intercepts data through the communication channel, no information about the data will be leaked.

Computing Security. Our system can calculate global update safely without requiring secret key and knowing individual contribution (Fig. 3).

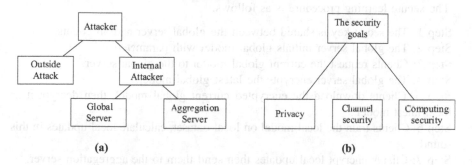

Fig. 3. (a). The kinds of attackers, (b). The security goals of our system

4 The Proposed System

4.1 Overview

Figure 4 illustrates the architecture of PPD-DL. There are N clients to learn a shared model maintained by the global server, each client has its own private dataset for training which is never uploaded to the global server. We utilize an auxiliary cloud server called aggregation server to aggregate locally-computed updates safely and then update the current global model. Throughout the learning process, all the communications (which we refer to that clients download current model from the global server, clients upload local updates to the aggregation server and the aggregation server uploads the global update to the global server) are ciphertexts. The global server cannot learn local update of each client and the aggregation server operates computation on ciphertexts, therefore no more information will be leaked to them.

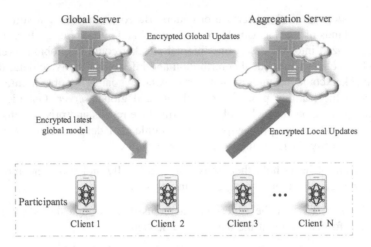

Fig. 4. The architecture of PPD-DL

The secure learning procedure is as follows.

Step 1: The secret key is shared between the global server and all clients.

Step 2: The global server initials global model with parameters.

Step 3: Clients request the current global model to the global server.

Step 4: The global server encrypts the latest global model.

Step 5: Clients download the encrypted current global model, then decrypt it as local latest model.

Step 6: Clients train the local model on local dataset, calculate local updates in this round.

Step 7: Clients encrypt local updates then send them to the aggregation server.

Step 8: The aggregation server aggregates all updates in cipher text and then sends encrypted result to the global server.

Step 9: The global server decrypts the aggregation of all local updates, calculates the average update then updates corresponding global model.

Repeat step 3 to 9 until to the end of training.

4.2   Privacy-Preserving Decentralized Deep Learning

Below we will specific elaboration the operations from the perspective of each key component of PPD-DL.

Clients. N clients participate in federated learning and each client trains the neural network in a circular fashion. Pseudo-code of the local training is given in Algorithm 1. On per round, each client requires encrypted global model C_{w_g}, runs SGD on the decrypted model and computes gradient $\nabla l(w^i; b^i)$ on its local data at the current model w^i, then uploads encrypted local update C_{w^i} to the aggregation server to aggregate the total updates. We assume that the clients perform local training in parallel and servers perform a synchronous update procedure in rounds of communication.

Algorithm 1: Clients

for client i in $1 \ldots N$ parallel **do**
    //download current global model
    receive C_{w^g}
    decrypt $w^g \leftarrow Dec(sk, C_{w^g})$
    //replace local model
    update $w^i \leftarrow w^g$
    run SGD on the local dataset, calculate gradients $\nabla l(w^i; b^i)$
    //update local model
    update $w^i \leftarrow w^i - \eta \nabla l(w^i; b^i)$
    encrypt $C_{w^i} \leftarrow Enc(pk, w^i)$
return C_{w^i} to the aggregation server

Aggregation Server. Algorithm 2 illustrates the aggregation server's pseudo-code. The aggregation server computes the sum of encrypted each client's local update. The aggregation server can apply a variety of homomorphic encryption algorithms for aggregation of the global update. In our scheme, we choose Paillier which is additive homomorphic encryption scheme to instantiate our system. The global server can obtain w_{sum} by decrypting C_{sum} without exposing each client's update and the aggregation server cannot get any sensitive information without secret key. The aggregation server can compute average update directly on ciphertexts instead of global server does. For efficiency, the global server computes average update to update global model on plaintexts.

Algorithm 2: Aggregation server

receive all clients update C_{w^i}
calculate $C_{sum} = C_{w^1} \oplus C_{w^2} \oplus C_{w^3} \oplus \cdots \oplus C_{w^N}$
return C_{sum} to global server

Global Server. The global server handles the whole learning process and Algorithm 3 shows the global server's pseudo-code. After initializing the global model, the global server enters the training loop. It receives encrypted aggregated update C_{sum} from the aggregation server, then compute average update w_{update} to update current global model. If the clients request, encrypted the latest model will be send to clients.

Algorithm 3: Global server

initializing the global model w^g
while not achieved approximate optimum **do**
    receive C_{sum} from aggregation server
    decrypt $w_{sum} \leftarrow Dec(sk, C_{sum})$
    calculate $w_{update} \leftarrow \frac{1}{N} w_{sum}$
    //update global model
    update $w^g \leftarrow w_{update}$
    if clients request current global model
        encrypt $C_{w^g} \leftarrow Enc(pk, w^g)$
        return C_{w^g} to clients

---

5 Analysis and Discussion

Correctness. We show that during each communication round, the global server can obtain correct aggregation of all clients' updates. In Paillier cryptosystem, encrypted local update of client i is $C_w i = Enc(pk, w^i) = g^{w^i} \cdot r^n \bmod n^2$, we have aggregation of all clients' updates as follow.

$$C_{sum} = \prod_{i=1}^{N} C_w i = \prod_{i=1}^{N} g^{w^i} \cdot r^n \bmod n^2$$
$$= g^{\sum_{i=1}^{N} W^i} \cdot r^{N \cdot n} \bmod n^2 = Enc(\sum_{l=1}^{N} W^i)$$

The global has $w_{sum} = Dec(sk, C_{sum}) = \sum_{i=1}^{N} w^i$. Thus, the global server obtains the correct global update after decrypting which is equal to the result computed on plaintexts.

Robustness. In the real word, client dropouts are common such as when the clients are mobile devices. If K of N clients participate in this round update and the rest are dropping out, the global update is the average of K clients' updates aggregates. No more additional operations should deal with client dropouts, therefore PPD-DL is robust to dropped-out clients.

Privacy. We desire for two types of privacy assurances when the global server is semi-honest and the aggregation server is semi-honest respectively. We assume that there is no collusion between the two cloud servers. If global server leaks the secret key to aggregation server, our discussion will be meaningless.

The Semi-honest Global Server. The local update of an individual client is invisible to global server who only get the aggregation of all clients' updates. Therefore, private data of each client cannot be reconstructed by individual local update.

The Semi-honest Aggregation Server. All operations of the aggregation server performed on ciphertexts. All received contents and calculated results are undecryptable.

Security. We desire for two types of security assurances for computing security and communication security respectively.

Computing Security. Paillier cryptosystem has been shown to provide semantic security against chosen-plaintext attacks (IND-CPA) which ensures that no bit of information is leaked from ciphertext. This guarantees the aggregation server for secure computing.

Channel Security. All the communications including the upload and download are performed on ciphertexts. Even if the adversary has intercepted the data exchanged in communication channel, it cannot derive anything meaningful without secret key.

Efficiency. With an auxiliary aggregation server, communication and computational overhead will increase and efficiency will decline. The extra overhead is acceptable in practice for the security.

PPD-DL can be extended to general neural networks. When users' data does not involve privacy, it can be sent to global server directly and build a pre-trained global model, which speeds up training. Our scheme is not suitable collaborative deep learning in [9], in which participates share a fraction of gradients. In such case, participates can upload encrypted gradients to the parameter server directly without an auxiliary aggregation server.

6 Conclusion

We design PPD-DL, a novel system which can provide more secure training method for federated learning through two non-collusion cloud servers. Even if two cloud servers are both curious, no more information will be leak to them who can compute safely among the training. Additionally, we ensure communication channel security in our system. PPD-DL protects privacy without declining the accuracy of deep learning in federated setting. In the future, we will implement PPD-DL with a specific application, analysis overhead and improve our system further.

References

1. Gurusamy, R., Subramaniam, V.: A machine learning approach for MRI brain tumor classification. CMC: Comput. Mater. Continua **53**, 91–108 (2017)
2. Cui, Q., McIntosh, S., Sun, H.: Identifying materials of photographic images and photorealistic computer generated graphics based on deep CNNs. CMC: Comput. Mater. Continua **55**, 229–241 (2018)
3. Li, C., Jiang, Y., Cheslyar, M.: Embedding image through generated intermediate medium using deep convolutional generative adversarial network. CMC: Comput. Mater. Continua **56**, 313–324 (2018)
4. McMahan, H.B., Moore, E., Ramage, D., Hampson, S., et al.: Communication-efficient learning of deep networks from decentralized data. arXiv preprint arXiv:1602.05629 (2016)
5. Melis, L., Song, C., De Cristofaro, E., Shmatikov, V.: Inference attacks against collaborative learning. arXiv preprint arXiv:1805.04049 (2018)
6. Gilad-Bachrach, R., Dowlin, N., Laine, K., Lauter, K., Naehrig, M., Wernsing, J.: Cryptonets: applying neural networks to encrypted data with high throughput and accuracy. In: International Conference on Machine Learning, pp. 201–210 (2016)
7. Hesamifard, E., Takabi, H., Ghasemi, M., Jones, C.: Privacy-preserving machine learning in cloud. In: Proceedings of the 2017 on Cloud Computing Security Workshop, pp. 39–43. ACM (2017)
8. Liu, J., Juuti, M., Lu, Y., Asokan, N.: Oblivious neural network predictions via minionn transformations. In: Proceedings of the 2017 ACM SIGSAC Conference on Computer and Communications Security, pp. 619–631. ACM (2017)
9. Shokri, R., Shmatikov, V.: Privacy-preserving deep learning. In: Proceedings of the 22nd ACM SIGSAC Conference on Computer and Communications Security, pp. 1310–1321. ACM (2015)

10. Bonawitz, K., et al.: Practical secure aggregation for privacy-preserving machine learning. In: Proceedings of the 2017 ACM SIGSAC Conference on Computer and Communications Security, pp. 1175–1191. ACM (2017)
11. Zhang, X., Ji, S., Wang, H., Wang, T.: Private, yet practical, multiparty deep learning. In: IEEE International Conference on Distributed Computing Systems, pp. 1442–1452 (2017)
12. Kamp, M., et al.: Efficient decentralized deep learning by dynamic model averaging. arXiv preprint arXiv:1807.03210 (2018)
13. Geyer, R.C., Klein, T., Nabi, M.: Differentially private federated learning: a client level perspective. arXiv preprint arXiv:1712.07557 (2017)
14. McMahan, H.B., Ramage, D., Talwar, K., Zhang, L.: Learning differentially private recurrent language models (2018)

Towards Edge Computing Based Distributed Data Analytics Framework in Smart Grids

Chunhe Song[1,2]([envelope]), Tong Li[3], Xu Huang[4], Zhongfeng Wang[1,2], and Peng Zeng[1,2]

[1] Chinese Academy of Sciences, Shenyang Institute of automation, Shenyang 110016, People's Republic of China
songchunhe@sia.cn
[2] Institutes for Robotics and Intelligent Manufacturing, Chinese Academy of Sciences, Shenyang 110016, China
[3] Liaoning Electric Power Research Institute, State Grid Liaoning Electric Power Co., Ltd., Shenyang 110000, People's Republic of China
[4] Shenyang Power Supply Company, State Grid Liaoning Electric Power Co., Ltd., Shenyang 110000, People's Republic of China

Abstract. Edge computing, as an emerging paradigm empower the network edge devices with intelligence, has become a prominent and promising future for Internet of things. Meanwhile, machine learning method, especially deep learning method has experience tremendous success recently in many application scenario. Recently, deep learning method applied in IoT scenario is also explored in many literatures. However, how to combine edge computing and deep learning method to advance the data analytics in smart grids has not been fully studied. To this end, in this paper, we propose ECNN (Edge-deployed Convolution Neural Network) in edge computing assisted smart grids to greatly enhance the ability in data aggregation and analytics. We also discuss how to train such network in edge computing distributively. Experiments shows the advantage of our paradigm.

1 Introduction

Although the prevalent of Internet of Things (IoT) is inevitable, it is also envisioned that IoT will be limited by the network bandwidth, and the IoT will become both provider and consumer of the data, which analyze, process, and store the data at the edge of Internet [1]. Thus, the conventional centralized cloud computing model has reveal its inherent problems. For example, the conventional paradigm could not process the multi-sources massive data at the edge of network in realtime; Both the delay and bandwidth has also come to a bottleneck to satisfy the requirements. Due to above reasons, the traditional cloud computing cannot efficiently support the IoT-based application services and thus, trigger to born of the new computing paradigm edge computing by moving the computation to the data producer side.

© Springer Nature Switzerland AG 2019
X. Sun et al. (Eds.): ICAIS 2019, LNCS 11632, pp. 283–292, 2019.
https://doi.org/10.1007/978-3-030-24274-9_25

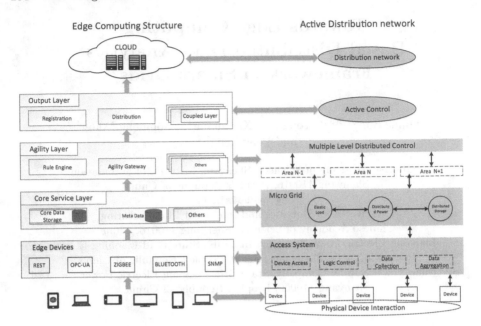

Fig. 1. Edge computing and smart grid system

Meanwhile, as the largest IoT system in real implementation, smart grids also come to the cross that how to improve the sensing ability with the power of artificial intelligence. Among also so called smart functions of smart grids, the data aggregation and analytics is of the most important and fundamental ones. However, the dumb end system has greatly limit the smart grids growing to real "Smart", as the AI algorithms require rather higher computation and sensing capacity of the end devices [2–4]. As such, we argue that, the edge computing paradigm could greatly solve such dilemma by deploying edge computing device close to the smart grids end system and also enable the high sensing and data aggregation functions. In fact, as shown in Fig. 1, edge computing paradigm is a very promising scheme to realized the so called Active Distribution Network of the smart grids, which proactively distributed and balance the power and actively collect the power from different kinds of power station, including not only the traditional ones but also the new power like wind, solar power and etc.

To realize such vision, in this paper, we design a new edge computing based distributed data analytics framework in Smart Grids. As is known to all that, the smart grids is a large scale distributed system with computing and data transmission ability. The framework of a large-scale distributed computing hierarchy provide new significance in the emerging era of IoT. We expected that most of data generated by the IoT devices must be processed locally at the devices or at the edge. Otherwise the amount of smart grid data would overwhelm the network bandwidth and lead to unacceptable processing delay. In comparison, the distributed computing paradigm offers opportunities for system scalability, data security and privacy, as well as less processing delay [5–7].

On the other hand, deep learning and CNN has illustrate its potential and tremendous advantage in machine learning tasks, especially like image process and etc. Recently, it also shows the effectiveness in sensor analytics. Thus, we are motivated to combine the deep learning and the edge computing to enhance the ability of smart grids. In this paper, we show that Edge-deployed Convolutional Neural Networks (ECNN) can systematically exploit the inherent advantages of a distributed computing hierarchy for CNN applications and achieve similar benefits.

In this paper, we mainly make following contributions:

- We design and propose a new edge computing based framework for smart grids.
- We have utilized the edge-deployed CNN (ECNN) as the core computing technique for our framework.
- We have analysis the advantage of our framework both quantitatively and qualitatively.

2   Related Work

2.1   Deep Learning

Deep learning [8] is firstly proposed as an extension of neural network [9] and with the flourish of the computing paradigm and resources, thus make the traditionally unrealized deep models feasible. Recent research has been paid on how to explore different structure to make such realization more accurate [10,11]. Recent proposed BNN has been shown to achieve good accuracy in MNIST and CIFAR-10 [12] by using less memory and small computation resources inference [13]. These models are especially promising in end devices. The researchers also use deep learning approaches to perform reinforce learning. In ECNN, we inspired by the federate learning [14] techniques and applied them in both the end devices, edge cloud and the central cloud, so that the inference and the training of the model could be performed.

2.2   Distributed Deep Learning

Current research on distributing deep learning is focused on the structure and the training efficiency. DistBelief [15] distribute large NNs over thousands of CPU cores during the training in 2012. Recently, several methods have been proposed to scale up deep NNs training over GPUs [16,17]. In 2017, Surat et al. [18] proposed an distributed deep neural networks structure to fit to embedded devices. It proposes the training and inference deployed over a distributed computing hierarchy, rather than processed in parallel over CPUs or GPUs in the cloud. Most recent proposed concept in follows the federated learning paradigm, which was proposed by Google [14]. Federated Learning is aiming at train a high-quality centralized model while training data remains distributed over the edge, which have unreliable and relatively slow network connections.

3   Edge-Deployed Convolutional Neural Networks

In this section we give an overview of the proposed edge-deployed deep neural network (ECNN) architecture and describe how is the training and inference in ECNN performed.

3.1   ECNN Architecture

Basically, the ECNN is a distributed CNN, where the first several layer of the CNN, which composed with a series of convolution layers with filters (kernels), Pooling, fully connected layers (FC) and apply Softmax function to classify an object. The edge cloud, and edge devices both own several layers of convolution layers and pooling layers. Meanwhile the local device could make the classification with the FC layers. Meanwhile, the cloud and edge also own their FC layers and the pooling layers.

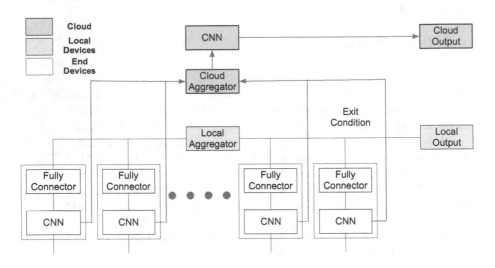

Fig. 2. ECNN structure for smart grid system

ECNN construct a CNN onto distributed smart-grid devices, edge-cloud, and the centralized cloud. Since ECNN relies on a combined CNN framework at all tiers in the neural network, the training and inference are greatly eased. Figure 2 is an overview of the ECNN architecture, which can be viewed as the standard CNN running in the edge and the cloud. In this case, sensor input captured on end devices will be sent to the cloud in form the features, the gradients or the original data.

This structure and the model could be performed in a single end device, by using first several layers of the CNN inference on the device. Then, using an exit condition, the local data could be used to perform local inference while the more data-intensive inference in a broad area will require the edge cloud or the central could to perform. In this case, the intermediate CNN output, e.g. the features or even the gradients, is sent to the cloud, where further inference is performed using additional layers and a final classification. Note that the features can are much smaller than the sensor input, and therefore drastically reduce the network communication cost.

3.2   Data Aggregation in ECNN

The data aggregation is the essential feature of ECNN, which render our framework fitting into the distributed smart grids. This feature could be used to perform cross area data inference and decision making. Basically, in this subsection, we mainly answer following question, how could we efficiently use the ECNN to aggregate the output from the each end device with balanced computation and communication cost to perform classification? We mainly answer this question by proposing several different schemes for aggregation. We basically utilize different pooling skill in the method to aggregate different features, which are as follows:

- Max Pooling. This method mainly ensemble the input by taking the max of each row. Formally, max pooling can be expressed as

$$\hat{e}_{max} = \max_{1 \leq i,j \leq n} e_{ij}, \qquad (1)$$

  where n is the number of inputs and c_{ij} is the element in i-th column and j-th row of the input matrix and $\hat{e}_{max}$ is the result of the max element.
- Average pooling (AP). AP aggregates the input vectors by taking the average of each component. This is written as

$$\hat{e}_{avg} = \sum_{i,j=1}^{n} \frac{e_{ij}}{n}, \qquad (2)$$

  where n is the number of inputs and e_{ij} is the element in i-th column and j-th row of the input matrix and $\hat{e}_{max}$ is the result of the max element. Averaging may reduce noisy input presented in some end devices.

3.3   ECNN Training

Although our structure pose a well constructed structure for edge-assisted deep learning, how to train them with the distributed big data is still unsolved. Thus, in this section, we propose a primary method to solve this problem.

Basically, the ECNN system can be trained centralized in a powerful the cloud. But one question is that how to determine the multiple exit points as shown in Fig. 2. At training stage, the loss function and the gradients of each exit is combined so that the entire NN could be jointly trained, and each exit determine the accuracy relative to its depth. In this work, we inspired by the work in [19, 20] and proposed a federated learning [14] alike method. We now describe formally how we train ECNNs.

Let y be a label vector, x be a sample and $\mathcal{C}$ be the set of all possible labels. In every exit point, we design a specific softmax objective function which can be written as

$$L(\hat{y}, y; \theta) = ||\hat{y} - y||^2 \tag{3}$$

$$\hat{y} = \text{softmax}(z) = -\frac{e^z}{\sum_{c \in \mathcal{C}} e_c^z}, \tag{4}$$

$$z = f_{\text{exit}_n}(x; \theta). \tag{5}$$

Here, f_{exit_n} is a function representing the computation of the neural network layers from an entry point to the n-th exit branch and θ represents the network parameters such as weights and biases of those layers.

Then the training could be performed wit the optimization problem as minimizing a weighted sum of the loss functions of each exit:

$$L(\hat{y}, y; \theta) = \sum_{n=1}^{N} \beta_n L(\hat{y}_{\text{exit}_n}, y; \theta)$$

where N is the total number of exit points and β_n is the associated weight of each exit. Usually, we define the weight of higher layer will be larger.

Note that each edge devices could jointly train the network with gradients exchange in the backward stage. The communication cost relies on the network size.

3.4 Inference of ECNN

Inference in ECNN is performed in several stages with exit thresholds T_i (where the T_i at each exit point i) which is a quantitative measure of how well is the prediction. Our basic idea is to construct the T_i by using a threshold as the confidence measure that determines whether to classify a sample at a exit point. This is enabled by searching the possible labeled set and while the max prediction value of the softmax is smaller the confidence level is also lower. The formal defined is as

$$\eta(\text{x}) = max[softmax(c_i)], \forall c_i \in \mathcal{C} \tag{6}$$

where $\mathcal{C}$ is the set of all possible labels and c_i is the elements. Note that the softmax out put is the probability between 0 and 1. Thus, the η has values between 0 and 1, when η close to 1 means that the ECNN is confident about the prediction; Meanwhile, η close to 0 implies not suitable. At each exit point, η is compared against T_i in order to determine if the sample should exit at that point.

At a given exit point, if the predictor is not confident in the result (i.e., $\eta > T$), the inference task will be transferred to the higher layer along with the features extracted in the edge until the cloud layer.

4 Analysis

In this section, we evaluate our method both theoretically and experimentally. In the theoretical part, we mainly analyze the most important part of the communication cost of ECNN inference. While the experiment part evaluate our method in terms of the prediction performance.

4.1 Communication Cost of ECNN

The total communication cost for an end device with the edge cloud and central cloud is formalized as follows

$$c = s \times z \times \mathcal{L} + (1 - s)f \times t, \tag{7}$$

where s is the portion of samples exited locally, $\mathcal{L}$ is number of possible labels, f is the number of pooling and FC filters, and t is the output size of a single filter for the final NN layer on the end-device. The constant z corresponds to the size of the data represent the feature extracted. The first term implies the probability that the sample to be transmitted from the end device to the edge cloud belongs.

The second term is the communication cost between edge cloud and the central cloud.

4.2 Numerical Results

We evaluate the combined ECNN with recognition accuracy and the training cost in trained environment with the samples we have collected. The data set using to running our framework is the CSI data collected using to identify the behavior and activity consist with 3 data sets, named fixed, semi, open. Such network are using to recognize 8 kinds of activities. We just simplify such task into 8 kind classification task (Fig. 3).

4.3 Accuracy Performance

We take the 80% of samples in each class as the training set, the rest as the test set. For the training set, we use 10-fold cross validation. From Fig. 4, we get that the average accuracy of activity model is 89.14%.

4.4 Training Cost

As is illustrated in Fig. 4, our model converge in different data set no greater than 10000 round of iteration. In data set fixed our model perform the best with only 3000 iteration to converge and the Loss is smaller than 0.6.

Dataset-1
Dataset-2
Dataset-2
Loss
Iteration
0.5
1
1.5
2
0
10000
20000
30000

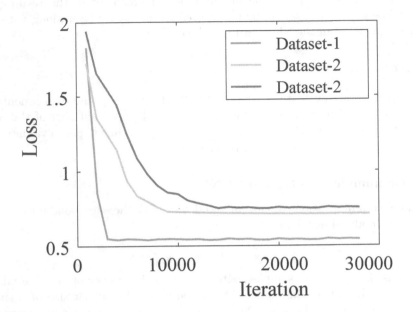

Fig. 3. The loss curve of ECNN

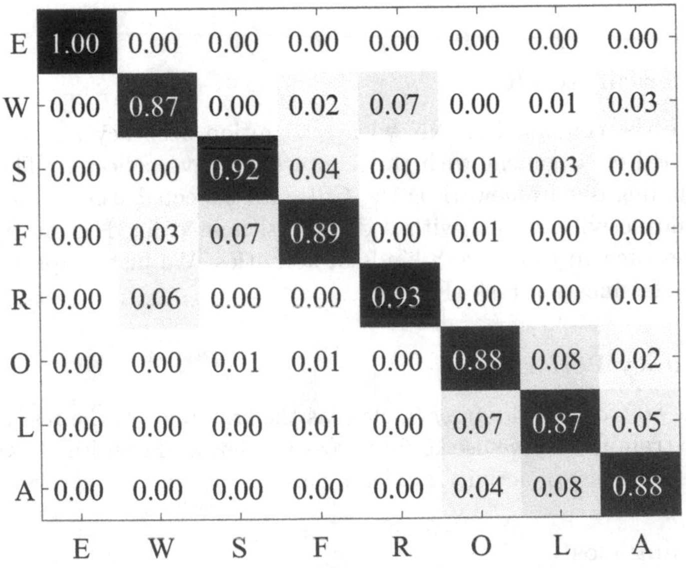

E W S F R O L A
E 1.00 0.00 0.00 0.00 0.00 0.00 0.00 0.00
W 0.00 0.87 0.00 0.02 0.07 0.00 0.01 0.03
S 0.00 0.00 0.92 0.04 0.00 0.01 0.03 0.00
F 0.00 0.03 0.07 0.89 0.00 0.01 0.00 0.00
R 0.00 0.06 0.00 0.00 0.93 0.00 0.00 0.01
O 0.00 0.00 0.01 0.01 0.00 0.88 0.08 0.02
L 0.00 0.00 0.00 0.01 0.00 0.07 0.87 0.05
A 0.00 0.00 0.00 0.00 0.00 0.04 0.08 0.88

Fig. 4. The recognition accuracy of our method

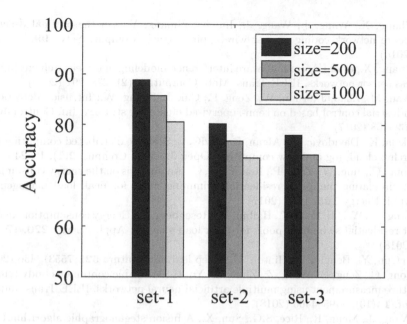

Fig. 5. The accuracy vs. the size of data set

4.5   Size of Data

According to the result illustrated in the Fig. 4 in different data set, we use different data size to train the model then use 10 folds to examine the accuracy. We find that, with only 1000 samples our model could achieve almost 90% accuracy. Plus, with no surprise, less data size lead to low prediction accuracy (Fig. 5).

5   Conclusions

In this paper we design and propose ECNN (edge-deployed Convolution Neural Network) in edge computing assisted smart grids to greatly enhance the ability in data aggregation and analytics. We also discuss how to train such network in edge computing distributively. Our method owning the advantage in communication cost and the prediction accuracy which fully utilized the distribution nature of the smart grid and the data compression and feature extraction ability of the CNN. We expect that our framework could greatly enhance the "smart" feature of the smart grids by providing low cost and high accuracy data analytics ability.

Acknowledgment. This work was supported by the State Grid Corporation Science and Technology Project (Contract No.: SG2NK00DWJS1800123).

References

1. Yi, S., Hao, Z., Qin, Z., Li, Q.: Fog computing: platform and applications. In: Hot Topics in Web Systems and Technologies, pp. 73–78 (2016)

2. Chang, X., Wang, J., Wang, J., Lu, K., Zhuang, Y.: On the optimal design of secure network coding against wiretapping attack. Comput. Netw. **99**(C), 82–98 (2016)
3. Chang, X., et al.: Accuracy-aware interference modeling and measurement in wireless sensor networks. IEEE Trans. Mob. Comput. **15**(2), 278–291 (2016)
4. Wan, M., Zhao, J., Yuan, W., Zeng, P., Cui, J., Shang, W.: Intrusion detection of industrial control based on semi-supervised clustering strategy. Inf. Control **46**(4), 462–468 (2017)
5. Skala, K., Davidovic, D., Afgan, E., SoviC, I.: Scalable distributed computing hierarchy: cloud, fog and dew computing. Open J. Cloud Comput. **2**(1), 16–24 (2015)
6. Song, C., Jing, W., Zeng, P., Rosenberg, C.: An analysis on the energy consumption of circulating pumps of residential swimming pools for peak load management. Appl. Energy **195**, 1–12 (2017)
7. Song, C., Wei, J., Peng, Z., Haibin, Y., Rosenberg, C.: Energy consumption analysis of residential swimming pools for peak load shaving. Appl. Energy **220**, 176–191 (2018)
8. LeCun, Y., Bengio, Y., Hinton, G.: Deep learning. Nature **521**(7553), 436 (2015)
9. Song, C., Zeng, P., Wang, Z., Zhao, H., Yu, H.: Wearable continuous body temperature measurement using multiple artificial neural networks. IEEE Trans. Industr. Inf. **14**(10), 4395–4406 (2018)
10. Wang, J., Meng, R., Rice, S.G., Sun, X.: A fusion steganographic algorithm based on faster R-CNN. CMC Comput. Mater. Continua **55**(1), 001–016 (2018)
11. Li, F., Sherratt, R.S., Zeng, D., Dai, Y., Wang, J.: Adversarial learning for distant supervised relation extraction. CMC Comput. Mater. Continua **55**(1), 121–136 (2018)
12. Rastegari, M., Ordonez, V., Redmon, J., Farhadi, A.: XNOR-Net: imagenet classification using binary convolutional neural networks. In: Leibe, B., Matas, J., Sebe, N., Welling, M. (eds.) ECCV 2016. LNCS, vol. 9908, pp. 525–542. Springer, Cham (2016). https://doi.org/10.1007/978-3-319-46493-0_32
13. Mcdanel, B., Teerapittayanon, S., Kung, H.T.: Embedded binarized neural networks (2017)
14. KoneČný, J., McMahan, H.B., Yu, F.X., Richtrik, P., Suresh, A.T., Bacon, D.: Federated learning: strategies for improving communication efficiency (2016)
15. Dean, J., et al.: Large scale distributed deep networks. In: International Conference on Neural Information Processing Systems, pp. 1223–1231 (2012)
16. Iandola, F.N., Moskewicz, M.W., Ashraf, K., Keutzer, K.: Firecaffe: near-linear acceleration of deep neural network training on compute clusters, vol. 37, pp. 2592–2600 (2015)
17. Dean, J.: Large scale deep learning (2014)
18. Teerapittayanon, S., McDanel, B., Kung, H.T.: Distributed deep neural networks over the cloud, the edge and end devices. In: 2017 IEEE 37th International Conference on Distributed Computing Systems (ICDCS), pp. 328–339. IEEE (2017)
19. Szegedy, C., et al.: Going deeper with convolutions, pp. 1–9 (2014)
20. Teerapittayanon, S., Mcdanel, B., Kung, H.T.: BranchyNet: fast inference via early exiting from deep neural networks, pp. 2464–2469 (2017)

Android Malware Identification
Based on Traffic Analysis

Rong Chen[1,2], Yangyang Li[1(✉)], and Weiwei Fang[2]

[1] Innovation Center and Mobile Internet Development and Research Center,
China Academy of Electronics and Information Technology, Beijing 100041, China
yli@csdslab.net
[2] Beijing Jiaotong University, Beijing 100044, China
{17127054,fangww}@bjtu.edu.cn

Abstract. As numerous new techniques for Android malware attacks have growingly emerged and evolved, Android malware identification is extremely crucial to prevent mobile applications from being hacked. Machine learning techniques have shown extraordinary capabilities in various fields. A common problem with existing research of malware traffic identification based on machine learning approaches is the need to design a set of features that accurately reflect network traffic characteristics. Obtaining a high accuracy for identifying Android malware traffic is also a challenging problem. This paper analyses the Android malware traffic and extract 15 features which is a combination of time-related network flow feature and packets feature. We then use three supervised machine learning methods to identify Android malware traffic. Experimental results show that the feature set we proposed can accurately characterize the traffic and all three classifiers achieve high accuracy.

Keywords: Malware traffic · Traffic analysis · Traffic classification · Machine learning

1 Introduction

With the development and popularization of smart phones, smart phones have become a very important part of people's life. It offers a wide variety of applications to meet people's daily needs [1], and more and more users store their private information in their smart phones. According to statistics from data Internet statistics company Statista, in 2016, there were 2.1 billion smart phone users worldwide, and the number is expected to grow to 2.87 billion in 2020 [2]. The widespread deployment of WIFI networks and the large number of applications available in the application market [3], compared with traditional network

This work was supported by the Fundamental Research Funds for the Central Universities of China under Grants 2017JBM021 and 2016JBZ006, and CETC Joint Fund under Grant 6141B08020101.

traffic, have enabled mobile devices not only to involve traditional communication activities (such as making voice calls and sending short messages), but
also to apply to more advanced scenarios such as finance, online games and
e-shopping. As mobile devices tend to store owners' private data [4] (such as
contacts, photos, videos and GPS locations), more and more attackers and traffic analysts are targeting the network traffic they generate in an attempt to mine
useful information. Google's Android has become the most popular mobile platform overtaking other operating systems. Such increasing popularity of Android
smart phones has attracted malicious app developers as well. According to the
statistics given in [5], among all malwares targeting mobile devices, the share
of Android malwares is higher than 46%. Another recent report also alerts that
Android malwares have grown around 400% since summer 2010 [6]. New techniques for Android malware attacks are emerging. Given this significant growth
of Android malware, there is a pressing need to effectively mitigate or defense
against them. In this paper, we focus on malware traffic and we extracted 15
features from raw network traffic. We propose a machine leaning model using
three supervised machine learning methods for android malware traffic identification. Organisation of paper is as follows. Section 2 overviews related work.
Section 3 demonstrates methodology. Section 4 is about experimental study and
results. Conclusion and Future Work are depicted in Sect. 5.

2   Related Work

Existing technology proposed for android malware classification falls into three
categories [7]: port-based identification [8], deep packet inspection (DPI) [9] identification and the machine learning (ML) identification [12]. Port-based identification was used in the past to associate applications with network connections,
but the accuracy of this method is decreasing with the increased use of dynamic
ports [10] and applications evading firewalls. Despite the decreased accuracy, port
numbers are often utilized as one of the packet features. Furthermore, port-based
identification is still quite often used to establish a ground truth for traffic identification experiments. Finsterbusch [11] summarized current main DPI-based traffic
identification methods. DPI technology is influenced by network traffic encryption measures. At present, the mainstream research mainly uses machine learning methods [13]. Machine learning approach of traffic identification attracts a
lot of research in academia [14–16], and related work mainly focused on how to
choose a better dataset. Dhote et al. [17] provided a survey on feature selection
techniques of internet traffic identification. There are generally two kinds of traffic
features that are mainly used in machine learning methods [18]. One is flow features, that is, the communication of the two sides of all the data packets reflected.
The other is packet features, which are the features of each packet. Wang [19],
Mauro [20] and Cheng [21] apply flow features to research P2P traffic, WebRTC,
Coull et al. [20] use packet features to research iMessage traffic. Korczynski [22]
and Koch [23] apply packet features to identify encrypted traffic. The corresponding classifiers are C4.5 decision tree; Naive Bayes and random forest respectively.

Aghaei et al. [24] proposed a identification method with flow features and C4.5 decision tree classifier on proxy traffic. Xu [25] proposed a identification method with only time related flow features on both regular encrypted traffic and protocol encapsulated traffic. A few researchers, such as, Du. [26] and Alshammari. [27] use combination of flow and packets features to identify [18] encrypted traffic. Most of the researches employ supervised machine learning Methods [31].

3   Methodology

3.1   Dataset

Arash [28] published CICAndMal dataset which includes four types of Android malware traffic. In this paper, we select three types of Android malware traffic from CICAndMal dataset. Each type of Android malware traffic includes 10 malware families and we randomly choose one pcap file from each malware family. Therefore, every malware traffic consists of 10 pcap files. And the benign traffic data also comes from Arash [29]. It consists of 173 pcap files which are generated by 1,500 benign Android applications from google play. Table 1 shows the detailed malware family of three types of malware traffic in our dataset. The size of our Android malware dataset is 3.2 GB, and the format is pcap.

Table 1. The details of Android malware families.

Traffic type	Malware families	
Adware	Dowgin family	Ewind family
	Feiwo family	Gooligan family
	Kemoge family	Koodous family
	Mobidash family	Selfmite family
	Shuanet family	Youmi family
Ransomware	Charger family	Jisut family
	Koler family	LockerPin family
	Simplocker family	Pletor family
	PornDroid family	RansomBO family
	Svpeng family	WannaLocker family
Scareware	AndroidDefender 17	AndroidSpy.277 family
	AV for Android family	AVpass family
	FakeApp family	FakeApp.AL family
	FakeAV family	FakeJobOffer family
	FakeTaoBao family	Penetho family

3.2 Model

In this paper, we propose an Android malware traffic identification model using a machine learning (ML) architecture. Figure 1 shows the overview of our proposed Android malware traffic identification method. Generally, this model consists of flow seperation, feature extraction and training machine learning classifiers.

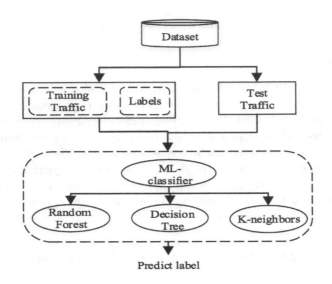

Fig. 1. The architecture of machine learning model.

A. Flow Seperation

Machine learning based traffic identification approach need to split continuous traffic to discrete units based on certain granularity at first [30]. The flow seperation module, We use flow and session which were also used by most researchers. Firstly, we apply five-tuples (source IP, source port, destination IP, destination port, transport layer protocol) to divide continuous network traffic into discrete flows. A session is a bi-directional flow that its source IP and destination IP can swap. For each flow, three packet series are considered: incoming packets only, outgoing packets only, and bi-directional traffic (i.e. both incoming and outgoing packets). A program written by Java languages are used to split continuous traffic to discrete flows. Before flows are passed on to the next stage, they are discarded if they contain any TCP retransmissions or other errors.

B. Feature Extraction

During the feature extraction, all traffic files (.pcap) are processed automatically generate feature sets (.csv). Feature extraction involves deriving 15 features from each flow. We extract simple packet features (e.g. packet length) and time-related flow feature from packets header portion of every session. These statistical features were computed using the Python pandas libraries. Subsequently, those features are labeled and then fed into supervised machine learning algorithms for classifying benign and malware traffic. The 15 selected features are showed in Table 2.

Table 2. Feature extracted from traffic flows.

ID	Feature	Description
1	Flow duration	Duration of the flow in Microsecond
2	flowBytesPerSecond	Number of flow bytes per second
3	total_opackets	Total packets in the outgoing direction
4	total_ipackets	Total packets in the incoming direction
5	min_opktl	Minimum size of packet in outgoing direction
6	max_opktl	Maximum size of packet in outgoing direction
7	mean_opktl	Mean size of packet in outgoing direction
8	std_opktl	Standard deviation size of packets in outgoing direction
9	min_ipktl	Minimum size of packet in incoming direction
10	max_ipktl	Maximum size of packet in incoming direction
11	mean_ipktl	Mean size of packet in incoming direction
12	std_ipktl	Standard deviation size of packets in incoming direction
13	min_flowpktl	Minimum length of a flow
14	max_flowpktl	Maximum length of a flow
15	mean_flowpktl	Mean length of a flow

C. Training Classifier

Machine learning can be used to automatically discover the rules by analyzing the data, and then the rules can be used to predict unknown data. Three classfiers were chosen because they are particularly suited for predicting classes (in our case, network traffic) when trained with the features that we extracted from network flows.

Random Forest algorithms achieve best performance. A Random Forest classifier is an ensemble method that uses multiple weaker learners to build a stronger learner. This classifier constructs multiple decision trees during training and then chooses the mode of the classes output by the individual trees. The construction process of random forest can be described as follows.

Algorithm 1. Random Forest Algorithm.

Require:

Training sample set T, Sample to be classified x

Ensure:

Sample label y

1: Random sampling of rows: assuming that the number of training set samples is N, the training set of a decision tree is constituted by random sampling N times in the way of putting back;

2: Column random sampling: in the attribute set of the training set (assuming that there are M attributes), randomly select the subset containing M (m l M) attributes;

3: Decision tree generation: select an optimal attribute in the sub-set of m attributes for complete splitting to construct the decision tree. No pruning is needed in the splitting process to maximize the growth of each decision tree;

4: Generate random forest: repeat steps 1-3 to grow multiple decision trees to generate forest;

K-Neighbors is one of the simplest and most well-known classification algorithms. It relies on the assumption that nearby data sets have the same label with high probability. The algorithm implementation is described as follows.

Algorithm 2. K-Neighbors Algorithm.

Require:

Training sample set T, Sample to be classified x, Number of neighbors k

Ensure:

Sample label y

1: first initialize the distance as the maximum distance;

2: calculate the distance dist between unknown samples and each training sample;

3: obtain the maximum distance max_dist in the current k closest samples;

4: If dist is less than max_dist, the training sample is taken as the k-nearest neighbor sample;

5: repeat steps 2, 3 and 4 until the distance between the unknown sample and all training samples was calculated;

6: count the occurrence times of each category in k nearest neighbor samples;

7: select the category with the highest occurrence frequency as the category of the unknown sample;

Decision tree is a prediction model, which represents a mapping between object attributes and object values. Each node in the tree represents the judgment condition of object attributes, and its branches represent the objects that meet the node conditions. The leaf nodes of the tree represent the predicted results to which the object belongs. The generation process of a decision tree is mainly divided into the following three parts: feature selection, constructing decision tree, decision tree pruning. The first is feature selection. Selecting an appropriate feature as the judgment node can quickly classify and reduce the depth of the decision tree. The goal of decision tree is to classify data sets according to corresponding class labels. In this paper, we use the gini coefficient ratio to select features. In the classification problem, assuming that there are K categories and the probability of the Kth category is P_k, the gini coefficient can be expressed as:

$$Gini(p) = \sum_1^k P_k(1 - P_k) = 1 - \sum_1^k (P_k)^2 \qquad (1)$$

According to the formula, the higher the degree of data mixing in the data set, the higher the gini index. When dataset D has only one category, the gini index has a minimum value of 0. If the selected attribute is A, then the calculation formula for the gini index of the data set D after splitting is as follows:

$$Gini_A(D) = 1 - \sum_1^k \frac{D_j}{D} Gini(D_j) \qquad (2)$$

Since the algorithm of decision tree is very easy to overfit, it must be pruned for the generated decision tree. There are many algorithms for pruning, and there is room for optimization in the pruning method of decision tree. There are two main ideas. One is pre-pruning, that is, when the decision tree is generated, the pruning is decided. The other is post-pruning, that is, construct the decision tree firstly, and then pruning through cross-validation. In our experiment, We chose the latter and got a good classification result.

4   Experiment and Results

Our experiments included two types of classification tasks, namely, binary classification and multi classification. Specifically, the binary classification task included benign and malware. The multi classification task included four types of classes, i.e., scareware, ransomware, adware and benign. Among all of the two experiments, the proportion of the training and test set is 8:2. Table 3 presents the distribution of traffic records in our dataset. We evaluate the performance of the three machine learning. In this section, we briefly introduce evaluation metrics for the performance analysis. Finally, we discuss experimental results of two experiments.

Table 3. Distribution of traffic samples in our dataset.

Type	Malware traffic			Benign traffic
	Adware	Ransomware	Scareware	Benign
Total Samples	34882	38159	34656	137105
Train Samples	27905	30527	2722	109684
Test Samples	6977	7632	6932	27421

4.1   Evaluation Metrics

In general, we use the confusion matrix to evaluate the performance of the machine learning algorithm. The confusion matrix contains three metrics, i.e., precision (P), recall (R), F-measure (F). These confusion metrics are made up of true positives (TP), true negatives (TN), false positives (FP) and false negatives (FN). Specifically, TP and TN are the number of instances predicted correctly as malware or benign, respectively. Accordingly, FP and FN are the number of instances incorrectly predicted as malware or benign.

Precision (P): Precision presents the percentage of all samples predicted as malware traffic that are truly malware.

$$P = \frac{TP}{TP + FP} \tag{3}$$

Recall (R): Recall presents the percentage of all malware traffic samples that are predicted to be truly malware.

$$R = \frac{TP}{TP + FN} \tag{4}$$

F1-score ($F1$): $F1$ value is the harmonic mean of precision and recall which can be better to evaluate the performance.

$$F1 = \frac{2PR}{P + R} \tag{5}$$

4.2   Experimental Result

Binary Classification: In this experiment, three types of malware traffic will be labeled as malware. Therefore, there are two classes benign and malware. All three machine learning algorithms are conducted to verify the combined features for malware identification. The results of binary classification are presented in Fig. 2. We found that the values of all the evaluation metrics of all three algorithms achieved were over 85%. These results implicate that the combined feature can be used to effectively classify Android malware and benign traffic. RandomForest is the best performer, with precision of 95%, recall of 95%, F1-value of 95%. And Decision Tree performs slightly worse, with precision of 93%, recall of 92%, F1-value of 92%. K-Neighbors performs the worst, with precision of 85%, recall of 86%, F1-value of 84%.

Multi Classification: On the basics of binary classification, we use the same algorithm to identify specific Android malware traffic, i.e., adware, ransomware, scareware. Experiments are conducted to evaluate the performance of RandomForest, Decision Tree, K-Neighbors. As observed from Fig. 3, the precision of three methods is higher than 80%. The evaluation metrics of RandomForest is the best with precision of 86%, recall of 85% and F1-value of 86%. The Decision Tree performs almost the same as RandomForest, with precision of 84%, recall of 84% and F1-value of 84%. The worst performance is from K-Neighbors algorithm with precision of 81%, recall of 81% and F1-value of 81%.

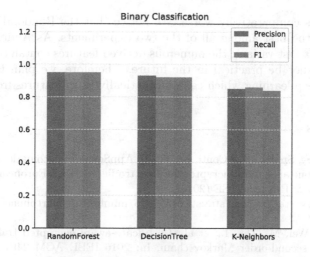

Fig. 2. The result of binary classification.

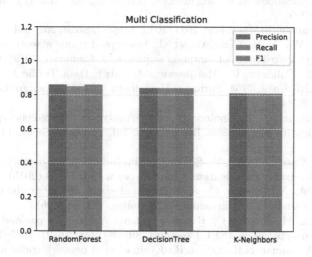

Fig. 3. The result of multi classification.

5   Conclusion and Future Work

In this paper, we have studied the time-related flow feature and packet feature
to address the challenging problem of characterization of android malware traffic
and identification of Android malware traffic. we proposed a set of feature and
Android malware identification model which contains three common machine
learning algorithms. The experimental results show that the proposed model
performs well when only classifying malware and benign traffic, with an average accuracy of 95%. When identifying specific malware and benign traffic, the

performance is comparatively worse. We notice that the RandomForest classifier performs the best among all of the two experiments. As Android malware application is a fast variant, the numerous derived features contained in existing datasets may not be practical in the future. Therefore, we plan to study the methods of deep learning which can automatically learn features from traffic.

References

1. Taylor, V.F., Spolaor, R., Conti, M., et al.: AppScanner: automatic fingerprinting of smartphone apps from encrypted network traffic. In: IEEE European Symposium on Security & Privacy. IEEE (2016)
2. https://www.statista.com/statistics/330695/number-of-smartphone-users-worldwide/
3. Shen, M., Wei, M., Zhu, L., et al.: Certificate-aware encrypted traffic classification using second-order Markov chain. In: 2016 IEEE/ACM 24th International Symposium on Quality of Service (IWQoS). ACM (2016)
4. Cui, J., Zhang, Y., Cai, Z., Liu, A., Li, Y.: Securing display path for security-sensitive applications on mobile devices. CMC Comput. Mater. Continua 55(1), 017–035 (2018)
5. Malicious mobile threats report 2011/2012. http://apo.org.au/node/29815
6. Gao, C.-X., Wu, Y.-B., Cong, W., et al.: Encrypted traffic classification based on packet length distribution of sampling sequence. J. Commun. 36(9), 65–75 (2015)
7. Biersack, E., Callegari, C., Matijasevic, M. (eds.): Data Traffic Monitoring and Analysis. LNCS, vol. 7754. Springer, Heidelberg (2013). https://doi.org/10.1007/978-3-642-36784-7
8. Conti, M., Mancini, L.V., Spolaor, R., et al.: Analyzing Android encrypted network traffic to identify user actions. IEEE Trans. Inf. Forensics Secur. 11(1), 114–125 (2016)
9. Bujlow, T., Carela-Espaiol, V., Barlet-Ros, P.: Independent comparison of popular DPI tools for traffic classification. Comput. Netw. 76, 75–89 (2015)
10. Madhukar, A., Williamson, C.: A longitudinal study of P2P traffic classification. In: IEEE International Symposium on Modeling. IEEE (2006)
11. Finsterbusch, M., Richter, C., Rocha, E., et al.: A survey of payload-based traffic classification approaches. IEEE Commun. Surv. Tutor. 16(2), 1135–1156 (2014)
12. Feizollah, A., Anuar, N.B., Salleh, R.: Evaluation of network traffic analysis using fuzzy C-means clustering algorithm in mobile malware detection. Adv. Sci. Lett. 24(2), 929–932 (2018)
13. Okada, Y., Ata, S., Nakamura, N., et al.: Application identification from encrypted traffic based on characteristic changes by encryption. In: 2011 IEEE International Workshop Technical Committee on Communications Quality and Reliability (CQR). IEEE (2011)
14. Gui, X., Liu, J., Chi, M., et al.: Analysis of malware application based on massive network traffic. China Commun. 13(8), 209–221 (2016)
15. Zuquete, A., Rocha, M.: Identification of source applications for enhanced traffic analysis and anomaly detection. In: IEEE International Conference on Communications (2012)
16. Kohout, J., Komrek, T., Tech, P., et al.: Learning communication patterns for malware discovery in HTTPs data. Exp. Syst. Appl. 101, 129–142 (2018)

17. Velan, P., Permk, M., Teleda, P., et al.: A survey of methods for encrypted traffic classification and analysis. Int. J. Netw. Manag. **25**(5), 355–374 (2015)
18. Alshammari, R., Zincir-Heywood, A.N.: An investigation on the identification of VoIP traffic: case study on Gtalk and Skype. In: International Conference on Network & Service Management (2010)
19. Wang, D., Zhang, L., Yuan, Z., et al.: Characterizing application behaviors for classifying P2P traffic. In: International Conference on Computing (2014)
20. Coull, S.E., Dyer, K.P.: Traffic analysis of encrypted messaging services: Apple iMessage and beyond. ACM SIGCOMM Comput. Commun. Rev. **44**(5), 5–11 (2014)
21. Mauro, M.D., Longo, M.: Revealing encrypted WebRTC traffic via machine learning tools. In: International Joint Conference on E-business & Telecommunications. IEEE (2016)
22. Korczynski, M., Duda, A.: Markov chain fingerprinting to classify encrypted traffic. In: Infocom. IEEE (2014
23. Koch, R., Rodosek, G.D.: Command evaluation in encrypted remote sessions. In: International Conference on Network & System Security. IEEE Computer Society (2010)
24. Aghaei-Foroushani, V., Zincir-Heywood, A.: A proxy identifier based on patterns in traffic flows. In: HASE, January 2015
25. Cheng, J., Ruomeng, X., Tang, X., Sheng, V.S., Cai, C.: An abnormal network flow feature sequence prediction approach for DDoS attacks detection in big data environment. CMC Comput. Mater. Continua **55**(1), 095–119 (2018)
26. Du, Y., Zhang, R.: Design of a method for encrypted P2P traffic identification using K-means algorithm. Telecommun. Syst. **53**(1), 163–168 (2013)
27. Alshammari, R., Zincir-Heywood, A.N.: Can encrypted traffic be identified without port numbers, IP addresses and payload inspection? Comput. Netw. **55**(6), 1326–1350 (2011)
28. Lashkari, A.H., Kadir, A.F.A., Taheri, L., Ghorbani, A.A.: Toward developing a systematic approach to generate benchmark android malware datasets and classification. In: Proceedings of the 52nd IEEE International Carnahan Conference on Security Technology (ICCST), Montreal, Quebec, Canada (2018)
29. Lashkari, A.H., Kadir, A.F.A., Taheri, L., Ghorbani, A.A.: Towards a network-based framework for android malware detection and characterization. In: Proceeding of the 15th International Conference on Privacy, Security and Trust, PST, Calgary, Canada (2017)
30. Xiao, B., Wang, Z., Liu, Q., Liu, X.: SMK-means: an improved mini batch K-means algorithm based on MapReduce with big data. CMC Comput. Mater. Continua **56**(3), 365–379 (2018)
31. Dhote, Y., Agrawal, S.: A survey on feature selection techniques for internet traffic classification. In: Computational Intelligence and Communication Networks, Jabalpur, pp. 1375–1380 (2015)

Unsupervised Traditional Chinese Medicine Text Segmentation Combined with Domain Dictionary

Qi Jia[1,2], Yonghong Xie[1,2], Cong Xu[1,2], Yue Zhou[1,2], and Dezheng Zhang[1,2(✉)]

[1] School of Computer and Communication Engineering,
University of Science and Technology Beijing, Beijing 100083, China
zdzchina@xs.ustb.edu.cn
[2] Beijing Key Laboratory of Knowledge Engineering for Materials Science,
Beijing 100083, China

Abstract. The literature in the field of traditional Chinese medicine (TCM) contains a large amount of knowledge of traditional Chinese medicine. Such knowledge plays an important role in the automatic diagnosis and treatment of TCM. In order to obtain the above knowledge, the word segmentation of TCM texts is crucial and fundamental. However, the corpus of TCM texts presents mostly in the form of classical Chinese, which is different from modern Chinese, but there are still some cases where the path of modern Chinese and classical Chinese comes in cross. So it is very difficult to use the current universal word segmentation. The lack of manually labeled corpus for TCM word segmentation which is also hard to get makes it difficult to use a supervised method to train the tokenizer applied in the Chinese medicine. In order to solve this problem, we use an unsupervised method which uses entropy as goodness together with traditional Chinese medicine domain dictionary to construct a TCM text-specific tokenizer. Finally, the effectiveness of this method has been proved through experiments on 280 MB TCM texts.

Keywords: Traditional Chinese medicine · Unsupervised word segmentation · Condition entropy · Domain dictionary

1 Introduction

TCM texts refer to ancient Chinese medicine books accumulated over thousands of years, as well as textbooks and literature in modern Chinese medicine fields. Although these Chinese medicine texts are consistent in the field of knowledge, there are big differences in the language formation. There are many differences in language morphology between ancient TCM literature and modern TCM literature, and different periods of ancient Chinese medicine literature also have differences. These unstructured texts data contain a large number of knowledge in the field of TCM, such as theory, experience of famous doctors, medical records, medicines and so on, which can be used in big data analysis in Chinese medicine field and intelligent clinical auxiliary treatment. Extracting such information from above text data, and then analyzing and mining the

© Springer Nature Switzerland AG 2019
X. Sun et al. (Eds.): ICAIS 2019, LNCS 11632, pp. 304–314, 2019.
https://doi.org/10.1007/978-3-030-24274-9_27

same by applying natural language processing technology is very necessary, and the word segmentation processing of TCM texts is a necessary and important basic task.

Currently, the word segmentation methods mainly include a dictionary-based method and a supervised-based sequence labeling method. The dictionary-based method usually combines the words in the dictionary with its frequency, and uses the maximum matching method in the forward and backward directions to cut the continuous character string. The problem of this method is that it is difficult to obtain a sufficient vocabulary for a specific domain and not able to solve the OOV problem neither. Supervised sequence labeling methods mainly use character-based labeled corpus as training data. Some methods such as HMM, CRF and deep learning have been used in sequence labeling tasks. These methods achieve a very good result in the public training data. However, these public training data is derived from the annotation of news. A tokenizer trained by such data won't have insufficient generalization ability when applied to a specific field. On the other hand, the labeled training data for the domain texts is difficult to obtain, and it is not enough to train a sufficiently effective tokenizer.

For domain texts in the case of only raw corpus available, the unsupervised word segmentation method can obtain a result that is little worse than the supervised method but acceptable in the absence of manual labeling data. Although the accuracy and recall are not as good as supervised method, it is also better than other universal word tokenizer and effective for basic texts analysis and mining needs such as text representation [1] and Sentiment Classification [2].

Our method is mainly to measure whether a character is the beginning of a word or the end of a word or neither beginning nor end, and the variation of entropy measured is used as the goodness for segmentation. At the same time, we used a domain dictionary to calculate the threshold of the goodness, avoiding the influence of artificial subjective definition of the threshold.

2 Related Work

Word segmentation systems trend to make use of three different types of information: the cohesion of the resulting units (e.g., Mutual Information [3]), the degree of separation between the resulting units (e.g., Accessor Variety [4]) and the probability of a segmentation given a string such as Goldwater et al. [5] and Mochihashi et al. [6]. The current unsupervised word segmentation method is usually based on linguistic assumptions, using a large number of raw corpus, constructing the goodness of statistical information to measure the probability that a string is a word. And then the optimal segmentation strategy is obtained through optimization based on the goodness. So building good goodness such as Mutual Information (MI) [7], normalized Variation of Branching Entropy (nVBE) [8] and Minimum Description Length (MDL) [9] is the key to unsupervised word segmentation. Jin et al. [10] introduce a classic approach which only relies on a separation measure inspired by a linguistic hypothesis that was proposed by Harris in 1955 [11]. Its main disadvantage is that the segmentation decision is very local and does not depend on adjacent segmentation. Zhao et al. [12] reviewed four classical goodness methods, and make a comparative analysis for three methods: Description Length Gain, Accessor Variety and Branching Entropy.

Chen et al. [13] used the idea of PageRank algorithm. They analogize words as a web page and together with mutual information to propose WordRank. Wang et al. [14] introduced a method that combines cohesion and separation measures in goodness, using string frequency and branch information entropy to construct goodness, and then optimizes segmentation results by iteration. Magistry et al. [8] regards normalized branch information entropy variation of Branching Entropy as a degree of goodness. These methods have good performance in general corpus and are also suitable for word segmentation in specific-domain texts.

The above methods mainly use statistical models to design goodness measures for candidate segmentation. In addition to using statistical models such as the n-gram model, there are now some use of neural language models to replace statistical models [15] in Chinese word segmentation. Qiu et al. [16] proposed a framework for sequence learning by incorporating cyclic self-learning training corpus. With that framework, Chinese word segmentation can be performed by a Bi-directional Long Short-Term Memory (Bi-LSTM) network. Qiu et al. [17] proposed a weakly supervised model by integrating the unigram language model and deep learning. This model is trained with words and frequencies and built by the Bi-directional Long Short-Term Memory (Bi-LSTM). So this model can get rid of additional manually labeling effort.

Traditional Chinese medicine, which was originated in the primitive society, has accumulated a large amount of books and literature in its continuous development. These TCM texts are large in data, complex in content, rich in carrier and diverse in writing. In classification, they can be divided into medical theory, herbal, medical records and so on. Most have been written in ancient times, such as the 《黄帝内经》 (The Yellow Emperor's Classic of Internal Medicine) in the Warring States Period, the 《伤寒论》 (Treatise on Exogenous Febrile Disease) in the Eastern Han Dynasty, and the 《本草纲目》 (Compendium of Materia Medica) in the Ming Dynasty, using classical Chinese or ancient people's spoken and lyrics. Their writing habit and expressions are quite different from modern Chinese. And there are many proper nouns and terminology, so it is difficult for universal tokenizer to perform well in TCM texts [18].

In order to solve the above problems, we calculate the variation of the conditional entropy using dictionary and get a threshold. Then we use an unsmooth variation of the conditional entropy as the beginning of the word. We adjust the goodness of the original branch entropy method. Thus, the purpose of the word segmentation of TCM texts is achieved.

3   Method

First, we state the definition the condition entropy of token sequence x_n in n-gram language model. For an n-gram sequence of length n, the condition entropy is defined as:

$$H(X|X_n) = -\sum_{x_n \in X_n} P(x_n) \sum_{x \in X} P(x|x_n) log P(x|x_n) \tag{1}$$

Where $P(x) = P(X = x)$ is the probability of occurrence of the token x, where $P(x) = P(X = x)$ is the probability of occurrence of the token x, $P(x|x_n) = P(X = x|X_n = x_n)$ is the probability of occurrence of the token x in condition of token sequence x_n.

According to the language observation of Bell et al. [12], $H(X|X_n)$ decreases as the growing length of token sequence n, such as Fig. 1 shows:

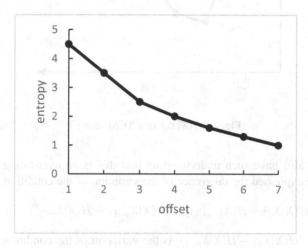

Fig. 1. $H(X|X_n)$ changing with length

we can observe that the condition entropy decreases as length increases. Jin et al. [10] use this, leverage the Branching Entropy as the goodness of boundary of a word, and this goodness works effectively in Chinese language. Specifically expressed as the difference of the conditional entropy:

$$H(X|X_{n+1}) - H(X|X_n) > \alpha \qquad (2)$$

if the difference is bigger than the threshold α, we consider x_{n+1} is the boundary of the word, then segment after x_{n+1}. However, we observe and discover the variation of the condition entropy that the variation of the conditional entropy in a reasonable word is relatively smooth, and if the variation of the entropy drops steeply, a form of a convex function will be formed like Fig. 2 in character "杀":

In Fig. 2, the variation of the condition entropy decreases sharply and our artificial word segmentation regards character "杀" as the first character of a word, and we consider that the steep drop of entropy reflect that the information of a substring suddenly trends to be "excessively certain". In a semantic perspective, this kind of "excessively certain" means that the semantic generalization ability of a substring produces a steep drop on this character. Therefore, we consider it destroying the generalization ability of the substring as a word, and compare to Fig. 1, Fig. 2 reflect a deviation of the condition entropy on character "杀". In the perspective of a language

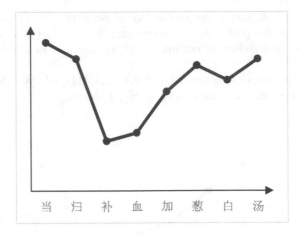

Fig. 2. $H(X|X_n)$ in a TCM string

model, we can also have such understanding that this is an over-fitting on this character. Then, we expressed the difference of the variation of the condition entropy with:

$$[H(X|X_n) - H(X|X_{n-1})] - [H(X|X_{n-1}) - H(X|X_{n-2})] > \beta \qquad (3)$$

in this formula, $[H(X|X_n) - H(X|X_{n-1})]$ is the variation of the condition entropy from x_{n-1} to x_n, $[H(X|X_{n-1}) - H(X|X_{n-2})]$ is the variation of the condition entropy from x_{n-2} to x_{n-1}, we define this difference as a goodness, when it is more than the threshold β, the character x_n is the first character of a word. We calculate the threshold β with the domain dictionary and the raw corpus.

First, we derive the word frequency through aligning the domain dictionary and the raw corpus. We select sentences that appear in words with a word frequency greater than 30 as the corpus for calculating the threshold β. For the interior of the word, we calculate it according to the conditional entropy calculated in the corpus. When the

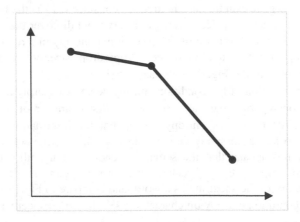

Fig. 3. The difference of the variation of the condition entropy of the first character in a word

situation as shown in Fig. 3 occurs, we calculate the difference of the variation of the condition entropy as k, taking the maximum k as the lower bound of the possible threshold β.

We can leverage dictionary to calculate the upper bound of the threshold β. For the words in aligning corpus, we take the forward two character of the word as contextual information and the first character of the word in a sentence. If the entropy situation as shown in Fig. 3 occurs, we calculate the difference of the variation of the condition entropy g and choose the minimum g as he upper bound of the threshold β. In practice, it is possible that the maximum k is greater than minimum g, if so, we select the next k and the next g instead, then take the mean as the threshold β.

After we confirm the threshold of the both of goodness, we set three kinds of word segmentation strategy as a label for each character:

- A(after): segment after the character
- B(before): segment before the character
- M(middle): the character in a word, no segment

and each time for the next segmentation, we take the word from the previous segmentation as a context to help measure the labeling of each character. For the segmentation threshold of the tail character, we use 0.1 as the threshold according [10], and for the first character of the word, we use the threshold obtained after a domain dictionary aligning with raw corpus. The specific strategy is as follows:

- Step 1. Add <bos> and <eos> respectively before and after the sentence.
- Step 2. Starting with the character that is not labeled with the segmentation strategy, the previous known word is connected as the current context character substring.
- Step 3. Calculate the condition entropy of current character with formula (1), if the length of substring is more than 3, formula (2) also need to calculate.
- Step 4. According to the current character goodness to confirm the segmentation strategy, then move to next character. If the strategy if M, add current character to substring, repeat Step 3–4 until A or B strategy occurs.
- Step 5. Go back to Step 2 until <eos>, the sentence segmentation complete.

Here, the calculation about entropy is based on Kenlm [19], which is a tool using raw corpus to generate n-gram language model.

4   Experience

In this section, we will apply the proposed method to segment the raw corpus of TCM texts for validating its performance. At the same time, we also using the other word segmentation tools and methods for comparison.

4.1   Datasets

We extract 1051 traditional Chinese medicine documents from the Internet as raw corpus, mainly traditional Chinese medicine literatures in various periods. These literatures include both ancient Chinese and modern Chinese. Each literature is between

0.3 and 3 MB in size, and the total size of the raw corpus is about 280 MB. We used Kenlm [19] to train the characters of N-gram language model, which is N = 4, and then use this language model to calculate conditional entropy.

At the same time, we prepare a traditional Chinese medicine dictionary, use string match to align these words and raw corpus for calculating the threshold of the variation of the condition entropy. When we matching a domain dictionary, blindly using it may introduce some align error because of word sense ambiguity. These errors will affect the calculating of the threshold. For example:

Table 1. Word sense ambiguity in the sentences

No.	Sentences	Word
1	齿血不止，浸醋含之。	齿血
2	凡咽喉病及满口牙齿血烂者皆以主之。	
3	甘温和血，辛温散内寒，苦温助心散寒。	和血
4	和血脉，收阴气，敛逆气。	

In this situation of Table 1, we can observe that the word "齿血" is not always a complete semantic unit in different sentences. In sentence 1, "齿血" is a word, but not in the sentence 2. Same case of "和血" happened on sentence 3 and 4. That is caused by the word sense ambiguity and will leads to an overlapped ambiguity in a sentence. Therefore, it is necessary to tailor the dictionary to avoid ambiguities. Based on this principle, we average Baidu-baike and Wikipedia to construct the original TCM dictionary, then exclude the undefined word to amend the dictionary as domain subset related. Finally, each word in the dictionary is a proper term of TCM and the length is between 2 and 4. After the corpus alignment, there are a total of 10941 words with a word frequency greater than 30 as shown in Table 2, and the aligned corpus has 4020857 sentences with a total size of 45 MB. After the statistics in the raw corpus, the threshold B is 0.024.

Table 2. The TCM dictionary after aligning in raw corpus

No.	Word	Frequency
1	太阳	55820
2	阳明	51150
3	发热	48525
4	小儿	48458
...	...	...
10939	紫茄	30
10940	宗脉所聚	30
10941	足厥冷	30

4.2 Comparison with Other Methods

In order to verify the validity of the method, we extracted 10,000 sentences from the text whose size is 1.12 MB and hand-labeled them as the test dataset. The results of the segmentation system are compared with the results of the manual segmentation, and the accuracy and recall rate are used to evaluate the effect of the word segmentation system. The accuracy rate P is the ratio of the number of words correctly segmented by the system to the total number of words segmented by the system, and the recall rate R is the ratio of the number of words correctly segmented by the system to the total number of words manually cut. In order to demonstrate the performance of our method, we also selected the current popular word segmentation tools and the unsupervised word segmentation method of [10] for comparison:

Ansj[1] is a popular text segmentation algorithm for Chinese corpus. It ensembles statistical modeling methods of Conditional Random Fields (CRF) based on the n-gram setting and Hidden Markov Models (HMMs). It using N-gram language model to do roughly cut of the shortest path, then plan the optimal path based on hidden Markov model and Viterbi algorithm, finally using CRF to implement new word discovery. There are five different modes of word segmentation: ToAnalysis, DicAnalysis, NlpAnalysis, IndexAnalysis, BaseAnalysis. We apply DicAnalysis mode to our test dataset.

Jieba[2] is a Chinese text segmentation method implemented in Python. It uses dynamic programming to find the maximum probability path to maximize the word segmentation based on word frequency. For the OOV words, the HMM model based on the Chinese characters is used. It has three modes to do Chinese text segmentation, including accurate mode, complete mode and search engine mode. We applying accurate mode to our test dataset.

LTPSeg [20] is a word segmentation module of LTP platform. A CRF model with a character tagging training data is used to segment Chinese words. All of the People's Daily (China) corpus is used as training data. It is a mainstream supervising word segmentation method.

The method of [10] is an unsupervised word segmentation method which is using the entropy of branching as the goodness. And the threshold of the goodness is calculated from a scaled raw corpus.

Except the method of [10], we use our dictionary to improve the performance of the other three methods to ensure the effectiveness of the comparison. The result is shown in Table 3. Some word segmentation errors of our method are shown in Table 4:

As it can be seen from Table 3, the word segmentation method in this paper performs well in terms of accuracy and recall rate, especially in the recall rate. According to the contrast experiments, we can see that Ansj, Jieba and LTP are not as good as the unsupervised word segmentation method in the raw corpus. It also shows that for these universal to tokenizers, the application effect in specific fields is more limited. On the basis of [10], this article adds the advantage of the first word as a

---

[1] https://github.com/NLPchina/ansj_seg.

[2] https://github.com/fxsjy/jieba.

Table 3. TCM word segmentation results comparison

Method	Prec.	Rec.	F1-Score
Ansj	0.750	0.746	0.748
Jieba	0.793	0.785	0.789
LTPSeg	0.831	0.806	0.818
Jin et al.	**0.906**	0.852	0.878
Ours	0.893	**0.912**	**0.902**

Table 4. Word segmentation errors

No.	Right Segmentation	Error Segmentation
1	瓶中**养花**\水\有\毒\伤人	瓶中\养\花\水\有\毒\伤人
2	功\专\补\五脏\之\阴	功专**补五脏**\之\阴
3	寒\客\肺中**作嗽者**\勿服	寒\客\肺中\作\嗽者\勿服
4	脾土**喜燥**\恶湿	脾土\喜\燥恶湿
5	飞\丝**入目**\及\一切\尘物\入目	飞\丝\入目\及\一切\尘物\入目

standard. And obtaining a good threshold through the domain dictionary avoids the subjective influence of manually setting the threshold, and the final effect is also able to acceptable for the needs of downstream text tasks. Meanwhile, we can see some errors in Table 4. These errors mainly happened due to the grain of the word segmentation. And there are also some ambiguities in results. These situation is related to the quality of the dictionary and the global information loss of the entropy calculation with N-gram language model. In further work, we will try to introduce more statistic feature and neural language model to improve the performance.

5 Conclusion

This paper implements an unsupervised word segmentation method for the text of Chinese medicine. On the basis of the branch entropy method, combined with the assumption of the difference of variation of the conditional entropy and the idea of semantic generalization, a new goodness is added to discover the first character of the word. In order to obtain a better goodness threshold, word frequency statistics are performed in the raw corpus based on the domain dictionary, and the text of the high frequency word is aligned for statistics. Then we use the measure of the goodness of each word to decide the segmentation strategy of each word in the sentence, and finally achieve the purpose of the word segmentation. It is proved by experiments that this method is better than the word segmentation method in the general field as well as the unsupervised word segmentation method before the improvement, which overcomes the difficulty of the segmentation of the raw corpus. However, although it has achieved certain results, it still has a certain gap with the performance of supervised learning based on general corpus. There are still many aspects can be improved for further improving the accuracy of the method, including using better language models and adopting more features.

Acknowledgment. This work is supported by the National Key Research and Development Program of China under Grant 2017YFB1002304. We would also like to thank the anonymous reviewers for their helpful comments.

References

1. Xiong, Z., Shen, Q., Wang, Y., Zhu, C.: Paragraph vector representation based on word to vector and CNN learning. CMC: Comput. Mater. Continua **55**(2), 213–227 (2018)
2. Zhang, Y., Wang, Q., Li, Y., Wu, X.: Sentiment classification based on piecewise pooling convolutional neural network. CMC: Comput. Mater. Continua **56**, 285–297 (2018)
3. Sproat, R., Shih, C.: A statistical method for finding word boundaries in Chinese text. Comput. Process. Chin. Orient. Lang. **4**(4), 336–351 (1990)
4. Feng, H., Chen, K., Deng, X., Zheng, W.: Accessor variety criteria for Chinese word extraction. Comput. Linguist. **30**(1), 75–93 (2004)
5. Goldwater, S., Griffiths, T.L., Johnson, M.: Contextual dependencies in unsupervised word segmentation. In: 44th Annual Meeting of the Association for Computational Linguistics Joint with the 21st International Conference on Computational Linguistics, pp. 673–680. Affiliated Organizations, Sydney (2006)
6. Mochihashi, D., Yamada, T., Ueda, N.: Bayesian unsupervised word segmentation with nested Pitman-Yor language modeling. In: the 47th Annual Meeting of the ACL Joint with the 4th International Joint Conference on Natural Language Processing of the AFNLP, Volume 1-Volume 1, pp. 100–108 (2009)
7. Chang, J.S., Lin, T.: Unsupervised word segmentation without dictionary. In: ROCLING 2003 Poster Papers, pp. 355–359 (2003)
8. Magistry, P., Sagot, B.: Unsupervized word segmentation: the case for Mandarin Chinese. In: Meeting of the Association for Computational Linguistics, Short Papers-Volume 2, pp. 383–387 (2012)
9. Magistry, P., Sagot, B.: Can MDL improve unsupervised Chinese word segmentation? In: 6th International Joint Conference on Natural Language Processing, Sighan Workshop, p. 2 (2013)
10. Jin, Z., Tanaka-Ishii, K.: Unsupervised segmentation of Chinese text by use of branching entropy. In: The COLING/ACL on Main Conference Poster Sessions, pp. 428–435 (2006)
11. Harris, Z.S.: From phoneme to morpheme. Language **31**(2), 190–222 (1955)
12. Zhao, H., Kit, C.: An empirical comparison of goodness measures for unsupervised Chinese word segmentation with a unified framework. In: 3th International Joint Conference on Natural Language Processing, Volume-I (2008)
13. Chen, S., Xu, Y., Chang, H.: A simple and effective unsupervised word segmentation approach. In: AAAI Conference on Artificial Intelligence, pp. 866–871. AAAI Press (2011)
14. Wang, H., Zhu, J., Tang, S., Fan, X.: A new unsupervised approach to word segmentation. Comput. Linguist. **37**(3), 421–454 (2011)
15. Bengio, Y., Ducharme, R., Vincent, P., Jauvin, C.: A neural probabilistic language model. J. Mach. Learn. Res. **3**(Feb), 1137–1155 (2003)
16. Qinjun, Q., Zhong, X., Liang, W.: A cyclic self-learning Chinese word segmentation for the geoscience domain. Geomatica **72**(1), 16–26 (2018)

17. Qiu, Q., Xie, Z., Wu, L., Li, W.: DGeoSegmenter: a dictionary-based Chinese word segmenter for the geoscience domain. Comput. Geosci. **121**, 1–11 (2018)

18. 杨海丰, 陈明亮, 赵臻. 常用中文分词软件在中医文本文献研究领域的适用性研究. 世界科学技术-中医药现代化 **19**(3), 536–541 (2017)

19. Heafield, K.: KenLM: faster and smaller language model queries. In: The Workshop on Statistical Machine Translation, pp. 187–197 (2011)

Research on the Efficiency and Application of Ship-Helicopter Cooperative Search

Yan Xu[1], Yan-jie Niu[1(⊠)], Wei-gang Fang[2], and Ting-ting Zhang[1]

[1] Army Engineering University, Nanjing 210000, China
Niuyanjie79@126.com
[2] Army Artillery and Air Defence Academy, Nanjing 210000, China

Abstract. In view of the maritime search and rescue problem, this paper analyzes the status and research results of maritime search and rescue, and uses the cooperative search of ship-ship as the main search method to study the optimization problem of search route. This paper designs three evaluation indexes of efficiency which include area searching time, key area searching time and the number of targets searched within a certain time, and builds three common mathematical models of cooperative parallel line search, spiral search and fan search. This paper compares the efficiency of the ship-helicopter cooperative searching routes through simulation analysis, then gives the suggestions of choosing the optimal cooperative searching route. Further research on the application of the three search routes to the actual rescue situation affected by the wind direction, the number of targets, and the presence or absence of location notification. It preliminarily designs the mode of combining UVAs and ships, trying to put forward feasible methods to improve the searching efficiency.

Keywords: Maritime search · Ship-helicopter cooperation ·
Simulation of searching route · Analysis · Application

1 Introduction

Maritime search and rescue refers to the process of searching and rescuing marine targets, maritime search is a key part as well as the prerequisite during this process. As the development of maritime trade, the exploitation of resource and so on, companying with frequent natural disasters such as tsunami, typhoon. The number of maritime accidents is staying at a high level, and the importance of improving maritime searching efficiency is increasing.

Due to the constraints of the character of targets, maritime search and rescue relys on ships and helicopters as searching tools to a large extent. When carrying out maritime search and rescue, ships have long endurance and great passenger capacity. But at the same time, the ship search also exists the limitation of low speed and low searching efficiency, it can be easily influenced by the sea condition, visibility, water depth and other objective conditions. The helicopter search and rescue, which has advantages of short preparation time, high response flexibility, wide search horizon, the ability of hovering when saving, and rapid speed of transitting. But helicopters have a

© Springer Nature Switzerland AG 2019
X. Sun et al. (Eds.): ICAIS 2019, LNCS 11632, pp. 315–326, 2019.
https://doi.org/10.1007/978-3-030-24274-9_28

short time of endurance and insufficient bearing capacity, which can hardly ensure the continuity and efficiency of searching and rescuing [1], and many other negative effects also can't be ignored, so make most of ship-helicopter cooperative search is very necessary.

According to the latest data from Ministry of Transport, Chinese Maritime Search and Rescue Center has dispatched 9,355 ships and 360 helicopters for searching and rescuing in 2017 [2]. Data shows the combination of search and rescue forces is obviously unbalanced. In fact, the number of helicopters for searching and rescuing in China is seriously inadequate to meet the requirements of the three-dimensional, coordinated and efficient search and rescue mode.

Taking ship-helicopter cooperation as the way of searching, this paper studies the optimization problem of searching routes. Through establishing the mathematical models of three commonly used searching routes and building the cooperative searching routes' modeling simulation, taking contrast research by quantitative analysis. The suggestions of the optimal allocation of searching power are proposed. Further study how to apply the combination of the three cooperative searching routes into reality. It preliminarily designs the mode of combining UVAs and ships, and trying to put forward feasible methods to improve the searching efficiency.

2   Search Method Resolution

Motion search refers to the process by which a search tool (or detector) dynamically searches for a stationary target. It also includes the situation where the target moves slowly (always in the search area). At present, the main equipment for sports search is ships and helicopters, mainly using ship search, helicopter search, and ship-machine collaborative search.

2.1   Ship Search

At present, the surface ship search mainly uses the method of visual force search for the surface search target, and searches by means of discrete detection. The areas on both sides of the ship are the visual observation range. Usually the ship search range is affected by many factors such as visibility, hydrometeorology and so on.

2.2   Helicopter Search

Helicopter search relies mainly on the visual force of the crew to search for continuous coverage of the sea surface. As shown in Fig. 1, the O point is the position of the helicopter, the two points A and C are the trailing edges of the left and right sides of the observer's viewport, and the B and D points are the leading edges of the left and right sides of the observer's viewport. For helicopter search, the eyesight search coverage area per unit time [7].

The search sweep width w of the helicopter increases as the height h increases, but when the altitude exceeds a certain value, the probability of finding the target begins to decrease. In addition, when the aircraft speed is increased, the search width will be

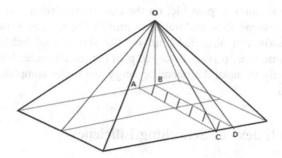

Fig. 1. Schematic diagram of helicopter search

reduced because the higher the flight speed, the shorter the time to observe the designated sea surface. Therefore, in order to ensure search efficiency during helicopter search, it is necessary to select an appropriate search height and cruising speed.

2.3 Collaborative Search

Collaborative search is a way to combine ship search and helicopter search to search together. At present, the use of helicopters is limited by many factors, among which the radius of maritime search and rescue is one of them. The radius of maritime search and rescue refers to the longest distance from the base, the helicopter can implement rescue and can safely return to the safe, that is, the maximum scope of helicopter rescue. In fact, the radius of assistance will change due to different rescue situations. In the case of the same distance, it will exceed the helicopter's endurance due to different factors such as specific sea conditions, search and rescue difficulty, resulting in the helicopter not being able to implement further. Search and rescue. Taking the helicopter's maritime search and rescue radius as the boundary, collaborative search can be divided into two situations: offshore search and offshore search.

In the offshore area, due to the rapid maneuvering speed of the helicopter, the search efficiency is much greater than that of the ship. If there is a danger, the helicopter should quickly reach the search and rescue area within the endurance, complete the search of the maximum effective range, and the search and rescue ship is completed after the preparation work is completed. Sailing at the maximum speed to the helicopter, the helicopter or the rescue helicopter can not be rescued. In the far-sea area, in order to improve search efficiency, the ship and helicopter collaborative search should be used as the main search method. Helicopter is the main search force. The ship plays the role of auxiliary search and rescue. It is used as a helicopter's endurance platform while searching and rescue. Reasonable design and selection of collaborative search routes can further improve the efficiency of search.

Ship search and helicopter search have their own advantages and disadvantages. In the search and rescue at sea, the implementation of the ship-machine collaborative search and rescue can better combine the advantages of the two search and rescue methods, and learn from each other's strengths. On the one hand, helicopters are used as the main search force, using its search speed and search range to quickly find targets and launch rescue as soon as possible; on the other hand, using surface ships as the main support force, using their endurance to provide supplies and transport for helicopters. The platform can also make up for the shortage of helicopter passenger capacity. At the same time, it is necessary to plan the search route. The two cooperate and cooperate closely to make the overall synergy and better complete the search and rescue work at sea.

3   Evaluation Indexs of Searching Efficiency

In actual cases, the ship search and helicopter search both mainly rely on visual observation for maritime targets, and realizing continuous coverage of the surface area by people's discrete visual observation. The efficiency of visual observation can be influenced by speed, visibility, hydrology and meteorology and so on. These complex external factors are simplified and quantified as the simulation parameters based on an ideal condition. What's more, it determines area searching time, key area searching time and the number of searched targets within a certain time as efficiency evaluation indexs.

3.1   Area Searching Time

Searching the same area, comparing the searching efficiency according to the time it takes to complete the search.

3.2   Key Area Searching Time

Assuming that the targets are distributed in the center of the searching area, carrying out the normal search in three cooperative searching routes, and stop once it finishes the search of the specified area. Comparing the searching efficiency according to the time it takes to complete the search.

3.3   The Number of Targets Searched Within a Certain Time

Searching a large area, and 100 targets were evenly distributed within the area. According to the cookie-cutter law, the discovery rate of those targets was set as the ideal value 1, which means it can be found only if within the coverage area. Comparing the searching efficiency according to the number of targets searched by the three cooperative routes in the specified time.

4   Modeling and Simulation

Cooperative search is a flexible combination of ship search and helicopter search, which can increase the searching efficiency effectively. According to **the *International Aviation and Maritime search and Rescue Manual***, the common search modes mainly include parallel line search, spiral search and fan search [4].

According to the theoretical search rate $Q_{th} = w * v$ (w represents the searching width, v represents the searching speed), the ratio of the search rates between ship and helicopter is approximately 1:15.

Since the efficiency of helicopter search is much higher than that of ship search, when developing cooperative searching routes within the specified period, the ships are mainly used to assist the helicopters to complete the maximum range of search.

For the three common search modes, the designed routes of the ship-helicopter cooperative search are shown in Fig. 2. The searching area is a square area whose sides are a, thick-line route Z represents helicopter's flying route, thin-line route J represents ships' route, point O is the starting position, point D is the approximate intersection location for helicopters and ships.

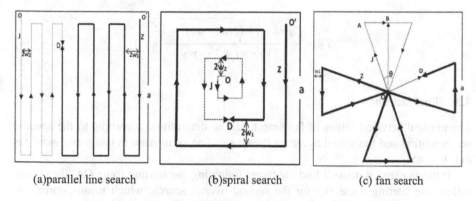

(a)parallel line search   (b)spiral search   (c) fan search

Fig. 2. The schematic diagram of search routes

4.1 Parallel Line Search

Parallel line searching route is designed as follow: a helicopter starting from point O', with velocity of V_Z, searching in route Z, the interval between two adjacent route is $2w_1$, and w_1 represents helicopter's width of unilateral visual cover, similarly, the ships search in route J with velocity V_J, the interval between two adjacent route is $2w_2$, and w_2 represents ship's width of unilateral visual cover.

The cover area of ship and helicopter:

$$2V_Z \cdot w_1 \cdot (t - \frac{a}{V'_Z}) + 2V_J \cdot w_2 \cdot t = a^2 \tag{1}$$

The time of parallel line search to cover the area:

$$T_1 = \frac{a^2 + \frac{2V_Z \cdot w_1 \cdot a}{V'_Z}}{2V_Z \cdot w_1 + 2V_J \cdot w_2} \tag{2}$$

4.2 Spiral Search

The principle of spiral searching route is similar to that of parallel line search. Taking repeatedly rotation into consideration which will affect the speed of the helicopter, and even produce observed blind area. The speed of the helicopter should be controlled about 90% of the original searching speed, to ensure the effectiveness of visual search.

The cover area of ship and helicopter:

$$\frac{9}{5} V_Z \cdot w_1 \cdot (t - \frac{\sqrt{(a - w_1)^2 + a^2}}{V_Z}) + \frac{9}{5} V_J \cdot w_2 \cdot t = a^2 \tag{3}$$

The time of spiral search to cover the area:

$$T_2 = \frac{\frac{5}{9} a^2 + w_1 \cdot \sqrt{(a - w_1)^2 + a^2}}{V_Z \cdot w_1 + V_J \cdot w_2} \tag{4}$$

4.3 Fan Search

The angle θ between routes of fan search can be determined according to the specific sea condition and the visual coverage range, etc. The simulation in this paper indicates that $\theta = 45°$.

If the fan search doesn't find the target following the starting route **OA**, then it can follow the starting route **OB** for the second overall search, which means starting to search after the entire route turns θ/n to the right direction. It continues the search only if the searching route does not repeat, **n** is the number of searching time. The larger the searching area is, the greater the value of **n** is to achieve full coverage, the value is decided by the minimum number of searching time to achieve full coverage.

The cover area of ship and helicopter:

$$s \approx 2(a - 2w_1)^2 \cdot \tan\frac{\theta}{2} + 8(a - 2w_1) \cdot w_1 \cdot \tan\frac{\theta}{2} \tag{5}$$

The total length of fan search everytime:

$$L = 4(a - 2w_1)(\tan\frac{\theta}{2} + \frac{1}{\cos\frac{\theta}{2}}) \tag{6}$$

The time of parallel line search to cover the area:

$$T_3 = \frac{nL}{V_Z + V_J} = \frac{4n(a - 2w_1)(\tan\frac{\theta}{2} + \frac{1}{\cos\frac{\theta}{2}})}{V_Z + V_J} \tag{7}$$

5 Simulation Analysis

Aiming at the above three cooperative searching routes, this paper conducts preliminary simulation analysis with MATLAB, trying to provide a basis for route selection and the distribution of searching power in cooperative search.

5.1 Simulation Conditions

In the simulated experiment, the visual observation doesn't consider the maritime condition, wind velocity, visibility, the size of the target and other complex external factors, then directly quantity them as ships and helicopters' speed and the effective range of searching, which embodied specifically in the effective visual detection width of parallel line search and spiral search, the steering angle of fan search, the speed of ships and helicopters, as well as other parameters.

5.2 Simulation Parameters

(See Table 1).

Table 1. Simulation conditions

Ships		Helicopters [5]	
Speed (km/h)	5	Speed (km/h)	150
Width of visual cover (km)	4	Width of visual cover (km)	10
Endurance (h)	500	Endurance (h)	4
		Refueling time once (h)	2

5.3 Simulation Results

(1) Comparing the time required for the three searching routes to cover the same area:

In Fig. 3, the horizontal axis represents the size of searching area, the vertical axis reprsents the searching time, sampling points represents the time for searching the size of 25×25 km^2, 50×50 km^2, 100×100 km^2, 200×200 km^2 area respectively. Make use of MATLAB simulation software, inputing parameters, then the corresponding results show the time in a certain searching route.

Three broken lines are fan search, spiral search and parallel line search from top to bottom, that is, fan search takes the most time and parallel line search takes the least time.

(2) Comparing the time of covering the central area with the side of 10 km when searching the square area whose sides are 100 km:

In Fig. 4, the horizontal axis represents three search modes, and the vertical axis represents the time taken for searching. Searching the square area whose sides are 100 km, assuming that the targets are distributed in the central area with the side of 10 km. Carrying out the normal search in three cooperative searching routes respectively, and

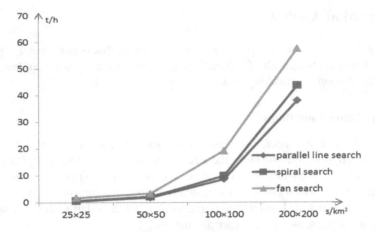

Fig. 3. The time of searching the same area

stop once it finishes the search of the central area. During the searching process, because the spiral search focuses on the central area, helicopter can carry out the inner circumference search, and reducing the speed to 80% of the set value, while the ship searches the peripheral area.

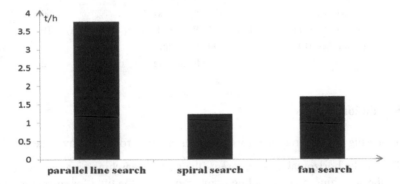

Fig. 4. The time of searching key area

Comparing the time of the three searching routes takes, the results show that the time of spiral search and fan search is less, and the time of parallel search is the longest.

(3) Comparing the number of searching targets in the same vast area within the same period:

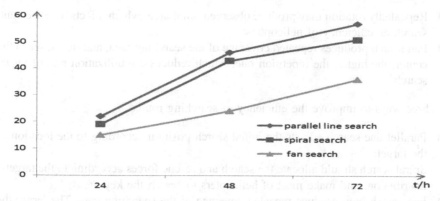

Fig. 5. The number of searching targets in the same time

In Fig. 5, it is assumed that 100 searching targets are evenly distributed in the large area whose sides are 1000 km. The horizontal axis is the searching time, and the vertical axis is the number of the searching targets. The number of targets found in the same time is compared according to the three search modes.

According to the simulation results, the three broken lines in the figure are parallel line search, spiral search and fan search from top to bottom. The former two results are similar, and the number of fan search is the lowest.

6   Analysis of Simulation Results

Through simulation analysis, the following conclusions are obtained:

1. The helicopter search is more efficient, so it is necessary to enhance its application in maritime search, and allow it to play the leading role. It's of vital importance to strengthen cooperative search of ships and helicopters, working out appropriate cooperative routes and to allocate search and rescue forces appropriately, in order to improve the searching efficiency.
2. Comparison of three searching routes:

(1) The searching efficiency of parallel line search is better than the other two overall and its applicability is larger;
(2) The searching efficiency of spiral search is relatively high, which is suitable for searching those accurate located areas, which aren't far away from the central position of the searching area;
(3) Fan search has more advantages for searching small area, if the position of the target is accurate (or the target is at a low speed), it can be used to search central circular area of the predicted area.

3. Comparing and analyzing the influencing factors of efficiency combined with the simulation process:

(1) Repeatedly rotation may produce observed blind area, which affects the speed and searching efficiency of helicopters;
(2) Fan search produces repeated coverage of the searching area, and the closer to the center, the higher the repetition rate, which reduces the utilization rate of visual search.

4. Three ways to improve the efficiency of searching routes:

(1) Parallel line search adjusts the initial search position according to the location of the target;
(2) Spiral search should allocate the search and rescue forces according to the targets' distribution, and make most of helicopters to search the key areas;
(3) Fan search may produce repeated coverage of the searching area. The larger the area is, the higher the repetition rate is. It 's necessary to fetch the searching area of proper size.

5. Suggestions about route selection in maritime search:

(1) Considering the searching area, when searching a large area, or carrying on patrol search, giving priority to the parallel line search and sprial search. If the target area is relatively concentrated on a area of small scale, giving priority to the sprial search and fan search;
(2) considering the searching time, the longer the searching time is, the advantage of parallel line search and spiral line search is more obvious, and the former is more obvious.

7 Prospect Forecast

7.1 Application of Combining the Three Cooperative Searching Routes

In the actual search, the flow velocity is known by hydrological data, and it isn't too long after the accidents.

When there is exact notification of the searching targets' location, it can be divided into two situations according to the wind direction:

The wind direction is relatively stable during this period

If there is a single target, the center of the circle point O is the reporting location(if there are several targets, taking the geometrical center of these targets as the point O), taking d [d = (time difference between informing and arrival) * (velocity)] as the radius of circle, taking the minimum wind direction line (GA) and the maximum wind direction line (GB) as tangents and intersect at the point G.

Taking d_1 [d_1 = time * (velocity + wind speed)] as the radius, draw arc intersect GA, GB at point E, F, arc EF acts as the search ending line. Taking d_2 [d_2 = time * (velocity-wind speed)], draw arc intersect FA, FB at point C, D, the CAD area is the key searching area.

The left fan-shaped area ① takes G as the starting point and GA as the starting direction, using fan search. In a circular area ② with a radius of point O, taking spiral or fan search. In the right peripheral fan area ③, the parallel line search is used to start from the inside, as shown in the Fig. 6:

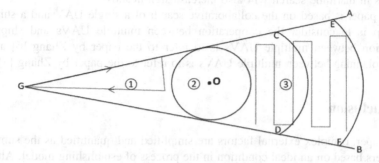

Fig. 6. Application of combined cooperative searching routes

The wind direction is unstable:

Conducting spiral or fan search of the area centered on the location of the notification (or geometric center of multiple targets);

If he searching targets have no specific location, taking the parallel line search, ships and helicopters start from the different side, near the area, enhancing the search if discover objective floaters.

7.2 Unmanned Aerial Vehicles Cooperate Ships with Searching

Unmanned Aerial Vehicle (UAV) is now in the period of great development, it's feasible to take UAV to cooperate ships with searching. Outside the ship perception coverage, forming continuous detection of peripheral area through sending back real-time images, to increase the cover width of ships. The UAVs carry out searching according to the ship's speed and its own searching speed on both sides of ships. In Fig. 7, it shows the cooperative unilateral route of the UAVs and ships: route J represents the ship sailing route, the dotted line W represents the UAV's route, w3 represents UAV's width of searching cover. Through this kind of cooperative search, it can significantly increase the ships' width of searching cover.

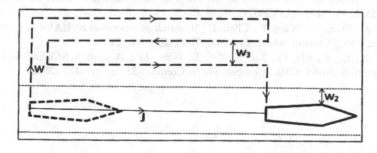

Fig. 7. Cooperative search of UAV's and ships

Nowadays high performance UAVs have about 30-minute endurance, maximum speed can reach to 65 km/h, remote control distance is up to 7 km. It's believed that the performance of the UAV will have a greater breakthrough, then its potential and prospects in maritime search will also increase significantly.

This paper is based on the collaborative search of a single UAV and a ship. The next step is to consider the cooperation between multiple UAVs and ships. The cooperation between multiple UAVs is to refer to the paper by Zhang [6] and the mission planning between multiple UAVs is to refer to the paper by Zhang [7].

8 Conclusion

In this paper, complex external factors are simplified and quantified as the simulation parameters based on an ideal condition in the process of establishing model. Although simplifies the model, it affects the complexity and precision of the model to a degree.

In the further analysis, various affecting factors can be gradually introduced to the process of modeling, such as add the searching probability, visibility and the targets' trajectory and so on, and further optimize the mathematical model to improve its precision, in order to provide more accurate basis for the route choice.

In addition, it is necessary to further think over the specific environmental conditions and influencing factors, and analyze the routes to further enhance their applicability when using the combined cooperative searching routes.

What's more, it is necessary to further study and improve the modes and methods of cooperative search of UAV and ship.

References

1. Wang, S., Li, W., Zheng, Y., Huang, Q.: Several key problems of warship-helicopter cooperation. Command Control Simul. **38**(1), 34–37 (2016)
2. Data source from: Chinese Maritime Search and Rescue Center. Ministry of Transport of the People's Republic of China. http//zizhan.mot.gov.cn/sj/zhongguohshsjzhx/shujutj_sjzhx/
3. Zhang, F.: Study on the optimal model of helicopter maritime search and rescue. Syst. Eng. Theory Pract. (03), 87–91 (2001)
4. International Maritime Organization: The International Aviation and Maritime Search and Rescue Manual. China Communication Press, Beijing (2003)
5. He, X.: Analysis and calculation of service range of the rescue helicopter. J. Dalian Maritime Univ. **33**(Suppl.), 122–125 (2007)
6. Zhang, Z., Zhang, J., Wang, P., Chen, L.: Research on operation of UAVs in non-isolated airspace. CMC: Comput. Mater. Continua **57**(1), 151–166 (2018)
7. Zhang, X., Li, Z., Liu, G., Xu, J., Xie, T., Nees, J.P.: A spark scheduling strategy for heterogeneous cluster. CMC: Comput. Mater. Continua **55**(3), 405–417 (2018)

Cellular Neural Network Based Contour Detection for Seismic Image

Jiangang Xie$^{(\boxtimes)}$, Guiying He, and Xiaohong Xiao

School of Artificial Intelligence, The Open University of Guangdong,
Guangzhou 510091, People's Republic of China
swordshadow@foxmail.com, 794119557@qq.com, 532325122@qq.com

Abstract. We apply a cellular neural network (CNN) based contour detection to exact the main reflective interface in seismic image. The seismic image is generated by reverse time migration (RTM) using the pseudospectral time domain (PSTD) method. According to Nyquist sampling theorem, the PSTD algorithm requires only two points per minimum wavelength rather than the traditional high order finite difference time domain (FDTD) which needs more than eight points per minimum wavelength to get the same accuracy. Thus, RTM using the PSTD algorithm can reduce the computing costs greatly when comparing with the traditional RTM based on the FDTD algorithm. To get more clear reflective interface in imaging result of reverse time migration, we use a contour detection algorithm based on CNN which calculates the template paramcters by the gray-scale and spatial relationship between the central pixel and the other neighboring pixels in the current local window. The simulation results shows that the proposed method have good efficiency and imaging quality, and the contour detection method makes the reflective interface easier to distinguish.

Keywords: Cellular neural network (CNN) · Contour detection ·
Seismic imaging · Reverse time migration (RTM) ·
Pseudospectral time domain (PSTD) method

1 Introduction

Contour detection is the first step of image analysis and object identification, thus it is an very important component in an image identification system or a machine vision system. Cellular neural network (CNN) is a simple and effective method for contour detection. CNN firstly presents by Chua in 1988 [7]. CNN is a nonlinear and local connected neural network which has fast computation speed and good parallel performance. CNN has been used in image processing [5]. Chua presents some interesting CNN templates for image processing Which include templates for contour detection [6]. In this work, we apply CNN to seismic image for contour detection and get a clear contour of the main reflective interface.

Reverse time migration (RTM) [2,12] has been widely used in seismic imaging and has been considered one of the best seismic imaging methods. However,

© Springer Nature Switzerland AG 2019
X. Sun et al. (Eds.): ICAIS 2019, LNCS 11632, pp. 327–337, 2019.
https://doi.org/10.1007/978-3-030-24274-9_29

RTM is still expensive in computation even in this days with rapid development of computer hardware.

The pseudospectral method (PSM) is a useful technique to reduce the costs of RTM. Baysal presents PSM firstly for seismic imaging [2]. The PSM uses the fast Fourier transform (FFT) to calculate the spatial derivatives, and thus possesses advantages of a higher accuracy and a smaller spatial sampling density when compared with the conventional second-order and high order finite difference time-domain method (FDTD) [11]. However, the periodicity limit of FFT will cause wraparound effect in the PSM. The PSTD algorithm is an important improvement of PSM which firstly proposed by Liu for scalar acoustic waves [15]. The PSTD algorithm use PML as the absorbing boundary condition which can not only absorb the outgoing waves but also remove the periodicity limitation of FFT. PML is originally proposed by Berenger for electromagnetic waves [3]. Chew et al. applies the PML to elastic waves [4], and Liu et al. extend the PML to acoustic waves [15,17]. In this work, we use RTM based on PSTD to get the seismic images.

In Sect. 2, we introduce the basic method of CNN based contour detection. In Sect. 3, we present the implementation of RTM based on the PSTD algorithm. In Sect. 4, we present three numerical examples of RTM and apply the CNN based contour detection on the seismic image.

2   Contour Detection

2.1   Cellular Neural Network Setting

For a cellular neural network with $M \times N$ cells and cell $C_{i,j}$, the standard CNN equation [5] is

$$
\begin{aligned}
x_{i,j} &= -x_{i,j} + \sum_{k,l \in S_r(i,j)} a_{k,l} y_{i+k,j+l} + \sum_{k,l \in S_r(i,j)} b_{k,l} u_{i+k,j+l} + Z_{i,j} \\
&= -x_{i,j} + \sum_{k=-r}^{r} \sum_{l=-r}^{r} a_{k,l} y_{i+k,j+l} + \sum_{k=-r}^{r} \sum_{l=-r}^{r} b_{k,l} u_{i+k,j+l} + Z_{i,j} \\
&(i = 1, 2, ..., M; \quad j = 1, 2, ..., N),
\end{aligned}
\tag{1}
$$

where $x_{i,j}$, $y_{i,j}$, $u_{i,j}$ and $z_{i,j}$ are scalars called state, output, input, and threshold of cell $C_{i,j}$; a_{kl} and b_{kl} are scalars called synaptic weights, and $S_{kl}(r)$ is the sphere of influence of radius r.

The output equation [5] is

$$
y_{i,j} = \frac{1}{2}(|x_{i,j} + 1| - |x_{i,j} - 1|) \quad (i = 1, 2, ..., M; j = 1, 2, ..., N).
\tag{2}
$$

For the CNN method, a suited template is of crucial importance. Different templates have great difference in image processing effect. When $r = 1$, a standard counter detection CNN template is defined as:

$$
A = \begin{pmatrix} 0 & 0 & 0 \\ 0 & 2 & 0 \\ 0 & 0 & 0 \end{pmatrix}, B = \begin{pmatrix} b_{-1,-1} & b_{-1,0} & b_{-1,1} \\ b_{0,-1} & b_{0,0} & b_{0,1} \\ b_{1,-1} & b_{1,0} & b_{1,1} \end{pmatrix}, Z = 4.7,
\tag{3}
$$

where parameter $b_{k,l}$ is defined by a nonlinear function $b_{k,l}(\triangle u_{i,j})$ ($\triangle u_{i,j} = u_{i,j} - u_{i+k,j+l}$) as following:

$$b_{k,l}(\triangle u_{i,j}) = \begin{cases} 0.5 & if \quad |\triangle u_{i,j}| > 0.45 \\ -1 & otherwise\,\sin(t) \end{cases} \tag{4}$$

2.2 Contour Detection of Seismic Image

For the CNN function, the numerical range of image point shall be $[-1, 1]$, but the seismic result generated by RTM is always not in this interval. Thus, before applying the CNN function, we must deal with the seismic imaging result as follows

$$I_n = -2 \times (\frac{I}{|I_{max}|} - 0.5), \tag{5}$$

where I is the origin value of seismic image, I_{max} is the maximum of seismic image. When applying the Eq. 2.2, the image value is normalization to $[-1, 1]$. We can directly use it as the input of CNN.

For the initial state, we set $X(0) = 0$. For the boundary condition, we use a constant boundary condition which sets all the cells out of the boundary to $u_{i,j} = y_{i,j} = 0$.

3 Reverse Time Migration

3.1 Implementation of PSTD

The acoustic equation of motion and mass conservation equation in a linear, inhomogeneous medium are:

$$\rho \frac{\partial \mathbf{v}}{\partial t} = -\nabla p, \tag{6}$$

$$\frac{\partial p}{\partial t} = -\rho c^2 \nabla \cdot \mathbf{v} + f_s(\mathbf{r}, t), \tag{7}$$

where ρ is the density, c is the sound speed, p is the pressure field, $\mathbf{v}$ is the particle velocity field, $f_s(\mathbf{r}, t)$ is the volume source density of pressure injection rate (Pa/s).

For the PSTD method, the spatial derivatives are calculated by pseudospectral derivative operator $D_{\eta, PS}$. The operator $D_{\eta, PS}$ on a function $f(\eta)$ for $\eta = x, y, z$ is defined as:

$$D_{\eta, PS}[u(j_\eta)] = \frac{i2\pi}{N_\eta^2} \sum_{m=-N_\eta/2}^{N_\eta/2-1} m\overline{u}(m) e^{i2\pi m j_\eta / N_\eta}, \tag{8}$$

where

$$\overline{u}(m) = \sum_{j_\eta=0}^{N_\eta-1} u(j_\eta) e^{i2\pi m j_\eta / N_\eta}. \tag{9}$$

The PSTD method is easy to implement, needs fewer calculation and can reach higher accuracy.

The traditional FDTD method uses a staggered grid in space discretization, the velocity and stress fields are set in edge, face center, and grid center respectively. While the PSTD method uses a central grid, the velocity and stress fields are set in the grid center. Thus the media properties in the center grid do not need to be averaged as it in the staggered grid.

Because the Fourier transform has an infinite order of accuracy for band-limited functions, and because for practical considerations most seismic imaging problem can be approximately treated as band-limited cases, the PSTD algorithm requires only two spatial sampling points per minimum wavelength at the highest frequency (PPW) [11,17], while the second-order FDTD needs more than 8 PPW for the first partial derivative wave equations [15]. So the PSTD algorithm can save about 75% PPW in each dimension theoretically. Compared with the second-order FDTD method in a 2D case, the implementation using the PSTD algorithm can save up to 93.75% memory. For a 3D case, the PSTD algorithm can save up to 98.44% memory. Of course, in the concrete implementation, some differences between the PSTD method and the FDTD method will also affect the exact amount of occupied memory, for example the FFT calculation needs some intermediate variable arrays.

For PSTD, the source must be spatially smoothed, because a point source represents a spatially discretized delta function which will cause the Gibbs phenomenon when we use FFT to calculate the space derivatives. We suggest to avoid the limit by stretching the point source to 3 to 5 cells in all directions [14–16].

In our work, the PML presented by Liu et al. [17] is used as ABC, which needs less calculation, fewer auxiliary parameters, and simpler implementation than other PML.

We use a constant velocity model to verify the performance of the PSTD method which can avoid the weaknesses of the traditional PSM. The model has a constant velocity of 2000 m/s and is a 2 km square in size.

Form the Fig. 1, we can find that the wraparound effect is well settled. There are not any folding waves or reflecting waves from the boundary layers in all three time steps.

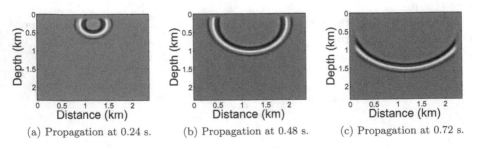

(a) Propagation at 0.24 s.   (b) Propagation at 0.48 s.   (c) Propagation at 0.72 s.

Fig. 1. Wave propagation in the constant velocity model by the PSTD method.

3.2   Implementation of RTM

Cross-correlation imaging condition multiply the source wavefield and the receiver wavefield at each time step to generate the seismic image [8]. However, for complex underground structures, the cross-correlation imaging condition may generate artifacts because of low frequency noise. Claerbout proposes cross-correlation normalized by the square of the source illumination strength to suppress the artifact close to the source [8]. Yang et al. introduce a time gating function to weight the result of RTM and suppress the artifact in radar imaging [19]. Xie et al. apply the time gating based RTM (TG-RTM) to acoustic RTM [18]. The TG-RTM takes advantage of the surrounding media information to estimate the occurring moment of dominating reflection. A time gating function is applied to the wavefield, and it can enhance the correlation of the two wavefields in time domain.

For a point at (x, y, z), two time thresholds $t_{m1}(x, y, z)$ and $t_{m2}(x, y, z)$ are defined as

$$t_{m1}(x, y, z) = \frac{d(x, y, z)}{v_{max}}, \tag{10}$$

and

$$t_{m2}(x, y, z) = min(tcoeff \times (t_w + \frac{d(x, y, z)}{v_{min}}), t_{max}), \tag{11}$$

where $d(x, y, z)$ is the distance between the imaging and source point at (x, y, z) in Cartesian coordinates, v_{max} is the maximum sound speed in the initial model, v_{min} is the minimum sound speed in the initial model, and t_w is the pulse width of source signal. $t_{m1}(x, y, z)$ is the minimum time that a source wave propagates from source to the imaging point (x, y, z), and $t_{m2}(x, y, z)$ is the maximum time that a source wave propagates from source to the imaging point (x, y, z). The $tcoeff$ is an empirical coefficient to zoom in the $t_{m2}(x, y, z)$ for complex models including turning or prismatic reflections which make the wavefield from source travel much longer than the straight ray path. The $tcoeff$ is one in general, but for complex models, it can be changed to a value larger than one. Reflection in location (x,y,z) can only occur in the interval $[t_{m1}(x, y, z)\ \ t_{m2}(x, y, z)]$.

A cross-correlation normalized by the square of the source illumination strength [8] is applied to the source and receiver wavefields at the moments between $t_{m1}(x, y, z)$ and $t_{m2}(x, y, z)$, which is given as

$$I_{TG}(x, y, z) = \frac{\sum_{t=t_{m1}}^{t_{m2}} S(x, y, z, t) R(x, y, z, t)}{\sum_{t=t_{m1}}^{t_{m2}} S^2(x, y, z, t)}. \tag{12}$$

In RTM, the forward modeling and back propagation are achieved by solving the two-way wave equations. The source wavefield is propagated forward in time (from t_0 to t_{max}) while the receiver wavefield is propagated backwards in time (from t_{max} to t_0). The imaging step needs to correlate the source field and receiver field at each time. Hence, the traditional RTM stores one of the wavefields to disk. It often becomes a bottleneck for the limited IO bandwidth. Dussaud and Clapp propose to propagate the source wavefield to the maximum recording time and then reverse the propagation (from t_{max} to t_0) to make it consistent with the receiver wavefield (from t_{max} to t_0) [9,10]. This approach saves only the source wavefield at boundaries of the computational domain and then re-injects them while doing the reverse propagation. It calculates the source wavefield propagation twice, but greatly reduces the occupied IO bandwidth and the used disk space. We apply this approach to our RTM. For the numerical examples in the next section, the receiver data for back propagation is synthetic data generated by a forward modeling using the exact velocity model. We place receiver arrays close to the surface of the exact model and record the wavefield of all time steps as synthetic data. Before using this synthetic data, we remove the direct wave from the data set by simply considering the relation between the arrival time of wavefield recorded by the receiver and the distance from the source to the receiver.

4   Numerical Result and Analysis

4.1   Irregular-Layer 2D Velocity Model

We make an irregular-Layer 2D Velocity Model to test the proposed RTM and contour detection method. The exact velocity model contains some horizontal layers and some abnormalities as Fig. 2a, and the initial velocity model contains only some horizontal layers as Fig. 2b. We use the Ricker wavelet with a center

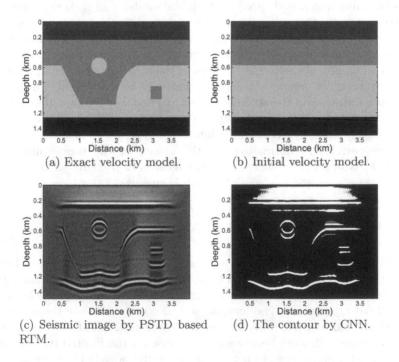

(a) Exact velocity model.

(b) Initial velocity model.

(c) Seismic image by PSTD based RTM.

(d) The contour by CNN.

Fig. 2. Irregular-layer 2D velocity model and seismic image.

frequency of $f_c = 20$ Hz as the source pulse. The maximum frequency of the source is about 55 Hz ($f_{max} = 2.75 f_c$) where the spectral magnitude is -40 dB below the peak.

Figure 2c is the seismic image generated by RTM based on the PSTD algorithm, and Fig. 2d is the contour detecting result when applies the CNN method to the seismic image in Fig. 2c. Form Fig. 2c, we can find that the seismic image is clear. Form Fig. 2d, we can find that the main reflective interface in the model has been enhanced. The greater contrast will be useful for intelligent identification.

4.2   SEG/EAGE 3D Salt Model

The "SEG/EAGE 3D Salt Model" which mainly contains a salt dome [1] is used as the first 3D example to test the imaging result of proposed method.

The total model area is $13.5 \times 13.5 \times 4.2$ km^3. The velocity varies from 1500 m/s to 4486 m/s. In this example, we adopts the Ricker source with a center frequency of 13.63 Hz. So the $\lambda_{min} = 40$ m. We set PPW $= 2$, $\Delta x = \Delta y = \Delta z = 20$ m and grid size $N_x \times N_y \times N_z = 676 \times 676 \times 210$. The whole simulation has 484 shots (22×22 shot arrays in x and y dimension) with an interval of 400 m. Each shot has 4920 m in x, y dimension and 4200 m in the z dimension. Each shot's source is set at $z = 80$ m and $x = y = 2460$ m. The whole simulation runs 5.25 s. The sensor arrays are set at the depth of 80 m with an equal spacing of 20 m. All the boundaries are PML.

In this numerical example, the initial model for this numerical example is an average of the exact model. We set the cell's velocity of the initial model with a average of cells in a square area of the exact model with a side length of 100 m. Figure 3 show the exact model, the seismic image and the contour generated by CNN. Figure 3a, b, and c are the slices of exact model in $x = 6000$ m, $y = 6000$ m and $z = 1800$ m respectively. We can verify the corresponding seismic imaging quality in Fig. 3d, e, and f, which are the slices of image in $x = 6000$ m, $y = 6000$ m and $z = 1800$ m. We can see that the areas of complex dip angles are reconstructed. Even the bottom boundary of salt dome is distinct. Figure 3g, h, and i is the result when applying the CNN method on the seismic result. We can see the main reflections in Fig. 3g and h is enhanced. But the result is bad in Fig. 3i, and it may cause by too small color difference in the origin seismic image.

4.3   SEG/EAGE 3D OverThrust Model

The "SEG/EAGE 3D OverThrust Model" is used for the second 3D model to test the imaging result [13]. The total model area of the overthrust model is 20 km $\times$ 20 km $\times$ 4 km. But for this numerical example, we uses only an area in size of 10 km $\times$ 10 km $\times$ 2.7 km in the top left corner of the whole model that includes the main overthrust structure, and the acoustics velocity varies from 2286 m/s to 5500 m/s.

In this numerical example, we also use an average of the exact model in a square area with a side length of 100 m to the initial model. We use the Ricker

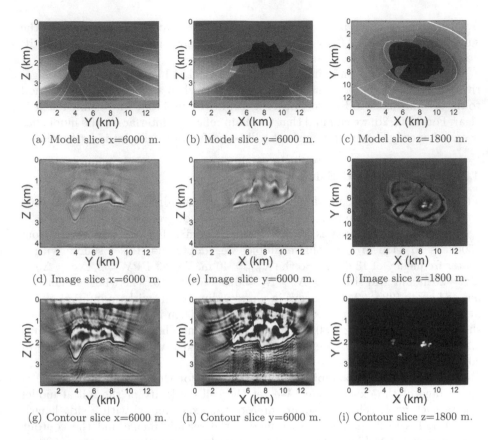

(a) Model slice x=6000 m.   (b) Model slice y=6000 m.   (c) Model slice z=1800 m.

(d) Image slice x=6000 m.   (e) Image slice y=6000 m.   (f) Image slice z=1800 m.

(g) Contour slice x=6000 m.   (h) Contour slice y=6000 m.   (i) Contour slice z=1800 m.

Fig. 3. SEG/EAGE 3D Salt Model at different cross sections. The top row is for the original velocity model, the middle row is for the RTM reconstructed images, and the bottom row is for the contour generated by CNN.

source pulse with a center frequency of 16.6 Hz, thus the maximum frequency is about 45.65 Hz. Within this frequency band, the minimum wavelength is $\lambda_{min} = 50$ m. The whole simulation has 3481 shots with an interval of 125 m starting from the upper left corner of the velocity model. Each shot has 2700 m in all three dimensions. The source of each shot is placed at $z = 100$ m and $x = y = 1350$ m. The total recording time is 2.993 s. The receiver arrays have an interval of 25 m and are also placed in the depth of 100 m. All the boundaries are PML.

The exact model, the seismic image and the contour generated by CNN are all showed in Fig. 4. The top row of Fig. 4 is the exact model, the middle row of Fig. 4 is for the RTM reconstructed images, and the bottom row of Fig. 4 is for the contour generated by CNN. When we compare the top and middle row of Fig. 4, we can find that the reconstructed images by RTM are clear enough and of high quality. We can also see in the bottom row of Fig. 4 the contour detection CNN method

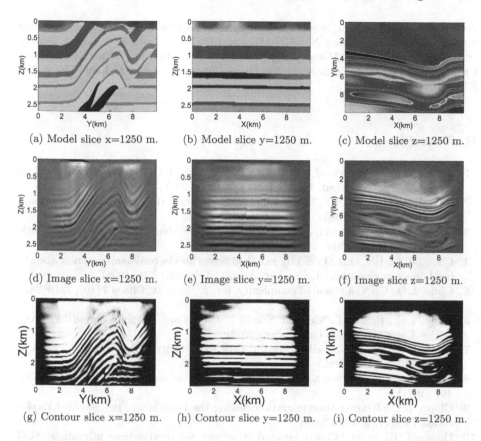

(a) Model slice x=1250 m.   (b) Model slice y=1250 m.   (c) Model slice z=1250 m.

(d) Image slice x=1250 m.   (e) Image slice y=1250 m.   (f) Image slice z=1250 m.

(g) Contour slice x=1250 m.   (h) Contour slice y=1250 m.   (i) Contour slice z=1250 m.

Fig. 4. SEG/EAGE 3D Overthrust Model at different cross sections. The top row is for the original velocity model, the middle row is for the RTM reconstructed images, and the bottom row is for the contour generated by CNN.

work fine. The main reflection interface in Fig. 4g, h and i is significantly enhanced. The contrast of image result is also improved.

5   Conclusion

The CNN based contour detection can generated high contrast image from the reconstructed seismic images. From the numerical result, we can clearly find the main reflective interface. When applying the CNN based contour detection, the reflecting interface has been enhanced. However, seismic image has some different characteristics when compared with the traditional application areas of CNN. The counter detection CNN template may need more study to fit for the seismic image. RTM based on the PSTD algorithm can significant reduce the computational cost when comparing with RTM based on traditional FDTD method.

Acknowledgments. This work was supported in part by National Natural Science Foundation of China (Grant No. 41504111) and by Undergraduate Teaching Quality and Reform Programme of Guangdong Province in 2015: Teaching Team Construction Project of Information Security in the Open University of Guangdong (Grant No. STZL201502).

References

1. Aminzadeh, F., Burkhard, N., Kunz, T., Nicoletis, L., Rocca, F.: 3-D modeling project: 3rd report. Lead. Edge **14**(2), 125–128 (1995)
2. Baysal, E., Kosloff, D.D., Sherwood, J.W.C.: Reverse time migration. Geophysics **48**(11), 1514–1524 (1983)
3. Berenger, J.P.: A perfectly matched layer for the absorption of electromagnetic waves. J. Comput. Phys. **114**(2), 185–200 (1994)
4. Chew, W.C., Liu, Q.H.: Perfectly matched layers for elastodynamics: a new absorbing boundary condition. J. Comput. Acoust. **4**(4), 341–359 (1996)
5. Chua, L.O.: CNN: a vision of complexity. Int. J. Bifurcat. Chaos **7**(10), 2219–2425 (1997)
6. Chua, L.O., Roska, T.: Cellular Neural Networks and Visual Computing. Cambridge University Press, Cambridge (2002)
7. Chua, L.O., Yang, L.: Cellular neural networks: theory. IEEE Trans. Circ. Syst. **35**(30), 1257–1290 (1988)
8. Claerbout, J.F.: Toward a unified theory of reflector mapping. Geophysics **36**(3), 467 (1971)
9. Clapp, R.G.: Reverse time migration: saving the boundaries. In: Stanford Exploration Project, p. 136 (2008)
10. Dussaud, E., et al.: Computational strategies for reverse-time migration. SEG Techn. Progr. Expanded Abs. **27**(1), 2267–2271 (2008)
11. Fornberg, B.: The pseudospectral method: comparisons with finite differences for the elastic wave equation. Geophysics **52**(4), 483–501 (1987)
12. Hemon, C.H.: Equations D'onde et Modeles. Geophys. Prospect. **26**(4), 790–821 (1978)
13. Lecomte, J.C., Campbell, E., Letouzey, J.: Building the SEG/EAEG overthrust velocity macro model. In: EAEG/SEG Summer Workshop-Construction of 3-D Macro Velocity-Depth Models, European Association of Exploration Geophysicists (1994)
14. Liu, Q.H.: The PSTD algorithm: a time-domain method requiring only two cells per wavelength. Microwave Opt. Technol. Lett. **15**(3), 158–165 (1997)
15. Liu, Q.H.: The pseudospectral time-domain (PSTD) algorithm for acoustic waves in absorptive media. IEEE Trans. Ultrason. Ferroelectr. Freq. Control **45**(4), 1044–1055 (1998)
16. Liu, Q.H.: Large-scale simulations of electromagnetic and acoustic measurements using the pseudospectral time-domain (PSTD) algorithm. IEEE Trans. Geosci. Remote Sens. **37**(2), 917–926 (1999)
17. Liu, Q.H., Tao, J.P.: The perfectly matched layer for acoustic waves in absorptive media. J. Acoust. Soc. Am. **102**(4), 2072–2082 (1997)

18. Xie, J., Guo, Z., Liu, H., Liu, Q.H.: GPU acceleration of time gating based reverse time migration using the pseudospectral time-domain algorithm. Comput. Geosci. **117**, 57–62 (2018)
19. Yang, H.N., Li, T.J., Li, N., He, Z.M., Liu, Q.H.: Time gating based time reversal imaging for impulse borehole radar in layered media. IEEE Trans. Geosci. Remote Sens. **PP**(99), 1 (2015)

Discovering New Sensitive Words Based on Sensitive Information Categorization

Panyu Liu[1,2], Yangyang Li[1(✉)], Zhiping Cai[2], and Shuhui Chen[2]

[1] Innovation Center and Mobile Internet Development and Research Center, China Academy of Electronics and Information Technology, Beijing 100041, China
ssslpy@163.com, yli@csdslab.net
[2] College of Computer, National University of Defense Technology, Changsha 410073, Hunan, China
zpcai@nudt.edu.cn

Abstract. Sensitive word detection has popped out nowadays as the prosperity of internet technologies emerges. At the same time, some internet users diffuse sensitive contents which contains unhealthy information. But how to improve sensitive information classification accuracy and find new sensitive words has been an urgent demand in the network information security. On the one hand, the sensitive information classification result inaccurate, on the other hand, all the research methods can not find the new sensitive information, in other word, it does not automatically identify new sensitive information. We mainly improved the existing outstanding machine learning classification algorithm, experimental results show that this method can significantly improve the classification accuracy. Beside, by researching word similarity algorithm base on *HowNet* and *CiLin*, we can realize expanding the database of sensitive words continually (i.e., discovery the new sensitive word). Through the methodologies mentioned above, we have got a better accuracy and realized new sensitive word discovery technology which will be analyzed and presented in the paper.

Keywords: Sensitive words · Sensitive information classification · Natural language processing · New word discovery

1 Introduction

With the advent of the Internet era, massive network information resources make it more and more convenient for people to obtain information, life communication, shopping financial management and so on. But at the same time when people get convenience [1], all kinds of pornography, violence, reaction, superstition and other illegal information also follow one another [2], it brought great harm to the people especially the youth, but it also brought great threats to the society [3]. In this regard, researchers engaged in information security have done a lot

This work was supported by CETC Joint Fund under Grant 6141B08020101.

of research and put forward a variety of sensitive information detection technology. Because the Internet features of resource sharing [4], real-time interactive, personalized and virtualization, it shortens the distance between people and promote the social contacting [5] development such as BBS, etc. However, network virtualization leading to people don't have to care about the composition of the conversation object [6]. Internet users can follow one's inclinations to express [7] their views, this phenomenon has led to uneven quality of online speech and even statements that endanger the social thought. Therefore, sensitive word detection technology is critical for the purification of network environment [8], especially for the national security of politic and Ideology.

Definition 1. *Sensitive Information: A word or phrase that has a sensitive political orientation (or anti-ruling party orientation), a violent orientation, an unhealthy color, or an uncivilized language. But some websites according to their own actual situation, set some only applicable to the site's special sensitive words. Sensitive word setting function is widely used in tieba or BBS [9].*

Definition 2. *Sensitive Information: In relevant laws and regulations, network sensitive information is defined in detail. It refers to the information distributed through the Internet which is not in compliance with the law and violates social ethics and morality and has a negative impact on society [10].*

After summarizing, we give our own definition of sensitive information according the need of function to achieved.

Definition 3. *Sensitive Information: In relevant network management regulations, sensitive information is a word or phrase that contain terror content, porn information, antisocialism or anticommunist, which distribute through the internet and has negative impact on society and country.*

Sensitive information is usually words or phrases with sensitive political tendencies, anti-social tendencies, violent tendencies, non-verbal or unhealthy tendencies. Relevant studies show that the deformation of some sensitive words cannot be handled correctly in the case of traditional algorithms [11], and the efficiency of simple text search and replacement is relatively low. In order to avoid filtering sensitive information, publishers usually take some measures. Such as the sensitive word "uniform seduction", it can replace sensitive words directly with Chinese pinyin and so on [12].

Extraction of sensitive information features is the key to study sensitive information filtering system [13]. Text feature extraction methods have been studied in depth, however, if it is directly applied to sensitive information feature extraction, problems such as low accuracy and poor self-adaptability will arise. According to relevant studies [14], currently sensitive information filtering technology mainly has the following key problems to be solved.

Sensitive information categorization is an important task in Natural Language Processing with many applications. Many researchers have adopted fuzzy matching method, it is useful in sensitive information identification from raw data. Recently, models based on machine learning have become increasingly popular. Up to now, BP neural network algorithm and belief-degree network are used to detect sensitive information. In this paper, we explore ways to scale these baselines to large corpus, in the context of text classification. Inspired by the recent work in feature selection, we show that classification models can train on a large words within five seconds, while achieving performance with the state-of-the-art.

2   Related Work

Because of the potential application value of sensitive information filtering, many scholars have carried out related research. Edel Greevy and others [15] using general text classification method researched on detecting and discovering related information about propaganda of racism on the Internet. Literature research studied the detection and tracking technology about Chinese hot topic in blog field and put forward the similarity calculation method of combing part of speech with word frequency. Tsou and others [16] carried on a classified research on the basis of the study of Chinese Beijing, Hong Kong, Shanghai, Taipei newspapers appraisal on four political figures (Kerrey, Bush, Junichiro Koizumi, Chen Shuibian). In literature [17], polar elements in the text by tagging corpus are first obtained, and then the measurements of the distribution of polar elements, the density of polar element and the intensity of semantic of polar elements are taken for each text, getting the results of texts according to nature of appraisal and degree of strength. Text classification model is highly dependent on the text feature extraction and similarity calculation. As there is no authoritative description of sensitive information features, common practice is to put sensitive words as sensitive information characteristics. In literature [18], it proposes a fusion of different algorithms and attempts to apply more natural language processing techniques to research. The filtering technology based on text content understanding can distinguish the actual meaning of the document dynamically and can achieve better filtering performance, but this is the bottleneck of Chinese word segmentation nowadays.

3   Methodology

3.1   Data Set

In the process of designing the model, we find that there are few text data sets marked as sensitive information in the public data sets currently. Because we employ supervised machine learning algorithm to extract features, if there are too few training sets with target labels, it will lead to inaccurate feature extraction, hence the data set is not meet our experiment requirements. In order to extract sensitive information features accurately, we decided to design a crawler system to crawl data sets which contains sensitive news website. Python, as a simple programming language, has many advantages for the development of crawler. When parsing the HTML source, the beautiful soup library is provided with minimal code to filter the HTML tags and extract the text. Pandas are used for data collection and storage. All the data used in the experiment from the web sites [19]. The total number of sensitive news is 14080. In the stage of data preprocessing, we divide all the sensitive data further. We screened out the news with the political orientation label from crawled sensitive news. Table 1 is description of the total number of crawled news, which is obtained from the Web pages.

Table 1. The total number of sensitive news.

Classification of scientific news	Number of sensitive news
Anti-communist news	1208
Corruption news	4560
Spy news	3750
Malignant events news	250
Civil rights news	2002

Collecting data by crawl technology has been done, we get the data that satisfy the corpus requirements. In order to better utilize this raw sensitive data, we have designed Algorithm 1 to deal with this raw data. The algorithm manifest the process of data screening data tagging data statistics and natural language processing.

3.2 Experiment

Sensitive News Feature Extraction and Model Training. Attention should be paid when extracting feature words in the raw data. Usually, the high-frequency words have higher weight. But the word frequency is not the single factor that affects the weight. In Chinese, the occurrence rates of words are very different. The utilization rates of some words are not high, but they have certain word frequency in a certain text, they are likely to represent the event described by the subject of the text [20]. In the contrary, some high-frequency words have high frequency in all texts; they may not be able to represent the event described by the subject of the text. So we use the TF/IDF algorithm to calculate the weight of words in the text.

$$W_{j,d} = \frac{TF_{j,d} \times \ln\left(N/DF_{j,d}\right)}{\sum_{i=1}^{m} \left[TF_{j,d} \times \ln\left(N/DF_{j,d}\right)\right]^2} \tag{1}$$

Among them, $W_{j,d}$ expresses the weight of feature word j in sentence d, $DF_{j,d}$ expresses the number of sentences in which feature word j appears, N is the total sentences, and $TF_{j,d}$ expresses the occurrences of j in d. Text Categorization, whose core is to build a function from a single text to category, is an important technology of data processing [21], divided into supervised learning, unsupervised learning, semi-supervised learning, enhance learning and deep learning [22].

Algorithm 1. Preprocessing of raw sensitive data for training data

---

1: $sensitivelabel = set()$
2: $length = Constant$
3: $Equalcorpus = \varnothing$
4: **for** each $new \in corpus$ **do**
5:     **if** $new \in$ corpus **then**
6:         **if** Length $t \geq 1$ **then**
7:             $new \Leftarrow [: Constant]$
8:             $sensitivelabel \Leftarrow new[lable]$
9:             $Equalcorpus \Leftarrow new$
10:        **else**
11:            $continue$
12:        **end if**
13:    **else**
14:        $continue$
15:    **end if**
16: **end for**
17: $T \Leftarrow T \cup [t]$
18: **return** T
19: **for** each $item \in Equalcorpus$ **do**
20:    $result = item.strip()$
21:    $result = segment$
22: **end for**
23: **return** $result$

Algorithm 2. Sensitive News Feature Extraction

1: $MAX\_SEQUENCE\_LENGTH = Constant1$
2: $EMBEDDING\_DIM = Constant2$
3: $TEST\_SPLIT = Constant3$
4: $TRAIN\_TEXTS = OPEN\_FILE1()$
5: $TEST\_TEXTS = OPEN\_FILE2()$
6: $ALL\_TEXTS = TRAIN\_TEST + TEST\_TEST$
7: $CountVector = Initialize(ALL\_TEXTS)$
8: $TFIDFTRANSFORMER = Initialize()$
9: $COUNT\_TRAIN = CountVector.fit\_transform(TRAIN\_TEXTS)$
10: $COUNT\_TEST = CountVector.fit\_transform(TEST\_TEXTS)$
11: $TRAIN\_DATA = TFIDFTRANSFORMER.fit(COUNT\_TRAIN).transform(COUNT\_TRAIN)$
12: $TEST\_DATA = TFIDFTRANSFORMER.fit(COUNT\_TEST).transform(COUNT\_TEST)$
13: $X\_TRAIN = TRAIN\_DATA$
14: $Y\_TRAIN = TRAIN\_LABELS$
15: $X\_TEST = TEST\_DATA$
16: $Y\_TEST = TEST\_LABELS$

This algorithm for title classification of scientific news is an algorithm of Chinese text categorization and bases on title of scientific news. we respectively designed algorithm to extract sensitive news feature (Algorithm 2)and to train classification model and prediction (Algorithm 3)

Algorithm 3. Classification Model Training and Prediction

```
 1: TRAIN_ALGORITHMS ⇐ ML_NN_ALGORITHMS_SETS
 2: x_TRAIN = TRAIN_DATA
 3: y_TRAIN = TRAIN_LABELS
 4: x_TEST = TEST_DATA
 5: y_TEST = TEST_LABELS
 6: for each ALGORITHM ∈ TRAIN_ALGORITHMS do
 7:    MODEL_ALGORITHM = ALGORITHM.initialize()
 8:    MODEL_ALGORITHM.FIT(x_TRAIN, y_TRAIN)
 9:    MODEL_SAVE = JOBLIB.DUMP(MODEL_ALGORITHM, FILE_PATH)
10:    return MODEL_SAVE
11: end for
12: MAX_SEQUENCE_LENGTH = CONSTANT
13: ISOMETRIC_LIST = ∅
14: TEST_LIST = ∅
15: TEST_CONTENT ⇐ file_open(test_corpus)
16: ISOMETRIC ⇐ TEST_CONTENT[: MAX_SEQUNECE_LENGTH]
17: for each new ∈ ISOMETRIC do
18:    new = new.strip()
19:    OUTSTR = news.segment()
20:    return OUTSTR
21: end for
22: MODEL_SETS = ∅
23: for each model ∈ read().MODEL_SAVE do
24:    MODEL_SETS ← model
25: end for
26: for each MODEL ∈ MODEL_SETS do
27:    PREDICT_MODEL ⇐ MODEL
28:    PREDICT_MODEL.TRANSFORM(OUTSTR)
29:    TFIDFTRANSFORMER ⇐ INITIALIZE()
30:    TEST_DATA = TFIDFTRANSFORMER.fit_transform()
31:    PRES = PREDICT_MODEL(TEST_DATA)
32:    NUM, SUM = ZERO
33:    PREDS = PRES.TOLIST()
34: end for
35: for each I ∈ PREDS do
36:    if Value I ≥ 1 then
37:       SUM = SUM + 1
38:    else
39:       continue
40:    end if
41: end for
```

New Sensitive Word Discovery. We get sensitive news after the Chinese word segmentation. The first step is to filter out all the words that contains one word in the segmented sensitive news, because it is difficult for single words to become new sensitive words. Secondly, we designed an algorithm to combine each word in sensitive news with every word in the database of sensitive words, in order to reduce the number of total words, this paper further filter out common stop words. The second step is to combine each word from sensitive words library and each word from segmented news. For example, suppose the number of sensitive lexicon words is m and the number of pre-processed sensitive news words is n, then the total number after pairing is $m * n$. We combine the *HowNet* and the *CiLin* to calculate the similarity of each pair of word. However, due to the difference in the structure and nature of *HowNet* and *CiLin*, it's inaccurate if calculate the similarity of each pair word simply. In order to achieve our goals better. We design two weights between the two words. The process are described in Algorithm 4 as follow.

Algorithm 4. Discovering new sensitive word

1: $sensitivewords \Leftarrow sensitvedictionary$
2: $HowNet = HowNetdict$
3: $CiLin = CiLindict$
4: $weight1 = Constant1$
5: $weight2 = Constant2$
6: $wordgroup = \varnothing$
7: **for** each $text \in corpus$ **do**
8:     **if** $new \in corpus$ **then**
9:         **if** Length $t \geq 2$ **then**
10:            **for** each $word \in sensitivewords$ **do**
11:                $wordgroup \Leftarrow pair(new.word, word)$
12:                $similarityvalue1 \Leftarrow HowNet(wordgroup)$
13:                $similarityvalue2 \Leftarrow CiLin(wordgroup)$
14:                $pip \Leftarrow similarity1 \times weight1 + similarity \times weight2$
15:            **end for**
16:        **else**
17:            $continue$
18:        **end if**
19:    **else**
20:        $continue$
21:    **end if**
22: **end for**
23: **if** value $pip \geq threshold$ **then**
24:    **return** $wordgroup$
25: **end if**

---

4   Result and Discussion

The analysis of the experiment results in Table 2 shows that other methods such as Naive Bayes are not very effective in classification of sensitive information. The classification effect of decision tree is better than that of naive bayes. The classification of sensitive news is different from the classification of general news. Sensitive news classification does not have a large amount of corpus for classifier learning and training. Therefore, naive bayes algorithm has no ideal decision tree for sensitive news classification. The establishment of decision tree is a top-down induction process. The decision tree is generated according to the continuous division of each feature. The similarity calculation method based on $HowNet$ and the similarity calculation method based on $CiLin$ can complement each other in natural language processing applications. Because of the different application goals of $HowNet$ and $CiLin$, there is a big difference in the entries. Please refer to literature for details. Despite the continuous optimization and expansion of the *HowNet* and *CiLin*, there are still great differences between them in many aspects due to the differences in structure and properties. Therefore, we combine the *HowNet* and *CiLin*, it can effectively improve the accuracy of new sensitive words discovery. The pearson correlation coefficient calculated without any preprocessing is 0.825. Compared to other word similarity calculations, the new sensitive discovery algorithm calculations are relatively good.

Table 2. Contrast effect of different classification.

Classifier	Precision	Recall	F-measure
Decision tree	0.98	0.96	0.97
Naive Bayes	0.88	0.86	0.85
SVM	0.75	0.74	0.74
KNN	0.60	0.56	0.53
LSTM	0.72	0.70	0.73

5   Conclusion

Sensitive information feature extraction and classification is the foundation and key of the sensitive information filtering model. It is varies according to dataset. This article improve the accurate of classification sensitive information base on unique supervised categorization machine learning and deep learning technology. It also proposes a method to detect sensitive information based on web information extraction. This paper mainly utilize the existing outstanding decision tree classification algorithm. By experimental results analysis, this method can obviously increase the sensitive news classification accuracy. In addition, we apply word similarity calculation algorithm combine *HowNet* with *CiLin*, we can expand the lexicon of sensitive words continually, in other word, through the methodologies mentioned above, this method have got a better accuracy and realized new sensitive word discovery technology.

References

1. Wu, S.: Research on Synthesis Governance of Internet Harmful Information. Beijing University of Posts and Telecommunications, Beijing (2011)
2. Greevy, E., Alan, F.S.: Classifying racist texts using a support vector machine. In: Proceedings of the 27th Annual International ACM SIGIR Conference, New York, USA, pp. 468–469 (2004)
3. Wu, O., Hu, W.: Web sensitive text filtering by combining semantics and statistics. In: Proceedings of IEEE NLP-KE 2005, pp. 215–259. IEEE Press (2005)
4. Guo, X., He, T.: Survey about research on information extraction. Comput. Sci. **42**, 14–17 (2015)

5. Xia, Y., Wong, K.F., Li, W.: A phonetic-based approach to Chinese chat text normalization. In: Proceedings of the 21st International Conference on Computational Linguistics and 44th Annual Meeting of the Association for Computational Linguistics, Sydney, Australia, pp. 993–1000 (2006)
6. Shen, B., Zhao, Y.-S.: Optimization and application of OPTICS algorithm on text clustering. J. Convergence Inf. Technol. (JCIT) 8(11), 375–383 (2013)
7. Wang, S., Wang, L.: An implementation of FP-growth algorithm based on high level data structures of Weka-JUNG framework. J. Convergence Inf. Technol. (JCIT) 5(9), 287–294 (2010)
8. Che, W., Li, Z., Liu, T.: A Chinese language technology platform. In: COLING: Demonstration Volume, Beijing, China, pp. 13–16 (2010)
9. Pan, L., Zhu, Q.: An identification method of news scientific intelligence based on TF-IDF. In: International Symposium on Distributed Computing and Applications for Business Engineering and Science, pp. 501–504 (2015)
10. Epochtimes homepage. http://www.epochtimes.com/gb/ncid277.htm. Accessed 4 Oct 2018
11. He, W., Guozhong, W., Liliang, L.: Fast automatic elimination of vertical parallax of multiview images. In: IEEE 10th International Conference on Signal Processing Proceedings, pp. 1004–1007 (2010)
12. Metwally, A., Agrawal, D., El Abbadi, A.: Efficient computation of frequent and top-k elements in data streams. In: Eiter, T., Libkin, L. (eds.) ICDT 2005. LNCS, vol. 3363, pp. 398–412. Springer, Heidelberg (2004). https://doi.org/10.1007/978-3-540-30570-5_27
13. Lim, E.-P., Nguyue, V.-A., Jindal, N., et al.: Detecting product review spammers using rating behaviors. In: Proceedings of the 19th ACM International Conference on Information and Knowledge Managment (CIKM 2010) (2010)
14. Sebastiani, F.: Machine learning in automated text categorization. ACM Comput. Surv. 34(1), 147 (2002)
15. Liu, T.Y., Yang, Y., Wan, H., Zeng, H.J., Chen, Z., Ma, W.Y.: Support vector machines classification with a very large-scale taxonomy. SIGKDD Explor. Newsl. 7(1), 36–43 (2005)
16. Brank, J., Grobelnik, M.: Training text classifiers with SVM on very few positive examples. Technical report, MSR-TR-2003-34, Redmond: Microsoft Research (2003)
17. Tang, Y., Lian, H., Zhao, Z., Yan, X.: A proxy re-encryption with keyword search scheme in cloud computing. CMC: Comput. Mater. Continua 56(2), 339–352 (2018)
18. Cui, J., Zhang, Y., Cai, Z., Liu, A., Li, Y.: Securing display path for security-sensitive applications on mobile devices. CMC: Comput. Mater. Continua 55(1), 017–035 (2018)
19. Liu, W.Y., Song, N.: A fuzzy approach to classification of text documents. J. Comput. Sci. Technol. 18(5), 640–647 (2003)
20. Ng, V., Dasgupta, S., Arifin, S.M.N.: Examining the role of linguistic knowledge sources in the automatic identification and classification of reviews. In: Proceeding of the COLING/ACL Poster Sessions (2006)
21. Blitzer, J., Dredze, M., Pereira, F., et al.: Boom-boxes and blenders: domain adaptation for sentiment classification. In: Proceedings of the Association for Computation Linguistic (ACL) (2007)
22. Asur, S., Huberman, B.A., Szab, G., Wang, C.: Trends in social media: persistence and decay. In: Adamic, L.A., Baeza-Yates, R.A., Counts, S. (eds.) Proceedings of the 5th International AAAI Conference on Weblogs and Social Media, pp. 434–437. The AAAI Press, Menlo Park (2011)

A Dynamic Event Region Tracking Approach Based on Node Calibration

Xiang Yu[1,3], Hui Lu[2(✉)], Le Wang[2(✉)], and Dapeng Man[4]

[1] School of Electronics and Information Engineering, Taizhou University,
Taizhou 318000, China
1267013@qq.com
[2] Cyberspace Institute of Advanced Technology, Guangzhou University,
Guangzhou 510006, Guangdong, China
{luhui,wangle}@gzhu.edu.cn
[3] National University of Defense Technology, Changsha 410000, China
[4] College of Computer Science and Technology, Harbin Engineering University,
Harbin 150000, China
6765279@qq.com

Abstract. The tracking technology is one of the most important research fields of wireless sensor networks (WSNs). However, this research is mostly used to track a single target, and there are few researches on continuously varying event region tracking. In addition, the energy limit of wireless nodes throttles the development of WSNs tracking technologies. Therefore, we start with reducing the energy consumption of the sensor nodes, and research on the continuously varying event region tracking method. We propose a dynamic event region tracking approach based on the node calibration which includes sensor node sleep-wake up mechanism and sensor node message feedback mechanism. Experimental results show that this method not only reduces the energy consumption, but also increases the region tracking accuracy. In consequence, the performance of tracking continuously varying event region is greatly improved.

Keywords: Wireless sensor networks · Dynamic event region tracking · Sleep-wake up · Feedback

1 Introduction

Dynamic event region tracking is the process that estimates the region of continuous event based on the attributes of interested events [1]. It is an important research topic in wireless sensor networks, and is mainly applied in the areas where people cannot directly monitor the event, such as fire, gas and chemical leakage. The factors that hinder its application are the same as those of WSNs, which include the energy limit of the sensor nodes, unfixed topology and loose infrastructures [2]. Furthermore, the accuracy is neglected in many algorithms, which largely decreases the tracking performance.

© Springer Nature Switzerland AG 2019
X. Sun et al. (Eds.): ICAIS 2019, LNCS 11632, pp. 347–357, 2019.
https://doi.org/10.1007/978-3-030-24274-9_31

The classes of the research on dynamic event region tracking include: (1) based on sensor node sensing [3–5]. In reference [6], the tracking is based on the whole region of the event, which takes advantage of all the sensor nodes within the event region to sense the event and transmit information. But it also wastes a lot of node energy. In reference [7–9], to provide detection results at each time step, a distributed event region tracking algorithm is proposed. The system dynamics and the information collected from neighbors are used to predict the underlying hypothesis at each sensor node and local observation is used for update. Mean field approximation is adopted in the algorithm for tractability. In reference [10], the event boundary is tracked via cluster structure. In each cluster, the sensors sense event information and transmit the information to the cluster head, then the cluster head identifies the event boundary sensor node based on boundary estimation function. However, it will construct the cluster twice which will definitely increase energy consumption when constructing the two-layer cluster structure. In reference [11], the proposed distributed boundary node selection algorithms allow B-nodes to self-select based on available 1-hop information extracted from nodes' simple geometrical and statistical features.

In this paper, we propose a dynamic event boundary tracking method NGEBTM based on node calibration. We start from decreasing the energy consumption of the sensor nodes and increasing the estimation accuracy of dynamic event boundary nodes. A sensor node sleep-wake up mechanism and an information feedback mechanism of the estimation nodes are proposed. We also set up an evaluation system for the estimation of region sensor node energy and the estimation accuracy of the boundary nodes.

2 Event Boundary Estimation

The aim of boundary sensor estimation is to save energy by turning the sensor nodes which are far away from the event boundary into sleep state [11]. As a result, one of the difficulties when estimating boundary nodes is how to choose a proper node to act as the event boundary node of the next moment, and the boundary is composed of many boundary nodes. When estimating the boundary, the boundary sensor nodes are selected to wake up the neighbor nodes so as to construct the boundary of dynamic events. The boundary nodes at moment t are denoted as $bn(t)_1$, $bn(t)_2$, ..., $bn(t)_i$, $bn(t)_{i+1}$, ..., $bn(t)_n$, and these sensor nodes communicate with each other, also construct an event boundary. As shown in Fig. 1, $bn(t)_i$, $bn(t)_{i+1}$, are two boundary sensor nodes at t moment, and the boundary nodes $bn(t+1)_i$, $bn(t+1)_{i+1}$, at $t+1$ moment is obtained via boundary estimation algorithm. Therefore, the boundary nodes at $t+1$ moment communicate with each other and the boundary at $t+1$ moment is consequently constructed.

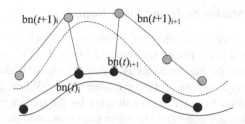

Fig. 1. The structure of boundary estimation

3 Algorithms on Sensor Node

3.1 Boundary Sensor Node Selection Algorithm

At the initial moment, the event boundary sensor nodes should be determined before boundary tracking [12–14].

(a) Determination of Neighbor Nodes

The determination of neighbor nodes provides the coordinates of the needed nodes, which is the prerequisite.

The sensor node that has detected event is put into the event detection node table (check_table), and the nodes in that table which can communicate within one hop are put into the neighbor node table (n_table) of the corresponding node.

(b) Determination of Event Boundary Nodes

The three nodes' coordinates can be used as the coordinates of the three vertexes of a triangle. The distance between two arbitrary vertexes is calculated using Eq. (1), and then the perimeter of the triangle is calculated using Eq. (2). Finally, the area of the initial triangle is calculated based on Heron's formula (Eq. (3)). The node to be detected together with two arbitrary nodes which are selected from the three vertexes are calculated, which determines the node's position relative to the initial triangle.

$$D_{UBiUBj} = \sqrt{(X_i - X_j)^2 + (Y_i - Y_j)^2} \tag{1}$$

$$L = \frac{1}{2}(D_{UB1UB2} + D_{UB1UB3} + D_{UB2UB3}) \tag{2}$$

$$S_{\triangle UB1UB2UB3} = \sqrt{L(L - D_{UB1UB2})(L - D_{UB1UB3})(L - D_{UB2UB3})} \tag{3}$$

D_{UB1UB2} denotes the edge length of the triangle, and L denotes the perimeter of the triangle. To judge whether node B, the node to be detected, is boundary node or not, $S_{UB1UB2UB3}$ and $S_{BUB1UB2} + S_{BUB1UB3} + S_{B1UB2UB3}$ are calculated respectively and compared as the following steps based on GCENS algorithm.

3.2 Estimation of Master Node and Slave Node

After the boundary sensor node selection, a master node which serves as estimation node together with two slave nodes are selected by NGEBTM in order to make the communication between the master nodes available. The salve nodes are located within the communication range of two different master nodes. When the slave nodes are connected, the estimation boundary is constructed by the master nodes.

Competition mechanism is adopted to select the master nodes. After confirming the boundary nodes, the nodes will send master node information to the next hop neighbor immediately. The first node which sends information successfully will become the master node. After being confirmed, the master nodes will broadcast slave node information to all the neighbor nodes, and the node which receives information from two different master nodes will become the estimation slave node. In this way, it is guaranteed that the slave node is located within the communication range of two different master nodes, which can help the master nodes communicate. As shown in Fig. 2, the black nodes are master nodes and the yellow ones are slave nodes. The yellow nodes are within the communication radiuses of the black ones.

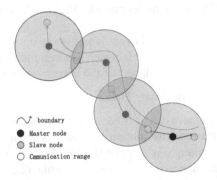

Fig. 2. Selection of master and slave nodes (Color figure online)

3.3 Boundary Node Estimation, Sleep-Wake up and Calibration Mechanism

(a) Boundary Node Estimation

Each node has a neighbor descriptor table, which contains the neighbor node's id, state, position, detection target indicator and timestamp. In the initial phase of the event, the neighbor descriptor table is initialized, and the neighbor node detection target indicator and timestamp are empty. Two adjacency master nodes transmit and receive boundary estimation pairing request via the slave node, and then construct an estimation node pair. In order to estimate the event boundary sensor nodes at the next time, each master node calculates the event changing speed and direction with the neighbor node event detection information in the neighbor descriptor table. As shown in Fig. 3, assume the history position of one neighbor node i of the master node N is (x_n, y_n), and the

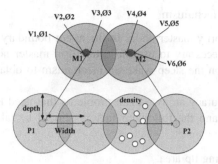

Fig. 3. Principle of master node estimation

position of the current master node M is (x_m, y_m). The event changing speed and direction that the master node detects at the current moment are shown in Eqs. (4) and (5):

$$v_i = \frac{\sqrt{(x_m - x_m)^2 + (y_n - y_n)^2}}{t_{current} - t_{history}} \tag{4}$$

$$\theta_i = \cos^{-1} \frac{x_m - x_n}{\sqrt{(x_m - x_n)^2 + (y_m - y_n)^2}} \tag{5}$$

where v_i, θ_i are the data that node i detects.

Usually, a master node has several neighbor nodes, so the master node can receive various node detection data from different directions. In order to make the estimation data more accurate, their mean value is calculated as follows:

$$v_m = \frac{1}{n} \sum_{i=1}^{n} v_i, \theta_m = \frac{1}{n} \sum_{i=1}^{n} \theta_i \tag{6}$$

The event changing speed and direction that the current node detects are obtained after the calculation. And the coordinate of the estimation boundary node at the next moment can be calculated by Eqs. (7) and (8):

$$x_{m+1} = x_m + v_m t \cos(\theta_m) \tag{7}$$

$$y_{m+1} = y_m + v_m t \sin(\theta_m) \tag{8}$$

In Fig. 6, the distance $\overline{M1M2}$ between M1 and M2 represents the current event boundary, and the estimation boundary of $\overline{P1P2}$ can be calculated from the above algorithm.

(b) Sleep-Wake up Mechanism

Since only the minority master nodes of the event boundary can be obtained from the above steps, it is necessary to use the estimation master nodes to wake up their neighbor nodes based on the sleep-wake up mechanism to obtain the complete event boundary.

The energy and accuracy are two main problems that need to be considered when waking up the nodes, and the following factors should be taken into consideration specifically:

(1) The width of waking up area.
(2) The depth of waking up area.
(3) The node density of waking up area.

(c) Boundary Nodes Estimation Feedback Mechanism

Evaluating estimation tracking algorithm is important for increasing the accuracy of node estimation. The estimation feedback mechanism for boundary nodes can inform the change of estimation accuracy of sensor nodes in time. A threshold of tracking accuracy μ is set as shown in Eq. (9).

$$\mu = \frac{number\ of\ estimated\ boundary\ nodes}{number\ of\ actually\ detected\ boundary\ nodes} \times 100\% \tag{9}$$

The estimation accuracy is calculated with t time interval during tracking. When estimation accuracy is less than or equal to μ, the system will immediately use the estimation sleep-wake up mechanism to adjust the depth, width and node density of the waking up area. The detailed process is as follows.

Assumes the width of waking up area is W, the depth is D, the node density is U, and the sensing range of the sensor nodes is R, it can be seen that U has smaller impact on the estimation accuracy from experiments, so U is ignored when adjusting the estimation area. The factor is set to be $W + D, 0 \leq W \leq R, 0 \leq D \leq R$, in which R is the initial value. It can be seen from experiments that the relationships between width, depth and estimation accuracy are proportional relationship and inverse relationship respectively. As a result, when estimation accuracy downgrades, we can make the accuracy increase by decreasing the value of $W + D$.

4   Experimental Results Analysis

4.1   Design Network Simulation Environment

The network simulation environment is generated randomly using Setdest in NS2 [13]. 200 wireless sensor nodes are deployed in the network area of 1600×1600, in which Leach is selected to be the route protocol and the simulation time is 500 ms. The energy consumption rate of the sensor nodes in sleeping and waken up states are 3 µA and 15 µA, and the receiving and transmitting energy consumption are 29 mA and

42 mA respectively. The initial area of the event is a circle, whose central coordinate is (800, 800), the radius is 500 and the time of happening is 100 ms. The properties of the sensor network are configured that include node index, bandwidth, time delay, type of the queue and initial node energy. Sink node is added into the topology area with the coordinate of (0, 0).

The position of the event will change as time goes on. The evaluation data of the algorithm's performance is obtained based on the initialized number of sensor nodes and the energy at different time comparing with the number of detected nodes and the rest of energy when the event boundary is detected. Then we get the performance evaluation of the algorithm by judging the various performance evaluation parameters.

Nine groups of data is given based on the time of event, and the time of data extracted are 100 ms, 150 ms, 200 ms, 250 ms, 300 ms, 350 ms, 400 ms, 450 ms, 500 ms.

4.2 Parameters of Evaluation

(1) **Energy consumption of the nodes.** The sum of energy consumption of all the active and sleeping nodes.
(2) **Boundary node accuracy.** The estimated number of boundary nodes by NGEBTM algorithm and the actual number of boundary nodes.

4.3 Experimental Result Analysis

The experiments contain the comparison of energy consumption and estimation accuracy with and without NGEBTM algorithm, and the impact of the width, depth and node density of the estimation area on the energy consumption and the accuracy of event boundary node estimation.

(a) Comparison of Energy Consumption and Node Accuracy with and without NGEBTM Algorithm

The energy consumption change of the nodes with the increasing of simulation time is shown in Fig. 4. It can be seen that the energy consumption performance of NGEBTM algorithm with sleep-wake up mechanism is obviously better than the network with all nodes active. As shown in Fig. 5, the node estimation accuracy before adding feedback mechanism into NGEBTM algorithm is about 80%, but after adding feedback mechanism, it is about 90% which has an obvious improvement.

(b) Impact of Width of Estimation Area on Energy Consumption and Accuracy

The impact of the width of the estimation area on the energy consumption of the sensor nodes and boundary node estimation accuracy are shown in Figs. 6 and 7. As shown in Fig. 6, the energy consumption decreases as the width of the estimation area increasing. It is because when the estimation width decreases, the distance of node communication will become larger and the energy consumption will increase. On the contrary, the boundary node estimation accuracy increases when increasing the width of estimation area as shown in Fig. 7. It indicates that a small width of estimation area

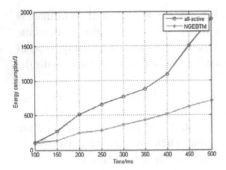

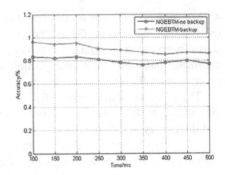

Fig. 4. Before and after NGEBTM

Fig. 5. Feedback mechanism influence on accuracy

brings about a high accuracy of detecting boundary nodes. As a result, the change of the width of the estimation area has a proportional impact on boundary node estimation accuracy and has an inversely proportional impact on the energy consumption of the sensor nodes.

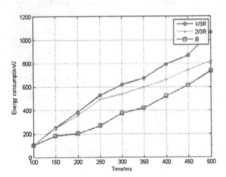

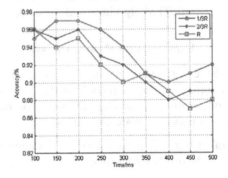

Fig. 6. Energy consumption

Fig. 7. Boundary node estimation accuracy

(c) Impact of Depth of Estimation Area on Energy Consumption and Accuracy

The impact of the estimation area depth on the energy consumption and boundary node estimation accuracy are shown in Figs. 8 and 9. The energy consumption becomes larger with the estimation area depth increasing at the same simulation time as shown in Fig. 8. It is because when the estimation area depth becomes larger, the distance of node communication will become larger and the energy consumption will increase. On the contrary, the boundary node estimation accuracy decreases when increasing the estimation area depth as shown in Fig. 9.

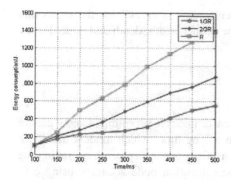

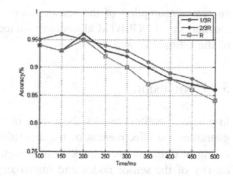

Fig. 8. Energy consumption

Fig. 9. Boundary node estimation accuracy

(d) Impact of Estimation Area Node Density on Energy Consumption and Accuracy

The impact of the estimation area node density on the energy consumption and boundary node estimation accuracy are shown in Figs. 10 and 11. As Fig. 10 depicts, the energy consumption that selects all the neighbor nodes of the estimation node is higher than that of selecting certain boundary nodes (slave nodes). And from Fig. 11 we can see that the difference of impact on accuracy between selecting the neighbor nodes which contain all the estimation nodes and selecting the neighbor nodes is very small. As a result, the impact of the estimation area density on the node estimation accuracy is very small.

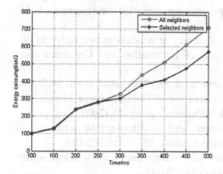

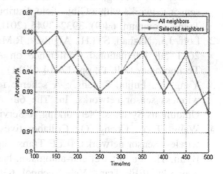

Fig. 10. Energy consumption

Fig. 11. Boundary node estimation accuracy

4.4   Summary

It can be concluded from the experiments above that the node sleep-wake up mechanism can save the energy of the sensor node at a large extent and the estimation feedback mechanism can improve the boundary node estimation accuracy very well. In addition, the width, depth and node density of estimation area have large impact on the energy consumption of the sensor nodes. Therefore, it is crucial for the estimation mechanism of NGEBTM algorithm to select the proper width, depth and node density of the estimation area.

5 Conclusion

In wireless sensor networks, the energy of the sensor nodes is very limited and it cannot guarantee the effectiveness of the algorithm in a long time, which hinders the application of dynamic event tracking techniques. In this paper, we research on saving the energy of the sensor nodes and improving the estimation node accuracy using estimation node information feedback mechanism, which improves the performance of tracking continuously varying event region.

Since the number of boundary nodes is small in our estimation algorithm, and the definition of event boundary is a little fuzzy, it is easy to lose the event boundary information. Resolving the above weakness is our future work.

Acknowledgement. The research is supported by the National Natural Science Foundation of China under Grant No. 61572153, No. U1636215 and No. 61871140, and the National Key Research and Development Plan (Grant No. 2018YFB0803504).

References

1. Wang, T.-Y., Yang, M.-H., Wu, J.-Y.: Distributed detection of dynamic event regions in sensor networks with a Gibbs field distribution and gaussian corrupted measurements. IEEE Trans. Commun. **64**(9), 3932–3945 (2016)
2. Lotf, J.J., Nazhad, S.H.H., Alguliev, R.M. (eds.): A survey of wireless sensor networks. In: 2011 5th International Conference on Application of Information and Communication Technologies (AICT), pp. 12–14 (2011)
3. Yang, Y., Fujita, S. (eds.): A scheme for efficient tracking of dynamic event region in wireless sensor networks. In: The 6th Annual International Conference on Mobile and Ubiquitous Systems: Networking & Services, MobiQuitous, pp. 13–16 (2009)
4. Wang, T.-Y., Cheng, Q.: Collaborative event-region and boundary-region detections in wireless sensor networks. IEEE Trans. Signal Process. **56**(6), 2547–2561 (2008)
5. Byun, H., Yu, J.: Cellular-automaton-based node scheduling control for wireless sensor networks. IEEE Trans. Veh. Technol. **63**(8), 3892–3899 (2014)
6. Lee, W., Yim, Y., Park, S., Lee, J., Park, H., Kim, S.H. (eds.): A cluster-based continuous object tracking scheme in wireless sensor networks. In: 2011 IEEE Conference on Vehicular Technology (VTC Fall), pp. 5–8 (2011)
7. Wu, T., Cheng, Q.: Online dynamic event region detection using distributed sensor networks. IEEE Trans. Aerosp. Electron. Syst. **50**(1), 393–405 (2014)
8. Wu, T., Cheng, Q.: Adaptive bandwidth allocation for dynamic event region detection in wireless sensor networks. IEEE Trans. Wireless Commun. **13**(9), 5107–5119 (2014)
9. Wu, T., Cheng, Q.: Distributed dynamic event region detection in wireless sensor networks. In: Proceedings of the IEEE Conference on Prognostics and System Health Management Conference (PHM), Montreal, QC, Canada, pp. 1–8 (2011)

10. Chang, W.R., Lin, H.T., Cheng, Z.Z. (eds.): CODA: a continuous object detection and tracking algorithm for wireless ad hoc sensor networks. In: The 5th IEEE Consumer Communications and Networking Conference, pp. 10–12 (2008)
11. Rafiei, A., Abolhasan, M., Franklin, D., Safaei, F. (eds.): Boundary node selection algorithms in WSNs. In: 2011 IEEE 36th Conference on Local Computer Networks (LCN), pp. 4–7 (2011)
12. Chraim, F., Erol, Y., Pister, K.: Wireless gas leak detection and localization. IEEE Trans. Ind. Informat. **12**(2), 768–779 (2016)
13. Gao, Z., Xia, S., Zhang, Y., et al.: Real-time visual tracking with compact shape and color feature. Comput. Mater. Continua **55**(3), 509–521 (2018)
14. Wang, J., Ju, C., Gao, Y., et al.: A PSO based energy efficient coverage control algorithm for wireless sensor networks. CMC Comput. Mater. Continua **56**(3), 433–446 (2018)

A Graph Updating Method of Data Theft Detection Based on Rough Set

Xiang Yu[1], Le Wang[2(✉)], Shuang Chen[1(✉)], and Yanbo Li[3]

[1] School of Electronics and Information Engineering,
Taizhou University, Taizhou 318000, China
1267013@qq.com, 474192094@qq.com
[2] Cyberspace Institute of Advanced Technology,
Guangzhou University, Guangzhou 510006, China
wangle@gzhu.edu.cn
[3] School of Computer Science, Heilongjiang Institute of Engineering,
Harbin 150000, China
282506364@qq.com

Abstract. In recent years, the problem of data theft is becoming more and more serious. This paper provides a graph update method of data theft detection based on rough set DLD-RGU to prevent the leakage of sensitive data. This method builds a clustering model of sensitive text data by training samples, and then constructs a sensitive word graph structure, periodically calculates the importance of sensitive words and latent sensitive words to update the sensitive word graph, adapts to the change of incremental sensitive data, and improves the detection effect. Experiments on real data sets and simulation data sets show that DLD-RGU can adapt to sensitive content changes, update the sensitive word graph in time, and accurately identify the key words of confidential text containing sensitive content.

Keywords: Information security · Data theft · Rough set · Graph

1 Introduction

The emergence of information technology such as the Internet and big data provides people with a variety of valuable information, but also intensifies the difficulty of information processing. According to IDC (Internet Data Center), the volume of global data will increase 50-fold by 2020. How to prevent the leakage of confidential data while making full use of data is a difficult problem.

Open and diverse information sources also give some malicious information theft opportunities, or through direct replication, the disguise of leakage and other illegal means of stealing data, which will threaten the national security, social order, business operations, etc. It is urgent and important to develop advanced text data leak detection and protection technology to filter text containing sensitive content.

This paper presents a data theft detection method DLD-RGU based on rough set, which can prevent the leakage of sensitive text data. DLD-RGU constructs the clustering model based on the training set data, constructs the sensitive word graph, uses

© Springer Nature Switzerland AG 2019
X. Sun et al. (Eds.): ICAIS 2019, LNCS 11632, pp. 358–367, 2019.
https://doi.org/10.1007/978-3-030-24274-9_32

the rough set importance calculation method, and incrementally updates the sensitive word graph according to the sensitive content changes, enables the sensitive word graph to reflect the sensitive content change promptly and accurately.

2 Related Work

According to the survey, about 51% of computer attacks are caused by insiders, the most common of which are intellectual illegal theft, non-subjective and deliberate disclosure of privacy and sensitive data, illegal theft of customer information and other data such as financial data. In addition, the survey shows that more than 67% of organizations believe that illegal theft from inside will be more dangerous than attacks from outside [1, 2].

In foreign countries, the research on data theft and its protection methods started earlier, which can be traced back to the access control model proposed to solve the problem of internal user privilege abuse [3]. Requirements for user access control were defined in the first computer security evaluation standard published in 1983. With the research of the problem, specific practical solutions, such as some software and hardware solutions, have been put forward [4].

Hardware solutions focus on encrypting or disabling communications, and even passive solutions such as removing USB interfaces [5]. Compared with hardware solutions, software solutions have higher research value and richer results. At present, software solutions are mostly content-based approaches. Content-based methods can be further divided into Rule-based methods and Classifier-based methods according to their implementation approaches [6]. The method based on rule implementation defines a series of targeted rules according to the sensitive words that may appear in the file in advance, scans the file to be detected and matches the sensitive words with the rules, and then determines the sensitive level of the file. The research on this method has matured and been applied on a number of commercial products [7]. Classifier-based methods involve a series of machine learning methods and classifier models, such as Naive Bayes Classifier and Support Vector Machine [8]. In this class, a file is represented as a space vector model, and a classifier is constructed and trained by a known file, and further identify whether an unknown file contains sensitive data or not.

Rule-based systems are too precise in dealing with such information leakage detection and processing problems [9]. As a result, a document that contains only one or a few secrecy may be ignored by such a system. Nowadays, this rule-based approach is not universally applicable because of this high false positive rate [10]. In addition, because most documents are non-confidential, and statistical-based classifiers focus on the most important features of data, classifiers such as support vector machines or naive Bayesian classifiers are not ideal for detecting such documents [11–13].

In view of this, this paper proposes a data theft detection method based on rough set theory and sensitive word graph update strategy. Firstly, the training documents are clustered, the classified contents are extracted, and the sensitive words are extracted according to the corresponding rules and integrated into a graph. When identifying whether the document under test is a confidential document, the sensitive words are searched in the document under test to reduce false positive misjudgment. When the confidentiality of the document set changes or new documents are added to the training set, the sensitive words can be updated according to the new situation, and redundant words and interference words can be reduced by the importance calculation method of rough set, then the graph structure can be updated. Finally, the sensitive words in the graph can be used to judge whether the document under test contains confidential information or not.

3   The Detection Approach for Data Theft Based on Graph Updating

In view of the traditional software-based data theft protection methods keep low false alarm rate while it is difficult to ensure a low level of false negative rate, and cannot effectively deal with the disguises in complex situation, which is difficult in data theft detection. The proposed solution DLD-RGU (Data Leakage Detection based on Rough reductions and Graph Updating) combines the advantages of rule-based detection method and classifier-based detection method. It uses classifier-based method for reference, clusters text according to topics, and detects the files of different topics to ensure the correct results. Meanwhile, based on the core idea of sensitive word recognition, the importance of sensitive words which represent sensitive data is analyzed and calculated, the influence of redundant words and interference words is reduced, and the disguised sensitive data is identified [14–17].

3.1   Confidential Document Clustering Model

In the training phase, the text is preprocessed firstly, and then the training documents are clustered to get a set of confidential documents containing sensitive contents under different topics. The corresponding set of sensitive words is analyzed and the sensitive word graph is constructed. The specific process is illustrated in Fig. 1.

(1) text preprocessing

Text preprocessing includes removal of stop words, removal of interference words and other steps. In the field of natural language processing, these preprocessing methods are very mature. In this paper, we first construct a list of stop words, remove interference words and stop words. And then extract the stem.

Filtering stop words is one of the important steps in text processing. Filtering out high-frequency words with low information content can reduce text processing time, save storage space and improve detection accuracy. Based on the RANKSNL multi-lingual stop words database, this paper collects and checks the stoppage word list manually.

Stem extraction in this paper adopts Porter Stemmer Algorithms which is widely used in information retrieval system proposed by Martin Porter.

(2) text clustering

At present, clustering analysis technology is very mature in data mining and machine learning. In this paper, TF-IDF weight is chosen as the vector space model.

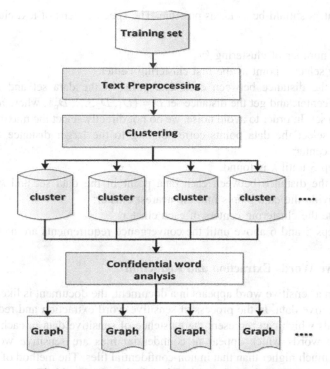

Fig. 1. The model of confident documents clustering

Latent Semantic Indexing (LSI) is used to reduce the dimensionality. k-means with Euclidean distance employed as the metric, is used to cluster the file sets.

Vector Space Model (VSM) is a statistical model for document representation, which is widely used and has good effect. VSM maps each document to a point in a vector space stretched by a set of normalized orthogonal term vectors, and all the document classes and unknown documents can be represented by the term vectors in this space. TF-IDF weight is a comprehensive representation of the local weight and global weight of a phrase in the document vector.

Latent semantic index usually faces a large number of files in data theft detection. Due to the high dimensionality of VSM, it is not enough to extract features only by extracting stem and removing stop words. Therefore, this paper uses latent semantic index method to reduce the dimension in text clustering phase. Latent semantic indexing (LSI) uses singular value decomposition to identify associated patterns in unstructured text sets. To establish a connection between words that appear in the same context, LSI can extract the specific content of a text, not just the specific sensitive words.

k-means clustering This paper chooses the distance-based k-means clustering algorithm for training text clustering, whose advantage is fast and concise. In order to reduce the dependence of algorithm results on the selection of initial clustering centers, the principle of selecting initial clustering centers is that the distance between initial clustering centers should be as far as possible. The specific steps of text clustering are as follows:

- Select the number of clustering k;
- Randomly select a point as the first clustering center;
- Calculate the distance between each data point in the data set and the nearest clustering center, and get the distance set $D = \{D_1, D_2, ..., D_n\}$, where n is the size of the data set. In order to avoid noise, we do not directly select the maximum value, randomly select the data points corresponding to the larger distance as the new clustering center;
- Repeat step 3 until k is found;
- Calculate the distance between each data point in the data set and k clustering centers, divide the data points into the nearest cluster;
- Recalculate the clustering centers of each cluster.
- Repeat steps 5 and 6 above until the convergence requirements are met.

3.2 Sensitive Words Extraction and Reduction

Usually, when a sensitive word appears in a document, the document is likely to be the carrier of sensitive data. In the process of sensitive word extraction and reduction, the sensitive words which can represent the existence of sensitive data in each cluster are detected. The words which appear in confidential files are sensitive words whose probability is much higher than that in non-confidential files. The method of calculating the score of sensitive words is shown in Eq. 1, where P_{cVM} and P_{ncVM} are the occurrence probabilities of entries t in secret file model and ordinary file model respectively.

$$\forall t \in cVM, \quad score + = P_{cVM}(t)/P_{ncVM}(t) \tag{1}$$

The calculation method of importance of sensitive words is shown in Eq. 2, where C denotes a set of sensitive words, D is a set of confidential files, and $Impt\,(a_i)$ is used to indicate the importance of the sensitive word a_i in C. In the confidential file set D, $Pos_c\,(D)$ denotes the portion of files that are correctly classified with sensitive words set C. $|U|$ denotes the set of all files.

$$Impt\,(a_i) = (||(Pos_C\,(D)| - |Pos_{C-a_i}(D)|)/|U| \tag{2}$$

3.3 Build Sensitive Words Graph

At the end of the training phase, each cluster constructs a set of sensitive words that can be represented and stored as a graph. In the graph, the sensitive word node records the content of the sensitive word and takes the calculated score of the sensitive word as the node weight. Two sensitive words connected by edges in a sensitive word graph. When multiple sensitive words appear in a paragraph are close to each other, it is more likely that the text contains confidential content. The weighted edges connect sensitive words whose distance is lower than threshold. The example of sensitive word diagram is shown in Fig. 2.

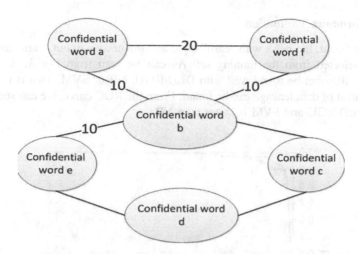

Fig. 2. The graph of sensitive words

3.4   Document Content Detection

In the detection phase, the system analyzes and calculates the detected documents, and then obtains the sensitive score of the documents. According to the sensitive score, it determines whether the documents contain confidential content. Firstly, the detected text is transformed into the vector of TF-IDF weight in the vector space model through the preprocessing step, and then the detected file is associated with the nearest one by the cosine similarity measure. Generally, only one similar cluster may not be able to detect the disguised sensitive content, because the disguised sensitive content carrier may mix the sensitive content into the file of a cluster, making it as a whole similar to the file in the same clusters.

4   Experimental Analysis

To further verify the effectiveness of the proposed method, Reuters-21578 is selected as the dataset to verify the algorithm. Reuters-21578 was manually sorted out and classified from the news released by Reuters News Agency in 1987 and distributed among 22 documents. All the documents contain category descriptions of news texts. The dataset consists of five subsets of five groups of news reports in the Reuters. Since a piece of news may belong to several different categories, choosing content under a single subject as sensitive data does not affect its existence in other categories. In the experiment, we select the economic subset of 10000% news text which contains 135 categories such as "inventory", "money supply" and "gold" to verify the performance of the algorithm, and select the news text of the topic "earn" as a confidential file or sensitive data carrier.

4.1   Performance Evaluation

In this experiment, the news with "earn" topic and the news without "earn" topic were randomly selected from the training set. As can be seen from Fig. 3, the original confidential files can be found well with DLD-RGU, NB or SVM. That is to say, the potential threat of data leakage can be found. From the ROC curve, we can see that the effect of DLD-RGU and SVM is better than NB.

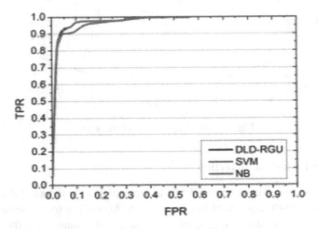

Fig. 3. Performance evaluation of original confidential files

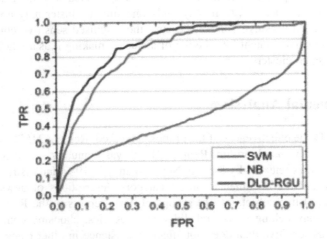

Fig. 4. Performance evaluation of files mixed with confidential contents

As can be seen from Fig. 4, SVM is obviously inferior to other methods because of the statistical characteristics of the algorithm for detecting the contents of a large number of confidential documents which are copied and mixed in ordinary files, and

DLDRGU is better than NB when the sensitive information is too small and fragmented to be detected. In summary, DLD-RGU still performs steadily and works well.

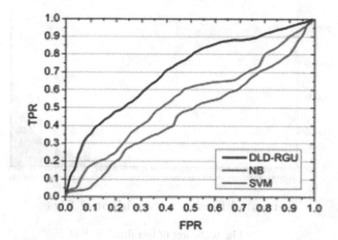

Fig. 5. Performance evaluation of files mixed with the revised confidential contents

As can be seen from Fig. 5, DLD-RGU is superior to SVM and NB in detecting the contents of confidential files that have been rewritten and mixed with ordinary files, which is attributed to the importance calculation and update strategy of sensitive words. Although sensitive content has been deliberately rewritten, many key terms still need to be retained or replaced by other words, while key terms or other words rewritten after the importance will still be higher. Therefore, DLD-RGU is still stable, and its detection effect is better than NB and SVM

4.2 False Negative Rate and False Alarm Rate

In this experiment, 931 news were selected as test files, 380 test files were marked as carriers of sensitive data, and the remaining 51 test files were marked as sensitive to 931 test cases. Sensitivity score statistics are shown in Fig. 6. Sensitivity scores of horizontal axis test files increase from left to right, and there is a significant difference between sensitive data carriers and ordinary files in the test results.

In the middle of the horizontal axis, there is an interlacing phenomenon between ordinary files and sensitive data carriers. In this experiment, 6 out of all 380 sensitive data carriers scored below 100 points. Of all the 551 ordinary documents, 15 scored higher than 100, and the false positive rate in the experiment was not higher than 2.8%. The above data show that the false alarm rate and false negative rate of the model have reached the expected demand. Finally, other relevant data in the experiment are given. The total sensitivity score for all sensitive data carrier test files was 515330.48.

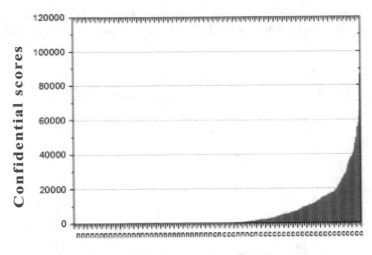

n-normal files   c-confidential files

Fig. 6. Scores of test files

5 Conclusion

Aiming at the problem of data theft which is becoming more and more serious in recent years, this paper presents a new graph update method of data theft detection based on rough set, DLD-RGU. Firstly, the k-means text clustering algorithm is used to construct the text data model, and then the sensitive word graph is constructed by detecting the importance of sensitive words. Experiments on real data sets show that DLD-RGU can accurately identify classified text containing sensitive content in different forms. How to further reduce the false alarm rate and improve the efficiency of confidential content detection is our future research direction.

Acknowledgement. The research is supported by the National Natural Science Foundation of China under Grant No. 61572153, No. U1636215 and No. 61871140, and the National Key Research and Development Plan (Grant No. 2018YFB0803504).

References

1. Aggarwal, C.C.: Social Network Data Analytics. Springer, New York (2011). https://doi.org/10.1007/978-1-4419-8462-3
2. Goyal, A., Bonchi, F., Lakshmanan, L.V.S.: On minimizing budge and time in influence propagation over social networks. Soc. Netw. Anal. Min. 1–14 (2012)
3. Alassi, D., Alhajj, R.: Effectiveness of template detection on noise reduction and websites summarization. Inf. Sci. **219**(0), 41–72 (2013)
4. Katz, G., Elovici, Y., Shapira, B.: CoBAn: a context based model for data leakage prevention. Inf. Sci. **262**, 137–156 (2014)
5. Information week global security survey. Technical report, Information Week (2004)

6. Böhme, R.: Security metrics and security investment models. In: Echizen, I., Kunihiro, N., Sasaki, R. (eds.) IWSEC 2010. LNCS, vol. 6434, pp. 10–24. Springer, Heidelberg (2010). https://doi.org/10.1007/978-3-642-16825-3_2

7. Hyde, R., Angelov, P., MacKenzie, A.R.: Fully online clustering of evolving data streams into arbitrarily shaped clusters. Inf. Sci. **382**, 96–114 (2017)

8. Raychaudhuri, S., Sutphin, P.D., Chang, J.T., et al.: Basic microarray analysis: grouping and feature reduction. Trends Biotechnol. **19**(5), 189–193 (2001)

9. CSO Magazine: Software Engineering Institute Cert Program at Carnegie Mellon University and Deloitte. 2010 Cybersecurity Watch Survey (2010)

10. Cohen, W.W.: Learning rules that classify email. In: AAAI Spring Symposium on Machine Learning in Information Access, pp. 18–25 (1996)

11. Belkin, N.J., Croft, W.B.: Information filtering and information retrieval: two sides of the same coin. Commun. ACM **35**(2), 29–38 (1992)

12. Jiang, F., Fu, Y., Gupta, B.B., et al.: Deep learning based multi-channel intelligent attack detection for data security. IEEE Trans. Sustain. Comput. https://doi.org/10.1109/tsusc.2018.2793284

13. Tian, Z., Cui, Y., An, L., Su, S.: A real-time correlation of host-level events in cyber range service for smart campus. IEEE Access **6**, 35355–35364 (2018)

14. Cui, Q., McIntosh, S., Sun, H.: Identifying materials of photographic images and photorealistic computer generated graphics based on deep CNNs. Comput. Mater. Continua **55**(2), 229–241 (2018)

15. Wang, X., Xiong, C., Pei, Q., et al.: Expression preserved face privacy protection based on multi-mode discriminant analysis. CMC Comput. Mater. Continua **57**(1), 107–121 (2018)

16. Chen, Y., Yin, B., He, H., et al.: Reversible data hiding in classification-scrambling encrypted-image based on iterative recovery. CMC Comput. Mater. Continua **56**(2), 299–312 (2018)

17. Wang, C., Feng, Y., Li, T., et al.: A new encryption-then-compression scheme on gray images using the Markov random field. Comput. Mater. Continua **56**(1), 107–121 (2018)

A Tutorial of Graph Representation

Yuanyuan Chen, Hui Lu, Jing Qiu[✉], and Le Wang[✉]

Cyberspace Institute of Advanced Technology (CIAT), Guangzhou University,
Guangzhou 510006, China
2899617212@qq.com, {luhui,qiujing,wangle}@gzhu.edu.cn

Abstract. With the development of network technology, graphs exist widely in real life, such as social networks, communication networks, biological networks, etc. Analyzing the structural of these graphs will have a far-reaching impact on various network applications. For example, node classification, link prediction, clustering, visualization. Traditional graph representation methods suffer a lot of space and time cost. In recent years, a category of technology which convert nodes into a low-dimensional vector has emerged. In this paper, First, we briefly introduce the development and challenges of graph representation algorithms. Then we introduce the existing methods of graph representation in the literature. It is mainly divided into three parts: node embedding, embedding based on heterogeneous graph, subgraph embedding. Node embedding algorithms are mainly divided into four categories: matrix factorization-based algorithms, random walk based algorithms, deep learning based algorithms and the algorithm based on the role of node structure. In addition, we also introduce LINE algorithms, embedding based on heterogeneous graph and sub-graph (whole graph) embedding algorithms. Finally, we introduce the related applications of graph embedding and the summary of this paper.

Keywords: Graph representation · Node embedding · Random walk ·
Deep learning · Heterogeneous graph

1 Overall Overview

1.1 Introduction

Graphs are widely used in real life. For example, the social network, the communication networks, the biological networks. Analyzing the structural of these graphs will have a far-reaching impact on the application of the networks. For example, node classification [1, 2] technology can predict which community an individual belongs to. Link prediction [3] technology can predict the missing links between nodes and the links that may appear in the future. However, the traditional methods of analyzing graph structure suffer a lot of space and time cost. Recently, the main direction of studying graph structure is to transform the node in the graph into a vector with low dimension. According to different applications of embedding vectors, we also have edge embedding, subgraph, or whole graph embedding. In this paper, we mainly introduce three parts: node embedding, embedding based on heterogeneous graph, subgraph embedding.

X. Sun et al. (Eds.): ICAIS 2019, LNCS 11632, pp. 368–378, 2019.
https://doi.org/10.1007/978-3-030-24274-9_33

Node embedding algorithms are classified into four categories: matrix factorization-based algorithms [4], random walk based algorithms, deep learning based algorithms and the algorithm based on the role of node structure. Besides, we will introduce heterogeneous graph embedding method and sub-graph (whole graph) embedding method. Matrix factorization-based algorithms mainly include Locally Linear Embedding (LLE) [5], Laplacian eigenmaps [6] and so on. Random walk based algorithms mainly include deepwalk [7], node2vec [8]. Deep learning methods mainly include SDNE [9], DNGR [10] and GCN [11]. The specific classification is shown in Fig. 1.

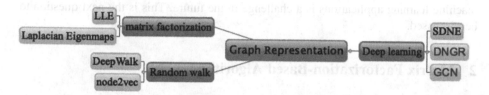

Fig. 1. Classification of node embedding

1.2 A Brief History of Graph Representation

Early graph representation mainly uses the form of adjacency matrix. However, when the network structure is very complex and the number of nodes is huge, this method will suffer a lot of space and time cost. After that, with the development of natural language processing, a new method of graph representation that converts node in a graph into a low-dimensional dense vector has emerged. This method is also called node embedding. The main idea of early node embedding algorithm is the reduction of vector dimensions. That is to say, all nodes in the constructed similarity graph are transformed into a d dimensional vector and d is far less than the number of nodes. For this dimension reduction, there a principal component analysis (PCA) [12] and multidimensional scaling (MDS) [13]. Local Linear Embedding (LLE) [5], Laplacian eigenmaps (LE) [6]. Because the decomposition matrix is used here to get node embedding. When the network structure is large enough, the storage of the matrix will generate much space and time cost. The method based on random walk solves this problem adequately. It uses local structure information of nodes with no more than two hops. Based on this idea, there are deepwalk algorithm [7], node2vec algorithm [8], LINE algorithm [14, 15]. However, the above method can only deal with the linear structure information of the graph. There are many nonlinear relationships between the existing network nodes. In the last two years, the method of deep learning can make full use of the nonlinear structural information of graphs. Deep learning methods mainly include SDNE [9], DNGR [10] and GCN [11].

1.3   Challenges

Scalability: Nowadays, the Network structure usually includes millions of nodes and edges. Effective processing of millions of nodes and edges while preserving the global structure information of graphs is a challenge in the future.

Preservation of information: Nodes in the network structure often contain various attribute information. Such as emotions, hobbies, beliefs and other information. How to preserve this attribute information in the embedded vectors of nodes is a challenge in the future.

Applicability: The low dimensional vectors in the embedded space are used as inputs to machine learning tasks. How to generate node embedding based on specific machine learning applications is a challenge in the future. This is the next question to be discussed.

2   Matrix Factorization-Based Algorithms

This method uses the factorize matrix to get the embedding vectors of nodes. The main idea is to use a series of reconstructed graphs as input graphs and factorize matrices to generate low-dimensional vectors. Although the algorithm based on matrix factorization can convert the nodes in the graph into a low-dimensional space [16], when the network structure becomes large enough, the storage of the matrix in memory will suffer a lot of space and time cost, which becomes the inherent defect of this algorithm. In the following sections, we will introduce the specific algorithms.

2.1   Locally Linear Embedding (LLE)

The main idea of LLE [5] algorithm: The representations of nodes and their neighbors are in a latent manifold. A node can be linearly combined by its neighbor nodes, as shown in formula (1). Minimizing loss function can get node vectors in embedded space, as shown in formula (2). This algorithm is mainly applicable to undirected graphs.

$$Y_i \approx \sum_j W_{ij} Y \tag{1}$$

$$\phi(Y) = \sum_i |Y_i - \sum_j W_{ij} Y_j|^2 \tag{2}$$

2.2   Laplace Eigenmaps (LE)

The main idea of Laplace eigenmaps [6] algorithm: The higher the weight between the nodes, the more similar the two nodes are. Therefore, when embedding nodes, the distance between the two nodes in the embedding space should be closer. That is, they have similar vector representation. The square of the Euclidean distance between the two vectors should be smaller. The algorithm is mainly applicable to undirected weighted graphs.

$$\phi(Y) = \frac{1}{2} \sum_{i,j} (Y_i - Y_j)^2 W_{ij} \tag{3}$$

$$= Y^T L Y \tag{4}$$

In the formula (3) and formula (4) above, the formula $L = D - W$ represents the Laplacian diagram of graph G.

3   Random Walk Based Algorithms

A random walk algorithm is used to construct the vector representation in the embedding space by using the neighborhood structure of nodes. Compared with the algorithms based on matrix decomposition, it only needs to store the neighborhood structure information of nodes in memory, which has certain advantages. This type of algorithm is applicable to situations where the network structure is too large to save the global structure information of the graph.

3.1   Deepwalk

The main idea of the deepwalk [7] algorithm: Nodes are embedded by using the idea of word embedding in the neural network language model. The nodes in the graph are analogous to the words in the language model. A series of random walk sequences are analogous to sentences. The method of solving node embedding is similar to skip-gram [17] model in general. Random walk algorithm is used to obtain the context nodes of the nodes and to maximize the likelihood function. Then it uses skip-gram model to obtain the embedding vectors.

Visualization of deepwalk algorithm is shown in Fig. 2.

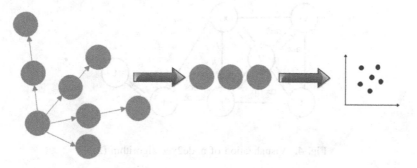

Fig. 2. Visualization of deepwalk algorithm

3.2   Node2vec

Node2vec [8] algorithm is developed on the basis of deepwalk algorithm. Deepwalk algorithm adopts unbiased random walk while node2vec algorithm adopts completely random walk strategy. It has two different random walk methods, breadth-first search (BFS) and depth-first search (DFS). The concrete implementation of the algorithm is shown in the following Fig. 3:

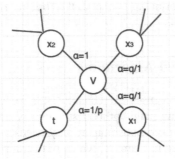

Fig. 3. Visualization of node2vec algorithm (1)

In the Fig. 3 above, the value of the parameter α on the edge is proportional to the probability of the edge to be taken in the next step. First, from t node to v node, t is the last hop node, and v is the current node. P is expressed as a return probability parameter, which controls the probability of revisiting t node in the next hop. The probability value is proportional to $1/p$. Q is expressed as leaving probability parameter, which controls the probability of visisting other nodes in the next hop. The probability value is proportional to $1/q$. The visualization of the algorithm is shown in the following Fig. 4.

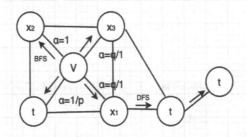

Fig. 4. Visualization of node2vec algorithm (2)

As shown in the above Fig. 4, the breadth-first search (BFS) tends to visit neighbor nodes in the next hop. It mainly explores local structural information of graphs.

The depth-first search (DFS) tends to visit the farther nodes. It is mainly used to explore the global structure information of graphs.

3.3   Large-Scale Information Network Embedding (LINE)

LINE [14, 15] algorithm is suitable for large-scale information networks and can be applied to different type of graph. The specific algorithm is roughly as follows.

LINE algorithm uses first-order proximity to preserve the local structure information of graphs and second-order proximity to preserve the global structure information of graphs. First-order proximity is applied to directly connected nodes. The greater the weight of the edge between the two nodes, the more similar the two nodes are. Second-order proximity considers that if the neighborhood structure of the two nodes is similar, the similarity between the two nodes is higher. The first-order proximity [15] can be used for undirected graphs, and the second-order proximity [18] can be used for directed graphs and undirected graphs. The solution procedure of the two methods is similar.

3.4   Hierarchical Representation Learning for Networks (HARP)

In summary, the above three algorithms do not make full use of the global structure information of graphs. Deepwalk and node2vec can only use the local structure information of graphs by using random walk. LINE algorithm uses first-order and second-order similarity to preserve only two-hop structure information of graphs. HARP [19] algorithm can deal with the above drawback. HARP algorithm combines the similar nodes and edges in the large graph and converts them into small graphs. Learning node representation from small graphs can make better use of the global structure information of graphs.

4   Deep Learning Based Algorithms

4.1   Structural Deep Network Embedding (SDNE)

The main idea of SDNE [9] algorithm: SDNE algorithm is a semi-supervised deep model and can be used to capture the nonlinear relationship between nodes [20]. The algorithm mainly includes two parts: supervised and unsupervised. Supervised first-order proximity is used to preserve local structure information of the network and unsupervised second-order proximity is used to preserve global structure information of the network. The algorithm uses simultaneous optimization of first-order and second-order proximity.

4.2   Deep Neural Networks for Learning Graph Representations (DNGR)

The main idea of DNGR [10] algorithm: Firstly, we use random surfing model to obtain probabilistic co-occurrence matrix from the weighted graph. Then we use probabilistic co-occurrence matrix to obtain positive pointwise mutual information

(PPMI) matrix. Finally, the vector representation of node in the graph is obtained by stacked denosing autoencoders.

DNGR algorithm uses random sorting of all vertices in the graph, and then randomly selects one vertex in the graph as the current vertex. The algorithm uses a matrix to contain the transition probability between different nodes in the graph. Instead of using SVD algorithm to establish linear mapping between PPMI matrix [21, 22] and output vectors, stacked denosing autoencoders are used to establish a non-linear mapping between PPMI matrix and output vectors. Stacked denosing autoencoders has a certain degree of robustness. The specific process of the algorithm is shown in the following Fig. 5.

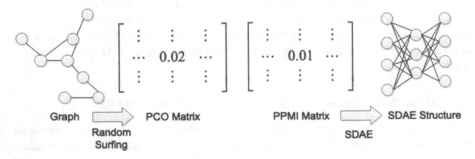

Fig. 5. Visualization of DNGR algorithm

4.3   Graph Convolutional Network (GCN)

The main idea of GCN [23, 24] algorithm: It is a deep learning method used in graph structure. After CNN is applied in the field of image, it can make up for the problem that CNN can't be applied to Non Euclidean data. GCN makes convolutional neural network applied in graph structure. It carries out end to end training, and make full use of the feature information of the node and the structural information of its neighborhood. The algorithm can be used to extract Non Euclidean data, and use convolution to gather information around neighbors.

4.4   Structure-Based Node Embedding

In some networks, the structure of nodes plays an important role. For example, the role of individuals in social networks. However, previous methods often fail to make full use of the structural role of nodes to generate node embedding. Stru2vec [25, 26] algorithm can solve this problem.

5 Heterogeneous Graph

In many real networks, many networks contain different types of nodes and edges. For example, A question answering system website. There are three kinds of nodes, the questioner, the respondent, and the answer [27]. There are different types of edges between them. In recommendation system, users and recommended items are two different of nodes, corresponding to different types of edges. The Metpath2vec [28] algorithm can be used to obtain node embedding in heterogeneous graph [29–31]. The general idea of this algorithm is to use meta-path-based random walks to obtain sampling sequence. Then a heterogeneous skip-gram [17] model to obtain node embedding.

6 Embedding Subgraph

The main idea of subgraph embedding [32]: A series of nodes and edges in a graph are equated to a subgraph. A low dimensional vector is used to represent the whole subgraph. When the structure between two subgraphs is similar, the distance between these two subgraphs should be closer. When subgraph is embedded, the graph kernel is used to represent the subgraph as a vector. The subgraph embedding algorithm is generally supervised, so the embedded vectors can be used to classify subgraphs.

One of the methods of embedding subgraph is to apply convolution method. And then the subgraph embedding is generated by aggregating the node embedding corresponding to a subgraph. Sum-based approaches [33] is to use this idea to obtain subgraph embedding.

7 Application

The node embedded vector of the graph can be used as input to the machine learning task. The specific application of graph representation can be divided into four categories: node classification, link prediction, visualization and clustering.

Node classification [2]: Classifying nodes is a semi-supervised problem. In real networks, only a small number of nodes have labels. Labels in different types of networks are usually different. In social networks, labels can be a person's hobby. In Web networks, labels represent what type of content the web page belongs to. By training the nodes with labels, a reasonable label can be predicted for nodes without labels.

Link prediction [34]: According to the existing network structure, we can predict the missing edges between nodes, or the edges may appear in the future and find some false edges between nodes. This application is widely used in biological networks. Link prediction method can predict the existence of edges between nodes at less cost.

Visualization [35–37]: Low-dimensional vectors represented in embedded space are transformed into two-dimensional vectors and displayed in two-dimensional space. This dimension reduction method usually has PCA and t-SNE [38]. In the visualization process, it can be observed that the relationship between nodes in the graph.

Clustering [39]: The similar nodes in the network are divided into the same category. For example, web pages with similar content are divided into the same categories [40]. In biological networks, proteins with similar functions are divided into the same categories [41, 42].

8 Summary

8.1 Conclusions

We review the algorithms for graph representation. We first introduce the algorithm of node embedding. Then we introduce the algorithm of heterogeneous graph representation. Finally, we introduce the algorithm of subgraph embedding.

Factorization is a traditional technique for matrix decomposition, but it needs to preserve all the information of the matrix. This will result in high space and time cost for the large networks. On this basis, random walk based network representation solves this problem well. Random walk only needs to represent the local structural characteristics of nodes, and it is an online algorithm. The lINE algorithm is expanded on the basis of deepwalk algorithm. The algorithm utilizes the local and global structure information of the graph. And the weighted directed graph or undirected graph can be adequately processed. In order to deal with the nonlinear structural features of graphs, a deep learning method is introduced. SDNE method makes full use of the first-order and second-order proximity of LINE algorithm, and optimizes them at the same time. It obtains not only the local structure information but also the global structure information of the graph. Driven by CNN, GCN has emerged in the analysis of graph structure. In addition, we introduce the method of generating node embedding using node structure information and the embedding of subgraph.

8.2 Future Directions

First of all, with the development of network, the network usually includes billions of nodes and edges. Large-scale network processing is the current problem. And how to make full use of the global structure of the network for embedding nodes becomes a challenge.

Secondly, most of the existing nodes in the graph contain various attribute information. In the node embedding, not only the structural information of graph should be preserved, but also the attribute information of node should also be fully utilized, which is a research direction in the future.

Finally, node embedding vector is widely used in machine learning, such as natural language processing, data mining and other fields. Therefore, how to generate node embedding vectors based on specific applications will be a research direction in the future.

Acknowledgement. This research was funded in part by the National Natural Science Foundation of China (61871140, 61872100, 61572153, U1636215), the National Key research and Development Plan (Grant No. 2018YFB0803504).

References

1. Wang, X., Cui, P., Wang, J., Pei, J., Zhu, W., Yang, S.: Community preserving network embedding. In: AAAI, pp. 203–209 (2017)
2. Bhagat, S., Cormode, G., Muthukrishnan, S.: Node classification in social networks. In: Aggarwal, C. (ed.) Social Network Data Analytics, pp. 115–148. Springer, Boston (2011). https://doi.org/10.1007/978-1-4419-8462-3_5
3. Wei, X., Xu, L., Cao, B., Yu, P.S.: Cross view link prediction by learning noise-resilient representation consensus. In: WWW, pp. 1611–1619 (2017)
4. Belkin, M., Niyogi, P.: Laplacian eigenmaps and spectral techniques for embedding and clustering. In: NIPS (2002)
5. Roweis, S.T., Saul, L.K.: Nonlinear dimensionality reduction by locally linear embedding. Science **290**(5500), 2323–2326 (2000)
6. Belkin, M., Niyogi, P.: Laplacian eigenmaps and spectral techniques for embedding and clustering. In: NIPS, vol. 14, pp. 585–591 (2001)
7. Perozzi, B., Al-Rfou, R., Skiena, S.: DeepWalk: online learning of social representations. In: Proceedings 20th International Conference on Knowledge Discovery and Data Mining, pp. 701–710 (2014)
8. Grover, A., Leskovec, J.: node2vec: scalable feature learning for networks. In: Proceedings of the 22nd International Conference on Knowledge Discovery and Data Mining, pp. 855–864. ACM (2016)
9. Wang, D., Cui, P., Zhu, W.: Structural deep network embedding. In: Proceedings of the 22nd International Conference on Knowledge Discovery and Data Mining, pp. 1225–1234. ACM (2016)
10. Cao, S., Lu, W., Xu, Q.: Deep neural networks for learning graph representations. In: AAAI, pp. 1145–1152 (2016)
11. Kipf, T.N., Welling, M.: Semi-supervised classification with graph convolutional networks. arXiv preprint arXiv:1609.02907
12. Svante, W., Esbensen, K., Geladi, P.: Principal component analysis. Chemometr. Intell. Lab. Syst. **2**(1–3), 37–52 (1987)
13. Kruskal, J.B., Wish, M.: Multidimensional Scaling, vol. 11. Sage, London (1978)
14. Tang, J., Qu, M., Wang, M., Zhang, M., Yan, J., Mei, Q.: Line: large scale information network embedding. In: Proceedings of the 24th International Conference on World Wide Web, pp. 1067–1077. ACM (2015)
15. Ahmed, A., Shervashidze, N., Narayanamurthy, S., Josifovski, V., Smola, A.J.: Distributed large-scale natural graph factorization. In: Proceedings of the 22nd International Conference on World Wide Web, pp. 37–48. ACM (2013)
16. Kruskal, J.B.: Multidimensional scaling by optimizing goodness of fit to a nonmetric hypothesis. Psychometrika **29**(1), 1–27 (1964)
17. Mikolov, T., Chen, K., Corrado, G., Dean, J.: Efficient estimation of word representations in vector space. CoRR, vol. abs/1301.3781 (2013)
18. Cao, S., Lu, W., Xu, Q.: GraRep: learning graph representations with global structural information. In: KDD (2015)
19. Chen, H., Perozzi, B., Hu, Y., Skiena, S.: HARP: hierarchical representation learning for networks. arXiv preprint arXiv:1706.07845 (2017)
20. Kipf, T.N., Welling, M.: Variational graph auto-encoders. In: NIPS Workshop on Bayesian Deep Learning (2016)
21. Bullinaria, J.A., Levy, J.P.: Extracting semantic representations from word co-occurrence statistics: a computational study. Behav. Res. Methods **39**(3), 510–526 (2007)

22. Levy, O., Goldberg, Y., Dagan, I.: Improving distributional similarity with lessons learned from word embeddings. TACL **3**, 211–225 (2015)
23. van den Berg, R., Kipf, T.N., Welling, M.: Graph convolutional matrix completion. arXiv preprint arXiv:1706.02263 (2017)
24. Defferrard, M., Bresson, X., Vandergheynst, P.: Convolutional neural networks on graphs with fast localized spectral filtering. In: NIPS (2016)
25. Donnat, C., Zitnik, M., Hallac, D., Leskovec, J.: Learning structural node embeddings via diffusion wavelets. arXiv preprint arXiv:1710.10321 (2017)
26. Henderson, K., et al: RoIX: structural role extraction & mining in large graphs. In: KDD (2012)
27. Chang, S., Han, W., Tang, J., Qi, G., Aggarwal, C.C., Huang, T.S.: Heterogeneous network embedding via deep architectures. In: KDD (2015)
28. Dong, Y., Chawla, N.V., Swami, A.: metapath2vec: Scalable representation learning for heterogeneous networks. In: KDD (2017)
29. Nickel, M., Murphy, K., Tresp, V., Gabrilovich, E.: A review of relational machine learning for knowledge graphs. Proc. IEEE **104**(1), 11–33 (2016)
30. Schlichtkrull, M., Kipf, T.N., Bloem, P., vandenBerg, R., Titov, I., Welling, M.: Modeling relational data with graph convolutional networks. arXiv preprint arXiv:1703.06103 (2017)
31. Fang, H., Wu, F., Zhao, Z., Duan, X., Zhuang, Y., Ester, M.: Community-based question answering via heterogeneous social network learning. In: AAAI, pp. 122–128 (2016)
32. Li, C., Ma, J., Guo, X., Mei, Q.: DeepCas: an end-to-end predictor of information cascades. In: WWW, pp. 577–586 (2017)
33. Duvenaud, D., et al.: Convolutional networks on graphs for learning molecular fingerprints. In: NIPS (2015)
34. Backstromand, L., Leskovec, J.: Supervised random walks: predicting and recommending links in social networks. In: WSDM (2011)
35. De Oliveira, M.C.F., Levkowitz, H.: From visual data exploration to visual data mining: a survey. IEEE Trans. Visual Comput. Graphics **9**(3), 378–394 (2003)
36. Pan, S., Wu, J., Zhu, X., Zhang, C., Wang, Y.: Tri-party deep network representation. In: IJCAI, pp. 1895–1901 (2016)
37. Le, T.M.V., Lauw, H.W.: Probabilistic latent document network embedding. In: ICDM, pp. 270–279 (2014)
38. Maaten, L.V.D., Hinton, G.: Visualizing data using t-Sne. J. Mach. Learn. Res. **9**, 2579–2605 (2008)
39. Ester, M., Kriegel, H., Sander, J., Xu, X., et al.: A density-based algorithm for discovering clusters in large spatial databases with noise. In: KDD (1996)
40. White, S., Smyth, P.: A spectral clustering approach to finding communities in graphs. In: Proceedings of the 2005 SIAM International Conference on Data Mining, pp. 274–285. SIAM (2005)
41. Wang, C., Feng, Y., Li, T., et al.: A new encryption-then-compression scheme on gray images using the markov random field. Comput. Mater. Continua **56**(1), 107–121 (2018)
42. Chen, Y., Yin, B., He, H., et al.: Reversible data hiding in classification-scrambling encrypted-image based on iterative recovery. CMC Comput. Mater. Continua **56**(2), 299–312 (2018)

Ground-Based Cloud Images Recognition Based on GAN and PCANet

Liling Zhao[1,2]($\boxtimes$), Yi Lin[1,2], Zelin Zhang[1], and Siqi Wang[1]

[1] School of Automation, Nanjing University of Information Science and Technology, 219, Ningliu Road, Nanjing 210044, China
zhaoliling@nuist.edu.cn, zeroy_1@163.com,
zhangzelin19931116@163.com, 66250773@qq.com
[2] Jiangsu Key Laboratory of Big Data Analysis Technology,
Nanjing 210044, Jiangsu, China

Abstract. In order to improve the recognition accuracy of ground-based cloud image, a new algorithm based on deep learning is proposed. In our approach, a large number of cloud images are generated by Generative Adversarial Networks first. Then, based on the original and these generate cloud images, the deep features of cloud images are extracted automatically by multi-layer automatic sensing feature network, which increase the features description ability effectively. Finally, the Support Vector Machine (SVM) classifier is trained and the cloud image recognition is completed. Comparing with the methods such as gray level co-occurrence matrix (GLCM) and PCA with original database only, our approach combines the advantages of both GAN and PCANet, and the experiment results shows that the accuracy of cloud image recognition is significantly improved.

Keywords: Data set · Deep learning · Artificial features · Deep features · Cloud image · Recognition

1 Introduction

Because of the advantage of low cost and strong intuition, the ground-based cloud image has become an indispensable meteorological observation data for weather forecast and climate research [1]. While the meteorological observation of cloud image mainly rely on human vision and experience, the recognition of cloud image is always restricted to the low accuracy and low efficiency. In recent years, with the development of computer technology and the progress of image processing, automatic acquisition and analysis of meteorological information is becoming a useful supplement for weather experts. The Meteorological Service Automation becomes to be an important means to improve the weather forecast. Thus, the automatic classification of cloud image is need to be pay more attention and be an important aspect in the field of Meteorological Service Automation [2].

According to the criterion of surface meteorological observation and the requirements of numerical weather prediction, the cloud is divided into 10 families, 3 genera and 29 species [3]. Because of the formation and the development of cloud are very

© Springer Nature Switzerland AG 2019
X. Sun et al. (Eds.): ICAIS 2019, LNCS 11632, pp. 379–390, 2019.
https://doi.org/10.1007/978-3-030-24274-9_34

complex, mainly based on the interaction of temperature, humidity, air flow, condensation nuclei and other factors, the type and character is quite different. For example, some of the surface of cloud is smooth, and some shows many ups and downs of the spots and wrinkles, and some contains much fiber structure. The various of cloud images is shown in Fig. 1.

cumulus clouds   nimbostratus clouds   cirrus clouds

cumulus clouds   nimbostratus clouds   cirrus clouds

Fig. 1. Example of cloud images.

As is shown in Fig. 1, the nimbostratus cloud is gray white, like fog and evenly like the screen shape. The cloud base is relatively low, but not to the ground, it often shroud mountains and tall buildings. While, the nimbostratus cloud often shows smooth with uniform texture and its gray level difference is small. The cumulus cloud is chiseled, with top projection and flat base, which is composed of low layer air convection condensation. These information of cloud image shows spots and wrinkles texture, while the height of cloud is deferent, the gray level of the cloud image is also not the same. The cirrus cloud is made up of ice, and usually be white, but at the sunset time it often shows yellow or red with yellow, at the night it is dark grey then. The texture of the cirrus cloud image is fibrous, strip, feather, hook, anvil etc. The characteristic of cloud image is very complex and the expression form of the same cloud is very rich and varied. Moreover, the cloud information, development and change are also transient and difficult to reproduce. To effectively achieve the cloud automatic recognition, accurate feature extraction is the important key.

The aforementioned complexity of the cloud images motivate us to study a new way for richer features extracting and obtain a high accuracy classification results. Recently, the Deep Learning (DL) has been successfully applied in many research and it has become a hot topic in image processing and recognition. Influenced by these current deep learning networks, our approach combines the advantages of both GAN and PCANet. In our new approach, the number of the training cloud images are dramatically increased and the cloud image features are extracted automatically. These new improvements can provide sufficient amount of image data and effective features for classifier training. A high accuracy classification result are achieved in dataset SWIMCAT and it will be shown in Sect. 4.

2 Related Work

2.1 Generative Adversarial Networks

In 2014, the new framework for generating models through counteraction process estimation called Generative Adversarial Networks (GAN) is proposed. Essentially, GAN [4] is a probabilistic model for generation. Its purpose is to find out the statistical rules within the given observation data, and to generate new data similar to the observation data based on the obtained rules. The realization of this process requires training two deep networks, one is to generate calls network G, the other is to discriminate calls network D, through the confrontation and competition between the two networks, the best data generation affection is achieved. The optimization objective function of GAN is expressed by formula (1).

$$\min_{G} \max_{D} V(D, G) = \mathrm{E}_{x \sim p_x(x)}[\log D(x)] + \mathrm{E}_{z \sim p_z(z)}[\log(1 - D(G(z)))] \qquad (1)$$

Where, G is generate network, D is discriminate network, $p_x(x)$ is distribution function of original data, $p_z(z)$ is generated data. After several iterations, the two networks will achieve a balance. When the performance of both networks can not continue to improve, the probability distribution of generated data and the distribution of original data will be similar. In computer vision, the application of GAN has been very extensive [5–9]. For example, in the research of dataset generation, GAN can generate various facial expressions based on expressionless facial images [10], and generate images with famous painting styles on landscape images [11], or become a frontier method for generating images, sounds, and videos [12] etc. Inspired by these research, we considers that on the basis of the existing cloud image dataset, GAN can be used to generate any type of cloud image by random noise according to the requirements, which can effectively expand the original cloud image dataset, so as to prepare sufficient training data for the task of cloud image recognition based on deep learning.

2.2 Image Features Extraction

The features of cloud image is very complex, it can be summarized mainly as two types: spectrum feature and pattern feature [13]. The gray, brightness temperature, or solar radiation information and other reflection characteristics of the cloud can be defined spectral features; while the pattern features contain gray level information, gradient and edge, etc. Thus, the cloud brightness, shape, size, shadow and texture can be described by means of the spectral features, pattern features or the combination of these above. The commonly used methods of digital image feature extraction and description can be roughly divided into two categories: one feature extraction is on shallow level (based on artificial rules), and the other feature extraction is on deep level (based on deep learning). However, the description ability of artificial rules is limited to describe the so complex features of cloud images. It not only requires the meteorological experts' knowledge and experience, but also has the limited ability of description and low recognition rate.

Therefore, the accuracy of cloud image recognition can be further improved by using more effective methods to effectively extract the complex features of cloud image.

In recent years, getting rid of the limitation of artificial rule features and realizing automatic image feature mining has attracted wide attention. Especially in 1998, after LeNet [14] was first proposed, deep neural network happened to be applied in image feature extraction, which opened a new research door for image recognition [15–18]. In 2012 subsequently, the automatic extraction and expression of image features on ImageNet Dataset based on deep learning were realized by Hilton [19]. Weng [20] used multi-layer neural network to extract the features of satellite cloud images and improve the cloud recognition rate. Therefore, for cloud image with complex edge information, rich texture and geometric structure, if the ability and adaptability of features expression will be further improved, the cloud image recognition accuracy can be achieved a more satisfactory result. Thus, the feature extraction method based on deep learning can be applied.

3   Method

In this paper, we introduce two deep learning networks in cloud image recognition, that is GAN and PCANet. GAN is used to generate a large number of new cloud images to further expand the scale of training dataset and PCANet is used to automatically extract the cloud image deep features, then train a more effective classification model.

3.1   Data Preparing

We use GAN to generate cloud image to expand cloud image data set. The basic principle is shown in Fig. 2.

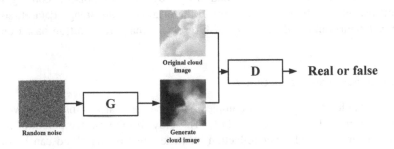

Fig. 2. The principles of cloud image generation

Firstly, two data parts are input into GAN network: one part is real cloud image, shown in formula (2), in which K_1 is the number of real cloud images, this part is directly input to D (Discriminator network) to obtain the discriminate results;

$$X_{ORG} = [X_1, X_2, \ldots, X_{K_1}] \tag{2}$$

The other part is random noise which is act as the input of G (Generator network) to generates cloud image. Then, the generated image is transmitted to D and a new discriminate result is obtained. In the process of iteration, generators and discriminators constantly confront each other, and eventually the two networks will achieve a dynamic equilibrium. That is, the generated image is close to the real image, and the discriminator can't identify which is the true and false images. The generated cloud image can be expressed as a formula (3), in which K_2 is the number of generated cloud images. When combine the real cloud image represented by formula (2) with the generated cloud image represented by formula (3), the expanded cloud image dataset can be expressed as formula (4), where N is the number of all cloud image in the new dataset.

$$X_{GAN} = [X_1, X_2, \ldots, X_{K_2}] \tag{3}$$

$$X = [X_{ORG}, X_{GAN}] = [X_1, X_2, \ldots, X_N] \tag{4}$$

3.2   Training

Deep feature extraction is an new application of deep learning theory in feature extraction, which has incomparable advantages over artificial rule features. In 2015, a light deep network PCANet [21] is proposed. PCANet combines the theoretical advantages of Convolutional Neural Networks (CNN) and Principal Component Analysis (PCA). It has effective deep features extraction of training samples and the reduction the convolution operation by PCA filtering than in traditional deep network. When all sample cloud images are expressed as PCANet features, it can provide a richer feature basis for cloud image recognition, and it is conducive for training the classifier. The basic principle of PCANet algorithm is shown in Fig. 3.

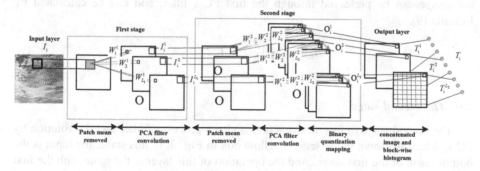

Fig. 3. The framework of PCANet (Color figure online)

Taking one cloud image as an example, PCANet needs to compute its block matrix first. According to the size of cloud image and the experience of deep learning sliding window selection, a square sliding window with $k_1 \times k_2$ pixels is selected in this paper. Every cloud image with the size $m \times n$ will be decomposed into $m \times n$ image blocks with the size of $k_1 \times k_2$. If the above operations is performed on all the cloud images in dataset, a matrix X with $N \times m \times n$ columns will be obtained, and every column indicate one image block with $k_1 \times k_2$ pixels. Thus, the ith block matrix is expressed as formula (5), and all the block matrixes are expressed as formula (6).

$$\bar{X}_i = [\bar{x}_{i,1}, \bar{x}_{i,2}, \ldots, \bar{x}_{i,mn}] \tag{5}$$

$$X = [\bar{X}_1, \bar{X}_2, \ldots, \bar{X}_K] \in \mathbb{R}^{k_1 k_2 \times K_{mn}} \tag{6}$$

Secondly, the deep features extraction PCANet contains three stage. In order to show its advantages over shallow feature extraction methods, the steps are described in detail below.

(a) **The first stage**

The first stage of feature extraction is a process of filter and convolution by PCA, which is shown in the first yellow box in Fig. 3. The numbers of filters required in the ith layer is assumed to be L_1 and a series of standard orthogonal matrix to minimize the reconstruction error is calculated from formula (7). By extracting the feature vectors corresponding to the first L_1 maximum eigenvalues of the covariance matrix X_h, the desired filters are formed, which can be calculated by formula (8).

$$\min_{V \in \mathbb{R}^{k_1 k_2 \times L_1}} \left\| X - VV^T X \right\|_F^2, \quad s.t. \ V^T V = I_{L_1} \tag{7}$$

$$W_L^1 = mat_{k_1,k_2}(q_L(XX^T)) \in \mathbb{R}^{k_1 \times k_2}, L = 1, 2, \ldots, L_1 \tag{8}$$

Then, each column of the feature vector above is arranged as a patch and L_1 patches with the size of $k_1 \times k_2$ are obtained. For each cloud images, the main information of the image can be preserved through the first PCA filter, and can be calculated by formula (9).

$$I_i^L = I_i * W_L^1, i = 1, 2, \ldots, K \tag{9}$$

(b) **The second stage**

The second stage of feature extraction is also a process of filter and convolution by PCA, which is shown in the second yellow box in Fig. 3. In this stage, the input is the output result of the first stage. And the operation of this layer is the same with the first layer. The result can be calculated by formula (10) and (11).

$$Y^L = [\bar{Y}_1^L, \bar{Y}_2^L, \ldots, \bar{Y}_K^L] \in \mathbb{R}^{k_1 k_2 \times K \tilde{m} \tilde{n}} \tag{10}$$

$$Y = [Y^1, Y^2, \ldots, Y^{L_1}] \in \mathbb{R}^{k_1 k_2 \times L_1 \tilde{m} \tilde{n}} \tag{11}$$

With the same processing, the filters of the second layer are composed with feature vectors corresponding to the covariance matrix and can be expressed by formula (12).

$$W_{L'}^2 = mat_{k_1,k_2}(q_{L'}(YY^T)) \in \mathbb{R}^{k_1 \times k_2}, L' = 1, 2, \ldots, L_2 \tag{12}$$

From the above two stages, there are L_1 filters in the first layer and L_2 filters in the second layer. Hence, for training each cloud image, there are $L_1 \times L_2$ characteristic matrix as outputs, which is expressed in formula (13).

$$O_i^{L'} = \{I_i^L * W_{L'}^2\}_{L'=1}^{L_2} \tag{13}$$

(c) *The output stage*

In order to reduce the amount of calculation data, every output must to be processed by binarization in the second stage and the output result contains only 1 or 0. Then, the hash coding is carried. As is shown in formula (14), the function $H(\,.)$ is a step function which can increase the difference in each feature:

$$T_i^L = \sum_{L'=1}^{L_2} 2^{L'-1} H(O_i^L) = \sum_{L'=1}^{L_2} 2^{L'-1} H(I_i^L * W_{L'}^2) \tag{14}$$

At last, the result of formula (8) is encoded by histogram encoding, and the feature extracted from one training cloud image is completed and the feature F_{hi} can be described with formula (15). Where *Bhist* is the histogram encoding, F_i is the results of image features, B is the number of image blocks.

$$F_i = \left[Bhist(T_i^1), \ldots, Bhist(T_i^{L_1})\right]^T \in \mathbb{R}^{(2^{L_2})L_1 B} \tag{15}$$

3.3 Classifier

After the expansion of cloud image dataset and the effective extraction of cloud images deep features, Support Vector Machine (SVM) will be the available classifier [22]. Because of the satellite cloud image recognition belongs to multi-classification problem, while the basic model of classical SVM support vector machine can only solve the problem of two-classification, so it is necessary to decompose the problem of multi-classification into many two-classification problems [23]. In this paper, the cloud image classification in our experiment is implemented by the Liblinear, a code package developed by Dr. Chih-Jen Lin of Taiwan University [24, 25].

3.4 Overview of Our New Algorithm

The innovation of this paper is that a cloud images recognition algorithm based on the combination of GAN and PCANet is proposed, which solves the problems of fewer dataset and the limitation of feature extraction based on artificial intelligent. The overall framework of our algorithm is shown in Fig. 4.

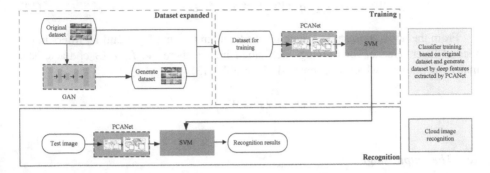

Fig. 4. The overall framework of our new method

In the first step, a large number of cloud images are generated by using GAN, and the original cloud image dataset are effectively expanded. Secondly, deep features of cloud images are extracted by a multi-layer perception neural network PCANet, which improves the feature expression ability of our algorithm. At last, the recognition of cloud image is implemented based on SVM.

The new algorithm mainly consists of three processes: dataset expansion, training process and classification. The specific steps are as follows:

(a) *dataset expansion*
    ① the original cloud images are composed of a real cloud image set, expressed as $X_{ORG} = [X_1, X_2, \ldots, X_{K_1}]$;
    ② generating cloud image set using GA, expressed as $X_{GAN} = [X_1, X_2, \ldots, X_{K_2}]$;
    ③ combining the real cloud image set and the generated cloud image set into the expanded dataset $X = [X_{ORG}, X_{GAN}] = [X_1, X_2, \ldots, X_N]$

(b) *training process*
    ① determine the number of network layers, filter size and filter number in each layer, etc. Based on the principle of PCANet, shown as formula (5)–(15), the deep features of each cloud image is extracted;
    ② obtaining the deep features of cloud images, expressed as $F_i = \left[Bhist(T_i^1), \ldots, Bhist(T_i^{L_1}) \right]^T \in \mathbb{R}^{(2^{L_2})L_1 B}$;
    ③ training SVM classifier based on the above features and corresponding labels;

(c) *classification*
    ① input: test image: x;
    ② using PCANet to extract the deep features F_x of test image x;
    ③ input the deep features F_x into the trained SVM classifier;
    ④ output: classification results of test image.

4 Experiments

4.1 Dataset

The original cloud image dataset are from SWIMCAT [26], we choose three class, such as cumulus clouds, stratus clouds and cirrus clouds, in our experiment. In order to expand the cloud image dataset, we select 80 cloud images as the original data in each class, and use GAN to generate 3000 cloud images for each class. The training dataset of our experiment is composed of the original image and the cloud image. With a lot of experiments, the Gauss mean noise input to G network is set to be a matrix [batch_size, 3, 3, 256], where batch_size is the number of per training, in our work batch_size is 8, 3 × 3 is the size of convolution filter, 256 is the number of convolution layer. The other main parameters of GAN are as follows: learning rate is 0.00008, error distance is 0.0002, activation function in every middle layers is ReLU, and tanh is in the last layer. Figure 5 shows the expanded dataset, and it can been seen that the original cloud images and the generate cloud images are similar. We choose 10% cloud images as testing images from dataset, and 90% as training images. The size of all the cloud images are zoomed to be 80 × 80 pixels.

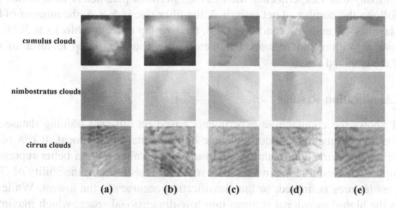

Fig. 5. Dataset of cloud image (a)–(b) generate cloud images by GAN, (c)–(e) original cloud images in SWIMCAT

4.2 Features Extraction

To illustrate the effectiveness of the proposed algorithm, two feature extraction methods of artificial rules are selected as the comparison. One is the Gray Level Co-occurrence Matrix, a classical feature extraction method, the other is PCA, a feature extraction method related to PCANet.

(a) **Simple features**

The features of ground-based cloud images can be described by GLCM (Gray Level Co-occurrence Matrix) [27], a famous artificial and simple feature extracted method. The main steps are as follows. First, GLCM is calculated separately in four angles, as 0°, 45°, 90°, 135°. Second, the four feature vectors, such as energy, entropy, contrast, correlation are extracted and calculated. Finally, the mean and standard deviation of each feature vectors in four directions are obtained. Thus, one cloud image consists 8 dimensional feature vectors and can be expressed as the formula (16). Where V_{GLCM} is the characteristics generated by the GLCM, M is the mean of the feature vectors, D is the standard deviation and the four subscripts are respectively indicate the energy, entropy, contrast, correlation.

$$V_{GLCM} = [M_{ener}, M_{ent}, M_{con}, M_{cor}, D_{ener}, D_{ent}, D_{con}, D_{cor}] \tag{16}$$

PCA (Principal Component Analysis) [28] is another method of feature extraction in our experiment, which is widely used in pattern recognition of the reduced dimension. In order to maximize the retention of the image feature information, the cumulative contribution rate of more than 90% of the principal component is selected as the final feature.

(b) *Deep features*

The deep features are extracted by PCANet, which is introduced in Sect. 3. Through many times experiments, the PCANet network parameters used in this paper are as follows:the number of net layer is 2, the filter size is 5 × 5, the number of filters in first layer is 40, and in second layer is 8, the overlap of feature blocks is 50%. With the above algorithm and network parameters, the abundant deep features of cloud images are obtained.

4.3   Classification Results

Table 1 shows the comparative experiments based on different training datasets and feature extraction methods under the same experimental environment. It can be seen that, the feature extraction method based on deep learning gives a better represent of the complex features of cloud images. The reasons are as follows: the ability of GLCM to express features is limited, so the classification accuracy is the lowest. While PCA projects the high-dimensional features into low-dimensional space, which maximizing the separation between classes and clustering within classes, PCA improves the classification accuracy. When using PCANet, the PCA method is cascaded into two layers in the framework of deep learning, the feature expression is further improved and the recognition rate is the highest. In addition, after expanding the training dataset, the recognition rate of each algorithm has been improved in different degrees, especially for the method based on deep learning. The result also shows that it is very important and necessary to expand the image dataset in deep learning algorithm. In terms of the algorithm time, because the classification step is carried out after network training, the trained network can be used offline in classification and recognition, so our new algorithm runs faster.

Table 1. Experimental results of cloud image recognition

		Feature dimension	Recognition accuracy	Time/S
GLCM	Original dataset	8	74%	85
	Expanded dataset	8	73.2%	88
PCA	Original dataset	305	73%	4019
	Expanded dataset	307	75.3%	4378
PCANet	Original dataset	4000	78.8%	48
	Expanded dataset	4800	83.3%	55

5   Conclusion

Cloud image automatic classification is an important part of Cloud Automatic Observation. It is one of the urgent problem of the atmospheric automatic detection. In this paper, we propose a feature extraction method based on deep learning. The new algorithm can provide more intrinsic characteristic which can't be described by a large number of artificial rules. The experiment use support vector machine classifier to classify three types of stratus, such as cumulus, cirrus and nimbostratus cloud. In the large data set of cloud images, the experiment results shows that our method has the higher accuracy in classification. Moreover, it can be predicted that with the increase of the data set the recognition rate of our method will be further improved.

Acknowledgement. This work was supported by the National Natural Science Foundation of China (Grant No. 61802199) and the Student Practice Innovation Training Program Fund of Nanjing University of Information Science and Technology (Grant No. 2017103000170).

References

1. Han, W.Y., Liu, L., Gao, T.C., et al.: Classification of whole sky infrared cloud image using compressive sensing. J. Appl. Meteorol. Sci. **02**, 231–239 (2015)
2. Gao, T.C., Liu, L., Zhao, S.J., et al.: The actuality and progress of whole sky cloud sounding techniques. J. Appl. Meteorol. Sci. **21**(1), 101–109 (2010)
3. China Cloud Image. Meteorological Press, Beijing (2004)
4. Goodfellow, I.J., Pouget-Abadie, J., Mirza, M., et al.: Generative adversarial nets. In: International Conference on Neural Information Processing Systems, pp. 2672–2680. MIT Press (2014)
5. Radford, A., Metz, L., Chintala, S.: Unsupervised representation learning with deep convolutional generative adversarial networks. Computer Science (2015)
6. Salimans, T., Goodfellow, I., Zaremba, W., et al.: Improved techniques for training GANs (2016)
7. Ledig, C., Wang, Z., Shi, W., et al.: Photo-realistic single image super-resolution using a generative adversarial network, pp. 105–114 (2016)
8. Brock, A., Lim, T., Ritchie, J.M., et al.: Neural photo editing with introspective adversarial networks (2016)

9. Tu, Y., Lin, Y., Wang, J., Kim, J.-U.: Semi-supervised learning with generative adversarial networks on digital signal modulation classification. CMC: Comput. Mater. Continua **55**(2), 243–254 (2018)

10. Yu, X., Porikli, F.: Ultra-resolving face images by discriminative generative networks. In: Leibe, B., Matas, J., Sebe, N., Welling, M. (eds.) ECCV 2016. LNCS, vol. 9909, pp. 318–333. Springer, Cham (2016). https://doi.org/10.1007/978-3-319-46454-1_20

11. Zhu, J.Y., Park, T., Isola, P., et al.: Unpaired image-to-image translation using cycle-consistent adversarial networks, pp. 2242–2251 (2017)

12. Fang, W., Zhang, F., Sheng, V.S., Ding, Y.: A method for improving CNN-based image recognition using DCGAN. CMC: Comput. Mater. Continua **57**(1), 167–178 (2018)

13. Wang, K., Zhang, R., Yin, D., et al.: Cloud detection for remote sensing image based on edge features and AdaBoost classifier. Remote Sens. Technol. Appl. **28**(2), 263–268 (2013)

14. Lecun, Y., Bottou, L., Bengio, Y., et al.: Gradient-based learning applied to document recognition. Proc. IEEE **86**(11), 2278–2324 (1998)

15. Taigman, Y., Yang, M., Ranzato, M., et al.: DeepFace: closing the gap to human-level performance in face verification. In: IEEE Conference on Computer Vision and Pattern Recognition, pp. 1701–1708. IEEE Computer Society (2014)

16. Sun, Y., Wang, X., Tang, X.: Deeply learned face representations are sparse, selective, and robust, pp. 2892–2900 (2014)

17. Szegedy, C., Liu, W., Jia, Y., et al.: Going deeper with convolutions, pp. 1–9 (2015)

18. Schroff, F., Kalenichenko, D., Philbin, J.: FaceNet: a unified embedding for face recognition and clustering, pp. 815–823 (2015)

19. Krizhevsky, A., Sutskever, I., Hinton, G.E.: ImageNet classification with deep convolutional neural networks. In: International Conference on Neural Information Processing Systems, pp. 1097–1105. Curran Associates Inc. (2012)

20. Weng, L.G., KongWB, X.I.A.M., et al.: Satellite imagery cloud fraction based on deep extreme learning machine. Comput. Sci. **45**(4), 227–232 (2018)

21. Chan, T.H., Jia, K., Gao, S., et al.: PCANet: a simple deep learning baseline for image classification? IEEE Trans. Image Process. **24**(12), 5017–5032 (2015)

22. Keerthi, S.S., Lin, C.J.: Asymptotic behaviors of support vector machines with Gaussian kernel. Neural Comput. **15**(7), 1667–1689 (2003)

23. Weston, B.J., Watkins, C.: Multi-class support vector machines. Department of Computer Science, Royal Holloway, University of London (2010)

24. Fan, R.E., Chang, K.W., Hsieh, C.J., et al.: LIBLINEAR: a library for large linear classification. J. Mach. Learn. Res. **9**(9), 1871–1874 (2008)

25. Lin, C.-J.: LIBLINEAR-a library for large linear classification [EB/OL], 10 August 2016. https://www.csie.ntu.edu.tw/~cjlin/liblinear/

26. Dev, S., Savoy, F.M., Lee, Y.H., et al.: WAHRSIS: a low-cost high-resolution whole sky imager with near-infrared capabilities. In: SPIE Defense + Security, 90711L (2014)

27. Zhang, Y.: A Course of Image Processing and Analysis. Posts & Telecom Press, Beijing (2009)

28. Zhou, Z.H.: Machine Learning. Tsinghua University Press, Beijing (2016)

Sparse Representation-Based Radiomics in the Diagnosis of Thyroid Nodules

Yunhua Cao[1], Ying Fu[2(✉)], and Guang Yang[1]

[1] School of Computer Science, Chengdu University of Information Technology,
Chengdu 610225, China
[2] Collaborative Innovation Center for Image and Geospatial Information,
Chengdu University of Information and Technology, Chengdu 610225, China
fuying@cuit.edu.cn

Abstract. Thyroid nodules are a disease with a high clinical incidence, but only about 5% of thyroid nodules are malignant. If they are detected and treated early, they can usually be completely cured. The diagnosis of benign and malignant thyroid nodules is for treatment. The choice of method is of great significance, so it is of great significance to correctly judge the benign and malignant thyroid nodules. Radiosurgery is a non-invasive diagnostic technique based on quantitative medical image analysis. However, current radionomics techniques do not have uniform standards for feature extraction, feature selection, and prediction. In this paper, we propose a radionomics system based on sparse representation for the diagnosis of benign and malignant thyroid nodules. First, we developed a feature extraction method based on dictionary learning and sparse representation, which takes advantage of the statistical properties of lesion regions, compared with traditional feature methods based on specified features and specific directions. Feature extraction is more comprehensive and effective. Then, I used a principal component analysis to reduce the extracted thyroid nodule features, and combined the potentially high-dimensional variables into linearly independent low-dimensional variables. Finally, I used the Naive Bayes classifier to classify the data obtained by dimensionality reduction. The total accuracy of the model is 93.3%, the sensitivity is 85.1%, the specificity is 98.6%. The classification result AUC value based on the sparse representation method is 0.920. Experimental results show that the proposed method has a good classification result.

Keywords: Thyroid nodules · Radiomics · Sparse representation · Classification

1 Introduction

Thyroid nodule refers to a mass produced by cells of goiter growing rapidly in an abnormal way under the influence of inducement. It can be divided into benign and malignant tumors. Benign thyroid nodules are more likely to occur in the affected area, leading to clinical diagnosis of patients with decreased vigilance, misdiagnosed as thyroid cancer, goiter and other adverse symptoms. In clinic, malignant nodules must be removed in time, while benign nodules only need regular follow-up observation, so

© Springer Nature Switzerland AG 2019
X. Sun et al. (Eds.): ICAIS 2019, LNCS 11632, pp. 391–401, 2019.
https://doi.org/10.1007/978-3-030-24274-9_35

the judgement of benign and malignant thyroid is very important. The medical diagnosis of benign and malignant thyroid nodules mainly adopts ultrasound-guided fine-needle puncture (FNAB) [1], which is an invasive examination. This examination is not only expensive and time-consuming, but also brings some painful experience to patients. At present, B-mode ultrasonography has become the most commonly used method to distinguish benign and malignant thyroid nodules because of its low price, non-invasive, non-radiation, real-time imaging and other advantages. However, there is no unified standard to judge benign and malignant thyroid nodules because of the subjective experience of doctors and the requirements of imaging equipment. With the epidemiological study, the incidence of thyroid malignant tumors has increased year by year, but with the continuous development of medical diagnostic technology, it is no longer difficult to obtain high-quality imaging and pathological data. Efficient and accurate interpretation of the results have become the key to improve the level of diagnosis [2].

Compared with traditional clinical medicine, which only interprets medical images from the visual level, image histology can deeply explore the biological nature of images and provide clinical decision support. Since Lambin et al. [3] put forward the concept of radiomics in 2012, more and more studies have tried to use the data extracted from radiomics to evaluate various phenotypes of tumors comprehensively, including histomorphology, cell molecules, genetic inheritance and other levels. Aerts et al. [4] extracted 440 image features from the CT images of 1019 patients with lung cancer and head and neck tumors, including the image gray distribution of the tumors, the shape and texture features of the tumors. The results showed that the heterogeneity of tumors captured by these imaging features was related to the pathological type, T stage and gene expression pattern of tumors, and was significantly related to the prognosis of patients. Yoon et al. [5] analyzed the CT features of 539 cases of lung adenocarcinoma, analyzed the size, location, volume, density and CT value of the tumor, and the relationship between the texture features based on pixels and gene expression patterns. It was found that these imaging features were significantly different between ALK gene positive group and ROS/RET fusion gene positive group. These studies suggest that the analysis of image feature data can effectively distinguish the molecular phenotype of tumor tissues. In recent years, more and more scholars have paid attention to imaging histology, explored the diagnosis, treatment and prognosis of tumors, and achieved a lot of results, which accelerated the clinical and transformation research of oncology.

Although image histology has achieved good results in medical image analysis, there are still some challenges in its key steps, such as feature extraction, feature selection and classification. Texture features based on gray level co-occurrence matrix (GLCM) and gray level run-length matrix (GLRLM) are usually used in image histology analysis [10–14]. However, these texture features represent the statistical relationship between adjacent pixel sets in specific directions, but they do not consider the relationship between multiple pixels in different directions at the same time. They ignore the local image structure which plays a key role in subsequent classification. At present, the extraction of image histology features depends on individual conditions and varies with diseases. The features designed for a particular disease are usually not suitable for the diagnosis of other diseases. Furthermore, there is a lot of redundancy in the extracted features to improve throughput, which also increases the risk of over-fitting for subsequent classification. In recent years, sparse representation has attracted more and more attention as the driving force of addressing image processing [15–18], data analysis and face recognition. Sparse representation has the following advantages in these applications. Firstly, sparse representation represents images by using adaptive learning dictionaries instead of traditional analytical dictionaries (e.g., discrete cosine transform, wavelet transform), which provide the ability to extract and represent various textures and details, especially for singular lines and surfaces [19]. In addition, these singular features in images usually play a decisive role in image classification. Furthermore, sparse representation can be regarded as a linear combination of some atoms in the supercomplete dictionary of natural signals [20, 21]. Therefore, based on effective sparse coding algorithm, sparse representation can accurately and effectively select the most basic features used to express data and delete redundant information. Effective use of intrinsic correlation in sparse coding phase will help to improve the accuracy of sparse solution and final classification.

In this paper, we propose a sparse representation based radiohistology system for the diagnosis of benign and malignant thyroid nodules. Firstly, we develop a feature extraction method based on dictionary learning and sparse representation, which trains the training image in dictionary and gets the representation. Then, I used principal component analysis (PCA) to reduce the dimension of the extracted thyroid nodule features [22], and synthesized the correlated high-dimensional variables into linear independent low-dimensional variables. Finally, I use naive bayes (NB)classifier to classify [23].

The rest of this paper is organized as follows: The second part gives the basic process and method background of the experiment. The third part presents the experimental results of the proposed method. The forth part presents the conclusion.

2 Method

In this section, we describe in detail the process of establishing a radiology system based on sparse representation. The overall framework of the method includes four important parts: image segmentation, feature extraction, feature selection and classification. First, select a part of the training sample image to train the feature extraction dictionary. Secondly, the patch based sparse representation method is used to extract texture features from training dictionaries. Furthermore, feature dimensionality reduction based on principal component analysis is used to reduce the dimension of extracted data features. Finally, a simple Bias classifier is used to classify the data obtained from dimensionality reduction, and the final result is obtained.

2.1 Image Segmentation

Medical image segmentation is a complex and key step in the field of medical image processing and analysis. Its purpose is to segment the part of medical image with some special meanings and extract relevant features, so as to provide reliable basis for clinical diagnosis and pathological research, and assist doctors to make more accurate diagnosis. After image preprocessing, a part of the image is selected as the region of interest (ROI) for segmentation. ROI can be segmented manually, semi-automatically or completely automatically. In recent years, many popular segmentation algorithms have been applied in medical imaging research. The most popular segmentation algorithms include region growing method [24, 25], level set method [26–31], graph cutting method [30–37], active contour method [38] and semi-automatic segmentation method. The region growing algorithm is fast, but if the image contains too much noise, it will produce undesirable "regions". In the field of image segmentation, graph cutting is a relatively new method, which constructs image-based graph and achieves the global optimal solution of energy minimization function. Because graph cutting algorithm tries to determine the global optimum, its cost is very high, and there is another problem in graph cutting that is over-segmentation. Because of the complexity of thyroid nodule image itself, a series of problems such as non-uniformity and individual differences need to be solved in the process of segmentation. Therefore, this paper combines the labeling of experienced doctors to perform manual segmentation to ensure the integrity of the lesion area. And then the region of interest (ROI) was segmented by Adobe Photoshop 2015, MATLAB R2016b 64 platform, as shown in Fig. 1 is a case related image.

2.2 Feature Extraction

Feature extraction is mainly about the selection of useful information in feature description of image. These features mainly include the intensity, shape, size and texture of the region of interest on the image. Medical images contain tens of thousands of features. It is easy to ignore some important features to judge benign and malignant by only relying on specific methods to extract certain features. Dictionary training can adaptively learn some unique structure and texture information from different kinds of images. If the test image belonging to class I is sparsely represented in the combination of each training dictionary, the representation coefficient associated with the first dictionary will be higher than that of other dictionaries, because the texture information contained in the second dictionary is more similar to the texture information of the test image. Therefore, the representation coefficient can be used as the feature of image classification.

Sparse coding is the key to realizing the sparse representation of over complete dictionary D, Assuming vector $y \in IR^n$, Existence of over complete dictionary $D \in IR^{n \times k}(k > n)$, The signal y can be approximated by a combination of baselines in a small number of dictionaries D. The corresponding sparse coefficient is x. That is $y \cong Dx$. The problem of solving x is converted to optimization:

$$\min_{x} ||y - Dx||_2^2 + \lambda||x||_1 \quad s.t. ||x||_0 \leq L \tag{1}$$

Among them, $x \in IR^k$ is the sparse coefficient of signal y to dictionary D. L is the constraint of sparsity of sparse coefficient x. $||x||_0$ is the l^0 norm of x. Represents the number of nonzero vectors in x, λ is a scalar regularization parameter.

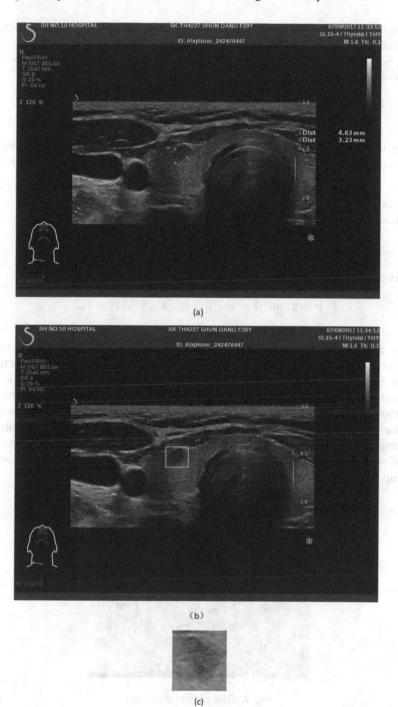

Fig. 1. Original image of thyroid nodule ultrasound image, doctor's annotation map and segmentation result. (a) original image of thyroid nodule ultrasound image; (b) doctor's annotation; (c) segmentation result

The over complete dictionary is the core of sparse expression, and the dictionary is generated by the K-SVD [39] algorithm. Hypothetical signal $Y = \{y_1, y_2, \ldots, y_m\} \in IR^{n \times m}$, Solving the over-complete dictionary corresponding to sparse decomposition can be equivalent to solving the optimal problem of formula 2:

$$\min_{D,X} ||Y - DX||_2^2 + \lambda ||X||_1 \quad s.t. ||X||_0 \le L \tag{2}$$

Among them, $X = \{x_1, x_2, \ldots, x_m\} \in IR^{k \times m}$, L is the largest number of non zero vectors in sparse x. The solution of formula 2 can be divided into the following steps:

(1) use Gauss random matrix to initialize the dictionary D and normalize each column unit.
(2) fixed dictionary D:

$$X = \arg\min_{X} ||Y - DX||_2^2 + \lambda ||X||_1 \tag{3}$$

(3) fix x, update dictionary D:

$$D = \arg\min_{D} ||Y - DX||_2^2 \quad s.t. ||D_i||_2^2 \le 1, i = 1, 2, \ldots, K \tag{4}$$

The above steps are iterated until the convergence condition is met, and a training dictionary is obtained. The inverse dictionary is obtained by using the obtained dictionary and the test picture, and the sparse coefficient is obtained by calculation. This result represents the texture feature that was finally extracted from the lesion area. The OMP algorithm was used in the inverse solution of the sparse expression model [40]. The dictionary that will be trained now is shown in Fig. 2. This training dictionary is obtained by taking 100,000 pictures from the training picture. Totally 512 dictionary atoms are learned with each atom of size 8 * 8. The small square areas are the basic structures that make up the whole tumor region.

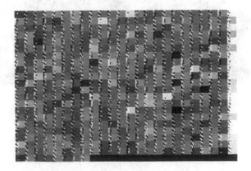

Fig. 2. The learned dictionary

2.3 Feature Reduction and Classification

Among the extracted features, many features are highly redundant. For the analysis and calculation of high-dimensional data, on the one hand, it is easy to fall into the dilemma of "dimension disaster". On the other hand, not all dimensions of data or concepts contain important prediction information. Because of the correlation between features, not all features are essential in classification. Redundant functions not only increase computational complexity but also have a negative impact on classification. Feature selection is the process of preprocessing the original data before using machine learning algorithm to construct the model. It is one of the research issues that attracts wide attention in the field of machine learning. In this experiment, a principal component analysis (PCA) based method was used for feature selection and then combined with a naive Bayesian(NB) classifier for classification. Good experimental results were obtained in this experiment.

2.4 Model Assessment

The performance of our classification system was evaluated in terms of classification accuracy (ACC), the sensitivity (SENS), and the specificity (SPE) and under receiver operating characteristic (ROC) curve (also known as area under curve(AUC)). They are defined as:

$$SENS = \frac{TP}{TP+FN} \tag{5}$$

$$SPE = \frac{FP}{TN+FP} \tag{6}$$

$$ACC = \frac{TP+TN}{TP+TN+FP+FN} \tag{7}$$

Where TP, TN, FP, and FN denote the true positives, true negatives, false positives and false negatives, respectively.

3 Experiment

In this section, to report the effectiveness of our proposed method in the differentiation of benign and malignant, we use a real clinical dataset from the Department of Medical Ultrasonics, the Tenth People's Hospital of Shanghai Tongji University, Shanghai, China. The dataset contains a total of 600 ultrasound images of thyroid patients. Of these, 480 were used to build a training set for the predictive model and 120 for the test set. According to the malignant degree information provided by the data set, it is divided into benign and malignant. The training set included 177 malignant thyroid nodules and 303 benign thyroid nodules. There were 47 cases of malignant thyroid nodules in the test group and 73 cases of benign thyroid nodules.

398   Y. Cao et al.

In this paper, we develop an image histology system based on sparse representation to solve the challenges in image histology. Firstly, we calibrate the thyroid lesion area of each ultrasound image by doctors who have many years of experience in thyroid ultrasound. Then we use Adobe Photoshop and MATLAB R2016b software to segment the thyroid lesion area manually to extract the relatively accurate image area. Secondly, we propose a sparse representation method based on dictionary learning to transform the tumor image into hyperphagia. Texture features of vomiting volume. Because the method uses the image structure based on adaptive learning to represent the texture features of the image, the statistical distribution of the small and medium texture structures in the tumor region can more effectively reflect the texture differences between the images. We use PCA dimension reduction method to obtain different feature spaces, and select the optimal feature space to determine the most accurate prediction. The feature space includes 50 quantized image features. Then, the default data were filled and normalized, and the naive Bayesian classification method was used to train the corresponding thyroid nodule prediction model. The sensitivity, specificity and accuracy were predicted. The total accuracy of the model is 93.3% (112/120), the sensitivity is 85.1% (40/47), the specificity is 98.6% (72/73), the area under the curve (AUC) is 0.920. Detailed data are shown in Fig. 3 is PR (precision-recall) curve and Fig. 4 is ROC curve.

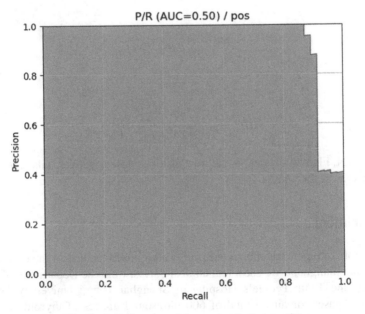

Fig. 3. P-R diagram of feature prediction results

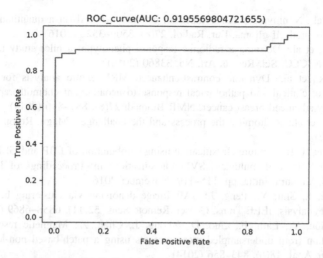

Fig. 4. ROC diagram of feature prediction results

4 Conclusion

This paper proposes a new radiotherapy framework for the prediction of benign and malignant thyroid nodules. The framework includes feature extraction based on sparse representation, feature selection based on principal component analysis, and naive Bayes-based classification. Sparse representation can accurately and effectively select the most basic features for expressing data and deleting redundant information, in sparse coding Effective use of intrinsic correlations at the stage will help improve the accuracy of sparse and final classifications. It is worth emphasizing that the proposed method is highly robust due to its automatic diagnosis; no intervention is required at any point throughout the process. In the future work, we will improve the automatic segmentation and classification methods to make the diagnosis of benign and malignant thyroid nodules more intelligent and accurate.

References

1. Li, W., Zhu, Q., Jiang, Y., et al.: Application of thin-layer liquid-based cytology smear in ultrasound-guided fine needle aspiration biopsy of thyroid. Union Med. J. **5**(1), 8–12 (2014)
2. Zhang, T., Qu, N., Zheng, P., et al.: Machine learning in the diagnosis and treatment of thyroid tumors. Chin. J. Cancer and so on
3. Lambin, P., Rios-Velaquez, E., Leijienaar, R., et al.: Radiomics: extracting more information from medical images using advanced feature analysis. Eur. J. Cancer **48**(4), 441–446 (2012)
4. Zhuangtiango: From radiography to radioimaging histology - Commemorating the 120th anniversary of the discovery of X-rays by Rontgen. Adv. Biomed. Eng. **36**(4), 189–195 (2015)
5. Yip, S., Aerts, H.: Applications and limitations of radiomics. Phys. Med. Biol. **61**(13), R150–R166 (2016)

6. Yu, J., et al.: Noninvasive IDH1 mutation estimation based on a quantitative radiomics approach for grade II glioma. Eur. Radiol. **27**(8), 3509–3522 (2016)

7. Aerts, H.J., et al.: Defining a radiomic response phenotype: a pilot study using targeted therapy in NSCLC. Sci. Rep. **6**, Art. No. 33860 (2016)

8. Teruel, J.R., et al.: Dynamic contrast-enhanced MRI texture analysis for pretreatment prediction of clinical and pathological response to neoadjuvant chemotherapy in patients with locally advanced breast cancer. NMR Biomed. **27**(8), 887–896 (2014)

9. Kumar, V., et al.: Radiomics: the process and the challenges. Magn. Reson. Imag. **30**(9), 1234 (2012)

10. Das, S., Jena, U.R.: Texture classification using combination of LBP and GLRLM features along with KNN and multiclass SVM classification. In: Proceedings of IEEE Conference CCIS, Mathura, India, pp. 115–119, November 2016

11. Xu, L., Li, J., Shu, Y., Peng, J.: SAR image denoising via clustering based principal component analysis. IEEE Trans. Geosci. Remote Sens. **52**(11), 6858–6869 (2014)

12. Qu, X., Hou, Y., Lam, F., Guo, D., Zhong, J., Chen, Z.: Magnetic resonance image reconstruction from undersampled measurements using a patch-based non-local operator. Med. Image Anal. **18**(6), 843–856 (2014)

13. Dong, W., Shi, G., Li, X., Ma, Y., Huang, F.: Compressive sensing via non-local low-rank regularization. IEEE Trans. Image Process. **23**(8), 3618–3632 (2014)

14. Dong, W., Zhang, L., Shi, G., Li, X.: Nonlocally centralized sparse representation for image restoration. IEEE Trans. Image Process. **22**(4), 1620–1630 (2013)

15. Rubinstein, R., Bruckstein, A.M., Elad, M.: Dictionaries for sparse representation modeling. Proc. IEEE **98**(6), 1045–1057 (2010)

16. Dong, W., Zhang, D., Shi, G.: Centralized sparse representation for image restoration. In: Proceedings of IEEE Conference ICCV, pp. 1259–1266, November 2011

17. Dabov, K., Foi, A., Katkovnik, V., Egiazarian, K.: Image denoising by sparse 3-D transform-domain collaborative filtering. IEEE Trans. Image Process. **16**(8), 2080–2095 (2007)

18. Hojjatoleslami, S., Kittler, J.: Region growing: a new approach. IEEE Trans. Image Process. **7**(7), 1079–1084 (1998)

19. Dehmeshki, J., Amin, H., Valdivieso, M., Ye, X.: Segmentation of pulmonary nodules in thoracic CT scans: a region growing approach. IEEE Trans. Med. Imaging **27**(4), 467–480 (2008)

20. Sethian, J.A.: Level Set Methods and Fast Marching Methods: Evolving Interfaces in Computational Geometry, Fluid Mechanics, Computer Vision, and Materials Science, 2nd edn. Cambridge University Press, Cambridge (1999)

21. Malladi, R., Sethian, J.A., Vemuri, B.C.: Shape modeling with front propagation: a level set approach. IEEE Trans. Pattern Anal. Mach. Intell. **17**(2), 158–175 (1995)

22. Ding, C., Huang, H., Yang, Y.: Description and classification of leather defects based on principal component analysis. J. Donghua Univ. (Engl. Ed.), 1–7 (2019)

23. Zhu, M.: Study on Bayesian Network Structure Learning and Reasoning. Xi'an University of Electronic Science and Technology (2013)

24. Gao, H., Chae, O.: Individual tooth segmentation from CT images using level set method with shape and intensity prior. Pattern Recogn. **43**(7), 2406–2417 (2010)

25. Chen, Y.T.: A level set method based on the Bayesian risk for medical image segmentation. Pattern Recogn. **43**(11), 3699–3711 (2010)

26. Krishnan, K., Ibanez, L., Turner, W.D., Jomier, J., Avila, R.S.: An opensource toolkit for the volumetric measurement of CT lung lesions. Opt. Express **18**(14), 15256–15266 (2010)

27. Osher, S., Sethian, J.A.: Fronts propagating with curvature-dependent speed: algorithms based on Hamilton-Jacobi formulations. J. Comput. Phys. **79**(1), 12–49 (1988)

28. Boykov, Y., Veksler, O., Zabih, R.: Fast approximate energy minimization via graph cuts. IEEE Trans. Pattern Anal. Mach. Intell. **23**(11), 1222–1239 (2001)
29. So, R.W.K., Tang, T.W.H., Chung, A.: Non-rigid image registration of brain magnetic resonance images using graph-cuts. Pattern Recogn. **44**, 2450–2467 (2011)
30. Xu, N., Bansal, R., Ahuja, N.: Object segmentation using graph cuts based active contours, vol. 42, pp. II-46–II53. IEEE (2003)
31. Slabaugh, G., Unal, G.: Graph cuts segmentation using an elliptical shape prior, pp. II-1222–II1225. IEEE (2005)
32. Liu, X., Veksler, O., Samarabandu, J.: Graph cut with ordering constraints on labels and its applications, pp. 1–8. IEEE (2008)
33. Ye, X., Beddoe, G., Slabaugh, G.: Automatic graph cut segmentation of lesions in CT using mean shift superpixels. J. Biomed. Imaging **2010**, 19 (2010)
34. Liu, W., Zagzebski, J.A., Varghese, T., Dyer, C.R., Techavipoo, U., Hall, T.J.: Segmentation of elastographic images using a coarse-to-fine active contour model. Ultrasound Med. Biol. **32**(3), 397–408 (2006)
35. He, Q., Duan, Y., Miles, J., Takahashi, N.: A context-sensitive active contour for 2D corpus callosum segmentation. Int. J. Biomed. Imaging **2007**(3), 24826 (2007)
36. Chen, C., Li, H., Zhou, X., Wong, S.: Constraint factor graph cut–based active contour method for automated cellular image segmentation in RNAi screening. J. Microsc. **230**(2), 177–191 (2008)
37. Suzuki, K., Kohlbrenner, R., Epstein, M.L., Obajuluwa, A.M., Xu, J., Hori, M.: Computer-aided measurement of liver volumes in CT by means of geodesic active contour segmentation coupled with level-set algorithms. Med. Phys. **37**, 2159 (2010)
38. Wang, L., Li, C., Sun, Q., Xia, D., Kao, C.Y.: Active contours driven by local and global intensity fitting energy with application to brain MR image segmentation. Comput. Med. Imaging Graph **33**(7), 520–531 (2009)
39. Wu, Q., Li, Y., Lin, Y., Zhou, R.: Weighted sparse image classification based on low rank representation. CMC Comput. Mater. Contin. **56**(1), 91–105 (2018)
40. Wang, R., Shen, M., Li, Y., Gomes, S.: Multi-task Joint sparse representation classification based on fisher discrimination dictionary learning. CMC Comput. Mater. Contin. **57**(1), 25–48 (2018)

Local Smoothing Constraint in Convolutional Neural Network for Image Denoising

Yonghong Guo[1](✉), Feng Jiang[2], Dongyang Zhao[1],
Zhaojing Wen[2](✉), and Shaohui Liu[2]

[1] Beijing Institute of Computer Application, Beijing, China
guoyonghong2004@163.com
[2] School of Computer Science and Technology, Harbin Institute of Technology,
Harbin, Heilongjiang, China
18s103172@stu.hit.edu.cn

Abstract. In this paper, we demonstrate that not only natural images but also their intermediate responses of convolutional neural networks (CNNs) have local smoothing priors. To imposing the local smoothing constraint, we design a local smoothing layer, which is able to suppress noises in a local receptive field. Further, we arrange the local smoothing layer in the early layers of CNNs to effectively capture context information, which is helpful to recovery image details. Experimental results validate that the proposed denoising method outperforms several state-of-the-art methods.

Keywords: Convolutional neural network · Denoise · Smoothing priors

1 Introduction

It is unavoidable to introduce noises in the process of image acquisition and transmission. However, most of high level tasks need images with high qualities as input. Therefore, image denoising plays a very important role in the field of image and video processing [1, 2]. In the literature, numerous image denoising methods [3–5] have been proposed. SUSAN filter [3] and bilateral filter [4] are two classical spatial filters applied to image denoising, which take into account both the space location and intensity similarity between neighboring pixels and assign larger weights to those pixels with smaller distance and larger similarity in a local region. BM3D [4] stacks some similar image patches to constitute a three dimensional array and sparsely represents them with a three dimensional wavelet basis or DCT basis.

For low level image restoration problems, it has been proved to be valuable to make full use of image priors. Currently the widely used prior models include local smoothing, nonlocal self-similarity and sparsity. The local smoothing prior reflects that the intensities of adjacent pixels are very similar. Total Variation (TV) [6], Mumford-Shah (MS) [7] and Markov random field [8] are three typical local smoothing models. The nonlocal self-similarity prior means that high level models (e.g., texture or structure) of natural images will be repeated. The nonlocal self-similarity prior of natural images is first used for texture synthesis [9], whose basic idea is to find some similar patches to determine the intensities of the degraded pixels. Buades et al. [10]

X. Sun et al. (Eds.): ICAIS 2019, LNCS 11632, pp. 402–410, 2019.
https://doi.org/10.1007/978-3-030-24274-9_36

expand this idea and propose an efficient nonlocal means (NLM) denoising method, which uses the average value of the pixels with similar structures as the recovered result. The sparse prior tells us that a natural image can be accurately represented by a small number of primary functions. A variety of works with sparsity as a regularization item have achieved great success [11].

In recent years, some works begin to take image priors into account in a deep learning framework. In [12, 13], Dong et al. show their proposed method has very strong relationship with traditional sparse coding based super resolution methods. In [14], Wang et al. show that a sparse coding model particularly designed for super-resolution can be incarnated as a neural network trained in a cascaded structure from end to end. The interpretation of the network based on sparse coding leads to much more efficient and effective training, as well as a reduced model size. Motivated by the sparsity-based dual-domain method, Wang et al. [15] design a deep network to imitate the sparse coding process. To the best of our knowledge, only the sparse prior has been considered in deep learning for image super resolution [12–14] and JPEG compressive image restoration [15]. Other image priors (e.g. local smoothing and nonlocal self-similarity) are unexplored in deep learning. Specifically, previous deep learning based image denoising methods do not take image priors into account so far. It is very interesting to explore the effectiveness of constraining image priors in deep learning for image denosing. In [25], Mahendran et al. proposed a general method to understand deep image representations by inverting them. Inspired from their work, we try to make statistical analysis on the convolutional neural network to find their interesting characteristic.

2 Local Smoothing Prior in CNNs

It is well known that natural images have a property of local smoothing. In this section, we give analysis and statistical results to show that the local smoothing prior also exists in the outputs of CNNs.

The local smoothing prior refers to that the intensities of adjacent pixels in the space domain are very similar. From a statistical perspective, local smoothing means that the responses of a set of high-pass filters will be very small. In a real world application, the widely used high-pass filters are the vertical and horizontal difference operators, i.e. $\mathcal{D}_v = \begin{bmatrix} 1 & -1 \end{bmatrix}^T$ or $\mathcal{D}_h = \begin{bmatrix} 1 & -1 \end{bmatrix}$. In this paper, we use these two operators to analyze the local smoothing characteristic of the outputs of CNNs. Given an input image p, the response x of a neuron w is expressed as:

$$x = w * p + b \tag{1}$$

Where $*$ is the convolution operation and b is the bias. Figure 1 shows the process of calculating the convolution response of a neuron. The right side refers to one channel of the previous layer, while the left side is the convolution output of one neuron in the current layer. P1 and P2 are two different receptive fields. Since there is a lot of overlaping between P1 and P2, they have very high correlation. Let $\sigma(P_1, P_2)$ be the similarity between P1 and P2. The convolution output of this neuron with respect to P1 and P2 can be calculated as $x_1 = w * P_1 + b$ and $x_2 = w * P_2 + b$, respectively.

Since there is high correlation between P1 and P2, then $x_1 \approx x_2$, i.e. x1 roughly equal to x2. In the other words, the outputs x1 and x2 are similar. It is the essence of local smoothing that neighborhood values are similar. In the other words, the convolutional outputs of the natural image will keep their local smoothing characteristic.

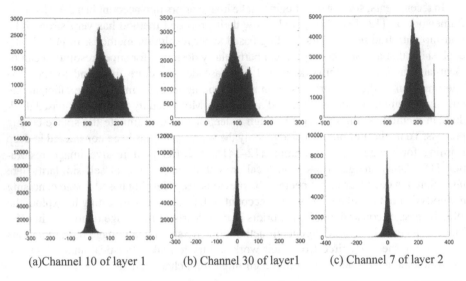

(a)Channel 10 of layer 1   (b) Channel 30 of layer1   (c) Channel 7 of layer 2

Fig. 1. Histograms and horizontal gradient histograms of some intermediate output of SRCNN. The first line is the three histograms while the second is these corresponding gradient histograms with respect to three channels of SRCNN. (a), (b), (c) are the 10th, 30th channels of layer 1 and 7th channel of layer 2, respectively.

3   Image Denoising with Local Smoothing Constraint CNNs

In the above section, our statistical results show that both natural images and their output from CNNs have the property of local smoothing. Inspired by these observations, we explore the use of the local smoothing prior in CNNs and propose an end-to-end CNN with local smoothing prior constraint for image denoising.

3.1   Proposed Network

In the domain of high level computer vision, it has been demonstrated the deeper network the better performance. But in the pioneer work SRCNN [12, 13], authors find that it is not deeper network better performance for image super resolution. It is not very clear what leads to this problem. In this paper, we use a local smoothing layer to make local smoothing constraint in front m mapping layers that helps us to train a deeper network. The deeper network has larger receptive fields. So our network can take more context into account for detail recovery. The configuration of the proposed method is outlined in Fig. 2. It contains feature extraction, shrinking, expanding, local smoothing, mapping and reconstruction layers. They can be shown in the following descriptions.

Feature Extraction Layer. The first feature extraction layer operates on the input noise image with n1 filters of size of $f_1 \times f_1 \times c$ where c denotes the number of channels of the noise image. In our experiments, we set $n_1 = 64$ and $f_1 = 3$. By doing convolution with these filters, each patch of the input noise image, which has the same size with the receptive field of a neuron, is represented as a high-dimensional feature vector. It should be noted that each output channel with respect to one neuron has local smoothing characteristics.

Shrinking & Expanding Layer. In order to reduce the running time of the local smoothing constraint layer, we add the shrinking and expanding layers in our network. The shrinking layer is used to reduce the feature dimension while the expanding layer performs the reverse operation. There are a lot of ways to perform the shrinking and expanding operations. For example, the convolution with larger than one stride will reduce about stride times for the output channels. The corresponding expanding operation will be deconvolution with the same stride. Another way is to use pooling as shrinking and unpooling as expanding operation. Inspired by Dong et al. [17], we adopt the 1×1 filter. Specifically, there are n_i filters of size of $1 \times 1 \times c_i$ for both the shrinking layer and expanding layer. For the shrinking operation, the number n_i of filters is less than the channel number c_i of the front layer, i.e. $n_i < c_i$. For the expanding operation, the number n_i of filters is larger than the channel number c_i of the front layer, i.e. $n_i > c_i$. In our experiments, we set $n_i = 16$ and $n_i = 64$ for shrinking and expanding layers respectively.

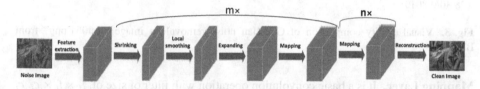

Fig. 2. Our Network Structure. It is an end-to-end mapping that inputs the noise image and output the clean one directly. The feature extraction layer uses multiple neurons to extract multiple feature channels. In order to reduce the running time of local smoothing constraint layer, the shrinking and expanding layer, which are of 1×1 filters, have also be added. We only do the local smoothing constraint before the first m mapping layers, while the remaining n mapping layers are cascaded simply. The final reconstruction layer output the clean image.

Local Smoothing Layer. For a degraded image, the property of local smoothing may be destroyed due to existing noise. Therefore, it is necessary to add local smoothing constraint in the convolutional network. It is well known that local smoothing can be obtained by convoluting the image with a low pass filter, whose output is the weighted sum of the adjacent pixels. It can be expressed as:

$$x'_1 = \sum_{y \in l} w(x_1, y) \cdot y \tag{2}$$

where I is the local neighbor of x1 and w is the filter kernel. There are many kinds of low pass filters, such as the normalized box filter, Gaussian filter, median filter and bilateral filter. They have their own strengths and weaknesses. It is hard to determine which one is better due to each neuron has its own characteristics. Considering the powerful learning ability of CNNs, we use the filter kernel learned by the network instead of the artificial design one. The local smoothing constraint is an elementwise operation that the output have the same size as the input. It is also need to be noted that the local smoothing constraint only operates on the single channel which is the output of the same neuron. In our experiment, the kernel size is 3×3.

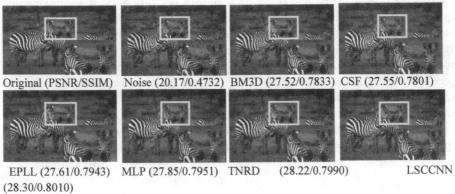

Original (PSNR/SSIM)   Noise (20.17/0.4732)   BM3D (27.52/0.7833)   CSF (27.55/0.7801)

EPLL (27.61/0.7943)   MLP (27.85/0.7951)   TNRD   (28.22/0.7990)   LSCCNN (28.30/0.8010)

Fig. 3. Visual quality comparison of Gaussian noise removal on image "test051.png" from BSD68

Mapping Layer. It is a basic convolution operation with filter of size of. $f_i \times f_i \times c_i$. c_i has the same size with the filter number of the layer in advance. In our experiment, we set the filter number n_i of each mapping operation to be 64. Therefore c_i is 64, too. To take more context into account for detail recovery, multiple mapping operations are used to increase the network receptive field. We only make the local smoothing constraint before the first m mapping layers, while the remaining n mapping layers are cascaded simply. It is well known that multiple small receptive fields cascaded will get a larger one. So it is wise to set $f_i = 3$.

Reconstruction Layer. We want to output a clean image with property of local smoothing. As most CNNs solve for low level problems, the final prediction is the convolution output of c filters of size of $f_r \times f_r \times c_r$. c equals to the number of the estimated clean image, i.e. c = 1 for gray image while c = 3 for color image. c_r has the same size with the filter number of the final mapping operation. We simply set $f_r = 3$.

3.2   Training

We now describe the objective to minimize in order to find optimal parameters of our model. Following most of CNN based image restoration methods, the mean square error is adopt as the cost function of our network. Our goal is to train an end-to-end mapping f that predicts values $\hat{y} = f(x)$, where x is a noise image and $\hat{y}$ is the estimate of the clean image. Given a training dataset $\{x_i, y_i\}_{i=1}^{N}$, the optimization objective is represented as:

$$\min_{\theta} \frac{1}{2N} \sum_{i=1}^{N} \|f(x_i; \theta) - y_i\|_F^2 \tag{3}$$

where θ is the network parameter needed to be trained, $f(x_i; \theta)$ is the estimated clean image with respect to noise image x_i. In the literature, people suggest to use the recently proposed Parametric Rectified Linear Unit (PReLU) as the activation function instead of the commonly-used Rectified Linear Unit (ReLU). In order to reduce parameters in our very deep network, ReLU is used after each convolution layer. We use the adaptive moment estimation (Adam) [26] to optimize all network parameters. For other hyper-parameters of Adam, we set the exponential decay rates for the first and second moment estimate to 0.9 and 0.999. We pad zero values around the boundaries before applying convolution to keep the size of all feature maps the same as the input. We initialize the convolutional filters using the same method as [27]. Our model is trained with the python toolbox on a Nvidia Titan X GPU.

4 Experimental Results

In this section, we evaluate the performance of the proposed method for image denoising on several datasets. We first describe datasets used for training and testing. Next, some training details are given. Finally, we show the quantitative and qualitative comparisons with six state-of-the-art methods. We name the proposed method as LSCCNN.

We compare our proposed LSCCNN with six state-of-the-art methods, namely BM3D [5], CSF [33], EPLL [34], MLP [19], TNRD [20] and WNNM [35]. For TNRD, we use its 7×7 filter model for comparison. The implementation codes are downloaded from the authors' websites and the default parameter settings are used in our experiments. We test the methods' performance on two noise level, i.e. 25 and 50. But to CSF and MLP, we just found their released models with respect to noise level 25, so their performance on noise level 50 will not be given.

Table 1 shows the PSNR and SSIM results of Gaussian noise removal by these six stat-of-the-art methods and ours on each image of Set5. In Table 2, we provide a summary of average PSNR and SSIM results of Gaussian noise removal by various algorithms on Set5, Set14 and BSD68. We highlight the best results with bold fonts. Both tables show that our method outperforms all the six compared state-of-the-art image denoising methods with respect to PSNR and SSIM. To noise level 25, we get 0.31 dB and 0.14 dB gain than TNRD and WNNM respectively. To noise level 50, we get 0.50 dB and 0.69 dB gain than TNRD and WNNM. It shows that our method reveals more advantages in high level noise. Figure 3 gives an example of qualitative comparison. It shows the visual quality comparison of Gaussian noise (here noise level is 25) removal on image "test051.png" from BSD68. Our method can recover much more image detail information such as the displayed enlarged ear part.

Table 1. The PSNR/SSIM results of Gaussian noise removal by various algorithms on Set5

Image	Level	Baby	Bird	Butterfly	Head	Woman	Average
BM3D [3]	25	31.75/0.8613	31.80/**0.8946**	28.35/0.9133	30.62/0.7287	30.74/0.9008	30.65/0.8597
	50	28.98/0.7897	28.30/0.8112	24.75/0.8412	28.46/0.6576	27.17/0.8301	27.53/0.7860
CSF [30]	25	31.03/0.8338	30.82/0.8600	28.56/0.9035	30.29/0.7154	29.89/0.8722	30.12/0.8370
	50	–	–	–	–	–	–
EPLL [31]	25	31.51/0.8561	31.37/0.8770	28.41/0.9106	30.48/0.7277	30.31/0.8896	30.42/0.8522
	50	28.51/0.7660	27.77/0.7824	25.10/0.8465	28.37/0.6395	26.99/0.8096	27.33/0.7688
MLP [17]	25	31.74/0.8621	31.81/0.8892	29.00/0.9125	30.60/0.7230	30.84/**0.9012**	30.80/0.8576
	50	–	–	–	–	–	–
TNRD [18]	25	31.76/**0.8625**	31.88/0.8907	29.30/0.9192	30.73/0.7324	30.76/0.9004	30.89/0.8610
	50	28.81/0.7861	28.10/0.7953	25.90/0.8393	28.68/0.6517	26.99/0.8096	27.78/0.7853
WNNM [32]	25	31.83/0.8626	32.21/**0.9034**	29.40/**0.9265**	30.59/0.7306	30.96/0.9072	31.00/**0.8661**
	50	28.89/0.7909	27.83/0.7930	25.08/0.8622	28.32/0.6454	27.43/0.8312	27.42/0.7793
LSCCNN	25	**32.24**/0.8623	**32.26**/0.8905	**29.91**/0.9175	**31.38**/**0.7553**	**31.23**/0.8996	**31.41**/0.8650
	50	**29.60/0.8035**	**28.83/0.8158**	**26.61/0.8660**	**29.36/0.6950**	**28.12/0.8477**	**28.51/0.8056**

Table 2. Average PSNR/SSIM of Gaussian noise removal by various algorithms on three datasets

Image	Level	Set5	Set12	BSD68	Average
BM3D [3]	25	30.65/0.8597	29.56/0.8227	28.56/0.8011	29.59/0.8278
	50	27.53/0.7860	26.39/0.7195	25.61/0.6860	26.51/0.7305
CSF [30]	25	30.12/0.8370	28.74/0.7942	28.32/0.7867	29.06/0.8060
	50	–	–	–	–
EPLL [31]	25	30.42/0.8522	29.24/0.8209	28.67/0.8121	29.44/0.8284
	50	27.33/0.7688	26.03/0.7053	25.67/0.6877	26.34/0.7206
MLP [17]	25	30.80/0.8576	29.50/0.8209	28.83/0.8124	29.71/0.8303
	50	–	–	–	–
TNRD [18]	25	30.89/0.8610	29.62/**0.8256**	**28.91/0.8151**	29.81/0.8339
	50	27.78/0.7853	26.45/0.7210	25.96/0.7019	26.73/0.7361
WNNM [32]	25	31.00/**0.8661**	29.85/0.8282	28.83/0.8156	29.98/**0.8366**
	50	27.42/0.7793	26.43/0.7276	25.78/0.7036	26.54/0.7368
LSCCNN	25	**31.41**/0.8650	**30.05**/0.8241	28.89/0.8131	**30.12**/0.8341
	50	**28.51/0.8056**	**27.13/0.7306**	**26.06/0.7087**	**27.23/0.7483**

5 Conclusion

In this paper, we first explore the essential attributes of the intermediate outputs of the convolutional neural network. Theoretical analysis and statistical results show that both natural image and the convolutional output of each neuron have the property of local smoothing. Based on this finding, a novel way to make local smoothing constraint in convolutional neural network is proposed. Due to image degradation destroys their local smoothing, we add local smoothing constraint to train a simple end-to-end network for image denoising. More prior information will be explored in the convolutional neural network in our future works.

References

1. Gurusamy, R., Subramaniam, D.: A machine learning approach for MRI brain tumor classification. CMC Comput. Mater. Continua **53**(2), 91–108 (2018)
2. Kan, X., Zhang, Y., Zhu, L., Xiao, L.: Snow cover mapping for mountainous areas by fusion of MODIS L1B and geographic data based on stacked denoising auto-encoders. CMC Comput. Mater. Continua. **57**(1), 49–68 (2018)
3. Smith, S.M., Brady, J.M.: SUSAN—a new approach to low level image processing. Int. J. Comput. Vis. **23**(1), 45–78 (1997)
4. Tomasi, C., Manduchi, R.: Bilateral filtering for gray and color images. In: Proceedings of IEEE International Conference on Computer Vision (ICCV), pp. 839–846 (1998)
5. Dabov, K., Foi, A., Katkovnik, V., et al.: Image denoising by sparse 3D transform-domain collaborative filtering. IEEE Trans. Image Process. **16**(8), 2080–2095 (2007)
6. Rudin, L.I., Osher, S., Fatemi, E.: Nonlinear total variation based noise removal algorithms. Physica D **60**, 259–268 (1992)
7. Mumford, D., Shah, J.: Optimal approximation by piecewise smooth functions and associated variational problems. Commun. Pure Appl. Math. **42**, 577–685 (1989)
8. Besag, J.: Spatial interaction and the statistical analysis of lattice systems. J. Roy. Stat. Soc.: Ser. B (Methodol.) **36**(2), 192–236 (1974)
9. Efros, A.A., Leung, T.K.: Texture synthesis by non-parametric sampling. In: Proceedings of International Conference on Computer Vision, vol. 2, pp. 1022–1038 (1999)
10. Buades, A., Coll, B., Morel, J.M.: A non-local algorithm for image denoising. Computer Vis. Pattern Recogn. **2**, 60–65 (2005)
11. Yang, J., Wright, J., Huang, T.S., et al.: Image super-resolution via sparse representation. IEEE Trans. Image Process. **19**(11), 2861–2873 (2010)
12. Dong, C., Loy, C.C., He, K., Tang, X.: Learning a deep convolutional network for image super-resolution. In: Fleet, D., Pajdla, T., Schiele, B., Tuytelaars, T. (eds.) ECCV 2014. LNCS, vol. 8692, pp. 184–199. Springer, Cham (2014). https://doi.org/10.1007/978-3-319-10593-2_13
13. Dong, C., Loy, C.C., He, K., et al.: Image superresolution using deep convolutional networks. IEEE Trans. Pattern Anal. Mach. Intell. **38**(2), 295–307 (2016)
14. Hui, T.-W., Loy, C.C., Tang, X.: Depth map super-resolution by deep multi-scale guidance. In: Leibe, B., Matas, J., Sebe, N., Welling, M. (eds.) ECCV 2016. LNCS, vol. 9907, pp. 353–369. Springer, Cham (2016). https://doi.org/10.1007/978-3-319-46487-9_22
15. Wang, Z., Liu, D., Chang, S., et al.: D3: deep dual-domain based fast restoration of JPEG-compressed images. In: Proceedings of the IEEE Computer Society Conference on Computer Vision and Pattern Recognition, pp. 2764–2772 (2016)
16. Dong, C., Deng, Y., Change, L.C., et al.: Compression Artifacts Reduction by a Deep Convolutional Network, pp. 576–584 (2015)
17. Dong, C., Loy, C.C., Tang, X.: Accelerating the super-resolution convolutional neural network. In: Leibe, B., Matas, J., Sebe, N., Welling, M. (eds.) ECCV 2016. LNCS, vol. 9906, pp. 391–407. Springer, Cham (2016). https://doi.org/10.1007/978-3-319-46475-6_25
18. Kim, J., Kwon Lee, J., Mu Lee, K.: Accurate image super-resolution using very deep convolutional networks. In: Proceedings of the IEEE Conference on Computer Vision and Pattern Recognition, pp. 1646–1654 (2016)
19. Burger, H.C., Schuler, C.J., Harmeling, S.: Image denoising: can plain neural networks compete with BM3D? In: Computer Vision and Pattern Recognition (CVPR), pp. 2392–2399 (2012)

20. Chen, Y., Pock, T.: Trainable nonlinear reaction diffusion: a flexible framework for fast and effective image restoration. IEEE Trans. Pattern Anal. Mach. Intell. **39**(6), 1256–1272 (2017)

21. Zhang, K., Zuo, W., Chen, Y., et al.: Beyond a Gaussian denoiser: residual learning of deep CNN for image denoising. arXiv preprint arXiv:1608.03981 (2016)

22. He, K., Sun, J., Tang, X.: Single image haze removal using dark channel prior. IEEE Trans. Pattern Anal. Mach. Intell. **33**(12), 2341–2353 (2011)

23. Zhang, J., Zhao, D., Gao, W.: Group-based sparse representation for image restoration. IEEE Trans. Image Process. **23**(8), 3336–3351 (2014)

24. Zeiler, M.D., Fergus, R.: Visualizing and understanding convolutional networks. In: Fleet, D., Pajdla, T., Schiele, B., Tuytelaars, T. (eds.) ECCV 2014. LNCS, vol. 8689, pp. 818–833. Springer, Cham (2014). https://doi.org/10.1007/978-3-319-10590-1_53

25. Mahendran, A., Vedaldi, A.: Understanding deep image representations by inverting them. In: Proceedings of the IEEE Conference on Computer Vision and Pattern Recognition, pp. 5188–5196 (2015)

26. Kingma, D.P., Ba, J.: Adam: A method for stochastic optimization. arXiv preprint arXiv: 1412.6980 (2014)

27. He, K., Zhang, X., Ren, S.: Delving deep into rectifiers: surpassing human-level performance on imagenet classification. In: IEEE International Conference on Computer Vision (ICCV), pp. 1026–1034 (2015)

28. Bevilacqua, M., Roumy, A., Guillemot, C., et al.: Low-complexity singleimage super-resolution based on nonnegative neighbor embedding. In: BMVC (2012)

29. Zeyde, R., Elad, M., Protter, M.: On single image scale-up using sparse-representations. In: Boissonnat, J.-D., et al. (eds.) Curves and Surfaces 2010. LNCS, vol. 6920, pp. 711–730. Springer, Heidelberg (2012). https://doi.org/10.1007/978-3-642-27413-8_47

30. Roth, S., Black, M.J.: Fields of experts. Int. J. Comput. Vis. **82**(2), 205 (2009)

31. He, K., Zhang, X., Ren, S., et al.: Delving deep into rectifiers: surpassing human-level performance on imagenet classification. In: Proceedings of the IEEE International Conference on Computer Vision, pp. 1026–1034 (2015)

32. Vedaldi, A., Lenc, K.: Matconvnet–convolutional neural networks for matlab. In: Proceedings of the 23rd ACM International Conference on Multimedia, pp. 689–692. ACM (2015)

33. Schmidt, U., Roth, S.: Shrinkage fields for effective image restoration. In: Proceedings of the IEEE Conference on Computer Vision and Pattern Recognition, pp. 2774–2781 (2014)

34. Zoran, D., Weiss, Y.: From learning models of natural image patches to whole image restoration. In: Computer Vision (ICCV), pp. 479–486 (2011)

35. Gu, S., Zhang, L., Zuo, W., et al.: Weighted nuclear norm minimization with application to image denoising. In: Proceedings of the IEEE Conference on Computer Vision and Pattern Recognition, pp. 2862–2869 (2014)

Perceptual Loss Based Super-Resolution Reconstruction from Single Magnetic Resonance Imaging

Guang Yang[1,2(✉)], Yunhua Cao[1,2], Xiaoyang Xing[1,2], and Min Wei[1,2]

[1] School of Computer Science,
Chengdu University of Information and Technology, Chengdu 610225, China
gooseon@163.com
[2] Collaborative Innovation Center for Image and Geospatial Information,
Chengdu University of Information and Technology, Chengdu 610225, China

Abstract. Magnetic Resonance Imaging (MRI) can provide anatomical images of internal organs to facilitate early diagnosis of the disease. But the inherent defects of medical imaging system make the acquisition of HR medical images face many problems. One way to solve these problems is to use super-resolution reconstruction technique. We design a feed-forward full connection convolution neural network, which includes five convolution layers and five residual blocks. In addition, loss function based on perception is also used to solve the problem caused by mean square error loss function which cannot meet the human visual sense very well. This method realizes build-in 4 times magnification reconstruction and avoids the checkerboard artifacts, which are often occurred when using deconvolution layers to up-sample images in convolution neural networks (CNN). The effectiveness of the method is verified by experiments, and both the visual and numerical results are improved.

Keywords: MRI · Super-resolution reconstruction · Deconvolution

1 Introduction

Magnetic resonance imaging technology is used to facilitate non-invasive medical treatment. Images are created with the use of strong magnetic fields, radiofrequency transducers, and computer-assisted image processing. It can produce a view of internal organs, particularly in structures such as the liver, brain and so on. However, it is not easy to obtain the desired resolution images because of the limitations of physical imaging systems, imaging environments and other factors such as noise and blur.

Many SR methods have proposed to greatly improve the sensitivity of MRI diagnostic imagine in recent years, it mainly includes two approaches: one is based on reconstruction [1], and the other one is based on the methods of learning [2]. Reconstruction based methods [3–6] usually use the regularization method to construct a priori constraint of a HR image, so HR images are estimated from LR images, and the problem is finally transformed into the problem of cost function optimization under constraint conditions. Learning-based methods have become a research hotspot in

© Springer Nature Switzerland AG 2019
X. Sun et al. (Eds.): ICAIS 2019, LNCS 11632, pp. 411–424, 2019.
https://doi.org/10.1007/978-3-030-24274-9_37

recent years. These methods exploit the relationship between HR and LR image pat-ches. After the learning progress, it can guide the reconstruction of LR images without prior knowledge anymore. Yang et al. [7] performed sparse representation of LR and HR image blocks, and found a LR and HR image block corresponding to a complete dictionary between the established contact; Rueda et al. [8] reconstructed HR brain MR images from LR brain MR images using sparse representation method. Dong et al. Deep neural network has proven to be very effective in computer vision fields. Deep convolutional network can learn the most suitable features of certain images without specific measure functions and outperform lots of traditional image processing meth-ods. Generative adversarial network (GAN) is becoming one of the highlights among these deep neural networks [23], different from the existing methods, convolution neural network (CNN) has universality [24]. [9] proposed a SR Convolutional Neural Network(SRCNN) to learn a nonlinear LR-to-HR mapping. Bahrami et al. [10] designed a five-story three-dimensional convolution neural network to reconstruct the 7T (Tesla) brain image from the 3T (Tesla) brain image; Oktay et al. [11] extend the SRCNN with an improved residual layer design and training object function, and show its application to cardiac MR images. Burgos et al. [12] proposed a method of local image similarity from the MR image reconstruction of CT images; Bahrami et al. [13] proposed a deep architecture CNN, which uses the appearance and anatomical features as input to nonlinearly map 3T MRI to 7T MRI.

Inspired by the work of [14, 15], Johnson et al. propose the use of perceptual loss functions for training feed-forward networks for SR tasks, and use in-network down-sampling to reduce the spatial extent of feature maps followed by in-network up-sampling to produce the final output image. But Odena et al. [16] propose that images generated by neural networks will produce checkboard artifacts, and this phenomenon was generated by the deconvolution operation, which also named transposed convolu-tion operation. Therefore, we combine two methods above and apply to the MRI single image SR reconstruction. Experimental results show that our method conquers the checkboard artifacts while using a feed-forward network for image transformation task.

The structure of this article is as follows: Sect. 2 shows that the phenomenon of checkerboard artifacts is easy to be generated in the convolution neural network, and then shows the MSE as the loss function of the network is not in accordance with human visual perception; Sect. 3 introduces the network structure, including Image transformation network, loss network and the optimization method. Section 4 carries on the experiment and the analysis. Section 5 arrives a brief conclusion.

2 Related Work

2.1 Build-In Up-Sampling and Checkerboard Artifacts

SRCNN [9] use a bicubic interpolation, a fixed up-sampling operator, to upscale input images to the desired size before passing it through the networks for prediction. This step increases unnecessary computational cost, and the deconvolution allows the up-sampling function to be learned jointly with the network. Several algorithms accelerate SRCNN by replacing the pre-defined up-sampling operator with sub-pixel convolution [17] or deconvolution convolution [18]. While using multiple of deconvolution, neural networks iteratively building a larger image out of a series of LR images. Images that generated from deconvolution operations often have checkerboard artifacts, as shown in Fig. 2, two patterns are multiplied, the unevenness gets squared. It is more obvious when the kernel size is not divisible by the stride [15]. We use the structure of the SRCNN and replace the fixed up-sampling operator by build-in deconvolutions, and we generate a HR image as shown in Fig. 1.

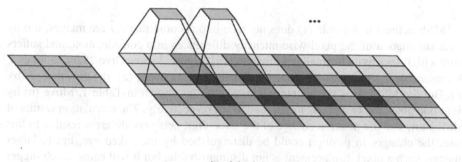

kernel size: 3×3

stride: 2

Fig. 1. Overlap in deconvolution.

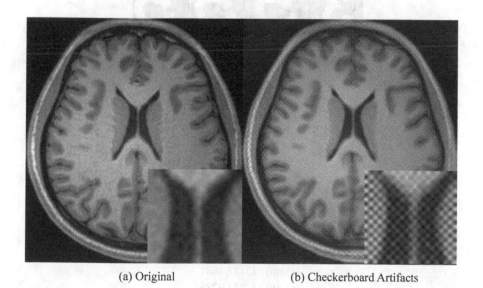

(a) Original   (b) Checkerboard Artifacts

Fig. 2. Checkerboard artifacts when using transposed convolution to reconstruct HR image from LR image

2.2 Mean-Squared Error Loss Function

Comparing reconstruction results require a measure of image quality. One commonly used measure is Mean-Squared Error (MSE). MSE is the cumulative squared error between the reconstruction image $\hat{I}(i,j)$ and original image $I(i,j)$, if both have shape $H \times W$, $I, \hat{I} \in \mathbb{R}^{H \times W}$, then the MSE is defined as:

$$MSE = \frac{1}{HW}(\hat{I} - I)^2 = \frac{1}{HW} \sum_{i=1}^{H} \sum_{j=1}^{W} (\hat{I}_{i,j} - I_{i,j})^2 \qquad (1)$$

MSE defined in formula (1) does not take into account that $I, \hat{I}$ are images, it only takes summation of the pixel-wise intensity differences into consideration, and suffers from a high sensitivity to small deformation [19]. Figure 3 shows five 28 by 28 images. A reasonable image metric presents smaller distance between (a), (b) than that of (b), (c). But the MSE gives the counterintuitive result, as shown in Table 1. Move (b) by right one pixel and two pixels to get (c) and (d) respectively. The calculation results of MSE show that the position change of the same digit gets very different results. In this case, the changes in position could be distinguished by the naked eye, but in larger images, such a pixel displacement is not distinguishable, but it will cause much bigger changes of MSE value.

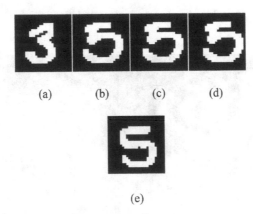

(a)   (b)   (c)   (d)

(e)

Fig. 3. Similar and dissimilar digits

Table 1. MSE of different digits pairs

Pair	MSE
(a), (b)	13187.4681
(e), (b)	13933.9286
(c), (b)	13933.9286
(d), (b)	8957.5255

Displayed equations are centered and set on a separate line.

The MSE loss function is also used to measure the average value of the predicted and true values of the model. Consider it as the performance of the model in the training set, when the model in the training set performance is not good, then the MSE will be higher. In the learning procedure, the mapping function f requires the estimation of a set of parameters $= \{w_i, b_i\}, i = 1, 2, \ldots, w_i$ and b_i are weights and biases of neurons that should be obtained. Given a set of HR images $\{y_i\}$ and their corresponding LR images $\{\hat{y}_i\}$, people often calculate the pixel-wise MSE of the reconstruction as an objective function to train the network:

$$J(\theta) = \frac{1}{n} \sum_{i=1}^{n} \|\phi_l(f(\hat{y}_i; \theta)) - \phi_l(y_i)\|^2 \tag{2}$$

Where n is the number of training samples. But MSE does not conform to the human visual senses, at the same time it is very sensitive to the deformation of the image, so only using MSE cannot measure the difference between the output of CNN and target real image well.

3   System Introduction

The system is composed of two components: image transformation network f and loss network $\varnothing$, the structure shown in Fig. 4.

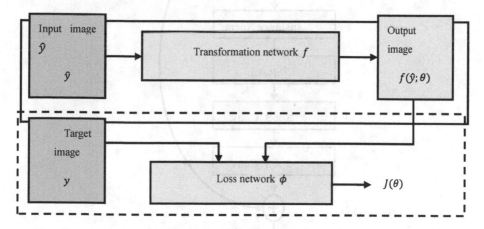

Fig. 4. System overview

The solid line part of Fig. 4 represents the process of image transformation, which realizes converting LR $\hat{y}$ image to HR $f(\hat{y}; \theta)$, where f is a trainable convolution neural network. The dotted line part uses a pre-trained network for image classification to calculate the perceptual loss. The loss network remains fixed during the training process, only transformation network is being studied during the training process.

3.1   Image Transformation Network

Feed-forward neural network divides neurons into different groups according to the order of receiving information. Each group can be viewed as a network layer where neurons in each layer receive the output of the previous layer of neurons as their input and then pass their output to the next level. The information in the entire network is spread in one direction. The feed-forward network can be regarded as a complex mapping of input space to output space through multiple combinations of simple non-linear functions.

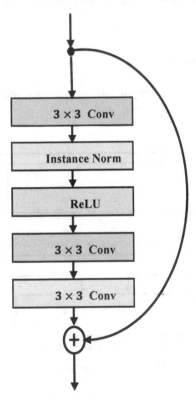

Fig. 5. Residual block structure

The image transformation network f is a fully connected feed-forward neural network, so at test-time, it can be applied to images of any resolution. The mapping function f is to convert LR medical image of size $H/4 \times W/4$ into a HR image of size $H \times W$. We find that the images pass through a certain depth of layers will appear the gradient dispersion, even if we use the batch normalization operation and this also causes high training mistake. The solution to this problem is to add residual blocks, where the input is the fast connection to the output of the activation layer. The residual block is proposed by He [20]. The idea is to use a standard feed-forward convolutional neural network and add a jump to the layers of the connection once. These are stride 1 convolution layers but the difference between these and normal convolutions layers is that we add the input of the network back to the generated output. Each time the residual block is skipped, the result of the skip is added to the input as the output result, the residual block designed as the structure of Fig. 5. Between the down-sampling and up-sampling layers, and we have 5 residual blocks.

The network also contains two (magnified) convolution layers, and then an image is enlarged to 4 times. We separate out up-sampling to a higher resolution from convolution to compute features by resizing the image (using bilinear interpolation) and then do a convolutional layer. The general method is to enlarge the image first and then pass it through the rest of the network, like SRCNN, but this will result in a lot of calculations. To avoid this situation, we put the enlarge convolution layers at the back of the network, so the up-sample layers are processed only on the small size of images and the calculation reduce a lot. The generated output must contain values that are all in the valid pixel range of 0 to 255, so we use a final non-linear layer which applies a scaled tanh function to each element in the output to produce a valid image as this is the final result of SR reconstruction. The exact architectures of all our networks show in Table 2.

Table 2. Network architectures

Layer	Parameters	Size
Input	-	$1 \times 1 \times 9$
Residual block	kernel size 9×9, filters 64, stride1	$64 \times 24 \times 24$
Residual block	filters 64, stride1	$64 \times 24 \times 24$
Residual block	filters 64, stride1	$64 \times 24 \times 24$
Residual block	filters 64, stride1	$64 \times 24 \times 24$
Residual block	filters 64, stride1	$64 \times 24 \times 24$
Residual block	filters 64, stride1	$64 \times 24 \times 24$
Residual block	kernel size 3×3, filters 64, stride 2	$64 \times 48 \times 48$
Residual block	kernel size 3×3, filters 64, stride 2	$64 \times 96 \times 96$
Residual block	kernel size 3×3, filters 1, stride 1	$1 \times 96 \times 96$

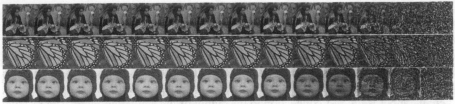

(a) Original (b) Relu1_1 (c) Relu1_2 (d) Relu2_1 (e) Relu2_2 (f) Relu3_1 (g) Relu3_2 (h) Relu3_3 (i) Relu4_1 (j) Relu4_2 (k) Relu4_3 (l) Relu5_1 (m) Relu5_2 (n) Relu5_3

Fig. 6. Use optimization to find an image that minimizes the MSE for each layer from the pretrained VGG-16 loss network $\emptyset$.

3.2 Loss Network

In the image classification task, the different layers in the network have different degrees of abstraction to the input image. In order to increase the space similarity between the output of the image transformation network and the real image, a pretrained convolutional neural network VGG16 [21] is introduced. It has a very uniform architecture that performs 3×3 or 2×2 convolution from beginning to end. As shown in Fig. 6, finding an image $\hat{y}$ that minimizes the MSE for early layers tends to produce images that are visually indistinguishable from $\hat{y}$ [16]. Image content and overall spatial structure that reconstruct from higher layers are preserved but color, texture, and exact shape are not.

When the image passes through the lower layer of VGG16, the pooling operation saves the content information of the image, and the absolute position information is weakened. Using this property, put the output of the SR reconstruction convolution neural network $f(\hat{y}; \emptyset)$ and the target image y into the VGG16 $\emptyset_l$ again, then using the MSE of $\emptyset_l(f(\hat{y}; \emptyset))$ and $\emptyset_l(y)$ as the loss function. In this way, not comparing by pixel, the similarity between the output of the network and the target image space is increased. Let $\emptyset_l(y)$ be the activations at the jth layer of networks $\emptyset$ for input y, then the loss function is defined as:

$$J(\theta) = \frac{1}{n} \sum_{i=1}^{n} \|\phi_l(f(\hat{y}_i; \theta)) - \phi_l(y_i)\|^2 \tag{3}$$

In the supervised machine learning task, the loss function can be used to estimate the difference between the predicted values and the real values of the model. It is a nonnegative function, and the loss function is to find the parameter θ to minimize the loss of J. In the application of SR reconstruction, the convolutional neural network is trained using the loss function defined by the formula (3). Making network output gets closer to the target image, but not a perfect match. The reconstructed image is more consistent with the visual characteristics of the human vision. In the process of training

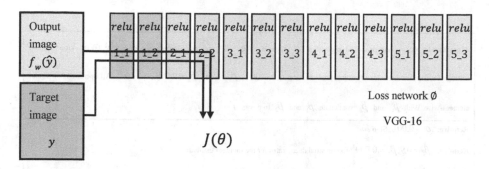

Fig. 7. Architecture of loss network

the network, the weights in the network are fixed, and the weights in the SR reconstruction network are constantly being revised in the training process. The network structure is shown in Fig. 7.

In order to prevent the over-fitting problems, the total variation regularization term is added after the loss function, and the parameter θ to be optimized is constrained. The objective function of the SR reconstruction can be expressed as the formula (4):

$$J(\theta) = \frac{1}{n}(\phi_l(f(\hat{y}_i; \theta)) - \phi_l(y_i))^2 + \lambda R_{tv}(f(\hat{y}_i; \theta)) \qquad (4)$$

where $\lambda = 0.001$ represents regularization factor. Here images are discrete, so TV norm is replaced by the finite-difference [16] approximation:

$$R_{tv}(x) = \sum_{i=1}^{H} \sum_{j=1}^{W} ((x_{i,j+1} - x_{i,j})^2 + (x_{i+1,j} - x_{i,j})^2)^{\frac{1}{2}} \qquad (5)$$

where $x_{i,j}$ represents the value of position (i, j) in x.

3.3 Network Optimization Method

The Adam optimization algorithm [22] is an extension to stochastic gradient descent and it computes a decayed moving average of the gradient and squared gradient (first and second-moment estimates) at each time step. The main advantage is that after bias correction, each iterative learning rate has a definite range, which makes the parameters more stable. The main steps of the algorithm are as follows:

Algorithm1: Adam, our proposed algorithm for stochastic. g_t^2 indicates the elementwise square $g_t \odot g_t$. Good default settings for the tested machine learning problems are $\alpha = 0.001$, $\beta_1 = 0.9$, $\beta_2 = 0.999$, $\epsilon = 10^{-8}$. All operations on vector element-wise. With β_1^t and β_2^t we denote β_1 and β_2 to power t.

Require: $\alpha = 0.001$: Step size

Require: $\beta_1 = 0.9, \beta_2 = 0.999$: Exponential decay rates for the moment estimates

Requires: $J(w)$: Stochastic objective function with parameters θ

Requires: w_0 : Initial parameter vector

$m_0 \leftarrow 0$ (Initialize 1st moment vector)

$v_0 \leftarrow 0$ (Initialize 2nd moment vector)

$t \leftarrow 0$ (Initialize timestep)

while w_t not converged **do**

$t \leftarrow t + 1$

$g_t \leftarrow \nabla_w J_t(w_{t-1})$ (Get gradient w.r.t. stochastic objective at timestep t)

$m_t \leftarrow \beta_1 \cdot m_{t-1} + (1 - \beta_1) \cdot g_t$ (Update biased first moment estimate)

$n_t \leftarrow \beta_2 \cdot n_{t-1} + (1 - \beta_2) \cdot g_t^2$ (Update biased second raw moment estimate)

$\hat{m}_t \leftarrow m_t / (1 - \beta_1^t)$ (Compute bias-corrected first moment estimate)

$\hat{n}_t \leftarrow n_t / (1 - \beta_2^t)$ (Compute bias-corrected second raw moment estimate)

$w_t \leftarrow w_{t-1} - \alpha \cdot \hat{m}_t / (\sqrt{\hat{n}_t} + \epsilon)$ (Update parameters)

end while

return w_t (Resulting parameters)

---

4 Experimental and Result

Learning-based methods are most effective when the data set is big enough. There are many large data sets in the field of natural images, such as ImageNet, but it is not easy to obtain large data sets in the field of medical images. The experimental data acquired from 35 young adults, the size of each image is 256×176, and the images are divided into two parts, one part for training, and the other one for testing. The training part of images is divided into image blocks of size 96×96, which are used as HR target images. The LR inputs are blurred from a Gaussian kernel of width $\sigma = 0.1$ and down sampled with bicubic interpolation of HR images. We train models with the upscaling factor 4 by minimizing feature reconstruction loss at layer relu2_2 from VGG-16 loss network $\varnothing$. We train the network with a batch size of 4 for 200k iterations using Adam with a learning rate 0.001.

Table 3. Network architectures of SRCNN

Layer	Parameters	Activation size
Input	-	$1 \times 32 \times 32$
Convolution layer	kernel size: 9×9 filters: 64 strides: 1	$64 \times 25 \times 25$
Convolution layer	kernel size 1×1 filters: 32 strides 1	$32 \times 25 \times 25$
Convolution layer	kernel size 5×5 filters: 1 stride 1	$1 \times 20 \times 20$

As a baseline model, we use SRCNN for its stable performance. SRCNN is a three-layer convolutional network trained to minimize per-pixel loss on 33×33 patches from the ILSVRC 2013 detection dataset. We change the size of the input patches, shown in Table 3. To account for the differences between SRCNN and our model in architecture, we train image transformation networks for 4 SR using MSE. At last, a bicubic interpolation method is also used for comparison.

It is shown from Table 4 that the experimental results using MSE as loss function or perceptual loss function are better than SRCNN [9] and bicubic method, which shows that the image transformation network designed in this paper is effective. The local magnification of the reconstructed results also shows that the artifacts of the checkerboard disappeared. The effectiveness of the method based on the perceptual loss SR reconstruction is also verified. It is worth noting that when we measure the difference by using the perceptual loss we ultimately use MSE, and we also note that PSNR of the test results also uses MSE, this may be one of the reasons for the high PSNR.

Visually, MSE loss methods result in some high-frequency information failing to be reconstructed, as shown in Fig. 8. In the result of the reconstruction of the perceptual loss method, most of the image details are restored and some noises are smoothed out, this is more in line with the human visual senses and visually validates the effectiveness of the method.

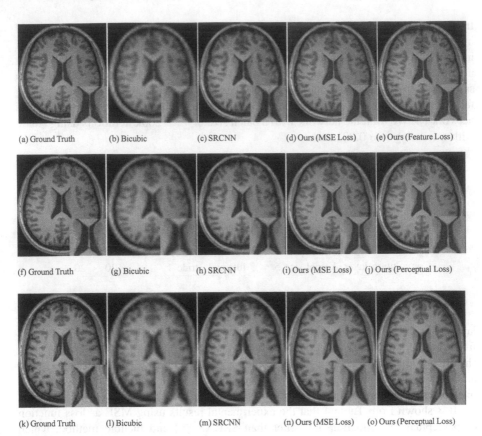

(a) Ground Truth (b) Bicubic (c) SRCNN (d) Ours (MSE Loss) (e) Ours (Feature Loss)

(f) Ground Truth (g) Bicubic (h) SRCNN (i) Ours (MSE Loss) (j) Ours (Perceptual Loss)

(k) Ground Truth (l) Bicubic (m) SRCNN (n) Ours (MSE Loss) (o) Ours (Perceptual Loss)

Fig. 8. SR results on different sizes from different human brain (the upscaling factor 4).

Table 4. PSNR (db) and SSIM result by different methods (the upscaling factor 4).

Test image	Methods	PSNR	SSIM
T1(a)	Bicubic	25.6570	0.7527
	SRCNN	27.1304	0.8173
	Ours (MSE loss)	29.5866	0.8803
	Ours (Perceptual loss)	30.0471	0.8820
T1(f)	Bicubic	25.0954	0.7674
	SRCNN	27.4621	0.8483
	Ours (MSE loss)	29.3266	0.8814
	Ours (Perceptual loss)	30.1098	0.9023
T1(k)	Bicubic	24.0340	0.7351
	SRCNN	26.2055	0.8268
	Ours (MSE loss)	28.7002	0.8879
	Ours (Perceptual loss)	29.5678	0.9067

5   Conclusion

In this paper, a feed-forward fully connected convolution neural network is designed to realize the SR reconstruction of a single medical image. At the same time, it avoids the problem that convolution neural networks can easily produce checkerboard artifacts. In order to get better image visual effect, a VGG16 image classification network was used to calculate the perceptual loss. It goes a step further than the pixel-wise MSE by using the lower layer extraction feature to calculate the MSE. The experimental results verify the validity of the method from the evaluation index and the visual perception. The results also have the good robustness to the size of the test image duo to the fully connected neural network. However, the algorithm requires a network to be trained independently to deal with various scales and also leads to heavier computation time and memory. In addition, different MRI data sets are required for different parts of the body, this leads to a limited scope of application. In the future, we can find a better way to measure the loss function of image perception difference and design the corresponding network for SR reconstruction.

Conflict of Interests.   The authors declare that there is no conflict of interests regarding the publication of this paper.

References

1. Panda, S.S., Prasad, M., Jena, G.: POCS based super-resolution image reconstruction using an adaptive regularization parameter (2011). arXiv preprint: arXiv:1112.1484
2. Glasner, D., Bagon, S., Irani, M.: Super-resolution from a single image. In: 2009 IEEE 12th International Conference on Computer Vision, pp. 349–356. IEEE (2009)
3. Stark, H., Oskoui, P.: High-resolution image recovery from image-plane arrays, using convex projections. JOSA A **6**(11), 1715–1726 (1989)
4. Irani, M., Peleg, S.: Improving resolution by image registration. CVGIP Graph. Models Image Process. **53**(3), 231–239 (1991)
5. Schultz, R.R., Stevenson, R.L.: A Bayesian approach to image expansion for improved definition. IEEE Trans. Image Process. **3**(3), 233–242 (1994)
6. Farsiu, S., Robinson, M.D., Elad, M., Milanfar, P.: Fast and robust multiframe super resolution. IEEE Trans. Image Process. **13**(10), 1327–1344 (2004)
7. Yang, J., Wright, J., Huang, T., Ma, Y.: Image super-resolution as sparse representation of raw image patches. In: IEEE Conference on Computer Vision and Pattern Recognition, CVPR 2008, pp. 1–8 (2008)
8. Rueda, A., Malpica, N., Romero, E.: Single-image super-resolution of brain MR images using overcomplete dictionaries. Med. Image Anal. **17**(1), 113–132 (2013)
9. Dong, C., Chen, C.L., He, K., Tang, X.: Image super-resolution using deep convolutional networks. IEEE Trans. Pattern Anal. Mach. Intell. **38**(2), 295 (2016)
10. Bahrami, K., Shi, F., Zong, X., Shin, H.W., An, H., Shen, D.: Hierarchical reconstruction of 7T-like images from 3T MRI using multi-level CCA and group sparsity. In: Navab, N., Hornegger, J., Wells, W.M., Frangi, A.F. (eds.) MICCAI 2015, Part II. LNCS, vol. 9350, pp. 659–666. Springer, Cham (2015). https://doi.org/10.1007/978-3-319-24571-3_79

11. Oktay, O., et al.: Multi-input cardiac image super-resolution using convolutional neural networks. In: Ourselin, S., Joskowicz, L., Sabuncu, M.R., Unal, G., Wells, W. (eds.) MICCAI 2016, Part III. LNCS, vol. 9902, pp. 246–254. Springer, Cham (2016). https://doi.org/10.1007/978-3-319-46726-9_29

12. Burgos, N., et al.: Attenuation correction synthesis for hybrid PET-MR scanners: application to brain studies. IEEE Trans. Med. Imaging **33**(12), 2332–2341 (2014)

13. Bahrami, K., Shi, F., Rekik, I., Shen, D.: Convolutional neural network for reconstruction of 7T-like images from 3T MRI using appearance and anatomical features. In: Carneiro, G., Mateus, D., et al. (eds.) LABELS/DLMIA 2016. LNCS, vol. 10008, pp. 39–47. Springer, Cham (2016). https://doi.org/10.1007/978-3-319-46976-8_5

14. Johnson, J., Alahi, A., Fei-Fei, L.: Perceptual losses for real-time style transfer and super-resolution. In: Leibe, B., Matas, J., Sebe, N., Welling, M. (eds.) ECCV 2016, Part II. LNCS, vol. 9906, pp. 694–711. Springer, Cham (2016). https://doi.org/10.1007/978-3-319-46475-6_43

15. Odena, A., Dumoulin, V., Olah, C.: Deconvolution and checkerboard artifacts. Distill **1**(10), e3 (2016)

16. Mahendran, A., Vedaldi, A.: Understanding deep image representations by inverting them. In: IEEE Conference on Computer Vision and Pattern Recognition, pp. 5188–5196 (2015)

17. Dumoulin, V., Visin, F.: A guide to convolution arithmetic for deep learning (2016)

18. Shi, W., et al.: Real-time single image and video super-resolution using an efficient sub-pixel convolutional neural network (2016)

19. Wang, L., Zhang, Y., Feng, J.: On the euclidean distance of images. IEEE Computer Society (2005)

20. He, K., Zhang, X., Ren, S., Sun, J.: Deep residual learning for image recognition, pp. 770–778 (2015)

21. Simonyan, K., Zisserman, A.: Very deep convolutional networks for large-scale image recognition. Comput. Sci. (2014)

22. Kingma, D.P., Ba, J.: Adam: a method for stochastic optimization. Comput. Sci. (2014)

23. Li, C., Jiang, Y., Cheslyar, M.: Embedding image through generated intermediate medium using deep convolutional generative adversarial network. CMC Comput. Mater. Contin. **56**(2), 313–324 (2018)

24. Yuan, C., Li, X., Jonathan Wu, Q.M., Li, J., Sun, X.: Fingerprint liveness detection from different fingerprint materials using convolutional neural network and principal component analysis. CMC Comput. Mater. Contin. **53**(3), 357–371 (2017)

DWI Fiber Tracking with Functional MRI of White Matter

Xiaofeng Dong[✉], Dan Xiao, and Zhipeng Yang

Chengdu University of Information Technology, Chengdu 610225, China
434726460@qq.com

Abstract. Tractography based on diffusion weighted imaging (DWI) is one of the tools for mapping the white matter structure of the brain. However, the accuracy of reconstructed fiber on the white matter boundary is constrained by the low resolution of DWI. In order to overcome this defect, we proposed a new DWI tractography algorithm combined with functional magnetic resonance (fMRI). Functional correlation tensor derived from fMRI signal anisotropy in the white matter was employed to describe the functional information of the fiber bundle firstly. Then the particle filter scheme was used to estimate the optimal directional probability distribution and reconstruct streamlines. Experiments on in-vivo data showed the fiber pathways under specific functions loading can be effectively reconstructed, and the accuracy of boundary region can be improved.

Keywords: Tractography · Functional MRI · White matter · Diffusion MRI · Particle filter

1 Introduction

DWI is the primary imaging method for non-invasive study of living brain tissue structures. The direction of fibers in white matter is indirectly estimated by measuring the diffusion of water molecules, with which the tractography algorithm map white matter trajectories [1].

Existing fiber tracking methods can be divided into two categories: deterministic fiber tracking methods and probabilistic fiber tracking methods [2]. The deterministic fiber tracking method starts from seed points and go forward following the diffusion direction distribution at each step. Then it repeats the process until the termination condition is satisfied. The probabilistic fiber tracking method mainly uses the prior information of the fiber to obtain the posterior probability distribution. The direction of each step is sampled from the probability distribution, and the probabilistic path from the seed point to the target area is finally obtained. Describe multiple possible paths in a probabilistic manner to overcome the difficulty of deterministic tracking for complex structure.

Compared to standard anatomical MRI images, dMRI has a lower spatial resolution because of the limited scanning time [3]. Partial Volume Effects (PVE) and angular discretization effects [4] caused by poor spatial resolution reduce fiber reconstructed accuracy in the boundary region. Moreover, the DWI signal decays rapidly in the junction area of white matter and gray matter (GM), which caused most of the fibers

X. Sun et al. (Eds.): ICAIS 2019, LNCS 11632, pp. 425–433, 2019.
https://doi.org/10.1007/978-3-030-24274-9_38

stop prematurely in the white matter without reaching the GM. Due to the uncertainly result, the structure and function of fibers in the cerebral gyrus cannot be comprehensive analyzed [5–8]. To this end, St-Onge, Yeh, and MI-Brain have conducted a series of studies based on the nerve fiber [9, 10].

fMRI is an imaging technique that estimates the functional property of the brain by measuring the blood oxygen level dependent (BOLD) in neuronal functional activity [11]. Previous studies of functional magnetic resonance imaging have been limited to gray matter. However, growing studies have found the BOLD signal in the white matter also contains cranial nerve activity, and the correlation between the neighborhood voxel signals is directional [2]. In addition, specific gray matter cortex and white matter nerve pathways are also associated with brain activity [12], which provides a new way to solve the reconstruction problem in boundary region.

Aiming at the problem of fiber reconstruction accuracy in the boundary region between white matter and gray matter, we propose a novel tractography algorithm using DWI and fMRI of white matter together. The function and structure information of WM were combined by particle filter fiber tracking frame to obtain more precise fiber distribution in the boundary region.

2   Methods

This paper assumes that the fiber trajectory has a Markov property, and each step depends only on the previous step and the current observation data. The observed value is the DWI signal of $\Omega \subset \mathbb{R}^3$ in the three-dimensional space of the brain. The fiber trajectory model consists of a series of displacement vectors in Ω, where the displacement vector is the parameter to be estimated. Assuming that the intensity of the DWI is U, given the position $x \in \Omega$, v_k is the unit direction vector in step k. In dynamic systems, states and observations are represented by $y_k = \{x_k, v_k\}$ and $z_k = \{U_{xk}\}$, and dynamic systems are defined by three densities: initialization, a priori, and maximum likelihood functions [13].

In step k, assume that the current step and the next step are independent of each other:

$$p(z_k, y_{k+1}|y_k) = p(z_k|y_k)p(y_{k+1}|y_k) \tag{1}$$

Due to the fiber trajectory given by (1) and the Markov [14] property of the independent condition, the fiber path can be modeled by a Markov chain. Therefore, dynamic systems are described only by the following densities:

$$p(y_k|y_{0:k-1}, z_{1:k-1}) = p(y_k|y_{k-1}) \tag{2}$$

$$p(z_k|y_{0:k}, z_{1:k-1}) = p(z_k|y_k) \tag{3}$$

Considering Eqs. (1), (2) and (3) and applying Bayes' theorem, we can get an expression of posterior density:

$$p(y_{0:k}|z_{1:k}) = p(z_k|y_k)p(y_k|y_{k-1})p(y_{0:k-1}|z_{1:k-1}) \tag{4}$$

The prior probability density reflects the proximity of the current tracking direction to the tracking direction of the previous step. The larger the value, the closer the two tracking directions are, and the further the deviation is. In this paper, the functional ODF constructed from the white matter fMRI signal is selected as the prior probability density function $p(y_k|y_{k-1})$.

Due to the influence of noise and other factors, there are uncertain components in the MRI dispersion information, and the observation probability density $p(z_k|v_k)$ is an indicator to measure such uncertainty. This paper chooses to use the Q-ball model to calculate fODF as the observed probability density $p(z_k|v_k)$.

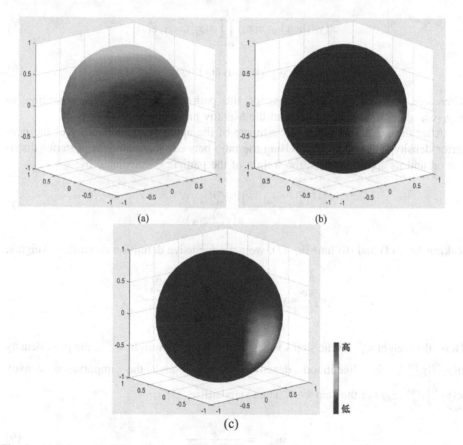

Fig. 1. (a) Prior probability density (b) Observation probability density (c) Posterior probability density

The posterior probability density function (c) in white matter and gray matter has an example of a fiber cross voxel, which is defined as the product of the prior probability density (a) and the observed probability density function (b), as shown in Fig. 1.

In 3D space, choose vMF distribution as the optimal importance density $p(y_{0:k-1}|z_{1:k-1})$.

Particle filtering sequentially samples a set of M paths starting from the starting point $x_0 \in \Omega$. At step $k = 0$, the M weighted particles are tracked forward from x_0. Given the set of particles $\{y_{0:k}^{(m)}, w_k^{(m)}\}_{m-1}^{M}$ at step k, the process of propagation to the next step $k+1$ is performed in three phases: prediction, weighting, and selection.

In the prediction phase, since the posterior probability $p(y_{0:k}|z_{1:k})$ cannot be evaluated, the importance density $\pi(y_{0:k}|z_{1:k})$ (which is an approximation of the posterior density) is used to simulate the vector at each point in the fiber path. Assuming the causal relationship of importance density, that is, for all $t \geq k$, $\pi(y_{0:k}|z_{1:t}) = \pi(y_{0:k}|z_{1:k})$, you can choose a recursive formula along the path [10] such as:

$$\pi(y_{0:k}|z_{1:k}) = \pi(x_0) \prod_{t=1}^{k} \pi(y_t|y_{0:t-1}, z_{1:t}) \tag{5}$$

$$\pi(y_{0:k}|z_{1:k}) = \pi(y_k|y_{0:k-1}, z_{1:k})\pi(y_{0:k-1}|z_{1:k-1}) \tag{6}$$

Therefore, in step k, the state y_k of the path $y_{0:k-1}$ is sampled according to $\pi(y_k|y_{0:k-1}, z_{1:k})$, taking into account the Markov property of the fiber path.

After the prediction phase, an estimate of the approximate reliability of the posterior density [15] is weighted. Using the ratio between the unknown posterior distribution and its approximation, the weight of the particle is calculated by:

$$w_k^{(m)} = \frac{p(y_{0:k}^{(m)}|z_{1:k})}{\pi(y_{0:k}^{(m)}|z_{1:k})} \tag{7}$$

Taking Eqs. (4) and (6) into Eq. (7), we get a recursive definition of particle weights:

$$w_k^{(m)} = w_{k-1}^{(m)} \frac{p(z_k|y_k^{(m)})p(y_k^{(m)}|y_{k-1}^{(m)})}{\pi(y_k^{(m)}|y_{0:k-1}^{(m)}, z_{1:k})} \tag{8}$$

Here, the weight $w_k^{(m)}$ in the step k is calculated using the weight $w_{k-1}^{(m)}$, the prior density $p(y_k^{(m)}|y_{k-1}^{(m)})$, the likelihood density $p(z_k|y_k^{(m)})$, and the importance density $\pi(y_k^{(m)}|y_{0:k-1}^{(m)}, z_{1:k})$ at the step $k-1$. Then standardize:

$$\tilde{w}_k^{(m)} = \frac{w_k^{(m)}}{\sum_{n=1}^{M} w_k^{(n)}} \tag{9}$$

The importance distribution of Eq. (6) will increase the variance of weights over time [16]. Therefore, in the early stages of the estimation process, a significant portion of the weight may drop rapidly. The purpose of the final phase selection is to avoid this degradation. Estimate the path using an estimate of the effective sample size (ESS) [16, 17]:

$$\hat{N}_{ESS} = \frac{1}{\sum_{m=1}^{M} (\tilde{w}_k^{(n)})^2} \tag{10}$$

When reduced below a fixed threshold, resampling should be performed to eliminate particles with lower weights [2].

3 Experimental Results

The test data collected functional images of visual stimuli from four adults. Visual stimuli were performed with an 8 Hz scintillation plate. The experiment was designed in the form of a square wave, with a 30 s fixed blank screen and then a 30 s chessboard flashing with repeated cycles. Acquisition parameters: T2*-weighted (T2* w) gradient echo (GE), echo planar imaging (EPI) The sequence collected three sets of BOLD signals, TR = 3 s, TE = 45 ms, matrix size = 80 × 80, FOV = 240 × 240 mm^2, 43-layer and 3 mm layer spacing, 145 volumes, 435 s. Each subject was scanned with the same parameters as above, and data acquisition was done under visual stimulation. At the same time, a single-shot, spin echo EPI sequence is used to collect diffusion weighted images (DWI) data: b = 1000 s/mm^2, 32 diffusion-sensitizing directions, TR = 8.5 s, TE = 65 ms, SENSE factor = 3, matrix size = 128 × 128, FOV = 256 256 mm^2, 68 layer and 2 mm layer spacing.

The collected data were preprocessed using SPM12. The fMRI signal is sequentially subjected to time layer correction, head motion correction, and FWHM = 4 mm Gaussian smoothing. If the head movement is more than 2 mm and the rotation is greater than 2°, the data will be rejected. The smoothed data of all subjects were registered to their respective DWI data spaces with reference to the DWI data of b = 0. The BOLD signal of all voxels is bandpass filtered by 0.01–0.08 Hz. This band contains the frequency of the experimental stimulus waveform (0.016 Hz). The T1w data was subjected to offset correction and segmentation to obtain white matter, gray matter and cerebrospinal fluid, and then jointly registered to the DWI image space with b = 0 DWI as a reference.

To verify the validity of the proposed algorithm, this study was tested on real brain data. The reconstructed structural pathway is traced from the lateral geniculate nucleus (LGN) to the visual radiation area with a step size of 0.5 pixels. If the advance to the target area or the direction changes by more than 90°, the tracking is stopped. Fiber tracking was performed 800 times for each case. The results of the tracking process are shown in Fig. 2. For comparison, tracking results without fMRI and with fMRI are shown in Fig. 2, respectively. The result is shown in Fig. 2 as the T1 image of the 27th layer. Large-area dispersed streamlines appear in the figure, most of which exit the visual radiation area, which may be due to the fact that the diffuse ODF is wider than the a posteriori ODF, resulting in probabilistic tracking that produces a large number of streamlines for all possible paths.

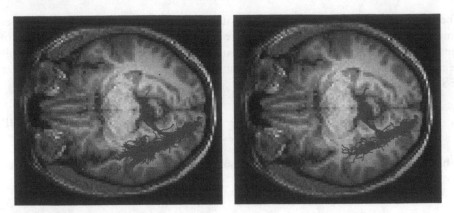

Fig. 2. Tracking results of LGN to the visual radiation area on different brain data. The image on the left has no fMRI and the image on the right has fMRI.

In order to evaluate the effect of adding fMRI on the fiber reconstruction accuracy in the boundary region between white matter and gray matter, fiber tracking experiments were performed on fiber bundles in the boundary region between white matter and gray matter. Figure 3 shows the results of 200 tracking imaging of different real brain data visual radiation areas, with a step size of 0.5 pixels, and stops tracking if it advances to the target area or the direction changes by more than 90°. For comparison, the tracking results without fMRI and with fMRI were shown in Fig. 3, respectively. The background of (a) and (b) is the T1 image of the 35th layer. The red box and the corresponding magnified area show the tracking results of boundary region between white matter and gray matter in the end point of the radiation. Compared with the tracking result without the added function signal, after adding the functional signal, the fiber bundle at the end point of the radiation is closer to boundary region between white matter and gray matter.

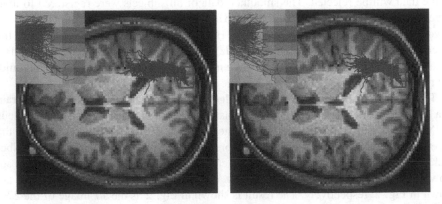

Fig. 3. Tracking reconstruction results of the radiation end point region: The red box and the corresponding magnified area are the tracking results of boundary region between white matter and gray matter in the radiation end point area. The image on the left has no fMRI and the image on the right has fMRI. (Color figure online)

Figure 4 is a comparison of the results of tracking the fiber in the radioactive area 800 times, with a step size of 0.5 pixels, and if the advancement to the target area or the direction change is greater than 90°, the tracking is stopped. For comparison, the tracking results without fMRI and with fMRI were shown in Fig. 4, respectively. The background of (a) and (b) is the T1 image of the 35th layer, the background of (c) (d) is the T1 image of the 32nd layer. The red box and the corresponding magnified area show the tracking results of boundary region between white matter and gray matter in the middle section of the radiation. Compared with the tracking result without the added function signal, after adding the function signal, the fiber bundle in the middle section of the radiation is closer to boundary region between white matter and gray matter.

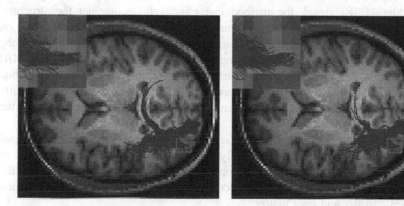

Fig. 4. Tracking reconstruction results of the mid-radiation area: The red box and the corresponding magnified area show the tracking results of boundary region between white matter and gray matter in the mid-radiation area. The image on the left has no fMRI and the image on the right has fMRI. (Color figure online)

Calculate the average length of the fiber by calculating the sum of the Euclidean distances of each segment, and invalid fibers (fibers that do not reach the gray matter or any ROI region are referred to as ineffective fibers) as a percentage of total fiber, and among the effective fibers, the fibers having a fiber length of 10 mm or more account for the percentage of the effective fibers, under the condition of adding the fMRI signal and not adding the fMRI signal (Table 1).

Table 1. Average length (mm), invalid fibers (%), Valid & fiber length $\geq$ 10 mm (%).

Tracking	Average length	Invalid fiber	Valid & fiber length $\geq$ 10 mm
Title (centered)	16.18	2.52%	10.21%
4th-level heading	17.65	2.21%	12.10%

4   Conclusion

Aiming at the problem of fiber reconstruction accuracy in boundary region between white matter and gray matter, this paper proposes a new DWI fiber tracking imaging algorithm based on fMRI of white matter, and combines particle filter theory to track and reconstruct imaging. This study provides a new way to solve the problem of fiber reconstruction accuracy in boundary region between white matter and gray matter, and can improve the accuracy of fiber tracking in boundary region between white matter and gray matter.

This study conducted a tracking experiment on real brain data. Firstly, the effectiveness of the proposed method is verified by tracking the LGN to the visual radiation area. By comparing the results of different brain data when adding fMRI signal and without adding fMRI signal, the method can effectively reconstruct the structural pathway from the lateral geniculate nucleus to the visual radiation area. Next, on different brain data, fiber tracking was performed on the middle and end regions of the radiation visual under the condition of adding the fMRI signal and not adding the fMRI signal. This method can improve the fiber tracking of boundary region between white matter and gray matter. Finally, the effectiveness and accuracy of the method are fully illustrated by analyzing the average fiber length and the ineffective fiber results of the tracking results on each data.

In summary, the method introduces the spatial correlation tensor of the fMRI signal anisotropy in the white matter and indirectly describes the geometrical information of the fiber bundle, which can effectively reconstruct the fiber nerve pathway of specific function and improve the fiber bundle reconstruction accuracy of boundary region between white matter and gray matter.

Acknowledgements. This study is Supported by Sichuan Science and Technology Program 2017RZ0012.

References

1. Conturo, T.E., Lor, N.F., Cull, T.S.: Tracking neuronal fiber pathways in the living human brain. Proc. Natl. Acad. Sci. U. S. A. **96**(18), 10422–10427 (1999)
2. Girard, G., Whittingstall, K., Deriche, R.: Towards quantitative connectivity analysis: reducing tractography biases. Neuroimage **98**, 266–278 (2014)
3. Friman, O., Farneback, G., Westin, C.: A Bayesian approach for stochastic white matter tractography. IEEE Trans. Med. Imaging **25**(8), 965–978 (2006)
4. Wu, X.D., Li, Y.B., Lin, Y., Zhou, R.L.: Weighted sparse image classification based on low rank representation. Comput. Mater. Contin. **56**(1), 91–105 (2018)
5. Behrens, T.E.J., Johansen Berg, H., Jbabdi, S.: Probabilistic diffusion tractography with multiple fibre orientations: what can we gain. Neuro Image **34**, 144–155 (2007)
6. Tournier, J.D., Susumu, M., Alexander, L.: Diffusion tensor imaging and beyond. Magn. Reson. Med. **65**, 1532–1556 (2011)
7. Basser, P.J., Pierpaoli, C.: Microstructural and physiological features of tissues elucidated by quantitative-diffusion-tensor MRI. J. Magn. Reson. **213**(2), 570–590 (2011)

8. Jbabdi, S., Heidi, J.B.: Tractography: where do we go from here. Brain Connect. **1**, 169–183 (2011)
9. St-Onge, E., Daducci, A., Girard, G., Descoteaux, M.: Surface-enhanced tractography (SET). NeuroImage **169**, 524 (2018)
10. Rheault, F., Houde, J.C., Descoteaux, M.: Visualization, interaction and tractometry: Dealing with millions of streamlines from diffusion MRI tractography. Front. Neuroinformatics **11**, 42 (2017)
11. Smith, R.E.: Anatomically-constrained tractography: improved diffusion MRI streamlines tractography through effective use of anatomical information. Neuroimage **62**, 1924–1938 (2012)
12. Ding, Z., Xu, R., Stephen, K.: Visualizing functional pathways in the human brain using correlation tensors and magnetic resonance imaging. Magn. Reson. Imaging **34**(1), 8–17 (2016)
13. Wu, X., Yang, Z.P., Bailey, S.: Functional connectivity and activity of white matter in somatosensory pathways under tactile stimulations. NeuroImage **152**, 371–380 (2017)
14. Wang, C.T., Feng, Y., Li, T.Z., Xie, H., Kwon, G.-R.: A new encryption-then-compression scheme on gray images using the Markov random field. Comput. Mater. Contin. **56**(1), 107–121 (2018)
15. Arulampalam, M.S., Maskell, S., Gordon, N., Clapp, T.: A tutorial on particle filters for online nonlinear/non-Gaussian Bayesian tracking. IEEE Trans. Signal Process. **50**(2), 174–188 (2002)
16. Ding, Z.: Detection of synchronous brain activity in white matter tracts at rest and under functional loading. Proc. Natl. Acad. Sci. **115**(3), 595–600 (2018)
17. Doucet, A., Godsill, S., Andrieu, C.: On sequential Monte Carlo sampling methods for Bayesian filtering. Stat. Comput. **10**(3), 197–208 (2000)

Multi-objective Investment Decision Making Based on an Improved SPEA2 Algorithm

Xi Liu[✉] and Dan Zhang

Glorious Sun School of Business and Management, Donghua University,
Shanghai 200051, China
1179195@mail.dhu.edu.cn

Abstract. An improved SPEA2 algorithm is proposed to optimize the multi-objective decision-making of investment. In the improved method, an external archive set is set up separately for local search after genetic operation, which guarantees the global search ability and also has strong local search ability. At the same time, the new crossover operator and individual update strategy are used to further improve the convergence ability of the algorithm while maintaining a strong diversity of the population. The experimental results show that the improved method can converge to the Pareto optimal boundary and improve the convergence speed, which can effectively realize the multi-objective decision making of investment.

1 Introduction

Enterprise investment planning is constrained by many conditions. The existing decision-making methods of production and investment projects in enterprises mainly include NPV method [1], payback period method [2], cost-benefit analysis [3], Monte Carlo simulation approach [4], probability tree method [5], dynamic programming method [6], incremental effect evaluation method [7,8] and so on. These methods have their own advantages and are widely used, whereas they also have shortcomings, which can not meet the criteria of reasonable and scientific evaluation. In addition, these methods are mainly based on single-objective decision-making, that is profit maximization. Single-objective decision-making method often fails to measure the whole scheme comprehensively, which makes decision-making difficult and even leads to wrong decision-making. While the investment of production projects of enterprises is influenced by many factors, and the reliability (project risk) is one of the important factors [9]. This paper establishes a multi-objective evaluation index system based on investment profit, investment risk and environmental costs, and makes multi-objective optimization decision for investment projects.

Evolutionary algorithm (EA) is a kind of adaptive global optimization probabilistic search algorithm which simulates the evolution process of organisms

© Springer Nature Switzerland AG 2019
X. Sun et al. (Eds.): ICAIS 2019, LNCS 11632, pp. 434–443, 2019.
https://doi.org/10.1007/978-3-030-24274-9_39

in natural environment. In recent years, many excellent multi-objective evolutionary algorithms (MOEA) have been proposed one after another, and good results have been achieved in solving multi-objective optimization problems. The representative algorithms are NSGAII [10], SPEA2 [11], PAES [12] and so on. The slow convergence speed and low precision of multi-objective evolutionary algorithm have become the fatal weakness that affects the performance of the algorithm. Most evolutionary algorithms expand the range of random search in order to prevent the algorithm from falling into local convergence, while the price of that is to weaken the ability of local search. The feasible solution space of multi-objective decision-making problem of enterprise investment is often very complex and non-linear [13]. It is not easy to converge to Pareto optimum when using traditional multi-objective optimization theory to optimize.

The existing local search algorithm is improved from hill climbing method. Local search algorithm has been widely used, and many improved algorithms [14,15] have been derived. But the simple local search is easy to fall into local optimum and the global search ability is limited. This paper proposes an improved SPEA2 algorithm based on local search for multi-objective decision-making of enterprise investment. That is to say, with strong global search capability, an external population dedicated to local search is set up separately for each iteration to generate a non-dominant set. Besides, this paper also improves the crossover operator and partially individual update strategy, which effectively improves the convergence ability of the algorithm. The results imply that this method can realize the optimization of multi-objective investment decision very well, and the convergence speed of the optimization results is faster and the results are more accurate than the traditional multi-objective optimization methods.

2   Methodology

Multi-objective optimization problems can be described as:

$$\min \ F(X) = (f_1(X), f_2(X), ..., f_m(X))$$
$$\text{s.t.} \ g_i(X) \leqslant 0, i = 1, 2, ..., p$$
$$h_j = 0, j = 1, 2, ..., q$$

where $X = [x_1, x_2, ..., x_n]$ is the decision variables, f_i is the ith optimization objection. Pareto domination is one of the main concepts of multi-objective optimization. The concepts of Pareto domination and Pareto solution set are as follows:

Pareto dominance: If A and B are any two different individuals in an evolutionary population, and A dominating B (A$\varPhi$B), the following two conditions must be satisfied:

(1) For all sub targets, A is not worse than B, that is $f_k(A) \leqslant f_k(B) \ k = 1, 2, ..., m$.

(2) There is at least one sub goal that makes A better than B, that is $\exists l \in \{1, 2, ..., m\}$, $f_k(A) < f_k(B)$.

Pareto-optimal set: The Pareto optimal solution set P^* is the set of all Pareto optimal solutions, which is defined as follows:

$$P^* \triangleq \{X^* | \neg \exists X \in X_f : X \Phi X^*\}, \tag{1}$$

where X_f is variable space.

2.1   The Basic Theory of SPEA2

SPEA2 is an efficient multi-objective optimization genetic algorithm proposed by Zitzler et al. It is based on the concept of Pareto domination for fitness allocation and selection operations, and uses niche method and external archiving elite retention mechanism. Although SPEA2 has some advantages over other multi-objective algorithms, its genetic evolution operation has strong randomness. In this way, the search range can be enlarged, the algorithm will not fall into local convergence, but the local search ability is insufficient. After reaching nearby

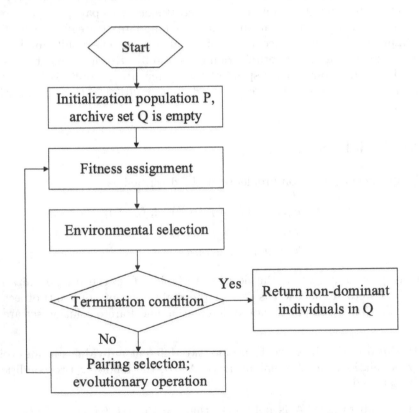

Fig. 1. The description of SPEA2 algorithm

regions of the Pareto optimal solution, the optimization efficiency of SPEA2 often decreases dramatically, and sometimes the Pareto optimal solution can not even be searched. The specific flowchart is shown in Fig. 1.

2.2   Improved SPEA2

In order to solve the problem of insufficient local search ability of current SPEA2 algorithm, a local search method is proposed.

Local Search Strategy. The standard SPEA2 evolutionary algorithm has strong randomness in genetic operation. Although this can increase the search range and avoid falling into local convergence, the local search ability is relatively poor. After reaching the nearby of Pareto optimal solution, the optimization efficiency of SPEA2 often decreases significantly, sometimes even fails to converge to the Pareto optimal solution, and the solution set is not always the global optimal. In order to preserve the global search capability of SPEA2 and enhance the local search capability, we set up a separate population L to store the non-dominant set generated by each iteration. In addition, local fine-tuning of the internal individual in L is carried out to enhance the ability of neighborhood search. For binary coding, local search is to select a mutation near the end of the chromosome. The specific operation is as Fig. 2.

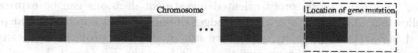

Fig. 2. The description of SPEA2 algorithm

The paternal population of the next iteration is composed of population L and population P after fine-tuning of local search operation. Using simultaneous evolution of two populations can exchange the genetic information carried by excellent individuals among populations to break the balance within the population and realize the search near the optimal solution set. The diversity of alternative populations is richer than that of standard algorithms, and the chances of finding the optimal solution set will be greatly increased.

Crossover Operator. Conventional crossover operators only perform partial gene recombination of two individuals according to a certain crossover probability. Obviously, the intersection of two individuals with high similarity is of little significance to population evolution, which will only bring population evolution to a standstill and increase the possibility of local convergence. In order to overcome this shortcoming, we judge the similarity of two individuals before crossing. It is only when the difference between two individuals reaches a certain degree that cross operation is carried out. In this paper, we use Euclidean distance of two chromosomes as a measure of individual similarity.

$$\text{Crossover} = \begin{cases} 1 & D_{ij} \geqslant T \\ 0 & D_{ij} < T \end{cases} \tag{2}$$

where D_{ij} represents the Euclidean space distance between two individuals, T is the similarity thresholds. Number 1 indicates that there can be a crossover operator between two individuals, and number 0 represents no crossover.

Individual Updating Strategy. In order to further enhance the diversity of the population and reduce the risk of falling into local optimum in iteration, we "re-select" some inferior individuals of the population according to a certain proportion every several algebras, delete them, and re-initialize some individuals to join the parent population. This method is conducive to maintaining population diversity, improving search performance and effectively preventing premature emergence.

In order to evaluate the convergence performance of the algorithm, a closer evaluation method for convergence index is used in this work [16].

3   Multi-objective Decision Making in Enterprise Investment

In the traditional sense, profit oriented investment decisions can be expressed as following. The annual investment budget of one enterprise in one n year plan period is b_i, $(i = 1, 2, ..., n)$, and there are m different projects that can be invested. d_{ij} is known to represent the profit from the jth $(j = 1, 2, ..., m)$ per unit investment project in year i. The goal is to maximize the total profit during the planned period. However, the profit based single objective decision often fails to take account of the complexity of investment. In this work, investment profits, investment risks and environmental cost of the project are considered in the investment decision making. In economics, environmental cost (EC) [17] can be understood as the consumption of energy corresponding to investment.

Table 1 shows the investment plan to be determined. I_{ij} represents the capital invested in the jth investment project in year i, R_i is the investment risk of ith project, E_i is the energy consumption per unit output of ith project. Thus, the optimization objective considering investment risk, investment profit and environmental cost can be expressed as:

$$\max \text{ Profit} = \sum_i \sum_j d_{ij} I_{ij}$$

$$\min \ [\text{Risk} = \sum_i \sum_j R_j I_{ij}, \text{EC} = \sum_i \sum_j E_j d_{ij} I_{ij}]$$

Among them, the total amount of investment in the ith year should not exceed the investment budget in the ith year, and the investment amount should not be

Table 1. Description of investment parameters

Year	Projects				
	1	2	$\cdots$	j	$\cdots$	m
1	I_{11}	I_{12}	$\cdots$	I_{1j}	$\cdots$	I_{1m}
2	I_{21}	I_{22}	$\cdots$	I_{2j}	$\cdots$	I_{2m}
$\vdots$	$\vdots$	$\vdots$	$\vdots$	$\vdots$	$\vdots$	$\vdots$
i	I_{i1}	I_{i2}	$\cdots$	I_{ij}	$\cdots$	I_{im}
$\vdots$	$\vdots$	$\vdots$	$\vdots$	$\vdots$	$\vdots$	$\vdots$
n	I_{n1}	I_{n2}	$\cdots$	I_{nj}	$\cdots$	I_{nm}
Risk	R_1	R_2	$\cdots$	R_j	$\cdots$	R_m
EC	E_1	E_2	$\cdots$	E_j	$\cdots$	E_m

negative. The above model is a general investment planning model, which can be slightly modified in practical application and extended to other economic activities (such as: selection of construction projects, utilization of foreign capital).

A specific investment plan is used as a case to discuss the specific application of ant colony algorithm. During the three-year planning period, an enterprise needs to invest four development projects as follows: Project A can be invested at the beginning of the first year to the third year. It is estimated that every 10,000 dollars of investment can make a profit of 2000 dollars from the investment projects, and the annual capital and profits of that year can b be reinvested into the investment plan. While project B needs to be invested at the beginning of the first year. After two years of investment, it can make a profit of 5000 dollars per 10,000 dollars, and it can be reinvested into the investment plan. However, the maximum investment for the project should not exceed 200,000 dollars. While project C needs to be invested at the beginning of the second year. After two years, every 10,000 dollars of investment can make a profit of 6000 dollars per year, but the amount of investment for this project should not exceed 100,000 dollar. While project D needs to be invested in the third year, with a profit of 4,000 dollars per 10,000 dollars, but the amount of investment for the project is limited to 150,000 dollar. During the entire planning period, the amount of investment that the enterprise can invest is 300,000 dollars. What needs to be solved is which kind of investment plan can make the enterprise obtain the maximum profit in the whole investment plan. However, there will be risks for every investment. Enterprises always expect the least risk when they invest. The risk parameters associated with each investment are $R = [0.1, 0.25, 0.5, 0.75]$. At the same time, enterprises expect the environmental cost of investment as low as possible. Here, the environmental cost coefficients are $E = [0.15, 0.3, 0.2, 0.4]$. The optimization objective can be expressed as:

$$\max \ \text{Profit} = 0.2I_{1A} + 0.2I_{2A} + 0.2I_{3A} + 0.5I_{1B} + 0.6I_{2C} + 0.4I_{2D}$$

$$\min \ \text{Risk} = 0.1(I_{1A} + I_{2A} + I_{3A}) + 0.25I_{1B} + 0.5I_{2C} + 0.75I_{2D}$$

$$\min \ \text{EC} = 0.15 \cdot (0.2I_{1A} + 0.2I_{2A} + 0.2I_{3A}) + 0.3 \cdot 0.5I_{1B} + 0.2 \cdot 0.6I_{2C} + 0.9 \cdot 0.4I_{2D}$$

$$\text{s.t.} \ I_{1A} + I_{1B} \leqslant 30$$

$$I_{2A} + I_{2C} \leqslant 30 - I_{1B} + 0.2I_{1A}$$

$$I_{3A} + I_{3D} \leqslant 30 + 0.5I_{1B} + 0.2I_{1A} + 0.2I_{2A} - I_{2C}$$

$$I_{2B} \leqslant 20; I_{2C} \leqslant 15; I_{3D} \leqslant 10$$

$$I_{1A} \geqslant 0; I_{2A} \geqslant 0; I_{2A} \geqslant 0; I_{1B} \geqslant 0; I_{2C} \geqslant 0; I_{3D} \geqslant 0.$$

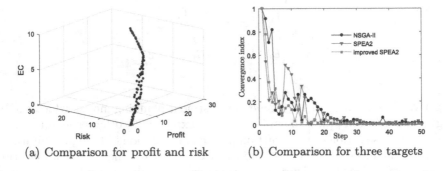

(a) Comparison for profit and risk   (b) Comparison for three targets

Fig. 3. Comparison of convergence results of different methods.

The proposed method is used to solve this problem. The model parameters are as follows: the initial population size is 300, the external archive size is 50, the crossover probability is 0.6, and the mutation probability is 0.3.

At present, environmental protection has become the consensus of the whole society. How to reduce carbon emissions per unit output while gaining profits is a problem that enterprises need to consider at present. Figure 3(a) gives Pareto boundaries for investment strategy optimization considering investment profits, investment risks and environmental costs. In order to more intuitively respond to the conclusions given in Fig. 3(a). Figure 4 shows the plane analysis of Fig. 3(a). As can be seen from Fig. 4, from a trend perspective, profit is positively related to risk and EC. After the profit reaches 230,000, the risk will accelerate. After the profit reached 220,000, EC rose rapidly. In addition, we can get an interesting phenomenon from Fig. 4. Under different investment strategies, sometimes the risk increases slightly, while the EC may reduce a lot, while the profit does not change much. This result is consistent with many industrial investment phenomena in reality.

Table 2. Investment strategy comparison (10000 dollars). Investment strategy I

Year	A	B	C	D
1	9.34	9.57		
2	2.98		5.22	
3	13.26			0.559

Table 3. Investment strategy comparison (10000 dollars). Investment strategy II

Year	A	B	C	D
1	13.60	2.41		
2	3.17		8.45	
3	18.10			0.148

Tables 2 and 3 give two different investment strategies. These two investment strategies are all Pareto optimal solutions. The profit, risk and environmental costs under Table 2 are 13.256, 7.529 and 3.252, while those under Table 3 are 13.304, 8.31 and 2.245. It can be seen that the total profit under the two investment strategies is similar, but the investment risk in second strategy is 10.36% higher than that in first strategy, but the EC in first strategy is 44.9% higher than that in second strategy. This shows that the choice of investment strategy has a great impact on the final results, which also shows the necessity of optimization model in this paper.

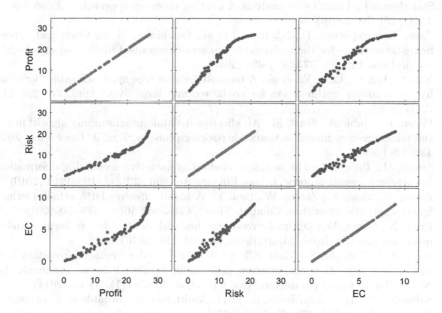

Fig. 4. The description of SPEA2 algorithm

4 Conclusion

Facing the high complexity of investment decision-making space, traditional multi-objective optimization methods pay too much attention to global search ability because of pursuing convergence speed and avoiding falling into local optimum, while local search ability is insufficient, which makes it difficult to converge to Pareto optimal boundary. To solve this problem, this paper uses an improved SPEA2 algorithm to optimize the multi-objective decision-making of enterprise investment. In this method, an external archive set is set up separately for local search after genetic operation, which guarantees the global search ability and also has strong local search ability. Through the optimization of investment by this method, a series of alternative Preto optimal investment schemes can be provided for decision makers, which can optimize environmental costs and profits within a certain risk tolerance range.

References

1. Ye, S., Tiong, R.L.K.: NPV-at-risk method in infrastructure project investment evaluation. J. Constr. Eng. Manag. **126**(3), 227–233 (2000)
2. Byung-cheol, K., Euysup, S., Reinschmidt, K.F.: Probability distribution of the project payback period using the equivalent cash flow decomposition. Eng. Econ. **58**(2), 112–136 (2013)
3. Soderbaum, P.: Benefit-cost analysis. A political economy approach. J. Econ. Issues **25**(1), 261–263 (2016)
4. Asta, S., Karapetyan, D., Kheiri, A., et al.: Combining Monte-Carlo and hyper-heuristic methods for the multi-mode resource-constrained multi-project scheduling problem. Inf. Sci. **373**, 476–498 (2016)
5. Xia, Y., Liu, C., Li, Y.Y., et al.: A boosted decision tree approach using Bayesian hyper-parameter optimization for credit scoring. Exp. Syst. Appl. **78**, 225–241 (2017)
6. Furini, F., Ljubic, I., Sinnl, M.: An effective dynamic programming algorithm for the minimum-cost maximal knapsack packing problem. Eur. J. Oper. Res. **262**, 438–448 (2017)
7. Smith, M., Taffler, R.: The incremental effect of narrative accounting information in corporate annual reports. J. Bus. Finance Account. **22**(8), 1195–1210 (2010)
8. Zhang, S., Yang, X., Zhong, W., Sun, Y.: A highly effective DPA attack method based on genetic algorithm. Comput. Mater. Continua **56**(2), 325–338 (2018)
9. Peng, X., Wang, W.: Optimal investment and risk control for an insurer under inside information. Insur. Math. Econ. **69**, 104–116 (2016)
10. Sadeghi, J., Sadeghi, S., Niaki, S.T.A.: A hybrid vendor managed inventory and redundancy allocation optimization problem in supply chain management: An NSGA-II with tuned parameters. Comput. Oper. Res. **41**(1), 53–64 (2014)
11. Salgueiro, Y., Toro, J.L., Bello, R., et al.: Multiobjective variable mesh optimization. Ann. Oper. Res. **258**(2), 1–25 (2016)
12. Knowles, J.D., Corne, D.W.: Approximating the nondominated front using the pareto archived evolution strategy. Evol. Comput. **8**(2), 149–172 (2014)
13. Lejeune, M.A., Shen, S.: Multi-objective probabilistically constrained programs with variable risk: Models for multi-portfolio financial optimization. Eur. J. Oper. Res. **252**(2), 522–539 (2016)
14. Bhuvana, J., Aravindan, C.: Memetic algorithm with preferential local search using adaptive weights for multi-objective optimization problems. Soft Comput. **20**(4), 1365–1388 (2016)

15. Wu, C., Zapevalova, E., Chen, Y., Li, F.: Time optimization of multiple knowledge transfers in the big data environment. Comput. Mater. Continua **54**(3), 269–285 (2018)

16. Michalewicz, Z., Deb, K., Schmidt, M., et al.: Test-case generator for nonlinear continuous parameter optimization techniques. IEEE Trans. Evol. Comput. **4**(3), 197–215 (2000)

17. Henri, J.F., Boiral, O., Roy, M.J.: Strategic cost management and performance: The case of environmental costs. Br. Account. Rev. **48**(2), 269–282 (2016)

Power Load Forecasting Based on Adaptive Deep Long Short-Term Memory Network

Junbo Wu[1], Ping Zhang[1], Zheng Zheng[1], and Min Xia[2(✉)]

[1] State Grid Henan Economics Research Institute, Zheng Zhou 450052, China
[2] School of Automation, Nanjing University of Information Science
and Technology, Nanjing 210044, China
xiamin@nuist.edu.cn

Abstract. Power load data has obvious timing dependence. Aiming at the time-dependent characteristics of power load, an adaptive depth long-term and short-term memory network model is proposed to predict power load. The model can extract sequential dependencies of load sequences effectively through deep memory networks. In addition, the input adaptive measurement of the model can solve the problem of amplitude change and trend determination, and avoid over-fitting of the network. The experimental results show that the model is superior to BP neural network, autoregressive model, grey system, limit learning machine model and K-nearest neighbor model. Adaptive depth LSTM network provides a new effective method for power load forecasting.

Keywords: Power load · Prediction analysis ·
Long short-term memory network · Deep learning

1 Introduction

The reliable operation of the power system is the basis for the development of all areas of the national economy. Power load forecasting is an important data basis for grid planning and production scheduling. Accurate load forecasting has become one of the important signs of smart grid [1]. The core of power load forecasting is the prediction algorithm. Power load forecasting is a typical time series forecast. The current main methods of load forecasting are based on optimization of mathematical fitting methods, grey system theory and machine learning methods [2].

The optimization-based mathematical fitting method is represented by an autoregressive model [3–5], mainly including Auto-Regressive and Moving Average (ARMA) and Auto-regressive Integrated Moving Average (ARIMA) methods. The regression-based model algorithm is simple, but the data stability requirements are relatively high, and the load prediction accuracy of this method is not high enough. In addition, the gray system theory is also widely used in load forecasting, and the gray theory has an advantage in modeling the stochastic wave uncertainty time series, so it is more suitable to model the load forecast [6]. However, it is difficult for gray systems to implement time series modeling of complex scenes, resulting in insufficient accuracy of load forecasting. Another type of load forecasting method is based on machine learning theory. At present, load forecasting based on machine learning mainly includes neural

© Springer Nature Switzerland AG 2019
X. Sun et al. (Eds.): ICAIS 2019, LNCS 11632, pp. 444–453, 2019.
https://doi.org/10.1007/978-3-030-24274-9_40

network [7, 8], support vector machine and wavelet analysis [9]. Among them, because the neural network has strong nonlinear fitting ability, it has advantages over other methods in load forecasting. However, current methods are difficult to extract timing dependencies of load time series.

In recent years, more and more studies have confirmed that Long Short-Term Memory (LSTM) can extract time series time series dependence [10], which is very suitable for load time series analysis. However, since LSTM lacks a systematic process of building a model, when the input data are very different from the training data, the prediction results are not always accurate, and the network may suffer from under-fitting or over-fitting. In order to solve this problem, this paper proposes a new mechanism, using input adaptive metrics, the output data are evolved from a hybrid mechanism. The adaptive metric of the input of the model can accommodate local variations in trends and amplitude. Most of the input to the network are close to historical data to avoid a sharp increase in prediction error due to large differences between the training data and the input data. In the proposed hybrid output mechanism, the prediction result can be adjusted by the relative error to make the prediction result more accurate.

2 Load Forecasting Model

2.1 Deep Long Short-Term Memory Network

Long Short-Term Memory Network (LSTM) contains a chained form of a repetitive neural network module. The internal structure of the LSTM repeating module is shown in Fig. 1, where each small rounded rectangle represents a layer of cyclic neural network with learnable parameters; The small circle represents the point-wise operation, where vector addition and point multiplication are used; σ represents the sigmoid activation function, tanh represents the tanh activation function (Fig. 2), C_{t-1} represents the state of the previous moment, and h_{t-1} represents the output of the previous moment, X_t Represents the output of the current moment, C_t represents the state of the current moment, and h_t represents the output of the current moment. The LSTM model consists of multiple such repeating modules.

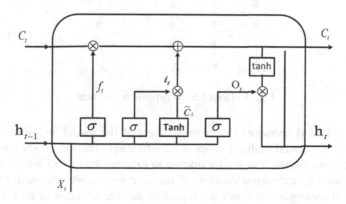

Fig. 1. Internal structure of the LSTM repeating module

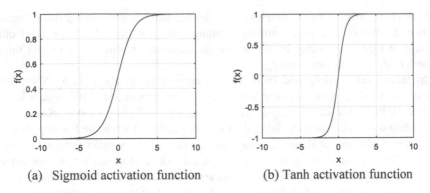

(a) Sigmoid activation function   (b) Tanh activation function

Fig. 2. Activation function

The LSTM method can be described as follows:

$$i_t = \delta(W_i \cdot [h_{t-1}, X_t] + b_i),$$
$$f_t = \delta(W_f \cdot [h_{t-1}, X_t] + b_f),$$
$$\widetilde{C}_t = \tanh(W_C \cdot [h_{t-1}, X_t] + b_c),$$
$$O_t = \delta(W_O \cdot [h_{t-1}, X_t] + b_O),$$
$$h_t = O_t \times \tanh(C_t),$$

where W_i, b_i are the connection weights and bias values of *sigmoid* layer in "Input gate" respectively. W_f, b_f are the connection weights and bias values of *sigmoid* layer in "Forget gate" respectively. W_C, b_c are the connection weights and bias values. O_t, b_O are the connection weights and bias values of *sigmoid* layer in "Output gate" respectively.

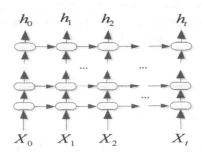

Fig. 3. Deep LSTM expansion structure

The deep LSTM enhances the expressiveness of the model and allows duplicate modules to be replicated multiple times at each moment. The loop body parameters of each layer are consistent, and the parameters in different layers are different. Figure 3 shows the time step expansion structure of the deep long short-term memory network. Each rounded rectangle represents the repeating module structure of an LSTM.

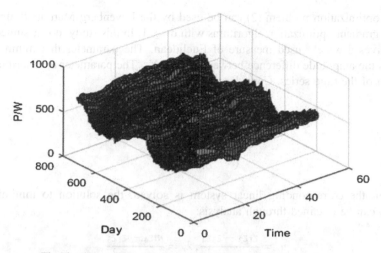

Fig. 4. Three-dimensional power load three-dimensional map

2.2 Adaptive Deep Long-Term Memory Network (AD-LSTM)

It is well known that artificial neural networks may exhibit under-fitting and over-fitting [11, 15]. A network that is not complex enough may be unable to fully detect the signal, which can lead to under-fitting. When a model is too complex, over-fitting usually occurs. For these two problems, over-fitting is more prominent when the signal data is sufficient and the network is complex enough. In order to avoid the occurrence of overfitting, an adaptive neural network model has been proposed. In this model, the after-the-fact data are used to modify the input data of the artificial neural network in the prediction process so that the input data is close to the learning data. Therefore, this algorithm can reduce the probability of overfitting. Based on the existing artificial neural network, this paper extends the adaptive neural network model (ADNN) of time series prediction. First, a strategy is used to initialize the input data y_t, y_{t-1}, y_{t-2},...., y_{t-m+1}, where m is the number of input nodes. This strategy uses adaptive metrics similar to the adaptive k-nearest neighbor approach. The data sets y_t, y_{t-1}, y_{t-2},...., y_{t-m+1} are compared with other parts of the same length in this time series. The comparison metrics in this paper select the Minkowski indicator:

$$L_M(Yt, Yr) = (|y_t - y_r|^d + |y_{t-1} - y_{r-1}|^d + \ldots + |y_{t-m+1} - y_{r-m+1}|^d)^{\frac{1}{d}} \tag{1}$$

The above equation gives the difference between Y_t and Y_r, but the difference in trend and amplitude does not appear. Trend and amplitude information are a critical factor in time series prediction. In this study, in order to solve this problem, an adaptive metric was introduced, and the algorithm is as follows:

$$L_A(Yt, Yr) = \min_{\lambda r, ur} f_r(\lambda_r, u_r) \tag{2}$$

The optimization problem (2) can be used by the Levenberg-Marquardt algorithm or other gradient optimization algorithms with d $\geq$ 1. In this study, d is assumed to be 2 and gives a widely used measure of Euclidean. The parameter that minimizes λ_r balances the amplitude difference between Y_t and Y_r. The parameter u_r determines the direction of the time series. Consider two equations:

$$\begin{cases} \dfrac{\partial f_r(\lambda_r, u_r)}{\partial \lambda_r} = 0, \\[2mm] \dfrac{\partial f_r(\lambda_r, u_r)}{\partial u_r} = 0. \end{cases} \tag{3}$$

When the corresponding linear system is solved, the solution to minimize the problem can be obtained through analysis:

$$u_r = \frac{z_1 z_2 - z_3 z_4}{m z_2 - z_3^2}, \lambda_r = \frac{m z_4 - z_1 z_3}{m z_2 - z_3^2},$$

at this time

$$z_1 = \sum_{i=1}^{m} y_{t-i+1}, \; z_2 = \sum_{i=1}^{m} y_{r-i+1}^2, \; z_3 = \sum_{i=1}^{m} y_{r-i+1}, \; z_4 = \sum_{i=1}^{m} y_{r-i+1} y_{t-i+1}.$$

Based on this strategy, an adaptive k-nearest neighbor method is chosen. The input vector of the first network (called the primary network) can be defined as:

$$input_v = (q_t^v, q_{t-1}^v, \cdots, q_{t-p+1}^v) = (\frac{y_t - u_{rv}}{\lambda_{rv}}, \frac{y_{t-1} - u_{rv}}{\lambda_{rv}}, \cdots, \frac{y_{t-p}+1 - u_{rv}}{\lambda_{rv}}) \tag{4}$$

Most input values can be used to approach historical data in this way. Since the difference between the training data and the input data is large, the prediction error is significantly increased. In order to get a more accurate y_t, y_{t-1}, y_{t-2}, $\cdots$, y_{t-p+1}, time series, use k sets of inputs, the output vector is $output_v = b_v$, $v = 1, 2,...,k$.

The mechanism of the mixed output is as follows:

$$y_{t+1} = \frac{1}{v} \sum_{v=1}^{k} T_v(\lambda_{r_v} b_v + u_{r_v}) \tag{5}$$

It is found from Eq. (5) that the prediction result of y_{t+1} is calculated by b_v $v = 1, 2, \cdots, k$, where T_v is a weight coefficient, which is set to the sequence similarity in the actual process. The algorithm steps of the proposed method are as follows.

Step 1: training two neural networks using historical data. In the first neural network, $y_i, y_{i-1}, y_{i-2}, \cdots y_{i-m+1}$ is the input training data and y_{i+1} is the output training data. In the second neural network, $L_A(Y_t, Y_{r_v})$, λ_{r_v}, u_{r_v} and $|t - r_v|$ are the inputs to the training and the relative error $\widetilde{RE_v}$ is the output of the training. The BP algorithm is used to train the two neural networks.

Step 2: Compare the data set $y_t, y_{t-1}, y_{t-2}, \ldots y_{t-m+1}$ and other parts of the time series using the adaptive metric distance of the Euclidean space based on Eq. (3).

Step 3: Select the K nearest neighbor classification algorithm and obtain λ_{r_v}, u_{r_v} based on Eq. (3). Initialize the input data $q_i^v, q_{i-1}^v, q_{i-2}^v, \ldots q_{i-m+1}^v, v = 1, 2 \ldots, k$ of the first network according to Eq. (4).

Step 4: Apply the first neural network and get the result output $output_v = b_v$, $v = 1, 2, \ldots, k$.

Step 5: Apply the mixing mechanism Eq. (5) and obtain the prediction result of y_{t+1}.

3 Power Load Forecasting Example Analysis

In order to verify the reliability of the method in this paper, this paper uses the public data set of EUNITE Network [12] for testing. EUNITE Network data set is real power load data with a sampling interval of 30 min. Figure 4 shows the 730-day load data for this data set. Figure 5 shows the 50-day single-day load data captured in this data set. The power load sequence has significant periodicity from the data characteristics. The periodic nature of the data is an important auxiliary feature for sequence prediction. This timing dependency provides a reliable piece of information for load forecasting.

In order to effectively utilize the timing dependence of load data, this paper uses an adaptive deep long short-term memory network to achieve load prediction. This method realizes the extraction of timing relationships through LSTM, and reduces the over-fitting of the network by using adaptive input. In order to compare the model with other methods, this paper uses normalized mean square error (NMSE) and mean absolute percent error (MAPE) as error criteria. In the existing literature, the correct rate of power load forecasting usually adopts MAPE as the evaluation index. In this paper, NMSE and MAPE are used to more effectively reflect the credibility of the algorithm. The normalized mean square error is described as:

$$
NMSE = \frac{\sum\limits_{i=1}^{M} (y_i - \tilde{y}_i)^2}{\sum\limits_{i=1}^{M} y_i^2},
\tag{6}
$$

where y_i is the real data, $\tilde{y}_i$ is the predict data, M is the number of the prediction data. The mean absolute percent error is defined as:

$$
MAPE = \frac{1}{M} \sum\limits_{i=1}^{M} \left| \frac{y_i - \tilde{y}_i}{y_i} \right| .100\%
\tag{7}
$$

In order to better prove the effectiveness of the proposed method, the method is compared with BP neural network, autoregressive model (ARMA), extreme learning machine model (ELM) [13] and gray system model (GM (1,1)) [14]. In order to reflect the advantages of this method for modeling time series relationships, this paper implements load forecasting from two scales: in days and in half an hour. When forecasting by daily load, the input of the BP network and the ELM is also the data of one week of the predicted data, and the fitting of the ARMA is also based on the data of the previous week.

Table 1. Comparison of daily load forecasting results by different methods

	ANN	AR	ELM	GM (1,1)	AD-LSTM
NMSE	0.041	0.059	0.039	0.049	0.013
MAPE	2.0%	2.4%	1.9%	2.3%	1.1%

Figure 6 shows a comparison of several methods when forecasted by day. It can be seen from Fig. 6 that the method of this paper has higher prediction accuracy than other methods, and can well predict the load. The specific numerical indicators of several methods are shown in Table 1. It can be seen from Table 1 that the ARMA has the worst effect, because the regression method is a linear fitting method and cannot effectively reflect the nonlinear relationship of the data. Although BP network and ELM network can achieve nonlinear fitting, but the timing information is not well utilized, the effect is not as good as the method in this paper.

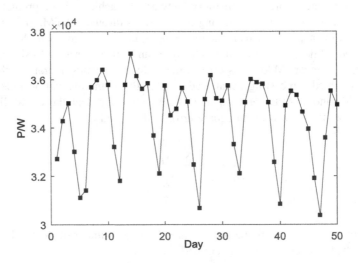

Fig. 5. Daily power load curve

Figure 7 shows a comparison of the effects of the load forecast based on half an hour. One of the cycles is shown in this paper. It can be seen from the simulation that the prediction accuracy of this method is better than other methods. Table 2 gives a comparison of the specific predictions of several methods.

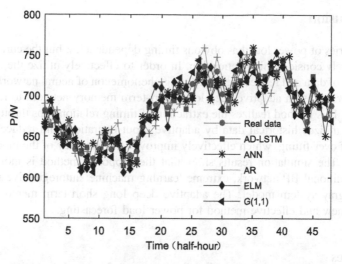

Fig. 6. Comparison of daily load forecasting by different methods

Table 2. Comparison of the results of different methods for half-hour load forecasting

	ANN	AR	ELM	GM (1,1)	AD-LSTM
NMSE	0.066	0.123	0.061	0.097	0.029
MAPE	1.8%	2.5%	1.7%	2.0%	0.9%

It can be seen from the above comparison test that whether it is predicted by day or half an hour, this method has advantages over other methods and can effectively realize load forecasting.

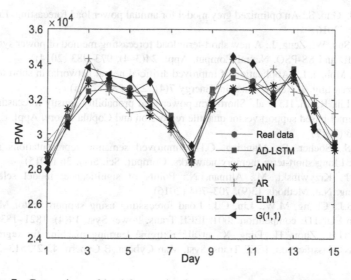

Fig. 7. Comparison of load forecasting by different methods for half an hour

4 Conclusion

The time series of power load has obvious timing dependencies, but the current related methods rarely consider this relationship. In order to effectively utilize the time series dependence of data and reduce the over-fitting phenomenon of neural network learning, this paper proposes an adaptive deep long short-term memory network to realize load forecasting. This method realizes the extraction of timing relationships through LSTM, and further utilizes historical data by adaptive input operation, and reduces the phenomenon of over-fitting, which effectively improves the accuracy of the model in load forecasting. The simulation results show that the proposed method is more accurate than the traditional BP network, extreme learning machine, autoregressive model and traditional gray system model. The adaptive deep long short-term memory network provides a new and effective method for power load forecasting.

References

1. Li, H.Z., Guo, S., Li, C.J., et al.: A hybrid annual power load forecasting model based on generalized regression neural network with fruit fly optimization algorithm. Knowl. Based Syst. **37**(2), 378–387 (2013)
2. Lee, W.J., Hong, J.: A hybrid dynamic and fuzzy time series model for mid-term power load forecasting. Int. J. Electr. Power Energy Syst. **64**, 1057–1062 (2015)
3. Wang, B., et al.: Research on hybrid model of garlic short-term price forecasting based on big data. Comput. Mater. Continua **57**(2), 283–296 (2018)
4. Hu, R., Wen, S., Zeng, Z., et al.: A short-term power load forecasting model based on the generalized regression neural network with decreasing step fruit fly optimization algorithm. Neurocomputing **221**(C), 24–31 (2017)
5. Bozkurt, Ö.Ö., Biricik, G., Tayşi, Z.C.: Artificial neural network and SARIMA based models for power load forecasting in Turkish electricity market. PLoS ONE **12**(4), e0175915 (2017)
6. Zhao, H., Guo, S.: An optimized grey model for annual power load forecasting. Energy **107**, 272–286 (2016)
7. Liu, Z., Sun, W., Zeng, J.: A new short-term load forecasting method of power system based on EEMD and SS-PSO. Neural Comput. Appl. **24**(3–4), 973–983 (2014)
8. Wei, S., Mohan, L.: Application of improved artificial neural networks in short-term power load forecasting. J. Renew. Sustain. Energy **7**(4), 279–288 (2015)
9. He, Y., Liu, R., Li, H., et al.: Short-term power load probability density forecasting method using kernel-based support vector quantile regression and Copula theory. Appl. Energy **185**, 254–266 (2017)
10. Tai, K.S., Socher, R., Manning, C.D.: Improved semantic representations from tree-structured long short-term memory networks. Comput. Sci. **5**(1), 36 (2015)
11. Lever, J., Krzywinski, M., Altman, N.: Points of significance: model selection and overfitting. Nat. Methods **13**(9), 703–704 (2016)
12. Chen, B.J., Chang, M.W., Lin, C.J.: Load forecasting using support vector Machines: a study on EUNITE competition 2001. IEEE Trans. Power Syst. **19**(4), 1821–1830 (2004)
13. Huang, G.B., Zhou, H., Ding, X., et al.: Extreme learning machine for regression and multiclass classification. IEEE Trans. Syst. Man Cybern. B Cybern. **42**(2), 513–529 (2012)

14. Li, L., Wang, H.: A VVWBO-BVO-based GM (1,1) and its parameter optimization by GRA-IGSA integration algorithm for annual power load forecasting. PLoS ONE **13**(5), e0196816 (2018)
15. Xiao, B., Wang, Z., Liu, Q., Liu, X.: SMK-means: an improved mini batch k-means algorithm based on mapreduce with big data. Comput. Mater. Continua **56**(3), 365–379 (2018)

Optimized White Matter Fiber Reconstruction Using Combination of Diffusion and Functional MRI

Dan Xiao$^{(\boxtimes)}$, Xiaofeng Dong, and Zhipeng Yang

Chengdu University of Information Technology, Chengdu 610225, China
553450016@qq.com

Abstract. Diffusion weighted MRI (DWI) is a primary tool for mapping structural connectivity of white matter tracts in the human brain. Recently, fiber reconstruction can be improved combing diffusion and functional MRI (fMRI) to obtain the optimal path. In this paper, we proposed an optimized white matter fiber reconstruction algorithm which used diffusion and functional MRI signals in white matter to track functional active pathways under specific neural activities. The experimental results demonstrated the method we proposed can be used to reconstruct the functional white matter fiber bundle, which is more reliable and robust than the existing method of fiber reconstruction.

Keywords: Diffusion weighted MRI · Fiber tractography ·
Optimized reconstruction · Function MRI

1 Introduction

Diffusion weighted MRI (DWI) is a non-invasive method for detecting the diffusion of water molecules in the white matter [1, 2]. The distribution of direction of fibers is indirectly calculated by estimating the voxel-wise diffusion orientation distribution functions (dODFs) [3]. DWI tractography can be achieved by transforming dODFs into fiber orientation distribution functions (fODFs) and delineating the anatomical tracts of white matter through inter-voxel connectivity. It can be gained insight into the mechanisms underlying brain development, aging and pathology by evaluating the tissue properties of white matter nerve fibers [4].

The existing DWI fiber reconstruction algorithms can be divided into local fiber reconstruction methods and global fiber reconstruction methods. The local fiber reconstruction method starts from the initial point and proceeds along the fiber direction to obtain the whole fiber path. The global fiber reconstruction method establishes the cost function on the interconnected fiber paths and uses the optimization technique to find the optimal fiber path. The global fiber reconstruction method can eliminate accumulated noise and local random noise and improve the reliability of long-distance imaging.

Jbabdi presented a method to obtain the optimal tract using Bayesian framework for global probabilistic tractography, incorporating prior information [5]. An evident drawback of such a paradigm, however, is that the priors available do not include the position or function information of fiber bundles. Moreover, it is complicated to find

© Springer Nature Switzerland AG 2019
X. Sun et al. (Eds.): ICAIS 2019, LNCS 11632, pp. 454–462, 2019.
https://doi.org/10.1007/978-3-030-24274-9_41

the optimal solution for whole brain. The tracts can only be estimated by heuristically sampling from the posterior distribution.

In 2012, Wu present an improved method to combine global probabilistic tractography with layered fiber clustering, using K-means clustering and improved Hubert statistics to divide the fiber path, which aims to approximate the optimal solution by iterative sampling and clustering on each fiber bundle, greatly promoting the clinical study of fiber bundle imaging in human complex neural networks [6]. It can be seen that the core of the global optimization class method is to calculate the evaluation equation, which determines whether the optimized structural connection is consistent with the real physiological structure.

Reconstructing structural connections with functional significance is the most fundamental problem in neuroscience research. Previous studies had combined the structural connections of DWI with functional magnetic resonance imaging based on gray matter to reconstruct white matter structure connections that connect multiple gray matter functional areas.

However, the current fusion studies were only a basic combination. The results only indicate that there are white matter fiber connections in specific gray matter functional areas, and the white matter structure itself has no functional properties. It has been found recently that functional MRI (fMRI) in white matter can be used to analyze the functional properties of nerve fibers by measuring the blood oxygen level dependent (BOLD) in the functional activities of white matter neurons, and has been successfully applied to pathological studies [7, 8].

At present, deep Learning is such a powerful tool that we have seen tremendous success in areas such as Computer Vision, Speech Recognition, and Natural Language Processing [9]. Deep convolutional networks are gradually emerging, and have great potential in the field of image processing such as image feature extraction and image classification. In recent years, they have achieved great success in the field of medical imaging and auxiliary diagnosis. Qi proposed a method of detecting photographic images and computer generated graphics using a deep neural network. The existing method is solved, and the defect of image feature classification cannot be analyzed in real time when the calculation is intensive [10]. This will also bring new ideas to the reconstruction of white matter fiber bundles in the future.

In this work, we integrate fMRI of white matter into DWI global optimization fiber reconstruction, using functional prior information fibers to reconstruct the optimal functional path. We obtain a Bayesian optimal path algorithm of the global optimization class instead of the existing methods. It breaks the framework of forming the optimal path only through the spatial position, and reconstructs the optimal path of brain information transmission when performing specific brain activities.

2 Method

2.1 DWI Optimization Method

The DWI data of the brain is defined as an undirected brain-graph $G = (V, E, w_E)$, where V is the node set of all DWI voxels nodes except cerebrospinal fluid (CSF), E is the edge set, and w_E is the weight of the edge. On the 3D image grid.

Each node is connected to its $3 \times 3 \times 3$ neighborhood by an edge $e \in E$, and each edge e is assigned a weight $w_E(e) \in [0, 1]$ to indicate the probability of a fiber bundle connecting its two endpoint nodes.

The likelihood value of a path is the product of all edge weights $w_E(e)$ on the path, namely:

$$\mathcal{L}(\pi_{v,v'}) = \prod_{i=1}^{n-1} w_E(v_i, v_{i+1}) \tag{1}$$

Where $v \in V$ and $v' \in V$ are two nodes in G, and $\pi_{v,v'}$ is the path connecting these two points, which can be expressed as a sequence of nodes $\pi_{v,v'} = [v_1, v_2, \ldots, v_n]$, where $v_1 = v, v_n = v', (v_i, v_{i+1}) \in E, i = 1, \ldots, n-1$. The cardinality of the path is equal to the total number of its nodes $|\pi_{v,v'}| = n$.

We use fODF $f : S^2 \rightarrow R_+$ in any direction θ on the unit sphere S^2 to obtain the probability that there exists a fiber along that direction, thereby indicating the diffusion information from the DWI.

For each voxel, we are interested in 26 adjacent voxel directions θ_i, with $i = 1, \ldots, 26$. The weight $w(\theta_i)$ in the direction $\theta_i \in S^2$ is obtained by calculating the fODF of the set C_i in all directions [11].

The weight $w(\theta_i)$ indicates the probability that the voxel is connected to the direction, which is approximated as:

$$w(\theta_i) = \int_{C_i} f(\theta)d\theta \approx$$
$$\sum_{\hat{\theta}_k \in S_i} \left(f(\hat{\theta}_k) \cdot \frac{Vol(S^2)}{N} \right) \tag{2}$$

As $w(\theta_i)$ is depends on the source node, the edge weight $w_E(v, v')$ is defined as the average between voxel v and voxel v':

$$w_E(v, v') = 1/2 \cdot (w(v \rightarrow v') + w(v' \rightarrow v)) \tag{3}$$

2.2   DWI Optimization Method

Despite the difficulty of fiber tractography using DWI, it is still the standard method for studying brain structural connectivity.

The structural connections based on DWI are often combined with functional connections based on fMRI, where a typical approach is to define gray matter regions of interests (ROIs) using resting or active fMRI. Then use it to guide fiber bundle tracking for specific functions and to analyze the relationship between structure and function.

However, this approach has a distinct disadvantage. DWI and fMRI have different signal sources and are used in different regions of the brain. This approach only provides an indirect combination of the two imaging modalities.

The bridge that fully fuses the two modal data is the white matter BOLD signal, which can characterize the functional state of the nerve fibers. The anisotropy of fMRI signals in white matter is modeled as a spatio-temporal correlation tensor that modulates the ODF derived from diffusion signals for tracking [12–14].

For each node $v \in V$ from the DWI image, the functional prior probability of the node in the path is indicated by $p_F(v) \in [0, 1]$, so that it can form the optimal path of brain information transmission according to its functional information when performing specific brain activities.

We propose an efficient algorithm that combines the Bayesian model along the edge of the brain-graph $G = (V, E, w_E)$ with $p_F : V \rightarrow \mathbb{R}_+$ representing the node function information.

The edge-joined Bayesian model can be constructed from the transformation of the previous node and edge $e \in E$ [15].

Given a single edge $e = (v, v') \in E$, the functional prior probability $P(e)$ is defined as the square root of the product of the functional probability $p_F(v)$ of the fiber bundle at point v and $p_F(v')$ at the v' point:

$$P(e) = \sqrt{p_F(v)p_F(v')} \tag{4}$$

An edge weight $w_E(e)$ is assigned to each edge of the image to represent the structural connectivity of the brain along the edge e.

We use the Bayes' theorem to calculate the posterior connectivity probability of the structure and function of brain along the edge e, and obtain a fiber optimized reconstruction method for solving the optimal path problem in the modified graph $\bar{G} = (V, E, \bar{w}_E)$ [16].

For any edge $e(v, v')$ there are:

$$\bar{W}_E(e) = -logP(e|w_E(e)) = \\ - log\left(\sqrt{p_F(v)} \cdot w_E(v, v') \cdot \sqrt{p_F(v')}\right) \tag{5}$$

For all $e_i = (v_i, v_{i+1})$, the edges are not related, and the path probability is expressed as:

$$\sum_{i=1}^{n-1} \bar{w}_E(e_i) = -log\left(\prod_{i=1}^{n-1} P(e_i|w_E(e_i))\right) \tag{6}$$

the path $\pi_{v,v'}$ with the path probability $P(\pi_{v,v'}|G)$ is the optimal path connecting v and v' in $\bar{G}$:

$$P(\pi_{v,v'}|G) = \prod_{i=1}^{n-1} P(e_i|w_E(e_i)) = \\ \sqrt{p_F(v_1)p_F(v_n)} \prod_{i=1}^{n-1} w_E(e_i) \prod_{i=2}^{n-1} p_F(v_i) \tag{7}$$

3 Discussion

3.1 Data Acquisition

Full brain MRI data were from healthy adult volunteers. The experimental instrument used a 3T Philips Achieva scanner with a 32-channel head coil.

The experimental set of T_2^*-weighted images were acquired from four adults with sensory stimulations which were designed in the form of a square wave [17].

The BOLD images were obtained using a gradient echo (GE), echo planar imaging (EPI) sequence with the following parameters: TR = 3 s, TE = 45 ms, matrix size = 80×80, FOV = 240 mm $\times$ 240 mm, 43 axial slices of 3 mm thick with zero gap, and 145 volumes. During the same imaging session, DWIs were acquired as well with TR = 8.5 s, TE = 65 ms, b = 1000 s/mm², SENSE factor = 3, matrix size = 128×128, FOV = 256×256, 68 axial slices of 2 mm thick with zero gap, and 32 diffusion-sensitizing directions.

To provide anatomical references, 3D high resolution T_1-weighted (T_1w) anatomical images were acquired in all cases and acquired using a multi-shot 3D GE sequence with a pixel size of 1 mm $\times$ 1 mm $\times$ 1 mm.

3.2 Image Preprocessing

The acquired data was preprocessed using SPM12.

All fMRI time series were sequentially subjected to time layer correction, head motion correction, and FWHM = 4 mm Gaussian smoothing.

The BOLD signals of all voxels are bandpass filtered by 0.01–0.08 Hz. This band contains the frequency of the experimental stimulus waveform at 0.016 Hz.

3.3 Optimized Reconstruction Experiment

Table 1 shows a quantitative comparison of the two methods, where the true positive parameter of the optimized algorithm is larger and the variance is smaller.

It can be seen that the optimized algorithm can obtain more concentrated and compact pathways when reconstructing the path of the functional activation state, which is more robust than the existing method.

Table 1. Mean and standard deviation of true positive scores from thalamus to sensory area

Algorithm	True positive scores
DWI	0.0732 ± 0.026
Optimized	0.2835 ± 0.011

Figure 1 demonstrates the tracking results from the thalamus to the sensory area where the red mark in the figure is the central posterior region of the brain.

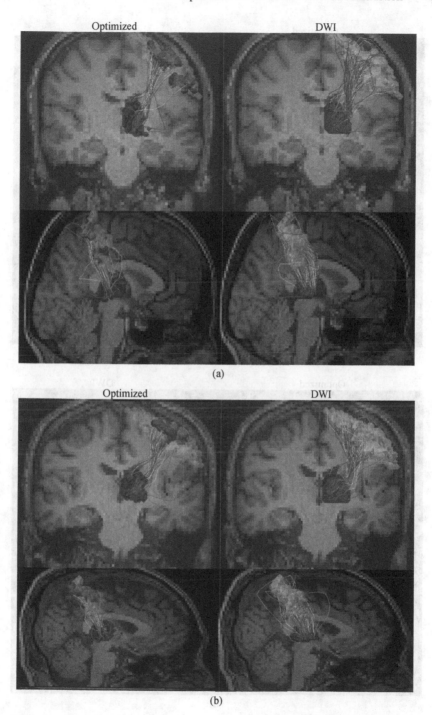

Fig. 1. Results of tracking from the thalamus to sensory area. There are 4 examples which the seed area is in gray color. The target ROI of traditional DWI method is in yellow color and activation area is in red. For each subject, the upper row is a coronal view and lower row is a sagittal view. Note that the streamlines are randomly colored for visual effect. (Color figure online)

Optimized   DWI

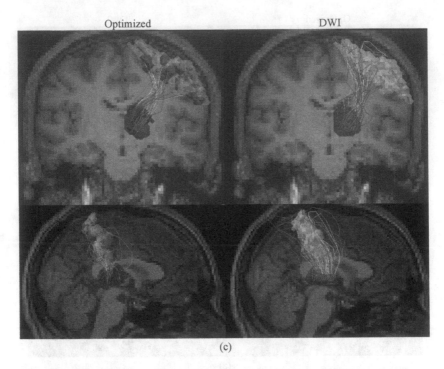

(c)

Optimized   DWI

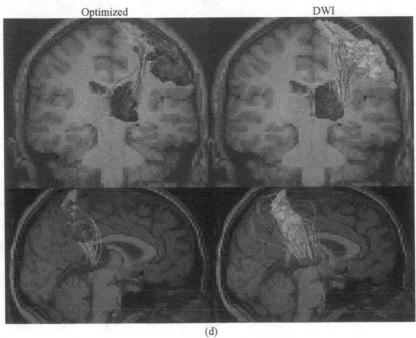

(d)

Fig. 1. (*continued*)

The central part of the brain is activated when the experimenter's palm is stimulated, which receives the pain, temperature, touch pressure, position and movement sensation of the contralateral trunk of the dorsal thalamus by physiological analysis.

As shown in Fig. 1, the traditional DWI algorithm is used to obtain the path of the large-area cortical region shown by yellow in the figure, and the proposed optimized algorithm merging functional signal of white matter can directly delineate structurally concentrated and functionally active fiber pathways.

4 Conclusion

In this paper we used functional information in white matter to delineate functionally active pathways and proposed an optimized white matter fiber reconstruction algorithm which used combination of diffusion and functional MRI signals in white matter to track functional active pathways under specific neural activities. Spatio-temporal correlation tensors model the functional properties in white matter, providing effective complementary information for tracking of DWI. This optimized reconstruction method is a useful complement to the study of the structural and functional relationships of the human brain.

We analyzed the fiber bundle pathways that connect the thalamus to the sensory region of the human brain. The central part of the back received the pain, temperature, touch pressure and movement sensation of the contralateral trunk of the dorsal thalamus, which was activated when the experimenter's palm was stimulated. The traditional DWI algorithm can't accurately find the path of functional activation state, and the optimized method of this work can accurately and effectively obtain the functional activity pathway of white matter fiber bundle, which indicated that this work can help solve the problem of difficult tracking of white matter functional structure.

However, the white matter fiber reconstruction optimization algorithm proposed in this paper will also face some technical challenges. Since the BOLD signal is susceptible to imaging artifacts, it is necessary to more efficiently detect weak BOLD signals in the white matter. With the advancement of image acquisition technology and the complicated artifact correction method and image quality improvement, the ability of the proposed optimization algorithm can be greatly improved.

In summary, we proposed a new white matter fiber bundle optimized reconstruction method based on the global optimized Bayesian optimal path algorithm, using the functional information in the white matter to obtain the brain when performing specific brain activities. The anisotropy of the fMRI signal in the white matter is modeled as a spatio-temporal correlation tensor and modulates the ODF derived from the diffused signal for tracking. The optimized reconstruction of DWI fibers incorporating white matter functional signals has great potential for reconstructing fiber pathways in specific functional loops.

Acknowledgments. This study is supported by Sichuan Science and Technology Program 2017RZ0012.

References

1. Johansen-Berg, H., Behrens, T.E.: Diffusion MRI: From Quantitative Measurement to in Vivo Neuroanatomy. Academic Press, Amsterdam (2013)
2. Conturo, T.E.: Tracking neuronal fiber pathways in the living human brain. Natl. Acad. Sci. U.S.A. **96**(18), 10422–10427 (1999)
3. Hagmann, P., Jonasson, L., Maeder, P.: Understanding diffusion MR imaging techniques: from scalar diffusion-weighted imaging to diffusion tensor imaging and beyond. RadioGraphics **26**(Suppl 1), 205–223 (2006)
4. Iwata, N.K., Kwan, J.Y., Danielian, L.E.: White matter alterations differ in primary lateral sclerosis and amyotrophic lateral sclerosis. Brain **134**(9), 2642–2655 (2011)
5. Jbabdi, S., Woolrich, M.W., Andersson, J.L.: A Bayesian framework for global tractography. NeuroImage **37**(1), 116–129 (2007)
6. Xi, W., Mingyuan, X., Jiliu, Z.: Globally optimized fiber tracking and hierarchical clustering - a unified framework. Magn. Reson. Imaging **30**(4), 485–495 (2012)
7. Tung-Lin, W., Feng, W., Adam, W.: Effects of anesthesia on resting state BOLD signals in white matter of non-human primates. Magn. Reson. Imaging **34**(9), 1235–1241 (2016)
8. Zhaohua, D., Yali, H., Bailey, S.K.: Detection of synchronous brain activity in white matter tracts at rest and under functional loading. Proc. Natl. Acad. Sci. U.S.A. **115**(3), 595–600 (2018)
9. Ya, T., Yun, L., Jin, W.: Semi-supervised learning with generative adversarial networks on digital signal modulation classification. Comput. Mater. Continua **55**(2), 243–254 (2018)
10. Qi, C., Suzanne, M., Huiyu, S.: Identifying materials of photographic images and photorealistic computer generated graphics based on deep CNNs. Comput. Mater. Continua **55**(2), 229–241 (2018)
11. Voronoi, G.: Nouvelles applications des paramètres continus à la théorie des forms quadratiques. Deuxième mémoire. Recherches sur les parallélloèdres primitifs. reine angew **134**, 198–287 (1908)
12. Zhaohua, D., Ran, X., Stephen, K.B.: Visualizing functional pathways in the human brain using correlation tensors and magnetic resonance imaging. Magn. Reson. Imaging **34**(1), 8–17 (2016)
13. Poupon, C., Clark, C.A., Frouin, V.: Regularization of diffusion-based direction maps for the tracking of brain white matter fascicles. NeuroImage **12**, 184–195 (2000)
14. Basser, P.J., Pierpaoli, C.: Microstructural and physiological features of tissues elucidated by quantitative-diffusion-tensor MRI. J. Magn. Reson., Ser. B **111**(3), 209–219 (1996)
15. Iturria-Medina, Y., Canales-Rodríguez, E.J., Melie-García, L.: Characterizing brain anatomical connections using diffusion weighted MRI and graph theory. NeuroImage **36**(3), 645–660 (2007)
16. Yendiki, A., Panneck, P., Srinivasan, P.: Automated probabilistic reconstruction of white-matter pathways in health and disease using an atlas of the underlying anatomy. Front. Neuroinf. **5**, 23 (2011)
17. Van Hecke, W., Emsell, L., Sunaert, S. (eds.): Diffusion Tensor Imaging. Springer, New York (2016). https://doi.org/10.1007/978-1-4939-3118-7

Convolutional Neural Networks for Scene Image Recognition

Yulian Li[1], Chao Luo[1], Hao Yang[1,2], and Tao Wu[1(✉)]

[1] School of Computer Science, Chengdu University of Information Technology,
Chengdu 610025, China
wut@cuit.edu.cn
[2] School of Information and Software Engineering,
University of Electronic Science and Technology of China, Chengdu, China

Abstract. Words are the most indispensable information in human life. It is important to analyze and understand the meaning of words. Compared with the general visual elements, the text conveys rich and high-level meaning information, which enables the computer to better understand the semantic content of the text. With the rapid development of computer technology, the research on text information recognition has made great achievements. However, in the face of dealing with text characters in natural scenes, there are certain limitations in the recognition of natural scene images. Because scene images have more interference and complexity than text, these factors make the identification of natural scene image texts facing many challenges. This paper focused on the recognition of natural scene image texts, and mainly studied a text recognition method based on deep learning in natural scene images. Firstly, text recognition is based on Kares using the Dense Convolutional Network (DenseNet) network model by using the existing standard test data set. Secondly, each character is classified using Softmax outputs to achieve the use of automatic learning. The characteristics of the context replace the manually defined features, which improve the recognition efficiency and accuracy. Lastly, the text recognition of the natural scene image is realized. And the method is suitable for problems encountered in medical images.

Keywords: Recognition · Deep learning · DenseNet · Softmax

1 Introduction

Words, as the crystallization of human wisdom, are one of the most important symbols of human civilization. Since ancient times, words have played an indispensable role in our lives. Text contains rich and accurate semantic information that is widely used in visual understanding-based tasks, so natural scene text detection and recognition becomes more and more important and becomes.

A research hotspot in computer vision and document analysis. In recent years, a large amount of research results and great research progress have been made in this field, but there are still many challenges, such as noise, blur and distortion, for text extraction and recognition in natural scene images. With the rapid development of computer technology and handheld mobile camera equipment and the popularity of

© Springer Nature Switzerland AG 2019
X. Sun et al. (Eds.): ICAIS 2019, LNCS 11632, pp. 463–474, 2019.
https://doi.org/10.1007/978-3-030-24274-9_42

web 2.0 technology, we have ushered in the era of media, everyone can shoot and upload pictures anytime, anywhere, resulting in a surge in the number of images containing various natural scenes. These massive natural scene images greatly exceed the intensity of manual processing, and automation of image management and retrieval is urgently required. In natural scene images or videos, it often contains a lot of text information, such as notices, road signs, and captions. The text contains rich and accurate semantic information that is widely used in visual understanding, such as: autopilot, blind navigation, license plate recognition, and text-based image retrieval. Extracting text information from natural scene images can help us to further understand the image and retrieve the required information from massive data, saving time and improving efficiency. Therefore, text detection and recognition in natural scenes are becoming more and more important. It has gradually become a very active research topic in computer vision and document analysis. Internationally, the emphasis on the detection and recognition of natural scene texts has gradually increased, and many well-known journals and conferences have included them in the agenda. To promote the development of this field, since 1991, the International Conference on Document Analysis and Recognition (ICDAR) has been held every two years. In recent years, researchers have done a lot of research and made great progress in this field. Although the traditional document text detection and recognition has matured, there are still many insurmountable text detection and recognition for natural scene images. Challenges such as noise, blur, distortion, and non-uniform illumination. Natural scene text detection and recognition belongs to the intersection of pattern recognition, computer vision, machine learning, etc., and the research results can promote the theoretical development of these fields. Therefore, text detection and recognition in natural scenes have important theoretical research and practical application value. Based on the in-depth analysis of the current progress and challenges in this field, this paper combines the current popular deep learning techniques to design and implement a text recognition method based on deep learning.

Text recognition is to obtain semantic information in a picture, and images containing semantic information are generally pre-cut. Since the natural scene image is very different from the document images, the conventional character recognition method cannot be directly applied to the text recognition in the scene image. In recent years, researchers have done a lot of research on text recognition in natural scenes. Text recognition is a process of transforming image information into a sequence of symbols that can be represented and processed by a computer. The text recognition task can be considered as a special translation process in which the image signal is translated into a natural language. This is similar to speech recognition and machine translation. From a mathematical point of view, they convert a set of input sequences containing a lot of noise into an output sequence of a given set of labels.

Yao et al. obtained a series of middle-level features by learning the sub-blocks of characters: strokelets, and then obtained the characters by Hough voting. Then, the random forest classifier is trained by the strokelet and HOG features for character recognition. Wang et al. trained a CNN character recognizer to obtain a character position confidence map by sliding the input image, and based on the confidence map, the characters were segmented and then identified by Bissacco et al. The two segmentation methods perform character segmentation on words, and then combine word search (Beam Search) and HOG feature-based character classifier to realize word recognition. This method is faster and more robust, but requires a lot of training data and can only recognize horizontal text lines.

Goel et al. used the entire text image to identify words. They used gradient-based feature maps to compare pre-made word images, and used dynamic k-nearest neighbors to determine the words contained in the current image [1], which relies on a fixed dictionary and pre-generated word images. In 2013, Rodriguez-Serrano et al. used an integrated fisher vector and a structured support vector machine framework to establish the relationship between pictures and the entire word encoding [2].

Multi-digit Number Recognition from Street View released by Google in 2013 [3]. This paper described a system for extracting numbers from streetscapes. The system used an end-to-end neural network, and the authors continued to explain how the same network could beat Google's own CAPTCHA SYSTEM with human-level accuracy, and Google's architecture have proven to work well for CAPTCHAS. In the original text, Goodfellow et al. first proposed using Maxout [4] as a nonlinear activation unit to construct a deep CNN to encode the entire image, and using multiple position-sensitive character-level classifiers [5] for text recognition. They have achieved great success in the identification of the street view number. They also applied the model to the 8-bit verification code recognition task and trained the model using synthetic training data. This method achieved a recognition rate of more than 96% in the Google Street View number recognition task. At the same time, it has obtained more than 99% recognition rate for the Google verification code task, and then obtained the state-of-the-art result in the text classification [6]. The disadvantage of Deep CNN [7] is that the maximum length of the predictable sequence is selected in advance, which is more suitable for the house number or license plate number (a small number of characters, and each character can be regarded as independent).

The two results published by Jaderberg et al. in 2014 made minor changes to the above model which the classifier for predicting the length of the character was eliminated, and the terminator was used to indicate the end of the text [8]. They then demonstrated that models trained using synthetic training data can be successfully applied to real-world identification problems. Encoding words [9] into vectors is a viable dictionary word recognition method, but in the case of no constraints, characters can be arbitrarily combined. When the number of characters is sufficient, the performance of the method based on fixed length vector coding is significantly degraded. However, there are still some shortcomings: some studies use deep learning techniques in the single-character identification step, but the overall framework still follows the traditional processing flow design, so the problems described in the introduction will still be encountered in other steps. Goodfellow et al.'s [10] research uses a pure neural network to directly complete the entire identification process and achieve industry-leading results. However, since they need to use a fixed-size image as an input and encode the input image as a fixed-length feature vector, the recognition accuracy of the model is significantly reduced in the case of many characters in the image. On the other hand, since their models do not explicitly position [11] and segment [12] the image, it is impossible to know where each character is located in the original image.

2 Related Work

There is a lot of work to study how to define a good set of text features [13], but most of the features of practical applications are not universal. In extreme cases, many features are almost ineffective or even impossible to extract, such as stroke features, shape features, and so on. On the other hand, defining and extracting artificial features [14] is also an extremely time consuming and labor intensive task. The pictures that usually need to be identified are divided into two categories. The simple texts with a clear background and the complex texts with blurred backgrounds and complex texts are very stressful and challenging [15].

This paper attempts to combine deep learning neural network technology with text recognition technology, and proposes an effective text recognition method to find a feasible new way to solve the difficulties in text recognition in natural scene images. The focus and difficulty of image recognition in natural scene images is the feature extraction of characters and the design of classifiers. In the research of character extraction method of characters, the effective feature information of characters is extracted by studying the characters, and these features are combined with traditional character statistical features and structural features to identify the characters in the corpus system.

Due to the characteristics of neural network and its potential in the field of image text recognition, this paper conducts in-depth research on the natural scene image text detection and recognition technology based on neural network, and proposes a natural scene image text detection based on neural network. And the recognition algorithm [16, 17], using DenseNet network [18] model based on Kares [19] to construct text recognition [20], using Softmax output to classify each character [21], combined with the corpus to find the word that matches the character feature [22]. The classification of the character is obtained, thereby improving the recognition efficiency and precision, and realizing the text recognition of the natural scene image. Experiments show that this method can obtain better natural scene image text detection and text recognition effects, and achieve an efficient deep learning framework. The framework can support a variety of neural network structures and provide a series of effective training. Strategy, using this framework to preliminarily verify the effectiveness of natural scene text recognition algorithm based on deep learning.

3 System Introduction

In this study, the data set was preprocessed by CTPN [23], then the text recognition model in the image was established by DensNet, and finally the text was classified by Softmax classification.

3.1 Data Reprocessing

This research is mainly aimed at the problem of text recognition in natural scene images. Firstly, the standard data set of VOC is made by using data set. The data needed by this research is obtained by CTPN method, as shown in Fig. 1. Then one is passed. A Chinese corpus containing 5990 characters is used to mark the obtained data set for subsequent model training.

Fig. 1. Training data

3.2 Basic Model

In this study, using a DensNet network model based on the Convolutional Neural Network (CNN) [24, 25], CNN is the basic framework of most network models. CNN is a standard feedforward multi-layer neural network inspired by biological processes. It uses a sparse connection and shared weighting strategy. It consists of a series of hidden convolutional layers and pool sampling layers, optionally following the fully connected layer, and is good at extracting useful. Local and global features are trained to classify. The standard CNN contains the layout of the convolutional layer and the pool sampling sublayer. Through this series of hidden layers, CNN uses the BP algorithm to train the weights. The main components of the network are shown in Fig. 2.

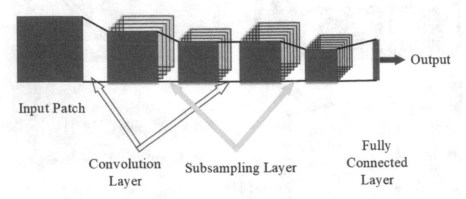

Fig. 2. CNN network main components

The main components of the hidden layer of the CNN network are described in detail below,

(1) Convolutional layer: Layer parameters consist of a set of learnable convolution kernels (filters). In the forward process, each convolution kernel moves incrementally over the width and height of the image matrix, and at each position, a dot product is computed between the number of convolution kernels and the local image matrix until convolution transformation (the mapping is completed), the completion of the original image. The BP algorithm is then applied to the gradient calculation.

(2) Activation function: This function increases the nonlinear nature of the decision function. Three common activation functions are commonly used, namely Sigmoid, hyperbolic tangent (tanh) and corrected linear unit (ReLU) functions.

(3) Pool sampling layer: This layer gradually reduces the amount of space represented by the image to reduce the number of parameters and computational load in the network. In practice, several nonlinear functions are often used to implement pools, such as maximum pools, mean pools, and random pools.

(4) Fully connected layer: Each node of the fully connected layer is connected to all nodes of the previous layer to combine the features extracted from the front. Due to its fully connected nature, the parameters of the fully connected layer are also the most common.

3.3   Text Recognition Model

This study uses the DenseNet network model to build our text recognition model based on Kares [26]. The biggest advantage of using DenseNet is to enhance the feature propagation and encourage feature reuse. The core idea is to create a cross-layer connection to connect the network. The middle and back layers are ideal for scene text recognition.

After DenseNet was proposed by Resnet [27], the variant network of ResNet emerged in an endless stream, each with its own characteristics, and the network performance also improved. DenseNet is mainly compared with ResNet and Inception networks. It has a new idea, but it is a new structure. The network structure is not complicated, but it is very effective. It completely surpasses ResNet in Cifar [28] indicators. It can be said that DenseNet absorbs the best of ResNet. Partly, and doing more innovative work here, the network performance is further improved. The connection is dense, the gradient disappears, the feature propagation is enhanced, feature reuse is encouraged, and the parameter quantity is greatly reduced.

DenseNet is a convolutional neural network with dense connections. In this network, there is a direct connection between any two layers. That is to say, the input of each layer of the network is the union of the output of all the previous layers, and the feature map learned by the layer is also directly transmitted to all layers behind it are used as input. Figure 3 is a map of DenseNet's dense block. The structure inside a block is as follows, which is basically the same as BottleNeck in ResNet: BN-ReLU-Conv (1×1)-BN-ReLU-Conv (3×3), and one DenseNet consists of multiple such blocks. The layer between each DenseBlock is called transition layers and consists of BN $\rightarrow$ Conv(1×1) $\rightarrow$ average Pooling(2×2).

$$x_l = H_l(x_{l-1}) + x_{l-1} \tag{1}$$

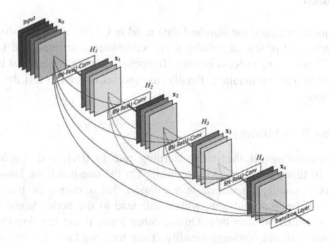

Fig. 3. DenseNet network model

The above formula is an expression of ResNet, where x_l represents the output of the l layer and H_l represents a nonlinear change, for ResNet, the output of layer $l - 1$ is the output of layer $l - 1$ plus a nonlinear transformation of the output of layer.

$$x_l = H_l([x_0, x_1, \ldots, x_{l-1}]) \tag{2}$$

The above formula is the expression of DenseNet, where $[x_0, x_1, \ldots, x_{l-1}]$ means that the output feature map of the 0 to $l - 1$ layer is concatenation, concatenation is the channel merge, and is the same as Inception [29], while the former ResNet is the sum of the values, the number of channels is unchanged, H_l includes convolution of BN, ReLU and 3 * 3.

3.4 Classifier

This experiment uses the Softmax classifier as the final output layer [7]. The Softmax function is based on Softmax regression, which is a supervised learning algorithm based on loss function of Softmax formula,

$$J(\theta) = -\frac{1}{m} \left[\sum_{i=1}^{m} \sum_{j=1}^{k} I\left\{ y^{(i)} = j \right\} \log \frac{e^{\theta_j^T x^{(i)}}}{\sum_{l=1}^{k} e^{\theta_l^T x^{(i)}}} \right] \tag{3}$$

Where $I\{\bullet\}$ represents an exponential function indicating whether $x^{(i)}$ is a class j. The function calculates the crossover loss based on the probability of the output of the Softmax function.

4   Experiment

In this experiment, we used the standard data used in CTPN, randomly divided all the data into 5 parts, and produced training sets, verification machines, and test sets in a ratio of 3:1:1. The training process iterates 50epoches, and the 1epoch test is performed after each 1epoch training iteration. Finally, the test set is used to test the accuracy of the training model.

4.1   Learning Rate Strategy

In this experiment, we set the initial learning rate to 0.01, and the learning rate decreased by 10 times for each epoch training. On the one hand, we know that if the learning rate is set too high, it will cause oscillation, that is, during the training process, the accuracy will be high and low, which will lead to the network not learning the characteristic information smoothly. On the other hand, if the learning rate is set too low, the network will not converge steadily. Therefore, we have adopted a strategy of decreasing learning rates.

4.2   Experimental Configuration

To complete this experiment, we used precision as the unit of measure. All experiments were implemented in Python 2.7 with the Tensorflow [30] and Keras frameworks. We trained the network M40 GPU on NVIDIA Tesla using the SGD [31] solver and model to perform the best test data set preservation for further analysis.

4.3   Experimental Procedure

4.3.1   Production Data Set

The VOC dataset format is a standard data format that is now used by many deep learning frameworks. We made all the images into a dataset in VOC format, which uses the folders Annotation, Image Sets, and JPEG Images. The folder Annotation mainly stores xml files, each xml corresponds to an image, and each xml stores the location and category information of each target of the mark, and the naming is usually the same as the corresponding original image; while Image Sets we only need Use the Main folder, which is stored in some text files, usually train.txt, test.txt, etc. The content of the text file is the name of the image that needs to be trained or tested (no suffix without path); In the JPEG Images folder, put the original image we have named according to the uniform rules. Input the prepared data set into the CTPN model for training, iterate 50epoches, input 30 pictures each time (batch size = 30), verify each time it is completed, and finally save the best model as the prediction model, and pass the prediction. The model gets the data set needed for text recognition. All the images obtained by CTPN are only intercepted into the demand area, and then combined with the Chinese corpus to make a training data set.

4.3.2   Training and Experimental Results

The prepared data set is input into the network for training, iterating 50epoches, inputting 30 pictures each time (batch size = 30), verifying each time it is completed, and finally saving the best model as a predictive model. The results of different model experiments are shown in Table 1. The experimental comparison results show that the LeNet result is 87.2, the NinNet test result is 82.4, the VGGNet test result is 93.3, and the DenseNet test result is 94.0. From the experimental results, the experimental results of VGGNet are good, but compared with the DenseNet experiment. The result is still a bit worse, and the experimental results will change due to environmental influences. The experimental results are shown in Fig. 4.

Table 1. The accuracy of predictive models of scene images

Model	Training sets	Testing sets	Accuracy/(%)
LeNet	254800	10000	87.2
NinNet	254800	10000	82.4
VGGNet	254800	10000	93.3
DenseNet	254800	10000	94.0

Detection took 5.327s for 3 object proposals
Mission complete, it took 6.225s

Recognition Result:

Humpsfor
60tards

Detection took 1.914s for 3 object proposals
Mission complete, it took 2.121s

Recognition Result:

MOOSE
(
CROSSINC

Detection took 1.334s for 2 object proposals
Mission complete, it took 1.488s

Recognition Result:

EXAMROOM10
Thera0yH00m

Detection took 1.044s for 4 object proposals
Mission complete, it took 1.514s

Recognition Result:

!269
Dr.ChisGreen
ztftifery
CASCOBAY//CHIROPRACTIC

Detection took 0.192s for 2 object proposals
Mission complete, it took 0.268s

Recognition Result:

MARKEISIREET

Detection took 0.257s for 3 object proposals
Mission complete, it took 0.444s

Recognition Result:

AVALON
HOUSE
STYLEEXPRESSION

Fig. 4. Experimental results

5 Conclusions

In this study, the relatively simple background of the text area can be well recognized, the background is relatively complicated, especially in the background, there are many pictures that interfere with the text, and it is easy to mark the text area with heavy background, which leads to misidentification and do optimization work. For text recognition, according to the data set produced above, the accuracy of the experiment can reach about 94.0%. The experiment proves that the text recognition model based on DensNet can well realize the text recognition in natural scene images.

Acknowledgments. This study was supported by the Scientific Research Foundation (KYTZ201718) of CUIT. (KYTZ201718).

References

1. Goel, V., Mishra, A., Alahari, K., et al.: Whole is greater than sum of parts: recognizing scene text words. In: International Conference on Document Analysis and Recognition, pp. 398–402. IEEE Computer Society (2013)
2. Rodriguez-Serrano, J.A., Perronnin, F.: Label embedding for text recognition. In: BMVC (2013)
3. Goodfellow, I.J., Bulatov, Y., Ibarz, J., et al.: Multi-digit number recognition from street view imagery using deep convolutional neural networks. Comput. Sci. (2013)
4. Goodfellow, I.J., Warde-Farley, D., Mirza, M., et al.: Maxout networks. arXiv preprint arXiv:1302.4389 (2013)
5. Yaeger, L.S., Lyon, R.F., Webb, B.J.: Effective training of a neural network character classifier for word recognition. In: Advances in Neural Information Processing Systems, pp. 807–816 (1997)
6. Jaderberg, M., Simonyan, K., Vedaldi, A., et al.: Synthetic data and artificial neural networks for natural scene text recognition. Eprint Arxiv (2014)
7. Zhang, K., Zuo, W., Chen, Y., et al.: Beyond a Gaussian denoiser: residual learning of deep CNN for image denoising. IEEE Trans. Image Process. **26**(7), 3142–3155 (2017)
8. Jaderberg, M., Simonyan, K., Vedaldi, A., et al.: Reading text in the wild with convolutional neural networks. Int. J. Comput. Vis. **116**(1), 1–20 (2016)
9. Burden, V., Campbell, R.: The development of word-coding skills in the born deaf: an experimental study of deaf school-leavers. Br. J. Dev. Psychol. **12**(3), 331–349 (1994)
10. Goodfellow, I.J., Bulatov, Y., Ibarz, J., et al.: Multi-digit number recognition from street view imagery using deep convolutional neural networks. arXiv preprint arXiv:1312.6082 (2013)
11. Harrington, S.J., Klassen, R.V.: Subpixel character positioning with antialiasing with grey masking techniques: U.S. Patent 5,701,365 23 December 1997
12. Shi, J., Malik, J.: Normalized cuts and image segmentation. IEEE Trans. Pattern Anal. Mach. Intell. **22**(8), 888–905 (2000)
13. Aghdam, M.H., Ghasem-Aghaee, N., Basiri, M.E.: Text feature selection using ant colony optimization. Expert Syst. Appl. **36**(3), 6843–6853 (2009)
14. Tian, J., Chen, D.M.: Optimization in multi-scale segmentation of high-resolution satellite images for artificial feature recognition. Int. J. Remote Sens. **28**(20), 4625–4644 (2007)

15. Fang, W., Zhang, F., Sheng, V.S., Ding, Y.: A method for improving CNN-based image recognition using DCGAN. CMC Comput. Mater. Continua **57**(1), 167–178 (2018)
16. Ye, Q., Doermann, D.: Text detection and recognition in imagery: a survey. IEEE Trans. Pattern Anal. Mach. Intell. **37**(7), 1480–1500 (2015)
17. Coates, A., Carpenter, B., Case, C., et al.: Text detection and character recognition in scene images with unsupervised feature learning. In: International Conference on Document Analysis and Recognition, pp. 440–445. IEEE (2011)
18. Huang, G., Liu, Z., Van Der Maaten, L., et al.: Densely connected convolutional networks. In: CVPR, vol. 1, no. 2, p. 3 (2017)
19. Bien, Z., Chung, M.J., Chang, P.H., et al.: Integration of a rehabilitation robotic system (KARES II) with human-friendly man-machine interaction units. Auton. Rob. **16**(2), 165–191 (2004)
20. Zhu, Y., Newsam, S.: DenseNet for Dense Flow, pp. 790–794 (2017)
21. Salakhutdinov, R., Hinton, G.E.: Replicated softmax: an undirected topic model. In: International Conference on Neural Information Processing Systems, pp. 1607–1614. Curran Associates Inc. (2009)
22. Krizhevsky, A., Sutskever, I., Hinton, G.E.: ImageNet classification with deep convolutional neural networks. In: Advances in Neural Information Processing Systems, pp. 1097–1105 (2012)
23. Tian, Z., Huang, W., He, T., He, P., Qiao, Yu.: Detecting text in natural image with connectionist text proposal network. In: Leibe, B., Matas, J., Sebe, N., Welling, M. (eds.) ECCV 2016. LNCS, vol. 9912, pp. 56–72. Springer, Cham (2016). https://doi.org/10.1007/978-3-319-46484-8_4
24. Oquab, M., Bottou, L., Laptev, I., Sivic, J.: Learning and transferring mid-level image representations using convolutional neural networks. In: Computer Vision and Pattern Recognition, pp. 1717–1724 (2014)
25. Zhang, Y., Wang, Y., Li, Y., Wu, X.: Sentiment classification based on piecewise pooling convolutional neural network. CMC Comput. Mater. Continua **56**(2), 285–297 (2018)
26. Krizhevsky, A., Hinton, G.: Convolutional deep belief networks on cifar-10. Unpublished Manuscript **40**(7) (2010)
27. Girshick, R.: Fast R-CNN. In: IEEE International Conference on Computer Vision, pp. 1440–1448. IEEE (2015)
28. Huang, F., Ash, J., Langford, J., et al.: Learning Deep ResNet Blocks Sequentially using Boosting Theory (2018)
29. Szegedy, C., Ioffe, S., Vanhoucke, V., et al.: Inception-v4, inception-resnet and the impact of residual connections on learning. In: AAAI, vol. 4, p. 12 (2017)
30. Abadi, M., Barham, P., Chen, J., et al.: Tensorflow: a system for large-scale machine learning. In: OSDI, vol. 16, pp. 265–283 (2016)
31. Bottou, L.: Large-scale machine learning with stochastic gradient descent. In: Lechevallier, Y., Saporta, G. (eds.) Proceedings of COMPSTAT 2010, pp. 177–186. Physica, Heidelberg (2010). https://doi.org/10.1007/978-3-7908-2604-3_16

A Classification Model of Power Equipment Defect Texts Based on Convolutional Neural Network

Junyu Zhou[1]($\boxtimes$), Guoming Luo[1], Chao Hu[2], and Yiguo Chen[2]

[1] Guangdong Power Grid Company Limited Foshan Power Supply Bureau,
Foshan 528000, China
Imkate_938@hotmail.com

[2] NARI Information and Communication Technology Co., Ltd.,
Nanjing 210033, China

Abstract. A large amount of equipment defect texts are left unused in power management system. According to the features of power equipment defect texts, a classification model of defect texts based on convolutional neural network is established. Firstly, the features of power equipment defect texts are extracted by analyzing a large number of defect records. Then, referencing general process of Chinese text classification and considering the features of defect texts, we establishes a classification model of defect texts based on convolutional neural network. Finally, we develop classification effect evaluation indicators to evaluate the effect of the model based on one case. Compared with multiple traditional machine learning classification models and according to the classification effect evaluation indicators, the proposed defect text classification model can significantly reduce error rate with considerable efficiency.

Keywords: Power text processing · Defect classification ·
Convolutional neural network

1 Introduction

During the long-term operation of power equipment, a large number of defect text data are recorded and accumulated through inspection and testing [1–3]. These textual data are stored in the system and often serve as a guide for the elimination or troubleshooting, and then cannot be further utilized. On the other hand, a large number of equipment defect classification tasks need to be done manually, which is not only inefficient, but also for some sub-health defects with strong ambiguity, the inspectors are often difficult to accurately judge due to the knowledge structure and experience limitations, so the classification accuracy is affected [4]. With the rapid development of Chinese text processing technology, it has become possible to automatically classify a large number of defective texts in the grid production management system by using Chinese text classification

© Springer Nature Switzerland AG 2019
X. Sun et al. (Eds.): ICAIS 2019, LNCS 11632, pp. 475–487, 2019.
https://doi.org/10.1007/978-3-030-24274-9_43

technology based on machine learning. The application of this technology can not only revitalize the textual information resources of the power system, but also lay a foundation for its further use, and can reduce or even eliminate the workload of manual classification, and improve the classification accuracy while ensuring that defects can be processed and reported in time.

In response to the application of machine learning in English power text data mining, foreign countries have conducted substation fault prediction through historical fault event records and weather data, and component and system fault risk prediction through faulty work orders [5,17]. Related research, but most of the models of these studies are based on traditional machine learning classification models, and rarely use deep learning-based classification models, such as convolutional neural networks. However, the research on Chinese power defect text classification methods is basically based on the traditional machine learning classification model, and there is no model design and improvement for the characteristics of power defect texts [6,7,18]. In general, most of the current research on the classification of power text machine learning is based on the traditional text classification model, and the classification model is not targeted.

In order to further explore the application of machine learning text classification model in power defect text classification, this paper explores the construction of machine learning model suitable for power device defect text classification based on convolutional neural network. Firstly, the characteristics of power defect texts are summarized from a large number of power defect records, which lays a foundation for the targeted processing of subsequent models. Then the limitations of traditional Chinese text classification are analyzed, and the power is constructed based on convolutional neural networks. The defect text classification model, combined with the characteristics of the power defect text, carries out targeted research on the preprocessing, text representation and classifier of the model. Finally, through the example, the error rate, serious deviation rate and classification efficiency of the classification The convolutional neural network-based model and the traditional machine learning classification model are comprehensively constructed. The feasibility and superiority of the power defect classification model based on convolutional neural network are proved.

The rest of this paper is organized as follows. Section 2 introduces the characteristics of the power equipment defect description text and Chinese text classification technology. Section 3 introduces a text classification model for power equipment defects based on convolutional neural networks. An example analysis is given in Sect. 4. Finally, the conclusion of this paper is given in Sect. 5.

2   Preliminaries

2.1   Power Equipment Defect Text

In order to provide the health level of the relevant equipment in the power system, in the daily maintenance and maintenance process, the defects of the power equipment need to be recorded, and the recorded contents usually include the type of the defective equipment, the name, the date of the defect discovery, the defect description, the defect classification, and the like. Thereby a large amount of power defect text is formed. Unlike other contents of the defect record, the defect description is recorded in the form of short text. There is no fixed format and structure, but it contains more important defect information, such as specific parts of the device, defects, specific phenomena, etc.

According to the classification criteria for power equipment defects, the defect classification can be divided into three categories: "general", "important" and "emergency" according to the severity of the defect. The classification work is generally done manually. Through the machine learning method, using the existing defect texts to train and mine the specific defect information contained in the defect description text, the automatic classification of defects can be realized.

Compared with the general Chinese text, the power device defect description text has the following characteristics: (1) The text of the defect description relates to the professional field of electrical equipment, contains a large number of electrical professional vocabulary, and may have different descriptions of the same component due to different experience and habits of the inspectors, such as "reservoir" and "oil pillow", etc. (2) Due to the complexity of the various defects and the difference in the level of detail recorded by the inspectors, the lengths of the texts of the various defects are very different, with the shortest of 4 words and the longest of more than 40 words. (3) A considerable part of the defect description text is mixed with words and numbers, such as "Pressure relief valve oil leakage, 1 min 15–20 drops". These fields containing quantitative information have an important and even decisive role in the classification of defect levels. (4) The large amount of data in the defect description text is conducive to the implicit rules in machine learning mining text, but it also puts forward certain requirements on the classification efficiency and storage overhead of the classification model [8].

2.2 Chinese Text Classification Technology

Chinese Text Classification Process. Text classification refers to the process of dividing text into predetermined text categories according to its content [12]. The Chinese text classification technology refers to the related technology of finding the correspondence between text features and text categories from a large number of existing Chinese text data by using machine learning methods, and using its laws to realize the automatic classification of new texts.

The construction of Chinese text automatic classification model based on machine learning is mainly divided into two stages, namely training stage and testing stage. In the training phase, the Chinese text is first preprocessed, including segmentation, clauses, word segmentation, and deactivation words. The specific preprocessing steps are related to the length of the text and the specific content of the text. Then the text is represented, that is, the text is converted. For the form that can be recognized and processed by the computer, the text is generally represented in the form of matrix or vector. The method of text representation is closely related to the extraction of text features, and also affects the effect of post-text classification [15]; The classifier classifies the text and outputs the predicted classification result; finally compares the given actual classification result with the result of the classifier prediction, if the prediction result reaches a preset standard, such as reaching a certain prediction accuracy or a certain degree If the number of iterations is equal, the training is completed. Otherwise, the relevant parameters of the classifier are adjusted according to the comparison result, and the classification is repeated, and the cycle prediction is achieved until the classification prediction result reaches the standard.

After the training is completed, the model is tested. In the test phase, the preprocessing and text representation are also performed first. The processing flow is the same as the training phase. Then, the classifier obtained in the training phase is used for classification, and compared with the given classification result, the performance of the classification model is evaluated. Subsequent applications provide a reference.

Traditional Chinese Text Classification Model. In the text representation stage, the traditional classification model uses the vector space model (VSM) to vectorize the text. The basic idea is to use matrix to represent the sentence set. Each line of the matrix represents the sentence vector of a sentence, and the matrix column Represents the characteristics of a sentence, and the number of features of each sentence is the same. According to different feature selection methods, there are many representation methods, such as Boolean representation, word frequency-reverse document frequency representation, potential Dirichlet distribution representation, etc. [13]. The feature selection of these methods is basically based on the frequency of each word in the sentence, regardless of the order of the words, such as "Main change site temperature is higher than the background display temperature" and "Main change background display temperature is higher than the field temperature". It is obviously different in sentence meaning, but after the word segmentation and VSM representation, it will be converted into the same sentence vector.

In the classification stage, the machine learning classifier used in the traditional text classification model includes Logistic Regression, Naive Bayes, Support Vector Machine, etc. The advantage is that the model complexity is low, so the training speed is relatively fast, which can be explained Stronger; but because the model level is shallow, the automatic extraction of text features can not be achieved, so the classification effect is greatly affected by the selection of artificial features.

3   Defect Text Classification Model of Power Equipment Based on Convolutional Neural Network

3.1   Text Preprocessing

Text preprocessing includes word segmentation and de-stopping words for the characteristics of power device defect text. Chinese text is different from English text, and there is no natural boundary between words and words. Therefore, Chinese text needs to be segmented before the text is represented. In this paper, the hidden Markov model is used, and the defect description text is segmented by means of a self-edited power equipment defect dictionary.

For some words that cannot characterize the severity of power equipment defects, such as the name of the substation, the relevant place name, etc., it needs to be removed as a stop word from the defect description text after the word segmentation to reduce the noise of the text. This paper establishes a stop word list, and after the word segmentation, compares the stop word list and removes the stop words in the defect description.

3.2 Distributed Text

The distribution was proposed by Hinton [15], and its representation is based on the hypothesis that "the semantics of words are characterized by their neighbors". According to this, the word can be represented by a distributed word vector.

First, referring to the neural network language model (NNLM) of Bengio et al. [9], a large number of preprocessed power equipment defect records are used as a corpus to train the word vector representation of each word. The semantic features of the words learned by NNLM. Taking the word vector with dimension 3 as an example, the word vector of the partially defective text is represented in the feature space, as shown in Fig. 1.

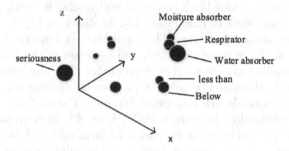

Fig. 1. Word vectors in feature space

Where, each dot represents a word vector, and the x, y, and z axes respectively represent three semantic feature dimensions of the word vector. It can be seen from Fig. 1 that the word vectors corresponding to words with similar meanings are relatively close in the feature space, while the words with large differences in word meanings are farther away from each other, that is, the word meanings can be characterized by word vectors. In practical applications, the size of the word vector dimension can be specified according to the corpus size, usually taking 100 300 dimensions. Each dimension represents a word feature automatically learned by the machine, and has no actual physical meaning.

Then, the word vector of the synonym is merged with reference to the power device term specification. For example, by training the defect corpus, the word vectors of "respirator", "hygrometer" and "hygroscopic" are obtained, and the three are very close in the feature space (the degree of proximity is characterized by the Euclidean distance of the vector). At the same time, in the specification of power equipment terms, the standard word "breathing device" of the part was found, so the word vector of "moisture absorber" and "hygroscopic device" was unified into the word vector of "respirator", thereby realizing Synonym word vectors are merged. The reason why only the words contained in the term specification are vector-merged is because other words are close in the feature space, such as "below" and "less than", but the semantics still have some differences, that is, they are synonyms. Therefore, the word vectors are not merged.

3.3 Convolutional Neural Network Classifier for Defect Text of Power Equipment

The convolutional neural network model was proposed by Lecun in 1989 [11], which refers to a neural network that uses convolution instead of general matrix multiplication at least in one layer of the network. The convolutional neural network has the characteristics of local perception and weight sharing, which greatly reduces the number of training parameters and improves the computational efficiency of complex networks.

The convolutional neural network can be used as a classifier to classify the vectorized defect description text and output the corresponding classification result. In this paper, a four-layer convolutional neural network is constructed with reference to the work of Kim et al. [19], as shown in Fig. 2.

The first layer is the input layer. The input layer is a matrix $I \in R^{s \times n}$ corresponding to the sentence to be classified, and each row of the matrix represents a vector corresponding to each word in the sentence. The number of rows s is the number of words in the sentence, and the number of columns n is the dimension of the vector. For example, All respirators discolor. The sentence is divided into "All+respirators+discolor" by word unit. Each word is then vectorized and converted into word vectors of equal dimension to form matrix I as the input layer of the convolutional neural network. During the training process, the stochastic gradient descent (SGD) method is usually used to fine-tune the word vector, making the word vector more suitable for the specific classification task [13], but because the deficient text is mixed with numbers and words, the same number is different. The semantic tendency in the defect text may be completely different, such as "temperature rises 5 °C" and "oil spill every 5 s". The larger the former, the more serious the defect, and the latter is opposite. The word vector is fine-tuned, which is not conducive to the judgment of severity. To this end, in the training process, the word vector of the number is fixed, and the other word vectors are fine-tuned to improve the generalization ability of the model.

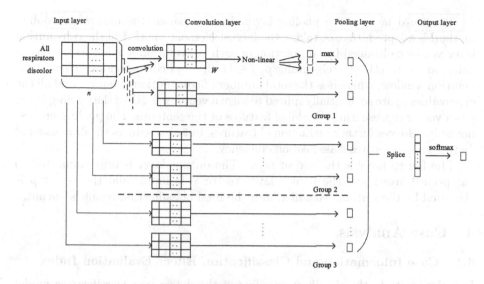

Fig. 2. Structure of convolutional neural network

The second layer is a convolution layer. The convolution matrix window $W \in R^{h \times n}$ with the same number of columns as I and the number of rows h is convoluted with each h row and n column matrix blocks of the input layer matrix I from top to bottom. Convolution result r_i:

$$r_i = W \cdot I_{i:i+h-1} \tag{1}$$

where $i = 1, 2, \cdots, s - h + 1$; $I_{i:i+h-1}$ represents the ith, h-row, n-column, matrix block from top to bottom; "$\cdot$" represents the point multiplication operation, that is 2 all elements of the same position in the matrix are multiplied and then summed. Therefore, a total of $s - h + 1$ convolutions are performed, and after each convolution, non-linearization is performed to obtain a non-linearized result c_i:

$$c_i = \mathrm{Re}\,LU(r_i + b) \tag{2}$$

where b is the bias term and its value can be automatically adjusted during training; $\mathrm{Re}\,LU$ is the modified linear unit function. Finally, a total of $sh + 1$ real numbers ci are obtained, and these real numbers are sequentially arranged to form a vector $c \in R^{s-h+1}$ of the convolutional layer. Due to the large change of the length of the defective text, different defective texts may be expressed by different numbers of words when expressing the same information. Therefore, this paper divides the convolution window into multiple groups. Figure 2 uses three types of groups. Different groups use convolutional windows of different sizes (different lines) to convolve with I to obtain different levels of words. Semantic features. In addition, there are multiple convolution windows in each group, and the element values between the respective convolution windows (matrices) are different in order to extract features in multiple aspects.

The third layer is the pooling layer. In this paper, the maximum pooling method is adopted, that is, taking the largest element $\max\{c\}$ in the convolution layer vector c obtained by convolution of each convolution window as the eigenvalue, and extracting the eigenvalue p_j $j \in \{1, 2, \cdots, \}$ corresponding to each convolution window, where w is the total number of convolution windows, and all the eigenvalues p_j are sequentially spliced to form a vector $p \in R^w$ of the pooling layer, p is a vector representing the global features of the sentence. The pooling process not only achieves further extraction of features, but also reduces the dimension of features and improves classification efficiency.

The fourth layer is the output layer. The output layer is fully connected to the pooled layer, and the pooled layer vector p is input, and the vector p is classified by the softmax classifier, and the final classification result is output.

4   Case Analysis

4.1   Case Information and Classification Effect Evaluation Index

In order to study the classification effect of the defect text classification model constructed in this paper on the defect text of power equipment, take the transformer defect record as an example to conduct experiments, select 4365 transformer defect record data of a power grid company from 2005 to 2015, and describe the defects of each data. Specific transformer defect information is recorded, and the defect levels have been manually classified. When training and testing the text classification task, all 4365 pieces of defect data were randomly arranged and divided into 5 equal parts, each containing 873 pieces of data. Four of the data were taken as a training set in turn, and one piece of data was used as a test set for 5-fold cross-validation.

When comparing the classification effect of the text classification model, the $Error$ indicator is introduced to reflect the error of the text classification. S_i represents the total number of texts in the ith test set. C_i represents the number of misclassified texts for the ith test set.

$$Error = \frac{\sum\limits_{i=1}^{5} \frac{C_i}{S_i}}{5} \tag{3}$$

In addition, since the information on the severity of defects contained in the "general" and "emergency" categories of defects is quite different, the "general" defects are misclassified as "emergency" or misidentified as "emergency" defects. "General", all indicate that the classification has a serious deviation, which is a serious misclassification. In order to reflect the deviation of the classification model from the severity information, a "severe deviation rate" indicator was introduced. SDR represents severe deviation rate, S_i represents the total number of texts in the ith test set, D_i represents the number of severely misclassified texts in the ith test set.

$$SDR = \frac{\sum\limits_{i=1}^{5} \frac{D_i}{S_i}}{5} \tag{4}$$

In practical applications, training set vector, word vector and classifier training can be completed offline and saved in the model parameters. It can be used directly during the test, no need to repeat training, so the online calculation time is only test time. Therefore, the training time and test time of the five cross-validations are averaged respectively, and the "training time-consuming" and "testing time-consuming" indicators are obtained to compare the offline calculation and online calculation efficiency of different classification models.

4.2 Parameter Settings

Since the convolutional neural network belongs to the deep learning model, the automatic learning and extraction of text features can be performed. Therefore, when the parameters of the word vector, the number of convolution windows of each group, etc. are changed within an appropriate range, the influence on the classification effect is Not obvious. Therefore, accurate numerical experiments on these parameters have limited significance. In the pre-experiment, these parameters are scanned by the control variable method to determine the appropriate range of parameters, and then a parameter value that makes the model classification less time-consuming is selected within the range.

In order to verify the effect of the structural parameters of the convolutional neural network model for the characteristics of the power defect text, this paper considers the three main factors of the word vector generation method, the word vector fine-tuning method, and the window size of each group. Three comparison models based on convolutional neural networks were compared with the constructed text classification model. The specific network parameter settings are shown in Table 1.

Table 1. Parameter setting of convolutional neural network models

Parameter	Model of this paper	Model 1	Model 2	Model 3
Word vector dimension	200	200	200	200
Generate word vector randomly	No	Yes	No	No
Group 1 window size (number of rows)	3	3	3	4
Group 2 window size (number of rows)	4	4	4	4
Group 3 window size (number of rows)	5	5	5	4
Number of windows each group	64	64	64	64

In addition, in order to compare the classification effect of the convolutional neural network classification model and the traditional classification model, several typical traditional machine learning methods are selected for comparative experiments. In the text representation phase, the VSM is represented by a Boolean representation, a TF-IDF representation, and an LDA representation.

The TF-IDF and LDA representations are done using the Python-based gensim toolkit. In the classification stage, the three kinds of machine learning classifiers, Logistic Regression, Naive Bayes and Linear SVM, are used to classify the sentence vectors. The Python-based sklearn toolkit is used for classification.

4.3 Analysis of Experiment Results

The convolutional neural network text classification model and the traditional text classification model are tested, and the misclassification matrix and computation time are counted. The statistical results are shown in Tables 2 and 3. Based on the statistical results of Tables 2 and 3, the following comparative analysis can be performed.

Table 2. Classification result statistics of convolutional neural network text classification models

Model	Error/%	SDR/%	Training time/s	Test time/s
This paper model	2.86	0.80	51.36	0.48
Model 1	3.94	1.1	42.74	0.49
Model 2	3.12	0.96	51.35	0.48
Model 3	3.69	1.03	50.44	0.46

Table 3. Classification result statistics of traditional text classification models

Model	Error/%	SDR/%	Training time/s	Test time/s
Boolean value + Logistic regression	8.29	1.28	18.18	0.039
TF-IDF + Logistic regression	7.10	1.33	20.38	0.033
LDA + Logistic regression	11.66	2.27	14.57	0.002
Boolean value + naive Bayes	10.49	1.35	17.64	0.034
TF-IDF + naive Bayes	9.85	1.31	19.67	0.028
LDA + naive Bayes	13.17	2.86	13.29	0.001
Boolean value + Linear SVM	8.02	1.24	18.41	0.047
TF-IDF + Linear SVM	6.99	1.17	20.49	0.031
LDA + Linear SVM	11.07	2.31	14.20	0.001

(1) Contrast of text representation methods for convolutional neural network classification models. It can be seen from the control comparison model 1 in Table 2 that the model training using the random generated word vector takes less time, but the error rate and the serious deviation rate are higher. It can be seen that the model of this paper learns the semantic features of words from the existing fault corpus and the specification of power equipment, which has a great effect on improving the accuracy of the model.

(2) Comparison of word vector fine-tuning methods for convolutional neural network classification models. It can be seen from Table 2, comparison model 2 that the method of using all vector trimming and the fine-tuning method for text and digital mixed text are similar in training and computational efficiency.

(3) Convolutional neural network classification model convolution window size selection comparison. It can be seen from the comparison model 3 in Table 2 that the convolution window of various sizes can adapt to the change of the length of the defect text, effectively improving the feature extraction effect, thereby reducing the error rate and the serious deviation rate. Since the model has the same total number of windows as the Table 2 3, that is, the number of training parameters is the same, the efficiency is close.

(4) Comparison of convolutional neural network classification models with traditional classification models. It can be seen from Tables 2 and 3 that the error rate of the convolutional neural network classification model is significantly lower than that of the traditional classification model, and the serious deviation rate is lower than the traditional classification model. The error rate of the convolutional neural network classification model constructed in this paper is as low as 2.86%, while the traditional classification model has a minimum error rate of 6.99%, which is 2.4 times that of the model. The classification model has a severe deviation rate of 0.80%, while the traditional classification model. The minimum is 1.17%. In addition, the classification model calculated in this paper takes a little longer than the traditional classification model. On the one hand, it is because the semantic features of the word arc learned by the iterative method in the word representation stage, while the traditional classification model only needs simple statistics; The structure of the convolutional neural network is more complex than the traditional model, and there are many training parameters, so the calculation process takes more time. However, in practice, the training time is offline calculation time-consuming, and the online calculation time only includes the test time. From Table 2, it can be seen that the classification time of 873 test texts can be controlled within 0.5 s, which is significantly higher than The efficiency of manual classification is feasible and practical in the classification of actual power defect texts.

5 Conclusions

A deep learning-based convolutional neural network model is introduced in the processing of power defect texts. The error rate, severe deviation rate and classification efficiency are used as indicators. The convolutional neural network text classification model and the traditional machine learning text classification model are comprehensive. In contrast, it provides a new method and idea for data mining research of other Chinese texts in power systems. Based on the convolutional neural network, combined with the characteristics of strong electrical equipment defect, large length difference, mixed text and numbers and large amount of data, the power defect text classification model is constructed in a targeted manner. The significant advantages of the model in classification accuracy and the feasibility of classification efficiency provide an effective means to improve the classification of power texts in machine learning.

References

1. Song, Y., Zhou, G., Zhu, Y.: Present status and challenges of big data processing in smart grid. Power Syst. Technol. **37**(4), 927–935 (2013)
2. Miao, X., Zhang, D., Sun, D.: The opportunity and challenge of big data's application in power distribution networks. Power Syst. Technol. **39**(11), 3122–3127 (2015)
3. Zhao, T., Zhang, Y., Zhang, D.: Application technology of big data in smart distribution grid and its prospect analysis. Power Syst. Technol. **38**(12), 3305–3312 (2014)
4. Cao, J., Chen, L., Qiu, J., et al.: Semantic framework-based defect text mining technique and application in power grid. Power Syst. Technol. **41**(2), 637–643 (2017)
5. Rudin, C., Waltz, D., Anderson, R., et al.: Machine learning for the New York City power grid. IEEE Trans. Patt. Anal. Mach. Intell. **34**(2), 328–345 (2012)
6. Ma, R., Wang, L., Yu, J., et al.: Circuit breakers' condition evaluation considering the information in historical defect texts. J. Mech. Electric. Eng. **32**(10), 1375–1379 (2015)
7. Qiu, J., Wang, H., Ying, G., et al.: Text mining technique and application of life-cycle condition assessment for circuit breaker. Autom. Electric Power Syst. **40**(6), 107–112 (2016)
8. Wang, X., Shi, Y., Zhang, J., et al.: Computation services and applications of electricity big data based on Hadoop. Power Syst. Technol. **39**(11), 3128–3133 (2015)
9. Bengio, Y., Ducharme, R., Vincent, P., et al.: A neural probabilistic language model. J. Mach. Learn. Res. **3**(6), 1137–1155 (2003)
10. Lai, S., Liu, K., He, S., et al.: How to generate a good word embedding. IEEE Intell. Syst. **31**(6), 5–14 (2016)
11. Lecun, Y., Bottou, L., Bengio, Y., et al.: Gradient-based learning applied to document recognition. Proc. IEEE **86**(11), 2278–2324 (1998)
12. Cai, S., Wang, P., Yang, Y., et al.: Review on augmented reality in education. China Remote Educ. Mag. **27**, 27–40 (2016)
13. Liang, G., Wellers, R., Zhao, J., et al.: The 2015 ukraine blackout: Implications for false data injection attacks. IEEE Trans. Power Syst. **32**(4), 3317–3318 (2017)
14. Dash, S., Reddy, K., Pujari, A.: Adaptive Naive Bayes method for masquerade detection. Secur. Commun. Netw. **4**(4), 410–417 (2011)
15. Wang, C., Zou, X.: A data cleaning model for electric power big data based on Spark framework. Electric. Measure. Instrum. **54**(14), 33–38 (2017)
16. Zhao, Y., Huang, J., Li, P.: Fault diagnosis on transformer based on weighted fuzzy C-means clustering algorithm. Shaanxi Electric Power **39**(9), 39–41 (2011)
17. Meng, R., Rice, S., Wang, J., Sun, X.: A fusion steganographic algorithm based on faster R-CNN. Comput. Mater. Continua **55**(1), 001–016 (2018)

18. Xiong, Z., Shen, Q., Wang, Y., Zhu, C.: Paragraph vector representation based on word to vector and CNN learning. Comput. Mater. Continua **055**(2), 213–227 (2018)
19. Kim, Y.: Convolutional neural networks for sentence classification. In: 2014 Conference on Empirical Methods in Natural Language Processing (EMNLP 2014), pp. 1746–1751, Doha (2014)

Research on Artificial Intelligence Technology in Computer Network Technology

Tingting Yang[1(⊠)] and Shuwen Jia[2]

[1] Institute of Information and Intelligence Engineering, University of Sanya,
Sanya, Hainan, China
yttl202@126.com
[2] Teaching Management Office, University of Sanya, Sanya, Hainan, China

Abstract. In recent years, with the rapid development of computer technology and economy in China, artificial intelligence has gradually become the new focus of the development of times, which promotes people's quality of life and the continuous progress of science and technology. Computer network technology and artificial intelligence share mutual benefit and common development which brings new growth points to people's life and social development. This paper analyzes the significance and difficulties of the research on artificial intelligence in computer network technology and studies its application.

Keywords: Computer · Network technology · Artificial intelligence

1 Introduction

With the improvement of computer network technology, artificial intelligence has become the most important technology development in the 21st century. China's economic development has laid a good foundation for the advancement of computer network technology, and the development of artificial intelligence has gradually become the focus of computer network technology. Artificial intelligence is an important technology that provides convenience for people's lives and production, replacing people's complex and tedious jobs, completing more complex content, improving people's quality of life, and laying a good foundation for the future development of science and technology in China.

2 Research on Artificial Intelligence Technology in Computer Network Technology

In recent years, artificial intelligence has been deeply and extensively developed in computer network technology. Computer networks have developed rapidly and become an important basis for artificial intelligence research, promoting the cross-development of artificial intelligence and various disciplines. Foreign research on artificial intelligence put forward the term Artificial Intelligence as early as the 1960s and gradually began to develop. The research of artificial intelligence in China started relatively late, but in the course of the vigorous development of computer networks in China, artificial

© Springer Nature Switzerland AG 2019
X. Sun et al. (Eds.): ICAIS 2019, LNCS 11632, pp. 488–496, 2019.
https://doi.org/10.1007/978-3-030-24274-9_44

intelligence has become an important part of the national plan. We have re-examined computer network technology, and the application of artificial intelligence theory and technology which influence scientific and technological development, as well as promote the application of science and technology in various fields such as finance, medical care, and education. Artificial intelligence is mainly based on human intelligence to complete its tasks. It cannot be separated from electronics, mathematics, and psychology. It also has a wide range of applications in finance, medicine, services, culture, tourism, and other industries. To achieve artificial control, enhance the rigid setting of parameters in traditional computer network technology, realize artificial control in psychology and cognition, enhance the self-consciousness of artificial intelligence, and be able to identify and apply them sensitively, artificial intelligence technology cannot be separated from the application of widespread computer network. It has freed people from the traditional practice of simple repetitive work to provide stable high-tech identification and application, so that the society and people's production and life can achieve intelligent development, improve production and management efficiency, promote the improvement of people's living standards and quality of life and enhance computer network technology further develop to new intelligence.

3 Problems in Research on Artificial Intelligence Technology in Computer Network Technology

The research and development of artificial intelligence technology is faced with many problems. There are many loopholes and deficiencies in computer and network technology. The hardware, firmware and software of the computer itself are insufficient, the connectivity of each system in the construction process is not high, and the system vulnerability is large, which brings bottleneck problems for practical application. Computer network technology is faced with threats such as viruses and hackers. It urgently improves network security and reliability, which will affect the development of artificial intelligence, and lag behind the development of intelligence.

3.1 Problems in Computer Technology

Computer technology has been gradually improving, but due to the uneven development of hardware and software, it has an impact on system storage and operation which influences the operation and development of artificial intelligence technology directly. Computer technology can dynamically share physical resources and resource pools, which leads to realization of the efficient use of resources, application of virtualization technology, and achievement of reduction of management costs by reducing the number of physical resources. Artificial intelligence technology needs the reliability and security of computers. The efficiency and performance of computer systems have gradually improved, and they can further carry out controllable security access and mission accomplishment, multilevel control, and achieve dual data isolation and service requirements. However, there are still insufficient security and limited reliability in in-depth management and limited reliability which will Influence the advancement and impact of computer technology. The combination of hardware, firmware, and software in computer technology is not close enough, and it is easy to cause insufficient throughput and analytical aging ability. At the same time, the shortage of relevant professionals and the bottleneck of technology improvement also affect computer technology. The problem of computer technology itself has become the further development of artificial intelligence technology.

3.2 Problems in Network Technology

Computer network technology is the product of the combination of communication technology and computer technology. It is a new leap in the development of science and technology. It connects and assembles independent and decentralized computers through network protocols, realizes information and resource sharing, and can make people enjoy the convenience brought by information transmission. Connecting media are mainly cables, optical fibers, and communication satellites, which enable the realization of centralized processing, maintenance, and management of data, as well as the conversion and exchange of information, and technology services of modern science. However, the depth and breadth of attacks by viruses and hackers on computer networks have gradually increased. The theft and destruction of information, and even the emergence of systems and networks, have caused serious deficiencies in safety and reliability. At the same time, due to the rapid development of hackers and viruses in recent years, the scope of destruction and capabilities has expanded, bringing serious implications to the development of artificial intelligence. Local area networks (LAN), wide area networks (WAN), public and private network information and resource control are not available. The relevant management level technology and level are limited, and the use of unreasonable network security and service impact has brought about considerable difficulties for the development of artificial intelligence. The limited use of communication channels in computer network technology, as well as the sharing and openness of the Internet, have many impacts on the security of the network. There are many security blank points, which have a deeper impact on computer network security.

4   Application of Artificial Intelligence Technology in Computer Network Technology

Artificial intelligence technology in computer network technology has gradually become an important direction for the future development of many industries and technologies. The field of artificial intelligence is gradually deepening, and the further development of artificial intelligence is realized through the current extensive and continuous improvement of computer network technology. Computer and network technology has different degrees of loopholes and deficiencies, and it is necessary for professionals and talents in various fields to continuously exploit their potential, give full play to their advantages, and realize the intelligent development of science and technology. China has a clear plan for the development of artificial intelligence technology. At the same time, it is necessary to increase investment in it and promote the construction of new industries, increase the training and application of talents in related fields, improve the scope of intelligent use, and realize the construction of artificial intelligence security systems. It is necessary to lay a good foundation for the intelligent development of robots.

In computer network security management system, the application of artificial intelligence is mainly embodied in intrusion detection intelligent firewall technology, data mining data fusion, artificial immunity and intelligent anti-spam. Intrusion detection technology and intelligent firewall technology are the core technology of artificial intelligence, and also an important part of computer network security. They intercepted irrelevant information in the network and prevent foreign intrusion, thus ensuring a safer and more reliable transmission of network resources and data. The application of data mining greatly improved the detection efficiency of network intrusion detection. Data fusion connected multiple sensors in the network, so that each sensor can work on its full capacity to ensure the security of the network and enhance the effectiveness and security of intrusion detection. Artificial immune technology assisted the recombination and mutation patterns of gene fragments to better identify invasive viruses, thus better prevent the invasion of viruses. Intelligent spam sending system identified and shielded spam on the network, and reduces the interference of mailboxes from spam.

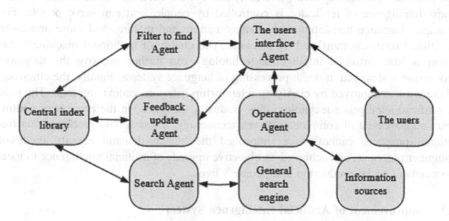

Fig. 1. Intrusion detection intelligent firewall technology

In computer network management system, the application of artificial intelligence is mainly embodied in the application of expert system database, artificial intelligence problem solving and agent technology (see Fig. 1). The comprehensive integration of expert database technology and artificial intelligence can make up for the shortcomings of traditional database technology in data processing and the weakness of artificial intelligence in logical reasoning and knowledge processing, thus greatly improving the efficiency. Artificial intelligence solutions have changed the way of answering, which was rather tedious in the past. By a very simple instruction, the computer can screen the information in the network, and automatically judge, filter, process and optimize the search information, and then find the best information, which greatly shorten the time of information searching and improve the utilization of network resources.

4.1 Expanding the Field of Artificial Intelligence Applications

With the continuous popularization and development of computer network technology, the Internet has developed rapidly around the world, enabling various countries and various fields of resources to share and transmit, reducing the management and physical costs of production and life, and continuously promoting the rapid development of human science and technology. In recent years, computer network technology has become stable. Artificial intelligence has become the main direction of development, and its application is faster and more efficient than the popularity of computer networks, becoming an indispensable requirement for social development and people's lives. Finance, medical care, education and other industries have also developed rapidly. For example, the rapid development of artificial intelligence in Alibaba enterprises. Many aspects of artificial intelligence services are realized, such as online payment, consultation and feedback information collection, which see the rapid development of artificial intelligence in China. The application field of artificial intelligence technology is also expanding rapidly at geometric speed, and it gradually penetrates into many fields and becomes an important direction for future service and development. Artificial intelligence technology can realize the interaction between computer and network systems, and carry out system environment and other interactions. Intelligence of replicator is controlled by people, and can serve people. For example, language translation is becoming mature and mature, and more and more traditional corpus is translated by machine. The quality of traditional machine translation is low. Artificial intelligence technology can further improve the language processing system and in-depth processing of language systems. Finally, the efficiency of the work is improved by clarifying relationship between context and tone. The field of artificial intelligence technology has gradually increased. In the process of continuous improvement of computer network technology, it has solved problems that traditional programs cannot solve, improved the human demand activity mode of computer programs, and achieved an objective upgrade of artificial intelligence to meet the needs of social production and people's lives.

4.2 Improvement of Artificial Intelligence System

In 2017, China issued Three-Year Action Plan for the Development of a New Generation of Artificial Intelligence Industry (2018–2020), striving to achieve a series of important breakthroughs in artificial intelligence iconic products by 2020. This shows the determination and planning direction of China's artificial intelligence system construction and development. Artificial intelligence technology in computer network technology is an important basis for promoting a new round of scientific and technological revolution and industrial transformation. It will promote technological progress in many industries and create important prerequisites for emerging industries. Artificial intelligence technology in computer network technology will be integrated into the manufacturing industry and public service systems, and the development of artificial intelligence industry will be realized, and the transformation and upgrading of the national and social industries will be achieved by using high-end smart products. Artificial intelligence in computer network technology is the key to realizing open sharing of resources and services, as well as the basis for resource exchange and development. Since the 20th century, computer network technology has developed rapidly and integrated into all walks of life in the world. With the application of artificial intelligence, we will speed up the development of industrialization and the deployment of systems to realize information exchange and development in manufacturing industries, finance, medical care, culture, transportation, agriculture, tourism and other industries, so as to increase productivity. The improvement of the overall structure and efficiency of the industry provide a reliable guarantee. By improving the construction of artificial intelligence systems in computer network technology, we will increase the application of video, language, and translation technologies, improve service capabilities, and meet the needs of smart Internet, smart service robots, smart drones, and medical impact assisted diagnosis. The complex understanding of the environment is further analyzed and applied, and the application of artificial intelligence technology such as human-computer interaction can be realized. It can develop the needs of the global intelligent model with large-scale and personalized development.

4.3   Application of Artificial Intelligence Network Security

The safety problem in computer network technology is always the industry's criticism. Artificial intelligence network security application is the key to promote intelligent development. With the popularization and upgrading of computer and network technology, the two major problems of hackers and viruses have become important factors that threaten network security. This problem in the development of artificial intelligence is also a bottleneck for the industry. The development and application of artificial intelligence network security and the management of computer network security is the key to network reliability. It improves its own risk management and makes reasonable judgments on viruses and hacker attacks through the application of artificial intelligence to the management of computer networks (see Fig. 2).

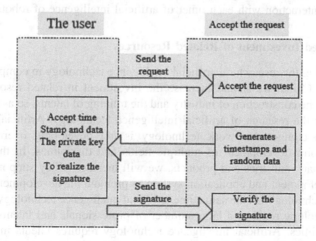

Fig. 2. Intrusion detection intelligent firewall technology

It is necessary to analyze and manage each element reasonably, and deal with the problem of harm to network health quickly, improve computer network security and reliability, and provide reliable help for the further development of artificial intelligence. Fuzzy and massive data are processed by analyzing the large data of artificial intelligence. Different types and forms of party data are classified and screened, and threats to network security are identified in a timely manner, and the efficiency and degree of automation of security monitoring are improved. The analysis, classification and fusion of the security relevance in the computer network system are necessary. Different means are taken to deal with security threats by using reasonable and sophisticated security analysis of a large number of data, a further assessment of the security situation of the network. The important network security application of artificial intelligence is mainly its own learning ability. The automation and learning ability of artificial intelligence is an important channel to deal with network threats. Security threats such as the monitoring of network security intrusion and the detection of malicious software form intelligent security protection strategies, which can actively carry out security defenses, and ensure the application of artificial intelligence technology in computer network technology.

4.4 Improved Intelligentization of Robots

With the continuous development of computer network technology in China, the ability of intelligent robots through artificial intelligence has also been continuously improved. In the important direction of scientific and technological development, the research on intelligent robots has gradually deepened, and the application of artificial intelligence to key technologies such as human-computer information exchange, operation, and writing has been adopted to realize the innovative application of public service, fire protection, medical treatment and other multi-industry systems. It can achieve high-precision and low-cost core infrastructure construction, improve the intelligence ability of robots, improve the application of artificial intelligence, and consolidate the development of the industry through the environmental perception, independent learning and interaction with each other of artificial intelligence of robots.

4.5 Increased Investment of Related Resources

While increasing the research on artificial intelligence technology in computer network technology in China, we should increase the investment in related resources; attach importance to the construction of industry and the training of talents, so as to lay a good foundation for the research of artificial intelligence technology. Artificial intelligence technology in computer network technology is not developing overnight, and it requires the joint development of multiple fields and disciplines. In the process of developing smart industries and products, we will increase policy support and form a complete development and application system to promote the development of artificial intelligence technology. At the same time, artificial intelligence technology in computer network technology requires a large number of professionals and talents with higher related capabilities. Artificial intelligence technology requires talents in many disciplines such as psychology and mathematics to advance together. In the process of application, high quality personnel are also needed for maintenance and information feedback to promote the continuous improvement and development of artificial intelligence technology. We will promote artificial intelligence products and industries through new materials, new processes and new design inputs to consolidate the hardware and software base, actively implement software application layouts, support the construction of open platforms, and comprehensively promote the research, development and application of artificial intelligence technologies in computer network technology. We will deepen the adjustment of China's industrial structure and promote the further development of China's economy and science and technology.

5   Conclusion

To sum up, the research on artificial intelligence technology in computer network technology is the most important issue in the development of our economy and science and technology. We are to solve the shortage of computer and network technology and improve the level of research and development and application of artificial intelligence technology. We shall expand the use of artificial intelligence, improve the construction of artificial intelligence systems, and promote the intelligent development of robots. We are to increase government investment in artificial intelligence, attach importance to supporting emerging industries, and promote new technologies and materials. We shall establish an information exchange platform for artificial intelligence and attach importance to the training of relevant personnel in multiple fields. The purpose of all the efforts is to realize the further adjustment of China's industrial structure and economic leapfrog development.

Acknowledgement. This work is supported by Hainan Provincial Natural Science Foundation of China (project number: 20166235), project supported by the Education Department of Hainan Province (project number: Hnky2017-57).

References

1. Quan, H.: Application and exploration of artificial intelligence in computer network technology. South. Agric. Mach. **49**(17), 43+47 (2008)
2. Zhaotong, Ma.: Analysis of the application of artificial intelligence in computer network technology. Comput. Fan **10**, 3 (2018)
3. Huchao, Z.: Practical analysis of the artificial intelligence in computer network technology. Comput. Fan **10**, 16–17 (2018)
4. Caihong, L., Huifang, W.: Artificial intelligence technology and its application in computer network. Sci. Technol. Innov. **25**, 74–75 (2018)
5. Cheng, J., Ruomeng, X., Tang, X., Sheng, V.S., Cai, C.: An abnormal network flow feature sequence prediction approach for DDoS attacks detection in big data environment. CMC Comput. Mater. Continua **55**(1), 095–119 (2018)
6. Hinton, G.E., Srivastava, N., Krizhevsky, A., et al.: Improving neural networks by preventing co- adaptation of feature detectors. Comput. Sci. **3**(4), 212–223 (2012)

 7. Le Cun, Y., Huang, F.J., Bottou, L.: Learning methods for generic object recognition with invariance to pose and lighting. In: Proceedings of the 2004 IEEE Computer Society Conference on Computer Vision and Pattern Recognition (CVPR 2004) (2004)
 8. Girshick, R., Donahue, J., Darrell, T., et al.: Rich feature hierarchies for accurate object detection and semantic segmentation. In: Proceedings of the IEEE Conference on Computer Vision and Pattern Recognition, pp. 580–587 (2014)
 9. Simonyan, K., Zisserman, A.: Very deep convolutional networks for large-scale image recognition. In: Proceedings of ICLR 2015 (2015)
10. Mensink, T., Verbeek, J., Perronnin, F., Csurka, G.: Metric learning for large scale image classification: generalizing to new classes at near-zero cost. In: Fitzgibbon, A., Lazebnik, S., Perona, P., Sato, Y., Schmid, C. (eds.) ECCV 2012. LNCS, pp. 488–501. Springer, Heidelberg (2012). https://doi.org/10.1007/978-3-642-33709-3_35
11. Russell, B.C., Torralba, A., Murphy, K.P., Freeman, W.T.: LabelMe: a database and web-based tool for image annotation. Int. J. Comput. Vision 77(1), 157–173 (2008)
12. Nair, V., Hinton, G.E.: Rectified linear units improve restricted Boltzmann machines. In: Proceedings of 27th International Conference on Machine Learning (2010)
13. LeCun, Y., Huang, F.J., Bottou, L.: Learning methods for generic object recognition with invariance to pose and lighting. In: Computer Vision and Pattern Recognition (CVPR 2004) (2004)
14. Endres, I., Hoiem, D.: Category independent object proposals. In: Daniilidis, K., Maragos, P., Paragios, N. (eds.) ECCV 2010. LNCS, vol. 6315, pp. 575–588. Springer, Heidelberg (2010). https://doi.org/10.1007/978-3-642-15555-0_42
15. Wang, X., Yang, M., Zhu, S., Lin, Y.: Regionlets for generic object detection. IEEE Trans. Pattern Anal. Mach. Intell. 37(10), 2071–2084 (2015)
16. Zeiler, M., Taylor, G., Fergus, R.: Adaptive deconvolutional networks for mid and high level feature learning. In: Computer Vision and Pattern Recognition (CVPR 2011) (2011)
17. Howard, A.G.: Some improvements on deep convolutional neural network based image classification. In: Proceedings of ICLR 2014 (2014)
18. Perronnin, F., Sánchez, J., Mensink, T.: Improving the fisher kernel for large-scale image classification. In: Daniilidis, K., Maragos, P., Paragios, N. (eds.) ECCV 2010. LNCS, vol. 6314, pp. 143–156. Springer, Heidelberg (2010). https://doi.org/10.1007/978-3-642-15561-1_11
19. Fei-Fei, L., Fergus, R., Perona, P.: Learning generative visual models from few training examples: an incremental bayesian approach tested on 101 object categories. Comput. Vis. Image Underst. 106(1), 178–187 (2007)
20. Fang, S., et al.: Feature selection method based on class discriminative degree for intelligent medical diagnosis. CMC Comput. Mater. Continua 55(3), 419–433 (2018)

Research on Detection Method of Unhealthy Message in Social Network

Yabin Xu[1,2]([✉]), Yongqing Jiao[2], Shujuan Chen[2], and Yangyang Li[3]

[1] Beijing Key Laboratory of Internet Culture and Digital Dissemination
Research, Beijing, China
[2] Beijing Information Science and Technology University,
Beijing 100101, China
xyb@bistu.edu.cn
[3] China Academy of Electronics and Information Technology,
Beijing 100041, China

Abstract. In order to avoid the release and dissemination of eroticism, gamble, drug and politically sensitive message in social network, and purify the network space, we propose a method to detect unhealthy message in social network. Firstly, the Naive Bayes model is used to classify the message released by the social network. Then, according to the features of all kinds of unhealthy message, the classification model of Support Vector Machine (SVM) is used to make further judgment. The comparative experiment results show that, the classification model of SVM has better precognitive effect than that of Naive Bayes and Decision Tree.

Keywords: Social network · Unhealthy message detection · Naive Bayes · Support vector machine

1 Introduction

With the emergent and rapid development of social network, people can communicate and comment without geographical constraints, conveniently and fast. According to the 39th China Internet Development Statistics Report, as of December 2016, the usage rate of WeChat friends circle and Weibo were respectively 85.8% and 37.1%.

Due to the features of convenience and fast and wide spread, the social network has become a tool for criminals to disseminate unhealthy messages about eroticism, gamble, drug and also politically sensitive message through social network. The spread of unhealthy message not only endanger the physical and mental health of Internet users, especially young people [1], but also impact the security and stability of a country. So, curbing the release and dissemination of unhealthy and sensitive message in social networks have become the extremely urgent problem which needs to be solved.

Therefore, how to quickly and efficiently detect the unhealthy message in social network can not only protect the users from the effect of unhealthy message, but also promote the healthy development of social network effectively. But the solving method is still a combination of artificial and mechanical identification, which is mainly

© Springer Nature Switzerland AG 2019
X. Sun et al. (Eds.): ICAIS 2019, LNCS 11632, pp. 497–508, 2019.
https://doi.org/10.1007/978-3-030-24274-9_45

because the effect of mechanical identification is limited. Therefore, to improve the accuracy and efficiency of machine identification has a huge development space.

2 Related Work

At present, the major social network platforms take measure of matching sensitive words as the basic means to detect unhealthy messages. However, the unhealthy message releasers will deform the sensitive words to avoid being detected. Therefore, the detection of pornographic, gamble, drugs and even politically sensitive content in social network only by detecting sensitive words is not enough.

Cohen [2] proposed a rule learning method for mail classification. He analyzed the particularity of e-mail messages and presented a new approach to learning sensitive words based on RIPER rules. Salvador Nieto Sanchez et al. of Louisiana State University use the OCAT mining algorithm for text classification [3]. This method uses the Boolean model to break down the text and ignores the weight of the word.

Wang [4] and others proposed a Naive Bayesian classification model based on five kinds of detection feature. But most features do not have robustness. Zhang [5] firstly used the regular expression to deal with special words or symbols, and then constructed a filtration model of unhealthy text in virtual community by using the algorithm of Bayesian and support vector machine. Fang [6] employed a multi-label classification framework and the method have better accuracy and lower FNR. Xiao [7] proposed a SMK-means which is achieved by Mini Batch K-means based on simulated annealing algorithm for anomalous detection of abnormal information.

Zhu [8] researched text filtration method based on synonym extension, and found synonyms through thesauruses and Internet mining for query expansion. Zhou [9] extracted the set of positive and negative features that can represent the content of the positive and negative text, and designed a new text weight calculation method.

Jinghong [10] analyzed the problem of pornographic message in social network. Huiyu [11] used a new neural network algorithm to design a real-time monitoring prototype system for unhealthy messages. Shao [12] proposed a kind of information filtration method based on semantic association. By calculating the relevant degree of meaning between the text and unhealthy semantic factors, which effectively overcome the drawbacks of traditional methods.

Meng [13] analyzed the application of semantic analysis technology in the field of counter-terrorism and showed the importance of semantics for sensitive content analysis. Liu et al. [14] adopted a sensitive content filtering approach based on a two-stage filtering model (topic information filtering and propensity filtering). In recent years, with the development of deep learning, Neerbeky [15] used recurrent neural networks to assign sensitivity scores to the semantic components of the sentence structure, enabling interactive detection of sensitive information.

From the above research, it can be seen that the current academic circles have carried out a number of research on the detection of unhealthy message on Internet, but the research on the detection of unhealthy message on social network is numbered. In addition, because the social network has their own characteristics, such as short text and colloquial. The detection method is different from the web page with the characteristics of long text, logical, written language, thus the method is more difficult.

In this paper, the method of identifying unhealthy message in social network is as follows. In the first step, we should preprocess the data by the methods of word segmentation, disambiguation, dereference, and so on, we use the Naive Bayesian method to classify the message of social network into four categories which is highly related to eroticism, gamble, drug and politically sensitive and other categories. We only care about the first four categories. In the second step, based on the feature extraction from unhealthy message in each category, the support vector machine (SVM) model determines if it is unhealthy message. If a certain type of unhealthy message is determined, the release of the message is rejected.

3 Classification of Released Message

This paper uses the naive Bayes method to classify the released content. The method is efficient, accurate and easy to implement [16]. The specific processing is as follows:

$C = \{c_1, c_2, \ldots, c_5\}$ denotes the collection of categories, $c_1 \sim c_4$ respectively stand eroticism, gamble, drug and politically sensitive categories, c_5 represents other categories. Each released content is represented by vector $d = \{t_1, t_2, \ldots, t_n\}$. We use D to denote the example set that contains all released contents, so the relationship is $d \in D$.

$p(c_i|d)$ represents the probability that the released content d belongs to category c_i. If the probability value of $p(c_i|d)$ is bigger, the released content is more likely belongs to the category c_i. According to Bayes formula, the probability that released content d belonging to category c_i is:

$$p(c_i|d) = \frac{p(d|c_i)p(c_i)}{p(d)} = \frac{p(d|c_i)p(c_i)}{\sum_{j=1}^{5} p(d|c_j)p(c_j)} \tag{1}$$

$P(c_i)$ is the probability that the category of released content is c_i. We suppose that $|D_c|$ is the number of all released contents, and $|D_{c_i}|$ is the number of the released content of category c_i. So we can get the following equation.

$$p(c_i) = \frac{1 + |D_{c_i}|}{|C| + |D_c|} \tag{2}$$

$p(d|c_i)$ can be calculated by formula (3):

$$p(d|c_i) = p((t_1, t_2, \ldots, t_n)|c_i) = \prod_{j=1}^{n} p(t_j|c_i) \tag{3}$$

Among them, $p(t_j|c_i)$ indicates the probability of occurrence of the word t_j in category c_i. According to the Multi-variable Bernoulli Model, among $d = \{t_1, t_2, \ldots, t_n\}$, $t_k \in (0, 1)$, $1 \leq k \leq n$, $t_k = 0$ means that t_k does not appear in the vector d. $t_k = 1$ means that t_k appears in the vector d. $|D_{c_{ik}}|$ denotes the number of released content that contains the word t_k and belongs to category c_i. In order to prevent the occurrence of zero probability, we can add a smoothing factor:

$$p_{ik} = p(t_k = 1|c_i) = \frac{|D_{c_{ik}}| + 1}{|D_{c_i}| + 2} \tag{4}$$

So we can get the following equation:

$$p(t_k|c_i) = p_{ik}^{t_k}(1 - p_{ik})^{1-t_k} = \left(\frac{p_{ik}}{1 - p_{ik}}\right)^{t_k}(1 - p_{ik}) \tag{5}$$

According to the formula (2)–(6), we can get the following

$$
\begin{aligned}
\hat{c}(d) &= \arg\max_{c_i \in C}\left\{p(c_i) \times \prod_{k=1}^{n}\left(\frac{p_{ik}}{1 - p_{ik}}\right)^{t_k}(1 - p_{ik})\right\} \\
&= \arg\max_{c_i \in C}\left\{\log\left(\frac{1 + |D_{c_i}|}{|C| + |D_c|}\right) + \sum_{k=1}^{n}\log(1 - p_{ik}) + \sum_{k=1}^{n}t_k \times \log\left(\frac{p_{ik}}{1 - p_{ik}}\right)\right\}
\end{aligned}
\tag{6}
$$

From Eq. (6), it can be seen that the words with $t_k = 1$ play a role in the classification. In other words, we can get the category c_i from the released content d, by seeking i to make the value of $\hat{c}(d)$ maximum.

The steps of content classification are as follows:

(1) We first take a piece of data from Content Category table, segment words, remove stop words, so we obtain $d = \{t_1, t_2, \ldots, t_k, \ldots, t_n\}$. Then we write $(t_k,$ Count, Category, Privacy Category) in the Word Category table, where the initial value of Count is 1. If $(t_k,$ Category, Privacy Category) is already in Word Category table, then we plus 1;
(2) We add the count of the corresponding category in the Category Table with 1;
(3) Repeat step (1), (2);
(4) Take a piece of data from the example set, preprocess and remove stop words and repeat words, so $d = \{t_1, t_2, \ldots, t_k, \ldots, t_n\}$. is obtained;
(5) Calculate the value of (2), (4), (6), and get i which makes $\hat{c}(d)$ maximum. Then c_i is the category of released content d.

4   Feature Recognition of Unhealthy Message

In this paper, after classifying all the content from the data set, we give a detailed feature identification process by taking pornographic category as an example.

4.1 Camouflage Feature Recognition of Sensitive Words

To avoid sensitive words being detected, most of the words in unhealthy message are disguised with the following characteristics. We need to adopt the corresponding processing method respectively:

(1) Recognition method of sensitive words with special symbols.

In unhealthy messages, criminals often separate sensitive words with special symbols to outsmart the detection. In order to determine the legitimacy of released messages, we can adopt the method of regular expression to match special symbols such as "*", "&" and others and remove them. Then we restore the sensitive words into the state of the normal combination. For example: for "practice 法*轮*功, you can keep fit", we use regular expressions to identify "*" and delete it. Then, we can get the sensitive word "法轮功" without word segmentation.

(2) Recognition method of sensitive words with pinyin instead of word.

In the released text with unhealthy content, sensitive words are often partly replaced by phonetic symbols, such as: "法lun功". For this case, literature [17] proposed a method to find the most similar word which can combine with adjacent words and establish a comparison table of phonetic alphabet and word. We accumulate the number of occurrence of the word in the text in order to count the frequency of sensitive words in documents. The words can be quickly matched with a phonetic alphabet. Therefore, we use this method to identify sensitive word in the pinyin instead of the word.

(3) Sensitive word recognition method of components.

Criminals often split words in sensitive words to avoid detection. For example, the "轮" in "法轮功" is splited into "车仑" to avoid detection. The literature [18] proposed a method, in which we firstly find components of Chinese characters appeared in released content, and judge whether the word adjacent to the right is a component of Chinese characters. If the word exists in the dictionary, the ability of combining the word with its adjacent word to form a sensitive word is found by using the word segmentation algorithm. If the word doesn't exist in the dictionary, we go to identify the next word. This article learn from this method.

4.2 Similarity Feature Recognition of Released Message

Unhealthy messages transmitted through such social network may be overwritten in a short period of time. They repeatedly release unhealthy message at different time to ensure that unhealthy messages are disseminated. So, we can take the mean of similarity of messages released by user as a feature of the unhealthy message.

We firstly delete url (links), @ (symbols), emotion faces, etc. Next, we segment words and remove the stop word. Finally, we calculate the similarity of released messages of a particular user in adjacent time, according to the TF-IDF algorithm and the cosine similarity. So we can take the mean of similarity value of all released content as a feature of unhealthy messages.

In the TF-IDF method, the term frequency (tf) refers to the frequency that a word appears in a given released message:

$$tf_{i,j} = \frac{n_{i,j}}{\sum_{k=1}^{k=m} n_{k,j}} \tag{7}$$

In Eq. (7), $n_{i,j}$ indicates the number of times word t_i appears in the released message d_j.

The inverse document frequency (idf) refers to the universal importance of a word, that is, the idf of a particular word is obtained through dividing the number of released messages by the number of released messages containing the word:

$$idf_i = log \frac{|D|}{1 + |\{j : t_i \in d_j\}|} \tag{8}$$

In Eq. (8), $|D|$ indicates the total number of released message, $|\{j{:}t_i \in d_j\}|$ indicates the number of released messages containing the word t_i.

The $tfidf_{i,j} = tf_{i,j} \times idf_i$ value of each feature word in the released message is used as the weight of the word $w_{i,j}$ to construct the vector space model, the j-th released message d_j is expressed as: $d_j = \{w_{1,j}; w_{2,j}; \ldots, w_{n,j}\}$.

In the vector space model, the cosine of the angle between the vectors is used to represent the message similarity of the two texts:

$$sim(d_i, d_j) = cos\theta = \frac{\sum_{k=1}^{n} w_{k,i} \times w_{k,j}}{\sqrt{\left(\sum_{k=1}^{n} w_{k,i}^2\right)\left(\sum_{k=1}^{n} w_{k,j}^2\right)}} \tag{9}$$

Then, we take the average value of similarity as the similarity of user release message:

$$Avg_{sim} = \frac{\sum_{i=1}^{n-1} sim(d_i, d_{i+1})}{total_{content} - 1} \tag{10}$$

4.3   Content Feature Recognition of Unhealthy Message

The Proportion of URL Links in Released Message. The outlaws usually release eye-catching keywords, add links to arouse the curiosity of ordinary users, and entice users to click the link so as to disseminate unhealthy messages. Therefore, the ratio of url link can also be used as one of the features of unhealthy messages.

We use U to indicate the percentage of the released messages containing url links to the total number of messages released by users.

The Proportion of Hot Topics in Released Messages. Lawless people always make use of some current hot topics of the time, and add some hot topics to their unhealthy message. This article uses H to represent the proportion of released messages containing hot topics to the total number of released messages.

The Number of @ in Released Messages. Lawless people often use this method of @ to push unhealthy messages directly to the concerned users. In this paper, we use M to express the mean of each released message included symbol @.

The Proportion of Picture Included in Released Messages. Criminals use very eye-catching pictures to attract normal users to click and link to an unhealthy information page. In this paper, we use P to indicate the mean of the picture number included in each message.

4.4   Feature Recognition of Unhealthy Message Releaser

Concern Degree of Unhealthy Message. The fan number of lawless people is usually less, and the concern degree tends to be low because the content is often involved in unhealthy message. In this paper, we use A to express the attention degree, that is, the proportion of the number of messages concerned by their fans to the total number of messages released by the user.

The Ratio of Numbers of Concerned Users to the Numbers of Followers. As garbage users often release unhealthy message, the number of fans is poor. But garbage users will concern a large number of users in order to achieve the purpose of expanding the scope of unhealthy messages. Therefore, the number of span users watching is far greater than the number of followers. In this paper, we use F to indicate the proportion of the number of concerned users to the number of fans.

5   Determination of Each Class of Unhealthy Message

In this paper, we need to identify the characteristics of the bad information in the four types of information to further determine whether it is bad information. We only take the eroticism class as example. According to the features determined in Sect. 4, we determine whether the content about pornographic is unhealthy message by using the support vector machine model.

According to the need of classification, this paper takes the classification of two kinds of data as an example. Given the training set $(\mathbf{x_i}, y_i), i = 1, 2, \ldots, l, \mathbf{x_i} \in R^n, \mathbf{x_i}$ represents the characteristic vector of the first i sample; $y \in \{\pm 1\}$, represents the category of the i-th sample hyperplane: $(\mathbf{w} \cdot \mathbf{x}) + b = 0$. In order to classify all samples in the data set correctly and possess the classification interval, it is necessary to satisfy the constraints: $y_i[(\mathbf{w} \cdot \mathbf{x_i}) + b] \geq 1, i = 1, 2, \ldots, l$. Classification interval is $2/\|\mathbf{w}\|$. So, the problem of constructing the optimal hyperplane is converted to the constraint condition (11):

$$min\emptyset(w) = \frac{1}{2}\|w\|^2 = \frac{1}{2}(w' \cdot w) \tag{11}$$

We introduce the Lagrange function to solve the constrained optimization problem. The problem of constrained optimization is determined by the saddle point of the Lagrange function, and the solution of the optimization problem is that the bias of the w and b at the saddle point is equal to 0. Therefore, we transform QP (quadratic programming) problem into following dual problem:

$$maxQ(a) = \sum_{j=1}^{l} a_j - \frac{1}{2}\sum_{i=1}^{l}\sum_{j=1}^{l} a_i a_j y_i y_j (x_i \cdot x_j) \qquad s.t. \sum_{j=1}^{l} a_j y_j = 0, \qquad (12)$$
$$a_j \geq 0, j = 1,2,\ldots,l.$$

The optimal solution can be obtained as: $\mathbf{a}^* = \left(a_1^*, a_2^*, \ldots, a_l^*\right)^{\mathrm{T}}$.
The optimal weight vector w^* and the optimal bias b^* are:

$$w^* = \sum_{j=1}^{l} a_j^* y_j x_j \qquad b^* = y_i - \sum_{j=1}^{l} y_j a_j^* (x_j \cdot x_i) \qquad (13)$$

In the above formula, the subscript $j \in \left\{j | a_j^* > 0\right\}$, we can get the optimal classification hyperplane $(\mathbf{w}^* \cdot \mathbf{x}) + b^* = 0$, and the optimal classification function is:

$$f(x) = sgn\{(w^* \cdot x) + b^*\} = sgn\left\{\left\{\sum_{j=1}^{l} a_j^* y_j (x_j \cdot x_i)\right\} + b^*\right\}, x \in R^n \qquad (14)$$

The goal of training based on SVM is to obtain the classification surface that optimizes the structural risk. The training process is as follows (12) ~ (14).

6   Experiment

6.1   Data Set and Data Preprocessing

The data set used in this paper is Datatang. The data set consists of user table and Weibo table. The preprocessing of the data set is as follows: Firstly, we carry on the Chinese word segmentation, delete stop word and other processing on content field of Weibo Table. Finally, we obtain a total of 8283398 experimental data of 1017553 users. In this paper, we sort them out manually that stop word dictionary containing 1893 stop words, the unhealthy dictionary containing 317 words and the health feature dictionary containing 523 words.

6.2   Evaluation Indicator

In this paper, bi represents unhealthy message, N_{bi} represents the number of unhealthy message bi, $\overline{bi}$ represents non-unhealthy message, which is normal message, $N_{bi \rightarrow bi}$ represents the number of unhealthy message bi correctly detected, $N_{bi \rightarrow \overline{bi}}$ represents the number of unhealthy message bi improperly detected, $N_{\overline{bi} \to bi}$ represents the number of error that $\overline{bi}$ is classified as bi, $N_{\overline{bi} \to \overline{bi}}$ represents the number of $\overline{bi}$ that is correctly detected. In this paper, the detection effect is measured by the recall rate, precision and comprehensive index F-Measure [19]. The three indicators are defined as follows (Table 1):

Table 1. Calculation method of each index.

Recall rate	Precision rate	F-Measure
$R = \dfrac{N_{bi \to bi}}{N_{bi}}$	$P = \dfrac{N_{bi \to bi}}{N_{bi \to bi} + N_{\overline{bi} \to bi}}$	$F = \dfrac{2 \times P \times R}{P + R}$

In addition, we introduce the ROC (Receiver Operating Characteristic curve) and AUC (Area Under roc Curve) in order to overcome the shortcomings of traditional evaluation indexes when measure the classifier under the condition that the positive and negative samples are not balanced. The ROC curve is measure by TPR (True Positive Rate) and FPR (False Positive Rate). TPR represents the probability of correctly detecting the positive case. FPR represents the probability that a negative example is divided into positive cases.

In the generated ROC space, the TPR is the vertical coordinate, and the FPR is the horizontal coordinate. The quality of the classifier can be measured directly with the AUC area, which is the area under the ROC curve. It can be seen from the ROC curve that the performance of the classification algorithm is better when the TPR grows rapidly, the ROC curve approaches the longitudinal axis quickly, and the area of AUC is large.

6.3 Experiment and Result Analysis

Classification Experiment on Released Messages. The data set used in this paper includes 8283398 data. After pretreatment and manual labeling respectively, we get 53998 piece of eroticism data, 47395 piece of gamble data, 51682 piece of drug data, 49257 piece of sensitive political data and 8081066 piece of data in other category. In this paper, naïve Bayes classifier in weka3.8.0 software package is used, and the experimental results are shown in Table 2:

Table 2. Experimental results of content classification.

Category	Recall	Precision	F-Measure
Eroticism	84.52%	83.10%	83.80%
Gamble	82.71%	81.61%	82.16%
Drug	84.11%	83.14%	83.62%
Political	83.77%	84.07%	83.92%
Others	80.94%	81.29%	10 point, italic

As we can see from Table 2, the recall rate of each category is more than 80%, the precision rate is above 81%, and F-Measure is above 81%. The results show that naive Bayes classifier has a good classification effect on multi-classification, and has little difference for different categories. It means that the performance is more stable.

Experiment on Unhealthy Message Judgement. (1) Experiment on balanced positive and negative samples.

The data set used in this article, has 54,000 data on pornography, where 10672 data include unhealthy message, 43328 data does not include unhealthy message, 5000 data are used as example set and other 5000 data are used as test set. This paper use SMO (SVM algorithm) classifier, the naïve Bayes classifier and the trees.J48 (C4.5 decision tree algorithm) classifier in weka3.8.0 software package to carry out experiment, and the experimental results are shown in Table 3:

Table 3. Experimental results of content classification.

Algorithm	Precision	Recall	F-Measure
SVM	82.7%	82.7%	82.7%
Naïve Bayes	72.3%	72.3%	72.2%
C4.5	78.5%	78.5%	78.5%

From the experimental result, we can see that the SVM algorithm is better than the naïve Bayes algorithm and the C4.5 algorithm. Therefore, the SVM algorithm selected in this paper is better than the other two algorithms in judging the unhealthy message in social network in the case of high dimension and small samples.

(2) Experiment on unbalanced positive and negative samples.

In unbalanced positive and negative samples experiment, 25000 data were used as example set and another 25000 data were used as test set. Among them, there are 5000 unhealthy messages and 20000 healthy messages. In this paper, SMO (SVM algorithm) classifier, naïve Bayes classifier, the trees.J48 (C4.5 decision tree algorithm) classifier in weka3.8.0 software package were carried out respectively, and we got respective ROC curve shown in Fig. 1:

In Fig. 1, curve (a) represents the C4.5 decision tree algorithm, and AUC = 0.851. Curve (b) represents the SVM algorithm, and AUC = 0.837. Curve (c) represents the Naïve Bayes algorithm, and AUC = 0.757. We can see that some of the points in the C4.5 decision tree algorithm and the SVM algorithm are coincident. The classification effect of C4.5 decision tree algorithm is better than that of support vector machine, although the difference is not great. The experimental results of support vector machine algorithm and C4.5 decision tree algorithm are much better than that of naive Bayesian algorithm. Also, the experimental results of support vector machine are much better than that of C4.5 decision tree algorithm in balanced experiment. So, it shows that the classification effect of the SVM algorithm is the best.

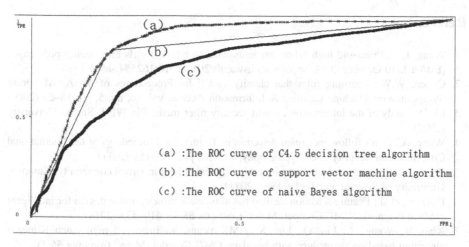

(a) :The ROC curve of C4.5 decision tree algorithm

(b) :The ROC curve of support vector machine algorithm

(c) :The ROC curve of naive Bayes algorithm

Fig. 1. The ROC curve.

7 Conclusion

The promotion and popularization of social network can effectively help people to establish and maintain the relationship with each other to meet the need of social contact. But there are many people with unhealthy habits to use social network to release unhealthy messages and illegal elements. They make use of the characteristics of social network to disseminate rapidly and widely in order to obtain unlawful gains or to achieve ulterior motives. So, in order to purify the cyberspace and suppress the spread of unhealthy message, the research on the detection of unhealthy message in social network is not only realistic but also far-reaching.

Based on the analysis of unhealthy messages of eroticism, gambling, drug and political sensitivity, this paper uses the Naive Bayesian method to perform multi-classification experiments on the characteristics of unhealthy message in social network. Then, based on the unique characteristics of various types of unhealthy message, the support vector machine algorithm, the C4.5 decision tree algorithm and the naive Bayesian algorithm are used in comparison experiments on balanced positive and negative samples and also unbalanced positive and negative samples. The experimental results show that the support vector machine algorithm is better than the other two classification algorithms.

Acknowledgement. This work was supported by the National Natural Science Foundation of China Nos. 61672101, the Beijing Key Laboratory of Internet Culture and Digital Dissemination Research (ICDDXN004)* and Key Lab of Information Network Security, Ministry of Public Security, No.C18601.

References

1. Wang, L.: 17-year-old high school students want to try rape girls after seeing porn pages [EB/OL], 10 October 2014. http://news.hsw.cn/s/2014/1010/162554.shtml
2. Cohen, W.W.: Learning rules that classify email. In: Proceedings of the AAAI Spring Symposium on Machine Learning & Information Access, vol. 96, no. 5, pp. 18–25 (2000)
3. Li, D.: Study of the information content security filter method in WEB, Shanxi University (2004)
4. Wang, A.: Don't follow me: spam detection in Twitter. In: Proceedings of the International Conference on Security and Cryptography, Athens, pp. 142–151 (2011)
5. Zhang, L.: Research on bad information filtering technology in virtual community, Kunming University of Science and Technology (2011)
6. Fang, S., et al.: Feature selection method based on class discriminative degree for intelligent medical diagnosis. CMC Comput. Mater. Continua 55(3), 419–433 (2018)
7. Xiao, B., Wang, Z., Liu, Q., Liu, X.: SMK-means: an improved mini batch K-means algorithm based on mapreduce with big data. CMC Comput. Mater. Continua 56(3), 365–379 (2018)
8. Zhu, X.: Research on adaptive text filtering system based on vector spatial model, Shandong Normal University (2006)
9. Zhou, J.: A bad text filtering method, University of Electronic Science and Technology of China (2016)
10. Jinghong, X., Yifei, L.: "Anti - pornography" in the social network age: status quo, problems and countermeasures. J. Beijing Univ. Posts Telecommun. (Soc. Sci. Ed.) 17(3), 9–13 (2015)
11. Huiyu, H., Congdong, L., Jiadong, R.: Real Time Monitoring Prototype System for Bad Information Based on Artificial Neural Networks. Comput. Eng. 32(2), 254–256 (2006)
12. Shao, X., Xu, Q.: Network camouflage bad information detection method of research and simulation. Comput. Simul. 29(2), 135–138 (2012)
13. Meng, X., Zhou, X.P., Wu, S.Z.: The application research of semantic analysis in the field of anti-terrorism. J. Intell. 36(3), 13–17 (2017)
14. Liu, M.Y., Huang, G.J.: Research on text filter model for information content security. J. Chin. Inf. Process. 31(2), 126–131 (2017)
15. Neerbeky, J., Assentz, I., Dolog, P.: TABOO: detecting unstructured sensitive information using recursive neural networks. In: IEEE, International Conference on Data Engineering. IEEE (2017)
16. Jiang, Z.: Research on micro-blogging privacy detection based on Bayesian, Harbin Engineering University (2013)
17. Wei, S.: Harmful information detection and filtering toward interactive web media, Dalian Maritime University (2009)
18. Huiling, W., Xiwei, G., Jianjing, S., et al.: Research on the text pre-processing to malicious information filtering. Microcomput. Inf. 22(12X), 58–60 (2006)
19. Yabin, J.X.: Privacy content detection method for the judgment documents. J. Chongqing Univ. Posts Telecommun. (Nat. Sci. Ed.) 27(5), 639–646 (2015)

Image Authentication by Single Target Region Detection

Huanrong Tang, Zhuosong Fu, Jianquan Ouyang$^{(\boxtimes)}$, and Yunhua Song

Key Laboratory of Intelligent Computing and Information
Processing Ministry of Education, College of Information Engineering,
Xiangtan University, Xiangtan 411105, China
throng@126.com, 328149901@qq.com, oyjq@xtu.edu.cn,
syh_xtu@163.com

Abstract. Digital image has been widely used in people's daily life, and image authentication technology is more and more important. This paper proposes an image authentication method based on convolutional neural nets, which performed better compared with the VGG and Alex-Net. A single target region detection method under the attention model is proposed and it helps a lot in distinguish the source images and the derived images with watermarks or mosaic.

Keywords: Image authentication · CNN · Single target region detection

1 Introduction

With the continuous development of modern digital technology, digital images have been widely used in our daily life and work, but digital images have also brought some problems while bringing convenience to people. The acquisition of images is much easier and the retouching technology is very popular, people who learn a little skill can easily process an image, such as cropping, adding watermarks, etc., and then release the processed image with the identity of "new image", which is very detrimental to the protection of intellectual property and the filtering of junk image. Although some processed images can be distinguished by human easily, the extremely large data size makes the manual discriminating process costly. It is important to find a way to identify whether an image comes from another image efficiently and automatically [1].

In 1993, Friedman proposed the concept of a "trusted digital camera" which used traditional cryptographic hashes to identify image sources. In 1996, Professor S.F. Chang proposed an image recognition method based on image block histogram at the ICIP conference. In 2000, researchers at the Microsoft Research Institute collaborated with the University of Illinois to publish relevant papers at the ICIP conference. Since 2001, various universities and research institutes in China have successively carried out related research in the field of image identification, The research results such as image recognition technology based on texture recognition, image source identification algorithm based on hybrid feature extraction, image source identification technology based on passive forensics enhance Chinese scientific research ability in this field

© Springer Nature Switzerland AG 2019
X. Sun et al. (Eds.): ICAIS 2019, LNCS 11632, pp. 509–515, 2019.
https://doi.org/10.1007/978-3-030-24274-9_46

continuously [2]. Modern image identification technology is based on the feature extraction method, that is, under the guidance of prior knowledge, extract the commonality of specific objects, which is used to identify the identification of specific objects, to distinguish different objects or classify objects. Although image recognition based on artificial extraction features has achieved good results, from the development of these technologies, a better authentication algorithm often wins on feature extraction, which means that limitations of manually extracted image features always exist. Humans are usually confined to fixed thinking and neglect certain important factors. The introduction of the deep learning method is expected to break through the limitations of human extraction features. The self-gaming training of the Alpha-zero also confirms that the deep learning and reinforcement learning methods can achieve results which are not readily available with human experience.

2   Proposed Image Authentication Scheme

2.1   United Convolutional Neural Nets

Convolutional neural network is a kind of artificial neural network, which has become a research hotspot in the field of image recognition. Its weight-sharing network structure makes it more similar to biological neural networks, reducing the complexity of the network model and reducing the number of weights. This advantage is more obvious when the input of the network is a multi-dimensional image, so that the image can be directly used as the input of the network, avoiding the complicated feature extraction and data reconstruction process in the traditional recognition algorithm, and the network structure is highly invariant for panning, scaling, tilting or other forms of deformation. These characteristics of the convolutional neural network are very suitable for the problems studied in this paper.

In this paper, the nets are expected to recognize the image after the process like clipping, adding watermark, blurring, etc. from a certain source image. Different from the simple image classification work, in this paper the images classified as one kind will have large differences on the surface data, such as the blurred image and the watermarked image, so it is necessary to extract relatively more advanced features, which means a deeper number of layers is required for normal structure, and it makes the load of the computer increase sharply and will be plagued by the disappearance of the gradient, which is negative to training. Inspired by the inception structure of Google Net [3], this paper parallels multiple shallow networks to extract different features of images through different settings of convolutional layers in each shallow network, and then uses several layers of fully connected layers to combine the extracted features and finally get the feature layer for identification [4]. The scheme is depicted in Fig. 1.

Each CNN has 4 convolutional layers and 4 max-pool layers. From CNN-1 to CNN-4, the convolutional kernel size is 2×2, 3×3, 5×5, 7×7 respectively. Convolutional layers don't change the data size using zero-padding and each pool layer half the width and height of input. FC1 has 1024 neurons, FC2 has 512 neurons, FC3 has 256 neurons and the Feature layer is a 128-D vector. The full scheme can be regarded as 2 independent parts, CONV part and FC part, so the size of feature map

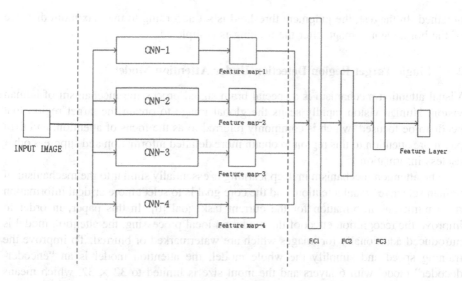

Fig. 1. Scheme of nets

depends on the input size and the FC part can adjust the size of weight matrix to fit the feature map. For 2 datasets with different size of image, the first layer of FC part should be retrained. Cross entropy is used as the loss function during the training step.

2.2   Improved Euclid Distance

Euclidean distance is a common method for measuring the distance between two sets of data in multidimensional space and can be described as the following formula:

$$d = \sqrt{(x_1 - y_1)^2 + (x_2 - y_2)^2 + (x_3 - y_3)^2 + \cdots + (x_n - y_n)^2} \tag{1}$$

According to the research content of this paper, there must be considerable differences between the two images that are completely irrelevant, and the difference between the homologous images is small. It's better that the distance measurement function can accommodate the difference between the homologous images as much as possible. Therefore, the improved Euclidean distance is proposed. As mentioned above, a 128-dimensional feature vector is finally obtained. When calculating the Euclidean distance, the smallest value among the adjacent four dimensions is selected and included in the calculation, which can be described as the following formula:

$$d = \sqrt{\min_{i \in [1,4]} (x_i - y_i)^2 + \min_{i \in [5,8]} (x_i - y_i)^2 + \cdots + \min_{i \in [125,128]} (x_i - y_i)^2} \tag{2}$$

This makes the distance measurement function more inclined to accommodate the difference between the two images. For different source images, even if such an operation is performed, a distance far greater than the homologous image will be obtained. In the test, the judgment threshold is set according to the maximum distance of the homologous image after the training is completed.

2.3 Single Target Region Detection Under Attention Model

Visual attention mechanism is a special brain signal processing mechanism of human vision. Human vision rapidly scans the global image to obtain the target region that needs to be focused, which is commonly referred to as the focus of attention, and then pay more attention to this region to obtain more detailed information and suppress other useless information [5].

The attention mechanism in deep learning is essentially similar to the mechanism of human selective visual attention, and the core goal is to select more critical information from numerous information for the current task goal [6]. In this paper, in order to improve the recognition effect of the model on local processing, the attention model is introduced additionally for images which are watermarked or blurred. To improve the training speed and simplify the whole model, the attention model is an "encoder-decoder" model with 6 layers and the input size is limited to 32 × 32, which means when the model gets the recognition signal of local processing, within the range of 32 × 32 pixels with the current signal point as the center, the attention model is embedded into the first convolutional layer and the second convolutional layer of the overall convolutional model to adjust the weight of this part region on the feature graph. The structure of "encoder-decoder" model can be found in Fig. 2.

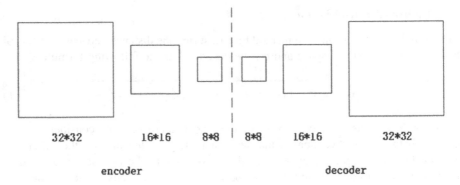

| 32*32   16*16   8*8 | 8*8   16*16   32*32 |

encoder   decoder

Fig. 2. "encoder-decoder" model

3 Experiment and Results

In the experiment, five types of images were selected, including flowers, figures, airplanes, birds, and ships. For each type 20 images were selected randomly, and every image was randomly cropped, watermarked, and partially blurred generating 200 images respectively. The examples can be found in Fig. 3.

A dataset with 60020 images was constructed. The image size was uniformly adjusted to 128 * 128. Each image is labeled with a 6-dimensional vector with the first

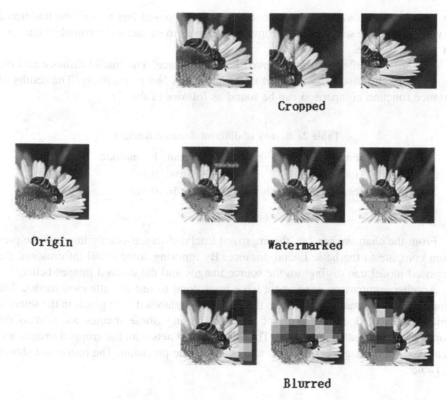

Fig. 3. Examples of generating fake images

5 dimensions representing the category and the 6th dimension denoting the source. When the loss is no longer falling, the 128-dimensional vectors of all source image are saved and set the classification threshold. Then 200 derived images and 200 non-derivatized images are randomly selected for testing. In this paper, Alex-Net, ZF-Net and VGG network structures are selected for comparison experiments. The experimental results are as follows (Table 1):

Table 1. Results of different networks

Net	prec	recall	F1_measure
Alex-Net	0.538	0.560	0.549
ZF-Net	0.542	0.534	0.538
VGG	0.574	0.592	0.583
Proposed Net	0.629	0.656	0.642

According to the results, our model exactly have improved the effect of distinguishing the source images and the derived images. The Alex-Net and ZF-Net have similar depth and structure, so they also get similar scores. VGG focuses on increasing the layers, and actually get an improvement. The proposed Net widens the traditional networks and unite several simple convolutional nets to extract more complete features, get a highest score.

To verify the effect of the improved Euclid distance. The Euclid distance and the improved Euclid distance were used in the proposed Net respectively. The results of distance function comparison can be found as follows (Table 2):

Table 2. Results of different distance function

Function	prec	recall	F1_measure
Euclid distance	0.533	0.596	0.563
Improved Euclid distance	0.629	0.656	0.642

From the chart we can see, the improved Euclid distance exactly improve the prec score compare to the basic Euclid distance. By ignoring some detail information, the proposed model can distinguish the source images and the derived images better.

Another comparison experiment have been done to test the attention model. The images with watermark or mosaic in the dataset are relabeled. The pixels in the selected region are labeled as the signal of local processing, these images are sent to the proposed net with attention model. Then test the two nets with the cropped images and local processed images respectively and calculate the precision. The results are shown in Table 3.

Table 3. Results of attention model

Model	Cropped images	Images with watermark or mosaic
No attention model	0.527	0.572
Attention model	0.524	0.635

The results show the attention model can help the whole model recognize the watermark and mosaic, but it doesn't work on cropped images, which meets the expectation.

4 Conclusion

According to experimental results, proposed method has a certain degree of improvement compared with using VGG or Alex-Net network directly for Image authentication, but the overall accuracy is low, there is still much room for improvement. The improved Euclidean distance proposed in this paper can improve the accuracy to a certain extent. And the single target region detection under attention model can also help the model recognize the images with watermarks or mosaic. To achieve better effects, more efforts are needed.

Acknowledgement. This research has been supported by NSFC (61672495), Scientific Research Fund of Hunan Provincial Education Department (16A208), Project of Hunan Provincial Science and Technology Department (2017SK2405), and in part by the construct program of the key discipline in Hunan Province.

References

1. Wu, W.C.: Quantization-based image authentication scheme using QR error correction. Eurasip J. Image Video Process. **2017**(1), 13 (2017)
2. Shojanazeri, H., Wan, A.W.A., Ahmad, S.M.S., et al.: Authentication of images using Zernike moment watermarking. Multimedia Tools Appl. **76**(1), 1–30 (2017)
3. Szegedy, C., Vanhoucke, V., Ioffe, S., et al.: Rethinking the inception architecture for computer vision. In: Computer Vision and Pattern Recognition, pp. 2818–2826. IEEE (2016)
4. Papandreou, G., Kokkinos, I., Savalle, P.A.: Untangling local and global deformations in deep convolutional networks for image classification and sliding window detection. Eprint Arxiv (2014)
5. Meng, R., Rice, S.G., Wang, J., Sun, X.: A fusion steganographic algorithm based on faster R-CNN. CMC Comput. Mater. Continua **55**(1), 001–016 (2018)
6. Xiong, Z., Shen, Q., Wang, Y., Zhu, C.: Paragraph vector representation based on word to vector and CNN learning. CMC Comput. Mater. Continua **055**(2), 213–227 (2018)

Security Approaches and Crypto Algorithms in Mobile Cloud Storage Environment to Ensure Data Security

Micheal Ernest Taylor[1](✉) and David Aboagye-Darko[2](✉)

[1] School of Computer and Software, Nanjing University of Information Science
and Technology, Nanjing 210044, Jiangsu, People's Republic of China
delen007@live.com
[2] Department of Information Technology,
University of Professional Studies, Accra, Ghana
aboagye.david@upsamail.com

Abstract. Mobile Cloud Storage Architecture is a promising service platform provided by CSPs to store and access resources on-demand via the internet. Information and data stored on these large storage platforms can be well managed than locally stored. Cloud storage services use deduplication for saving bandwidth and storage. However, using these services pose lots of doubts and challenges in the minds of its users in relation to security, privacy, reliability and integrity of their stored data and information. An adversary can exploit side-channel information in several attack scenarios when deduplication takes place at the client side, leaking information on whether a specific plaintext exists in the cloud storage. In this paper, different security techniques and algorithms adopted to enhance security, reliability and integrity of data and information stored in the cloud are discussed. Also, an analysis of trending issues with regards to security of data and information stored in the cloud as well as the reliability and integrity of these storage platforms provided by CSPs are discussed extensively..

Keywords: Mobile cloud storage · Security · Techniques · Data

1 Introduction

Issues of data security and privacy have become more pervasive in mobile cloud storage, unlike traditional computer systems, as a result of four main functions of mobile cloud storage systems; measured service and on-demand self-service, elasticity of resources, ubiquitous sharing of resources and integration of digitization. Users access data and computing resources with little or no knowledge of where data is stored or which machines are responsible for the execution of tasks. This makes users question the reliability, privacy and security of data in mobile cloud storage systems which, to a large extent, influences its appropriation. People access the internet via mobile devices such as smart phones and tablets. These mobile devices are consistently being appropriated in organizational and human activities which induce the need for human mobility. The capabilities and functional essence of these mobile devices serve as a platform for advanced computing, faster connectivity, dynamic configuration and

© Springer Nature Switzerland AG 2019
X. Sun et al. (Eds.): ICAIS 2019, LNCS 11632, pp. 516–524, 2019.
https://doi.org/10.1007/978-3-030-24274-9_47

access to several computing resources regardless of the temporal or the spatial state of the user or the data. However, issues of data security and privacy emerge whenever computing resources are accessed over a network or are handled by "third parties", as evidenced in the mobile cloud ecosystem.

Paradoxically, the increase in the use of the internet via mobile devices has given rise to web based malicious threats that undermine the reliability and security of mobile cloud data. [1] Acknowledge the challenges implied by data protection and security in mobile cloud storage architecture and argue for further examination of security approaches and crypto algorithms in mobile cloud storage to ensure data security.

Mobile cloud computing is today's most fascinating technology because of its elasticity and cost efficiency. This technology holds the potential to reduce the requirements of expensive computing infrastructure for IT-based solution and services that industries use. Furthermore, it promises to provide a flexible IT architecture which is accessible through the internet on handheld devices [2] such as smart phones and tablets (Fig. 1).

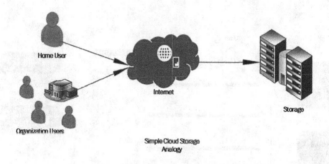

Fig. 1. Cloud storage analogy

In mobile cloud computing, data processing and storage occurs independent of the mobile device. This is due to the fact that mobile devices do not have large storage capacities. Storing data on cloud can be problematic due to data insecurities. As internet enabled mobile devices (including smart phones and tablets) are proliferated, web based malicious threats continue to increase, making security issues more complex. Therefore, data security is imperative in mobile cloud environments.

2   Cloud Storage Architecture

Cloud storage architectures are regarded as catalysts for more technological breakthroughs because of its features; ubiquitous sharing of resources, measured service, elasticity of resources, integration of digitalization and internet technologies. Cloud storage architectures are mainly about delivering storage on-demand using a highly scalable and multi-tenant approach. Generally, a cloud storage architecture consists of a front-end that disseminates an API to communicate with the backend storage. Cloud storage architecture has three main components which are:

i. In old-fashioned storage systems, this API is the SCSI protocol. However, in the cloud, this is known as surfacing protocol. At this layer, there are web services, file-based Internet SCSI or iSCSI front ends. This layer is the first communication point between the user and the service provider. Users access technological resources using their credentials.
ii. The medium component layer, known as the storage controller, interconnects and communicates from the front API to the storage at the backend. This layer is characterized by diversity of features including replication, and traditional data placement algorithms with geographical location.
iii. The back-end consists of physical storage for data. This may be a central protocol that runs dedicated programs or a traditional back-end to the physical disks as illustrated in Fig. 2.

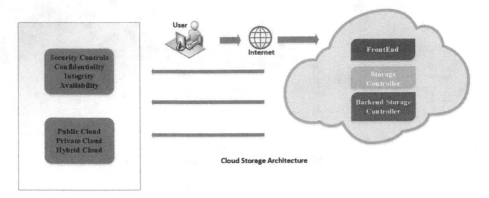

Fig. 2. Cloud storage architecture

2.1 Security Concerns of Cloud Storage

Privacy and security issues continually confront cloud storage systems. A fundamental goal of cloud vendors is to ensure that clients do not experience security issues such as data loss or unauthorized access. Malicious users or hackers can access data in the cloud storage system and impersonate a legitimate user, thereby altering the entire cloud system. In consequence, countless users using the compromised cloud system will have challenges such as inconsistent and inefficient service delivery. Security challenges that confront cloud storage systems include: data theft, data integrity, privacy issues, data loss, data availability, vendor level security and user level security.

The modern generation of cloud computing services do not provide any privacy against untrusted cloud operators hence they are not supposed to store important information such as medical records, financial records or high impact business data.

The main use of encryption is to provide privacy through the idea of all useful information about plaintext. Encryption renders data unusable in the sense that one does not get easy access to it.

3   Related Works

In [6], the authors presented a protocol that uses the services of a third-party auditor or checker not only to verify and authenticate the integrity of data stored on remote servers but also in retrieving and getting the data back as soon as possible, with all sections intact. The core advantage of this scheme is the use of digital signature to ensure the integrity of local data. However, the overall process is quite problematic and complex as the keys and data are also encrypted and decrypted respectively.

The authors in [7] dealt with the security of data during transmission. The distress in this is the encryption of data, so that confidentiality and privacy can be easily achieved. They used EAP-CHAP along with the Rijndael Encryption Algorithm. Gampala et al. [10] proposed elliptic curve cryptography to provide confidentiality and authentication of the data between clouds. It is a public key cryptosystem. An elliptic curve over a field K is a nonsingular cubic curve in two variables f (x, y) = 0. Elliptic Curve groups for cryptography are examined with field of Fp and F2m. Public key is used for encryption signature verification and private key is used for decryption signature verification in this technique. As the data storing process is done outside, security is the major concern. Singh et al. [11] propose Public Key Cryptographic technique to provide security of the user's data on the cloud server. This technique contains three primary services.

4   Data Security Techniques

Data security is the practice of protecting data from unauthorized access, use, modification, destruction or deletion. It is a level of information security that is concerned with protecting data stores, knowledge repositories and documents. The following table is common data security techniques and considerations (Table 1).

Table 1. Data security techniques

Security Technique	Explanation
Data anonymization	This is the process of removing personally identifiable information from data. It is done in order to release information in such a way that the privacy of individuals is maintained. For example, student's data may be released for the purposes of research and contact in case of emergency with all names, postal codes and other identifiable data removed. The following are common types of data anonymization
Data authentication	The process of confirming the origin and integrity of data. The term is typically related to communication, messaging and integration. Data authentication has two elements: authenticating that you are getting data from the correct entity and validating the integrity of that data

(continued)

Table 1. (*continued*)

Security Technique	Explanation
Data masking	The process of replacing real data with structurally similar fake data for purposes such as testing and training. Creating test data from scratch is extremely resource intensive and may result in data that does not reflect production realities. As such, it is common for organizations to use real data for testing. Data masking is typically used to remove anything personally identifiable or confidential in data
Data purging	Permanently deleting data such that it cannot be recovered by standard methods. The term is most commonly applied to databases but is used by other business softwares as well
Degaussing	The reduction, elimination or reorientation of a magnetic field. It began as a series of techniques for reducing the magnetic signatures of ships during WWII. Degaussing is also used as a means of physically destroying data on magnetic media such as a hard drive

5 Data Integrity Technique

In [4], authors examined data confidentiality and access control. Authors of this work proposed a scheme for trusted authority. It offers key to data owner (DO) and generates incremental message authentication code (MAC) of the file offered by DO. DO requests storage service provider (SSP) for a file. It accesses the policy then encrypted file is sent to Decryption Service provider (DSP). DSP sends this file to DO as well as trusted authority. The trusted authority again generates MAC and checks it for equality with previous MAC stored. If these two MAC match then integrity of file is verified and result is transferred to DO.

5.1 Mobile Cloud

In this paper [5], authors proposed a new mobile cloud framework known as Mobicloud. ESSI plays an important role in Mobicloud. It is a virtual machine designed for an end user having full control of the information stored in its virtual hard drive. The authors presented a new mobile framework through trust management and private data isolation.

- **Mobile Cloud Trust Management:** The trust management model of mobile cloud comprises identity management, key management and security policy enforcement. It uses user centric identity management that allows an individual full control for identities. It also infers that a user has control over the data sharing over the internet and can also transfer and delete the data when necessary. The authors introduced an integrated solution involving identity-based cryptography and attribute-based data access control to construct the trust management system for mobile cloud. The authors proposed a fully functional identity-based encryption scheme which has a chosen cipher text security in random oracle model.

6 Security Principles and Algorithms of Cryptography

Cryptography can facilitate the integration of Cloud Computing by increasing the number of privacy related companies. The primary level of privacy cryptography can help Cloud computing is safe and secure storage. Cryptography is the science of storing messages securely by converting the raw data into unreadable formats [8]. Currently, cryptography is considered as a collection of three algorithms; Symmetric-key algorithms, Asymmetric key algorithms and Hashing [9]. The main problems in Cloud computing are related to data security, backup data, network traffic, file storage system and security of host. Cryptography is considered as an appropriate way to resolve such issues.

For safe and secure communication between the guest domain and the host domain, or from hosts to management systems, encryption technologies, such as Secure HTTP, encrypted VPNs and TLS should be used. Encryption minimizes attacks such as man-in-the middle attacks, spoofing attacks, and session hijacking. Cloud computing provides clients with computing facilities and infrastructure needed to store data and run applications. While the advantages of cloud computing cannot be overemphasized, it also introduces new security challenges as cloud operators are supposed to manipulate data for clients without necessarily being fully trusted.

Cloud data storage augments the menace of data leakage and does not give access to unauthorized users. Cloud data management cannot be trusted entirely by data owners. This is because data processes and computations may compromise the privacy of users. To overcome the above issues, cryptography is being proposed as a means to ensure data security, privacy and trust in cloud computing.

6.1 Symmetric Key Algorithms

Symmetric uses single key, which works for both encryption and decryption. The symmetric systems provide a two channel system to their users which ensures authentication and authorization. Symmetric-key algorithms are those algorithms which use only one key for one or both. The key is kept as secret. Symmetric algorithms have the advantage of not taking in too much of computation power and it works with very high speed in encryption.

Symmetric-key algorithms are divided into two types: Block cipher and Stream cipher. In block cipher, input is taken as a block of plaintext of fixed size depending on the type of symmetric encryption algorithm. A key of fixed size is applied to a block of plain text. In effect, an output block of the same size as the block of plaintext is obtained. In case of stream cipher one bit is encrypted at a particular time. Some popular symmetric-key algorithms used in cloud computing includes: Data Encryption Standard (DES), TripleDES, and Advanced Encryption Standard (AES).

- *Advanced Encryption Standard (AES):* In cryptography, the Advanced Encryption Standard [12] is a type of symmetric-key encryption algorithm. Each of the ciphers have a 128-bit block size and having key sizes of 128, 192 and 256 bits, respectively. AES algorithm ensures that the hash code is encrypted in a secure manner. AES has a block size of 128 bits. Its algorithm is as follows:

Key Expansion, Initial Round - Round Keys are added. Rounds, Sub Bytes—a no uniform substitution step where each byte is substituted with another according to a table. Rows are shifted—a transposition step where each row of the state is shifted cyclically for a certain number of steps. Columns are mixed—a mixing operation which operates on the columns of the state, combining the four bytes in each column 8. Add Round Key— each byte of that particular state is combined with the round key; each round key is derived from the given cipher key using a key schedule. Final Round, Sub Bytes, Shift Rows, Add Round Key.

- **Data Encryption Standard (DES):** The Data Encryption Standard (DES) is a block cipher and comes under symmetric key cryptography found in January 1977 by the National Institute of Standards and Technology, named as NIST. At the encryption site, DES simply takes a 64-bit plaintext and creates a 64-bit cipher text, at the decryption process, it takes a 64-bit cipher text and creates a 64-bit plaintext, and same 56 bit cipher key is used for both encryption and decryption. The encryption process is made using two permutations (P-boxes), which we call initial and final permutation, and sixteen Fiestel rounds. Each round uses a different sort of 48-bit round key which is generated from the cipher key according to a predefined algorithm.

- **Blowfish Algorithm:** Blowfish also comes under symmetric block cipher that can be used as a substitute for DES. It takes a variable-length key, starting from 32 bits to 448 bits, making it considerably better for both domestic and exportable use. Blowfish was designed in 1993 by Bruce Schneier as a free, fast substitute to existing encryption algorithms. Since then it has been verified considerably, and it is gradually gaining popularity as a strong encryption algorithm. Blowfish is unpatented and license-free, and is available free for all uses.

6.2   Asymmetric Key Algorithms

It is comparatively a new concept, unlike symmetric cryptosystem. Different keys are used for encryption and decryption. This is a property which makes this scheme different from symmetric encryption scheme. Each receiver possesses a decryption key, generally referred to as his private key. Receiver needs to generate an encryption key, referred to as his public key. Generally, this type of cryptosystem involves trusted third parties which officially declares that a particular public key belongs to a specific person or entity only.

- **Diffie-Hellman Key Exchange:** Whitfield Diffie and Martin Hellman introduced a key exchange protocol with the help of the discrete logarithm problem in 1976. In this key exchange protocol, the sender and receiver will manage to set up a secret key to their symmetric key system, using an unsafe channel. For instance, to set up a key Alice chooses a random integer aE[1; n] computes ga. Similarly Bob computes gb for random bE [1; n] and sends it to Alice. The secret key is gab, which Alice computes by computing (gb)a and Bob by computing (ga)b. Diffie-Hellman Protocols depend on security concepts such as DDH, DHP, DLP.

- **Elgamal Encrytion:** Taher Elgamal postulated the Elgamal encryption scheme (also known as Elgamal encryption) in 1985. This algorithm can be considered as an extension of Diffie-Hellman Key Exchange protocol. This algorithm is premised on the complexity of two problems namely, the Diffe-Hellman (DH) problem and the discrete logarithm problem. Elgamal encryption is ideal in an instances where homomorphic multiplication operations are required on encrypted data.

- **Predicate-Based Encryption (PBE):** As part of its cryptographic operations, PBE presents opportunities for selective fine-grained access control. In PBE, cipher texts and scheme entities are characterized by attributes. These attributes detail aspects of the data being encrypted, the environment and entities. When the attributes of the cipher-text matches that of the decrypting entity, decryption of the cipher-text will be possible by the entity. In order to ensure "a match" or "alignment", access polices (predicates) must indicate:

  i. *The kind of attributes (authorized) which entities should have to facilitate decryption and access to the plain-text.*
  ii. *The relationship that exists between the attributes.*

- **Identity Based Encrytion (IBE):** In 1984, Adi Shamir proposed an encryption scheme which enables public keys to be an arbitrary string. Fundamentally, this algorithm was aimed at making certificate management in e-mail systems simple. In IBE encryption, public keys are generated from ASCII strings or a known identity value. This leads to the generation of corresponding private keys by the private key generator (PKG). This encryption algorithm is essential in situations where authentication of prior key distribution is inappropriate as a result of technical constraints.

- **Attribute Based Encrytion (ABE):** This encryption algorithm uses generalizations based on IBE algorithm schemes and general styled predicates as Boolean formula. This covers operations including disjunction, conjunction and thresholds. The attributes may not necessarily point to the identity of an entity or even to the entity itself [13]. However, it may refer to non-identity aspects such as TCP/IP addresses and ports numbers.

7 Conclusion

This paper discusses different security techniques which ensure data storage security. Cloud security is a critical concept spiraling as one of the interesting research areas as a result of the potential benefits it presents as well as the numerous challenges associated with it. Security algorithms which can be implemented in cloud storage include symmetric algorithms such as DES, Triple-DES, AES, Blowfish. However, security algorithms which allow linear searching on decrypted data are required for cloud computing, because they ensure data safety [14]. This paper argues that cryptography should be considered as an appropriate means of ensuring cloud security. This paper will be helpful to researchers who work on cloud data storage security.

References

1. Purushothaman, D., Abburu, S.: An approach for data storage security in cloud computing. Int. J. Comput. Sci. **9**(1), 100–105 (2012)
2. Guha, V., Shrivastav, M.: Review of information authentication in mobile cloud over SaaS and PaaS layer. Int. J. Adv. Comput. Res. **39**(1), 119–121 (2013)
3. Vasu, R.: Techniques for efficiently ensuring data storage security in cloud computing. IJCTA **2**(5), 1717–1721 (2011)
4. Garg, P., Sharma, V.: Secure data storage in mobile cloud computing. Int. J. Sci. Eng. Res. **4** (4), 1154–1159 (2013)
5. Shimpi, A.S., Chander, R.P.: Secure framework in data processing for mobile cloud computing. Int. J. Comput. Sci. Inf. **2**(3), 73–76 (2012)
6. Chandar, R., Kavitha, M.S., Seenivasan, K.: A proficient model for high end security in cloud computing. Int. J. Emerg. Res. Manage. Technol. **5**(10), 697–702 (2014)
7. Singla, S., Singh, J.: Cloud computing security using authentication and encryption technique. IJARCET **2**(7), 2232–2235 (2013)
8. Stinson, D.: Cryptography: Theory & Practice. Chapman and Hall Publications, Boca Raton (2006)
9. Nigoti, R., Jhuria, M., Singh, S.: A survey of cryptographic algorithms for cloud computing. Int. J. Emerg. Technol. Comput. Appl. Sci. **4**(1), 141–146 (2013)
10. Gampala, V., Inuganti, S., Muppidi, S.: Data security in cloud computing with elliptic curve cryptography. Int. J. Soft Comput. Eng. **2**(3), 138–141 (2012)
11. Singh, K., Kharbanda, L., Kaur, N.: Security issue occurs in cloud computing and their solution. Int. J. Comput. Sci. Eng. **4**(5), 945–949 (2012)
12. Bokefode, J.D., Ubale, S.A., Pingale, S.V., Karane, K.J., Apate, S.S.: Developing secure cloud storage system by applying AES and RSA cryptography algorithms with role bases access control model. Int. J. Comput. Appl. **118**(12), 36–47 (2015)
13. Sujatha, R., Ramakrishnan, M., Duraipandian, N., Ramakrishnan, B.: Optimal adaptive genetic algorithm based hybrid signcryption algorithm for information security. CMC **55**(3), 523–539 (2018)
14. Cheang, C.F., Wang, Y., Cai, Z., Xu, G.: Multi-VMs intrusion detection for cloud security using Dempster-Shafer theory. CMC **57**(2), 297–306 (2018)

Probe-Polling: A Polling Based MAC Protocol for Energy Harvesting Wireless Sensor Networks

Yu Han[1(✉)], Guangjun Wen[1], Chu Chu[1], and Jian Su[2]

[1] School of Information and Communication Engineering,
University of Electronic Science and Technology of China, Chengdu, China
YuHan.UESTC@outlook.com
[2] Nanjing University of Information and Technology, Nanjing, China

Abstract. By enabling nodes to harvest energy from their surrounding environments, Energy Harvesting Wireless Sensor Networks (EH-WSNs) solves the energy-supply problem faced by traditional battery-powered WSNs. Without the needs of battery replacement and recharge, EH-WSNs is environment-friendly and has an infinite lifetime in theory. Different form battery-powered WSNs MAC protocols which take the energy conservation as the most important principle, EH-WSNs MAC protocols are designed to maximize the network performance under certain energy harvesting conditions. In this paper, A MAC protocol named Probe-Polling was proposed for EH-WSNs based on polling scheme. Probe-Polling can effectively decrease the network bandwidth waste due to collision by using probe packets sent by polled sensors. The proposed MAC is implemented and evaluated using MATLAB. The result shows that Probe-Polling performs well in both throughput and fairness, and has a low inter-arrival time.

Keywords: EH-WSNs · Polling · Medium access control · Probe packet

1 Introduction

Wireless Sensor Networks (WSNs) has been largely used in modern lives, such as health monitoring, transport controlling, animal protecting, etc. Energy supply is the most critical issue faced by WSNs [1–4]. Traditional WSN nodes are battery-powered. Once the energy depleted, the nodes will be "dead," which will sharply degrade network performance. Replacing batteries will bring additional cost and even be impossible in remote areas. To solve this problem, researchers introduced the concept of Energy Harvesting Wireless Sensor Networks (EH-WSNs) [5, 6]. In EH-WSNs sensor nodes can harvest energy from their surrounding sources and power themselves using the energy harvested. Consequently, EH-WSNs breaks the bottleneck of lifetime constraint due to energy and is environment-friendly.

Traditionally, MAC protocols designed for WSN should take the energy conservation as the most critical focal principle, a large number of strategies and schemes have been proposed to improve the sensor energy efficiency to extend the network lifetime as much as possible. With the ability of energy harvesting, the concern related

© Springer Nature Switzerland AG 2019
X. Sun et al. (Eds.): ICAIS 2019, LNCS 11632, pp. 525–536, 2019.
https://doi.org/10.1007/978-3-030-24274-9_48

to lifetime is eliminated. The primary design aspiration of MAC protocols used for EH-WSNs has turned to maximize the network performance under the energy harvesting rates which sensors can realize [7]. In [8], the author proposed a receiver-initiated MAC protocol named ODMAC, which is suitable for EH-WSNs with low traffic conditions. Nodes under ODMAC can independently adjust their duty cycles to achieve ENO-Max state (the energy harvested and consumption are perfect balanced) to maximize the network performance. However, ODMAC does not take the variation of energy harvesting rate into account. Thus the performance may be attenuated severely in real scenarios. By taking the RF energy charging characteristic into account, Authors in [9] introduced RF-MAC to optimize the energy delivery to sensor nodes, while minimizing disruption to data communications. RF-MAC performs better than traditional CSMA MAC protocols in the simulation whereas RF-MAC has a high requirement of nodes' hardware, which makes RF-MAC hard to implement. In [10], through the experiments of energy harvesting process under different real environments, the author points out that the energy harvesting time of every charging cycle is random and hard to predict. Then a probabilistic polling algorithm (PP-MAC) for single-hop WSNs is proposed. PP-MAC specifically exploits the dynamic characteristic of the energy charging process to achieve a better overall network performance compared to other protocols.

Sink node in PP-MAC periodically broadcasts a polling packet contains a contention probability parameter P to all the sensor nodes in the network. Sensor nodes which energy reaches the threshold will start listening to the channel and generate a random number between 0 and 1 upon receiving a polling packet. If the generated number is smaller than P, the node will transmit a full-size data packet to the sink. Else, the polling packet will be disregard. The sink node adjusts P according to the result of data packet reception: increase P if no data received, decrease P if a collision happens. Thanks to this mechanism, PP-MAC has good scalability and behaves well in different network densities and energy harvesting rates.

Admittedly the P adjust mechanism is proved to be effective. However, collision can only be reduced but not eliminated. When the network density or energy harvesting rate is relatively high, the channel bandwidth waste caused by collision will prevent the performance of PP-MAC to be improved. To save the bandwidth wasted by collision, in this paper, we proposed Probe-Polling, an enhanced polling protocol drove form PP-MAC. The basic idea of Probe-Polling is to let sensor nodes use short probe packet instead of the long data packet when responding polling packet. Sink node judge the channel condition using the received Probe packet and feedback the information with a broadcast ACK packet. Sensor node will continue to transmit its data packet only if the ACK indicates the channel is free. Thus if a collision happens, the bandwidth wasted in PP-MAC will be saved, and the network will start a new polling cycle immediately. Simulation result shows that Probe-Polling achieves a higher throughput and lower inter-arrival time compared to PP-MAC.

The rest of this paper is organized as follows: Sect. 2 gives a detailed description of the proposed Probe-Polling protocol. And then we present the simulation results in Sect. 3. Finally, we conclude our work in Sect. 4.

2 Probe-Polling for EH-WSNs

2.1 System Overview

In this paper, we pay attention to single hop wireless sensor networks with one sink and several sensor nodes. Sink connects with power lines, so it always has enough energy to work continuously and plays a role of sensor data collection. Sensor nodes have the ability of energy harvesting, they communicate with sink and upload their sensing data using the energy harvested.

In real scenarios, the sensors' effective energy harvesting rate and their working power usually suffer a colossal mismatch. Therefore duty cycling is widely used in EH-WSNs. In this paper, we assume sensor nodes employ an harvest-use energy management scheme for its simplicity and easy to implement. Sensor nodes will turn to receive mode immediately and always have a data packet needed to upload once their energy reaches the threshold E_f which we will describe later. When the operation is over, sensor nodes will return to the charging mode and waiting for their energy reaches the E_f again. The energy mode of sensor nodes is shown in Fig. 1.

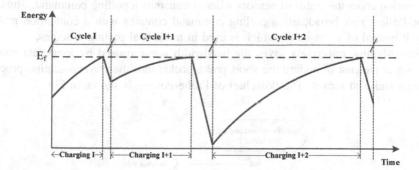

Fig. 1. Three charging cycles of a sensor node are displayed. In cycle I, the node did not respond to the polling command; in cycle I + 1, the node successfully transmitted its data packet to sink; in cycle I + 2, the node sent a probe packet to sink and received an ACK which implied a collision, it then stopped to transmit the data packet to sink.

We consider the network area is circular with a radius of 50 m; the sink locates in the center of the cycle. The max distance of communication between the sink and sensor nodes is 50 m, which can guarantee the reliable transmission. Thus we assume that the collision is the only reason for reception failure at the sink side. To judge the performance of the proposed protocol, we consider three crucial metrics namely Network Throughput(S), Fairness(F), and Inter-arrival time(Γ). S is termed as the rate of successful data packets receipted by the sink. Fairness represents the balance degree of the network and is quantified using the classic Jain's fairness metric in this paper, let R_i be the rate of data packets received from sensor i, the Fairness can be calculated using the following equation:

$$F = \frac{\left(\sum\limits_{i=1}^{n} R_i\right)^2}{n\left(\sum\limits_{i=1}^{n} R_i^2\right)} \tag{1}$$

The Inter-arrival time indicates how fast one sensor can successfully access the channel and is computed using:

$$\Gamma = \frac{\left(\sum\limits_{i=1}^{n} \frac{1}{R_i}\right)}{n} \tag{2}$$

2.2   Probe-Polling Detailed

Probe-Polling is designed for single-hop EH-WSN. Experiments in [10] have shown that the energy harvesting process of sensors is random. Sink in EH-WSNs has no information about the status of sensors when it transmits a polling command. Thus, in Probe-Polling sink broadcasts a polling command contains with a contention probability P instead of a sensor ID which is used in traditional polling schemes.

Probe-Polling effectively saves the bandwidth waste caused by long data packet collision at the cost of adding the short probe packet into the communication process between sink and sensor. The flowchart of Probe-Polling is shown in Fig. 2.

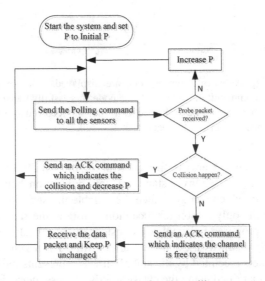

Fig. 2. Flowchart of probe-polling

Sensors which energy reaches the threshold will turn to receive state. Every sensor will generate a random number between 0 and 1 separately upon receiving the polling packet and compare the number with P contained in polling packet. The sensor will transmit a short probe packet to sink only of the generated random number is smaller than P and wait for an ACK packet. Otherwise, the sensor will ignore the polling packet and turn to the charging state waiting for its energy reaches E_f again.

Sink will judge the channel state by receiving the probe packet. After broadcasting a polling packet, the sink will turn to the receive state and wait for the probe packet. If only one probe packet is received, the sink will transmit an ACK packet which indicates the channel is free, the sensor which receives the ACK will upload its data packet to sink and then turns to the charging state for energy harvesting. If more than one sensors transmit probe packets to sink, a collision will be detected at sink side; then an ACK which indicates the channel is in collision will be sent by the sink, sensors which receive the ack will not upload their data packets and turn to the charging state immediately. If sink receives no probe packet throughout the carrier sense time, it will terminate the current polling cycle. We give an example of Probe-Polling in Fig. 3.

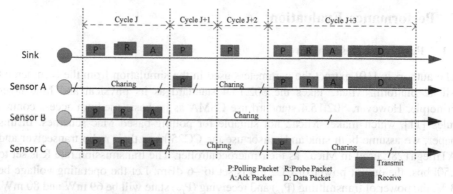

Fig. 3. Four polling cycles are displayed. In cycle J, sensor B and sensor C transmitted a probe packet to sink thus caused a collision. In cycle J + 1, only sensor A received the polling packet. However its generated random number was bigger than P, therefore ignored the poll. In Cycle J + 2, there was no sensor in receiving state. In Cycle + 3, sensor A and sensor C received the poll packet; however only sensor A transmitted a probe packet to sink. Sink feedback an ack packet indicated the channel was free. Thus the data packet was successfully uploaded.

Sink will adjust the parameter P in every polling cycle based on the transmission condition of its previous cycle. Specifically, sink will increase P if there is no node transmit probe packet during the last cycle. On the other hand, sink will decrease P if a collision is detected during the last cycle. If sink receives a data packet successfully, it will keep P unchanged. Authors in [10] introduced four specific adjustment schemes, namely additive-increase with multiplicative-decrease (AIMD), multiplicative-increase with multiplicative-decrease (MIMD), additive-increase with additive-decrease (AIAD), and multiplicative-decrease with additive-decrease (MIAD). Let P_{inc} be the increaser and P_{dec} be the decreaser. Name the linear factor as P_{lin}, the multiplicative-increase factor as

P_{mi}, and the multiplicative-decrease factor as P_{md}. Define the P_i as the contention parameter of the ith polling cycle. Then we can get:

$$P_{inc} = \begin{cases} P_{lin} & \text{for AIMD or AIAD} \\ P_{mi} * P_i & \text{for MIMD or MIAD} \end{cases}$$

$$P_{dec} = \begin{cases} P_{lin} & \text{for AIAD or MIMD} \\ P_{md} * P_i & \text{for AIMD or MIMD} \end{cases} \tag{3}$$

$$P_{i+1} = \begin{cases} \max(P_i + P_{inc}, 1) & \text{if no reply} \\ P_i & \text{if success} \\ \min(P_i - P_{dec}, 0) & \text{if collision} \end{cases} \tag{4}$$

Different P adjustment schemes will have different effects on the network performance. To make the Probe-Polling perform as well as possible, We tested different attempts and found that an AIMD scheme with P_{lin} as 0.01 and P_{md} as 0.1 showed the best overall performance in simulation.

3 Performance Evaluation

3.1 Parameter Description

The authors in [10] extract the parameters used in the simulation from the commercial Mica2 platform. Mica2 takes the 802.15.4 standard as its physical and Mac layer principle. However, 802.15.4 standard use CSMA as its basic medium access control rules [11], which makes Mica2 not suitable for polling-based Mac schemes. In this paper, we assume both sink and sensor use the CC2500 as their radio transceiver and ATmega128L used in Mica2 as their microcontroller. The transmission rate R is set to 250kbps, the output power of CC2500 is set to –6 dBm. Let the operating voltage be 3 V, the power of transmitting (P_{tx}) and receiving (P_{rx}) state will be 69 mW and 80 mW. The power during hardware turnaround (P_{ta}) is estimated to be the average of P_{tx} and P_{rx}, thus to be 74.5 mW.

Figure 4 shows the packet format of Probe-Polling. Considering the polling and ack packet's data filed size are 8 bytes and 1 byte separately. The total length of polling (S_{poll}) and ack (S_{ack}) packet are 15 bytes and 8 bytes. Every sensor has 100 bytes data needed to upload once it wakes up. We split the data and put the first byte into the data field of probe packet and the remainder into the data field of data packet. Thus the total length of probe (S_{pro}) and data (S_{data}) packet are 8 bytes and 106 bytes. Given the packet length and transmission rate, we can get the transmit time of polling (T_{poll}), ack (T_{ack}), probe (T_{pro}), and data (T_{data}) packet: 0.48 ms, 0.26 ms, 0.26 ms, 3.4 ms. The carrier sense time (T_{cca}) and hardware turnaround time (T_{ta}) are 96us and 21.5us according to the datasheet of CC2500.

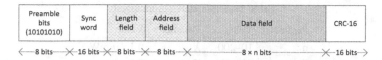

Fig. 4. Packet format of probe-polling

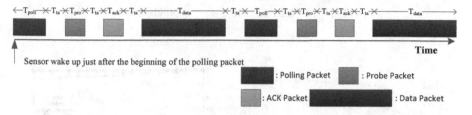

Fig. 5. The transmission timing of two successive polling cycles

To make sure that the sensor can receive at least one polling packet once it wakes up from the charging state. The energy threshold E_f should be chosen strictly. Figure 5 showed the timing information of two successive polling cycles. Imagine a sensor wakes up just after the beginning of a successful polling cycle and will successfully upload its data in the next polling cycle. Thus the energy it needed during its awake period should be the energy threshold E_f, and can be calculated using the following equation:

$$E_f = (2 * T_{poll} + T_{pro} + 2 * T_{ack} + T_{data} + 4 * T_{ta}) * P_{rx} + 3 * T_{ta} * P_{ta} + (T_{pro} + T_{data}) * P_{tx}$$

(5)

The network is deployed in a circular region with the radius to be 50 m. Sink locates the center of the circle, and nodes are randomly spread. Based on the experiment results from PP-MAC, we assume that the energy harvesting rate of the sensor in every second is a continuous variable with an expectation λ and independent from each other. To check the protocol performance under different network sizes, we set λ at 2 mW and vary the number of sensors(n) from 10 to 200. After that, we set the network size to be 100 and vary the λ from 0.1 mW to 10 mW to check the protocol performance under different energy harvesting environments. Every simulation runs 100 s, and each plotted point in the following graphs of results are the average over ten simulation runs.

Table 1 gives a summarized of the parameters used in the simulation.

3.2 Performance Under Different Network Sizes

To check the protocol's performance under different networks sizes. In this section, we let the average energy harvesting rate λ at 2 mW and vary the number of sensors from 10 to 200. Two other protocols namely PP-MAC and ID-Polling are included to make a

Table 1. Parameters summarized

Parameter	Value	Parameter	Value
n	10–200	λ	0.1-10 mW
P_{rx}	80 mW	T_{pro}	0.26 ms
P_{tx}	69 mW	T_{data}	3.4 ms
P_{ta}	74.5 mW	T_{ta}	21.5 μs
T_{poll}	0.48 ms	T_{cca}	96 μs
T_{ack}	0.26 ms	R	250 kbps

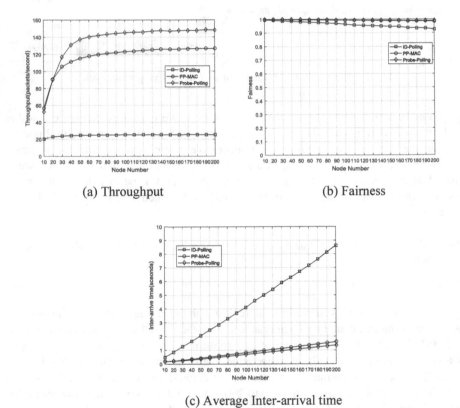

(a) Throughput   (b) Fairness

(c) Average Inter-arrival time

Fig. 6. Network Performance under different network sizes (λ = 2 mW)

comparison with Probe-Polling. PP-MAC has been proved to have a better overall performance than both slotted and unslotted CSMA under single-hop EH-WSNs. ID-Polling is a widely used protocol, in EH-WSNs it is hard for the sink to know the state of a particular sensor. Thus we assume ID-Polling randomly choose a sensor ID in every polling cycle. The simulation results are shown in Fig. 6.

From Fig. 6 we can get that when the node number is small (less than 30), the network throughput and inter-arrival time of Probe-Polling and PP-MAC are similar, that is because when the network size small, both of them has a low collision probability, the advantage of Probe-Polling is weakened. However, when the network size becomes larger, the collision probability will be increased. Thus Probe-Polling will have a higher throughput and lower inter-arrival time than PP-MAC by reducing the bandwidth waste caused by collision.

3.3   Performance Under Different Energy Harvesting Rates

Sensors will get varying average energy harvesting rates with different kinds of energies they harvest. In real scenarios, the average rate λ will also be variable when the environment changes. To check the network performance under different energy harvesting conditions, we fix the network size to 100 and change the λ from 0.1mW to 10 mW. Figure 7 shows the simulation results.

From Fig. 7 we can get that when the average energy harvesting rate is low (less than 0.4 mW), the network throughput and inter-arrival time of Probe-Polling and PP-MAC are similar. However, with the improvement of λ, Probe Polling will present a better performance than PP-MAC.

Give a deep insight into this phenomena, both small network sizes and low average harvesting rates will make the network have only a small number of awake sensors in every polling cycle. Thus the P will converge to a relative big value, and the collision probability will be tiny. In those conditions, the advantage of Probe-Polling will be suppressive. And the performance of Probe-Polling and PP-MAC will become similar. However, when the network sizes and average harvesting rates increase, the number of awake sensors in every polling cycle will be improved, resulting in pulling up the collision probability. Probe-Polling can effectively reduce the bandwidth waste caused by collision. Thus it will perform better than PP-MAC in those conditions.

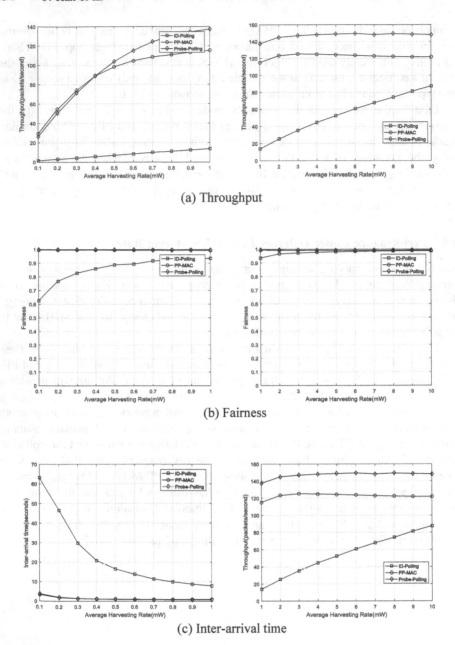

(a) Throughput

(b) Fairness

(c) Inter-arrival time

Fig. 7. Network Performance under different average energy harvesting rates (n = 100)

4 Conclusion

In this paper, we focus on single-hop EH-WSNs. To reduce the network bandwidth waste caused by collision, we propose a polling based Mac protocol namely Probe-Polling. The core concept of Probe-Polling is using the short probe packet for sink to detect the channel condition before sensor transmits their long data packet, and terminate the current polling cycle once collision happens. Thus the wasted bandwidth caused by long data packet collisions will be effectively saved. We evaluate the proposed protocol under different network scenarios and make a comparison with other protocols. The results show that Probe-Polling achieves high throughput and fairness as well as low inter-arrival times and performs better than other protocols.

For future works, we will develop the Probe-Polling to take the data packet's priority into account. We believe that the probe packet which used in Probe-Polling could carry the priority information and will be a suitable solution for multi-priority sensor networks.

Acknowledgment. This work was supported in part by the National Natural Science Foundation of China under project contracts No.61601093, No.61791082, No.61701116, No.61371047, in part by Sichuan Provincial Science and Technology Planning Program of China under project contracts No.2016GZ0061 and No.2018HH0044, in part by Guangdong Provincial Science and Technology Planning Program of China under project contracts No.2015B090909004 and No.2016A010101036, in part by the fundamental research funds for the Central Universities under project contract No.ZYGX2016Z011, and in part by Science and Technology on Electronic Information Control Laboratory.

References

1. Wei, Y., Heidemann, J., Estrin, D.: An energy-efficient MAC protocol for wireless sensor networks. In: International Conference on Computer Communications, pp. 1567–1576. IEEE (2002)
2. Huang, P., Xiao, L., Soltani, S., Mutka, M.W., Xi, N.: The evolution of MAC protocols in wireless sensor networks: a survey. IEEE Commun. Surv. Tutorials **15**(1), 101–120 (2013)
3. Wang, J., Ju, C., Gao, Y., Sangaiah, A.K., Kim, G.: A PSO based energy efficient coverage control algorithm for wireless sensor networks. Comput. Mater. Continua **56**(3), 433–446 (2018)
4. Liu, X.D., Liu, Q.: A dual-spline approach to load error repair in a HEMS sensor network. Comput. Mater. Continua **57**(2), 179–194 (2018)
5. Zhi, A.E., Seah, W.K.G., Tan, H.P.: A study of MAC schemes for wireless sensor networks powered by ambient energy harvesting. In: International Conference on Wireless Internet, pp. 78. ACM, The United States (2008)
6. Ramezani, P., Pakravan, M.R.: Overview of MAC protocols for energy harvesting wireless sensor networks. In: International Symposium on Personal, Indoor, and Mobile Radio Communications, pp. 2032–2037. IEEE (2015)
7. Basagni, S., Conti, M., Giordano, S., Stojmenovic, I.: Mobile Ad Hoc Networking: Cutting Edge Directions, 2ed edn. Wiley, Hoboken (2013)

8. Fafoutis, X., Dragoni, N.: ODMAC: an on-demand MAC protocol for energy harvesting wireless sensor networks. In: Symposium on Performance Evaluation of Wireless Ad Hoc, Sensor, and Ubiquitous Networks, pp. 49–56. ACM, Florida (2011)
9. Naderi, M.Y., Nintanavongsa, P., Chowdhury, K.R.: RF-MAC: a medium access control protocol for re-chargeable sensor networks powered by wireless energy harvesting. IEEE Trans. Wireless Commun. 13(7), 3926–3937 (2014)
10. Zhi, A.E., Tan, H.P., Seah, W.K.G.: Design and performance analysis of MAC schemes for wireless sensor networks powered by ambient energy harvesting. Ad Hoc Netw. 9(3), 300–323 (2011)
11. Ramachandran, I., Das, A.K., Roy, S.: Analysis of the contention access period of IEEE 802.15.4 MAC. ACM Trans. Sens. Netw. 3(1), 4 (2007)

An Dynamic Protocol for the Quantum Secure Multi-party Summation Based On Commutative Encryption

Wen Liu[1,2(✉)] and Min-Yao Ma[3]

[1] School of Computer Science and Cybersecurity,
Communication University of China, Beijing, China
lw_8206@163.com
[2] Key Laboratory of Convergent Media and Intelligent Technology,
Communication University of China, Ministry of Education, Beijing, China
[3] Department of Mathematics and Computer Science,
Guizhou Education University, Guiyang, China

Abstract. A dynamic protocol for the quantum secure multi-party summation based on commutative encryption is proposed. Without using the entangled character, joint measurement, n parties can encrypt their private information and privately get the summation of their private information using commutative encryption. Any m parties can dynamically participate and drop out the proposed protocol. Correctness analysis shows that the proposed protocol can be used to get the summation of their private information correctly. Security analysis shows that the proposed protocol can resist the general active attacks from an outside eavesdropper. And it can overcomes the problem of information leakage. In theory, our protocol can be used to build complex secure protocols for other multiparty computations and also lots of other important applications in distributed networks.

Keywords: Quantum secure multi-party summation · Dynamic · Commutative encryption · Correctness · Security

1 Introduction

Many quantum cryptographic protocols, such as quantum key distribution (QKD) [1–7], quantum secret sharing (QSS) [8–11], quantum stegonagraphy [12],

Supported by the National Natural Science Foundation of China (Grant No.61502437,Grant No.61773352); The China Scholarship Council(No.201707055033); The Fundamental Research Funds for the Central Universities (Grant No.2018CUCTJ017); The Science and Technology Program of Guizhou Province (No.QianKeHeJiChu[2016]1115); The Science and Technology Platform and Talent Team Project of Guizhou Province (No. QianKeHePingTaiRenCai [2017]5501; QianKe-HePingTaiRenCai [2016]5609); The Youth Science and Technology Talent Program of Department of Education of Guizhou Province (No. QianJiaoHeKYZi[2016]220).

X. Sun et al. (Eds.): ICAIS 2019, LNCS 11632, pp. 537–547, 2019.
https://doi.org/10.1007/978-3-030-24274-9_49

private quantum computation [13], and so on, have been proposed to solve various secure problems.

Secure multi-party summation problem was introduced by Goldreich in [14] and it is a important problem in secure multi-party computation. In the problem of secure multi-party summation, we supposed that there are n parties $P_1, P_2, .., P_n$ and they want to correctly calculate a summation function using their private information $x_1, x_2, ..., x_n$. It is a fundamental primitive of secure multi-party computation and can be applied in secret sharing, electronic voting, secure sorting, data mining and so on.

Secure multi-party summation problem has been extended to the quantum field and some researchers have investigated this problem based on quantum states. In 2006, a multi-party summation protocol with the two-particle N-level entangled states was proposed by Hillery et al. [15]. In 2007, a secure quantum addition module $n + 1$ based on non-orthogonal single states was presented by Du et al. [16]. In 2010, a quantum summation protocol with the multi-particle entangled GHZ states was presented by Chen et al. [17]. Then, Zhang et al. employed single photons in both polarization and spatial-mode degrees of freedom to design a quantum summation protocol [18] and proposed a quantum summation protocol based on the genuinely maximally entangled six-qubit states [19]. In 2016, a quantum summation protocol based on quantum Fourier transform and CNOT gate operators was presented by Shi et al. [20]. In 2017, Liu et al. [21] used Pauli matrices operations to encode information and Hadamard matrix to extract information and present a quantum secure multi-party summation protocol.

In this paper, we proposed a dynamic secure multi-party quantum summation protocol based on commutative encryption. In our protocol, n parties can privately get the result of $x_1 + x_2 + ... + x_n$ using the rotation operations and single-state measurement, which are easier to be realized with current technologies. The participants can dynamically be added or deleted in our protocol and it is more flexible in practice. Compared to other previous protocols, our protocol is simple and the entangled character, joint measurement of quantum states are not needed. The security of the presented protocol is also proved to be secure against both outside and participant attacks.

The structure of this paper is as follows: we propose a quantum dynamic multi-party summation protocol based on commutative encryption in Sect. 2; and we analyze the correctness and security of this protocol in Sect. 3. A brief discussion and the concluding summary are given in Sect. 4.

2   The Quantum Dynamic Secure Multi-party Summation Protocol based on Commutative Encryption

2.1   Quantum Commutative Encryption Scheme

Before presenting the protocol, we firstly give a description of the quantum commutative encryption scheme [22, 23]. Note that binary data can be encoded by using horizontal and vertical polarization (i.e., the horizontally polarized photon $|0\rangle$ represents zero in a binary representation and the vertically polarized photon $|1\rangle$ represents one). And, all transmitted polarized photons are encrypted before the transmission. The secret key is defined as a set of angles $K = \{\theta_i : 0 \le \theta_i < \pi, i = 1, 2, 3, ..., n\}$ for an n-bit message, where the subscript indicates the position of the bit in the message where the encryption with the angle θ_i is applied, and the rotation operation as encryption (i.e., a process o f disguising to hide its original polarization). Let $E_K[M]$ be an encryption of data M with a secret key K. Then, in order to read the disguised photons correctly, the receiver must rotate the transmitted photon by the angle θ_i in the opposite direction of what the sender rotated. This operation is defined as decryption. Let $D_K[M]$ be an decryption of data M with a secret key K. These operations can be represented mathematically as shown below.

In the following discussion, without losing generality, we can assume that a message M is a single photon encoded as $M : |\psi_0\rangle = |0\rangle$ for simplicity. By using the Jones matrix representation, the rotation operation can be represented by the following matrix:

$$R(\theta) = \begin{pmatrix} \cos\theta & \sin\theta \\ -\sin\theta & \cos\theta \end{pmatrix} \tag{1}$$

A sender encrypts the data qubit $|\psi\rangle$ with θ_A. (θ_A is randomly chosen and is shared between a sender and a receiver prior to the communication.)

$$\begin{aligned} E_K[M] = R(\theta_A)|0\rangle &= \begin{pmatrix} \cos\theta_A & \sin\theta_A \\ -\sin\theta_A & \cos\theta_A \end{pmatrix}\begin{pmatrix} 1 \\ 0 \end{pmatrix} \\ &= \begin{pmatrix} \cos\theta_A \\ -\sin\theta_A \end{pmatrix} = \cos\theta_A|0\rangle - \sin\theta_A|1\rangle = |\psi_1\rangle \end{aligned} \tag{2}$$

The sender sends the superposition states $|\psi_1\rangle$ to a receiver.

Before the receiver measures the received photon, he needs to rotate the received photon by θ_A in the opposite direction o f what the sender rotated. This decryption can be represented as follows:

$$\begin{aligned} R(-\theta_A)|\psi_1\rangle &= \begin{pmatrix} \cos(-\theta_A) & \sin(-\theta_A) \\ -\sin(-\theta_A) & \cos(-\theta_A) \end{pmatrix}\begin{pmatrix} \cos\theta_A \\ -\sin\theta_A \end{pmatrix} \\ &= \begin{pmatrix} \cos^2\theta_A + \sin^2\theta_A \\ \sin\theta_A \cdot \cos\theta_A - \cos\theta_A \cdot \sin\theta_A \end{pmatrix} = \begin{pmatrix} 1 \\ 0 \end{pmatrix} = |0\rangle. \end{aligned} \tag{3}$$

The main advantage of this encryption/decryption scheme is that a receiver does not have to decrypt a ciphertext in the same order as it was encrypted with different secret keys when data is encrypted more than once (e.g., i times) as follows.

$$\begin{aligned} E_{\theta_1}[E_{\theta_2}[...E_{\theta_{i-2}}[E_{\theta_{i-1}}[E_{\theta_i}[M]]]...]] &= E_{\theta_1}[E_{\theta_2}[...E_{\theta_{i-2}}[E_{\theta_{i-1}}[R(\theta_i).|\psi\rangle]]...]] \\ &= E_{\theta_1}[E_{\theta_2}[...E_{\theta_{i-2}}[R(\theta_{i-1}).R(\theta_i).|\psi\rangle]...]] \\ &= E_{\theta_1}[E_{\theta_2}[...E_{\theta_{i-2}}[R(\theta_{i-1}+\theta_i).|\psi\rangle]...]] \\ &= R(\theta_1 + \theta_2 + ... + \theta_{i-2} + \theta_{i-1} + \theta_i).|\psi\rangle \end{aligned} \tag{4}$$

Evidently, the encrypted data are irrespective of the order of encryptions. Also, the commutative relation of decryptions is trivial. In short, even if a sender encrypts a message with K_1 and then encrypts it with K_2, a receiver can decrypt the ciphertext with K_1 and then decrypt it with K_2.

$$D_{K_1}[D_{K_2}[E_{K_2}[E_{K_1}[M]]]] = D_{K_1}[D_{K_2}[E_{K_1}[E_{K_2}[M]]]] = M \tag{5}$$

Another notable feature o f this encryption scheme is that the original message (plaintext) in the encrypted data (ciphertext) can be modified without decrypting the ciphertext if the plaintext is known. For example, let us assume that the plaintext is a single bit, say, logic-one(i.e.,$M = |1\rangle$). Now, Alice encrypts it as $E_\theta[M] = R(\theta).|1\rangle = \sin\theta|0\rangle + \cos\theta|1\rangle$. If Alice wants to change the plaintext from logic-one to logic-zero after encryption, Alice rotates the quantum state by 90 degrees(i.e., $\pi/2$ radians).

$$
\begin{aligned}
R(\pi/2).E_\theta[|1\rangle] &= R(\pi/2).R(\theta)|1\rangle = R(\pi/2 + \theta)|1\rangle \\
&= \begin{pmatrix} \cos(\pi/2 + \theta) & \sin(\pi/2 + \theta) \\ -\sin(\pi/2 + \theta) & \cos(\pi/2 + \theta) \end{pmatrix} \begin{pmatrix} 0 \\ 1 \end{pmatrix} \\
&= \begin{pmatrix} -\sin(\theta) & \cos(\theta) \\ -\cos(\theta) & -\sin(\theta) \end{pmatrix} \begin{pmatrix} 0 \\ 1 \end{pmatrix} = \begin{pmatrix} \cos(\theta) \\ -\sin(\theta) \end{pmatrix} \\
&= \cos(\theta)|0\rangle - \sin(\theta)|1\rangle = R(\theta).|0\rangle = E_\theta[|0\rangle]
\end{aligned}
\tag{6}
$$

By using this technique, receivers can perform exclusive-OR (XOR) operations between the encrypted states and classical bits without decrypting if the receiver needs it for some applications. For instance, suppose the input is 1, we have $K_2 = \pi/2$, then

$$
\begin{aligned}
E_{\pi/2}E_{K_1}|0\rangle &= E_{K_1}R(\pi/2)|0\rangle = E_{K_1}|1\rangle = E_{K_1}|1 \oplus 0\rangle \\
E_{\pi/2}E_{K_1}|1\rangle &= E_{K_1}R(\pi/2)|1\rangle = E_{K_1}|1\rangle = E_{K_1}|1 \oplus 1\rangle
\end{aligned}
\tag{7}
$$

where $\oplus$ denotes the addition module 2.

2.2   The Basic Scheme

Supposed that there are n parties, $P_1, P_2, ..., P_n$, where P_j has a secret sequence $I_j = (I_j^1, I_j^2, ..., I_j^L)(j = 1, 2, ..., n)$. They can calculate the summation $\oplus\sum_{j=1}^n I_j$, where $\sum \oplus$ denotes the addition module 2. In this case, one player, suppose that the player P_1 can act as TP. The detail of our quantum dynamic secure multiparty summation protocol is described as follows:

(1) P_1 randomly generates a secret key $\theta_1 = \theta_1^1\theta_1^2, ..., \theta_1^L$, where $\theta_1^1\theta_1^2, ..., \theta_1^L$. It prepares a L-length sequence of photons $|\psi_1^1\rangle|\psi_1^2\rangle, ..., |\psi_1^L\rangle$ according to its secret sequence I_1, if $I_1^i = 0$, $|\psi_1^i\rangle = |0\rangle$; if $I_1^i = 1$, $|\psi_1^i\rangle = |1\rangle$. P_1 uses θ_1 to encrypt $|\psi_1^1\rangle|\psi_1^2\rangle, ..., |\psi_1^L\rangle$ and gets the result states $R(\theta_1^1)|\psi_1^1\rangle \otimes ... \otimes R(\theta_1^L)|\psi_1^L\rangle$, where $R(\theta_1^i)(i = 1, 2, ..., L)$ is the rotation operation.

P_1 prepares L' particles, which are randomly chosen from four photon states $|+y\rangle, |-y\rangle, |+\rangle, |-\rangle$ and randomly inserts the sequences S_1' of L' particles into the result states $R(\theta_1^1)\,|\psi_1^1\rangle \otimes ... \otimes R(\theta_1^L)\,|\psi_1^L\rangle$ to form a new states sequence S_1. P_1 records the insert positions sequence Po_1 and sends S_1 to P_2.

For $j = 2, ..., n$:

(2) After receiving S_{j-1}, P_{j-1} and P_j perform the eavesdropping check. P_{j-1} announces the insert positions Po_{j-1} and the measuring bases of S_{j-1}'. If the insert particle is $|+y\rangle$ or $|-y\rangle$, the measuring basis is $|+y\rangle$ or $|-y\rangle$ basis; if the insert particle is $|+\rangle$ or $|-\rangle$, the measuring basis is X basis. Then P_j chooses the L' particles from S_{j-1} according to the insert positions Po_{j-1} and measures these particles according to the measuring bases. P_{j-1} and P_j can find the existence of an eavesdropper by a predetermined threshold of error rate according to their measuring results. If the error rate exceeds the threshold they preset, they abort the scheme. Otherwise, they discards the measured photons in S_{j-1} and continue to the next step.

(3) P_j performs the commutative encryption on the photons $R(\theta_1^1)(\left|\psi_1^1 \oplus \overset{j-1}{\underset{K=2}{\oplus}}\right.$

$\left. I_k^1 \right\rangle \otimes ... \otimes R(\theta_1^L)(\left|\psi_1^L \oplus \overset{j-1}{\underset{k=2}{\oplus}} I_k^L \right\rangle)$ according to his secret sequence I_j: if $I_j^i = 0$, the encryption key $\theta_j^i = 0$; if $I_j^i = 1$, the encryption key $\theta_j^i = \pi/2$.

After performing the commutative encryption, the photons $R(\theta_1^1)(\left|\psi_1^1 \oplus \overset{j-1}{\underset{K=2}{\oplus}}\right.$

$I_k^1 \otimes ... \otimes R(\theta_1^L)(\left|\psi_1^L \oplus \overset{j-1}{\underset{k=2}{\oplus}} I_k^L \right\rangle)$ become $R(\theta_1^1)(\left|\psi_1^1 \oplus \overset{j}{\underset{k=2}{\oplus}} I_k^1 \right\rangle) \otimes ... \otimes R(\theta_1^L)(|\psi_1^L \oplus$

$\overset{j}{\underset{k=2}{\oplus}} I_k^L \rangle$.

P_j prepares L' particles, which are randomly chosen from four photon states $|+y\rangle, |-y\rangle, |+\rangle, |-\rangle$ and randomly inserts the sequences S_j' of L' particles into the result states $R(\theta_1^1)(\left|\psi_1^1 \oplus \overset{j}{\underset{k=2}{\oplus}} I_k^1 \right\rangle) \otimes ... \otimes R(\theta_1^L)(\left|\psi_1^L \oplus \overset{j}{\underset{k=2}{\oplus}} I_k^L \right\rangle)$ to form a new states sequence S_1. P_j records the insert positions sequence Po_j and sends S_j to P_{j+1}(if $j = n$, P_n send S_n to P_1).

(4) When P_1 has received the photons from P_n, he first does eavesdropping check with P_n. If there is no eavesdropper, he gets photons $R(\theta_1^1)(\left|\psi_1^1 \oplus \overset{n}{\underset{k=2}{\oplus}} I_k^1 \right\rangle) \otimes ... \otimes R(\theta_1^L)(\left|\psi_1^L \oplus \overset{n}{\underset{k=2}{\oplus}} I_k^L \right\rangle)$ and uses the secret key $\theta_1 = \theta_1^1\theta_1^2, ..., \theta_1^L$ to decrypt these photons $R(-\theta_1^1)R(\theta_1^1)$

$(\left|\psi_1^1 \oplus \overset{n}{\underset{k=2}{\oplus}} I_k^1 \right\rangle), ..., R(-\theta_1^L)R(\theta_1^L)(\left|\psi_1^L \oplus \overset{n}{\underset{k=2}{\oplus}} I_k^L \rangle)$. P_1 measures $\left|\psi_1^1 \oplus \overset{n}{\underset{k=2}{\oplus}}\right.$

$I_k^1 \rangle, ..., \left|\psi_1^L \oplus \overset{n}{\underset{k=2}{\oplus}} I_k^L \right\rangle$ and gets the summation of n parties' secret information.

2.3 Add Participants

We assume m participants $P_{n+1}, ..., P_{n+m}$ want to join the old n participants $P_1, P_2, ..., P_n$ before the step(4) of the basic protocol. Each participant of $P_{n+1}, ..., P_{n+m}$ has a secret sequence $I_j = (I_j^1, I_j^2, ..., I_j^L)(j = n+1, n+2, ..., n+m)$. The protocol of adding participants is described as follows:

For $j = n+1, ..., n+m$:

(1) After receiving S_{j-1}, P_{j-1} and P_j perform the eavesdropping check.

(2) P_j performs the commutative encryption on the photons $R(\theta_1^1)(\left|\psi_1^1 \oplus \overset{j}{\underset{k=2}{\oplus}} I_k^1\right\rangle) \otimes ... \otimes R(\theta_1^L)(\left|\psi_1^L \oplus \overset{j-1}{\underset{k=2}{\oplus}} I_k^L\right\rangle)$ according to his secret sequence I_j: if $I_j^i = 0$, the encryption key $\theta_j^i = 0$; if $I_j^i = 1$, the encryption key $\theta_j^i = \pi/2$.

After performing the commutative encryption, the photons $R(\theta_1^1)(\left|\psi_1^1 \oplus \overset{j}{\underset{k=2}{\oplus}} I_k^1\right\rangle) \otimes ... \otimes R(\theta_1^L)(\left|\psi_1^L \oplus \overset{j-1}{\underset{k=2}{\oplus}} I_k^L\right\rangle)$ become $R(\theta_1^1)(\left|\psi_1^1 \oplus \overset{j}{\underset{k=2}{\oplus}} I_k^1\right\rangle) \otimes ... \otimes R(\theta_1^L)(\left|\psi_1^L \oplus \overset{j}{\underset{k=2}{\oplus}} I_k^L\right\rangle)$.

P_j prepares L' particles, which are randomly chosen from four photon states $|+y\rangle, |-y\rangle, |+\rangle, |-\rangle$ and randomly inserts the sequences S_j' of L' particles into the result states $R(\theta_1^1)(\left|\psi_1^1 \oplus \overset{j}{\underset{k=2}{\oplus}} I_k^1\right\rangle) \otimes ... \otimes R(\theta_1^L)(\left|\psi_1^L \oplus \overset{j}{\underset{k=2}{\oplus}} I_k^L\right\rangle)$ to form a new states sequence S_1. P_j records the insert positions sequence Po_j and sends S_j to P_{j+1}(if $j = n+m$, P_{n+m} send S_{n+m} to P_1).

(3) When P_1 has received the photons from P_{n+m}, he first does eavesdropping check with P_{n+m}. If there is no eavesdropper, he gets photons $R(\theta_1^1)(\left|\psi_1^1 \oplus \overset{n+m}{\underset{k=2}{\oplus}} I_k^L\right\rangle) \otimes ... \otimes R(\theta_1^L)(\left|\psi_1^L \oplus \overset{n+m}{\underset{k=2}{\oplus}} I_k^L\right\rangle)$ and uses the secret key $\theta_1 = \theta_1^1 \theta_1^2, ..., \theta_1^L$ to decrypt these photons:$R(-\theta_1^1)R(\theta_1^1) (\left|\psi_1^1 \oplus \overset{n+m}{\underset{k=2}{\oplus}} I_k^1\right\rangle), ..., R(-\theta_1^L)R(\theta_1^L) (\left|\psi_1^L \oplus \overset{n+m}{\underset{k=2}{\oplus}} I_k^L\right\rangle)$. P_1 measures $\left|\psi_1^1 \oplus \overset{n+m}{\underset{k=2}{\oplus}} I_k^1\right\rangle, ..., \left|\psi_1^L \oplus \overset{n+m}{\underset{k=2}{\oplus}} I_k^L\right\rangle$ and gets the summation of $n+m$ parties' secret information.

2.4 Delete Participants

Without loss of generality, we assume the original participants are $P_1, P_2, ..., P_n$, and m participants $P_2, P_3, ..., P_m + 1$ want to leave. The protocol of deleting participants is described as follows:

(1) Before P_1 decrypts photons $R(\theta_1^1)(\left|\psi_1^1 \oplus \overset{n}{\underset{k=2}{\oplus}} I_k^1\right\rangle) \otimes ... \otimes R(\theta_1^L)(\left|\psi_1^L \oplus \overset{n}{\underset{k=2}{\oplus}} I_k^L\right\rangle)$, $P_2, P_3, ..., P_m + 1$ can leave the protocol.

For $j = 2, 3, ..., m + 1$:

(2) P_j performs the commutative encryption on the photons $R(\theta_1^1)(\left|\psi_1^1 \oplus \overset{n}{\underset{k=2}{\oplus}}\right.$

$\left. I_k^1 \oplus \overset{j-1}{\underset{k=2}{\oplus}} I_k^1 \right\rangle) \otimes ... \otimes R(\theta_1^L)(\left| \psi_1^L \oplus \overset{n}{\underset{k=2}{\oplus}} I_k^L \oplus \overset{j-1}{\underset{k=2}{\oplus}} I_k^L \right\rangle)$ according to his secret
sequence I_j(if $I_j^i = 0$, the encryption key $\theta_j^i = 0$; if $I_j^i = 1$, the encryption
key $\theta_j^i = \pi/2$).

After performing the commutative encryption, the photons $R(\theta_1^1)(\left| \psi_1^1 \oplus \overset{n}{\underset{k=2}{\oplus}} \right.$

$\left. I_k^1 \oplus \overset{j-1}{\underset{k=2}{\oplus}} I_k^1 \right\rangle) \otimes ... \otimes R(\theta_1^L)(\left| \psi_1^L \oplus \overset{n}{\underset{k=2}{\oplus}} I_k^L \oplus \overset{j-1}{\underset{k=2}{\oplus}} I_k^L \right\rangle)$ become $R(\theta_1^1)(\left| \psi_1^1 \oplus \overset{n}{\underset{k=2}{\oplus}} I_k^1 \oplus \right.$

$\left. \overset{j}{\underset{k=2}{\oplus}} I_k^1 \right\rangle) ... \otimes R(\theta_1^L)(\left| \psi_1^L \oplus \overset{n}{\underset{k=2}{\oplus}} I_k^L \oplus \overset{j}{\underset{k=2}{\oplus}} I_k^L \right\rangle)$.

P_j prepares L' particles, which are randomly chosen from four photon
states $|+y\rangle, |-y\rangle, |+\rangle, |-\rangle$ and randomly inserts the sequences S_j' of L' particles

into the result states $R(\theta_1^1)(\left| \psi_1^1 \oplus \overset{n}{\underset{k=2}{\oplus}} I_k^1 \oplus \overset{j}{\underset{k=2}{\oplus}} I_k^1 \right\rangle) \otimes ... \otimes R(\theta_1^L)(\left| \psi_1^L \oplus \overset{n}{\underset{k=2}{\oplus}} I_k^L \right.$

$\left. \oplus \overset{j}{\underset{k=2}{\oplus}} I_k^1 \right\rangle)$ to form a new states sequence S_j. P_j records the insert positions
sequence Po_j and sends S_j to P_{j+1}(if $j = m + 1$, $P_m + 1$ send S_j to P_1).

P_{j+1} has received the photons from P_j, he also needs to do the eavesdropping
check like the eavesdropping check in the basic scheme.

(3) P_1 decrypts $R(\theta_1^1)(\left| \psi_1^1 \oplus \overset{n}{\underset{k=2}{\oplus}} I_k^1 \overset{m+1}{\underset{k=2}{\oplus}} I_k^1 \right\rangle) \otimes ... \otimes R(\theta_1^L)(\left| \psi_1^L \oplus \overset{n}{\underset{k=2}{\oplus}} I_k^L \overset{m+1}{\underset{k=2}{\oplus}} I_k^L \right\rangle)$
and gets the summation of $n - m$ parties' secret information.

3   Analysis

3.1   Correctness Analysis

In the step(1) of our basic protocol, P_1 gets $E_{\theta_1}(|\varphi_1^1\rangle |\varphi_1^2\rangle, ..., |\varphi_1^L\rangle) = R(\theta_1^1) |\psi_1^1\rangle$
$\otimes ... \otimes R(\theta_1^L) |\psi_1^L\rangle$. P_1 sends the encrypted states to P_2.

$P_2, P_3, ..., P_n$ choose the encryption key according to their secret sequences
and sequentially execute the commutative encryption on the encrypted states
of P_1. After $P_2, P_3, ..., P_n$ sequentially perform the commutative encryption,
they get the new states $R(\theta_n^1)R(\theta_{n-1}^1)...R(\theta_2^1)R(\theta_1^1)(|\psi_1^1\rangle) \otimes ... \otimes R(\theta_n^L)R(\theta_{n-1}^L)...$
$R(\theta_2^L)R(\theta_1^L)(|\psi_1^L\rangle)$.

If there is no eavesdropper between these parties, the new states according to Eq. (7) become as follows:

$$
\begin{aligned}
&R(\theta_n^1)R(\theta_{n-1}^1)...R(\theta_2^1)R(\theta_1^1)(|\psi_1^1\rangle) \otimes ... \otimes R(\theta_n^L)R(\theta_{n-1}^L)...R(\theta_2^L)R(\theta_1^L)(|\psi_1^L\rangle) \\
&= R(\theta_n^1)R(\theta_{n-1}^1)...R(\theta_1^1)(|\psi_1^1 \oplus I_2^1\rangle) \otimes ... \otimes R(\theta_n^L)R(\theta_{n-1}^L)...R(\theta_1^L)(|\psi_1^L \oplus I_2^L\rangle) \\
&= R(\theta_1^1)(|\psi_1^1 \oplus I_2^1 \oplus ... \oplus I_{n-1}^1 \oplus I_n^1\rangle) \otimes ... \otimes R(\theta_1^L)(|\psi_1^L \oplus I_2^L ... \oplus I_{n-1}^L \oplus I_n^L\rangle) \\
&= R(\theta_1^1)\left(\left|\psi_1^1 \oplus \bigoplus_{k=2}^{n} I_k^1\right\rangle\right) \otimes ... \otimes R(\theta_1^L)\left(\left|\psi_1^L \oplus \bigoplus_{k=2}^{n} I_k^L\right\rangle\right)
\end{aligned}
\tag{8}
$$

When P_1 checks the eavesdropper, he can use his secret key to decrypt and measure the new states. Then he can get $\bigoplus_{k=1}^{n} I_k^1, ..., \bigoplus_{k=1}^{n} I_k^L$.

In the protocol of adding participants, there are m participants want to join the quantum dynamic secure multi-party summation protocol. They performs the commutative encryption on $R(\theta_1^1)\left(\left|\psi_1^1 \oplus \bigoplus_{k=2}^{j} I_k^1\right\rangle\right) \otimes ... \otimes R(\theta_1^L)\left(\left|\psi_1^L \oplus \bigoplus_{k=2}^{j-1} I_k^L\right\rangle\right)$ according to his secret sequence I_j, the new states according to Eq. (7) become as follows:

$$
\begin{aligned}
&R(\theta_{n+m}^1)...R(\theta_{n+1}^1)R(\theta_n^1)...R(\theta_1^1)(|\psi_1^1\rangle) \otimes ... \otimes R(\theta_{n+m}^L)...R(\theta_{n+1}^L)R(\theta_n^L)...R(\theta_1^L)(|\psi_1^L\rangle) \\
&= R(\theta_{n+m}^1)...R(\theta_1^1)(|\psi_1^1 \oplus I_2^1\rangle) \otimes ... \otimes R(\theta_{n+m}^L)...R(\theta_1^L)(|\psi_1^L \oplus I_2^L\rangle) \\
&= R(\theta_1^1)\left(\left|\psi_1^1 \oplus \bigoplus_{k=2}^{n+m} I_k^1\right\rangle\right) \otimes ... \otimes R(\theta_1^L)\left(\left|\psi_1^L \oplus \bigoplus_{k=2}^{n+m} I_k^L\right\rangle\right)
\end{aligned}
\tag{9}
$$

When P_1 checks the eavesdropper, he can use his secret key to decrypt and measure the new states. Then he can get $\bigoplus_{k=1}^{n+m} I_k^1, ..., \bigoplus_{k=1}^{n+m} I_k^L$.

In the protocol of deleting participants, m participants want to leave the quantum dynamic secure multi-party summation protocol. They performs the commutative encryption on $R(\theta_1^1)\left(\left|\psi_1^1 \oplus \bigoplus_{k=2}^{j} I_k^1\right\rangle\right) \otimes ... \otimes R(\theta_1^L)\left(\left|\psi_1^L \oplus \bigoplus_{k=2}^{j-1} I_k^L\right\rangle\right)$ according to his secret sequence I_j, the new states according to Eq. (7) become as follows:

$$
\begin{aligned}
&R(\theta_{m+1}^1)...R(\theta_2^1)R(\theta_n^1)...R(\theta_1^1)(|\psi_1^1\rangle) \otimes ... \otimes R(\theta_{m+1}^L)...R(\theta_2^L)R(\theta_n^L)...R(\theta_1^L)(|\psi_1^L\rangle) \\
&= R(\theta_1^1)\left(\left|\psi_1^1 \oplus \bigoplus_{k=2}^{n} I_k^1 \oplus \bigoplus_{k=2}^{m+1} I_k^1\right\rangle\right) \otimes ... \otimes R(\theta_1^L)\left(\left|\psi_1^L \oplus \bigoplus_{k=2}^{n} I_k^L \oplus \bigoplus_{k=2}^{m+1} I_k^L\right\rangle\right) \\
&= R(\theta_1^1)\left(\left|\psi_1^1 \oplus \bigoplus_{k=m+2}^{n} I_k^1\right\rangle\right) \otimes ... \otimes R(\theta_1^L)\left(\left|\psi_1^L \oplus \bigoplus_{k=m+2}^{n} I_k^L\right\rangle\right)
\end{aligned}
\tag{10}
$$

When P_1 checks the eavesdropper, he can use his secret key to decrypt and measure the new states. Then he can get $I_1^1 \oplus \bigoplus_{k=m+2}^{n} I_k^1, ..., I_1^L \oplus \bigoplus_{k=m+2}^{n} I_k^L$.

3.2 Security Analysis

Firstly, we show that the outside attack is invalid to our protocol. Secondly, we show that the n parties can not get any information about the private information of others.

3.3 Outside Attack

We analyze the possibility of the outside eavesdropper to get information about $I_1, I_2, ..., I_n$ in every step of protocol. In the basic scheme, the chance of attack from the outside eavesdropper is to attack the quantum channel in Step (1)(3). In Step (1)(3), the outside eavesdropper can attack the quantum channel when

$$P_i \text{ sent } R(\theta_1^1)(\left| \psi_1^1 \oplus \bigoplus_{k=2}^{j} I_k^1 \right\rangle) \otimes ... \otimes R(\theta_1^L)(\left| \psi_1^L \oplus \bigoplus_{k=2}^{j} I_k^L \right\rangle) \text{ to } P_{i+1}.$$ Because of

the use of nonorthogonal decoy photons, we performed eavesdropper checking process in Step (2)(4) and several kinds of outside attacks, such as the intercept-resend attack, the measure-resend attack, the entangle-measure attack, were detected with nonzero probability. Anyone who do not know the insert positions and bases of decoy particles cannot distinguish the decoy particles and the signal particles. For some special attacks, such as the photon-number-splitting (PNS) attack, the decoy-photon Trojan horse attack and the invisible photon Trojan horse attack, participants can defeat these attacks by using some beam splitters to split the sampling signals chosen for eavesdropping check before their operations and inserting filters in front of their devices to filter out the photon signal with an illegitimate wavelength. So, our quantum protocol is robust against outside attack.

3.4 Participant Attack

The term "participant attack", which emphasizes that the attacks from dishonest users are generally more powerful and should be paid more attention to, is first proposed by Gao et al. in Ref. [24] and has attracted much attention in the cryptanalysis of quantum cryptography [25–30]. We analyze the possibility of the n parties to get information about $I_1, I_2, ..., I_n$ in our protocol. We firstly analyze the case that P_i wants to learn the private information of other $n - 1$ parties. Secondly, we analyze the case that P_1 wants to learn the private information of $P_2, ..., P_n$.

Case 1: P_i wants to learn the private information of other $n - 1$ parties.

In our protocol, P_i can get $R(\theta_1^1)(\left| \psi_1^1 \oplus \bigoplus_{k=2}^{j} I_k^1 \right\rangle) \otimes ... \otimes R(\theta_1^L)(\left| \psi_1^L \oplus \bigoplus_{k=2}^{j} I_k^L \right\rangle)$. The secret key θ_1 is randomly chosen by P_1. Without the secret key, P_i cannot decrypt and measure these phones. So P_i cannot infer any information about the private information of other $n - 1$ parties.

Case 2: P_1 wants to learn the private information of $P_2, ..., P_n$.

In our protocol, P_1 knows the secret key θ_1 and also gets phones $R(\theta_1^1)(\left| \psi_1^1 \oplus \right.$ $\left. \bigoplus_{k=2}^{j} I_k^1 \right\rangle) \otimes ... \otimes R(\theta_1^L)(\left| \psi_1^L \oplus \bigoplus_{k=2}^{j} I_k^L \right\rangle)$. P_1 decrypts and measures these photons.

Although he can get the summation of n parties' secret information, he cannot exactly know $I_i(i = 1, 2, ..., L)$. So P_1 cannot infer any information about the private information of $P_2, ..., P_n$.

4   Discussion and Conclusions

In summary, we have put forward a dynamic quantum protocol to compute secure multiparty summation. In our protocol, n parties use the commutative encryption to encrypt the photons which include the private information of $P_1, P_2, ..., P_n$. And P_1 decrypts and measures the photons to get $\bigoplus_{k=1}^{n} I_k^1, ..., \bigoplus_{k=1}^{n} I_k^L$. Any m parties can participate and quit this protocol. Our protocol can not only withstand outside attacks, but also preserve the privacy of $P_1, P_2, ..., P_n$'s information. Furthermore, our quantum summation protocol can be generalized to compute lots of secure multiparty numerical computations.

References

1. Bennett, C.H., Brassard, G.: Quantum cryptography: public key distribution and coin tossing. In: Proceedings of IEEE International Conference on Computers, Systems, and Signal Processing, pp. 175–179 (1984)
2. Ekert, A.K.: Quantum cryptography based on Bell's theorem. Phys. Rev. Lett. **67**, 661–663 (1991)
3. Bennett, C.H., Brassard, G., Mermin, N.D.: Quantum cryptography without Bell's theorem. Phys. Rev. Lett. **67**, 557–559 (1992)
4. Deng, F.G., Long, G.L.: Controlled order rearrangement encryption for quantum key distribution. Phys. Rev. A **68**, 042315 (2003)
5. Gao, F., Guo, F.Z., Wen, Q.Y., Zhu, F.C.: Quantum key distribution without alternative measurements and rotations. Phys. Lett. A **349**, 53–58 (2006)
6. Guo, F.Z., Gao, F., Wen, Q.Y., Zhu, F.C.: A two-step channel-encrypting quantum key distribution protocol. Int. J. Quantum Inf. **8**, 1013–1022 (2010)
7. Gao, F., Guo, F.Z., Wen, Q.Y., Zhu, F.C.: Quantum key distribution by constructiong nonorthogonal states with Bell states. Int. J. Mod. Phys. B **24**, 4611–4618 (2010)
8. Karlsson, A., Koashi, M., Imoto, N.: Quantum entanglement for secret sharing and secret splitting. Phys. Rev. A **59**, 052307 (1999)
9. Xiao, L., Long, G.L., Deng, F.G., Pan, J.W.: Efficient multiparty quantum-secret-sharing schemes. Phys. Rev. A **69**, 162–168 (2004)
10. Deng, F.G., Zhou, H.Y., Long, G.L.: Bidirectional quantum secret sharing and secret splitting with polarized single photons. Phys. Lett. A **337**, 329–334 (2005)
11. Sun, Y., Wen, Q.Y., Gao, F., Chen, X.B., Zhu, F.C.: Multiparty quantum secret sharing based on Bell measurement. Opt. Commun. **282**, 3647–3651 (2009)
12. Qu, Z., Zhu, T., Wang, J., Wang, X.: A novel quantum stegonagraphy based on brown states. CMC Comput. Mater. Continua **56**(1), 47–59 (2018)
13. Liu, W., Chen, Z., Liu, J., Su, Z., Chi, L.: Full-blind delegating private quantum computation. CMC Comput. Mater. Continua **56**(2), 211–223 (2018)

14. Goldreich, O., Micali, S., Wigderson, A.: How to play any mental game. In: Proceedings of the Nineteenth Annual ACM Symposium on Theory of Computing, p. 218. ACM, New York (1987)
15. Hillery, M., Ziman, M., Buek, V., Bielikov, M.: Phys. Lett. A **349**(1–4), 75 (2006)
16. Du, J.Z., Chen, X.B., Wen, Q.X., Zhu, F.C.: Secure multiparty quantum summation. Acta Phys. Sin-Ch. Ed. **56**, 6214–6219 (2007)
17. Chen, X.B., Xu, G., Yang, Y.X., Wen, Q.Y.: An efficient protocol for the secure multi-party quantum summation. Int. J. Theor. Phys. **49**, 2793–2804 (2010)
18. Zhang, C., Sun, Z.-W., Huang, X.: Three-party quantum summation without a trusted third party. Int. J. Quantum Inf. **13**(2), 1550011 (2015)
19. Zhang, C., Sun, Z., Huang, Y.: High-capacity quantum summation with single photons in both polarization and spatial-mode degrees of freedom. Int. J. Theor. Phys. **53**(3), 933–941 (2014)
20. Shi, R., Yi, M., Zhong, H., Cui, J., Zhang, S.: Secure multiparty quantum computation for summation and multiplication. Sci. Rep. **6**, 19655 (2016)
21. Jakobi, M., et al.: Practical private database queries based on a quantum-key-distribution protocol. Phys. Rev. A **83**(2), 022301 (2011)
22. Kanamori, Y.: Quantum encryption and authentication protocols. Ph.D thesis, University of Alabama in Huntsville (2006)
23. Sun, Z., Huang, J., Wang, P.: Efficient multiparty quantum key agreement protocol based on commutative encryption. Quantum Inf. Process. **15**, 2101 (2016)
24. Gao, F., Qin, S.J., Wen, Q.Y., et al.: A simple participant attack on the Bradler-Dusek protocol. Quantum Inf. Comput. **7**, 329 (2007)
25. Qin, S.J., Gao, F., Wen, Q.Y., et al.: Cryptanalysis of the Hillery-Buzek-Berthiaume quantum secretsharing protocol. Phys. Rev. A **76**, 062324 (2007)
26. Lin, S., Gao, F., Guo, F.Z., et al.: Comment on multiparty quantum secret sharing of classical messages based on entanglement swapping. Phys. Rev. A **76**, 036301 (2007)
27. Lin, S., Wen, Q.Y., Gao, F., et al.: Improving the security of multiparty quantum secret sharing based on the improved Bostroem-Felbinger protocol. Opt. Commun. **281**, 4553 (2008)
28. Gao, F., Guo, F.Z., Wen, Q.Y., et al.: Comment on experimental demonstration of a quantum protocol for Byzantine agreement and liar detection. Phys. Rev. Lett. **101**, 208901 (2008)
29. Song, T.T., Zhang, J., Gao, F., et al.: Participant attack on quantum secret sharing based on entanglement swapping. Chin. Phys. B **18**, 1333 (2009)
30. Guo, F.Z., Qin, S.J., Gao, F., et al.: Participant attack on a kind of MQSS schemes based on entanglement swapping. Eur. Phys. J. D **56**, 445 (2010)

Optimal Resource Allocation for Energy Harvesting Cognitive Radio Network with Q Learning

Xiaoli He[1,2(✉)], Hong Jiang[1(✉)], Yu Song[1,3], Xiufeng Yang[1], and He Xiao[1]

[1] School of Information Engineering, South West University of Science and Technology, Mianyang 621010, Sichuan, China
hexiaoli_suse@hotmail.com
[2] School of Computer Science, Sichuan University of Science and Engineering, Zigong 643000, China
[3] Department of Network Information Management Center, Sichuan University of Science and Engineering, Zigong 643000, China

Abstract. In order to improve the utilization of available resources in wireless networks, this paper studies the resource allocation problem of underlay cognitive wireless network based on energy harvesting (EH-CRN). Our goal is to maximize the capacity of the EH-CRN by allocation optimal power while considering interference, SINR, energy conservation, and quality of service (QoS) guarantees. A Q-learning EH resource allocation algorithm based on reinforcement learning (QLRA-EHCRN) is proposed to solve the non-convex nonlinear programming optimization problem. Theoretical analysis and simulation results show that the proposed algorithm can effectively improve the system capacity, reduce the average delay, and improve the resource utilization of EH-CRN.

Keywords: Cognitive Radio Networks · Resource allocation · Energy harvesting · Q learning · Reinforcement learning

1 Introduction

With the rapid development of wireless communication technology and the widespread use of new mobile terminal devices, wireless communication has occupied an irreplaceable position in various fields. It is worth noting that the limited and unrecoverable radio frequency spectrum resources are increasingly lacking in the demand for rapidly growing wireless communication technology applications. The basic idea of solving the problem of lack of spectrum resources is to maximize the utilization of existing spectrum. Cognitive Radio (CR) technology can make full use of the idle spectrum resources of the spectrum resources in time and space to get the attention and research of researchers. The CRN (Cognitive Radio Networks), which combines CR technology with the wireless communication network, brings a new dawn to the development of the future wireless communication technology. In the CRN, the SU improves the spectrum utilization rate through Dynamic Spectrum Access (DSA) technology. Most of the CRN network nodes are powered by batteries, all of which face the problem of limited energy

© Springer Nature Switzerland AG 2019
X. Sun et al. (Eds.): ICAIS 2019, LNCS 11632, pp. 548–560, 2019.
https://doi.org/10.1007/978-3-030-24274-9_50

on the node itself. How to prolong the network lifetime and maintain the communication network stability becomes extremely critical.

Thus, to extend the lifetime of these low-power nodes, the concept of energy harvesting (EH) has been proposed and used in the research of wireless sensor networks (WSNs), CRNs and cellular networks. EH technology is a green energy technology that converts environmental energy sources (e.g., solar, wind, vibration, tidal, and radio frequency) into electrical energy [1]. However, due to the variability of the environment and the lack of maturity of energy conversion technology, this new EH technology has a strong randomness. Therefore, in the EH CRN communication, how to effectively manage and utilize the harvested energy to meet the network transmission needs is a real problem.

1.1 Related Work

Recently, the focus of research on EH CRN communication is mainly on resource allocation, relay selection, outage probability and access mode [2–5]. In the [2] study, the secondary user (SU) used multiple primary user (PU) transmitters to harvest energy and communicated with the access point with the harvested energy. In order to avoid interference, a communication protocol for EH was proposed. Analyzed the SU's recent EH time, power allocation and channel selection strategy. For the centralized and distributed architecture in heterogeneous cognitive radio networks, [3] studied the joint transmission of time and power allocation. Joint optimization problems are often used in CRN research [4]. Under fair constraints, the optimization problem was modeled to maximize the total capacity of the SU. The dynamic optimal joint transmission time and power allocation scheme for heterogeneous cognitive radio networks was proposed. [5] investigated the combined effect of perceived probability, access probability, and energy queue capacity on the maximum achievable throughput. For the extreme cases where the energy queue capacity was infinite or very small, if the channel sensing probability was properly selected and the optimal perceptual probability was derived, the maximum achievable throughput was not affected by the channel access probability.

All of the above researches consider that in the EH CRN, the SU converts the interference signal of the PU into energy for its own data transmission. The model designed is the frequency at which multiple EH-SUs multiplex a PU. In this multiplexing mode, the channel resources of the PU will be completely occupied by the EH-SU, and the amount of energy harvested by one PU is very low. In order to improve the spectrum efficiency and EH rate, this paper mainly studies the resource allocation problem under multiple EH-SUs multiplexing multiple PUs channel resources.

1.2 Contribution

In this study, unlike previous research work, our goal is to optimize the resource allocation (RA) of EH CRN to maximize the throughput of EH-SU. Therefore, we evaluate the RA problem of underlay CRN under multiple constraints (i.e., interference temperature, QOS guarantee, power limitation and energy conservation). More specifically, our main contributions to this work are summarized below:

- First, this paper considers the EH CRN RA problem. Therefore, multiple EH-SUs are allowed to multiplex spectrum resources of multiple PUs in the optimization problem.
- Subsequently, the established optimization problem is a non-convex nonlinear programming problem. Thus, a Q learning resource allocation algorithm for EH-CRN (QLRA-EHCRN) is proposed to obtain the optimal solution and improve the overall performance of the network.
- Finally, we provide numerical results to evaluate the effectiveness of our proposed RA algorithm QLRA-EHCRN. The numerical simulation results show that the proposed algorithm can obtain better theoretical optimal performance in the scenario with higher signal-to-noise-to-interference ratio (SINR). In addition, these tasks can effectively prolong the network lifetime, and also provide some insights for CRN research.

1.3   Organization of the Paper

The rest of this paper is organized as follows. Section 2 establishes system and network model, including EH model and mathematical modeling. Section 3 presents a solution to the problem. Numerical results are addressed. in Sect. 4. Finally, Sect. 5 concludes this paper.

2   System and Network Model

2.1   System Model

As shown in Fig. 1, we consider the scenario where multiple SUs share the uplink spectrum resources of the two PUs. We are investigating the underlay mode of CRN, so as long as the interference of the SUs to the PU does not exceed the interference temperature, the SUs can reuse the spectrum of the PU. At the same time, regardless of the spectrum allocation process, only the power control problem after allocation is considered.

In Fig. 1, the PU is powered by a conventional battery. Each EH-SU has a transmitter and a receiver. It is assumed that the EH-SU transmitter has an EH function and is equipped with an infinite capacity battery to store the harvested power. Since the signal decoding process at the receiver is ultra-low power consumption, this paper does not consider the power distribution of the EH-SU receiver. At the same time, the transmission process of the whole system is the case of time slot transmission.

Suppose there are M PUs and N EH-SUs in the EH CRN. So there are N cognitive links in the network, and any EH-SU communication link will interfere with PU and other EH-SUs. Similarly, the PU will also interfere with all EH-SUs. Unlike a typical OFDMA system, the sub-channel selection of the EH-SU depends not only on its channel gain,

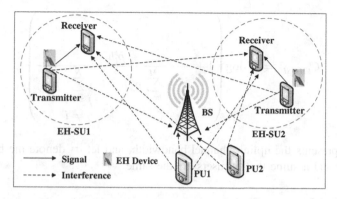

Fig. 1. System model of underlay CRN: PUs and EH-SUs share the uplink link scenario

but also on the interference of the PU and the neighbor EH-SU. According to the system assumption, in the t time slot, the signal at the receiver of PU and EH-SU can be written as:

$$PUR_m^t = \sqrt{p_m^t} h_{mB} x_{mB} + \underbrace{\sum_{i=1}^{N} \sqrt{p_i^t} h_{iB} x_{iB}}_{EH-SU_i \; interference \; to \; PU_m} + n_0 \qquad (1)$$

$$EH-SUR_i^t = \sqrt{p_i^t} h_i x_i + \underbrace{\sum_{m=1}^{M} \sqrt{p_m^t} h_{mi} x_m}_{PU_m \; interference \; to \; EH-SU_i} + \underbrace{\sum_{\substack{j=1 \\ j \neq i}}^{N} \sqrt{p_j^t} h_{ij} x_j}_{neighbor \; EH-SU_j \; interference \; to \; EH-SU_i} + n_0 \qquad (2)$$

where in the t slot, p_m^t, p_i^t and p_i^t represent the transmission power of PU_m, $EH-SU_i$ and $EH-SU_j$, respectively. h_{mB} and h_{iB} indicate channel gain to base station of PU_m and $EH-SU_i$. h_i, h_{mi} and h_{ij} indicate channel gain between $EH-SU_i$ sender and receiver, $EH-SU_i$ and PU_m, $EH-SU_i$ and $EH-SU_j$, respectively. x_{mB}, x_{iB}, x_i, x_m and x_j represent the transmission of data information. n_0 is the additive white Gaussian noise power with mean value of 0 and variance of σ^2 [6].

According to Shannon's theorem, the channel capacity of the main link and the EH-SU link in the t slot can be expressed as follows:

$$C_{PU_m}^t = W \log \left(1 + \frac{p_m^t h_{mB}}{\sigma^2 + \sum_{i=1}^{N} p_i^t h_{iB}} \right) \qquad (3)$$

$$C^t_{EH-SU_i} = W \log \left(1 + \frac{p^t_i h_i}{\sigma^2 + \sum\limits_{m=1}^{M} p^t_m h_{mi} + \sum\limits_{\substack{j=1 \\ j \neq i}}^{N} p^t_j h_{ij}} \right) \quad (4)$$

where W represents the uplink channel bandwidth, and let σ^2 denote the background noise power and assume that all users are the same.

2.2 EH Model

At present, solar energy is the main energy harvesting source in practical applications, in which the power density of solar energy is 10–15 mW/m³. Although solar energy has higher energy replenishment efficiency, it cannot be harvested at night or in rainy days due to the lack of illumination at night and the lack of light in rainy days, thus affecting the practicality of the network. Therefore, this paper assumes that the EH model of EH-SUs obeys the independent composite Poisson distribution shown by Eq. (1) in [11]. The EH model is shown in Fig. 2.

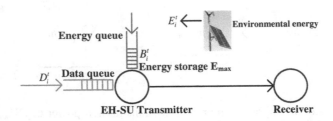

Fig. 2. EH model

In the time slot with a total length of T, each time slot is fixed. Under the time slot t, the average energy of the E^t_i unit is reached and stored in the battery B^t_i, and D^t_i unit data is transmitted. Assuming that the battery is not leaking, store all the harvested energy into the battery. All arrivals known by transmitter beforehand. The energy of the P^t_i unit is used for transmission in each time slot, and the residual energy of the battery in each time slot is:

$$B^t_i = E^t_i + B^{t-1}_i - P^t_i \leq E_{\max} \quad (5)$$

In addition, the limited capacity of the battery must be considered and battery overflow should be avoided. The battery capacity is large enough that each input energy can be stored in the battery. The maximum storage capacity (size) of the battery is $E_{\max}$, where energy harvested above this capacity is lost due to the battery being full.

After the transmission of the $t-1$ time slot is completed, the energy used by the node for transmission in the t slot is

$$P_i^t \leq \min\{B_i^t, P_{EH-SU}^{\max}\} \tag{6}$$

where $P_{EH-SU}^{\max}$ is the system maximum power of the EH-SU. Equation 5 represents the storage causality, and Eq. 6 is energy capacity. In addition to energy causality and battery overflow, the node's data arrival process should also be considered. Therefore, data causality is limited

$$D_i^t + C_{EH-SU_i}^{t-1} - C_{EH-SU_i}^t \leq D^{\max} \tag{7}$$

where $D^{\max}$ is the system maximum data buffer. In this case, the storage and consumption of energy is used only for communication. At the same time, the base station knows the energy status information and channel status information of all the nodes, and the base station can control the power of the user through the information [12].

2.3 Mathematical Modeling

On this basis, by constructing an optimization model, an optimal resource allocation algorithm can be found to maximize the throughput of the entire system. Before considering the transmission rate requirements of the guaranteed PU, this paper considers the total transmission rate of all EH-SU communication links in the optimized network under the time slot t. The optimization target expression is as follows:

$$\mathbf{P1}: \quad \max_{\{p_i^t\},\{P_m^t\},T} \sum_i^N C_{EH-SU_i}^t \tag{6a}$$

$$s.t. \ 0 \leq p_i^t \leq \min\{B_i^t, P_{EH-SU}^{\max}\}(t=\{1,2,\cdots T\}, i=\{1,2,\cdots N\}) \tag{6b}$$

$$C_{EH-SU_i}^t \geq C_{EH-SU}^{th} \tag{6c}$$

$$\sum_{t=1}^T p_i^t \leq \sum_{t=1}^T E_i^t (t=\{1,2,\cdots T\}, i=\{1,2,\cdots N\}) \tag{6d}$$

$$\sum_{i=1}^N p_i^t h_{iB} \leq I^{th} (i=\{1,2,\cdots N\}) \tag{6e}$$

$$D_i^t + C_{EH-SU_i}^{t-1} - C_{EH-SU_i}^t \leq D^{\max} \tag{6f}$$

$$0 \leq p_m^t \leq P_{PU}^{\max} (t=\{1,2,\cdots T\}, m=\{1,2,\cdots M\}) \tag{6g}$$

$$C_{PU_m}^t \geq C_{PU}^{th} \tag{6h}$$

(6b) represents that the power of the $EH - SU_i$ must be lower than the available energy. (6g) indicates that the power of the PU_m cannot exceed the maximum transmit power. The $C^t_{EH-SU_i}$ and $C^t_{PU_m}$ are the channel capacity of the i th EH-SU and the m th PU, which are obtained by Eqs. (3) and (4), respectively. (6c) and (6h) denote that the transmission rate of $EH - SU_i$ and PU_m should reach the minimum transmission rate thresholds $C^{th}_{EH-SU_i}$ and $C^{th}_{PU_m}$, respectively. Meanwhile, (6d) means that the energy consumed for data transmission cannot exceed the harvested energy at the allocated time and transmission power. (6e) demonstrates the transmission power of the $EH - SU_i$ cannot exceed the interference temperature at the PU transmitter. (6f) is a data causal constraint that can reduce data buffer overflow [13].

3   Problem Solution Method

The optimization goals and constraints (6c), (6f) and (6h) in problem **P1** are all related to the channel capacity. The channel capacity $C^t_{EH-SU_i}$ and $C^t_{PU_m}$ are Shannon expressions for $\{p^t_i\}$ and $\{p^t_m\}$, which are non-convex functions. Therefore, the problem **P1** is a non-convex problem. At the same time, in order to maximize resource utilization, this paper proposes a Q learning resource allocation algorithm for EH-CRN (QLRA-EHCRN) to obtain a solution to this problem. The base station can dynamically allocate power according to the real-time change of the channel state and the energy state. When the channel state is good and the energy is sufficient, the user allocates more resources, otherwise allocates less resources to achieve the long term resource utilization of the system. QLRA-EHCRN algorithm specific steps are as follows.

3.1   Q Learning

This paper uses Q Learning, the most widely used algorithm in reinforcement learning (RL). The basic principle of Q learning is that after an action is taken by an agent, it causes the state of the environment to change, and the effect of this change can be quantified as a reward. The value of the return value can reflect the award or punishment to evaluate the movements of the agent. The agent selects the next action based on the return value and the current state of the environment. The principle of selection is to increase the probability of being a positive reward value until convergence.

Q learning consists of basic elements such as environmental state set S, action set A, reward function R, state transition probability $P^a_{ss'}$, and strategy π. At time t, agent obtains the environmental state $s \in S$ and selects action $a \in A$ according to the current policy π. After the environment is affected by action a, it changes to the new environmental state $s' \in S$ according to probability $P^a_{ss'}$. At the same time, the return value R is generated and fed back to agent. Agent updates policy π according to R and s', and proceeds to the next iteration. The ultimate goal of agent is to find the best strategy π^* for all states s to maximize the expected long-term cumulative return. The cumulative reward expectation value can be calculated by Eq. 7.

$$V^{\pi}(s) = \mathbb{E}_{\pi}\left[R_{i,t}^n | S_t = s\right] = \sum_{a \in A} \pi(s,a)\left[R_{ss'}^a + \gamma \sum_{s' \in S} P_{ss'}^a V^{\pi}(s')\right] \tag{7}$$

where $\gamma \in [0,1]$ is the discount factor, which is used to measure the impact of future rewards on cumulative rewards. The greater the value of γ, the more emphasis is placed on past experience, otherwise the more attention is paid to immediate interests. $R_{ss'}^a$ is the return value of the new state s' when the action a is performed in the state s. According to the Bellman optimal equation, the maximum value can be obtained as follows:

$$\begin{aligned} V^{\pi^*}(s) &= \max_{a \in A}\left[R_{ss'}^a + \gamma \sum_{s' \in S} P_{ss'}^a V^{\pi^*}(s')\right] \\ &= R_{ss'}^a + \max_{a \in A} \gamma \sum_{s' \in S} P_{ss'}^a V^{\pi^*}(s') \end{aligned} \tag{8}$$

The $\pi(s,a)$ value corresponds to a Q value, which is expressed as $Q^{\pi}(s,a)$:

$$Q^{\pi}(s,a) = R_{ss'}^a + \gamma \sum_{s' \in S, a' \in A} P_{ss'}^a Q^{\pi}(s',a') \tag{9}$$

$$\begin{aligned} Q^{\pi^*}(s,a) &= \max\left[R_{ss'}^a + \gamma \sum_{s' \in S} P_{ss'}^a \max Q^{\pi^*}(s',a')\right] \\ &= R_{ss'}^a + \max_{a \in A} \gamma \sum_{s' \in S} P_{ss'}^a \max Q^{\pi^*}(s',a') \end{aligned} \tag{10}$$

Through the Bellman optimal equations, the optimal action policy π^* can be solved as follows:

$$\pi^*(s,a) = \arg_{\pi} \max_{u \in A} Q^*(s,a), \{R^*(s,a) \geq R^{\pi_i}(s,a), \pi_i \in \pi\} \tag{11}$$

At each t time slot, Q learning updates the Q value in an iterative manner. The update process is as follows:

$$Q_{t+1}(s,a) \leftarrow (1-\alpha)Q_t(s,a) + \alpha\left[r_t + \gamma \max_{a \in A} Q_t(s',a')\right] \tag{12}$$

where $\alpha \in [0,1)$ is the learning rate. So when $t \to \infty$, $\alpha \to 0$, $Q_t(s,a)$ converges to $Q_t^*(s,a)$. The optimal strategy π^* can be obtained by using Eq. (11).

3.2   Q Learning for EH-CRN

In this paper, each EH-SU transmitter is an agent, which is the resource allocator. When the Q learning algorithm is applied to the EH-CRN, factors such as system state S, action A, and reward R need to be connected to the actual access model. The specific process is as follows.

- State set S: The system state contains Energy State Information (ESI), Channel State Information (CSI), and Queue Status Information (QSI) of the data to be transmitted. More specifically, at t time slot S is defined as follows:

$$S = \{\tilde{E}^t, \tilde{B}^t, \tilde{H}^t, \tilde{D}^t\} \tag{13}$$

where $\tilde{E}^t = \{\tilde{E}_1^t, \tilde{E}_2^t, \tilde{E}_3^t\}$ represents the ability to harvest energy, which is normalized into three levels (i.e., $\tilde{E}_1^t = low, \tilde{E}_2^t = medium, \tilde{E}_3^t = high$). $\tilde{B}^t = \{\tilde{B}_1^t, \tilde{B}_2^t, \cdots \tilde{B}_N^t\}$ indicates the existing energy of the battery. $\tilde{H}^t = \{0, 1\}$ is the channel state. If the CSI is perfect (ideal), that is, there is no CSI delay, quantization error and CSI feedback error, then $\tilde{H}^t = 0$. Conversely, if the CSI is imperfect (non-ideal), then $\tilde{H}^t = 1$. $\tilde{D}^t = \{\tilde{D}_1^t, \tilde{D}_2^t, \cdots \tilde{D}_N^t\}$ denotes the queued data.

- Action set A: $A = \{\tilde{P}^t\}$ represents the ratio of the power allocated by the EH-SU at the time t to the total transmission power of the system. Where $\tilde{P}^t = \{0 \leq \tilde{P}_i^t \leq 1, \forall i\}$.
- Transition probability $P_{ss'}^a$: According to the system model, the transition probability $P_{ss'}^a$ at time t to the next state $s' \in S$ at time $t + 1$ is:

$$P_{ss'}^a = \mathbb{P}\left(s^{t+1} = \{\tilde{E}_i^{t+1}, \tilde{B}_i^{t+1}, \tilde{H}_i^{t+1}, \tilde{D}_i^{t+1}\} = s' \big| s^t = \{\tilde{E}_i^t, \tilde{B}_i^t, \tilde{H}_i^t, \tilde{D}_i^t\} = s, a^t = a\right) \tag{14}$$

- Reward R: For the network scenario, the channel capacity is used as a reward function. We can find the optimal power control of the EH-SU by calculating the cumulative return value of the channel capacity to maximize system throughput. The description of $C_{EH-SU_i}^t$ is shown in Eq. (4) and the total discounted reward can be calculated as:

$$R^t = \sum_{t=1}^{T} \gamma^t \sum_{i=1}^{N} C_{EH-SU_i}^t = \sum_{t=1}^{T} \gamma^t \sum_{i=1}^{N} W \log \left(1 + \frac{p_i^t h_i}{\sigma^2 + \sum_{m=1}^{M} p_m^t h_{mi} + \sum_{\substack{j=1 \\ j \neq i}}^{N} p_j^t h_{ij}} \right) \tag{15}$$

Action strategy is a core part of Q learning. The choice of action strategy needs to solve the balance problem of exploration and exploitation. The control parameters corresponding to different strategies change with time. Common methods include ε-greedy strategy and Boltzmann mechanism. This paper chooses ε-greedy strategy as the action selection strategy. Calculate the Q function value according to Eqs. (9) and (10). According to the action strategy, the maximum cumulative return value is obtained as follows:

$$Q_t(s,a) = Q_{t-1}(s,a) + \alpha \left[R^t + \gamma \max_{a \in A} Q_{t-1}(s',a') - Q_{t-1}(s,a) \right] \quad (16)$$

3.3 Algorithm Implementation Steps

The specific steps of the EH-CRN resource allocation algorithm (QLRA-EHCRN) based on Q learning in reinforcement learning proposed in this paper are shown in Algorithm 1.

Algorithm 1 QLRA-EHCRN based Power Control Algorithm

Initialize: $t \leftarrow 0$, T, α, γ, ε, N, M

for $i = 1$ to N do

    Exchange causal knowledge and observe the current state s_i^t based on $\tilde{E}_i^t, \tilde{B}_i^t, \tilde{H}_i^t, \tilde{D}_i^t$

    Select the transmission power p_i^t based on the ε-greedy strategy

    While $i \neq N$ and $EH - SU_i$ is harvesting energy **do**

        Transmit using the selected transmission power p_i^t based on equation (6)

        Calculate B_i^t, D_i^t using equation (5) and equation (7)

        Calculate the corresponding discounted reward R_i^t using equation (11)

        Exchange causal knowledge and observe the next state s_i^{t+1}

        Select next transmit power p_i^{t+1} using the ε-greedy strategy

        Update the Q value $Q_{t+1}(s,a), s \in S, a \in A$ according to equation(12)

        Update the value function R_i^{t+1} and share with the neighbors

        $t \leftarrow t+1$

    End while

End for

---

4 Simulation Result

In this section, we analyze the performance of QLRA-EHCRN resource allocation algorithm based on RL through MALAB R2015b simulation. The effectiveness of the algorithm is verified by algorithm estimation and algorithm comparison. The simulation parameter table is shown in Table 1.

Assuming that the entire network coverage is 50 m × 50 m, one BS, two PUs and six EH-SU pairs (i.e., transmitter and receiver) are randomly distributed. The system is deployed in a Rayleigh fading environment, and channel state information (CSI) is comprised of perfect CSI and imperfect CSI (we choose the perfect CSI for this simulation). Assuming that the system has completed the allocation of subcarriers, the focus of our research is to perform power control of the EH-SUs at different energy arrival rates.

Table 1. Comparison table of system parameters

Parameters	Value	Parameters	Value
Channel	Rayleigh	Maximum data $D^{\max}$	3
Spectrum bandwidth W	2 MHz	Battery maximum capacity $E_{\max}$	200 W
Number of PUs M	2	PUs maximum power $P_{PU}^{\max}$	7 dBm
Number of EH-SUs N	8–20	EH-SUs maximum power $P_{EH-SU}^{\max}$	3 dBm
Noise power σ^2	−80 dBm/Hz	PUs minimum capacity C_{PU}^{th}	1 bps/Hz
Interference temperature I_{th}	3 dBm	EH-SUs minimum capacity C_{EH-SU}^{th}	1 bps/Hz
Learning rate α	0.3, 0.5, 0.7	Path-loss parameter	3.5
Discount factor γ	0.3, 0.5, 0.7	Greedy ε	0.3

Firstly, we change the learning rate α and discount factor γ to verify the capacity change of the system with different EH-SUs. Secondly, it is compared with the classical water-filling power allocation algorithm (WFPA) and the EH resource allocation (EHRA) algorithm of literature [2].

4.1 Algorithm Performance Estimation

As shown in Fig. 3, when the QLRA-EHCRN algorithm has different discount factors γ, the CRN capacity becomes larger as the number of EH-SUs increases. At the same time, it can be observed that when the same number of EH-SUs, the discount factor γ is high and the capacity is larger. For example, when the number of EH-SUs is 20 and the discount factor $\gamma = 0.7$, the capacity is maximized.

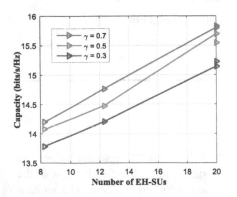

Fig. 3. Capacity VS. number of EH-SUs with different γ.

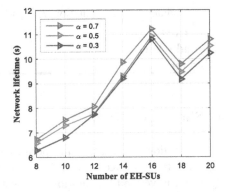

Fig. 4. Network lifetime VS. number of EH-SUs with different α.

Figure 4 shows the relationship between network lifetime and the number of EH-SUs. We can see from Fig. 4 that when the number of EH-SUs is between 8 and 16, the network lifetime increases with more EH-SU access. When the number of EH-SUs is 16 and 18, the energy consumption increases due to the increase of the node distance, and the network lifetime decreases. After the energy harvested by the EH-SU increases, the network lifetime also increases. At the same time, it can be seen that an increase in the learning rate α will also affect the improvement of the network lifetime.

Through Figs. 3 and 4, we can get that in the QLRA-EHCRN algorithm, both the discount factor γ and the learning rate α will affect the capacity and lifetime, but the impact on the optimal power allocation is small. The performance of QLRA-EHCRN is verified by comparison with other algorithms (i.e., EHRA, WFP) next.

4.2 Algorithm Performance Comparison

Figure 5 shows the effect of three power control algorithms on CRN capacity. As the number of EH-SUs increases, our proposed algorithm QLRA-EHCRN can achieve higher capacity and improve system throughput. The main reason for this phenomenon is that EH is not considered in the WFPA algorithm, while the EHRA algorithm considers EH, but the algorithm is not adaptive.

Figure 6 represents the effect of the three algorithms on the average delay. It can be seen that the two algorithms (QLRA-EHCRN, EHRA) with energy harvesting have a smaller average delay and a slower change. The EH can provide energy to the EH-SU, ensuring sufficient energy and reducing network transmission delay.

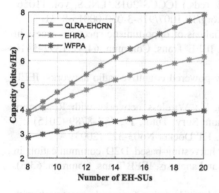

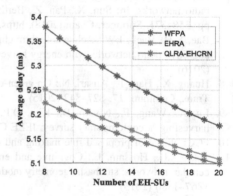

Fig. 5. Capacity VS. number of EH-SUs with different Power control algorithm.

Fig. 6. Average delay VS. number of EH-SUs with different Power control algorithm.

5 Conclusions

This paper proposes an intelligent power control resource allocation algorithm to establish a resource allocation model for OFDMA uplink multi-user communication system based on dynamic energy harvesting. EH-SU has EH function. Under multi-constraint conditions, the system is built as a multi-user Markova decision process with the goal of maximum system capacity. In order to maximize system capacity, we propose a Q learning method based on reinforcement learning (QLRA-EHCRN) to dynamically allocate power.

Acknowledgments. This work was partially supported by National Natural Science Foundation of China (No. 61771410), by Postgraduate Innovation Fund Project by Southwest University of Science and Technology (No. 18ycx115), by 2017, 2018 Artificial Intelligence Key Laboratory of Sichuan Province (No. 2017RYY05, No. 2018RYJ03), and by Horizontal Project (No. HX2017134, No. HX2018264).

References

1. Ku, M.-L., Li, W., Chen, Y., Liu, K.J.R.: Advances in energy harvesting communications: past, present, and future challenges. IEEE Commun. Surv. Tutor. **18**(2), 1384–1412 (2016)
2. Tran, H.V., Xuan, T.Q., Tran, H.V., et al.: Optimal energy harvesting time and power allocation policy in CRN under security constraints from eavesdroppers. In: IEEE International Symposium on Personal. IEEE (2018)
3. Xie, R., Ji, H., Si, P., et al.: Optimal joint power and transmission time allocation in cognitive radio networks. In: IEEE Wireless Communication & Networking Conference. IEEE (2010)
4. He, X., Jiang, H., Song, Y., et al.: Joint optimization of channel allocation and power control for cognitive radio networks with multiple constraints. Wirel. Netw. 1–20 (2018)
5. Fanzi, Z., Jisheng, X.: Leasing-based performance analysis in energy harvesting cognitive radio networks. Sensors **16**(3), 305–320 (2016)
6. He, X., Jiang, H., Song, Yu., Xiao, H.: Optimal resource allocation for underlay cognitive radio networks. In: Sun, X., Pan, Z., Bertino, E. (eds.) ICCCS 2018. LNCS, vol. 11066, pp. 358–371. Springer, Cham (2018). https://doi.org/10.1007/978-3-030-00015-8_31
7. Bae, Y.H., Baek, J.W.: Achievable throughput analysis of opportunistic spectrum access in cognitive radio networks with energy harvesting. IEEE Trans. Commun. **64**(4), 1399–1410 (2016)
8. Huang, X., Han, T., Ansari, N.: On green-energy-powered cognitive radio networks. IEEE Trans. Commun. **17**, 827–842 (2015)
9. Lu, X., Wang, P., Niyato, D., Kim, D.I., Han, Z.: Wireless networks with RF energy harvesting: a contemporary survey. IEEE Commun. Surv. Tutor. **17**, 757–8789 (2015)
10. FCC: Notice of proposed rule making and order. ET Docket No03-322 (2003)
11. Sakr, A.H., Hossain, E.: Cognitive and energy harvesting-based D2D communication in cellular, networks: stochastic geometry modeling and analysis. IEEE Trans. Commun. **63**(5), 1867–1880 (2015)
12. Liu, Y., Yang, Z., Yan, X., et al.: A novel multi-hop algorithm for wireless network with unevenly distributed nodes. CMC **58**(1), 79–100 (2019)
13. Wang, J., Ju, C., Gao, Y., et al.: A PSO based energy efficient coverage control algorithm for wireless sensor networks. CMC **56**(3), 433–446 (2018)

Facial Expression Recognition Based on Complete Local Binary Pattern and Convolutional Neural Network

Pingping Yu[1], Yaning Nie[1], Ning Cao[2(✉)], and Russell Higgs[3]

[1] School of Information Science and Engineering,
Hebei University of Science and Technology, Shijiazhuang, China
chinanieyaning@163.com
[2] College of Internet of Things, Wuxi Institute of Technology, Wuxi, China
ningcao2008@hotmail.com
[3] School of Mathematics, University College Dublin, Dublin, Ireland
russell.higgs@ucd.ie

Abstract. Facial expression recognition is a challenging problem in computer vision as changes in the background and location of the same person may also lead to difficulties in the recognition. In order to improve the poor effect of facial expression recognition algorithms due to it's easy to be affected by illumination and posture in real life environment, a facial expression recognition algorithm based on CLBP and convolutional neural network is proposed. The algorithm uses HOG feature and Adaboost algorithm to cut out images with face and eyes, extracts CLBP fusion feature images, constructs a seven-layer convolutional neural network model with two convolutional and pooling layers, two full connection layers and one Softmax classification layer to recognize six expressions of anger, aversion, fear, happiness, sadness and surprise. Four sets of comparative experiments are designed on the public data set CK+, a recognition rate of 98.60% is achieved, better than the existing mainstream methods.

Keywords: Computer vision · Face expression recognition ·
Complete local binary pattern · Convolutional neural network

1 Introduction

In the communication of human society, facial expression plays an important role, it is also one of the important characteristics for human emotional recognition. Facial expression recognition is a complex system. Ekman [1] et al. proposed Facial Action Coding System (FACS) in 1978. The system divided the facial region into 43 motion units according to the anatomical characteristics of human faces. It analyzed the dynamic characteristics of these motor units and the characteristics of the facial regions they represent and defined six basic human facial expressions, anger, sadness, surprise,

This research has been financially supported by grants from the Hebei Provincial Education Department Youth Fund (No. QN2018095)

X. Sun et al. (Eds.): ICAIS 2019, LNCS 11632, pp. 561–572, 2019.
https://doi.org/10.1007/978-3-030-24274-9_51

happiness, aversion and fear by combining the units, becoming one of the more widely used technologies in facial expression at that time. Since the 1990s, facial expression recognition algorithms have become more systematic [2]. Facial feature extraction should minimize the variety of extracted features, and at the same time, maximize the identification of differences of feature types. One method is to calculate the relative position offset between the five sense organs, but it often loses important information by using smaller data features, and the recognition rate is unsatisfactory. The other is to construct classifier to extract the whole. The better method is to use SVM [3, 4], Gabor wavelet [5] and local binary mode [6], etc. Facial expression recognition is the last step. Through the combination and analysis of features extracted by classifier, facial expression can be inferred. These methods depend on the advantages and disadvantages of feature algorithm classifier design and the number of features as well as human understanding of explicit features of expression, thus limiting the improvement of expression recognition rate.

With the improvement of the computer data processing level and the rise of in-depth learning, it is possible to process large amounts of data. "End-to-end" learning mode is the fundamental idea that deep learning is different from traditional machine learning [7]. In the whole learning process of neural network, manual classifier is not used, but to construct deep learning model to obtain output directly from input of original data. This is also the most important aspect that distinguishes in-depth learning from other traditional algorithms. Convolutional Neural Network (CNN) has shown its tremendous advantages in the field of image recognition. CNN can realize data parallel processing and has achieved higher recognition rate than traditional manual extraction algorithms in the fields of handwritten numeral recognition [8], object recognition and so on. However, in the field of facial expression recognition, its recognition scope is limited, and the use of deep network is not conducive to the promotion and transplantation of methods. In this paper, a high recognition rate is maintained, and at the same time, the complexity of network structure is reduced, an algorithm combining artificial features and convolutional neural network is proposed, and a complete verification method is provided. The following parts of this paper are arranged as follows: the second part introduces the related work in the field of expression recognition; the third part designs an expression recognition system based on CBLP and convolutional neural network; the fourth part designs a comparative experiment and analyses the results.

2   Related Work

In the past decade, unprecedented leaps have been made in the field of facial expression recognition. The following highlights the methods closely related to the paper.

Meunier et al. [9] proposed a feature method using gradient histogram, that was to firstly extract facial features using the three feature extractors LBP, PCA [10] and HOG [11], and then classify static facial images using SVM. In their study, anger, fear, happiness, disgust and sadness were classified and 70% recognition rate was obtained. Shan et al. [12, 13] made an in-depth study to the local binary model. The authors used LBP to extract features from images, obtained two-dimensional coded feature vectors of facial expressions, then carried out recognition by combining template matching, linear regression and machine learning algorithm of SVM. Georgesc [14] proposed a method combining manual feature and deep neural network, which realized facial expression recognition by CNN and bag-of-visual-words (BOVW) model. After integrating the functions of the two types, the author used a local learning framework to predict the output attributes of each test image. [15] designed ConvNet architecture, which was implemented in four phases, each of which contained different layers. In the first two stages, the maximum pooling rule and normalization were used in the pooling layer behind the convolutional layer, then average pooling strategy was used after the second convolutional layer, and in the last stage, the Softmax layer with seven outputs was used, representing the probability of seven expressions. Levi et al. [16] combined LBP feature with convolutional neural network, used local learning to extract the features of the image to be recognized in advance, which showed that the recognition effect of the combination of CNN and handmade function was better than that of single CNN model.

The combination algorithm in the above research often increases the complexity of the algorithm, but at the same time, it can only improve the recognition rate to a small extent. And the recognition effect depends on the choice of classifier combination by the algorithm designer, which is not conducive to improving the generalization of the combination algorithm. Further more, the large-scale convolutional neural network used in traditional facial expression recognition algorithm is prone to over-fitting, which further restricts the improvement of recognition rate.

3 Facial Expression Recognition System

This part mainly focuses on image preprocessing, CLBP (Complete local binary pattern) feature extraction and convolutional neural network construction stage in the process of facial expression recognition. In the data preprocessing stage, the face is calibrated and cut for downsampling. In the CLBP operator feature extraction stage, CLBP operator is used to extract series fusion features as training set and test set of neural network. The construction stage of convolutional neural network is to construct seven-layer convolutional neural network to train and recognize the pre-processed data set.

3.1 Data Preprocessing

The data preprocessing flow is shown in Fig. 1.

Fig. 1. Image preprocessing flow.

Face Detection. Using HOG feature algorithm and by counting gradient change at the edge of the target to obtain the histogram, counting and analyzing the histogram of each gradient to obtain the edge features of the face image to be detected, using integral image to make accelerated operation on HOG features to obtain weak classifier, using AdaBoost method [17] to carry out cascade operation on weak classifier so as to achieve fast and accurate face detection.

Image Clipping. There are many interference information in the recognition of facial expressions from the face images obtained by preliminary detection, such as ears, hair and forehead. These background information may lead to the decline of classification accuracy. Therefore, according to the distance between eyes, 0.3 reduction factor is selected in the vertical direction, and 0.6 reduction factor is used in the horizontal direction. After cutting the image, the information unrelated to the expression recognition area is removed and the size of the image is reduced, which greatly reduces the workload of training neural network in later stage.

Downsampling. The downsampling operation is to further reduce the image size while keeping the position of each image's facial organs (eyebrows, eyes, nose, mouth, etc.) unchanged. The final image is 32 * 32 pixels.

3.2   CLBP Feature Extraction

Local Binary Pattern (LBP) is an effective operator for extracting local image texture. Take the neighborhood central pixel as the threshold value, compare the gray value of eight adjacent pixels with it. If the surrounding pixel value is larger than the central pixel value, the pixel position is marked as 1, otherwise it is 0. When the neighborhood contains eight other pixels, the binary string is regarded as an eight-bit binary number between 0 and 255, and the result is equal to the pixel value. It's shown in Fig. 2 below.

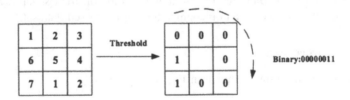

Fig. 2. LBP extraction method.

Formula (1) defines the process:

$$LBP(X_P, Y_P) = \sum_{P=0}^{P-1} 2^P s(I_P - I_C) \tag{1}$$

In the formula, (X_P, Y_P) represents the central position of the area, the pixel value is I_P, I_C represents other pixel values in neighborhood area, $S(X)$ is a sign function. When $X \geq 0$, $S(X)$ is 1, otherwise, $S(X)$ is 0.

The features extracted by LBP are only in a small area, which obviously cannot meet the needs of image size change. In order to solve this problem, Guo et al. [18] proposed a complete LBP operator, which consists of two parts: the central pixel LBP operator (CLBP-Center, CLBP_C) and the local difference sign-Magnitude Transform (LDSMT). LDSMT operators are divided into symbolic LBP operators (CLBP-Sign, CLBP_S) and numerical LBP operators (CLBP-Magnitude, CLBP_M), as shown in the Fig. 3:

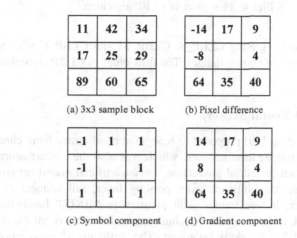

(a) 3x3 sample block   (b) Pixel difference

(c) Symbol component   (d) Gradient component

Fig. 3. CLBP operator.

The difference between the gray values of the central pixel and the neighboring pixel is calculated to be: $d_P = I_P - I_C$.

$$d_P = s_P \times m_P$$
$$s_P = \text{sgn}(d_P) \qquad (2)$$
$$m_P = |d_P|$$

In the formula, $s_P = \begin{cases} 1 & d_P \geq 0 \\ -1 & d_P < 0 \end{cases}$ indicates the symbol of d_P, m_P indicates the size of d_P.

The calculation formulas of CLBP_M coding and CLBP_C coding are shown in formula (3) and formula (4) (Fig. 4):

$$F_{CLBP\_M} = \sum_{P=0}^{P-1} 2^P s(m_P, c), s(x, c) = \begin{cases} 1 & x \geq c \\ 0 & x < c \end{cases} \qquad (3)$$

$$F_{CLBP\_c} = \sum_{P=0}^{P-1} s(I_c, c_I), s(x, c_I) = \begin{cases} 1 & x \geq c_I \\ 0 & x < c_I \end{cases} \qquad (4)$$

In the formula, c is the mean value of m_P in local image, c_I is the gray mean value of local image.

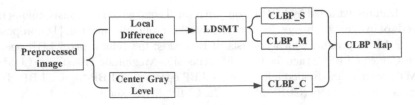

Fig. 4. Flow chart of CLBP algorithm.

A joint histogram integrating CLBP_S, CLBP_M and CLBP_C is established to characterize the features of texture images. The flow chart of CLBP algorithm is shown in (4).

3.3   Convolutional Neural Network

In the 1990s, Lecun et al. [19] proposed to recognize handwritten bank check number at that time by back propagation network, which was also the earliest neural network model applied in actual industrial production. LeNet artificial neural network is composed of input layer, convolutional layer, pooling layer, full connection layer and Softmax output layer. It was trained with pictures in MINIST handwritten digital library as training set, and obtained a very high recognition rate of 99.2% at that time. In this paper, LeNet-5 network is improved. The structure of convolutional neural network is shown in Fig. 5.

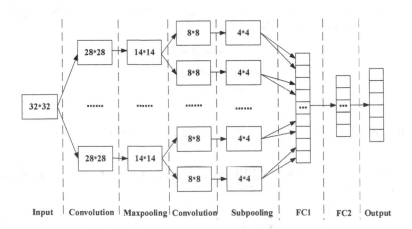

Fig. 5. Convolutional neural network structure.

Convolutional Layer. Convolution in convolution layer is the mathematical operation of convolution kernel in image matrix. Figure 6 shows the 5 * 5 image input matrix and its corresponding 3 * 3 convolution kernel. Assuming that the stride of convolution operation is 1, multiply the parameters in the convolution kernel by the input matrix parameters of the corresponding position from the upper left corner of the image, and the results are obtained. Then calculate from left to right and from top to bottom in one stride to obtain the convolution characteristics of 3 * 3. Through convolution operation, the convolutional layer can get the edge information of the input image [20]. We can learn the shape and texture of the image by adjusting the size and stride of the convolution kernel in the convolutional layer.

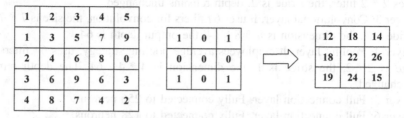

Fig. 6. Convolution operation.

Pooling Layer. The pooling layer is actually a kind of downsampling. It has three functions: feature invariance, feature dimensionality reduction and overfitting avoidance. The feature invariance makes the original features of the image more obvious. Feature dimensionality reduction reduces the dimensionality in the spatial range, which can greatly reduce the computational load of the network on the premise of guaranteeing the original features. The existence of over-fitting is due to the over-learning of more information and redundant information in the given samples, which leads to a high degree of matching in the training process. However, the poor performance in the test set results in a decline in the generalization of the network.

Activation Function. Activation function plays a role in increasing the non-linear expression ability of convolutional neural network model. ReLU function can accelerate the convergence of stochastic gradient method and avoid the occurrence of gradient saturation phenomenon. The formula of ReLU function is as follows:

$$R(x) = \begin{cases} x & x \geq 0 \\ 0 & x < 0 \end{cases} \tag{5}$$

Full Connection Layer and Softmax Layer. The function of the full connection layer is to transform the dimension from high dimension to low dimension while retaining useful information. Softmax calculates the probability of the final output, which is between 0 and 1. Softmax output layer formula is as follows, where n represents the number of outputs.

$$f(z_j) = \frac{e^{z_j}}{\sum_{n=1}^{n} e^{z_k}} \quad j = 1, \bullet \bullet \bullet, k \tag{6}$$

The detailed structure of CNN:

Layer 0: Input layer. It inputs 32 * 32 gray LBP feature image.

Layer 1: Convolutional layer. It calculates the output of the neurons in the regions associated with the input, and calculates the weight of the region connected to each neuron. It uses 32 filters with the size of 5 * 5, the stride is 1, the padding is 0, the dimension is 28 * 28 * 32, and the depth is 32.

Layer 2: Pooling layer. It employees the maximum pooling strategy, that is, to take the maximum point in the pooling area as the value after pooling. Maximum pool uses 2 * 2 filter, the stride is 2, depth remains unchanged.

Layer 3: Convolutional layer. It uses 64 filters for convolution, the size is 7 * 7, the stride is 1, the dimension is 8 * 8 * 64, the output depth is 64.

Layer 4: Pooling layer. It employees average pooling strategy, uses 64 filters, the size is 2 * 2, the stride is 1, the dimension is 4 * 4 * 64. The depth remains unchanged.

Layer 5: Full connection layer. Fully connected to 256 neurons.

Layer 6: Full connection layer. Fully connected to 128 neurons.

Layer 7: Softmax layer. It has 6 neurons, which are used to predict six types of output of facial expressions.

4 Experiment and Analysis

The hardware platform involved in the experiment is Intel Core i5-8500 3.0 GHz CPU and NVIDA GeForce GTX 1080Ti GPU. Software platform is Python 3.5, opencv3.2 and TensorFlow deep learning framework under Win10.

4.1 Data Set

CK+ (Extended Cohn-Kanade dataset) data set is used in the experiment. CK+ data set includes 593 image sequences of 123 persons, the images are captured from videos in the camera from the beginning to the peak of the expression. The images in the data set are 640 × 480 pixel gray images and eight numbers of 0–7 are used as labels to mark neutrality, anger, contempt, disgust, fear, happiness, sadness and surprise expressions respectively, of which six expressions excluding neutrality and contempt are selected for the experiment. In the experiment, 770 original pictures are selected in CK+ concentration, on which basis, we expand the data and increase the number of training samples. By avoiding the occurrence of over-fitting, the generalization ability of network model is improved. The expansion method adopted in this experiment is to rotate the original image at −30°, −15°, 15°, and 30°, 3850 images are obtained, among which, 3350 images are used as training data, 500 images are used as test sets that are divided into 6 groups for independent verification. Figures 7 and 8 are examples of six expressions and rotating images.

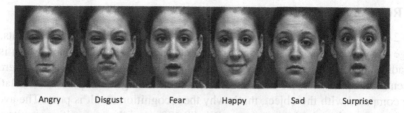

Angry   Disgust   Fear   Happy   Sad   Surprise

Fig. 7. CK+ database facial expression examples.

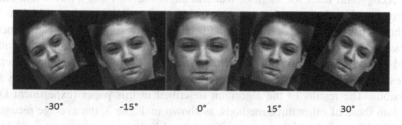

-30°   -15°   0°   15°   30°

Fig. 8. Image rotation.

4.2   Experiment

Four comparative experiments were designed to verify the validity, all of them used CK+ database, and the parameters were kept the same during the training process. The final results were expressed by the average and maximum values of the recognition.

In experiment A, a database without any interference or image preprocessing was used, and training and test was carried out after extracting LBP features.

In experiment B, a database without any image preprocessing operation was used as training set and test set of convolutional neural network (CNN). The parameters during the training process are shown in Table 1.

Table 1. Training parameter.

Parameter	Value
Loss function	SGD
Momentum	0.90
Learning rate	0.01
Epochs	500

Experiment C was carried out on the basis of experiment B, it used a data set after clipping as the training set and test set to train the neural network.

Experiment D was the extraction process after adding CLBP operator to the data set of experiment C. The other experimental processes were consistent with that in experiment C.

4.3   Result Analysis

Table 2 shows the recognition results of six expressions by the four experiments. The average recognition rate obtained in experiment A is 48.64%. The main reason is that the traditional LBP operator uses matching algorithm, it looks for the differences between classes, easy to lose texture details, and the change of expression is relatively subtle compared with the object, that's why the recognition result is poor. The average recognition rate obtained in experiment B is 80.40%, and the recognition results of six kinds of expressions are significantly higher than that of experiment A. In experiment A, the recognition rates for sadness, fear and anger are 28.72%, 24.07% and 32.30% respectively, while the recognition rate obtained by using CNN reaches as high as 70%. This shows that CNN network has great advantages over single classification method. The average recognition rate obtained in experiment C is 83.16%. Compared with the method of using original data in experiment B, most of the information irrelevant to facial expression is removed after clipping of the image, thus it can better classify facial expressions. The results of the algorithm described in this paper (experiment D) are better than those of other three methods, as shown in Table 3, the average recognition rate is 92.83%, and the highest recognition rate of happiness expression is 98.6%.

Table 2. Recognition results of the four experimental schemes.

	Angry	Disgust	Fear	Happy	Sad	Surprise
A	32.30%	62.78%	24.07%	70.64%	28.72%	73.30%
B	70.15%	84.40%	67.00%	93.78%	75.65%	91.40%
C	72.64%	87.84%	71.68%	94.10%	83.41%	89.28%
D	92.42%	94.55%	84.29%	98.60%	89.84%	97.28%

Table 3. Average and maximum recognition results of the four experimental.

	Average	Best
A	48.64%	73.30%
B	80.40%	93.78%
C	83.16%	94.10%
D	92.83%	98.60%

In order to further detect the expression recognition ability of the algorithm described in this paper, a hybrid matrix is established. Among them, the accuracy rate of happiness and surprise is higher than 97%, and the recognition rate of sadness is the lowest, only 82.48%. The main reason is that sad expressions are easily confused with anger and fear, that is, the three expressions are of high similarities (Table 4).

In order to compare the recognition effect of this method with other methods, this paper lists the methods of artificial extraction and deep learning. Under the same environment and the same number of experiments, the recognition results are shown in Table 5. It can be seen from Table 5 that the recognition rate of the manual extraction method is lower than that of the deep learning method. The method based on CBLP and convolutional neural network has excellent performance in CK+ data set.

Table 4. The hybrid matrix in the experiment.

	Angry	Disgust	Fear	Happy	Sad	Surprise
Angry	85.29%	3.37%	0	3.59%	7.75%	0
Disgust	3.60%	94.34%	2.06%	0	0	0
Fear	6.29%	0.00%	87.55%	2.02%	1.04%	3.10%
Happy	1.08%	0	0	97.74%	0.96%	0.22%
Sad	4.50%	6.20%	5.33%	1.49%	82.48%	0
Surprise	0.00%	0	0.00%	0	1.30%	98.70%

Table 5. Comparison of the algorithms.

Category	Algorithm source	Method	Recognition rate
Manual methods	Meunier [9]	LBP+PCA+HOG+SVM	70.00%
	Shan [12]	Gabor+LBP	85.00%
Deep learning methods	Georgescu [14]	BOVW+CNN	87.76%
	Levi [16]	LBP+CNN	97.81%
	Our method	CLBP+CNN	98.60%

5 Conclusion

This paper presents a facial expression recognition algorithm based on CBLP and convolutional neural network, which has the following advantages: using HOG feature and AdaBoost algorithm to recognize the face area, preprocess the face, cut out the image with face and eye position, remove the background information, and reduce the calculation of subsequent steps; using CLBP to extract image texture features, extract not only difference sign feature CLBP_S, but also difference magnitude feature CLBP_M and gray feature of the center pixel CLBP_C; considering not only the relationship between the central pixel and the surrounding pixel, but also the role of the central pixel; using CLBP fusion feature images to construct a seven-layer convolutional neural network model to recognize six expressions, further improves the recognition rate.

By designing four comparative experiments, this method achieves 98.60% recognition rate on the public data set CK+, shows the advantages of the algorithm in recognition effect, analyses the rationality of the design of the algorithm based on the relationship between expressions. At the same time, the main artificial recognition algorithm and the deep network algorithm are compared, and the results are better than those of the existing mainstream methods. In the future work, we can focus on the recognition of dynamic expression sequence, such as fear in anger, joy in surprise and etc.

References

1. Ekman, P., Friesen, W.V.: Facial Action Coding System: A Technique for the Measurement of Facial Movement. Consulting Psychologists Press, Palo Alto (1978)
2. Xie, X., Yuan, T., Zhou, X., Cheng, X.: Research on trust model in container-based cloud service. CMC: Comput. Mater. Continua 56(2), 273–283 (2018)
3. Wang, B., et al.: Research on hybrid model of garlic short-term price forecasting based on Big Data. CMC: Comput. Mater. Continua 57(2), 283–296 (2018)
4. Cortes, C., Vapnik, V.: Support-vector networks. Mach. Learn. 20(3), 273–297 (1995)
5. Praseeda Lekshmi, V., Sasikumar, M.: Analysis of facial expression using Gabor and SVM. Int. J. Recent Trends Eng. 1(2), 47–50 (2009)
6. Choi, S.E., Lee, Y.J., Lee, S.J., Park, K.R., Kim, J.: Age estimation using a hierarchical classifier based on global and local facial features. Pattern Recognit. 44(6), 1262–1281 (2011)
7. Krahenbuhl, P., Doersch, C., Donahue, J., Darrell, T.: Data-dependent initializations of convolutional neural networks. In: International Conference on Computer Vision, pp. 1–12, November 2015. http://arxiv.org/abs/1511.06856
8. LeCun, Y., Bottou, L., Bengio, Y., Haffner, P.: Gradient-based learning applied to document recognition, vol. 86, no. 11, pp. 2278–2324 (1998)
9. Dahmane, M., Meunier, J.: Emotion recognition using dynamic grid-based HoG features. In: IEEE International Conference on Automatic Face & Gesture Recognition and Workshops, pp. 884–888. IEEE (2011)
10. Yang, J., Zhang, D.D., Frangi, A.F., et al.: Two-dimensional PCA: a new approach to appearance-based face representation and recognition. IEEE Trans. Pattern Anal. Mach. Intell. 26(1), 131–137 (2004)
11. Wang, X., Han, T.X., Yan, S.: An HOG-LBP human detector with partial occlusion handling. In: IEEE, International Conference on Computer Vision, pp. 32–39. IEEE (2009)
12. Shan, C., Gong, S., Mcowan, P.W.: Facial expression recognition based on local binary patterns: a comprehensive study. Image Vis. Comput. 27(6), 803–816 (2009)
13. Lucey, P., Cohn, J.F., Kanade, T., et al.: The extended Cohn-Kanade dataset (CK+): a complete dataset for action unit and emotion-specified expression. In: Computer Vision and Pattern Recognition Workshops, pp. 94–101. IEEE (2010)
14. Georgescu, M.I., Ionescu, R.T., Popescu, M.: Local learning with deep and handcrafted features for facial expression recognition (2018)
15. Kahou, S.E., Michalski, V., Konda, K., et al.: Recurrent neural networks for emotion recognition in video. In: ACM International Conference on Multimodal Interaction, pp. 467–474. ACM (2015)
16. Levi, G., Hassner, T.: Emotion recognition in the wild via convolutional neural networks and mapped binary patterns. In: ACM on International Conference on Multimodal Interaction, pp. 503–510. ACM (2015)
17. Zhu, J., Zou, H., Rosset, S., et al.: Multi-class AdaBoost. Stat. Interface 2(3), 349–360 (2006)
18. Guo, Z., Zhang, L., Zhang, D.: A completed modeling of local binary pattern operator for texture classification. IEEE Trans. Image Process. 19(16), 1657–1663 (2010)
19. Simard, P., LeCun, Y., et al.: Efficient pattern recognition using a new transformation distance. In: Advances in Neural Information Processing Systems, pp. 50–58. DBLP (1992)
20. Zhang, J., Lin, W., Dong, Y., et al.: A double-layer interpolation method for implementation of BEM analysis of problems in potential theory. Appl. Math. Model. 51, 250–269 (2017)

A Novel Malware Detection and Classification Method Based on Capsule Network

Shu-wei Wang(✉), Gang Zhou, Ji-cang Lu, and Feng-juan Zhang

China State Key Laboratory of Mathematical Engineering and Advanced
Computer, Zhengzhou 450001, China
star0452@126.com

Abstract. By using camouflage technologies such as code confusion, packing and signature, malware could escape the killing of anti-virus software with a high probability. To detect malware efficiently, traditional machine learning methods usually require complex feature extraction work in advance, CNN and other deep learning methods usually need a large number of labeled samples, all of these will affect the detection performance. For these problems, an improved deep learning method (ColCaps) based on malware color image visualization technology and capsule network is proposed in this paper to detect malware. Firstly, the malware is transformed into a color image. Then, the dynamic routing-based capsule network is used to detect and classify the color image. Without advanced feature extraction and with only a small number of labeled samples, ColCaps has better performances in cross-platform detection and classification. The experimental results show that, the detection accuracy of the proposed method on Android and Windows platforms is 99.3% and 96.5% respectively, which is 20% higher than that of the existing method. Meanwhile, the classification task in Drebin dataset has an accuracy of 98.2%, which is a significant improvement over the prior DREBIN.

Keywords: Deep learning · Malware detection · Malware classification · Capsule network

1 Introduction

With the advent of the era of big data, Internet technology and mobile internet technology have developed rapidly, and the number of malicious applications has also exploded exponentially, which brings unprecedented challenges to our network space. According to Symantec's 2018 Internet Security Threat Report (ISTR) [1], malware implant attacks increased by 200% in 2017 and new mobile malware variants grew by 54%. For business benefit, manufacturers are constantly making gray software applications that leak privacy data from smartphone devices. Millions of malicious code enters the Internet every day, but existing common network security detection technologies fail to detect them effectively, which will cause huge losses to individuals, businesses, institutions and even countries.

At present, there are a lot of research results in the field of malware detection, but some key problems still cannot be solved. For example, a large number of labeled

© Springer Nature Switzerland AG 2019
X. Sun et al. (Eds.): ICAIS 2019, LNCS 11632, pp. 573–584, 2019.
https://doi.org/10.1007/978-3-030-24274-9_52

samples are needed for training, the feature extraction in the early stage is too complicated and the accuracy of cross-platform malware detection is not higher. In order to solve these problems listed above, a cross-platform malware detection and classification method based on malware image visualization technology and deep learning technology is proposed in this paper. Using malware code color image generation technology and capsule network framework, the specially processed executable files (APK, DLL, EXE, etc.) are converted into color RGB images. And then, the generated uniform color images are sent into the capsule network to extract efficient features and train detection model. Finally, the trained capsule network model is used for the detection of unknown software and the homology classification analysis of malware. The method achieves cross-platform malware detection and classification. The classification accuracy in the Drebin dataset reaches 98.2%, and the detection accuracy for unknown software reaches 96.5% (Windows) and 99.3% (Android).

The main innovations of the proposed methods are as follows:

(1) Introducing malware code color image generation technology into the field of malware detection, which can completely store the feature information of malware in color image and effectively detect malicious code processed by code obfuscation technology.
(2) Using the capsule network to extract features of the color images generated by malware to learn and train. Compared with the CNN, the capsule network converts scalars into vectors, which can better store features and use routing algorithms for calculation. Then, the detection accuracy is further improved.
(3) The proposed malware detection model (ColCaps) based on color image generation technology and capsule network can realize cross-platform detection and classification for different types of files.

2   Existing Research

2.1   Traditional Static and Dynamic Malware Detection

Many technologies have been proposed to detect malicious software. Detection technology based on static analysis was first proposed, which judges whether the software was malicious or not by detecting the possible execution path, start-up mode, malicious behavior and other characteristics of binary code [2, 3]. At present, obfuscation techniques are becoming more and more complex. Feature-based static analysis techniques can be bypassed by multiple obfuscation techniques such as polymorphism, encryption and packaging [4], while software signature library-based detection methods cannot detect new unknown malware.

Another behavior-based dynamic detection technology came into being [5, 6]. Although this technology can avoid the interference of the confusing technology, it needs to dynamically monitor and track the executable program in the honeypot environment, which has the disadvantages of high computational resources and low execution efficiency, especially cannot cope with large-scale sample detection. So this technology cannot be applied to smart mobile device terminals.

2.2   Machine Learning-Based Malware Detection

In recent years, many machine learning-based algorithms have been proposed to detect malware and have achieved good results. Daniel et al. [9] designed a lightweight Android malware detection method to collect multiple functional features of the application and classified them with linear support vector machine SVM, but this method cannot be applied to Windows malware. Alam et al. [10] regarded malicious software images as feature vectors and used a random forest model to classify various malware families, but made errors for visually similar malware. Yerima et al. [12] built a Bayesian classification model by extracting program features with potentially malicious behavior from a large amount of static malicious code. The disadvantage is that the detection of new unknown Android malware is not good.

2.3   Deep Learning-Based Malware Detection

At present, deep learning-based malware detection technology has also developed rapidly [13–15]. Saxe et al. [14] proposed a deep learning network (DNN) detection method, which first extracts feature information from PE files, and then the feature vector is sent to a deep learning network with two hidden layers for training classification. This method has carried out complex feature extraction work in the early stage, so the model is slightly complicated. Jiang et al. [15] converted the executable file into grayscale image and used the trained CNN model to detect malware, but the detection accuracy of this method for Android malware is less than 80%.

It can be seen from above introduce that, there still are some key problems in traditional malware detection algorithm, machine learning classification algorithm and deep learning technology. For example, the detection rate of traditional detection algorithm in the face of code obfuscation, shelling, signature and other camouflage technology is significantly reduced. In the early stage of the machine learning algorithm, the feature extraction and screening of malware is too complicated and the cross-platform detection model is poorly versatile and so on. In order to solve those problems, this paper proposes a ColCaps framework model based on malware visualization technology and capsule network.

3   The Proposed Malware Detection Method: ColCaps

3.1   Overall Architecture of Malware Detection and Classification

By converting malware files into images, the complex feature extraction of malware's static decompiled files and dynamic behavior could be transformed into simple static image feature extraction. Then, the deep neural networks can be used for its simplicity and higher efficiency in image feature extraction. Compared with grayscale images, RGB images with more colors have better feature representation capabilities, while the capsule network has a stronger ability to recognize spatial relationships between objects in the image and rotated objects compared with CNN. Therefore, in this paper, the above advantages are used to combine malware color image generation technology with the capsule network framework for malware detection and classification.

The detection-classification model based on malware image visualization technology and capsule network mainly includes the following three parts: malware image visualization, construction and training of capsule network, malware detection and classification. The general process is shown in Fig. 1:

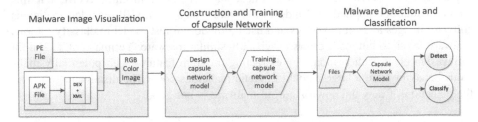

Fig. 1. Overall flow of malware detection and classification.

3.2 Malware Image Visualization Method

There are few researches on the visualization methods of malicious code. Nataraj et al. [16] first proposed to visualize malware binary code as grayscale image and classified malware according to the similarity of image texture. In this paper, a new malicious code visualization method is applied to convert binary code into RGB color image. Because RGB three-channel color image (24-bit pixels per sample) can save the feature information of malware with 16777216 colors, compared with only 256 colors (8-bit pixels per sample) of grayscale images, there is a stronger feature representation capability. The hexadecimal mapping technique is used to convert the binary code into RGB mode code in this paper. The conversion rules are as follows (Mapping every 8 bits to an integer value of RGB in sequence): (Ox868816 = (R: 134, G: 136, B: 22), Ox849A87 = (R: 204, G: 232, B: 207) etc.). According to the above rules, the benign and malware binary samples in PE files and APK files have been converted. Figure 2 is the benign and malicious sample images of the Windows and Android software. The third image is sample image of the DroidKungFu malware family. It can be seen clearly from the figures that, image samples from different software families have distinct texture features and the same malware family samples are very similar. Because software code from the same family contains similar API calls and code structures. So this method will provide an effective sample input for the detection and homology classification of the capsule network.

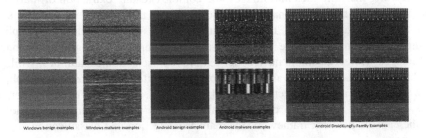

Fig. 2. Windows & Android software sample images.

3.3   Capsule Network Based on Dynamic Routing Algorithm

Unlike the existing deep neural networks such as CNN and RNN, the capsule network is not composed of neurons but by Capsule. Capsule [17] is a set of artificial neural networks that performs complex internal calculations on sample inputs, and the result is encapsulated in a small vector. Each Capsule is a carrier containing multiple neurons, which represents various properties of a particular entity appearing in the image. The capsule network consists of multiple layers consisting of two convolutional layers and a fully connected layer, then uses an iterative dynamic routing algorithm [18] to ensure a more accurate output of low-level capsule vectors to higher-level parent capsules. The above characteristics make the capsule network more efficient in image feature extraction and image classification accuracy.

Input and Output of Capsule Vectors. The color image is delivered to the model in the form of a multi-dimensional matrix, and the feature vector is obtained through the convolution layer processing. The capsule network first converts the feature input from the lower layer into the prediction vector through the weight matrix [19]. Then, similar to the artificial neural network, the summation matrix is obtained by weighted summation. Finally, the new nonlinear activation function of the vector (Squashing Function) [18] is used, this compression function converts the summation matrix to the output vector, which will become the input vector of the next higher-level feature. The related functions are defined as follows:

$$\hat{\mathbf{u}}_{j|i} = W_{ij}u_i, s_j = \sum_i c_{ij}\hat{\mathbf{u}}_{j|i}, \mathbf{v}_j = \frac{\|\mathbf{s}_j\|^2}{1 + \|\mathbf{s}_j\|^2} \cdot \frac{\mathbf{s}_j}{\|\mathbf{s}_j\|} \tag{1}$$

Where u_i is the feature vector input, W_{ij} is the weight matrix, $\hat{\mathbf{u}}_{j|i}$ is the prediction vector, s_j is the summation matrix, $\mathbf{v}_j$ is the vector output of capsule j ($\|\mathbf{v}_j\| \leq 1$), c_{ij} is a coupling coefficient determined by an iterative dynamic routing algorithm.

Dynamic Routing Algorithm. The essence of the dynamic routing protocol algorithm is to send the output of the low-level feature vector $\mathbf{v}_j$ to a certain high-level feature $\mathbf{v}_j$ that "agrees" to receive the output. This process is implemented by an iterative routing algorithm that dynamically changes the value of the weight parameter c_{ij}. Compared to CNN, the scalar output is replaced by the capsule vector output and the max pooling method is replaced by the routing protocol algorithm [20]. The number of capsule network parameters has increased accordingly and the high-level capsules can represent more complex target objects. The experiment also proves that the routing algorithm in the capsule network is better than the max pooling of CNN.

Loss and Reconstruction. The reconfiguration ability of the model reflects its robustness. The feedback mechanism can well preserve the information used for reconstruction throughout the training process. Like regularization, it can avoid the over-fitting of training data and facilitate the generalization of the capsule network [21].

$$(\text{Reconstruction Loss}) = (\text{Input image})^2 - (\text{Reconstructed image})^2 \tag{2}$$

$$(\text{Final Loss}) = (\text{Margin Loss}) + \beta(\text{Reconstruction Loss}) \tag{3}$$

Where $\beta = 0.0005$ in this paper.

3.4   The Detection and Classification Algorithm Based on Capsule Network

We design the malware detection and classification algorithm (ColCaps) based on the malware code visualization method and the capsule network, as shown in the Fig. 3:

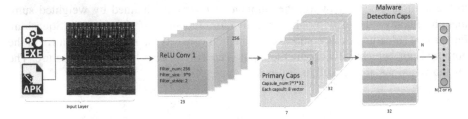

Fig. 3. Malware detection and classification algorithm based on capsule network (ColCaps).

(1) **The Input Layer of Model**. The malware training sample files are converted into RGB color image according to the method in Subsection 2.1. The downsampling algorithm is used to unify the RGB image of fixed format as the input of the model.

(2) **Primary Capsule Layer.** The capsule network contains two convolutional layers. The first convolutional layer collects low-level features of the input data, which contains 256 filters with a stride of 1, size of 9 and no padding. Using the ReLU function as a nonlinear activation function, the optimal drop out value is 0.7, which effectively avoids the gradient disappearance during training. The second convolutional layer contains the Capsule and the output is Primary Caps, which stores the low-level feature vectors.

(3) **Malware Detected Capsule Layer.** The Primary Capsule Layer and the Malware Detected Capsule Layer are fully connected and are vector to vector connections. Using the iterative routing protocol algorithm (Subsect. 3.3), the weight parameter C is calculated over three iterations and the vector V is output. When the model performs malware detection, the output is a two-category. When the model performs malware family classification, the output is an N-category.

4 Experiment and Results Analysis

4.1 Experiment Datasets and Environment

To better complete this experiment, the data sets consist of three projects. Drebin Dataset [25], VirusShare Dataset, MMCC Dataset (Microsoft Malware Classification Challenge on Kaggle) [26]. Meanwhile, a large number of top-ranked benign software programs were crawled and downloaded from Chinese mainstream Android application websites. As shown in Tables 1 and 2.

Table 1. Datasets for malware detection.

	#Malware	#Benign	Total
Windows	5,000	7,000	12,000
Android	4,000	6,000	1,0000

Table 2. Datasets for malware family classification.

	#Malware	#Family	Dataset
Windows	10,860	9	MMCC
Android	4,183	20	Drebin

The experimental hardware and software environment is as follows in Table 3.

Table 3. Software and hardware environment for experiment.

Hardware	#Information	Software	#Version
Cpu	Core i7-6700 3.4 GHz	**Python**	3.6
Memory	DDR4 2400 MHz 8G	**TensorFlow**	1.8
HDD	1 TB	**CUDA**	8.0
GPU	GTX 1070 Ti 8G	**cuDNN**	6.0

4.2 Evaluation Metrics

Through the experimental results, we measure the detection Accuracy (ACC), TPR (Recall) and Final Loss (Sect. 3.3), which are defined as follows:

$$\text{ACC} = \frac{TP + TN}{TP + TN + FP + FN}, TPR = \frac{TP}{TP + FN}, \text{FPR} = \frac{FP}{FP + TN} \qquad (4)$$

Where, TP is the true positives, FP is the false positives, TN is the true negatives, FN is the false negatives.

4.3   Experimental Results

TensorFlow's flexible architecture implements the ColCaps model perfectly, and the experimental results are obtained on the training samples and the verification samples, as shown in Table 4. It can be seen that on the Android and Windows platform, the detection accuracy ACC reached 99.3% and 96.5% respectively, and the classification accuracy also reached 98.2% and 95.2% respectively.

Table 4. Experimental results.

	ACC	Recall	FPR	Final loss	Epoch	Training time
Android malware detection task	99.3%	98.6%	1%	0.007	50	16.6 min
Windows malware detection task	96.5%	96.2%	2%	0.043	100	32.3 min
Android malware classification task	98.2%	–	–	0.025	80	82.7 min
Windows malware classification task	95.2%	–	–	0.023	100	138.3 min

In the malware detection experiment, the ACC and FinalLoss of the ColCaps model were statistically analyzed. The results are shown in Fig. 4:

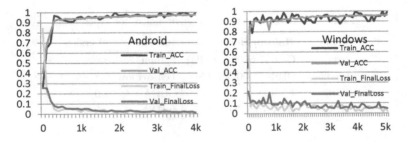

Fig. 4. ACC and final loss of malware detection task.

In the malware family classification experiment, the ACC and FinalLoss of the ColCaps model were statistically analyzed. The results are shown in Fig. 5 (The X axis is Step and the Y axis is ACC & FinalLoss).

As can be seen from the figures, the ColCaps achieved over 90% high detection accuracy at the beginning of training, indicating that the model's image feature collection ability and classification ability are very strong. Meanwhile, the final loss is reduced to a minimum of 0.007, indicating that the model's reconstruction and reduction ability is very high, and the restored image is almost the same as the original image. In the Android twenty-category experiment of Drebin Dataset, the total number of data samples is only 4,183, but the classification accuracy rate is 98.2%. It shows that the ColCaps can still achieve good training results in the case of a small number of data samples, avoiding the drawbacks of CNN requiring a large number of training samples. It can be obtained from the experimental results that the detection and classification accuracy of the Android malware are higher than that of the Windows platform, indicating that the ColCaps is more sensitive to the detection of Android malware.

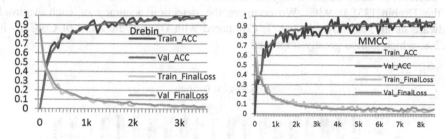

Fig. 5. ACC and final loss of malware family classification task.

4.4 Comparison with Related Approaches

In this section, we compare the existing research methods [15, 25, 27] in terms of malware detection and classification, all using the same data set or similar data sets of the same size.

In terms of malware detection, Jiang et al. [15] adopts gray-scale image texture and CNN-based detection methods. The datasets are of the same source, and our dataset is larger. The Android malware detection rate is increased by 20%, ACC is 99.3%, Recall is 79.5%, and Windows malware detection ACC is 97.6%, as shown in Fig. 6.

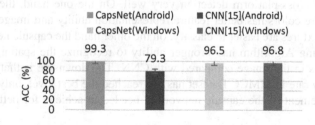

Fig. 6. Comparison of experimental results between ColCaps and CNN [15]

R2-D2 also uses CNN detection method [27], its detection accuracy is 93%, Recall is 96%, but the system cannot be used for Windows malware detection; Drebin uses the SVM detection method, the ACC is 94% [25]. The comparison of the three methods in ACC, TPR and FPR is shown in Table 5:

Table 5. Experimental results of comparing Drebin and R2-D2.

	Method	ACC	TPR	FPR
DREBIN	SVM	94%	–	1%
R2-D2	CNN	93%	96%	9%
ColCaps	Capsule network	99.3%	98.2%	1%

In terms of malware homology classification, the classification detection accuracy of the Drebin [25] is 93%. We compare the detection accuracy of each Android malware family, as shown in Fig. 7. Compared with Drebin, the ACC of ColCaps is 98.2%, which is also greatly improved.

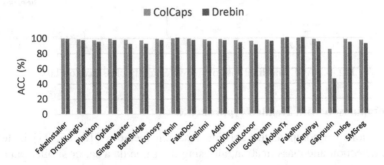

Fig. 7. The result of comparing DREBIN in each malware family.

We can see that the ColCaps based on capsule network performs better in malware detection and classification compared with the traditional machine learning classification algorithm SVM [15] and deep neural network CNN [25, 27], while it can solve the problem of cross-platform detection very well. On the one hand, the RGB color image with more colors has better feature representation ability and images with more distinct color textures are easier to classify, on the other hand the capsule network using Dynamic Routing Algorithm has stronger ability to recognize the spatial relationship between objects in the image compared with CNN. The downside is that the classification accuracy rate in MMCC Dataset has not reached the best level, only 95.2%, and further improvement of the capsule network is needed to achieve for better results.

5 Summary and Prospect

In this paper we present a ColCaps framework for cross-platform malware detection and classification based on malware image visualization technology and capsule network. This method first converts the software samples into three-channel RGB color images and then performs the capsule network model training, finally uses the trained ColCaps to automatically detect and classify a large number of malicious software samples. Experimental results show that the technology has the characteristics of high detection accuracy and low false alarm rate in cross-platform detection. It better solves the problem of low detection rate of Android malware processed through obfuscation and the defect that the CNN in deep learning needs a large number of training sample sets.

This paper focuses on the real malware detection and proposed a better performance algorithm. However, some scholars have proposed a GAN-based adversarial malware examples generation method recently, the adversarial malware examples are highly resistant to machine learning detection algorithm [23] and RNN-based sequence detection methods [24]. Liu et al. [28] craft adversarial examples by adding interference to the transformed data of malware images to deceive machine learning classification algorithms and CNN. Therefore, how to detect the adversarial malware examples and how to maintain high detection accuracy and robustness will be the direction for further research in the future.

References

1. Symantec: 2018-Internet-Security-Treat-Report. Symante (2018). https://www.symantec.com/content/dam/symantec/docs/reports/istr-23-executive-summary-en.pdf
2. Li, T., Dong, H., Yuan, C.: Description of Android malware feature based on Dalvik instructions. J. Comput. Res. Dev. **51**(7), 1458–1466 (2014)
3. Jieren, C., Ruomeng, X., Xiangyan, T.: An abnormal network flow feature sequence prediction approach for DDoS attacks detection in big data environment. CMC: Comput. Mater. Continua **55**(1), 095–119 (2018)
4. Okane, P., Sezer, S., McLaughlin, K.: Obfuscation: the hidden malware. IEEE Secur. Priv. **9**(5), 41–47 (2011)
5. Ki, Y., Kim, E., Kim, H.: A novel approach to detect malware based on API call sequence analysis. Taylor & Francis, Inc. (2015)
6. Enck, W., Gilbert, P., Han, S.: TaintDroid: an information-flow tracking system for realtime privacy monitoring on smartphones. In: Usenix Conference on Operating Systems Design & Implementation, pp. 393–407 (2014)
7. Zhou, Y., Wang, Z., Zhou, W.: Hey, you, get off of my market: detecting malicious apps in official and alternative Android Markets. In: Proceedings of Annual Network & Distributed System Security Symposium (2012)
8. Yan, L., Yin, H.: DroidScope: seamlessly reconstructing the OS and Dalvik semantic views for dynamic android malware analysis. In: Proceedings of the 21st USENIX Conference on Security Symposium, p. 29. USENIX Association (2012)

9. Yang, C., Xu, Z., Gu, G., Yegneswaran, V., Porras, P.: DroidMiner: automated mining and characterization of fine-grained malicious behaviors in Android applications. In: Kutyłowski, M., Vaidya, J. (eds.) ESORICS 2014. LNCS, vol. 8712, pp. 163–182. Springer, Cham (2014). https://doi.org/10.1007/978-3-319-11203-9_10

10. Alam, M., Vuong, S.: Random Forest classification for detecting Android malware. In: Proceedings of IEEE International Conference on Green Computing and Communications and IEEE Internet of Things and IEEE Cyber, Physical and Social Computing, pp. 663–669. IEEE Computer Society (2013)

11. Yerima, S., Sezer, S., Mcwilliams, G.: Analysis of Bayesian classification-based approaches for Android malware detection. Inf. Secur. IET 8(1), 25–36 (2016)

12. Yerima, S., Sezer, S., Mcwilliams, G.: A new Android malware detection approach using Bayesian classification. In: Proceedings of International Conference on Advanced Information NETWORKING and Applications, pp. 121–128. IEEE Computer Society (2013)

13. Yuhong, Z., Qinqin, W., Yuling, L., Xindong, W.: Sentiment classification based on piecewise pooling convolutional neural network. CMC: Comput. Mater. Continua 56(2), 285–297 (2018)

14. Saxe, J., Berlin, K.: Deep neural network based malware detection using two dimensional binary program features. In: Proceedings of the 10th International Conference on Malicious and Unwanted Software, pp. 11–20 (2015)

15. Jiang, C., Hu, Y., Si, K.: An malicious file detection method based on image texture and convolutional neural network. J. Comput. Appl. 1001–9081 (2018)

16. Nataraj, L., Karthikeyan, S., Jacob, G.: Malware images: visualization and automatic classification. In: Proceedings of International Symposium on Visualization for Cyber Security, pp. 1–7. ACM (2011)

17. Edgar, X., Selina, B., Yang, J.: Capsule network performance on complex data. arXiv preprint, arXiv:1712.03480 (2017)

18. Sara, S., Nicholas, F., Geoffrey, H.: Dynamic routing between capsules. In: Advances in Neural Information Processing Systems, pp. 3859–3869 (2017)

19. Dilin, W., Qiang, L.: An optimization view on dynamic routing between capsules. In: Proceedings of the 6th International Conference on Learning Representations (2018)

20. Hinton, G.E., Krizhevsky, A., Wang, Sida D.: Transforming auto-encoders. In: Honkela, T., Duch, W., Girolami, M., Kaski, S. (eds.) ICANN 2011. LNCS, vol. 6791, pp. 44–51. Springer, Heidelberg (2011). https://doi.org/10.1007/978-3-642-21735-7_6

21. Kumar, A.D.: Novel deep learning model for traffic sign detection using capsule networks. ArXiv preprint (2018)

22. Wongsuphasawat, K., Smilkov, D., Wexler, J.: Visualizing dataflow graphs of deep learning models in TensorFlow. IEEE Trans. Vis. Comput. Graph. 24(3), 1–12 (2018)

23. Hu, W., Tan, Y.: Generating adversarial malware examples for black-box attacks based on GAN. arXiv preprint, arXiv:1702.05983 (2017)

24. Hu, W., Tan, Y.: Black-box attacks against RNN based malware detection algorithms. arXiv preprint, arXiv:1705.0813 (2017)

25. Arp, D., Spreitzenbarth, M., Hübner, M.: DREBIN: effective and explainable detection of Android malware in your pocket. In: Network and Distributed System Security Symposium (2014)

26. Ronen, R., Radu, M., Feuerstein, C.: Microsoft malware classification challenge. arXiv preprint, arXiv:1702.10135 (2018)

27. Huang, D., Kao, Y.: R2-D2: color-inspired convolutional neural network (CNN)-based Android malware detections. arXiv preprint, arXiv:1705.04448 (2017)

28. Liu, X., Lin, Y., Li, H.: Adversarial examples: attacks on machine learning-based malware visualization detection methods. arXiv preprint, arXiv:1808.01546 (2018)

Application of Gradient Boosting Decision Tree in Wind Turbine Drivetrain Recognition

Cheng Qiang[1], Deng Aidong[1(✉)], Li Jing[1,2], and Zhai Yimeng[1]

[1] National Engineering Research Center of Turbo-Generator Vibration,
Southeast University, Nanjing, China
dnh@seu.edu.cn
[2] School of Information Engineering, Nanjing Audit University, Nanjing, China

Abstract. Dynamic and static components health are important factors to keep large rotatory machine safety and efficient work. The shaft and bearing are key components in wind turbine drivetrain, whose health detection and diagnosis are important parts of wind turbine operation condition assessments. This paper proposed a novel failure diagnostics algorithm based on Gradient Boosting Decision Tree (GBDT) framework to recognize Acoustic Emission (AE) source in wind turbine drivetrain and further to diagnose components operational condition. This method combined Gradient Boosting (GB) with Decision Tree (DT) to improve the ability of network ensemble learning and enhance model generalization. The AE date sampled from the test rig of wind turbine drivetrain rig, are classified by fault type included normal, bearing crack and shaft rubbing. The experimental results indicate that the average recognition of these three fault conditions is approximated 97.43%. It is an effective method to recognize the rubbing faults for the machine normal operation.

Keywords: Acoustic Emission · Gradient Boosting Decision Tree · Rotatory machine fault recognition

1 Introduction

As the demand of environmental protection, the wind energy severed as an important renewable energy exhibits a significant trend. Followed by this trend, wind turbines are constantly developed in the direction of the size increment and higher power ratings [1]. With more and more wind turbines in operation for a long time, wind farm operation and maintenance become more challenging [2]. Therefore, there is a need in the wind turbines for rotor incipient fatigue detection [3, 4]. By far, the most researches are focused on the different failure caused by various damages of the drivetrain using vibration and supervisory control and data acquisition (SCADA) methods.

SCADA system is already installed in wind turbines after delivered, which monitor vital equipment operational condition by several parameters such as temperature, power generation and blade rotation speed etc. This approach does not need any additional expense and then keeps maintenance more cost-effective [5]. However these different parameters of SCADA data sampled according to their own sampling frequency are under data consistency threat. Besides, some parameters of SCADA data

© Springer Nature Switzerland AG 2019
X. Sun et al. (Eds.): ICAIS 2019, LNCS 11632, pp. 585–594, 2019.
https://doi.org/10.1007/978-3-030-24274-9_53

setting inferior time resolution bring disadvantages wind turbine drivetrain failure detection. Vibration severed as another detection method is sensitive to incipient faults, which is widely used to detect faults in wind turbine drivetrain [6]. At present, some scholars have investigated vibration signal processing method to extract the health characteristics of rotatory machine such as wavelet analysis, empirical mode decomposition (EMD) and phase-space reconstruction and so on. However, vibration signal is not sensitive to weak faults occurred in early term and usually masked by background noise caused by mechanical vibration signals from rotating machinery [7].

In recent years, acoustic emission (AE) have been paid more attention to extract characteristics of weak fault occurred in early term. AE waveform are usually analyzed by some characteristic parameters such as: Hit accumulation, Amplitude distribution, Frequency distribution and Power Spectral Density (PSD) [8, 9]. Besides, combined with various classifiers, rotating machinery fault conditions and type can be diagnosed more detailed and accurate. Deng et al researched AE Waveform Factual Dimension algorithm, which is used into support vector machine (SVM) to recognize the rubbing fault recognition in the rotatory machine [10]. Thus, it is demonstrated that AE has t has beneficial prospects for applications in rotating machinery fault diagnosis field.

Neural network (NN), initially used for the processing procedure of the human behavior to perform difficult tasks, is an effective method to simulate complicated relationship between inputs and outputs. Then, several research institutes successfully used NN to construct various classification models to optimize the multivariable non-linear system [11]. Gradient boosting decision tree (GBDT) is a widely-used machine learning algorithm, due to its efficiency, accuracy, and interpretability [12]. Decision trees is a tree diagram which is used for making decisions to approximate the underlying complex nonlinear relationship in the data. Decision trees model given by gradient boosting is a sum of piecewise constant functions. With more complex trees, nonlinear relationship could be fit better and prediction accuracy could be higher [12].

In order to achieve a high performance of rotating machinery fault recognition algorithm using AE technology, this paper mainly focuses on the design of an novel DBGT algorithm, which adds ensemble learning method using boosting strategy into different decision trees models. DBGT is a kind integration framework of dynamic network by self-learning model adaptive weight so as to have the generalization effect. In this way, decision trees with self-learning residual and cascade structure to make the network scape from the local minima.

Generally, the function minima problem can be resolved by the Gradient Boosting Decision Tree. In this paper, the self-learning DBGT algorithm is innovatively used to resolve the function optimization problem in rotating machinery fault diagnosis.

2   Gradient Boost Decision Tree

Ensemble learning is a widely used machine learning algorithm to enhance model generalization. GBDT made by GB framework and DT classifier is a kind of ensemble learning method. DT is a flowchart-like structure to represent classification rules in paths from root to leaf, in which each internal node represents a "test" on an attribute, each branch represents the outcome of the test, and each leaf node represents a class label.

It can bucket continuous feature (attribute) values into discrete bins. GB framework implements machine learning algorithms stagewise additive expansions and steepest decent minimization. Gradient boosting of decision trees produces competitive, highly robust, and interpretable procedures for regression and classification [13].

LightGBM is further to improve decision efficiency and precision by change DT structure into one side sampling and exclusive feature bundling. It will select the leaf with max delta loss to grow, which is leaf wise tree growth. Holding leaf fixed, leaf-wise algorithms tend to achieve lower loss than level-wise algorithms. Leaf-wise may cause over-fitting when data is small, so LightGBM includes the max_depth parameter to limit tree depth.

The core points of the algorithm are that decision trees are learned by fitting the negative gradients in each iteration. GBDT takes nonparametric approach and applies numerical optimization in function space. Supposed a sample set $\{y_i, \mathbf{x}_i\}_1^N$, where $\mathbf{x} = \{x_1, \ldots, x_n\}$ is input variables, y_i is input label. It is considering $F(x)$ evaluated at each point $\mathbf{x}_i$ to be a parameter and seek to minimize. $\Psi(y, F(x))$ is the loss functions include squared error, absolute error for regression and negative binomial log-likelihood for classification.

$$\phi(F(x)) = [E_y(\Psi(y, F(x))|x] \tag{1}$$

The function $F(x)$ is considered to be a member of a parameterized class, which can be explained as additive expansions of functions $f(x)$:

$$F^*(x) = \sum_{m=0}^{M} f_m(x) \tag{2}$$

Where $f_0(x)$ is an initial guess, and $\{f_m(x)\}_1^M$ are increment function named steps or boosts, which is defined by the optimization method.

Steepest-decent is taken to be

$$f_m(x) = -\rho_m g_m(x) \tag{3}$$

With

$$g_m(x) = \left[\frac{\partial E_y(\Psi(y, F(x))|x]}{\partial F(x)}\right]_{F(x)=F_{m-1}(x)} \tag{4}$$

And

$$F_{m-1}(x) = \sum_{i=0}^{m-1} f_i(x) \tag{5}$$

The multiplier ρ_m by the line search is calculated as following:

$$\rho_m = \arg\min_{\rho} E_{y,x}\Psi(y, F_{m-1}(x) - \rho g_m(x)) \tag{6}$$

Given the current approximation $F_{m-1}(x)$ at the m-th iteration, the function $h(x; a)$ is the best greedy step towards the minimizing solution $F^*(x)$. Here $h(x; a)$ is used in place of the unconstrained one $g_m(x)$ in the steepest-decent strategy. This is the $h(x; a)$ most highly correlated with $g_m(x)$ over the data distribution. It can be obtained from the solution

$$a_m = \arg\min_{a,\rho} \sum_{i=1}^{N} [-g_m(x_i) - \rho h(x_i; a)]^2 \tag{7}$$

The approximation updated is taken (Table 1)

$$F_m(x) = F_{m-1}(x) + \rho_m h(x_i; a_m) \tag{8}$$

Table 1. GBDT model parameter learning.

Algorithm 1: Gradient Boost Decision Tree

$F_0(x) = \arg\min_{\rho} \sum_{i=1}^{N} \Psi(y_i, \rho)$

    For $m = 1$ to M do:

    $\tilde{y}_i = -\left[\dfrac{\partial \Psi(y_i, F(x_i))}{\partial F(x_i)}\right]_{F(x)=F_{m-1}(x)}, i = 1, N$

    $a_m = \arg\min_{a,\rho} \sum_{i=1}^{N}\left[\tilde{y}_i - \rho h(x_i; a)\right]^2$

    $\rho_m = \arg\min_{\rho} \sum_{i=1}^{N} \Psi(y_i, F_{m-1}(x_i) + \rho h(x_i; a_m))$

    $F_m(x) = F_{m-1}(x) + \rho_m h(x_i; a_m)$

    End For

End

---

3 Experiments and Result Analysis

The experiment rig of wind turbine drivetrain AE acquisition in rotatory machinery is shown in Fig. 1. Shaft rotational speed is controlled by frequency converter. And the AE acquisition system is used to record the AE data in accordance with the various damage degrees. AE acquisition system from PAC, UT-1000 AE sensors are mounted in the observation components housing contact filling coupling into surfaces. The acquisition sampling frequency is set at 1 MHz, the digital filter band is 1–200 kHz and the pre-amplifier is 40 dB.

Fig. 1. Fault AE in wind turbine drivetrain experiment rig

According to the different damage characteristics of wind turbine drivetrain rig, AE records of normal, bearing crack and shaft rubbing conditions can be divided into three classifications with 600 items for each.

AE signal severed as non-stationary signal, using its short and steady characteristic, AE timing signal is divided into several short frames. Since hamming window can improve signal spectrum leakage, hamming window is usually used for window plus frame processing of AE signal.

$$w(n) = \begin{cases} 0.54 - 0.46\cos[2\pi n/(N-1)], & 0 \le n \le (N-1) \\ 0, & \text{otherwise} \end{cases} \tag{9}$$

Based on framed AE signal, a feature vector is construed using the zero-crossing rate, kurtosis, short-time releasing energy and Mean amplitude difference features as shown in Table 2.

Tabel 2. Feature list of AE signal

Index	Feature description
1	Zero-crossing rate and its statistics
2	Kurtosis its statistics
3	Short-time releasing energy and its statistics
4	Mean amplitude difference and its statistics

In the experiment, the parameters settings are: the learning rate $\eta = 0.1$, the num_leaves $\alpha = 100$, the max_depth $h = 12$ and the number of trees is $n\_estimators = 3000$, the objective function is negative binomial log-likelihood for classification. The above network is carried out the experiments to detect fault conditions of the wind turbine drivetrain caused by dynamic and stationary components contact. Figure 2 give the precision performance of the used network. GBDT algorithm has early stopping regulation. As Initialization definition, number of estimators is set at 3000. While the GBDT algorithm achieved computational requirement at 235 iterations. It makes the conclusion that GBDT algorithm has excellent computational convergence, as boosting number increase, the loss function gradually converge close to 0. Also the average recognition of these three fault conditions is approximated 97.43%.

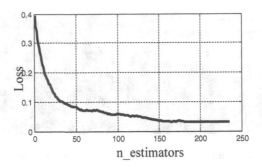

Fig. 2. The loss of GBDT algorithm

The Table 3 tabulated recognition rate of these three different fault conditions source in wind turbine drivetrain rig. The recognition rate of shaft rubbing achieves 100%, which is 0.46% and 1.67% higher than bearing crack and normal conditions. Besides, there are 1.67% for normal confusing shaft rubbing. It is because in the view of waveform variations, AE signals in shaft rubbing and normal conditions are approximate to same. While the short-time releasing energy is the critical factor to fault condition recognition.

Table 3. The accuracy of fault conditions recognition

	Normal	Bearing crack	Shaft rubbing
Normal	98.33%	0	1.67%
Bearing crack	0%	99.54%	0.45%
Shaft rubbing	0%	0%	100%

The Table 4 gives the computational performance of the different number leave. Using 100 number leave in GBDT, the computational consuming time reduces 38.86 s, recognition rate increase 9.28% than Using 100 number leave in GBDT. While 200 num_leave in GBDT, the computational consuming time reduces 1.02 s, recognition rate increase 0.07% than Using 100 num_leave in GBDT. In the view of consuming time and recognition rate, It is noted that 100 num_leave in GBDT achieves optimal solution. Therefore, the less deviation could be received by choosing the appropriate number of trees and number leave.

Table 4. Comparison of different number leave

num_leaves	Recognition rate	Time/s	Reach deviation goal
10	90.01%	143.09	Yes
100	99.29%	104.23	Yes
200	99.36%	103.21	Yes

4 Model Blending

Model blending is a very powerful technique to increase accuracy on a variety of ML tasks. For a problem, we use a different algorithm to get a lot of models g. Each model will have its own parts and some parts that are not good at it. If we can mix them, the new model may work well. Suppose we have got T models like g_1, g_2, ..., g_T, then we mix as a new model $G(x)$ as follows:

The simplest, directly in all models, choose the smallest model with the smallest verification error:

$$G(x) = \arg \min_{t \in 1,2,...T} E_{val}(g_t^-) \tag{10}$$

Take the opinions of all models directly and trust them equally, such as classification problems:

$$G(x) = sign(\sum_{t=1}^{T} 1 \cdot g_t(x)) \tag{11}$$

More recent than the previous case, giving each g a different number of votes, that is, they are no longer the same weight:

$$G(x) = sign(\sum_{t=1}^{T} \alpha_t \cdot g_t(x)) \tag{12}$$

This weight $\alpha_t \geq 0$ can be obtained by training.

A little more special, according to the characteristics of different data, to give different weights:

$$G(x) = sign(\sum_{t=1}^{T} q_t(x) \cdot g_t(x)) \tag{13}$$

Where $q_t(x) \geq 0$.

We can also use $g_t(x)$ as a feature transformation, so that we convert the original data to:(z_n, y_n), $z_n = (g_1(x_n), ..., g_T(x_n))$, Seeing exactly the same as linear regression, we can use linear regression to solve α directly.

$$\min_{\alpha_t \geq 0} \frac{1}{N} \sum_{n=1}^{N} (y_n - \sum_{i=1}^{T} \alpha_t g_t(x_n))^2 \tag{14}$$

Compared to LightGBM, XGBoost is also an optimized distributed gradient boosting library designed to be highly efficient, flexible and portable. It implements machine learning algorithms under the Gradient Boosting framework. XGBoost provides a parallel tree boosting (also known as GBDT, GBM) that solve many data science problems in a fast and accurate way.

Most decision tree learning algorithms grow trees by level (depth)-wise, like the following image, such as XGBoost (Fig. 3).

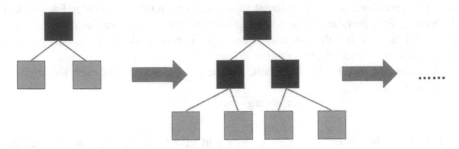

Fig. 3. Level-wise (XGBoost)

LightGBM grows trees leaf-wise (best-first). It will choose the leaf with max delta loss to grow. Holding leaf fixed, leaf-wise algorithms tend to achieve lower loss than level-wise algorithms (Fig. 4).

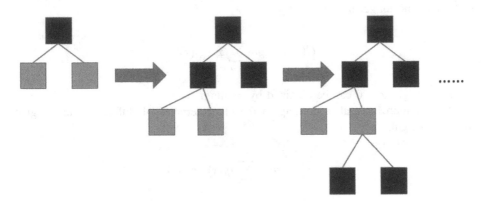

Fig. 4. Leaf-wise (LightGBM)

We set different parameters for different models. Here are some key parameters to set, such as learning_rate, num_leaves and max_depth, etc. The Table 5 gives specific setting parameters for each model.

Table 5. Different parameters of the five models

	Learning_rate rate	num_leaves crack	max_depth rubbing
LightGBM1	0.1	50	3
LightGBM2	0.05	100	2
LightGBM3	0.05	150	1
XGBoost1	0.1	100	3
XGBoost2	0.05	150	2

Finally, we use the stacking strategy for model blend. Each training set is obtained through bootstrapped sampling on the entire training data set, and a series of classification models are obtained, which are called Layer 1 classifier, and then the output is used to train the Layer 2 classifier. One of the underlying ideas is that the training data has to be learned correctly (Fig. 5).

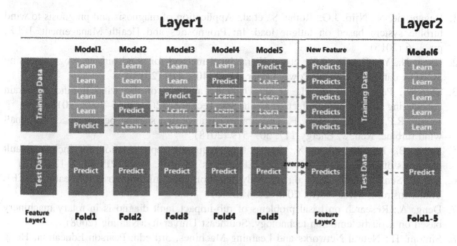

Fig. 5. Framework of stacking strategy

After model blending, the Table 6 tabulated recognition rate of these three different fault conditions source in wind turbine drivetrain rig. Compared with Table 3, the results of the blending performs better.

Table 6. The accuracy of Fault conditions recognition

	Normal	Bearing crack	Shaft rubbing
Normal	99.17%	0	0.83%
Bearing crack	0%	100%	0%
Shaft rubbing	0%	0%	100%

5   Conclusions

The essay researches on the operating condition recognition from AE signal source in wind turbine drivetrain rig based on decision tree model, adding the gradient boosting frame which integrates learning independent sub models. For the defect of falling into local minimum in decision tree, gradient boosting decision tree uses cascade learning model residuals method to improve the capability of searching global optimization effectively. The algorithm has more essential description of the AE features of wind turbine drivetrain operating condition. Therefore, it has superiority in fault diagnosis applications.

Acknowledgments. This work is supported by the National Nature Science Foundation of China (no. 51875100). The authors would like to thank anonymous reviewers and the associate editor, whose constructive comments help improve the presentation of this work.

References

1. Beganovic, N., Njiri, J.G., Rothe, S., et al.: Application of diagnosis and prognosis to wind turbine system based on fatigue load. In: Prognostics and Health Management. IEEE, pp. 1–6 (2015)
2. Chen, N., Yu, R., Chen, Y., et al.: Hierarchical method for wind turbine prognosis using SCADA data. IET Renew. Power Gener. **11**(4), 403–410 (2017)
3. Shi, W., Park, Y., Park, H., et al.: Dynamic analysis of the wind turbine drivetrain considering shaft bending effect. J. Mech. Sci. Technol. **32**(7), 3065–3072 (2018)
4. Jerson, R.P., David, H., Erb, F.: Drivetrain resistance and starting performance of a small wind turbine. Renew. Energy **117**, 509–519 (2018)
5. Yang, B., Liu, R., Chen, X.: Sparse time-frequency representation for incipient fault diagnosis of wind turbine drive train. IEEE Trans. Instrum. Meas. **PP**(99), 1–12 (2018)
6. Jin, X., Sun, Y., Que, Z., et al.: Anomaly detection and fault prognosis for bearings. IEEE Trans. Instrum. Meas. **65**(9), 2046–2054 (2016)
7. Deng, A.: Research on basal problems of rub-impact fault diagnosis in rotary machinery based on acoustic emission technology. Southeast University, Nanjing (2008)
8. Simom, H.: Neural Networks and Learning Machines, 3rd edn. Pearson Education, Hong Kong (2009)
9. Pinetro, J., Klempnow, A., Lescano, V.: Effectiveness of new spectual tools in the anomaly detection of rolling element bearings. J. Alloys Compd. **2000**(310), 276–279 (2000)
10. Li, J., Deng, A., Yang, Y., et al.: A new iterative near-field coherent subspace method for rub-impact fault localization using AE technique. J. Mech. Sci. Technol. **31**(5), 2035–2045 (2017)
11. Dunne, F., Simley, E., Pao, L.Y.: LIDAR wind speed measurement analysis and feed-forward blade pitch control for load mitigation in wind turbines: January 2010–January 2011. Office of Scientific & Technical Information Technical Reports (2011)
12. De Vito, L.: LinXGBoost: Extension of XGBoost to Generalized Local Linear Models (2017)
13. Friedman, J.H.: Greedy function approximation: a gradient boosting machine. Ann. Stat. **29**(5), 1189–1232 (2001)
14. Meng, R., Rice, S.G., Wang, J., Sun, X.: A fusion steganographic algorithm based on faster R-CNN. CMC: Comput. Mater. Continua **55**(1), 001–016 (2018)
15. Cui, J., Zhang, Y., Cai, Z., Liu, A., Li, Y.: Securing display path for security-sensitive applications on mobile devices. CMC: Comput. Mater. Continua **55**(1), 017–035 (2018)

Implementation of MD5 Collision Attack in Program

Yuying Li, Xiaohan HeLu, Mohan Li, Yanbin Sun, and Le Wang[(✉)]

Cyberspace Institute of Advanced Technology (CIAT), Guangzhou University,
Guangzhou 510006, China
2945488593@qq.com, 18878628303@163.com,
limohan.hit@gmail.com, sunyanbin@jnu.edu.cn,
wangle@gzhu.edu.cn

Abstract. Md5 [1] has been widely used because of its irreversibility, but its security is also questionable. Since Professor Wang [2] pointed out that MD5 is unsafe, Md5 collision and various attack algorithms began to appear and were used in large quantities. In the paper of Bai Honghuan's MD5 fast collision algorithm [3], the characteristics of MD5 collision were proposed, he pointed out that when the MD5 values of two different files are the same, the files are added with the same prefix, and their MD5 values are still the same. Similarly, when the same suffix is added, MD5 values is still the same, and a program is tested to verify the result.

This paper first studies the principle of MD5 algorithm [4], then points out the process of MD5 collision through Fastcoll tool, and experiments on a simple C language program using Bai Honghuan's method to verify that the program can be collided by MD5. So the method of double encryption or multiple encryption for this phenomenon, it is equivalent to adding two locks or more locks to the data. The data is first encrypted by sha-256 to obtain a hash value, and then Md5 encryption is performed on the hash value. This method does not change the fact that MD5 can be collided and attacked, but in this case it will increase the difficulty of generating two different programs with the same MD5 value through the MD5 prefix attack. In the current situation, the possibility of SHA-256 being cracked is small. When the MD5 value (SHA-256 of the modified program) is collided, but if program is changed, the SHA-256 value is also modified, finally the MD5 value will be different. According to this conclusion, if data is complex encrypted multiple times by SHA-256 and MD5, it will be more difficult to crack.

Keywords: Md5 algorithm · Fastcoll · SHA-256 · Multiple encryption

1 Introduction

1.1 Research Background

Whether it is a business or an individual, the daily input and output of information is particularly large. And with the development of the Internet, the flow of information is increasing, and the demand for information is getting higher and higher. Our dependence on information also requires the transmission of information to be large and efficient.

X. Sun et al. (Eds.): ICAIS 2019, LNCS 11632, pp. 595–604, 2019.
https://doi.org/10.1007/978-3-030-24274-9_54

However, the security of information has been greatly threatened. How to ensure the security of various data transmitted in the network, how to make data security from the sender to the receiver have become an urgent problem to be solved.

As data is being threatened more and more, it has also led to the development of cryptography. Cryptography is broadly divided into cryptographic coding and crypt-analysis. Cryptography will study data encryption as the core to ensure data authentication, integrity, confidentiality, non-repudiation, etc. Cryptography has generally gone through three phases:

The first stage is the ancient encryption stage, the most representatives are the single-table substitution and mult table substitution cryptosystem. The origins of classical cryptography can be traced back to ancient wars thousands of years ago. How to spread intelligence without being discovered by the enemy is a big problem. Therefore, current cryptography focuses on how to transmit messages in secret. This stage does not have much Inference formula. They are relatively simple, and people only need to encrypt them manually. For example, ancient people write information on the body and hide information in poetry or painting, which is not easy to find;

The second phase is the mechanical phase, also known as the classical code. This stage mainly relies on encryption equipment to achieve automatic encryption through machinery. The most representative is the Enigma rotation device invented by the German Scherbius during World War II. In the second phase, the popularity of computers and communication devices has driven people's demand for data information protection, resulting in a relatively famous encryption system, symmetric cryptosystem: DES data encryption standard;

The third phase is the modern password phase, which also becomes the computer phase. People don't have to face the cost of expensive electronic devices because computers have gained a lot of popularity. At the same time, modern mathematics has also been developed. Modern mathematics and electronic computers provide the most powerful weapon for cryptography, making cryptography calculations more precise and efficient. This phase can be said to be the most active phase. Various cryptographic theories have been introduced, and a large number of cryptographic algorithms and many common encryption standards have emerged. But at the same time there have been various attacks.

1.2   Research Status

Hash function is equivalent to a compression mapping, which can convert the data of arbitrary length into the data of fixed length to ensure the integrity of information transmission. As a hash function, Md5 algorithm plays a vital role in data security [5]. And because it does not require users to pay copyright fees and its own characteristics: computability, anti-modification and irreversibility, MD5 is very popular [6]. However, there are several attacks on Md5: running dictionary, which requires a large amount of plaintext to store database, birthday attack and differential attack, and Md5 collision. In 2004, Professor Wang Xiaoyun made a report on the decoding of MD5 at the International Cryptography Conference held in the United States, which caused a sensation [7]. Professor Wang Xiaoyun's modular aberration analysis of hash function combines modular aberration and difference or two operations to construct Md5 collision. In the literature [2], the author studies and analyses the collision research proposed by Professor Wang Xiaoyun, and improves the algorithm on this basis which improves the collision probability of MD5 and greatly accelerates the search speed. In the literature [3], the author has doubts about the security of MD5, so the collision of MD4 and MD5 is analyzed, and finally the prefix collision algorithm of MD5 selection is improved.

2 Md5 Algorithm

2.1 Md5 Introduction

Md5 (Message Digest Algorithm) as an irreversible encryption algorithm, belongs to a hash function applied in the field of computer security and it is one of the most secure algorithms at present. So let's start with the introduction of hash function. Hash function can map plaintext data of arbitrary length to a fixed length hash value. And Md5 inherits the characteristics of hash:

Comprebility: No matter how long the plaintext length is, it always can be compressed to a fixed length MD5 value.

Easy computability: It is easy to calculate MD5 value of data.

Irreversibility: It is difficult to deduce plain text from known MD5 values.

Because of the above characteristics, we can conclude that MD5 value is easy to store, low cost and high security. Therefore, MD5 is widely used.

2.2 Algorithm Analysis

2.2.1 Message Padding

First of all, we need to know that the operation object of md5 is binary data. If it is not, it must be converted to binary to operate. Then we need fill the binary data, the filling method is: Fill in the binary data, the first bit is 1, followed by 0, until M1 mod 512 = 448, M1 is the length of filled binary data and M is the original binary data.

2.2.2 Adding Data Length

A result of the first step, the obtained binary data M1 is added by 64-bit binary data. The 64-bit binary data is the length of the original data. If the original message length is greater than 2^64 bits, the lower 64 bits are taken. So the added data is a multiple of 512.

2.2.3 Introducing Magic Numbers and Function Operations

In the c language, the constant is called a magic number, and the magic number is just a specific number, which does not mean any meaning. The four standard magic numbers are:

A=0x67452301
B=0XEFCDAB89
C=0X98BADCFEL
D=0X10325476L

The logic function is:

F(X,Y,Z)=(X&Y)|((~X)&Z)
G(X,Y,Z)=(X&Z)|(Y&(~Z))
H(X,Y,Z)=X^Y^Z
I(X,Y,Z)=Y^(X|(~Z))
FF(a,b,c,d,Mj,s,ti): a=b+((a+(F(b,c,d)+Mj+ti)<<< s)
GG(a,b,c,d,Mj,s,ti): a=b+((a+(G(b,c,d)+Mj+ti)<<< s)
HH(a,b,c,d,Mj,s,ti):a=b+((a+(H(b,c,d)+Mj+ti)<<< s)
II(a,b,c,d,Mj,s,ti): a=b+((a+(I(b,c,d)+Mj+ti)<<< s)
$ti = 2^{32}*abs(sin(i))$ The integer part.

Calculating signs:
&: And, only when both numbers are 1, the operation result is 1, and the others are 0;
|: Or, as long as one of the two numbers is 1, the result is 1, and the others are 0;
~: No, if it is 1, the result is 0. If the operand is 0, the result is 1.
^: XOR, if the two numbers are the same, the result is 0, otherwise it is 1;
<<: Indicates left shift, number << 1 equivalent number multiply by 2.

2.2.4   Data Processing

The data is processed in groups of 512, and each group can be divided into 16 groups, which are recorded as M_j (j = 0, 1 … 15), and the operation is started.

ZZ(a, b, c, d, M0, s, ti)
ZZ(d, a, b, c, M1, s, ti)
ZZ(c, d, a, b, M2, s, ti)
ZZ(b, c, d, a, M3, s, ti)
ZZ(a, b, c, d, M4, s, ti)
ZZ(d, a, b, c, M5, s, ti)
ZZ(c, d, a, b, M6, s, ti)
ZZ(b, c, d, a, M7, s, ti)
ZZ(a, b, c, d, M8, s, ti)
ZZ(d, a, b, c, M9, s, ti)
ZZ(c, d, a, b, M10, s, ti)
ZZ(b, c, d, a, M11, s, ti)
ZZ(a, b, c, d, M12, s, ti)
ZZ(d, a, b, c, M13, s, ti)
ZZ(c, d, a, b, M14, s, ti)
ZZ(b, c, d, a, M15, s, ti)

In the first round ZZ(a, b, c, d, Mj, s, ti) = FF(a, b, c, d, Mj, s, ti). In the second round ZZ(a, b, c, d, Mj, s, ti) = GG(a, b, c, d, Mj, s, ti). In the third round ZZ(a, b, c, d, Mj, s, ti) = HH(a, b, c, d, Mj, s, ti). In the fourth round ZZ(a, b, c, d, Mj, s, ti) = II(a, b, c, d, Mj, s, ti).

After the execution, the next set of operations is performed, and after the run is completed, the final obtained values are combined in order, and the Md5 value is obtained.

The part of 2.2.1, 2.2.2, 2.2.3, 2.2.4 can be expressed by Fig. 1.

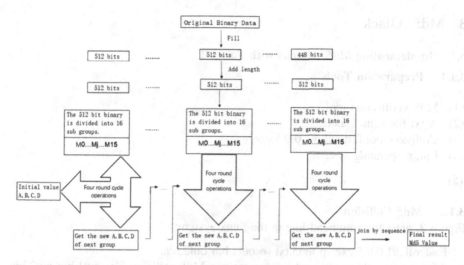

Fig. 1. MD5 algorithm diagram

2.3   Application

Password Encryption

We need a password to log in to the website, QQ, WeChat and bank debit. If the password is leaked, it will have serious consequences. Md5 can be used to protect the password. The data stored in the database can be the Md5 value of the password or the Md5 value of the username and password or the Md5 value of the half password. In this case, even if the attacker obtains the information of the database, the password of the user cannot be obtained due to the irreversibility of the Md5.

Data Integrity

Md5 can be used to verify the integrity of the data. The integrity of the data refers to the accuracy and reliability of the data. When transmitting data including the md5 value of the data, the receiver can determine whether the data is modified during transmission by calculating Md5.

Search

Md5 can be used for web search, why is it that the result of typing "md5" and typing "hash" in the search box are different? Because their md5 value is not the same, the database can be queried according to Md5.

Digital Signatures

Digital signatures are similar to physical signatures. This means that the sender of the message adds a data that electronically proves his identity and the data being transmitted. The identity of the sender is verified to prevent the sender from denying. This data segment that can verify identity can be implemented by Md5.

3 Md5 Attack

3.1   Implementing Md5 Attacks with Fastcoll

3.1.1   Preparation Tools

(1) Md5 verification tool,
(2) A txt file named a.txt,
(3) Collision tool:fastcoll_v1.0.0.5.exe
(4) Linux operating system

(5)

3.1.2   Md5 Collision

Figure 2, enter the command line in the linux system:

Fastcoll_v1.0.0.5.exe -p md5.txt -o out1.bin out2.bin.
After running this command we can get two Md5 collision files:out1.bin out2.bin.

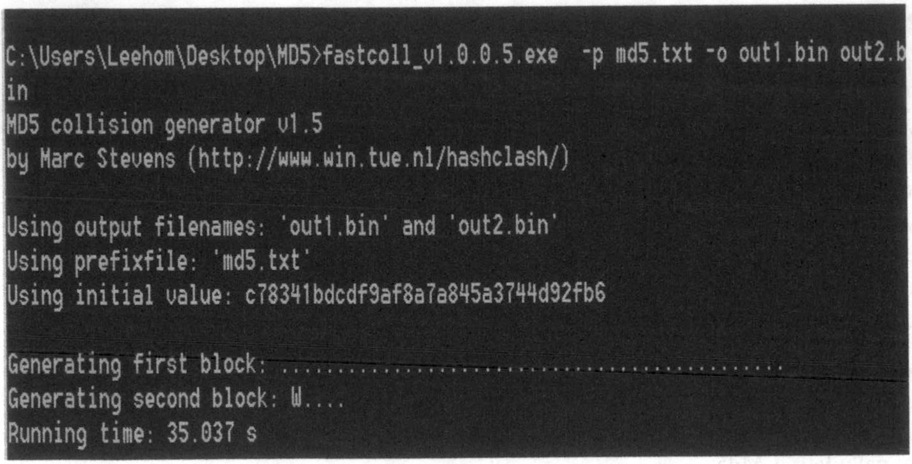

```
C:\Users\Leehom\Desktop\MD5>fastcoll_v1.0.0.5.exe  -p md5.txt -o out1.bin out2.b
in
MD5 collision generator v1.5
by Marc Stevens (http://www.win.tue.nl/hashclash/)

Using output filenames: 'out1.bin' and 'out2.bin'
Using prefixfile: 'md5.txt'
Using initial value: c78341bdcdf9af8a7a845a3744d92fb6

Generating first block: ......................................
Generating second block: W....
Running time: 35.037 s
```

Fig. 2. Fastcoll command

3.1.3   Verify Md5 Value

We verify whether the Md5 values of out1.bin and out2.bin with the MD5 verification tool. In the following pictures Figs. 3 and 4 you can find that md5 values are same, but SHA1 and CRC32 values are different.

```
MD5:  33F51944F121615D5CAD6DDD96FCED22
SHA1: 7D39962992DDA9CB32ECD40C8598D69E5DB88177
CRC32: 49F34C77
```

Fig. 3. MD5 value of out1.bin

```
MD5:  33F51944F121615D5CAD6DDD96FCED22
SHA1: 9980258E4D27DBD553DE131235CD9BD7A33E2AEE
CRC32: 2F70C2C5
```

Fig. 4. MD5 value of out2.bin

3.2   Md5 Collision with MD5collgen

3.2.1   Generate Two Different Files

Figure 5, command: $ md5collgen -p prefix.txt -o out1.bin out2.bin
   $ diff out1.bin out2.bin

```
root@kali:~/Documents/md5_patch# md5collgen -p prefix.txt -o out1.bin out2.bin
MD5 collision generator v1.5
by Marc Stevens (http://www.win.tue.nl/hashclash/)

Using output filenames: 'out1.bin' and 'out2.bin'
Using prefixfile: 'prefix.txt'
Using initial value: 49864b4219078e0b7de435cca097df55

Generating first block: ................................................
...................
Generating second block: S10.............
Running time: 60.3232 s
```

Fig. 5. Difference of out1.bin and out2.bin

3.2.2   Verify if that Two Different Files Have the Same MD5 Value

command: $ md5sum out1.bin
   $ md5sum out2.bin

We can find md5 values of out1.bin and out2.bin are same. They all are
"B6alla56bdde4c22f7208f47860a9176".

3.3   MD5 Collision of Executable Files

3.3.1   Problem Description and Target

```
Source code:
#include <stdio.h>
unsigned char xyz[100] = {
    /* The actual contents of this array are up to you */
};
int main(){
    int i;
    for (i=0; i<100; i++){
        printf("%x", xyz[i]);
    }
    printf("\n");
}
```

Our target is that using the above source code to create two different versions of the binary, the program's XYZ array contents are different, but the executable has the same hash value.

3.3.2   Create File A.exe

Exe file function: create an array of length 200, which stores 200 A to fill XYZ.

3.3.3   Prefix Collision

Use the A.exe prefix file for MD5 conflicts. After the collision, it will appear out1.bin and out2.bin, we can see their binary data in the pictures of Figs. 6 and 7. Their file suffix are different. So we create two different programs with same md5 value out2.bin:

```
71 FB E5 D4 E8 75 69 E9 94 BF E9 6E 40 C2 50 3C
64 EE 1F 6A 94 A2 4B D3 28 B2 82 21 66 F6 33 D8
A3 DB B5 D7 00 CD F9 0B EB 05 C3 DB E7 DF F8 1A
32 4E 49 9E EE 91 EB 86 A9 A5 4A F1 F5 5D 4C D4
E1 AA C4 B7 13 F9 48 91 21 92 AB DC 2F 0D AB 43
4E 39 C2 6D 01 BB E0 20 D5 FB F4 CC CC 31 5D 22
4B 67 1F F6 39 A6 A2 94 AD 6F B4 CF 54 45 6A C8
EC E7 95 95 FC AE 73 9D A9 99 36 15 D8 7C 79 4E
```

Fig. 6. out1.bin

We can find Md5(out1.bin) = Md5(out2.bin), we know the characteristic of MD5: if Md5(x1) = Md5(X2), then Md5(x1+x) = Md5(x2+x) and Md5(x+x1) = Md5(x+x2).

```
71  FB  E5  D4  E8  75  69  E9  94  BF  E9  6E  40  C2  50  3C
64  EE  1F  EA  94  A2  4B  D3  28  B2  82  21  66  F6  33  D8
A3  DB  B5  D7  00  CD  F9  0B  EB  05  C3  DB  E7  5F  F8  1A
32  4E  49  9E  EE  91  EB  86  A9  A5  4A  71  F5  5D  4C  D4
E1  AA  C4  B7  13  F9  48  91  21  92  AB  DC  2F  0D  AB  43
4E  39  C2  ED  01  BB  E0  20  D5  FB  F4  CC  CC  31  5D  22
4B  67  1F  F6  39  A6  A2  94  AD  6F  B4  CF  54  C5  6A  C8
EC  E7  95  95  FC  AE  73  9D  A9  99  36  95  D8  7C  79  4E
```

Fig. 7. out2.bin

So we replace the array part of the A.exe file with file suffix of the out1.bin and replace the array part of the A.exe file with file suffix of the out2.bin. Then we can get two different programs B.exe and C.exe. Their Md5 values will still be same because of the characteristic of MD5, but we need to verify.

3.3.4 Verify the Executable File

If we run B.exe and C.exe, we can get different results. So A.exe and B.exe are different programs. But whether the Md5 values is same. Then we begin to verify the MD5 values of the executable exe files. They are same and they all are BEF3AA74-DE604C29537F10418A408DFC, you can see the md5 values of B.exe and C.exe (Figs. 8 and 9).

```
MD5:  BEF3AA74DE604C29537F10418A408DFC
SHA1:  9B78F0BABB332B243CC85F6D22DE2CA36351292E
CRC32:  C7E542B4
```

Fig. 8. Md5 value of B.exe

```
MD5:  BEF3AA74DE604C29537F10418A408DFC
SHA1:  D9BAD90AA7EEBEE39FC85FF20B7F8E616D9BC766
CRC32:  667DCDA7
```

Fig. 9. Md5 value of B.exe

4 Double Encryption and Mixed Encryption

The mean of double Encryption is that the data is first encrypted by SHA-256 to obtain a hash value, and then Md5 encryption is performed on the hash value to obtain a MD5 value. This MD5 value still can be used to verify the integrity of the information. The advantage of Md5 is not change, the change is the difficulty of Md5 cracking. The data will be hard to be brute force because of SHA-256. And for the prefix attack, even if you get the files with the same MD5 value and two different data. The data is also difficult to modify, because when adding the same prefix or suffix, SHA-256 will inevitably change, so the MD5 value will inevitably change. Mixed encryption means that data is complex encrypted multiple times by SHA-256 and MD5. It also can increase the difficulty of MD5 collision attacks.

As mentioned by the part of abstract, this method does not change the fact that MD5 can be collided and attacked, but in this case it will increase the difficulty of generating two different programs with the same MD5 value through the MD5 prefix attack. So this method is feasible.

5 Summary

We are increasingly demanding encryption algorithms, Md5 is a very good encryption algorithm. The paper explains the principles and applications of the MD5 algorithm, as well as examples of MD5 collisions, and a method of double encryption or multiple encryption are mentioned for this phenomenon. But due to the complexity of the MD5 algorithm. MD5 is still safe for the time being, after all, there are very few collisions. But due to the complexity of the MD5 algorithm. MD5 is still safe at the moment, after all, there are few collisions.

Acknowledgement. This research was funded in part by the National Natural Science Foundation of China (61871140, 61872100, 61572153, U1636215), the National Key research and Development Plan (Grant No. 2018YFB0803504).

References

1. Rivest, R.L.: The MD5 Message Digest Algorithm, Request for Comments (RFC)1321, Internet Activities Board, Internet PrivacZ Task Force, April 1992.3RIPEMD-1281
2. Wang, X., Yu, H.: How to break MD5 and other hash functions. Springer, Heidelberg (2005)
3. Bai, H.: The study of quick Md5 collision algorithms, 7 July 2010
4. Stevens, M.: On collisions for md5. Master's thesis, Eindhoven University of Technology, June 2007
5. Yang, Y., Chen, Y., Chen, Y., et al.: A novel universal steganalysis algorithm based on the IQM and the SRM. CMC Comput. Mater. Continua **56**(2), 261–272 (2018)
6. Tang, Z., Ling, M., Yao, H., et al.: Robust image hashing via random Gabor filtering and DWT. Comput. Mater. Continua **55**(2), 331–344 (2018)
7. Gao, Z., Xia, S., Zhang, Y., et al.: Real-time visual tracking with compact shape and color feature. Comput. Mater. Continua **55**(3), 509–521 (2018)

Automatic Discovery Mechanism of Blockchain Nodes Based on the Kademlia Algorithm

Liwen Zheng, Xiaohan Helu, Mohan Li, and Hui Lu[✉]

Cyberspace Institute of Advanced Technology (CIAT),
Guangzhou University, Guangzhou 510006, China
18800160613@163.com, 18878628303@163.com,
limohan.hit@gmail.com, luhui@gzhu.edu.cn

Abstract. The emergence of the Ethereum platform has led to the unprecedented development of blockchain technology. Ethereum ensures that blockchain technology becomes the core technology of Bitcoin, and users can expand and develop other applications on the Ethereum platform. P2P networks are applied in Ethereum to achieve peer-to-peer communication in transactions, with nodes being equal to each other and without trust. Ethereum is a peer-to-peer distributed network. Inter-node communication does not pass through a trustworthy intermediary, and each node can get the latest data by sending requests to its neighboring nodes. Each node acts as both a server and a service provider. This mode guarantees the data synchronization of all the nodes in Ethereum, so it is very important to study the automatic discovery of nodes. This paper mainly analyzes the automatic discovery mechanism of nodes based on the Kademlia algorithm, including principle of the protocol, the process of communication handshake and the specific algorithm mechanism. At last, we used the Mist wallet to observe the results of automatic discovery of nodes in the Ethereum client's, and used Python to do a simple experiment for automatic discovery of Ethereum nodes.

Keywords: Blockchain · Ethernet node · Discovery of nodes · Kademlia algorithm

1 Research Background

Blockchain is a decentralized database, a non-tamperable and unforgettable distributed ledger [1]. Under normal circumstances, both parties to the transaction will rely on a third party, which is called a trustworthy intermediary. For example, in a bank transfer transaction, the bank is just the trustworthy intermediary. In this trading mode, the book of transactions record is managed by the intermediary, and what the blockchain does is the direct peer-to-peer communication, without involving any intermediary to achieve decentralization. All nodes on the network are equal to each other. The blockchain data is maintained by all nodes, and each participating node can obtain a copy of the complete ledger. The blockchain has the following typical characteristics:

© Springer Nature Switzerland AG 2019
X. Sun et al. (Eds.): ICAIS 2019, LNCS 11632, pp. 605–616, 2019.
https://doi.org/10.1007/978-3-030-24274-9_55

- Decentralization: Blockchain can be viewed as a distributed database. One of the most important features is the decentralized and distributed storage.
- De-trusting: Transactions in the blockchain are open and transparent, and each node can trade without mutual trust.
- Programmable features: The blockchain system now offers a flexible scripting code system that allows users to provide decentralized projects such as the smart contracts in Ethereum.

Because of its high security, high reliability, and anonymity, the emerging perspective of the blockchain has gradually attracted people's attention. The main application of the blockchain is still bitcoin. Although bitcoin technology is very successful, its limitations are also obvious. For example, generation time of a block is about 10 min, which will greatly limit the number of transactions completed during per unit time. So a 12-s generation time is necessary for Ethereum developers to run smart contracts. In other words, developers can develop blockchain applications on an Ethereum framework. Developers and users can assume that it has no license to be modified. It can be said that all transactions are transparent on the Ethereum platform. So we can consider Ethereum as a huge and shared computer system [4].

Ethereum applies blockchain technology and P2P network, and it is a peer-to-peer decentralized virtual machine. PCs only need to install Ethereum client to become a virtual node of Ethereum, and all of the virtual nodes form a supercomputer system together [2]. Under the mode of a peer-to-peer network, even if several nodes has get off line or been attacked, other nodes can still exist in the whole system. So its resistance of risk and tolerance of fault are very high [6]. The Kademlia protocol is applied to the inter-nodes communication of Ethereum. The main function is to establish and maintain communication between nodes [7]. This paper will mainly study the automatic discovery mechanism of blockchain nodes which is based on the Kademlia algorithm.

2 Kademlia Protocol

Kademlia is a distributed hash table (DHT) technology, but when compared with other DHT implementation technologies, such as Chord, CAN, Pastry, etc., Kademlia has established a new DHT topology based on XOR. Compared with other algorithms, it improves the speed of routing query greatly. More details about Kademlia Protocol will be introduced in the following parts [8].

2.1 Operation Command of Kademlia Protocol

In the Ethereum network, the inter-nodes communication protocol in the Kademlia network is mainly composed of the following commands:

- Ping: This command probes a node to determine whether it is online.
- Pong: This command is the response of the Ping.
- FindNode: This command is used to query the node that is close to the target node.

- Neighbors: This command is the response of the FindNode. When a node receives a FindNode message from another node, it will send a Neighbors message which carries the information its neighbor node.

2.2 Handshake Based on Kademlia Protocol

In the Ethereum network, when the PING-PONG handshake between two nodes passes, the corresponding node is considered to be online, and the following figure is a flow chart describing the process of the handshake between two nodes (Fig. 1):

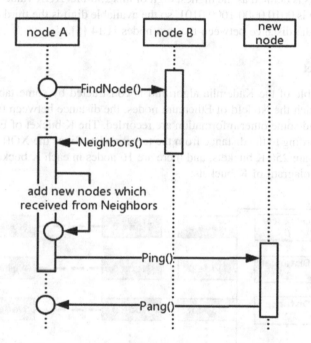

Fig. 1. The flow chart of handshake based on Kademlia protocol

The following process can be derived from the above figure:

- The current node A sends a FindNode message to the Node B indicating that it wishes to query its neighboring nodes.
- After receiving the FindNode message, the Node B sends a Neighbors message to the sending node A, which contains the information of its neighbor nodes.
- After receiving the Neighbors message, Node A will add the nodes carried in the Neighbors message to its own node list, which are recorded as new nodes and node A will send a Ping message to the new nodes.
- If a new node sends a Pong message to node A to prove that it is alive, node A will consider the new node as its neighboring node.

3 Automatic Discovery Mechanism of Nodes Based on Kademlia Algorithm

3.1 Method to Calculate Distance Between Two Nodes in Ethereum

The Ethereum system will generate a unique identifier called NodeID (512-bits) for each node and will use the sha3 algorithm to generate a 256-bits hash value for the 512-bits NodeID. Then the system will manipulate the hash values of two nodes by XOR operation, which will generate a 256-bits XOR value. And the distance between these two nodes is defined as the highest digit of this 256-bits XOR value. For example, the XOR value is 0010 0000 1000 0101, so the available digit is the third digit from the left, and then the distance between the two nodes is 14 [5].

3.2 K-bucket

The routing table of the Kademlia algorithm is constructed by some tables called "K bucket", in which the NodeId of Ethereum nodes, the distance between two nodes, the target node, and some other information are recorded. The K bucket of Ethereum sorts the nodes according to the distance from the target nodes. Since the XOR value is up to 256 bits, there are 256 K buckets, and there are 16 nodes in each K bucket. Figure 2 is the schematic diagram of K buckets:

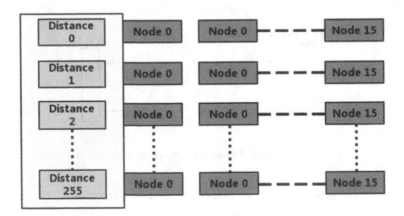

Fig. 2. K bucket

3.3 The Process of Discovering Neighboring Nodes

Ethereum applies the P2P network, and the automatic discovery mechanism of its neighboring nodes is based on the Kademlia algorithm. The flowchart of the process to discover neighboring nodes automatically is as follows:

As it can be seen from Fig. 3, when the system is started for the first time, a local node is randomly generated, and its NodeID is recorded as LocalID. Then the system will read the information of public nodes. After completing the process of Ping-Pong

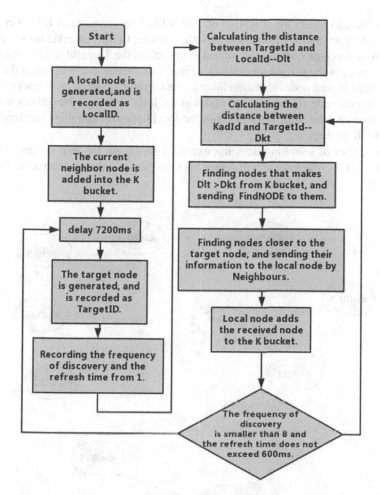

Fig. 3. Flowchart of discovering nodes

handshake, the Ethereum system will add the current neighboring nodes to the K buckets, and K buckets will be refreshed every 7200 ms. The refreshing process of K buckets is as follows:

- The Ethereum system generates a NodeId of target node randomly, which is recorded as TargetId. The frequency of discovery and the refresh time will be recorded from 1, and then the system will calculate the distance between the target node and the local node, which is recorded as Dlt.
- The NodeId of a node which is in the K buckets is recorded as KadId. The Ethereum system will calculate the distance between the target node and a node in the K buckets. This distance is recorded as Dkt.

- Nodes that can satisfy the condition of "Dlt > Dkt" are recorded as K-bucket nodes. Then the target node will send a FindNode message to the K-bucket nodes, and the FindNode message contains the information such as the TargetId of the target node.
- After a node in the K buckets receives a FindNode message, it will repeat the above three steps to find nodes that are closer to the target node from its K buckets. Then the K-bucket node will send these nodes to the local node by a Neighbors message.
- After receiving the Neighbors message, the local node will add these received nodes into the K buckets.
- If the number of searching does not exceed 8 times and the refresh time does not exceed 600 ms, the system will return back to the second step to execute the loop (Fig. 4).

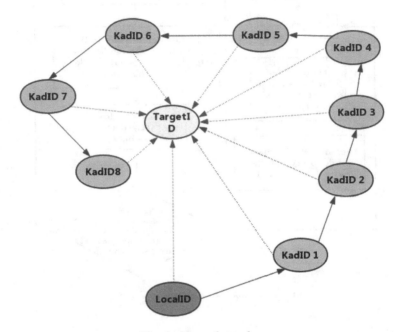

Fig. 4. Network topology

It can be seen from the network topology diagram of the Kademlia algorithm above that, in the process of discovering neighboring nodes, the Ethereum network will converges on the distance to the randomly generated target node, instead of converging to the local node.

4   Testing Results

4.1   Discovering Nodes Automatically Through Mist Wallet

Mist wallet is a full-node wallet client. If you want to trade, you need to synchronize the block information; and if you don't want it to synchronize the block information, you can set it as a light sync mode. In the full sync mode, block synchronization is performed to find neighboring nodes [3]. It can be seen from Figs. 5 and 6 that my account is connected to 4 neighboring nodes. Besides, 2,682,391 remote blocks have been synchronized locally.

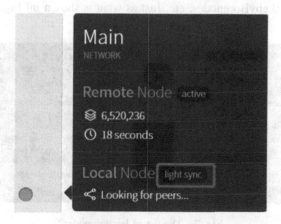

Fig. 5. Light sync mode

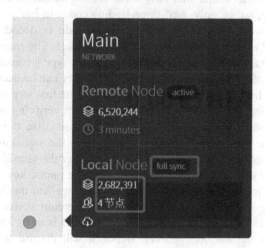

Fig. 6. Fill sync mode

4.2   Discovering Ethereum Nodes Automatically with Python

This section can be divided into three parts to display:

Firstly, the RLPx specification describes how to discover nodes. In the first part, we use the RLPx protocol to send packets through the 30303 port by default, using the function of encode and decode in rlp library to do the RLPx encoding, and to convert this object into a message. Then we use the UDP protocol to send the messages out. There are four messages defined in the RLPx protocol: PingNode, Pong, FindNeighbors, and Neighbors.

By analyzing the source code of go-ethereum, we learned that Ethereum has a list of leading nodes for different networks in it, such as MainnetBootnodes, TestnetBootnodes, RinkebyBootnodes, etc. Just as what is shown int Fig. 7 below:

```
var MainnetBootnodes = []string{
    // Ethereum Foundation Go Bootnodes

    // US-WEST
    "enode://78de8a0916848093c73790ead81d1928bec737d565119932b98c6b100d944b7a95e94
f847f689fc723399d2e31129d182f7ef3863f2b4c820abbf3ab2722344d@191.235.84.50:3030
3", // BR
    "enode://158f8aab45f6d19c6cbf4a089c2670541a8da11978a2f90dbf6a502a4a3bab80d288a
fdbeb7ec0ef6d92de563767f3b1ea9e8e334ca711e9f8e2df5a0385e8e6@13.75.154.138:3030
3", // AU
    "enode://1118980bf48b0a3640bdba04e0fe78b1add18e1cd99bf22d53daac1fd9972ad650df5
2176e7c7d89d1114cfef2bc23a2959aa54998a46afcf7d91809f0855082@52.74.57.123:30303
    ", // SG
```

Fig. 7. The list of leading nodes

After testing, it was found that only three leading nodes in the mainnet can be pinged successfully, so we only used three leading codes in our project.

Secondly, the work after pinging the leading node is decoding, which means unpacking the RLP encoded message into a python object. The messages in the RLPx specification are arranged as "hash || signature || packet-type || packet-data", and if the hash and signature of the message are both available, they can be decoded into different types of messages. In this process, packet decoding is the first step to be implemented, followed by verifying the secp256k1 signatures. Before verifying the secp256k1 signatures, the secp256k1 library should be used to de-serialize the signature into an object, and then the public key can be retrieved from the signatures. After that, the public key can be used to verify the signatures. And after the secp256k1 signatures are verified, a PublicKey object can be created to store the public key.

The last part is to dispose the FindNeighbors message and the Neighbors message to find neighboring nodes. After analyzing the go-ethereum source code, we learned that we should check whether the request source fromID is in its known-nodes record in order to process the findnode packet. If not, it will discard that request. So the leading node must be pinged first. When the leading node receives a ping, it will respond to a pong first. Then it will send a ping and wait for us to respond a pong. Once we respond a pong, our nodeID will enter the list of known-nodes of the leading node.

The FindNeighbors message can then be sent and the information of neighboring node sent back by the leading node can be received. Finally, the received neighboring nodes will be put into the recode. And we can change our ip address every once in a while to prevent Ethereum from refusing to be connected (Fig. 8).

```go
func (t *udp) findnode(toid enode.ID, toaddr *net.UDPAddr, target
    encPubkey) ([]*node, error) {
    // If we haven't seen a ping from the destination node for a
    while, it won't remember
    // our endpoint proof and reject findnode. Solicit a ping
    first.
    if time.Since(t.db.LastPingReceived(toid)) > bondExpiration {
        t.ping(toid, toaddr)
        t.waitping(toid)
    }

    nodes := make([]*node, 0, bucketSize)
    nreceived := 0
    errc := t.pending(toid, neighborsPacket, func(r interface{})
        bool {
        reply := r.(*neighbors)
        for _, rn := range reply.Nodes {
            nreceived++
            n, err := t.nodeFromRPC(toaddr, rn)
            if err != nil {
                log.Trace("Invalid neighbor node received", "ip",
                    rn.IP, "addr", toaddr, "err", err)
                continue
            }
            nodes = append(nodes, n)
        }
```

Fig. 8. Source code of udp.go in Go-ethereum

The code running results are listed as follows:

From Fig. 9 we can see that the current number of neighboring nodes is 27, and the source ip address is 191.235.84.50. After receiving neighboring nodes, the current number of neighboring nodes is 33. So there are four newly added neighboring nodes.

It can be seen in Fig. 10 that the ip of a neighboring node received previously is 23.240.248.126. There are 12 newly added nodes sent by the neighboring node in the list, and the node whose ip is 37.187.90.108 is one of the 12 nodes. It also can be seen that this node can be pinged successfully.

The final result can be seen in Fig. 11 that the node whose ip is 85.143.174.95 is the neighboring node sent by the leading node. And we can find new neighboring node by considering it as a new leading node.

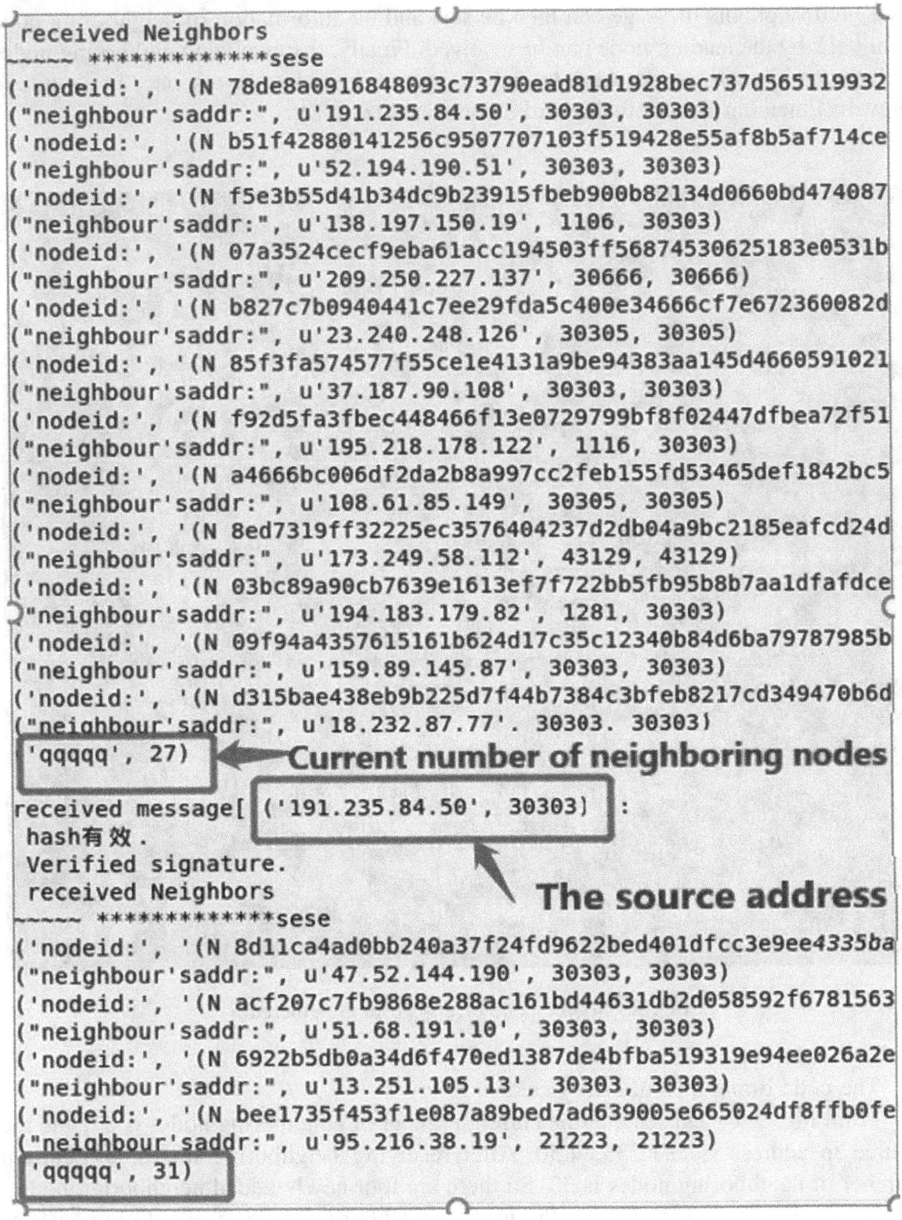

```
received Neighbors
~~~~ **************sese
('nodeid:', '(N 78de8a0916848093c73790ead81d1928bec737d565119932
("neighbour'saddr:", u'191.235.84.50', 30303, 30303)
('nodeid:', '(N b51f42880141256c9507707103f519428e55af8b5af714ce
("neighbour'saddr:", u'52.194.190.51', 30303, 30303)
('nodeid:', '(N f5e3b55d41b34dc9b23915fbeb900b82134d0660bd474087
("neighbour'saddr:", u'138.197.150.19', 1106, 30303)
('nodeid:', '(N 07a3524cecf9eba61acc194503ff56874530625183e0531b
("neighbour'saddr:", u'209.250.227.137', 30666, 30666)
('nodeid:', '(N b827c7b0940441c7ee29fda5c400e34666cf7e672360082d
("neighbour'saddr:", u'23.240.248.126', 30305, 30305)
('nodeid:', '(N 85f3fa574577f55ce1e4131a9be94383aa145d4660591021
("neighbour'saddr:", u'37.187.90.108', 30303, 30303)
('nodeid:', '(N f92d5fa3fbec448466f13e0729799bf8f02447dfbea72f51
("neighbour'saddr:", u'195.218.178.122', 1116, 30303)
('nodeid:', '(N a4666bc006df2da2b8a997cc2feb155fd53465def1842bc5
("neighbour'saddr:", u'108.61.85.149', 30305, 30305)
('nodeid:', '(N 8ed7319ff32225ec3576404237d2db04a9bc2185eafcd24d
("neighbour'saddr:", u'173.249.58.112', 43129, 43129)
('nodeid:', '(N 03bc89a90cb7639e1613ef7f722bb5fb95b8b7aa1dfafdce
("neighbour'saddr:", u'194.183.179.82', 1281, 30303)
('nodeid:', '(N 09f94a4357615161b624d17c35c12340b84d6ba79787985b
("neighbour'saddr:", u'159.89.145.87', 30303, 30303)
('nodeid:', '(N d315bae438eb9b225d7f44b7384c3bfeb8217cd349470b6d
("neighbour'saddr:", u'18.232.87.77', 30303, 30303)
'qqqqq', 27)         Current number of neighboring nodes

received message[ ('191.235.84.50', 30303) ]:
 hash有效.
 Verified signature.
 received Neighbors          The source address
~~~~ **************sese
('nodeid:', '(N 8d11ca4ad0bb240a37f24fd9622bed401dfcc3e9ee4335ba
("neighbour'saddr:", u'47.52.144.190', 30303, 30303)
('nodeid:', '(N acf207c7fb9868e288ac161bd44631db2d058592f6781563
("neighbour'saddr:", u'51.68.191.10', 30303, 30303)
('nodeid:', '(N 6922b5db0a34d6f470ed1387de4bfba519319e94ee026a2e
("neighbour'saddr:", u'13.251.105.13', 30303, 30303)
('nodeid:', '(N bee1735f453f1e087a89bed7ad639005e665024df8ffb0fe
("neighbour'saddr:", u'95.216.38.19', 21223, 21223)
'qqqqq', 31)
```

Fig. 9. Step 1

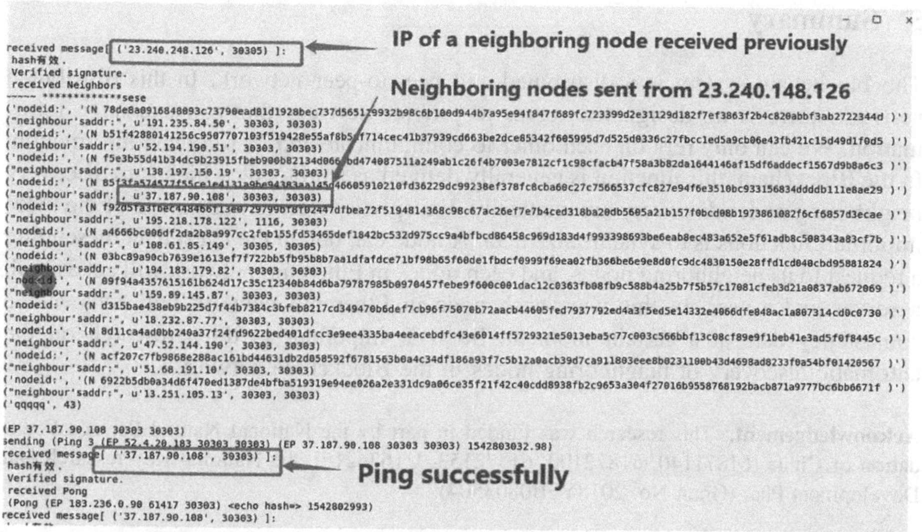

Fig. 10. Step 2

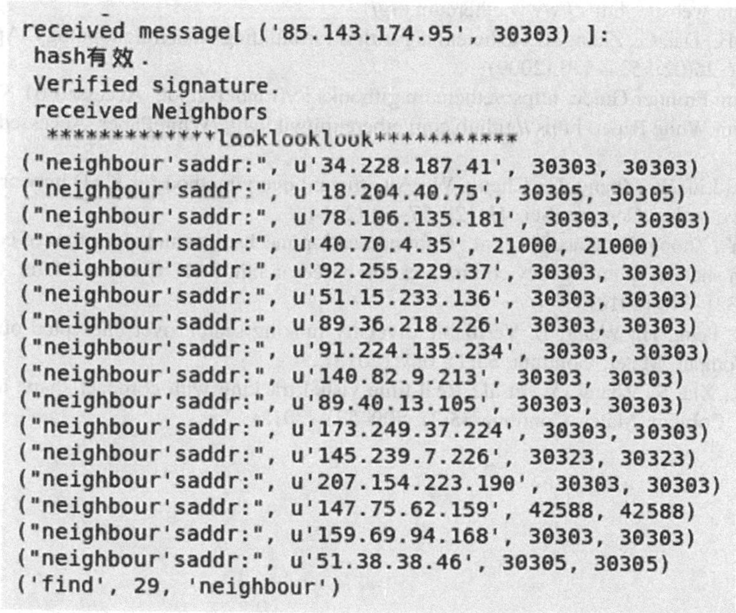

Fig. 11. Result

5 Summary

The blockchain system is a distributed and peer-to-peer network. In this distributed network, there is no designated server to provide services that can exchange information. We can only rely on each other to communicate and disseminate information. In the Blockchain, this function is generally defined as a protocol, which is to discovery neighboring nodes discovery automatically. Except discovering nodes, one of the more important functions is to synchronize data. A node can obtain the latest data by sending a request to its neighboring nodes, and each nodes in Ethereum network will act as both a server and a user. In this way, each node in Ethereum network will achieve the consistency data at a certain moment. So it is important to do a research on the automatic discovery of neighboring nodes in the Blockchain network.

Acknowledgement. This research was funded in part by the National Natural Science Foundation of China (61871140, 61872100, 61572153, U1636215), the National Key research and Development Plan (Grant No. 2018YFB0803504).

References

1. Ethereum website. https://www.ethereum.org/
2. Zhang, H., Dai, C., Zhang, C.: Efficient algorithm for building Kademlia topology. Appl. Res. Comput. **26**(02), 534–536 (2009)
3. Ethereum Frontier Guide. https://ethereum.gitbooks.io/frontier-guide. Accessed 01 Nov 2018
4. Ethereum White Paper. https://github.com/ethereum/wiki/wiki/WhitePaper. Accessed 01 Nov 2018
5. Yan, H., Liu, W., Zhang, G., Cheng, W.: An efficient query method for KAD networks based on active nodes. Comput. Sci. **41**(12), 57–59 (2014)
6. Jiang, Y., Zhong, X., Guo, Y., et al.: Communication mechanism and algorithm of composite location analysis of emergency communication based on rail. CMC Comput. Mater. Continua **57**(2), 321–340 (2018)
7. Liu, Y., Peng, H., Wang, J.: Verifiable diversity ranking search over encrypted outsourced data. Comput. Mater. Continua **55**(1), 037 (2018)
8. Gao, Z., Xia, S., Zhang, Y., et al.: Real-time visual tracking with compact shape and color feature. Comput. Mater. Continua **55**(3), 509–521 (2018)

Monochromatic Mutual Nearest Neighbor Queries Over Uncertain Data

Yifei Chen[1(✉)], Liling Zhao[2], and Pengjiang Mei[2]

[1] Binjiang College, Nanjing University of Information Science & Technology,
333 Xishan Avenue, Wuxi 214105, China
ch_yi_f@l26.com
[2] School of Automation, Nanjing University of Information Science
& Technology, 219 Ningliu Road, Nanjing 210044, China
zhaoliling@nuist.edu.cn, 1486222106@qq.com

Abstract. As a variant of nearest neighbor queries, mutual nearest neighbor (MNN) search has important applications. In this paper, we formalize the MNN queries in uncertain scenarios, namely the UMNN queries, which return data objects with non-zero qualifying guarantees of being the query issuers' MNNs. We also present some properties of UMNN problems. To process UMNN queries efficiently, we develop two approaches which employ techniques including best-first based uncertain NN retrieval with minimal maximum distance bounding, existing uncertain reverse NN search with geometric pruning, and make use of the reusing technique. An empirical study, based on experiments performed using both real and synthetic datasets, has been conducted to demonstrate the efficiency and effectiveness of developed algorithms under various settings. The experiments also testify the correctness of properties that we proposed as for the monochromatic UMNN problem.

Keywords: Uncertainty · Mutual nearest neighbor · Query processing

1 Introduction

Uncertainty is an inherent characteristic of location-based services [1] and moving object data management [2]. In recent years, nearest neighbor query processing and its variants in uncertain scenarios have increasingly drawn extensive attention from research community, such as uncertain nearest neighbor (UNN) queries [3], uncertain reverse nearest neighbor (URNN) queries [4] and so on. In this paper, we propose a novel query problem, namely uncertain mutual nearest neighbor (UMNN) search on a monochromatic dataset.

MNN search has important practical relevance to several applications, such as pattern recognition, decision making [5] and data mining [6]. Given a dataset D and a query issuer q, an MNN query retrieves the objects in D that are the NNs to q and meanwhile have q as their NNs. For example, soldiers A, B, C and D in Fig. 1(a) are executing tasks separately. For some reason, we need to assign a best partner to A, who can provide the support to A as soon as possible in emergency and vice versa. This equals an MNN search on a monochromatic dataset. If their locations are exact points

© Springer Nature Switzerland AG 2019
X. Sun et al. (Eds.): ICAIS 2019, LNCS 11632, pp. 617–629, 2019.
https://doi.org/10.1007/978-3-030-24274-9_56

as shown in Fig. 1(a), then C is the MNN of A. However, computing an MNN in the uncertain scenario is more complicated than its precise counterpart. All the possible locations of an uncertain object distribute in an "uncertainty domain" [7], for example the disc in Fig. 1(b), following some probability density function. If A, B, C, D are located at a_1, b_1, c_1 and d_1 respectively, then D is A's MNN. However, C is A's MNN when object A lies in a_2. In fact, an object might appear at any location in its uncertainty domain. Therefore, the existing algorithms for precise datasets are inapplicable in uncertain scenarios.

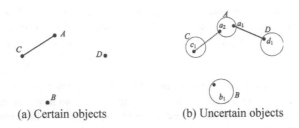

(a) Certain objects   (b) Uncertain objects

Fig. 1. An example of MNN problem.

Recently, the concept of bichromatic UMNN queries which considers two datasets is introduced [8]. The query issuer is from an uncertain dataset and retrieves the top-k probabilistic MNNs from a crisp point dataset. However, our paper focuses on monochromatic UMNN search on one dataset. Not only the query issuer but also data objects are uncertain. Motivated by the significance of MNN retrieval in uncertain scenarios and the lack of efficient algorithms, we provide a formal definition and develop processing algorithms in this paper. In the sequel, Sect. 2 formalizes the UMNN problem and analyses its properties. Section 3 elaborates query processing approaches for problems in Euclidean space. Section 4 demonstrates experimental results and reports findings. Finally, Sect. 5 concludes the paper with some directions for future work.

2 Preliminaries

Given an uncertain dataset D, assume each data object $o \in D$ can be represented by an uncertainty region, denoted as $o.ur$, in which o locates at position x_o with probability $o.pdf(x_o) \geq 0$ [4, 7]. The UMNN query is defined as follows.

Definition 1. *Given a query object* $q \in D$, *an UMNN query retrieves the data objects* $o \in D\backslash\{q\}$ *such that*:

$$P_{MNN}(q,o) = E(pr\{\forall o' \in D\backslash\{q,o\}, dist(q,o) \leq dist(q,o') \land dist(o,q) \leq dist(o,o')\})$$
$$> 0$$

$$(1)$$

where dist(q, o) is the Euclidean distance from q to o. Equation (1) is equal to the following,

$$P_{MNN}(q,o) = \int\limits_{n(q,o)}^{f(q,o)} pr\{dist(q,o) = r\} \cdot \prod_{\forall o' \in D \setminus \{q,o\}} pr\{dist(q,o') \geq r\} \cdot pr\{dist(o,o') \geq r\} dr$$

$$(2)$$

where $n(q, o)$ and $f(q, o)$ are the minimum and maximum distances from q to o respectively. $pr\{\cdot\}$ represents the probability of something is true.

The UMNN query has two important properties which make it different from UNN and URNN search.

Property 1. *MNN is symmetric. As for $\forall o, q \in D$, we have $o \in MNN(q) \Leftrightarrow q \in MNN(o)$, where $MNN(q)/MNN(o)$ is the set of q's/o's MNNs.*

According to Definition 1 and the symmetry of Euclidean distance, Property 1 obviously holds. Neither the UNN nor the URNN problem is symmetric.

Property 2. *Given a query issuer q, the number of q's MNNs varies as the data distribution of D or uncertainty regions of objects change.*

For some objects, their MNNs are unique; some objects have more than one MNN; whereas some objects have no MNN. This property makes UMNN search different from UNN retrieval, because any uncertain object has at least one NN. Taking the definitions of UMNN, UNN [3] and URNN [4] into consideration, we elicit the following theorems, lemmas and corollaries that contribute to the basis of our approaches.

Theorem 1. *MNN(q) is a subset of NN(q), i.e., $MNN(q) \subseteq NN(q)$, where $NN(q)$ is the set of q's NNs.*

Proof. The probability that an object o is q's NN is as [3]

$$P_{NN}(q,o) = E(pr\{\forall o' \in D \setminus \{q,o\}, dist(q,o) \leq dist(q,o')\})$$

$$= \int\limits_{n(q,o)}^{f(q,o)} pr\{dist(q,o) = r\} \cdot \prod_{\forall o' \in D \setminus \{q,o\}} pr\{dist(q,o') \geq r\} dr \qquad (3)$$

Since $pr\{\cdot\} \in [0, 1]$, we have

$$P_{MNN}(q,o) = \int\limits_{n(q,o)}^{f(q,o)} pr\{dist(q,o) = r\} \cdot \prod_{\forall o' \in D \setminus \{q,o\}} pr\{dist(q,o') \geq r\} \cdot pr\{dist(o,o') \geq r\} dr$$

$$\leq \int\limits_{n(q,o)}^{f(q,o)} pr\{dist(q,o) = r\} \cdot \prod_{\forall o' \in D \setminus \{q,o\}} pr\{dist(q,o') \geq r\} dr = P_{NN}(q,o).$$

That is to say, as for any $o \in MNN(q)$, $P_{MNN}(q, o) \leq P_{NN}(q, o)$. So $MNN(q) \subseteq NN(q)$. $\square$

Corollary 1. *If $o \in MNN(q)$, then $o \in NN(q)$ and $q \in NN(o)$.*

Proof. According to Theorem 1, $o \in NN(q)$ when $o \in MNN(q)$. As the symmetry of MNN (Property 1), $q \in MNN(o)$ if $o \in MNN(q)$. So $q \in NN(o)$. Corollary 1 holds. $\square$

Theorem 2. *$MNN(q)$ is a subset of $RNN(q)$, i.e., $MNN(q) \subseteq RNN(q)$, where $RNN(q)$ is the set of q's RNNs.*

The proof is analogous to that of Theorem 1 and is omitted due to page limitations.

Corollary 2. *If $o \in MNN(q)$, then $o \in NN(q)$ and $o \in RNN(q)$.*

Proof. According to Theorem 1, if $o \in MNN(q)$, then $o \in NN(q)$. According to Theorem 2, if $o \in MNN(q)$, then $o \in RNN(q)$. Hence, Corollary 2 holds. $\square$

The evaluation of Eq. (2) can be simplified with Lemma 1.

Lemma 1. *Supposing $\zeta_{q,o} = \min(minf(q), minf(o))$, where $minf(q)$ is the minimum of the maximal distances from q to all the other objects in D, namely $minf(q) = \min\limits_{o' \in D \setminus \{q\}} (f(q, o'))$; the definition of $minf(o)$ is analogous. Then we have*

$$P_{MNN}(q,o) = \int_{n(q,o)}^{\zeta_{q,o}} pr\{dist(q,o) = r\} \cdot \prod_{\forall o' \in D \setminus \{q,o\}} pr\{dist(q, o') \geq r\} \cdot pr\{dist(o, o') \geq r\} dr$$

$$(4)$$

Proof. We denote the integration function by $G(r)$ for simplification, and transform Eq. (2) into

$$P_{MNN}(q,o) = \int_{n(q,o)}^{\zeta_{q,o}} G(r)dr + \int_{\zeta_{q,o}}^{f(q,o)} G(r)dr \qquad (5)$$

If $\zeta_{q,o} = minf(q)$, then $\int_{\zeta_{q,o}}^{f(q,o)} G(r)dr = \int_{minf(q)}^{f(q,o)} G(r)dr$. There are two cases:

- If $minf(q) = f(q, o)$, then $\int_{minf(q)}^{f(q,o)} G(r)dr = 0$.
- If $minf(q) < f(q, o)$, then there is an object $w \in D \setminus \{q, o\}$, s.t. $minf(q) = f(q, w)$. As for w, $pr\{dist(q, w) \geq r\} = 0$ when $r \in [f(q, w), f(q, o)]$, so $\int_{minf(q)}^{f(q,o)} G(r)dr = 0$.

Analogously, $\int_{minf(o)}^{f(q,o)} G(r)dr = 0$ when $\zeta_{q,o} = minf(o)$. Accordingly, the part after "+" in Eq. (5) is always equal to 0. Lemma 1 holds. $\square$

Lemma 2. *As for any object $o' \in D$, if $o' \notin S_n(o)$, then o' has no contribution to $P_{MNN}(q, o)$. $S_n(o)$ is the set of influencing objects of o, and $S_n(o) = nn(q) \cup nn(o) - \{q, o\}$, where $nn(q)/nn(o)$ is the candidate set of q's/o's NNs.*

Proof. If $o' \notin S_n(o)$, then as for $\forall x_q \in q.ur$, $\forall x_o \in o.ur$ and $\forall x_{o'} \in o'.ur$, we have $dist(x_q, x_{o'}) > \zeta_{q,o}$ and $dist(x_o, x_{o'}) > \zeta_{q,o}$ [9]. Hence, $pr\{dist(q, o') \geq r\}$ and $pr\{dist(o, o') \geq r\}$ always equal 1 when $r \in [n(q, o), \zeta_{q,o}]$ in Eq. (4). So o' has no influence on $P_{MNN}(q, o)$. $\square$

According to Lemma 2, the evaluation of $P_{MNN}(q, o)$ can be simplified as

$$P_{MNN}(q,o) = \int_{n(q,o)}^{\varsigma_{q,o}} pr\{dist(q,o) = r\} \prod_{\forall o' \in S_n(o)} pr\{dist(q,o') \geq r\}pr\{dist(o,o') \geq r\}dr \quad (6)$$

3 UMNN Query Processing

In this section, we develop two processing approaches for UMNN queries based on the above corollaries. We utilize R-tree as the index of datasets [4] in the rest of paper.

3.1 Approach MN

$MNN(q)$ is a subset of $NN(q)$ according to Corollary 1. As the pseudo-code in Algorithm 1, we first conduct an UNN search to retrieve $nn(q)$, the candidate set of q's NNs, and then verify each object $o \in nn(q)$. The verification can be accomplished again via an UNN search to check whether $q \in nn(o)$. If yes, it means that o is possibly an MNN of q. At the same time, $S_n(o)$ is constructed after the retrieval of $nn(o)$. If $P_{MNN}(q, o)$ is greater than 0, then o is finally returned as a result. This approach obtains MNN candidates through Multiple UNN searches, so it is named as MN. Operator NNFind in line 3 and NNFind_InSecond in line 8 are employed to conduct the first UNN search and the following verification. Obviously, UNN search is a basic operator in algorithm MN. We can approximate the irregular uncertainty domain with its minimal bounding circle (MBC) without introducing false reports or missing result objects. If there is no special specification, we use the MBCs of uncertainty domains when dealing with the minimum/maximum distance computation in the rest of paper.

Algorithm 1. MN

Input: D: dataset; q: query object
Output: RS: result set, the form of element in RS is (o,p)
1:    initialize the min-heap H_{rfn}, the form of elements in H_{rfn} is (e,key)
2:    $S_{temp}=\emptyset$
3:    $nn(q)$=NNFind(q, root, H_{rfn}) // H_{rfn} preserves the pruned objects or nodes
4:    **for** each object o in $nn(q)$ **do**
5:        insert $(o,n(q,o))$ into H_{rfn}
6:        $S_{temp} = \bigcup_{e \in Hrfn}$
7:    **for** each object o in $nn(q)$ **do**
8:        $nn(o)$ =NNFind_InSecond(o, S_{temp})
9:        **if** $q \in nn(o)$ **then**
10:           evaluate $P_{MNN}(q,o)$ according to Equation (6)
11:           **if** $P_{MNN}(q,o) > 0$ **then**
12:               insert $(o, P_{MNN}(q,o))$ into RS
13: **return** RS

We present the pseudo-code of operator NNFind in Algorithm 2. Given a query object q, we traverse the R-tree in a best-first manner, by maintaining a min-heap H whose entry is in the form (E, key), where E is a node and key is the minimal distance from q to E (intuitively, an object closer to q would result in smaller $minf(q)$) at line 5 in NNFind.

Algorithm 2. NNFind

Input: *root*: the root of R-tree indexing the dataset; q: query issuer; H_{rfn}: a min-heap

Output: $nn(q)$: candidates of q's UNNs

1: initialize the min-heap H, the form of elements in H is (e, key)
2: insert $(root, 0)$ into H
3: $minf = \infty$ // $minf$ is the global minimum of the maximal distances
4: **while** H is not empty **do**
5:    de-heap the top entry (E, d_t) from H
6:    **if** $d_t > minf$ **then break**
7:    **if** E is not a leaf node **then**
8:      **for** each entry e in E **do**
9:        $D_e = f(q,e)$, $d_e = n(q,e)$
10:       **if** $D_e < minf$ **then**
11:         $minf = D_e$, insert (e, d_e) into H
12:       **else if** $d_e < minf$ **then**
13:         insert (e, d_e) into H
14:       **else**
15:         insert (e, d_e) into H_{rfn} //e is pruned and preserved in H_{rfn}
16:     **else** //E is a leaf node
17:       **for** each entry e in E **do**
18:         **if** $e \neq q$ **then**
19:           $D_e = f(q,e)$, $d_e = n(q,e)$
20:           **if** $D_e < minf$ **then**
21:             $minf = D_e$, insert e into $nn(q)$
22:             delete the objects $o \in nn(q)$ that satisfy $n(q,o) > minf$ and insert them into H_{rfn}
23:           **else if** $d_e < minf$ **then**
24:             insert e into $nn(q)$
25:           **else**
26:             insert (e, d_e) into H_{rfn}
27:         **else** // $e = q$
28:           insert $(q, 0)$ into H_{rfn}
29: **while** H is not Empty **do**
30:   de-heap the top entry (E, d_t) from H and insert it into H_{rfn}
31: **return** $nn(q)$

By using locally available nodes accessed in NNFind, we design an operator NNFind_InSecond as shown in Algorithm 3 to verify each object o in $nn(q)$. Instead of scanning the dataset from scratch like NNFind, NNFind_InSecond starts the traversal based on a local view, S_{temp}, of dataset.

Algorithm 3. NNFind_InSecond

Input : p: query object;

S_{temp}: the set including the objects and nodes have been visited in NNFind

Output : $nn(p)$: NN candidates of p

1: initialize the min-heap H, the form of elements in H is (e,key)

2: $minf=\infty$

3: **for** each element e in S_{temp} **do**

4:   **if** e is a data object and $e{\neq}p$ **then**

5:    $D_e=f(p,e)$, $d_e=n(p,e)$

6:    **if** $D_e< minf$ **then**

7:     $minf = D_e$, insert e into $nn(p)$

8:    **else if** $d_e< minf$

9:     insert e into $nn(p)$

10: **else**

11:   **if** e is a node **then**

12:    $D_e=f(p,e)$, $d_e=n(p,e)$

13:    **if** $D_e< minf$ **then**

14:     $minf = D_e$; insert (e,d_e) into H

15:    **else if** $d_e< minf$ **then**

16:     insert (e, d_e) into H

17: lines in the following is the same with lines 4~13, 16~21 and 23~24 of Algorithm 2, but the query object is p here

36: delete the objects in $nn(p)$ whose minimal distances from p are greater than $minf$

37: **return** $nn(p)$

3.2 Approach *NR*

The second approach is the same with Algorithm 1 in lines 1–6 as shown in Algorithm 4. The operator RNNFind(q, H_{rfn}) in line 7 retrieves the RNN candidate set, $rnn(q)$, which is guaranteed to be a superset of the final result set of UMNN retrieval. Corollary 2 ensures that q's MNN candidates is in the intersection of $nn(q)$ and $rnn(q)$. So in the "for" statement, each object o in $rnn(q)$ are verified whether it is one of q's NN candidates. If it is, then o is an MNN candidate. In the following, $nn(o)$ is obtained by operator NNFind_InSecond(o, S_{temp}) and is utilized to construct the set of influencing objects $S_n(o)$. This approach obtains candidates by once UNN search and once URNN search, so it is denoted by *NR*. The operator RNNFind in line 7 is an URNN retrieval based on the GP technique [4].

Algorithm 4. *NR*

Input: dataset D; query object q

Output: result set RS, the form of element in RS is (o,p)

1:~6: lines 1~6 are the same with Algorithm 1 // find NN candidates of q

7:     $rnn(q)$= RNNFind(q, H_{rfn})

8:     **for** each object o in $rnn(q)$ **do**

9:       **if** $o \in nn(q)$ **then**

10:       $nn(o)$=NNFind_InSecond(o, S_{temp})

11:       evaluate $P_{MNN}(q,o)$ according to Equation (6)

12:       **if** $P_{MNN}(q,o) > 0$ **then**

13:         insert $(o, P_{MNN}(q,o))$into RS

14:    **return** RS

Rule 1 (*Geometry Pruning, GP*). *Given a query object q, an object o' can be safely pruned as for the RNN of q, if o'.ur completely falls in some PR(o), where PR(o) = {p|p is a point in Euclidean space satisfying f(o, p) < n(q, p), as for o∈D\{q, o'}}.*

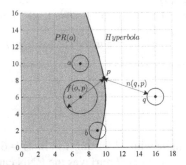

Fig. 2. An example of GP rule.

Supposing $q.ur$ and $o.ur$ are discs, then we obtain a hyperbola according to $n(q, p) = f(o, p)$ as shown in Fig. 2. Uncertainty regions of other shapes can be transformed into MBCs. Any point p' in the part on the left of the hyperbola, namely the shadow region, makes $f(o, p') < n(q, p')$. Object a completely falls in this part, which indicates that a is definitely closer to o than to q and a can be safely pruned. While object b intersects the hyperbola, so it cannot be discarded.

Algorithm 5 describes operator RNNFind which is on the base of GP rule and reusing technique. Instead of scanning the dataset from scratch [4], RNNFind starts the traversal based on a local view of the dataset preserved by the heap H_{rfn}. Consequently, only the accesses to nodes not locally available are necessary.

Algorithm 5. RNNFind

Input: q: query issuer

    H_{rfn}: the min-heap peserving the items that have been pruned or visited

Output: $rnn(q)$: candidate set of q's URNNs

1:    $O_{cand}=\varnothing$
2:    **while** H_{rfn} is not empty **do**
3:      de-heap the top entry (E,d_t) from H_{rfn}
4:      **if** $GP(E, O_{cand})$= false **then**
5:        **if** E is data item **then**
6:          **if** $E != q$ **then**
7:            $O_{cand}= O_{cand}\cup\{E\}$
8:            mark the objects that can be prune by GP rule about E in O_{cand}
9:        **else** // E is a node
10:         **for** each entry e in E **do**
11:           **if** $GP(e, O_{cand})$= false **then**
12:            insert $(e,n(q,e))$ into H_{rfn}
13:    insert objects without being marked in O_{cand} into $rnn(q)$
14:    **return** $rnn(q)$

---

4 Experimental Evaluations

In this section, the efficiency and effectiveness of proposed approaches are evaluated through experiments. All the algorithms are implemented in C++, and the experiments are conducted on a ThinkPad with Intel Core 3 2.13 GHz CPU and 2.92 GB available main memory, running Microsoft Windows 7 Ultimate Edition.

4.1 Experimental Setup

Given a set D of points, we generate uncertain data to simulate a database storing the positions of mobile clients [7]. Specially we use two real datasets, *CA* and *LB* available at http://www.rtreeportal.org. We also generate synthetic datasets following uniform distribution (*ui*), Gaussian distribution with 10 hotspots (*ga*) and two real digital road networks: the Oldenburg (*ol*) and the Singapore (*sg*) city map respectively [10]. For all the datasets, the workspace is normalized to $[0, 10^5]$ on every dimension. We will execute a workload of 100 queries in order to measure their average performance. We randomly select one target object in datasets as the query object. We inspect the performance of algorithms according to wall clock time which consists of CPU time and I/O cost [4, 7]. In the following, we denote the CPU time of two approaches by MNc and NRc, and denote the I/O time by MNi and NRi respectively. We also present the numbers of candidates and result objects to facilitate analysis and comparison.

4.2   Performance Study

The first set of experiments studies the effect of uncertainty on the performance of the algorithms using the real datasets. We vary r_{max}, the global maximal radius of uncertainty domains, between 100 and 500. The overhead increase with the growth of r_{max} in Figs. 3 and 4. The expansion of uncertainty regions leads to the increase of the maximal distances and the decrease of the minimal distances between objects. More objects become candidates as presented in Fig. 5 and more objects contribute to the final probabilities. These lead to more time spent on finding candidates, evaluating probabilities and I/O. The number of result objects also increases in Fig. 5. This is accord with Property 2, namely the size of uncertainty region has influence on the number of MNNs. Additionally, the percentage of result objects in candidates decreases. This indicates that the rate of false hits increases with the growth of uncertainty.

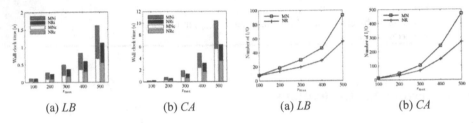

(a) *LB*   (b) *CA*   (a) *LB*   (b) *CA*

Fig. 3. Time cost vs r_{max}.   **Fig. 4.** Number of I/O vs r_{max}.

As shown in Fig. 4, the I/O overhead of approach *NR* is always less than that of *MN*. According to Fig. 5, *NR* introduces less false hits than *MN* does, which indicates that the former has better pruning capability than the latter has. Hence the time spent on probability evaluation of the former is always less than that of the latter. Therefore, *NR* outperforms *MN*.

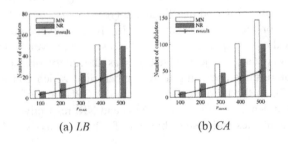

(a) *LB*   (b) *CA*

Fig. 5. Cardinalities of result and candidate set vs r_{max}.

The next set of experiments explores how the size of the dataset *#obj* influences query processing. We employ four synthetic datasets: *ui*, *ga*, *ol* and *sg* respectively by varying *#obj* from 25 K to 100 K and fixing r_{max} to 300. The distributions of datasets when *#obj* equals 100 K are demonstrated in Fig. 6.

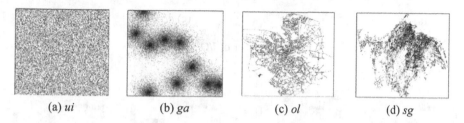

(a) *ui*   (b) *ga*   (c) *ol*   (d) *sg*

Fig. 6. Distribution of datasets.

The effect of varying *#obj* is similar but not as significant as that of varying r_{max}. As for four datasets, the overheads increase when *#obj* grows as shown in Figs. 7 and 8. The numbers of candidates and results also rise as demonstrated by Fig. 9. This is accord with Property 2. The reason is that the larger *#obj* is, the more objects are in the unit area when the size of space is fixed. The query objects are randomly chosen from the set of data objects, so their locations follow the underlying dataset distribution. Accordingly, the number of candidates and the number of objects contributing to the probabilities increase with the growth of *#obj*, which leads to the ascending time cost.

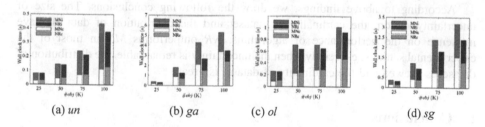

(a) *un*   (b) *ga*   (c) *ol*   (d) *sg*

Fig. 7. Time cost vs *#obj*.

Four synthetic datasets are the same in the settings of *#obj* and r_{max}, whereas the performance of the same algorithm is distinctively different on these datasets as shown in Figs. 7 and 8. Overheads are the highest on the dataset *ga* and they are the lowest on the dataset *un*. It is obvious that the distribution of *ga* is the most skewed among four datasets, while *un* is the most uniform. This indicates that the more skewed the data distribution is, the more overheads are incurred. The reason is that there are more objects around the query issuers when the distribution of dataset is skewed. Accordingly, candidates and objects contributing to the final probabilities are more. These lead to the growth of CPU time and number of I/O. The data distribution significantly affects the size of result sets. There are much more result objects when dataset is skewed.

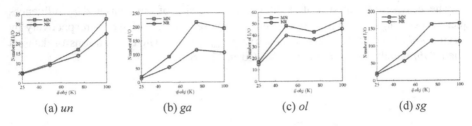

Fig. 8. Number of I/O vs *#obj*.

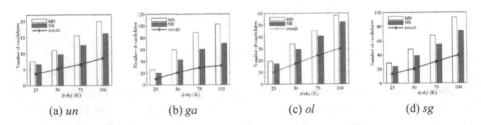

Fig. 9. Cardinalities of result and candidate set vs *#obj*.

Additionally, the distribution of dataset also has effect on the superiority of two approaches. As shown in Figs. 7 and 8, the superiority of *NR* is the most significant on dataset *ga*, then on *sg*, *ol*, and *un*. This indicates that the more skewed the dataset is, the better *NR* performs than *MN* does when other settings are the same.

According to above findings, we draw the following conclusions. The size of uncertainty region, the cardinality of dataset and the distribution of data all have influence on the performance of algorithms. *NR* outperforms *MN* in most of the experimental settings, especially when the uncertainty is remarkable, the distribution of dataset is skewed and the cardinality of dataset is great.

5   Conclusions

In this paper, we provide a formal definition of monochromatic MNN problems in uncertain scenarios and present some properties. According to the characteristics that the set of query object *q*'s MNNs is a subset of *q*'s NNs and is also a subset of *q*'s RNNs, we design two algorithms *MN* and *NR*. An experimental study upon real and synthetic datasets confirms that *NR* outperforms *MN* significantly under most settings. The performance improvement is due to the fact that *NR* adopts the GP rule to achieve better pruning capability. Our experiments verify that uncertainty, cardinality and distribution of datasets have influence on the performance of algorithms.

The proposed properties and algorithms are applicable to the problem in Euclidean space. A promising direction for future work may concern their extension to other metric space, such as the road network. We also intend to investigate efficient algorithms for handling UMNN queries over uncertain moving objects.

References

1. Liu, W., Luo, X., Liu, Y., Liu, L., Liu, M., Shi, Y.Q.: Localization algorithm of indoor Wi-Fi access points based on signal strength relative relationship and region division. CMC Comput. Mater. Continua **55**, 71–93 (2018)
2. Yang, X., Xiao, G., Wang, B., Chen, M.: The management of uncertain moving objects. Commun. CCF **4**, 21–31 (2009)
3. Cheng, R., Kalashnikov, D.V., Prabhakar, S.: Querying imprecise data in moving object environments. IEEE Trans. Knowl. Data Eng. **16**, 1112–1127 (2004)
4. Lian, X., Chen, L.: Efficient processing of probabilistic reverse nearest neighbor queries over uncertain data. VLDB J. **18**, 787–808 (2009)
5. Fang, S., Cai, Z., Sun, W., Liu, A., Liu, F., Wang, G.: Feature selection method based on class discriminative degree for intelligent medical diagnosis. CMC Comput. Mater. Continua **55**, 419–433 (2018)
6. Gao, Y., Zheng, B., Chen, G., Li, Q.: On the efficient mutual nearest neighbor query processing in spatial databases. Data Knowl. Eng. **68**, 705–727 (2009)
7. Tao, Y., Xiao, X., Cheng, R.: Range search on multidimensional uncertain data. ACM TODS **32**, 1–54 (2007)
8. Liang, Y., Zhang, Y., Zhou, S., Bai, W.: Top-k probabilistic mutual nearest neighbor query on uncertain data. Appl. Res. Comput. **28**, 2485–2487 (2011)
9. Chen, Y.: Query processing over locationally uncertain moving objects. Nanjing University of Aeronautics and Astronautics, Nanjing (2012)
10. Chen, S., Jensen, C.S., Lin, D.: A benchmark for evaluating moving object indexes. PVLDB **2**, 1574–2585 (2008)

Network-Embedding Based Storage Location Assignment in Mobile Rack Warehouse

Jing Qiu[1], Yaqi Si[2], Yuhan Chai[2], Yan Liu[2], Dongwen Zhang[2], Hao Han[3], and Le Wang[1(✉)]

[1] Cyberspace Institute of Advanced Technology (CIAT), Guangzhou University, Guangzhou 510006, China
qiujing.ch@gmail.com, wangle@gzhu.edu.cn
[2] Department of Information Science and Engineering, Hebei University of Science and Technology, Shijiazhuang 050000, China
siyaqi@stu.hebust.edu.cn, chyuhan_smile@163.com, apillowhill@gmail.com, zdwwtx@hebust.edu.cn
[3] Beijing Jizhijia Technology Co., Ltd., Beijing 100000, China
hanhao_st@163.com

Abstract. As mobile rack warehouses become more and more popular in e-commerce era, traditional storage location assignment strategy which optimize the space, retrieval speed, utilization ratio is no longer suitable for such situation. Current mobile rack warehouse often using random strategy to put goods onto racks. However, this strategy doesn't consider the relationships between goods, which are implied in order information. In this paper, a Network-Embedding based method is proposed to cluster goods into different groups, which helps to create storage location assignment strategy. First, we build the relationship network between goods based on the history orders data. Then, we train the goods representations through the network embedding model. At last, we find the strong-related goods by K-means algorithm, and put them onto the same rack. The experimental results show the method we proposed is more efficient than random strategy.

Keywords: Network-Embedding · Mobile rack · Warehouse · Cluster

1 Introduction

Recently, e-commerce platforms are developed rapidly as Internet is more and more popular in people's daily life. There are hundreds of e-commerce platform in China so far, and according to the statistic of these platforms, China's top 2 platforms, TaoBao and JingDong, completed 812 million and 240 million orders respectively in November 11, 2017 [1, 2]. Therefore, how to pick and send these orders efficiently gets a lot of concern by warehouse management.

In traditional warehouse management, orders are often generated by retailers, companies and supermarkets such as Wal-Mart. Warehouses will usually receive a small number of orders which has a large number of goods, and the strategy is often to optimize the space by arranging goods with various shapes, weight onto a proper

© Springer Nature Switzerland AG 2019
X. Sun et al. (Eds.): ICAIS 2019, LNCS 11632, pp. 630–639, 2019.
https://doi.org/10.1007/978-3-030-24274-9_57

location in the rack [3]. However, in the situation of e-commerce, the quantity of orders is often large while less than one hundred goods are contained in an order. Warehouses in such situations often pick orders using a pipeline system, and adopt the random, catalog, class and frequency strategies to retrieval good's location more quickly [4].

Recent years, mobile racks become more and more popular in warehouse picking system. Robots will move racks which contains target goods to workers, and workers only concentrate on the orders that he need to deal with [5]. In such situation, some limits in traditional warehouse has changed. For example, the distribution of goods in different racks is more important than the location of goods in a rack. Therefore, a new strategy is needed for mobile rack warehouses.

In this paper, we proposed a network embedding based method which arranges the location of goods based on the history orders. First, the relationships between goods are built from orders. Then, we get the representation of goods by network embedding algorithm. At last, we cluster the representation of goods using K-means [19], then goods are put onto different racks according to the clusters. We evaluated the racks-moved number of embedding method and random method. The results show that our method move less racks to process a batch of orders.

The remainder of this paper is organized as follows. In Sect. 2, we introduce the relation work in mobile rack storage location assignment. Section 3 illustrates the method we used to assign good's location. Section 4 present our experiment result on a company's data. And Sect. 5 discuss our conclusion and future work we will continue.

2   Related Work

Traditional storage location assignment strategy often discuss how to optimize the location of the goods so as to store more goods, make the rack more stable etc. in a warehouse. For example, [6] proposed a random method to store goods based on the remain location in a warehouse. [7] proposed a model based on the shape, weight and other features to optimize the utilization ratio of warehouse and solved the problem using heuristic algorithm.

In e-commerce situation, there are mainly two classes of method. The first class is finding how the to retrieval good's location quickly in a warehouse. For example, [8] store goods based on the goods classes, and help workers using visualization tools. Another class of methods research how to balance the workload of workers in different pipelines. For example, [9] proposed a genetic algorithm to optimize the space and balance of workload in pipelines.

The distinction of mobile rack warehouse and traditional warehouse is that robots can retrieval the racks that contain target goods and move the racks to picking workers automatically. [10] proposed a model to optimize the path length that robot walks in picking orders based on the order sequences and rack locations. [11] proposed a model to put similar goods in same rack using association rules. As the classic example beer&diaper in data mining shows, putting goods which has strong relationship together can save customer's time. However, association rules method can only find the local relationships between goods. For example, if we find another association rule toothpaste&&toothbrush, we don't know should we put toothpaste && toothbrush and beer&diaper together or not. [12] use clustering method to find similar goods and put similar goods onto same rack. But the features used for clustering are frequency and label, and such features neglect the inner relationship between goods.

In this paper, our core idea is that we first build the global relationships between all goods, then find goods which have strong relationships using Network-Embedding, and put the strong-related goods onto same racks at last. As we all know, graph or network is the most-used method to describe the relationships between entities, and if we want to take advantage of the information hided in the network, we need to map the edges and nodes into a special space that computers can understand. Network embedding is a type of popular deep learning methods that learn the low dimension features representation of the nodes and apply these features to many tasks such as classification, clustering, link prediction, visualization and so on. The main idea of Network-Embedding is find a mapping function to transform the nodes in the network into a vector representation. DeepWalk [14] is the first method that learns the representation of networks by deep learning. As the deep learning method word2vector [15] in natural language processing does, DeepWalk take nodes in networks as the word in a document, and the random walk path is a generated sentence in a document. Once the document is generated, the process of DeepWalk is just the same as word2vector, and it use Skip-gram or CBOW neural network to train the embedding of words which is also the embedding of nodes in the network. Node2vec [16] extend DeepWalk by introducing biased random walk which composed BFS (Breadth First Search) and DFS (Depth First Search), and learn the parameters by Semi-Supervised Learning method. LINE [13] defined a probability model that make sure the adjacent nodes and similar nodes has similar representations. The model has two parts to describe the similarity between nodes. The first part is the joint probability of adjacent nodes and the second part is the conditional probability of adjacent nodes. When the max likelihood probability is achieved, we get the representation of the nodes. CENE [17] takes the content of the nodes as special nodes, and the whole network has two types of edges: node-text, node-node. The optimization objective is to minimize the loss of two types of edges. CANE [18] uses the contexts of edges to model the network. An edge has two contexts: text context which contains the content representation vector, structure context which contains the representation vector of adjacent nodes. The text embedding could get by context-free method in which a node play the same role for the embedding of adjacent nodes, and context-aware method in which a node play different roles. In the experiment section of this paper, we use LINE as our network embedding method since we don't have the text information.

At last, we need to get a cluster of one by one according to the clustering algorithm. There are many methods of clustering, such as, hierarchical methods, partition-based methods, density-based methods, grid-based methods, model-based methods, FCM. There are other clustering methods, such as quantum clustering, kernel clustering, and spectral clustering. There are two main types of hierarchical clustering: combined hierarchical clustering and split hierarchical clustering, which are well interpretable, but have high time complexity. The method based on partitioning: The principle is simple. Imagine that you have a bunch of scatter points that need to be clustered. The desired clustering effect is that "the points in the class are close enough, the points between the classes are far enough", which is for large The data set is also simple and efficient, time complexity, low space complexity, and most importantly, the result is easy to be locally optimal when the data set is large. Density-based method: It is not sensitive to noise, and can find clusters of arbitrary shapes. The result of clustering of shortcomings has a great relationship with parameters. Network-based approach: speed is fast, because its speed is independent of the number of data objects, but only depends on the number of cells in each dimension in the data space, but the parameters are sensitive, unable to process irregularly distributed data, dimensions Disaster, etc. Model-based approach: the classification of "classes" is not so "hard", but is expressed in the form of probabilities. The characteristics of each class can also be expressed by parameters, but the execution efficiency is not high, especially the number of distributions and the amount of data. Fuzzy-based clustering: The algorithm will be good for clustering data that satisfies the normal distribution. In addition, the algorithm is sensitive to isolated points, but the performance of the algorithm depends on the initial aggregation because it cannot ensure that the FCM converges to an optimal solution. Class center [19, 20]. Here we use the K-means algorithm for clustering. K-means is one of the more classical clustering algorithms in the partitioning method. Because of its high efficiency, the algorithm is widely used in clustering large-scale data. The K-means algorithm uses K as a parameter to divide n objects into k clusters, which makes the clusters have higher similarity, and the similarity between clusters is lower [21]. It is this feature that we chose K-means as a clustering algorithm, and the goods placed on one shelf have a high degree of similarity.

3 Methodology

In this section, we first introduced the detail working process in a mobile rack warehouse. Then, we introduced the random method which assign goods to racks in current warehouse system. At last, we introduced the proposed Network-Embedding method and discussed the characteristic of two methods.

3.1 Storage Assignment in Mobile Rack Warehouse

Our works are aimed at the problem in the intelligent warehouse of A company. The warehouse designed by A company is shown as Fig. 1. The warehouse is divided into several separated regions and each region consists of several racks to store goods. And every rack has five levels where each level can store 20 types of goods. A region is managed by several human-controlled stations, and equipped with several robots which can move target racks for workers in parallel. The station is designed as a client to receive and process orders and each station is controlled by a picking worker. There is a screen on each station to display the orders and goods that system assigned to the worker, and there is also a sowing wall in front of the station which has 24 boxes to store goods of orders. One box should only contains goods of a single order, and the warehouse system will push orders to stations when orders arrive.

The process to pick an order by a station is as followed: (1) warehouse system schedules robots to move all racks that contain target goods to the station; (2) picking workers put every order's goods to the corresponding box; (3) when all goods of one

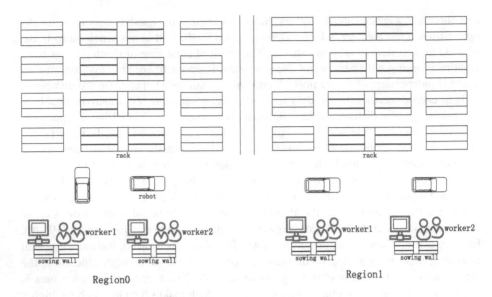

Fig. 1. Warehouse in A company.

order is picked to the corresponding box, system will package the goods in the order and empty the box for next order.

Without loss of generality, we assume that a station in A company processes 24 orders every time instead one by. When a batch of orders is processed by a station, the system dispatches another batch of orders to the station. Because workers have assistant tools to pick goods in a rack, we assume that the location of goods in a rack doesn't matter to the processing time, and the time to pick all the 24 orders is fixed. Therefore, the cost of processing a batch of orders is how many racks are moved in this process.

Suppose K types of goods exist in the warehouse and M racks are located in the warehouse. All goods in the warehouse is formalized as $G = \{g_i \mid 0 < i <= K\}$, where g_i stands for the ith good. The process of storage location assignment is to divide G into M groups: $P = \{p_j \mid 0 < j <= M\}$, where $p_j = \{g_l \mid 0 < l <= (K/M)\}$ means the goods assigned to j^{th} rack. The assignment strategy should help the system to move as less racks as possible, when processing the orders.

3.2   Random Method

A company adopted random method to assign the location of goods for the moment. The merits of random method is that goods are distributed in every racks uniformly and therefore the workload of every station is almost equal. Random method first concatenate all goods into a sequence, and shuffles the sequence randomly. Then, we need to divide the random sequence into racks based on the capacity of every rack. The pseudo-code of random method is as followed.

Algorithm 1 Random method

Input: G, M   **Output:** list of goods
1: disorder_sequence = shuffle(G) //shuffle the goods
2: groups = divide(G, M) //divide goods into M groups
3: return groups

Although random method can balance the workload of stations, the relationships between goods are not well taken advantaged by this method. Therefore strong-related goods may scattered in several racks and picking an order may consequently need to move more racks to the stations. From the point of the process that an order is generated, random method assumes that goods in an order are random distributed, which means goods in an order have no relationships with each other. However, this assumption is obviously contrary to the fact that users often buy goods based on some purpose, and he will buy related goods in an order. Therefore, we proposed a method based on the global relationships between goods, and learn the strong relationships from history orders.

3.3   Network-Embedding Method

In mobile rack warehouses, the process that an order is processed consists of two parts: dispatching order and picking order. Dispatching order refers to the process that when orders arrive, the system decide which station to process these orders. Picking order refers to the process that after a station receives a task, robots move the corresponding racks to the station.

The less racks moved to process an order, the more efficient a method is. We assume that there are some relationships network between goods. For example, a pen and a notebook may have the same function to a person and he may buy a notebook after he buy a pen. And when a consumer book an order, he may first pick one good, and then pick other goods that are connected with this good in the network. We also assume that the goods in an order share some strong relationships with each other. Therefore, if we could build the relationships network between goods from history data, and find the strong relationships between goods, then putting the strong relationships into same rack will speed up the process of picking this order.

The way we build the relationship between goods is as followed: (1) we extract all the good pairs that emerge in the same order and count the number in all orders. If two goods are in one pairs, we could say the two goods may have some relationship. (2) considering that occasional relationship often have a lower co-occurrence frequency, we remove the pairs whose frequency is lower than some threshold. (3) considering that a dense network can't distinct the strong and weak relationship, we compute the backbone of each edges in the relationships network, and finally simplify the network by removing some unimportant relationships.

The way we find strong relationship is as followed: (1) get the network-embedding of the relationships network using LINE [13]. (2) use K-means [22, 23] method to cluster the node in the network based on the embedding vector in step 1, and the goods in one cluster are the goods with strong relationship [24]. At last, we sort the clusters based on the size of a cluster, and divide the sorted sequence to racks. The pseudo-code of our method is as followed.

Algorithm 2 Network-Embedding method

Input: G, M   **Output:** list of goods
1: network = co-occurrence pairs (G) // find the co-occurrence pairs
2: frequency_filter(network) // filter low frequency pairs
3: backbone_filter(network) // filter the unimportant relationships
4: embedding = LINE(network) // train the embedding of network using LINE
5: clusters = K-means(embedding) // cluster goods into groups using K-means algorithm
6: sorted_sequence=sort(cluster) // sort clusters based on how many goods it contains
7: groups=divide(sorted_sequence, M) // divide the sorted sequence into racks
8: return groups

---

4   Experiment

In this section, we first introduced the data set used in our experiment, then we explain the baseline used to compare random method and network-embedding method. At last, we show the results of two methods using different parameters and discuss the factor that affects the result.

4.1   Data Set

The data set used in this experiment is provide by A company which builds auto robots and warehouse systems for e-commerce companies. The provided data is the received orders in a real warehouse between a couple of weeks, and the data format is shown in Table 1. As is shown in the table, one order is identified by a 'order_id' field, and about 2–20 goods identified by a 'good_id' field are contained in one order. The data set has 47660 orders and 4454 goods.

Table 1.   Data format in our experiment.

order_id	good_id
001	5001
001	5002
002	1001
002	1002

4.2   Baseline

As described in Sect. 3.1, we assume the key factor that affects the time of processing an order is how many racks are moved in this process. For simplicity, we don't consider the affection of different dispatching order strategies to this process, and we also assume that warehouse system dispatches a batch of orders to the station randomly. Therefore, our baseline is defined as followed:

$$W = \sum_{i=1}^{|O|} \sum_{o \in O_i} \sum_{p \in P} r_{op} \tag{1}$$

where O stands for the order groups which is corresponding to all the sowing walls; $O = \{O_1, O_2, O_3, ...\}$, where O_i stands for the ith group of orders; $o \in O_i$ is an order in i^{th} group, and $p \in P$ is a rack in the warehouse. $r_{op} = 1$ when order o contains the goods in rack p, and $r_{op} = 1$ when doesn't contains. Our objective is to find a good-rack mapping to minimize W.

4.3   Result

In this section, we compare the results of random method and network-embedding method. We use 46660 orders as training set, and the remaining 1000 orders as test set. In the process of test, we divide the test set into groups, and each of them has 24 orders. And the result is as follows.

Result of Two Methods. In our experiment, there are 4454 goods and 223 racks in warehouse, and each rack has 20 goods. In network-embedding method, we get 1065 goods to build the relationship network, and we cluster 60 groups. Concatenate with the remain 3383 goods, we get the final storage location assignment. The result of two methods is shown as Table 2. We can see from the result that the network-embedding method can promote about 20% of the efficiency than random method. And the promotion of network-embedding method is stable in different order number. Because we only build the relationship network of 25 percents of 4454 goods, we believe if we could build a more typical network, we can further promote the result.

Table 2. Racks moved in test set.

Order number	1000	700	500	200	100
Good number	1576	1383	1203	885	575
Rack number	5353/**4140**	3746/**2888**	2731/**2080**	1170/**929**	573/**447**

Affection of Parameter. We perform several experiments by using various network embedding vector dimensions and cluster numbers. The result is shown as Table 3. As the result shows, when we take different cluster number and vector dimension, the rack-moved number is almost not changed, and the cluster number and vector dimension have little affection to the result.

Table 3. Racks moved in with different parameters.

	1000	700	500	200	100
5d_K10	4434	3066	2224	989	488
5d_K30	4428	3085	2246	978	489
5d_K60	4442	3105	2255	988	498
10d_K10	4423	3077	2251	986	490
10d_K30	4453	3097	2254	983	488
10d_K60	4423	3109	2255	984	498
20d_K10	4431	3099	2227	990	492
20d_K30	4429	3101	2262	971	486
20d_K60	4488	3124	2272	995	494

There are two major reasons for this phenomenon: (1) the relationship network we build is not very dividable for goods and the goods number used to build the network is small comparing the entire number, thus the result clusters we get in the step of find strong relationship have little difference with each other. (2) the K-means method only take advantage of the embedding of nodes which is not suitable for a network clustering problem, and we could use a community detection algorithms. (3) in our built network, no node context is provided to give further information and some of relationship described in the good's attribute is not obtained in our method.

5 Conclusion and Future Work

In e-commerce era, mobile rack warehouses face the challenge of large quantity of small orders and most warehouses with mobile racks assign goods to racks using random method. In the paper, we proposed a network-embedding based method to solve the storage location assignment problem. First, we build the relationship network between goods based on history orders. Then, we learn the network-embedding using LINE, and we use K-means to find strong-relationship goods based on the embedding of the relationship network. It turns out that, our method perform 20% more efficient than random method.

In the future, we will optimize our method from three aspects: (1) we will try to solve these problem using constrained optimization methods by defining a objective function similar to Eq. (1) and minimize the objective using genetic algorithm (2) we could speed the entire picking system by integrating with dispatching orders strategy. For example, we could cluster the orders and sent each cluster to one station (3) we will study other method to build the relationship network so as to get better network-embedding.

Acknowledgment. This research was funded in part by the National Natural Science Foundation of China (61871140, 61872100, 61572153, U1636215, 61572492, 61672020), the National Key research and Development Plan (Grant No. 2018YFB0803504), and Open Fund of Beijing Key Laboratory of IOT Information Security Technology (J6V0011104).

References

1. Alibaba Data. https://dt.alibaba.com/
2. Jingdong Data. https://wx.jdcloud.com/
3. Dongxizhe: The studying on storage space optimization model and algorithms. Harbin Institute of Technology (2006)
4. Yangjingxiang: Research on the optimization of storage location assignment and order-picking routing in a shelf-type warehouse. Beijing Jiaotong University (2016)
5. Boysen, N., Briskorn, D., Emde, S.: Parts-to-picker based order processing in a rack-moving mobile robots environment. Eur. J. Oper. Res. **262**(2), 550–562 (2017)
6. Petersen, C.G., Aase, G.: A comparison of picking, storage, and routing policies in manual order picking. Int. J. Prod. Econ. **92**(1), 11–19 (2005)
7. Quintanilla, S., Pérez, Á., Ballestín, F., et al.: Heuristic algorithms for a storage location assignment problem in a chaotic warehouse. Eng. Optim. **47**(10), 1405–1422 (2014)
8. Muppani, V.R., Adil, G.K.: A branch and bound algorithm for class based storage location assignment. Eur. J. Oper. Res. **189**(2), 492–507 (2008)
9. Pan, C.H., Shih, P.H., Wu, M.H., et al.: A storage assignment heuristic method based on genetic algorithm for a pick-and-pass warehousing system. Comput. Ind. Eng. **81**(C), 1–13 (2015)
10. Boysen, N., Briskorn, D., Emde, S.: Sequencing of picking orders in mobile rack warehouses. Eur. J. Oper. Res. **259**(1) (2016)
11. Yafei, L., Dong, X., Wang, F., et al.: Application of association rule based on apriori algorithm in slotting distribution in warehouse of vehicles and equipment. J. Ordnance Eng. Coll. (2016)
12. Li, X.: Research on the join optimization of slotting distribution and order batch for mobile rack warehouse. Tsinghua University (2016)
13. Tang, J., Qu, M., Wang, M., Zhang, M., Yan, J., Mei, Q.: LINE: large-scale information network embedding. In: Proceedings of WWW, pp. 1067–1077 (2015)
14. Perozzi, B., Al-Rfou, R., Skiena, S.: DeepWalk: online learning of social representations (2014)
15. Bengio, Y., Schwenk, H., Senécal, J., et al.: Neural probabilistic language models. J. Mach. Learn. Res. **3**(6), 1137–1155 (2003)
16. Grover, A., Leskovec, J.: node2vec: scalable feature learning for networks (2016)
17. Sun, X., Guo, J., Ding, X., et al.: A general framework for content-enhanced network representation learning (2016)
18. Tu, C., Liu, H., Liu, Z., et al.: CANE: context-aware network embedding for relation modeling. In: Meeting of the Association for Computational Linguistics (2017)
19. Hartigan, J.A., Wong, M.A.: Algorithm AS 136: a K-means clustering algorithm. J. Roy. Stat. Soc. **28**(1), 100–108 (1979)
20. Xu, R., Wunsch, D.: Survey of clustering algorithm. IEEE Trans. Neural Networks **16**(3), 645–678 (2005)
21. Yi, H., Sam, K.: Learning assignment order of instances for the constrained k-means clustering algorithm. IEEE Trans. Syst. Man Cybern. Part B Cybern. **39**(2), 568–574 (2009)
22. Xiao, B., Wang, Z., Liu, Q., et al.: SMK-means: an improved mini batch K-means algorithm based on MapReduce with big data. Comput. Mater. Continua **56**(3), 365–379 (2018)
23. Xiong, Z., Shen, Q., Wang, Y., et al.: Paragraph vector representation based on word to vector and CNN learning. CMC Comput. Mater. Continua **55**, 213–227 (2018)
24. Gao, Z., Xia, S., Zhang, Y., et al.: Real-time visual tracking with compact shape and color feature. Comput. Mater. Continua **55**(3), 509–521 (2018)

Efficient PatchMatch-Based Image Registration and Retargeting for Cartoon Animation

Chuanyan Hao$^{(\boxtimes)}$, Bo Jiang, Weiming Wu, Sijiang Liu, and Liping He

Nanjing University of Posts and Telecommunications, Nanjing 210023, China
hcy@njupt.edu.cn

Abstract. Image registration and retargeting has been playing a significant role in creating sorts of visual effects in animation production pipeline, attracting plenty of researchers working on. However, previous methods are slow due to physically or geometrically based complicated computations and often rely on user assistants or external devices to capture the motion data, reducing their practicability. In this paper, we propose a novel approach to capture a path motion contained in a source animation in a fully automatic manner and reuse it to new characters with different appearances. The key idea is to employ visual difference based random search procedure to automatically track the motion and combine the moving least square based deformation technique to endue the new object with the captured motion. Our experiments demonstrate that our method achieves good results with high quality and performance.

Keywords: Data-driven approach · PatchMatch · Image registration · Motion retargeting

1 Introduction

Motion capture and retargeting is pioneered by [4] where a specific motion in a sequence of images is tracked and then transferred to a new animation. This technique bridges the gap between traditional animation and computer animation so that given a motion pattern, computer created animations can be easily reused and transferred to different domains and characters. Therefore, automation of this drawing process is greatly in demand and many investigations have been conducted recently on this topic, including image morphing and deformation [9,17], image registration [7,15] and retargeting [4,7,15]. In this paper, we are also interested in how to capture and reuse a motion pattern to other cartoon characters, as shown in Fig. 1 in which the left column is the source image (a red cartoon fish) and its animation video represented by picked frames. The right one is the target image and the transferred motion to another character (a blue cartoon whale).

Supported by NSFC 61702278, 61802197 and 61602252 and Natural Science Foundation of Jiangsu Province of China (No. BK20160902, BK20160964, BK20160967).

X. Sun et al. (Eds.): ICAIS 2019, LNCS 11632, pp. 640–651, 2019.
https://doi.org/10.1007/978-3-030-24274-9_58

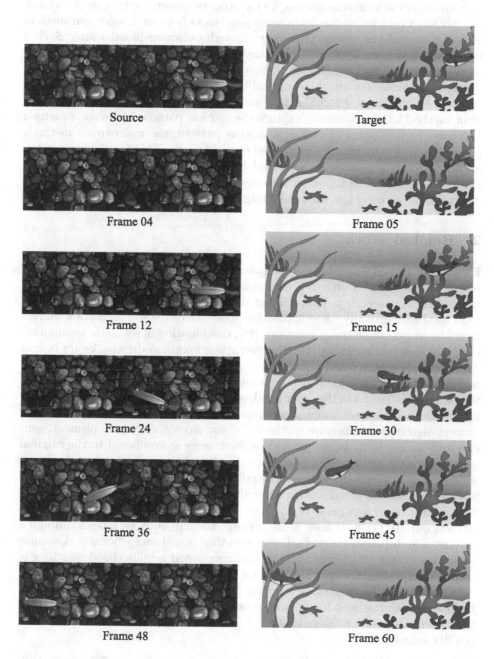

Fig. 1. An example of our work (Color figure online).

Different from most previous approaches which always capture motions by user inputs or data capture devices, we focus on an automatic treatment to track the motion. Considering the dense correspondences between frames, our method attempts to find the motion trajectory through exemplar-based search. Such a framework has been applicable for many hot issues such as texture synthesis, image inpainting and completion, image registration, motion field simulation, dense correspondences matching, optical flow calculation and lots of other applications. Among them, PatchMatch [3] enlightened us to present a fast and efficient method to automatically capture the motion pattern in a source cartoon sequence. In the aspect of reusing a motion pattern, the mainstream methods prefer physically or geometrically based computations. This type of approaches are often too complicated to solve and limited to some kind of physical phenomena or geometrical topology. In hence, inspired by the approaches of image deformation, we complete the retargeting based on the algorithm in [12].

2   Related Work

Exemplar Based Matching Methods for Cartoon Images. Matching correspondences between images is always a challenging task attacking the attentions of many researchers in the recent decades. As for cartoon images, earlier work used geometrically based approaches to match or register animation characters, like simple affine transformations [18], combination of semantic assumption [14], and skeleton matching [11]. However, their common drawbacks are lack of dense correspondences and restricted to specific applications. Although De Juan and Bodenheimer [8] employ dense correspondences in their work, its initialization is fully by hand. On the other hand, we observe that exemplar-based matching methods have been more popular in various research fields. For instance, current algorithms on texture synthesis [16] are simple, easy to implement, general and having brilliant results and performances as compared to the original parametrization models. Then amounts of subsequent researches become flourishing, including data-driven scenes completion [6], visual tracking through color features [5], steganography using reversible texture synthesis [19], and motion field simulation by synthesis [10,13]. Among them, the PatchMatch [3] algorithm attracts our attention. It finds dense correspondences between images through a random search procedure and achieves real-time speed and efficiency. A similar work to ours is in [15] where a visual similarity based neighborhood matching is proposed to obtain the new locations for point movements. However, it is very slow because of the exhaustive searches for finding the dense correspondences. Therefore, with the deep investigations on PatchMatch algorithm, we propose a grid-based PatchMatch algorithm to fast and efficiently track the motion pattern in a 2D animation.

Deformation Techniques. Deformation or warping techniques have been studied for years and proven to be a powerful tool to produce various visual effects, as surveyed in [17]. More recently, the concept of rigid-as-possible transformations have been introduced by [1]. Then Igarashi et al. [7] proposed a point-based image deformation method which generates as-rigid-as-possible deformations for cartoon-like images by minimizing a number of local scaling and shearing. To keep as-rigid-as-possible, this method solves a linear system on the triangulated mesh of the input image, whose size is equal to the number of vertices in the mesh, leading to intensive computation and possible discontinuities. Accordingly, Schaefer et al. [12] proposed an improved deformation algorithm based on Moving Least Squares (MLS), which solves a smaller linear system at each vertex of a uniform grid. Such a much smaller solution of equations can create very fast deformations with globally smooth and handle tens of thousands of vertices in real-time. After investigating on it, our approach adopts the MLS based deformation technique to derive the continuous motion pattern in our task. The necessary modification is to enable the precomputation for the points after deformed.

3   Our Approach

The core idea of our method is to sample point movements from shape consistency by search and matching, so that transformations can be calculated on points by using an improved computation based on Moving Least Square (MLS) algorithm [12]. A key observation is that such a workflow of PatchMatch [3] can bring significant benefit to motion tracking since it can find dense correspondences between images fast and efficiently, catering for automating the capture of motion information in an animation or a video. Another point lies on a fact that Moving Least Squares based method [12] provides a simple closed form solution to yield fast deformations since the precomputation on the input pivots could be conducted firstly. This simple calculation therefore can be improved in our task because points after transformed could be obtained in advance as well.

3.1   Automatic Motion Sampling Based on PatchMatch

Considering that cartoon characters or scenes are often drawn with clearly defined lines and a finite number of colorful regions which are easy to recognize compared with the NNF problem in [3], and that the next stage only needs a small number of sampling points as the inputs, our matching process tends to simplify the PatchMatch algorithm by finding the best correspondence on grid points rather than each pixel of the image.

Firstly, we embed the source frames in a uniform partitioned grid with a span of d pixels to obtain these points, as shown in Fig. 2 where the dashed green lines, one the left image, are used to indicate the original pixels, the blue lattice is for the uniform grid and the yellow points represent the vertices on the crosses of the grid in the frame of F_i, while on the right, the magenta blocks are the matched patches corresponding to the blue grids in the neighbor frame of F_{i+1}, also starting at the left corner of a block as the same yellow points shown. Formally, given a pair of neighbor frames $F_i, F_{i+1} \subset R^2$ and a collection of vertices $V = \{v_j\}$ on their meshes with the location of $P = \{p(v_j)\}$, our goal is to determine the motion of each vertex. Let $p(v_j^i)$ be the original position of the current vertex v_j in frame F_i and $p(v_j^{i+1})$ be its corresponding location in frame F_{i+1} after the animation playing from frame F_i to F_{i+1}, the motion could be derived as $M = p(v_j^{i+1}) - p(v_j^i)$. In order to find the new location $p^{i+1}(v_j)$ for the vertex v_j in its neighbor frame F_{i+1}, our approach carries out the neighborhood propagation and random search steps iteratively in scanline order on odd iterations and reverse scanline order on even iterations alternatively.

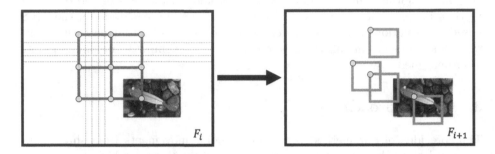

Fig. 2. Our simplified search process.

After the initialization on the vertices of the grid, each point is examined in the loop by neighborhood matching. For the current vertex v_j, we denote that its neighborhood range yields to its spatially adjacency according to the uniform grid. That is, as the propagation step, for the current block B_j^i starting at the left corner of the grid point $v_j^i(x, y)$ in F_i, our method sets up a candidate set $S(v_j^i)$ in F_{i+1} for B_j^i with a shift of d pixels or one grid as its initial neighbors. For the sake of coherence, we also add its relative neighbors to the candidate set in terms of the k-coherence algorithm [2]. So here, the candidate set is defined as $S(v_j^i) = \{(B_j^{i+1} + \triangle) \cup (B_{j+\triangle}^{i+1} + \triangle)\}$ where $\triangle$ takes the values of $(0, 0)$, $(d, 0)$, $(0, d)$, $(-d, 0)$, $(0, -d)$ as the displacements. As shown in Fig. 3, the current block B_j^i (red) and its neighbors $B_{1,2,3,4}$ (cyan) with one grid width in frame F_i are on the left image, and respectively, the magenta and blue blocks on the right image are for their best matches examined during the previous iteration, then the green blocks around the magenta one and those one grid cell shifting to the left, or right, or up, or down of the blues are all sent to the candidate set. Now the new location $p(v_j^{i+1})$ in the propagation step can be determined by the following minimization,

$$\arg\min \sum_{B_k \in S_j^i} |B(p(v_j^i)) - B_k(p(v_j^{i+1}))|^2 \qquad (1)$$

where k takes values from 1 to s, given s is the number of the candidates in S_j^i, i from 1 to f, the number of the frames and j from 1 to n, the number of the vertices in the grid, and $|\cdot|^2$ is the visual measurement to compare the blocks.

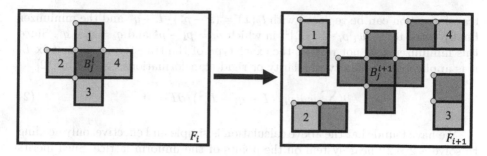

Fig. 3. The candidate set in propagation step.

Next, $p(v_j^{i+1})$ is going on to be updated in the randomized search step. Also like PatchMatch [3], a sequence of random sampled blocks around their vertices are evaluated in a set of exponentially decreasing windows centering at the current best $p(v_j^{i+1})$ and starting from a maximum search radius such as the boundary of the frame. The decrement ratio among these windows is generally set to $0.5 \times n$, the number of vertices. The visual criteria follows Eq. 1 as well only with the B_k being picked up from search windows rather than the candidate set. Thanks to the good identifiability of cartoon images, we also limit the maximum search radius to cover the most relative neighborhoods so to avoid some ambiguous choices and to reach higher efficiency. At last, this algorithm converges within a fixed number of iterations although convergence criteria changes depending on different drawings and the motion data of the rest pixels is filled by using bilinear interpolation.

3.2   Motion Calculation and Retargeting on MLSD

The Moving Least Squares algorithm is a deformation technique that allows to compute a map $\mathcal{F} : R^2 \mapsto R^2$ from the transformation of a set of N pivots p in the new positions q, which could be points or line segments as described in [12]. The map $\mathcal{F}$ is smooth, preserving the identity, that is, when $p = q$ the map is the identity and ensuring that the pivots p are transformed in the new one q, that is $f(p) = q$. Taking point as an example for the pivot, this method requires a user inputs as the pivots points p_i. Assume q_i is the set of the new positions corresponding to the p_i after user dragging, the authors [12] state a simple minimization computation that can solve, for each point on the R^2 plane, the best linear transformation (affinity, similarity or rigid transformation), moving the points according to a set of weights of the transformed p_i to q_i. Such a minimizer is explained as $\sum_i w_i |l_v(p_i) - q_i|^2$, where weight $w_i = 1/|p^i - v|^{2\alpha}$.

On the other side, an affine transformation l_v is generally composed of two parts, a linear transformation matrix L and a translate T, that is $l_v(x) = xL + T$. Now, the minimizer can be written as $\sum_i w_i |(p_i) \cdot L + T - q_i|^2$. In order to solve it, let its derivatives with respect to T be zero, as in Eq. 2, then T can be obtained as $T = q^* - p^* \cdot L$ with $p^* = \sum w_i p_i / \sum w_i$, $q^* = \sum w_i q_i / \sum w_i$. So the affine transformation can be replaced with $l_v(x) = (x - p^*) \cdot L + q^*$ and the minimizer finally turns to $\sum_i w_i |\hat{p}_i \cdot L - \hat{q}_i|^2$, in which $\hat{p}_i = p_i - p^*$ and $\hat{q}_i = q_i - q^*$. Since this minimizer does not restrict the exact type of the transformation matrix L, it is applicable for affinity, similarity or rigid transformations, as said in [12].

$$\partial(\sum_i w_i |(p_i) \cdot L - q_i + T|^2)/\partial T = 0 \tag{2}$$

We have found that the above calculation is simple and effective, only needing to solve a 2×2 linear system on the points of the uniform lattice. Such merits would be practicable for our task where relatively dense points are passed to the linear system and allow us to transfer motions between each pair of frames rather than between key frames. Further on, taking the simple affine transformation as an example, rotation matrix L can be obtained by directly introducing the classic normal equations solution as $L = (\sum_i \hat{p}_i^T w_i \hat{p}_i)^{-1} \sum_j w_j \hat{p}_j^T \hat{q}_j$. Now the deformation $\mathcal{F}_a(v)$ becomes the one in Eq. 3. More detail calculations and proofs and their extension to similarity or rigid transformations could refer to [12], we do not discuss too much here.

$$(v - p^*)(\sum_i \hat{p}_i^T w_i \hat{p}_i)^{-1} \sum_j w_j \hat{p}_j^T \hat{q}_j + q^* \tag{3}$$

The important thing lies on that Schaefer et al. [12] further on optimized their algorithm by picking up a precomputation item on the known points, that is the original user inputs. However, in our implementation, this step is given up because the initial positions p_i and the new positions q_j are all known from the matching stage. Therefore, we keep Eq. 3 and separate it to independent parts so that a parallel scheme can be performed. Thanks to the higher performance and dense enough points.

4   Results and Discussions

This section demonstrates our experiments and makes some discussions on the performances. We have tested our approach on several cartoon animations. All the capture and retargeting results presented in this section are generated on the laptop of Intel Core i5 CUP double @ 2.30 GHz with 8 GB memory. Figures 4, 5, and 6 show some results of our system where the first row is a sequence of frames of the source animation, the second row is the corresponding path motion automatically captured by our method, and the last one or two rows are sequences of frames after transferring the path motions to the target animations. Our experiments test several types of path lines and it can be seen that our approach can track the path motion successfully even if there are rotations happening through the path. More details can refer to Table 1.

Then we show a simple analysis of the performance of our algorithm. We optimize the parameters of our method on a set of different input animations using the qualitative criterion: root-mean-square-error (RMSE) between the corresponding deformed frame and the target one. It turns out that a set of constant

Table 1. Performance illustration.

Source	Frames	Size	Matching	Retargeting
Fish(Figure 4)	60	700 × 200	7.8s	63s–70s
Fish(Figure 5)	100	700 × 400	14.3s	96–110s
Basketball(Figure 6)	100	550 × 400	11.2s	67s

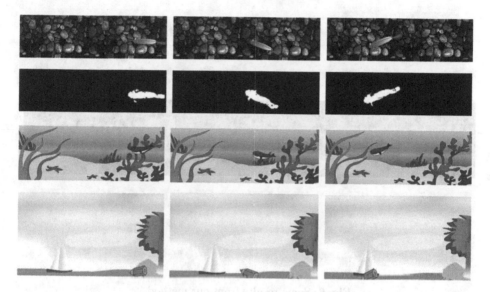

Fig. 4. Some results from our method.

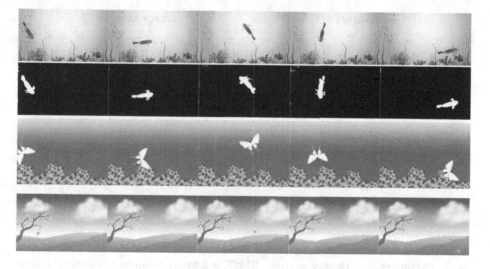

Fig. 5. Some results from our method.

parameters works well for most input exemplars: $d, r, n, w = 3, 8, 70, 16$, here d is the grid spacing, r is the search radius, n is the iterations (Depending on the input animations, slight differences available for iterations, average 70 for convergence.) and w is the patch size. Figure 7 demonstrates the robustness of our method. We also make a comparison between our implementation and the work in [15] for the matching procedure to find the correspondence among frames as

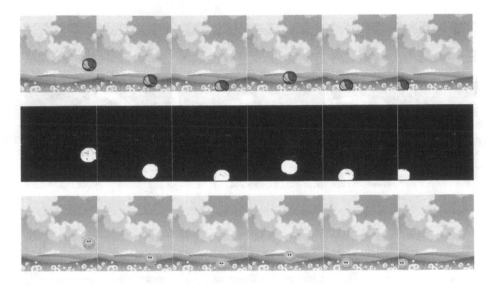

Fig. 6. Some results from our method.

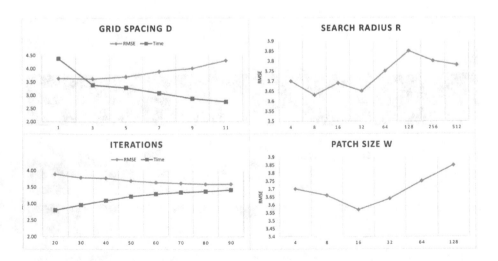

Fig. 7. Parameter performance analysis. RMSE is for root-mean-square-error and time is rewritten by log(2).

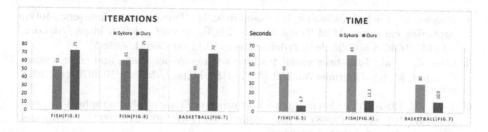

Fig. 8. Comparison with other method.

shown in Fig. 8, where it seems our approach many demand more iterations, but since each iteration is much faster in the random search model, our algorithm is still faster.

5   Conclusion and Future Work

This paper demonstrates a simple and effective method to automatically track and capture the path motion in a cartoon animation, which is later be transferred to the target character or scene. This task is achieved by two stages, a simplified PatchMatch-based randomized search algorithm and the MLS-based deformation system. Thanks to the match stage, dense enough points can be passed on to the deformation stage, which enables the effective computation to be carried out between each pair of frames. Correspondingly, owing to the deformation stage, noises in the motion data are accepted. The experiments also show that our method can work in a successful manner. However, we also need to present the limitations of this work. As observed in the results, the motion data is not completely smooth but with some noises, so our implementation first clears these noises by simple clustering. On the other hand, this framework now is just investigated on relatively simple characters which do not have shape changes of themselves because a complex cartoon includes too much challenging problems, such as how to make sure each part of it, like body, head, leg even toes, and how to capture the complicated actions of the each part and so on.

References

1. Alexa, M., Cohen-Or, D., Levin, D.: As-rigid-as-possible shape interpolation. In: Proceedings of the 27th Annual Conference on Computer Graphics and Interactive Techniques, SIGGRAPH 2000, pp. 157–164. ACM Press/Addison-Wesley Publishing Co., New York, NY, USA (2000). https://doi.org/10.1145/344779.344859
2. Ashikhmin, M.: Synthesizing natural textures. In: Proceedings of the 2001 Symposium on Interactive 3D Graphics, I3D 2001, pp. 217–226 (2001). https://doi.org/ 10.1145/364338.364405, http://doi.acm.org/10.1145/364338.364405
3. Barnes, C., Shechtman, E., Finkelstein, A., Goldman, D.B.: Patchmatch: A randomized correspondence algorithm for structural image editing. ACM Trans. Graph. **28**(3), 24:1–24:11 (2009)

4. Bregler, C., Loeb, L., Chuang, E., Deshpande, H.: Turning to the masters: Motion capturing cartoons. ACM Trans. Graph. **21**(3), 399–407 (2002). https://doi.org/10.1145/566654.566595, http://doi.acm.org/10.1145/566654.566595
5. Gao, Z., et al.: Real-time visual tracking with compact shape and color feature. Comput. Mater. Continua **55**, 509–521 (2018). https://doi.org/10.3970/cmc.2018.02634
6. Hays, J., Efros, A.A.: Scene completion using millions of photographs. Commun. ACM **51**(10), 87–94 (2008). https://doi.org/10.1145/1400181.1400202, http://doi.acm.org/10.1145/1400181.1400202
7. Igarashi, T., Moscovich, T., Hughes, J.F.: As-rigid-as-possible shape manipulation. ACM Trans. Graph. **24**(3), 1134–1141 (2005). https://doi.org/10.1145/1073204.1073323, http://doi.acm.org/10.1145/1073204.1073323
8. de Juan, C.N., Bodenheimer, B.: Re-using traditional animation: Methods for semi-automatic segmentation and inbetweening. In: Proceedings of the 2006 ACM SIG-GRAPH/Eurographics Symposium on Computer Animation, SCA 2006, pp. 223–232. Eurographics Association, Aire-la-Ville, Switzerland (2006), http://dl.acm.org/citation.cfm?id=1218064.1218095
9. Lee, S.Y., Chwa, K.Y., Shin, S.Y.: Image metamorphosis using snakes and free-form deformations. In: Proceedings of the 22nd Annual Conference on Computer Graphics and Interactive Techniques, SIGGRAPH 1995, pp. 439–448. ACM, New York (1995). https://doi.org/10.1145/218380.218501, http://doi.acm.org/10.1145/218380.218501
10. Ma, C., Wei, L.Y., Guo, B., Zhou, K.: Motion field texture synthesis. ACM Trans. Graph. **28**(5), 110:1–110:8 (2009)
11. Qiu, J., Seah, H.S., Tian, F., Chen, Q., Wu, Z., Melikhov, K.: Auto coloring with enhanced character registration. Int. J. Comput. Games Technol. **2008**, 2:1–2:7 (2008). https://doi.org/10.1155/2008/135398
12. Schaefer, S., McPhail, T., Warren, J.: Image deformation using moving least squares. ACM Trans. Graph. **25**(3), 533–540 (2006). https://doi.org/10.1145/1141911.1141920, http://doi.acm.org/10.1145/1141911.1141920
13. Schödl, A., Szeliski, R., Salesin, D.H., Essa, I.: Video textures. In: Proceedings of the 27th Annual Conference on Computer graphics and Interactive Techniques, SIGGRAPH 2000, pp. 489–498. ACM Press/Addison-Wesley Publishing Co., New York, NY, USA (2000)
14. Sýkora, D., Buriánek, J., Žára, J.: Unsupervised colorization of black-and-white cartoons. In: Proceedings of the 3rd International Symposium on Non-photorealistic Animation and Rendering, NPAR 2004, pp. 121–127. ACM, New York, NY, USA (2004). https://doi.org/10.1145/987657.987677, http://doi.acm.org/10.1145/987657.987677
15. Sýkora, D., Dingliana, J., Collins, S.: As-rigid-as-possible image registration for hand-drawn cartoon animations. In: Proceedings of the 7th International Symposium on Non-Photorealistic Animation and Rendering, NPAR 2009, pp. 25–33. ACM, New York, NY, USA (2009). https://doi.org/10.1145/1572614.1572619, http://doi.acm.org/10.1145/1572614.1572619
16. Wei, L.Y., Lefebvre, S., Kwatra, V., Turk, G.: State of the art in example-based texture synthesis. In: Eurographics 2009, State of the Art Report, EG-STAR. Eurographics Association (2009), http://www-sop.inria.fr/reves/Basilic/2009/WLKT09
17. Wolberg, G.: Image morphing: A survey. Visual Comput. **14**(8), 360–372 (1998). https://doi.org/10.1007/s003710050148

18. Xie, M.: Feature matching and affine transformation for 2d cell animation. Visual Comput. **11**(8), 419–428 (1995). https://doi.org/10.1007/BF02464332
19. Zhou, Q., et al.: Steganography using reversible texture synthesis based on seeded region growing and lsb. Comput. Mater. Continua **55**, 151–163 (2018). https://doi.org/10.3970/cmc.2018.055.151

Author Index

Printed in the United States
By Bookmasters